The Papers of
George Washington

The Papers of
George Washington

W. W. Abbot and Dorothy Twohig, *Editors*

Philander D. Chase and Beverly H. Runge, *Associate Editors*

Beverly S. Kirsch and Debra B. Kessler, *Assistant Editors*

Confederation Series

1

January–July 1784

W. W. Abbot, *Editor*

UNIVERSITY PRESS OF VIRGINIA

CHARLOTTESVILLE AND LONDON

This edition has been prepared by the staff of
The Papers of George Washington
sponsored by
The Mount Vernon Ladies' Association of the Union
and the University of Virginia
with the support of
the National Endowment for the Humanities,
the Andrew W. Mellon Foundation,
and the J. Howard Pew Foundation Trust.

THE UNIVERSITY PRESS OF VIRGINIA
Copyright © 1992 by the Rector and Visitors
of the University of Virginia

First published 1992

Library of Congress Cataloging-in-Publication Data
Washington, George, 1732–1799.
    The papers of George Washington. Confederation series / W. W.
Abbot and Dorothy Twohig, editors; Philander D. Chase and Beverly
H. Runge, associate editors; Beverly S. Kirsch and Debra B.
Kessler, assistant editors.
        p.   cm.
    Includes indexes.
    Contents: 1. January–July 1784
    ISBN 0-8139-1348-9 (v. 1).
    1. Washington, George, 1732–1799—Archives.   2. Presidents—
United States—Archives.   3. United States—History—Confederation,
1783–1789.   I. Abbot, W. W. (William Wright), 1922–   .
II. Twohig, Dorothy.   III. Title.   IV. Title: Confederation series.
E312.7   1992
973.4'1'092—dc20   91-3171
                                                              CIP

Printed in the United States of America

Frontispiece: George Washington by Joseph Wright (1756–
1793). Oil on panel, 35.8 x 30.4 cm. (14 ⅛ by 12 in.). Cour-
tesy of the Historical Society of Pennsylvania. See source
note in George Washington to Joseph Wright, 10 January
1784.

This volume is dedicated to
Francis L. Berkeley, Jr., David Shannon,
and Edgar F. Shannon, Jr.

Contents

NOTE: Volume numbers refer to the *Confederation Series.*

Editorial Apparatus

Transcription of the documents in the volumes of *The Papers of George Washington* has remained as close to a literal reproduction of the manuscript as possible. Punctuation, capitalization, paragraphing, and spelling of all words are retained as they appear in the original document. Dashes used as punctuation have been retained except when a period and a dash and another mark of punctuation appear together. The appropriate marks of punctuation have always been added at the end of a paragraph. When a tilde is used in the manuscript to indicate a double letter, the letter has been doubled. Washington and some of his correspondents occasionally used a tilde above an incorrectly spelled word to indicate an error in orthography. When this device is used the editors have corrected the word. In cases where a tilde has been inserted above an abbreviation or contraction, usually in letter-book copies, the word has been expanded. Otherwise, contractions and abbreviations have been retained as written except that a period has been inserted after an abbreviation when needed. Superscripts have been lowered. Editorial insertions or corrections in the text appear in square brackets. Angle brackets ⟨ ⟩ are used to indicate illegible or mutilated material. A space left blank in a manuscript by the writer is indicated by a square-bracketed gap in the text [ ]. Deletion of material by the author of a manuscript is ignored unless it contains substantive material, and then it appears in a footnote. If the intended location of marginal notations is clear from the text, they are inserted without comment; otherwise they are recorded in the notes. The ampersand has been retained and the thorn transcribed as "th." The symbol for per (℔) is used when it appears in the manuscript. The dateline has been placed at the head of a document regardless of where it occurs in the manuscript.

Since GW read no language other than English, incoming letters written to him in foreign languages generally were translated for his information. Where this contemporary translation has survived, it has been used as the text of the document and the original version has been included either in the notes or in the CD-ROM edition of the Papers. If there is no contemporary translation, the document in its original language has been used as the text. All of the documents printed in this volume, as well as other ancillary material usually cited in the notes, may be found in the CD-ROM edition of Washington's Papers (CD-ROM:GW).

Individuals mentioned in the text have been identified whenever possible at their first substantive mention and will not be identified at length in future volumes.

Symbols Designating Documents

AD	Autograph Document
ADS	Autograph Document Signed
ADfS	Autograph Draft Signed
ADf	Autograph Draft
AL	Autograph Letter
ALS	Autograph Letter Signed
D	Document
DS	Document Signed
Df	Draft
DfS	Draft Signed
LS	Letter Signed
LB	Letter-Book Copy
[S]	Signature clipped (used with other symbols: e.g., AL[S], Df[S])

Repository Symbols and Abbreviations

Arch. Aff. Etr.	Archives du Ministère des Affaires Etrangères, Paris (photocopies and microfilm at Library of Congress)
CD-ROM:GW	See "Editorial Apparatus"
CSmH	Henry E. Huntington Library, San Marino, Calif.
Ct	Connecticut State Library, Hartford
CtHi	Connecticut Historical Society, Hartford
CtY	Yale University, New Haven
DLC	Library of Congress
DLC:GW	George Washington Papers, Library of Congress
DNA	National Archives

DNA:PCC	Papers of the Continental Congress, National Archives
DNGS	National Genealogical Society, Washington, D.C.
DSI	Smithsonian Institution, Washington, D.C.
DSoCi	Society of the Cincinnati, Washington, D.C.
InU	Indiana University, Bloomington
MA	Amherst College, Amherst, Mass.
MdAN	U.S. Naval Academy, Annapolis
MdHi	Maryland Historical Society, Baltimore
MH	Harvard University, Cambridge, Mass.
MHi	Massachusetts Historical Society, Boston
MHi-A	Adams Papers, Massachusetts Historical Society, Boston
N	New York State Library, Albany
NAlI	Albany Institute of History and Art
NcD	Duke University, Durham, N.C.
NcRSC	North Carolina Society of the Cincinnati, Raleigh
NhD	Dartmouth College, Hanover, N.H.
NHi	New-York Historical Society, New York
NIC	Cornell University, Ithaca, N.Y.
NjMoNP	Washington Headquarters Library, Morristown, N.J.
NjP	Princeton University, Princeton, N.J.
NN	New York Public Library, New York
NNebgGW	Washington's Headquarters (Jonathan Hasbrouck House), Newburgh, N.Y.
OHi	Ohio State Historical Society, Columbus
OMC	Marietta College, Marietta, Ohio
PEL	Lafayette College, Easton, Pa.
PHC	Haverford College, Haverford, Pa.
PHi	Historical Society of Pennsylvania, Philadelphia
PPAmP	American Philosophical Society, Philadelphia
PPRF	Rosenbach Foundation, Philadelphia
P.R.O.	Public Record Office, London
PU	University of Pennsylvania, Philadelphia
PWacD	David Library of the American Revolution, Washington Crossing, Pa.
RG	Record Group (designating the location of documents in the National Archives)
RHi	Rhode Island Historical Society, Providence
RPJCB	John Carter Brown Library, Providence
ScHi	South Carolina Historical Society, Charleston
Vi	Virginia State Library and Archives, Richmond
ViFaCt	Fairfax County Courthouse, Fairfax, Va.

ViAlL   Washington Lodge No. 22, A.F. and A.M.,
                 Alexandria, Va.
ViHi   Virginia Historical Society, Richmond
ViMtV   Mount Vernon Ladies' Association of the Union
ViWC   Colonial Williamsburg, Williamsburg, Va.

Short Title List

Adams, *Works of John Adams.*   Charles Francis Adams, ed. *The Works of John Adams, Second President of the United States: With a Life of the Author, Notes and Illustrations.* 10 vols. Boston, 1850–56.

Addison, *Cato.*   *The Works of the Late Right Honorable Joseph Addison, Esq.* 4 vols. London, 1761.

Alden, *Sayre.*   John R. Alden. *Stephen Sayre, American Revolutionary Adventurer.* Baton Rouge, La., 1983.

Allen, *Massachusetts Privateers.*   Gardner Weld Allen. *Massachusetts Privateers of the Revolution.* Collections of the Massachusetts Historical Society, vol. 77. Cambridge, Mass., 1927.

Allis, *William Bingham's Maine Lands.*   Frederick S. Allis, Jr., ed. *William Bingham's Maine Lands, 1790–1820.* 2 vols. Publications of the Colonial Society of Massachusetts. Boston, 1954.

Billias, *Gerry.*   George Athan Billias. *Elbridge Gerry, Founding Father and Republican Statesman.* New York, 1976.

Boyd, *Jefferson Papers.*   Julian P. Boyd et al., eds. *The Papers of Thomas Jefferson.* 22 vols. to date. Princeton, N.J., 1950—.

Brown, "Dismal Swamp Canal."   Alexander Crosby Brown. "The Dismal Swamp." *The American Neptune: A Quarterly Journal of Maritime History,* (1945), 203–21.

Burnett, *Letters.*   Edmund C. Burnett, ed. *Letters of Members of the Continental Congress.* 8 vols. Washington, D.C., 1921–36. Reprint. Gloucester, Mass., 1963.

Butterfield, *Adams Diary and Autobiography.*   L. H. Butterfield et al., eds. *Diary and Autobiography of John Adams.* 4 vols. Cambridge, Mass., 1961.

Butterfield, *Rush Letters.*   L. H. Butterfield, ed. *Letters of Benjamin Rush.* 2 vols. Princeton, N.J., 1951.

Buxton, "History of the South Church, Peabody."   Bessie Raymond Buxton. "History of the South Church, Peabody." Essex Institute, *Historical Collections,* 87 (1951), 341–72.

Calendar of Virginia State Papers.   William P. Palmer et al., eds. *Calendar of Virginia State Papers and Other Manuscripts.* 11 vols. Richmond, 1875–93.

Campbell, *Friendly Sons of St. Patrick and the Hibernian Society.*   John

H. Campbell. *History of the Friendly Sons of St. Patrick and of the Hibernian Society for the Relief of Emigrants from Ireland.* Philadelphia, 1892.

Chastellux, *Travels in North America.* Howard C. Rice, ed. *Travels in North America in the Years 1780, 1781, and 1782 by the Marquis de Chastellux.* 2 vols. Chapel Hill, N.C., 1963.

Collins, *Witherspoon.* Varnum Lansing Collins. *President Witherspoon, a Biography.* 2 vols. Princeton, N.J., 1925.

Conway, *Paine.* Moncure Daniel Conway. *The Life of Thomas Paine with a History of His Literary, Political, and Religious Career in America, France, and England.* 2 vols. New York, 1892.

Conway, *Writings of Paine.* Moncure Daniel Conway, ed. *The Writings of Thomas Paine.* 4 vols. New York, 1902–8. Reprint. New York, 1969.

Cook, *Washington's Western Lands.* Roy Bird Cook. *Washington's Western Lands.* Strasburg, Va., 1930.

Diaries. Donald Jackson and Dorothy Twohig, eds. *The Diaries of George Washington.* 6 vols. Charlottesville, Va., 1976–79.

Early Proceedings of the American Philosophical Society. *Proceedings of the American Philosophical Society, Held at Philadelphia, for Promoting Useful Knowledge.* Vol. 22. Philadelphia, 1885.

Eisen, *Portraits of Washington.* Gustavus A. Eisen. *Portraits of Washington.* 3 vols. New York, 1932.

Fabian, *Wright.* Monroe H. Fabian. *Joseph Wright, American Artist, 1756–1793.* Washington, D.C., 1985.

Fitzpatrick, *Writings of Washington.* John C. Fitzpatrick, ed. *The Writings of George Washington from the Original Manuscript Sources, 1745–1799.* 39 vols. Washington, D.C., 1931–44.

Gordon, *History.* William Gordon. *The History of the Rise, Progress, and Establishment, of the Independence of the United States of America: Including an Account of the Late War; and of the Thirteen Colonies, from Their Origin to That Period.* London, 1788.

Griffin, *Boston Athenæum Collection.* Appleton P. C. Griffin, comp. *A Catalogue of the Washington Collection in the Boston Athenæum.* Cambridge, Mass., 1897.

Hawes, *McIntosh Papers.* Lilla Mills Hawes, ed. *The Papers of Lachlan McIntosh, 1774–1799.* Collections of the Georgia Historical Society, vol. 12. Savannah, 1957.

Hays, *Calendar of Franklin Papers.* I. Minnis Hays, ed. *Calendar of the Papers of Benjamin Franklin in the Library of the American Philosophical Society.* 2 vols. Philadelphia, 1906–8.

Heitman, *Officers of the Continental Army.* Francis B. Heitman. *Historical Register of Officers of the Continental Army during the War of the Revolution, April, 1775, to December, 1783.* Washington, D.C., 1893.

Hening. William Waller Hening, ed. *The Statutes at Large; Being a*

Collection of All the Laws of Virginia from the First Session of the Legislature, in the Year 1619. 13 vols. 1819–23. Reprint. Charlottesville, Va., 1969.

House of Delegates Journal, 1781–1785.   *Journal of the House of Delegates of the Commonwealth of Virginia; Begun and Held in the Town of Richmond, in the County of Henrico, on Monday, the Seventh Day of May, in the Year of Our Lord One Thousand Seven Hundred and Eighty-One.* Richmond, 1828.

Hume, *Society of the Cincinnati.*   Edgar Erskine Hume, ed. *General Washington's Correspondence concerning the Society of the Cincinnati.* Baltimore, 1941.

Hutchinson and Rachal, *Madison Papers.*   William T. Hutchinson, William M. E. Rachal, Robert A. Rutland, J. C. A. Stagg, et al., eds. *The Papers of James Madison.* 17 vols. Chicago and Charlottesville, Va., 1962–91.

Idzerda, *Lafayette Papers.*   Stanley J. Idzerda, Robert R. Crout, et al., eds. *Lafayette in the Age of the American Revolution: Selected Letters and Papers, 1776–1790.* 5 vols. to date. Ithaca, N.Y., 1977—.

JCC.   Worthington C. Ford et al., eds. *Journals of the Continental Congress.* 34 vols. Washington, D.C., 1904–37.

Jones, "Snickers."   Ingrid Jewell Jones. "Edward Snickers, Yeoman." *Proceedings of the Clarke County Historical Association,* 17 (1971–75), 1–62.

Journal of Massachusetts Senate.   "Journal of Senate, 1783–84." Vol. 4. Boston, 1830. Microfilm Collection of Early State Records.

Journal of N.C. House of Commons.   *The Journal of the House of Commons. At a General Assembly Begun and Held at Hillsborough, on the Nineteenth Day of April, in the Year of Our Lord One Thousand Seven Hundred and Eighty-Four. . . .* Hillsborough, N.C., 1784.

Journal of the Assembly of the State of New-York, at Their First Meeting of the Seventh Session.   *Journal of the Assembly of the State of New-York, at Their First Meeting of the Seventh Session, Begun and Holden at the City-Hall in the City of New-York, on Tuesday the Sixth Day of January, 1784.* New York, 1784.

Journal of Virginia Council.   Wilmer L. Hall, ed. *Journals of the Council of the State of Virginia.* 5 vols. Richmond, 1969–82.

Ledger A.   Manuscript Ledger in George Washington Papers, Library of Congress.

Ledger B.   Manuscript Ledger in George Washington Papers, Library of Congress.

"Letters of the Reverend William Gordon."   William Gordon. "Letters of the Reverend William Gordon, Historian of the American Revolution, 1770–1799." *Proceedings of the Massachusetts Historical Society,* 63 (1929–30), 303–613.

Life of Washington.   John Marshall. *The Life of George Washington, Commander in Chief of the American Forces, during the War Which Established the Independence of His Country. And First President of the United States.* 5 vols. Philadelphia, 1804–7. Reprint. 2 vols. Philadelphia, 1850.

McDowell, *Irish Public Opinion.*   R. B. McDowell. *Irish Public Opinion, 1750–1800.* London, 1944.

Meade, *Churches of Virginia.*   William Meade. *Old Churches, Ministers, and Families of Virginia.* 2 vols. Philadelphia, 1910.

Memoirs of the Historical Society of Pennsylvania.   *Memoirs of the Historical Society of Pennsylvania.* 14 vols. Philadelphia, 1826–95.

Minutes of the Pennsylvania Assembly.   *Minutes of the First Session of the Eighth General Assembly of the Commonwealth of Pennsylvania.* Philadelphia, 1783.

Morris, *Jay Papers.*   Richard B. Morris and Ene Sirvet, et al., eds. *John Jay, the Winning of the Peace: Unpublished Papers, 1780–1784.* Vol. 2. New York, 1980.

N.C. State Records.   Walter Clark, ed. *The State Records of North Carolina.* Winston and Goldsboro, N.C., 1895–1905.

Papers, Colonial Series.   W. W. Abbot et al., eds. *The Papers of George Washington*: Colonial Series. Charlottesville, Va., 1983—.

Papers, Presidential Series.   W. W. Abbot et al., eds. *The Papers of George Washington*: Presidential Series. Charlottesville, Va., 1987—.

Papers, Revolutionary War Series.   W. W. Abbot et al., eds. *The Papers of George Washington*: Revolutionary War Series. Charlottesville, Va., 1985—.

PCC.   Papers of the Continental Congress, 1774–89. RG 360, National Archives.

Phillips, "Salem Ocean-Borne Commerce."   James Duncan Phillips. "Salem Ocean-Borne Commerce." Essex Institute, *Historical Collections*, 75 (1939), 249–74.

Reitz, "An Unpublished Correspondence of George Washington." S. C. Bosch Reitz. "An Unpublished Correspondence of George Washington." *Journal of American History*, 24 (1930), 48–58.

Rutland and Rachal, *Madison Papers.*   Robert A. Rutland and William M. E. Rachal, J. C. A. Stagg, et al., eds. *The Papers of James Madison.* 17 vols. Chicago and Charlottesville, Va., 1962–91.

Scribner and Tarter, *Revolutionary Virginia.*   William J. Van Schreeven, Robert L. Scribner, and Brent Tarter, eds. *Revolutionary Virginia: The Road to Independence.* 7 vols. Charlottesville, 1973–83.

6 *Stat.*   Richard Peters, ed. *The Public Statutes at Large of the United States of America.* Vol. 6. Boston, 1948.

Syrett, *Hamilton Papers.*   Harold C. Syrett et al., eds. *The Papers of Alexander Hamilton.* 27 vols. New York, 1961–87.

Tilghman Memoir.   Tench Tilghman. *Memoir of Lieut. Col. Tench Tilghman.* New York, 1971.

Truro Parish Vestry Book.   Manuscript on deposit at Library of Congress.

Va. Exec. Jls.   H. R. McIlwaine, Wilmer L. Hall, and Benjamin Hillman, eds. *Executive Journals of the Council of Colonial Virginia.* 6 vols. Richmond, 1925–66.

Van Winter, *American Finance and Dutch Investment.*   Pieter Jan van Winter. *American Finance and Dutch Investment, 1780–1805: With an Epilogue to 1840.* 2 vols. New York, 1977.

"Washington's Grants in West Virginia."   Edgar B. Sims. *Making a State.* Charleston, W.Va., 1956.

The Papers of George Washington
Confederation Series
Volume 1
January–July 1784

Circular Letter to the State Societies
of the Cincinnati

Sir   Mount Vernon Jany 1st 1784

After taking all the various circumstances into mature consideration, I have thought proper to appoint the City of Philadelphia to be the place for the general meeting of the Society of Cincinnati on the first monday[1] in May next, agreeably to the original Institution—The object of this Letter is to communicate timely information thereof, that proper notice may be given to the Delegates of your State Society, whose punctual attendance will be expected at the time & place before mentioned.

Having made this communication, I have only to suggest that it may perhaps be preferable to give the necessary notice to your Delegates by Letter, rather than by a public Notification; I would however wish that whatever mode is adopted, measures may be taken to prevent a possibility of failure in the communication. I am &ca

Go: W——n

P.S. Be pleased to acknowledge the receipt of this Letter.

DfS, DSoCi. GW wrote to Henry Knox on 20 Feb. 1784 that it was "amongst" his "first Acts after I got home, to write to the President of each State Society, appointing Philadelphia (& the first Monday in May) for the general meeting of the Cincinnati." The draft of the circular letter printed here, which is in David Humphreys' hand, was originally dated December 1783 and then changed to 1 Jan. 1784. It lists the thirteen states, with checks after all but Delaware and the four southern states. The letters that GW sent by Lt. Col. Benjamin Walker to the states north of Virginia are dated 28 Dec. 1783, and those he sent to the three states to the south are dated 1 Jan. 1784. Among the copies of the circular letter found are those to the presidents of the state societies: Rhode Island (Nathanael Greene), RHi; Connecticut (Jedediah Huntington), in Hume, *Society of the Cincinnati*, 42; New York (Alexander McDougall), NHi; New Jersey (Elias Dayton), PPRF; Pennsylvania (Arthur St. Clair), OHi; North Carolina (Jethro Sumner), DLC:GW, NcRSC; and South Carolina (William Moultrie), DSoCi. In addition, John Sullivan of New Hampshire acknowledged the receipt of the circular letter on 12 Mar. 1784; Benjamin Lincoln of Massachusetts, on 2 Mar.; James Tilton of Delaware, on 20 Jan.; William Smallwood of Maryland, on 10 Feb.; and Lachlan McIntosh of Georgia, on 20 April (second letter). For further information on the Society of the Cincinnati, formed in 1783 by officers in the Continental army, see General Meeting of the Society of the Cincinnati, 4–18 May 1784, printed below.

1. "Monday" was inserted above the word "day," and "day" was inadvertently not crossed out.

To Richard Varick

Dear Sir,   Mount Vernon Jany 1st 1784
From the moment I left the City of New York until my arrival at this place,[1] I have been so much occupied by a variety of concerns that I could not find a moment's leizure to acknowledge the receipt of your favors of the 4th & 7th Ultimo.[2]

The public and other Papers which were committed to your charge, and the Books in which they have been recorded under your inspection, having come safe to hand,[3] I take this first opportunity of signifying my entire approbation of the manner in which you have executed the important duties of recording Secretary, and the satisfaction I feel in having my Papers so properly arranged, & so correctly recorded—and beg you will accept my thanks for the care and attention which you have given to this business. I am fully convinced that neither the present age or posterity will consider the time and labour which have been employed in accomplishing it, unprofitable spent.

I pray you will be persuaded, that I shall take a pleasure in asserting on every occasion the sense I entertain of the fidelity, skill, and indefatigable industry manifested by you in the performance of your public duties; and of the sincere regard & esteem with which I am—Dr Sir Yr Most Obedt & affe Servt

Go: Washington

ALS, NAlI; LB, DLC:GW.

Lt. Col. Richard Varick (1753–1831) of the 1st New York Regiment, who was Benedict Arnold's chief aide at the time Arnold's treason was discovered in the fall of 1780, became GW's recording secretary in May 1781. On 4 April 1781 GW wrote to Samuel Huntington, president of the Congress, that because his papers—"valuable documents which may be of equal public utility and private satisfaction"—were still "in loose sheets; and in the rough manner in which they were first drawn," he wished to employ "a set of Writers . . . for the sole purpose of recording them." It must be done, he wrote, "under the Inspection of a Man of character in whom entire confidence can be placed"

(DNA:PCC, item 152). After Congress gave its approval of the undertaking, GW wrote Varick, on 25 May 1781, putting him in charge of the project. He presented Varick with detailed and precise instructions for sorting into six classes, ordering, registering, and filing all of his official letters, orders, and instructions, as well as letters written to him, which were not to be transcribed. Varick was to hire "Clerks who write a fair hand, and correctly" to copy all of GW's official papers except incoming letters. Varick was to return to GW the original documents, properly docketed and arranged, as well as the transcripts. Varick at Poughkeepsie in the summer of 1781 began sorting the documents, and by September 1781 he had three clerks hard at work. In August 1783, two years after the work began, Varick and his clerks finally brought the transcripts up to date, and Varick delivered to GW twenty-eight completed volumes: six volumes of letters to Congress, fourteen of letters and orders to his officers, four of letters to civil officers, one of letters to foreigners, two volumes of councils of war, and, finally, one volume of his private correspondence which Varick and GW had decided should also be transcribed. Varick and one or more clerks continued to sort and copy GW's papers, which GW and his staff continued to send to Varick until December 1783 when Varick decided to "bid a happy Adieu to public Services & return to the pleasant, tho fatiguing, Amusement of a City Lawyer" (Varick to GW, 18 Nov. 1783).

1. GW bade an emotional farewell to his officers at Fraunces's tavern in New York on 4 December. He did not arrive at Mount Vernon until Christmas Eve, having stopped at New Brunswick and Trenton and having spent a week in Philadelphia before finally attending Congress at Annapolis to resign his commission on 23 December. This was the first time he had been at Mount Vernon "since the 4th of May 1775," except during the Yorktown campaign when he spent one day there going down and "took 3 or 4" in October 1781 on his way back north (GW to George William Fairfax, 10 July 1783).

2. On 17 Nov. 1783 GW instructed Varick to "forward all his Papers, recorded and unrecorded, to New York before the first of Decr next" (David Humphreys to Varick, NHi: Richard Varick Papers). All of GW's papers dated before 1 Oct. 1783, along with Varick's transcripts of them, had recently been sent to Mount Vernon (see note 3). The bundle of papers for 1 to 23 Oct. sent to Varick for transcribing had not arrived at Poughkeepsie and were thought to have been stolen. On 18 Nov. Varick reported "that the Packet of lost letters was found in a Swamp, but that the Letters were too wet" to be brought to GW, and so Varick went into New York from Poughkeepsie with what of GW's papers were still in his possession. On 4 Dec. Varick wrote GW that he had copied the drafts of the indexes to 1 Oct. for the last seven volumes of the transcripts and had "folded, sorted & properly endorsed & packed up in several Bundles" the papers still in his hands. He promised to submit his final account as soon as he could settle with the clerk, Taylor. Three days later Varick wrote that the "lost papers are just come to Hand & I have folded but not had Time to number them; they are in their respective Bundles. The Letter to me was not open'd, but in perfect order & Muddy." By 13 Dec. these papers too were on their way to Mount Vernon (see note 3).

3. GW began preparing to transport his papers to Mount Vernon as early as 18 June 1783, at which time he wrote to Daniel Parker in New York from Newburgh: "For the purpose of Transporting my Books of records & Papers with safety, I want Six strong hair Trunks well clasped and with good Locks" as well as "a label (in brass or copper) containing my ⟨na⟩me, & the year on each." Determined from the beginning to send his papers by land and not risk shipping by sea, GW in early October 1783 had at his headquarters near Princeton six wagons with teams to transport his papers, thinking it "probable that not less than 4 or 5 will do" (GW to Timothy Pickering, 8 Oct. 1783). Not until 9 Nov. did GW order Lt. Bezaleel Howe to conduct the wagons loaded with the papers, "which are of immense value to me," to Philadelphia and Wilmington, "& thence through Baltimore, Bladensburgh, George Town, and Alexandria to Mount Vernon." It is not known what day Howe got to Mount Vernon, but the remaining papers dated after 1 Oct. (see note 2) probably did not arrive long before GW did on 24 Dec. and may have arrived even shortly after that (see GW to Samuel Hodgdon, 13 Dec., and Hodgdon to GW, 18 Dec. 1783).

To Brühl

Sir,   Mount Vernon 3d Jany 1784

In forwarding the Letter of the Count de Solms[1] you have done a most acceptable office by bringing me acquainted with so venerable & dignified a character; You have also given me an occasion of experiencing your great politeness, & of expressing my obligations for it.

I must now take the liberty of committing to your charge a Letter directed to the Count; it is the harbinger of the Portrait which is intended to be presented to him,[2] in conformity to his request & your permission, & which will be likewise addressed to your care by my friend the Honorable Robt Morris of Philadelphia.[3] I have the honor to be &ca

          G: Washington

LB, DLC:GW.

At some time after becoming a clerk for GW in 1789, Bartholomew Dandridge (d. 1802), the nephew of Martha Washington, began entering in a letter book letters that GW had written since leaving the army at the end of 1783. He also copied a few personal letters written before 1784. The last letter that Dandridge copied in the letter book is dated 23 Jan. 1787, at which point George Washington Craik began copying.

GW had no secretary after his return to Mount Vernon in December 1783 until William Shaw came to work for him in the summer of 1785. All of the letters that Dandridge copied that were dated before Shaw's arrival he must have taken from GW's own drafts or retained copies, virtually all of which are missing. Perhaps they were discarded by Dandridge once they were entered into the letter book.

Aloys Friedrich, Graf von Brühl (1739–1789), a privy councilor to the elector of Savoy, at this time was the elector's envoy in London.

1. Brühl's letter to GW is from London, dated 4 Sept. 1783; the enclosed letter from Solms is dated 9 July 1783.

2. See GW to Solms, this date, and notes.

3. See GW to Robert Morris, 10 Jan. 1784.

From Henry Knox

My dear General.   West point [N.Y.] 3 January 1784

I did not leave New York untill the 18th ultimo, it being the earliest period that we were able consistent with the wish of Governor Clinton to withdraw the troops from thence. Indeed we then left nearly one hundred men, who are since releived by a company of light infantry, of the regiment retained in Service. In addition to which there is a sub., and about twenty artillery men.[1]

I have discharged all the troops but those specified in the enclosed return,[2] & I beg that your Excellency would accept of my letter to Congress, a copy of which is enclosed, as a report of that business.[3] I thought it would be best to write particularly to Congress, as it was probable that you were at Mount-Vernon, and it might cause much delay in writing to them through You. I have to request therefore that you will have the goodness to consider this as a private letter.

It having been established, that the objects of the War, being accomplished, and the service at an end, no officer could claim to be in the new arrangement upon the mere principle of seniority. And this was confirmed beyond a doubt by what was understood to be the opinion of the officers, who generally entertained the idea that it was optional with themselves to continue, or not, as suited their circumstances without having their certificates for the ultimate reward of their Services, delayed, or denied. The New Hampshire Officers agreed among themselves who should officer the two companies from that State. The nomination, of the officers for the remaining seven companies from the Massachusetts line were entirely left to the field Officers. And the Artillery officers were taken nearly as they stood upon the list. Were it not for the peculiar situation of the officers, discharged in the midst of a severe season, without pay and in some instances without subsistence Money, I believe the reduction would have been effected with as much facility as any that have preceeded it. The discontents however I beleive have not been great, except in the instance of Colonel Michael Jackson, whose affections, and views, appear to have been fixed to continue in service.[4]

Whatever may be the sentiments of any person respecting my agency in this necessary business I can truly assert, a regard to the public good, has been my sole object without favor or partiality.

There are two or three officers who have families which from the particular state of their circumstances cannot be removed this Winter—To these I have ordered rations to the first of March, or subsistence money as it may be. And perhaps there are some so infirm, as to be in the same predicament.

I shall expect to hear from Your Excellency respecting the time, and place, at which the general society shall meet in May next, and upon any other subject which you may think proper.[5]

I beleive I did not mention to your Excellency my idea of the pay for the offices which might be associated vizt The duties of the secretary at War, Master of ordnance and the charge or command of any troops which might be retained in service. It appears to me and I hope that I estimate fairly the expences and trouble, that the pay & emoluments of a Major General, in a seperate department, free of any encumbrances would not be an unreasonable appointment—should Congress think proper, to honor me with an offer of these offices associated together, I should be willing to accept them upon the above terms. But I should do Injustice to myself and family to accept of any employment which would not prevent my involving myself.[6]

Having brought the affairs here, nearly to a close, I shall soon depart for Boston, for which place Mrs Knox and her little family, set out from New York on the 16th Ultimo.[7] I should do violence to the dictates of my heart were I to suppress entirely its sensations of affection & gratitude to you for the innumerable instances of your kindness and attention to me, and although I can find no words equal to their warmth I may venture to assure you that they will remain indelibly fixed. I beg you to present my sincere regards, to Mrs Washington and ardent wishes for her health and felicity, and I devoutly pray that the Supreme Being would continue to afford you his efficient protection. I am my dear General Your truly affectionate

H. Knox

ALS, DLC:GW; ADfS, MHi: Knox Papers.

Maj. Gen. Henry Knox (1750–1806) was GW's choice to take command of the army in New York when GW departed on 4 Dec. 1783. Knox returned to West Point from New York City with the army on 18 Dec. and in accordance with GW's instructions continued to disband the army there. By this time he had organized the remnants of GW's army in a regiment under Col. Henry Jackson and a small corps of artillery, both composed of men of long-term enlistments. On 9 Jan. when Knox set out from West Point for Boston, Colonel Jackson took command at the post. As secretary general of the newly formed Society of the Cincinnati, Knox kept in close touch during the spring with his friend GW who was president of the society.

1. In a memorandum written on the back of the return described in note 2, Knox noted that there was left in New York City a subaltern with twenty-one men in addition to a company of Henry Jackson's regiment.

2. The enclosed return dated 4 Jan. reports that there were in Henry Jackson's infantry regiment 38 officers, 5 on the staff, 67 noncommissioned officers, and 527 rank and file; in the corps of artillery, 13 officers, 25 noncommissioned officers, and 100 rank and file. The copy of the return in the Knox Papers (MHi) reports 12 instead of 13 commissioned officers in the artillery.

3. In his letter to the president of the Congress of this date, which he enclosed, Knox reported: "In consequence of directions from His Excellency General Washington the several lines which composed the troops in this quarter are dissolved; and one regiment of infantry, commanded by Brig. Gen. Henry Jackson, and fully officered, consisting of five hundred rank and file, is formed of the men whose times of service do not expire until 1785—and a corps of artillery under the command of Major [Sebastian] Bauman, of about one hundred and twenty. The returns of the troops retained in service, No. 1, are enclosed, specifying the States to which the men belong.

"One company of infantry will be detached to Springfield [Mass.], as a guard to the valuable public stores deposited at that place. Another company and a small detatchment of artillery will be stationed at New York, at the request and under the orders of His Excellency Governor [George] Clinton, to remain there until the powers of the civil government are fully established. And a detachment of artillery now at Albany and its neighbourhood, are ordered to Fort Schuyler, to guard certain stores which were sent there this Summer past, with an intention of taking possession of the posts on the western lakes, and which it is presumed may be again wanted for the same purpose. The remainder of the infantry and corps of artillery will be stationed in this garrison and its immediate dependencies" (MHi: Knox Papers).

The remainder of the letter is concerned largely with supplies, arms, and the like. Knox explains that it is on GW's directions that he continues "to superintend the posts and military affairs of this department until the pleasure of Congress shall be known," and that he has GW's permission to leave shortly for New England to attend to his private affairs.

4. Knox is referring to his forming of Henry Jackson's regiment. The regiment was made up of men from New Hampshire and Massachusetts. See note 3. For a sketch of Michael Jackson, see GW to Thomas Mifflin, 19 Jan. 1784, n.1.

5. See Circular Letter to the State Societies of the Cincinnati, 1 Jan. 1784.

6. Congress made Knox secretary at war on 8 Mar. 1785.

7. See Knox to GW, 9 Jan. and 21 Feb. 1784.

To Solms

Sir,   Mount Vernon 3d Jany 1784

The Letter which you did me the honor to write from Konigstein on the 9h of July last came safely to my hands a few days ago, accompanied by one from Monsr le Conte de Bruhl.[1]

I must entreat, my General, that you will accept my best acknowledgments for the favorable opinion you are pleased to express of my military character, as well as for your great politeness in proposing to introduce my likeness amongst your collection of heroes. I must likewise be permitted to assure you with how much satisfaction I should have embraced & welcomed, at my Seat on the banks of the Patowmac, the venerable Soudart,[2] the noble Count de Solms, who has had the happiness to have served with, & to have been the friend & companion of those illustrious characters which now compose his inestimable collection, & into whose company, I am sensible it is no small honor, to have even my portrait admitted.

But as the distance, & circumstances will not permit me the pleasure of seeing you, I must be contented with giving the best demonstration of respect in my power; I have not delayed a moment therefore to comply with your wishes, but have employed a Gentleman to perform the work, who is thought on a former occasion to have taken a better likeness of me, than any other painter has done:[3] His forté seems to be in giving the distinguishing characteristics with more boldness than delicacy—And altho' he commonly marks the features very strongly, yet I cannot flatter you, that you will find the touches of his pencil extremely soft, or that the portrait will in any respect equal your expectations. Such as it may be (& for your sake, I would wish the execution was as perfect as possible) it will be forwarded from Philada, to the orders of the Count de Bruhl, as soon as it is finished. & I pray your acceptance of it as a token of the great veneration & esteem with which I have the honor to be Your &ca

G: Washington

LB, DLC:GW.

For most of his long life, Friedrich-Christoph, Graf zu Solms und Tecklenberg (1708–1789), had been in the service of the elector of Saxony (who until 1763 was also king of Poland), either as a military officer or as a high civil official. Humane and enlightened, he was a man of wide interests who wrote both history and poetry and boasted of a library of 10,000 volumes.

1. Solms wrote GW on 9 July 1783 that he had in his castle at Königstein on the Elbe a small collection of portraits of great men, including Prince Eugene, Maurice of Saxony, Frederick the Great, and Frederick's brother Henry. He now wished to add Washington's to the portraits of these men under whom he himself had "servi." For the identity of the comte de Brühl, see GW to Brühl, this date.

2. Solms referred to himself as an old soldier. In closing his letter of July 1783 he wrote: "Il faut bien que vous sachier aussi, qui est le vieux Soudart qui Vous importune—Eh Bien! C'est le Comte Solms, General d'Infantrie au Service de Saxe, Lieutenant General d'Infanterie au Service de S. M. tres Chretienne commandant de la forteresse de Konigstein, Commandeur des Ordres du Seraphin et de l'Epée du Suede, & le plus sincere Admirateur de l'Illustre Wasington" (DLC:GW).

3. The painter was Joseph Wright, who is identified in GW to Wright, 10 Jan. 1784. On 28 Aug. 1783 Charles Thomson, secretary of the Congress, sent Wright to GW's headquarters at Rocky Hill, N.J., with a copy of an act of Congress of 7 Aug. 1783 providing for the erection of an equestrian statue of GW. Thomson, describing Wright to GW "as an Artist skilled in taking Busts," asked GW to "admit him to try his talents." Wright did make busts of GW, although the equestrian statue was never erected, and it was at this time that Wright painted the "likeness" to which GW refers here. The portrait is reproduced in the frontispiece. See the source note in GW to Joseph Wright, 10 January.

To Robert Morris

Dear sir,   Mount Vernon 4th Jany 1784

Herewith I give you the trouble of receiving the account of my expenditures in Philadelphia, & on my journey home. If I recollect right, Colo. Cobb told me this was the mode you had suggested to him, as proper for my proceeding in this matter.

The hurry I was involved in the morning I left the City, occasioned my neglecting to take a memorandum of the amount of the last warrt which I drew on the Paymaster General, & obliges me *now* to exhibit two accounts that I may be sure that one of them is right. The reason is this—I gave Colo. Cobb the balance which was due to me on the last account, vizt £7.16.8. to found the warrant, but in the hurry we were both in, he neither asked, nor did I tell him that it was lawful money (that is, Dollars at 6/) & from the recollection of a circumstance which I did not advert to at the time I signed the warrant, I have reason to believe he considered it Pennsylvania money, & drew the warrant accordingly.[1]

Should this be the case, the account No. 2. is the one which ought to be presented at the Auditors Office, & vice versa. I must request the favor of you therefore my good Sir, to let one of your clerks examine the warrant which I drew, or[2] the Books of the Pay office to determine this point: and I shall be obliged to you for throwing the balance which may be found due to me on either, into the hands of Governor Clinton as soon as it is convenient; as he was kind enough to borrow money to answer my wants, for which I am now paying an interest of seven per Cent.[3]

Equally unexpected by them, as it appeared just in my eye[4] to do it, I have given my late Aids who attended me from the seat of my military command, one hundred dollars each, to bear their expences home—I could not think it reasonable that from their attachment to me, or from motives of etiquette, they should incur this charge themselves. Their finances I well knew were unable to bear it, altho' I had some difficulty to prevail on them to accept this aid. Cobb I would not suffer, (on account of his domestic & other concerns) to proceed any further than Philada with me, but his distance from thence home would be equal to those of the other Gentlemen, from this place—all stand therefore upon an equal footing in my allowance.[5]

I cannot close this Letter without a renewal of those sentiments of friendship & regard which I have always felt & professed for you; nor without those expressions of my sensibility for the many instances of polite attention & civilities which I have received from Mrs Morris & yourself, as result from a susceptible mind; particularly during my late stay in Philada.

I flatter myself it is unnecessary to repeat the assurances of the pleasure it would give Mrs Washington & me, to see you & Mrs Morris at this retreat from my public cares—& yet, if I obey the dictates of my inclination & wishes, I must do it: My best wishes, & respectful compliments, in which Mrs Washington joins me, are offered to you both; & with sincere & affection I am Dear sir, Your most obedient & very humble servt

G: Washington

LB, DLC:GW; copy, DLC:GW.

Robert Morris (1734–1806) in three weeks was to tender his resignation from the position of superintendent of finance for the Congress, but in May he was urged to remain in office, which he did through the summer. Morris was married to Mary White of Maryland.

1. GW's account, in his own hand, for the period 13 Dec. through 28 Dec. 1783 shows the payment to him of £217.16.8 (726⁸⁄₇₂ dollars) to balance the account on 13 Dec. and the subsequent expenditures by him of £213.8.4 (CSmH). Morris referred the matter of GW's account for 13–28 Dec. 1783 to the U.S. comptroller, James Milligan. Milligan concluded that GW was entitled to 857 5²⁄₉₀ dollars on his December account and transmitted a certificate for that amount to the superintendent of finance Morris, for GW (see Milligan to GW, 9 Mar. 1784). Morris then sent GW a warrant on U.S. Treasurer Michael Hillegas for 857 5²⁄₉₀ dollars, which GW endorsed and returned to Morris, assigning the warrant to George Clinton (see Morris to GW, 14 Feb., GW to Morris, 3 Mar., Clinton to GW, 27 Feb., and GW to Benjamin Walker, 24 Mar.). Milligan enclosed in his letter to GW of 9 Mar. a copy of GW's revised account for 13–28 December. See note 3 of Milligan's letter and note 3, GW to Milligan, 1 April.

2. The copy has "in" instead of "or." Perhaps GW intended to write "on."

3. See George Clinton to GW, 27 Feb. 1784, and notes.

4. The copy has "eyes" instead of "eye."

5. The aides were lieutenant colonels David Cobb, David Humphreys, and Benjamin Walker. GW's account for 13–28 Dec. 1783 (note 1) has an entry on 28 Dec. for $300, or £90, in payment to his aides of one hundred dollars each "to bear their Expens. back to their respective states—& not to be charged to them." The comptroller appended to the statement of GW's December accounts made on 6 Feb. by the clerk of accounts, William Ramsay, to the auditor, John D. Mercier, this note, also dated 6 Feb.: "His Excellency, by his letter to the Superintendant of Finance of the 4th of January 1784, a copy of which is herewith filed, observes that he had paid Colonels Humphreys, Cobb & Walker, his three Aids, each one hundred Dollars, to defray their Expences to their respective places of abode, within stated. As the General mentions these sums as presents or Gratuities, for which he expects, these Officers are not to be charged, the Comptroller is perfectly willing to comply with this reasonable desire. The Register will therefore not carry these sums to Account of those Gentlemen—J.M." (DLC:GW).

Letter not found: from Annis Boudinot Stockton, 4 Jan. 1784. On 18 Feb. GW wrote to Stockton: "The intemperate weather . . . prevented your letter of the 4th of last month from reaching my hands 'till the 10th of this."

To Jonathan Trumbull, Jr.

Dear Trumbull,   Mount Vernon Jany 5th 1784

Your obliging letter of the 15th of Novr did not reach me until some days after we had taken possession of the City of New York—The Scene that followed of festivity, congratulation, Addresses, and resignation must be my apology for not replying to it sooner.[1]

I sincerely thank you for the Copy of the Address of Govr Trumbull to the Genl Assembly & Freemen of your State—The Sentiments contained in it are such as would do honor to a Patriot of any Age or Nation! at least they are too coincident with my own, not to meet my warmest approbation. Be so good as to present my most cordial respects to the Governor and let him know that it is my wish the mutual friendship & esteem which have been planted & fostered in the tumult of public life, may not wither and die in the serenity of retirement: tell him we should rather amuse our evening hours of life, in cultivating the tender plants & bringing them to perfection before they are transplanted to a happier clime.[2]

Notwithstanding the jealous and contracted temper which seems to prevail in some of the States, yet I cannot but hope & believe that the good sense of the People will *ultimately* get the better of their *prejudices*; and that order & sound policy—tho' they do not come so soon as one would wish—will be produced from the present unsettled and deranged state of public Affairs. Indeed I am happy to observe that the political disposition is actually meliorating every day. Several of the States have manifested an inclination to invest Congress with more ample Powers—Most of the Legislatures appear disposed to do perfect Justice—and the Assembly of this Commonwealth have just complied with the requisitions of Congress, and I am informed without a dissentient voice. Every thing, my dear Trumbull, will come right at last as we have often prophesied— My only fear is we shall loose a little reputation *first*.

After having passed, with as much prosperity as could be expected, thro' the career of public life, I have now reached the goal of domestic enjoyment—in which state, I assure you, I find your good wishes most acceptable to me. The family at Mount Vernon joins in the same Complimts & Cordiality to you & yours with which I am—Dr Sir Yr Most Affecte & Obedt Servt

Go: Washington

ALS (photocopy), ViMtV; LB, DLC:GW.

Jonathan Trumbull, Jr. (1740–1809), was GW's secretary from June 1781 until the fall of 1783. During GW's presidency he served in the House of Representatives, from 1789 to 1795, and in the U.S. Senate, from 1795 to 1796.

1. In his draft of the letter of 15 Nov. 1783, Trumbull wrote in this vein: "so excessively jealous is the spirit of this State at present respecting the Powers of Congress & fullfillment of their Engagements; arizing principally for their Aversion to the Half Pay & Commutation granted to the Army . . . because it is but too true that some few are wicked eno' to Hope that by Means of this Clamor, they shall be able to rid themselves entirely of the whole public Debt by introducing so much Confusion & Disorder into our public Measures, as shall produce a general Abolition of the Whole—." He reassured GW, however, that "for myself I have not lost my Confidence in the final Issue of our political Establishments—And your Excellencys firmness & Resolution, I know to be superior to any desponding Ideas—"(CtY).

2. Jonathan Trumbull, Sr. (1710–1785), delivered the address (*An Address of His Excellency Governor Trumbull to the General Assembly and the Freemen of the State of Connecticut; Declining Any Further Election to Public Office . . .* [New London, 1783]) in October 1783 declining to stand for reelection to the governorship, an office he had held in Connecticut without interruption since October 1769. His address is a forceful plea for the state to "support and strengthen the fœderal union," urging the necessity of having "a Congress invested with full and sufficient authorities."

From David Humphreys

My dear General   Janry 6th 1784.

After your public Audience was concluded on the 23d of Decr[1] the President of Congress took me aside, and requested, "if any thing should occur to me in consequence of what had just been suggested in favor of the Gentlemen of General Washington's family who had continued with him to that moment, that I would communicate it to him in a Letter," and further observed, that he should take great pleasure in laying it immediately before Congress.

I have hesitated in deciding what was the best mode of making known my sentiments and wishes—for it is not a pleasing task to speak or write much respecting myself, and altho' my early studies, my opportunities of gaining experience from your example, my present habits and time of life, with some other circumstances, would have strongly inclined me to continue in some department of the public employment; yet I should not have presumed to offer my services, but for the generous encouragement which has been proffered, in consequence of your recommendations. My sense of that honorable notice and my readiness to obey the commands of Congress I have now determined to signify in a concise and respectful manner to them.

I do not know, however, whether it may appear too assuming in me, to mention in communication any particular department in which I could wish to serve the Public—but as Congress may probably in a short time have in their gift one or other of the following Appointments, viz., the office of Secretary of Foreign Affairs, the command of a Regiment in case of a Peace Establishment, or the nomination of a Secretary to one of their Commissions abroad; if there should be no impropriety in your farther interposition, and if the performance of the duties of either of those Offices should be deemed within the compass of my abilities, a suggestion of the kind (founded on the proffered encouragement of Congress) addressed even in your private character to the President, would be of sufficient avail.[2]

If also you could take the trouble of inclosing the copy of such a Letter to me, as a perpetual Memorial of your freindship and approbation, it would afford a gratification beyond which my wishes do not extend.

Perhaps I ask too much—but as your goodness has prompted, your indulgence will pardon the boldness of the request, and suppress whatever is improper in it.

In the mean time, permit me to return my best thanks for your obliging offer of being useful to me in future life, as well as for your kindness on every former occasion; and to testify with how great veneration and attachment I have the honor to be Dear Sir Your most faithful freind, and most Obed. humble Servant

D. Humphreys

ALS, DLC:GW.

As GW's aide-de-camp, David Humphreys (1752–1818) accompanied GW from New York to Virginia in December 1783. In the summer of 1784 Humphreys went to France as secretary to the Commission for Negotiating Treaties of Commerce with Foreign Powers composed of Thomas Jefferson, Benjamin Franklin, and John Adams. After his return to America in 1786 he was frequently at Mount Vernon and traveled with GW when GW went to New York to become president in 1789. During GW's presidency Humphreys served as a diplomat in various capacities. A graduate of Yale, he is regarded as one of the Connecticut Wits despite his lumbering prose and worse poetry.

1. GW resigned his commission in a public ceremony before Congress at Annapolis on 23 Dec. 1783 and then departed for Mount Vernon.

2. GW wrote to Thomas Mifflin, president of Congress, on 14 Jan. commending Humphreys as a suitable person to be made secretary of foreign affairs or a minister to another country. For Humphreys' appointment as secretary to Thomas Jefferson's commission to France, see Humphreys to GW, 18 May 1784. But see also Jacob Read to GW, 1 Feb. 1784.

From Lameth

Monsieur,   à Paris Le 6 janvier 1784.

Puis-je espérer que votre excellence voudra Bien Se rapeller encore quelqu'un qui ne peut jamais Oublier les Bontes flatteuses dont elle l'a honore, et qui ose aujourd'huy en Solliciter une nouvélle préuve.

L'amérique daigne admettre quelques officiers de L'armée De Rochambeau à L'association La plus honnorable, et La plus chére aux coeurs des françois, Puisquelle fixe L'époque de la Gloire immortelle de votre excellence, et qu'elle est pour Eux Le Gage de Son estime. L'amérique a cru devoir ne Comprendre dans cette Grace que les officiers Généraux, et Colonels de L'armée française; malgré ce que j'ai Souffert, et ce que je Souffrirai Probablement Le Réste de ma vie, pour La Liberté, et Le Bonheur de L'amérique, je n'ai Pas L'indiscrétion de demander à votre éxcellance qu'elle fasse en ma faveur une excéption qui pourait L'exposer à Des Réclamations, j'ose Seulement attendre de Sa Bonté une interprétation favorable au téxte même de la Loy portée par L'amérique: ma Position d'ailleurs est unique: elle ne peut être n'y Sous le rapport des Bléssures, n'y Sous celuy des Services celle d'aucun officier de L'armée francaise; que votre Excellence veuille Bien me perméttre de La luy éxposer. je suis parti de france avec le grade de Capitaine de Dragons; je n'avais pas L'age de demander à être fait Colonel: arrivé à L'amérique Mr Le Cte De Rochambeau m'a nommé premier aide Maréchal Gènéral des Logis de Son armée: j'avais obtenu de marcher comme volontaire en virginie, contre arnold, et je me Suis trouvé au Combat de Mr detouche du 16 mars. à new-yorck j'ai marché à L'avant Garde de Lauzun qui était chargée de Replier La Légion de De Lancey qui voulait troubler La Reconnaissance de votre Excellance. en quittant La Position de Philisbourg j'ai mené L'arriére Garde de L'armée. Le Passage de La Riviére du nord, ainsy que tous Les détails fatigans de notre marche, embarquement à annapolis, débarquement dans La Riviére de james ont en partie Roulé Sur moy. à L'investissement D'yorck j'ai marché avec L'avant Garde de L'armée qui a Protégé—La premiére Reconnaissance que votre Excellence a fait de cette place: Lors de L'ouverture de la Premiere parallelle, votre Excellence pourait Se rappeller que j'eu L'honneur de passer une partie de la nuit auprès de Sa personne: Pendant le Siége j'ai monté La tranchée comme officier de La Ligne: Enfin à l'attaque d'une des Redouttes de la Gauche des ennemis, marchant Comme volontaire avec les travailleurs qui formaient La tête de l'attaque, je Suis parvenu jusque Sur le parapet, et ai été assez heureux de faire couper La fraize avant de reçevoir deux coups de fusils dans les Deux Genoux. Je me rapellerai toute ma vie avec une tendre, et respectueuse reconnaissance L'extrême bonté qu'eut votre Excellence de venir me visiter Sur mon Lit de Douleurs.

Sur L'éxposé de mes Services, le Roy de france a Bien voulu m'accorder La croix de St Louis, et Le Grade de Colonel: mon Brevet est datté du mois de janvier, et ce n'est qu'au mois de fevrier que j'ai quitté L'amérique. *j'ai donc été Colonel à L'armée de M Le Cte De Rochambeau, en même tems qu'aide Maréchal General des Logis de Son armée, et me trouve dans Le Cas d'être Compris dans La distinction que L'amérique veut bien accorder aux Colonels.* Cependant Comme je n'en ai pas fait Le Service (et Comment aurais=je pu le faire, puisque mes Blessures m'ont retenu au Lit plusieurs mois après mon retour en france), Mr Le Cte De Rochambeau a poussé La rigoureuse éxactitude jusqu'à attendre pour me Comprendre La décision de votre Excellence: il a L'honneur de vous écrire pour La Solliciter favorable: Mr Le Mis de La fayette aura pareillement l'honneur d'écrire à votre Excellence, et de luy dire quil Pense que Mr Le Cte de Rochambeau aurait pu Sans donner d'éxtension à La Loy me Comprendre dans cette nomination cy. en éffet que votre excellence daigne Réfléchir un moment Sur ma position, elle Sentira combien il Serait Dur pour moy de voir des officiers qui n'ont Sèjourné que Deux mois à L'amérique, Sans y entendre un Coup de fusil, Recevoir une distinction militaire dont je Serais privé quoiqu'en étant Susceptible d'après La loy. quand les officiers francais ont autant à Se Louër des Bontés touchantes de L'amérique, votre Excellence ne permettera pas que celuy de tous qui a le plus Souffert pour elle, que celuy à qui vous avez Daigné montrer de L'intéret, et de L'estime, trouve toujours dans Ses Camarades des objets d'une Comparaison affligeante, et des motifs de Regrets qui ne finiraient plus, Si mon Oncle (Le Maréchal De Broglie) n'était absent, il aurait Surement eu L'honneur d'écrire dans cette circonstance à votre excellance pour me Recommander à Ses Bontés. Si, Comme je me plais à n'en pas douter, La décision de L'assemblée Généralle m'est favorable, j'aurai à m'applaudir de La Rigeur de Mr Le Cte De Rochambeau, Puisqu'elle m'aura valu, avec cette Grace, à la qu'elle j'attache Le plus grand prix, un témoignage plus Particulier de L'éstime de L'armée américaine, et de celle de votre Excéllence pour La qu'elle je donnerais ma vie. je Suis, avec une Réspectuéuse Reconnaissance, et une Profonde Vénération; De votre Excellance, Le très humble et très Obeissant Serviteur.

Le chr charles de Lameth. Col. De dragons.

ALS, DSoCi.

Charles-Malo-François, comte Charles de Lameth (1757–1832), was a captain of dragoons in Rochambeau's army when he was severely wounded while storming redoubt no. 9 at Yorktown on 14 Oct. 1781. He was commended by GW (GW to Lameth, 2 Jan. 1782) and promoted to colonel in January 1782. Because only general officers and colonels in the French army were eligible for election to the Society of the Cincinnati and, as Lameth explains here, his wounds forced him to return to France preventing his serving in America after being made colonel, he was asking that an exception be made in his case. Both Rochambeau, on 1 Mar. 1784, and Lafayette, on 9 Mar. 1784, urged that Lameth be elected to the society. A letter from Lameth was read on 6 May at the general meeting of the Society of the Cincinnati in Philadelphia, and on 17 May the general meeting approved Lameth's election. See Winthrop Sargent's Journal, doc. II in General Meeting of the Society of the Cincinnati, 4–18 May 1784, printed below.

To Jean de Neufville

Sir,   Mount Vernon 6th January 1784

I have had the honor to receive your Letter bearing date the 19th of August & find myself exceedingly indebted to your partiality in favor of my Country & myself, both personally, & as a citizen of the United States of America.

The disaster which has happen'd to the House with which you was connected must be very affecting to every true American, especially as your great zeal in the cause of liberty, & your unwearied efforts to promote the interests of the United States, are well known to the Citizens of this republic. I cannot but flatter myself however, that the successes of the new firm of de Neufville & Co. will equal their greatest expectations, & that they will meet with the patronage of all who may be favored with their acquaintance & correspondence.

Notwithstanding the embarrassments of our Finances, I am also of opinion, that justice will ultimately be rendered to all the public Creditors: indeed, it is very much to be regretted that any of our good friends should have suffered from the delay of it—The exigencies have been pressing, & the misfortunes arising therefrom to private individuals, perhaps inevitable; but the happy termination of the war, will I trust, soon afford an opportunity of retreiving the public credit, & enable Congress, & the State of South Carolina, to discharge the Debts which are due to your house.

I have had the pleasure of becoming acquainted with your son, & if it should be in my power to render him any services,[1] it will be extremely agreeable to, Sir Your most Obt hble Servant

G: Washington

LB, DLC:GW.

Jean de Neufville, an Amsterdam merchant with ambitions to act as a financial agent for the American states in Holland, in 1778 entered into a correspondence with the American agent William Lee. To strengthen his hand he also obtained a draft agreement from the city of Amsterdam for a commercial treaty with the United States, which the city soon repudiated and later had reason to regret. De Neufville's efforts probably contributed to Congress's decision in October and November 1779 to seek from the Dutch Republic a loan of ten million dollars and a treaty of commerce. The aspect of de Neufville's involvement in American affairs which eventually led "to the ruin of the Credit of his house" (de Neufville to GW, 19 Aug. 1783) was his dealings in 1780 and 1781 with Commodore Alexander Gillon, the Rotterdam-born agent whom the state of South Carolina sent to Europe to raise £500,000 for the purchase of ships. Upon arriving in Amsterdam from Prussia in December 1779, Gillon arranged to lease a newly built ship and authorized de Neufville to purchase, on credit, the necessary fitting and supplies for the privateer, which was to be renamed the *South Carolina*. Having difficulty raising money to pay de Neufville, Gillon turned for help to John Adams after Adams arrived in Amsterdam at the end of July 1780. Adams authorized de Neufville to float a loan for the United States. When de Neufville opened the loan on 1 Mar. 1781, only a few Dutch bankers were willing to subscribe. De Neufville got in touch with John Laurens in Paris, and Laurens as an agent of Congress agreed to provide Gillon £10,000 from the new French loan to pay for a part of his purchases and to make available up to £5,000 more to be used in getting Gillon's ship ready for sea. William Jackson (1759–1828), serving as Laurens's agent in Amsterdam, permitted de Neufville to spend far more than the £5,000 authorized for additional supplies, which only made matters worse. De Neufville and Gillon having reached a state of mutual distrust, Gillon in July 1781 put to sea in his privateer without endorsing any of the £10,000 in bills to his Dutch creditors, and de Neufville promptly sequestered the South Carolina holdings that Gillon left behind. See Van Winter, *American Finance and Dutch Investment*, 1 : 24–63.

According to the account that John de Neufville & Son had with the United States, dated at Amsterdam, 10 Aug. 1784, Congress had incurred obligations to de Neufville's company of 462,405.11 florins since 29 Dec. 1781, while de Neufville in turn had received in payment since 18 Dec. 1781 a total of 455,853.13 florins, leaving a balance owed to de Neufville of 6,551.18 florins. An account with the state of South Carolina of the same date shows charges incurred by the state through Gillon of 199,303.9.8 florins, none of which had been paid (DNA:PCC, item 78). Congress, "in consideration of particular services rendered the United States, during the war of their revolution, by the late John de Neufville," appropriated in 1797 "the sum of one thousand dollars to Anna de Neufville, widow of the said John de Neufville; a like sum for the use of Leonard de Neufville, his son; and a like sum for the use of Anna de Neufville, his infant daughter" (6 *Stat.* 29 [2 Mar. 1797]).

1. The son, Leonard de Neufville, was later declared insane. GW himself had further dealings with father and son and at one point consulted de Neufville about the possibility of the Dismal Swamp Company's securing a loan of £5,000 in Amsterdam (GW to Jean de Neufville, 8 Sept. 1785). For further information on the younger de Neufville, see the source note, Leonard de Neufville to GW, 29 June 1789.

To Clement Biddle

Dear Sir, Mount Vernon 8th Jan. 1784.
Be so good as to send me by the Post, or any other safe & expeditious conveyance, 70 Yards of livery lace three quarters,

or Inch wide; or any width between—Direct it to the care of the Postmaster in Alexandria. The lace should be red & white.[1]

I will thank you also for sending me, if an oppertunity should offer soon by Water, one hundred weight, or even a Barrel of good Coffee. Pray forwd the Acct between us that I may discharge the Balle if it is against me.[2] My Compliments in which Mrs Washington joins are offered to Mrs Biddle & Mrs Shaw.[3] I am—Dr Sir Yr Most Obedt Servt

Go: Washington

ALS, PHi: Washington-Biddle Correspondence; LB, DLC:GW.

Clement Biddle (1740–1814), Nathanael Greene's commissary general for forage from July 1777 to June 1780, was a Philadelphia merchant whom GW used as his factor, or commercial agent, in that city.

1. GW repeated the order for lace on 17 Jan. and 5 Feb.; on 10 Mar. he reported having received the lace after 1 March.

2. On 10 Mar. GW acknowledged receipt of Biddle's letters of 22 and 29 Feb., both of which are missing. He does not mention having received the account.

3. Rebekah Cornell Biddle was the daughter of Gideon Cornell, lieutenant governor and chief justice of Rhode Island at the time of his death in 1765. Mrs. Shaw was Sarah Biddle Penrose Shaw, Clement Biddle's sister, who was soon to marry her third husband, Rudolph Tillier (see GW to Biddle, 1 Feb. 1785).

From d'Estaing

[8 January 1784]

The Count De Estaing has the Honor to submit to His Excellency Gl Washington the four Memorials which have been sent to him since the last Letters He had the honor to address to him on the 25th of December 1783.[1]

Mr De Choin Colonel of Dragoons

Count De Kergariou Locmaria Captain of the Navy

Count Edwd Dillon, Colonel

Count Castellane Majestres, Captn of the Navy,[2] are [not] the only Gentlemen who solicited Count De Estaing to present their demand.

To participate the honor of this association inflames equally all the French Officers; and the motive for which I solicit in favor of the others are mentioned in the list of General Officers under whom they served.[3]

Translation, DSoCi; ALS, DSoCi. A transcription of the ALS is in CD-ROM:GW.

Charles-Hector, comte d'Estaing (1729–1794), as vice admiral in the French navy and senior naval officer in American waters during the Revolutionary War transported the first contingent of French land forces to Rhode Island in 1778 and participated in 1779 in the siege of Savannah. He supported the Revolution in France after 1789 and died on the gallows during the Reign of Terror.

1. On 25 Dec. 1783, d'Estaing wrote GW two letters, one personal and one official, about the regrettable failure of the Society of the Cincinnati to include in the society the captains in the French navy who had served in American waters while including their counterparts in the French land forces in America, the army colonels. In support of his argument for admitting the ship captains to the society, d'Estaing enclosed in his letters four *Mémoires* containing the names and an account of the service of (1) all the French navy captains who had served in America, (2) all the French navy captains who had served with d'Estaing in America, (3) the six senior naval officers whom d'Estaing considered most deserving of election to the society, and (4) the senior officers from the French land forces who had served with him at the siege of Savannah in 1779. The officers he named as most deserving were Le Bailli de Suffren (Pierre-André de Suffren Saint Tropez; 1729–1788), M. d'Albert de Rions (Charles-Hector, le comte d'Albert de Rions; 1728–1810), M. le chevalier de Borda (Jean-Charles de Borda; 1733–1799), M. le comte de Rumain (Charles-Marie de Trolong, chevalier du Rumain), M. de Bougainville (Louis-Antoine de Bougainville; 1729–1811), and M. le comte de Béthisy (Jules-Jacques-Eléonore de Béthisy; 1748–1816). At its general meeting in Philadelphia in May 1784, the Society of the Cincinnati confirmed that French naval captains were eligible for election to the French Society of the Cincinnati and decreed that the French society should determine the eligibility of its own members. See the letter from the society, 17 May 1784, in Winthrop Sargent's Journal, doc. II in General Meeting of the Society of the Cincinnati, 4–18 May 1784.

2. These are particularly deserving officers whose names d'Estaing is now adding to those he named on 25 Dec. 1783. See note 1. André-Michel-Victor, marquis de Choin (1744–1829), came to Rhode Island in 1778 as d'Estaing's aide-de-camp and took part in the siege of Savannah in 1779 before returning to France. Théobald-René, comte de Kergariou-Locmaria (1739–1795), commanded in American waters in 1778 the *Belle-Poule*, in 1780 the *Junon*, and thereafter the *Sibylle*, aboard which in 1783 he was severely wounded. His brother, the admiral Pierre-Joseph, marquis de Kergariou (b. 1736), also served in America during the Revolution. Edward, le comte Dillon (1750–1840), was one of several Dillons of Irish descent who served in America in the "régiment de Dillon" attached to the French fleet. He embarked for America in March 1779 in time to take part in the capture of Grenada, but he returned to France after breaking his arm and so did not participate in the siege of Savannah with his regiment commanded by his cousin Arthur Dillon (1750–1794). Henri-César, marquis de Castellane-Majastre (1733–1789), commanded the *Marseillais* in de Grasse's fleet at Yorktown in 1781.

3. See note 1. The French text of the last paragraph is: "Le desir de partager l'association enflamme presque également tous Les officiers françois qui
se flattent de pouvoir La'meriter, et les motifs des autres officiers qui sollicitent sont compris dans la précédente Liste, ou dans Les Listes des Généraux
sous lesquels ils ont servi." The letter is signed "Estaing."

From Benjamin Harrison

Richmond [Va.] Jany 8th 1784

I congratulate you my dear sir on your safe return to your
native country and to that domestic ease and happiness you
have so long earnestly wish'd for. Your disinterested virtue and
patriotism have raised you to a height of glory which no human
being can exceed, and stamp'd a value on your character superior if possible to the laurels you have gaind in the field, and the
glorious independence you have establish'd for your country.
That you may long enjoy in health and happiness the plaudits
of an admiring world, and the gratitude of your country, are
wishes too near my Heart to be withheld on the present occasion, altho', from the perfect knowledge I have of you, I should
fear the communication even from a friend might be construed
into flattery, if that friend was not too well known to you, to induce a suspicion of his being capable of such a vice. That you
have placed happiness within our reach is certain, but whether
we shall secure it or not seems to me problimatical; almost every
power in the union from Congress downwards appearing to
have lost sight of the greater objects, and our critical situation,
and to have given themselves over to an indolent security, to
party disputes, or to pursuits unworthy of a great nation. By
what means an alteration of conduct is to be brought about
Heaven alone can tell, or perhaps can bring about by another
friendly interposition. Examples are not wanting of confusions
producing order and happiness to nations, yet the experiment
is too dangerous to be tried, because they are not also wanting
to prove it has sometimes ended in despotism, Slavery, and
every human evil; the latter is much to be dreaded by us, as the
eyes of the world are on us, and tho' we were once the wonder
and envy of all, we are now sinking faster in esteem than we
rose, and without a total alteration of system, shall soon be the
object of their entire contempt which will revive the hopes of
Britain, and cause other nations to entertain thoughts that are

at present far from them; our safety will then alone depend on the rival powers not being able to agree on a division of the spoil. This is an interesting subject, and in a gloomy moment I may have carried it too far, tho' I think I am not altogether without a foundation for my fears, the example of Poland is too recent to be forgotten, or not to create apprehensions, that the same causes may produce the same effects.

A letter from Mr Jefferson dated the 24th of last month tells me that all business in congress is at an end by the going away of one member, and That they had but little hopes of geting nine States together to ratify the treaty in time for the stipulated exchange of it, and that it is to be apprehended if it is not done, that a variety of difficulties will arise before Great Britain can be brought to the same point again, be this as it may, it certainly behoves the States whose members are absent, and have so shamefully neglected their duty, to call them to account, and hold them up to that contempt and resentment they so richly deserve, for running the risk of again involving their country in war, and devastation, for the trifling consideration of a few weeks domestic enjoyments.

I have much more to say to you but this scrawl being already too lengthey, I shall postpone the rest till I have the pleasure of seeing you at mount Vernon, which I intend to do in the first part of the next month,[1] in the meantime I tender you and your good lady the compliments of the season, and am with sentiments of the most perfect esteem Dr Sir your most Obedient and most Humble Servant

Benja. Harrison

ALS, PHi: Sprague Collection.

Benjamin Harrison (c.1726–1791), of Berkeley, Charles City County, Va., was elected in November 1783 to his third and last one-year term as governor of Virginia.

1. Harrison was at Mount Vernon on 20 Mar. 1784. See GW to Henry Knox, 20 Mar. 1784. But see also GW to Thomas Jefferson, 24 Mar. 1784.

From Otho Holland Williams

Sir   Baltimore [Md.] 8th January 1784.

The inclosed Letter to Major Davidson, now one of the Council of this State, authenticates the address I had the honor to present at Annapolis.[1] The County Tyrone has been remarkable for a spirit of patriotism ever since the commenc[e]ment of the American revolution. In 1775, Mr Patterson, a merchant of this Town, tho' born in Ireland, traveled through that County and assures me that such was the admiration the Inhabitants had for the Americans that even common Innkeepers refused to be paid for his fare though they knew no more of him than that he was coming to this Country.[2] I trouble you with this among many anecdotes of the same sort because I think it the truest way of coming at the real Character of the people in general.

The Yankee club in Stewartstown, from what I can collect, is not unlike the old Whigg Club of Baltimore only that they had not perhaps so much cause to trespass against the rules of good Government. I beg the Honor of my best compliments to Mrs Washington and am with the sincerest Esteem and attachment Your most obedient Humble Servant

O. H. Williams

ALS, DLC:GW; LB, DLC:GW.

Otho Holland Williams (1749–1794) grew up in Frederick, Md., and went into business there. He arrived in Boston in 1775 as a lieutenant and left the army at the end of the war a brigadier general, having reached that rank during Nathanael Greene's southern campaign in 1781–82. He now was naval officer for the port of Baltimore, and he remained influential in Maryland politics until his death.

1. On 20 Dec. 1783, writing from Baltimore that he was too ill to go to Annapolis, John Davidson asked Williams to give GW an enclosed address that had just come to him from Philadelphia (MdHi: Otho H. Williams Papers). For the address from the Yankee Club of Stewartstown in Ireland, see GW to John Davidson, 20 Jan. 1784, n.1.

2. William Patterson (1752–1835), of county Donegal, Ireland, settled in Baltimore in 1778 where he soon became a leading merchant and, in 1803, the father-in-law of Jerome Bonaparte.

From Henry Knox

My dear General   West Point [N.Y.] 9th Jany 1784

I wrote you particularly on the 3d instant and enclosed you my report to Congress with the various returns. I have now finished the necessary arrangements for the winter and in a few hours I shall set out for Boston—The public interest has been my actuating principle in the cou[r]se of this business and I flatter myself will meet your approbation. I have found it necessary to direct that a few officers who are inevitably detained should for the present be permitted to draw their rations, as there is not any contract to my knowledge.

I shall hope for the pleasure of receiving a line from you at Boston. I beg you to present my sincere regards to Mrs Washington and I am my dear General Your Affectionate

H. Knox

ADfS, MHi: Knox Papers.

From Thomas Mifflin

Sir   Annapolis [Md.] 9th January 1784
I have the Honor to transmit to you an Act of Congress of the 5th Inst.; relative to a Proposal from the Secretary of the Polish Order of Knights of Divine Providence; containd in your Excellencys Letter of the 28th August last.[1] I have the Honor to be with the greatest Respect Your Excellencys most Obedt humble Servt

Thomas Mifflin

ALS, DLC:GW; LB, DNA:PCC, item 16.

Thomas Mifflin (1744–1800), born a Quaker in Philadelphia, was GW's aide-de-camp briefly in the summer of 1775 before becoming quartermaster general of the Continental army. He was one of the main supporters of the move in 1777 to have Horatio Gates replace GW as commander in chief. Elected president of the Congress on 3 Nov. 1783, he served until 3 June 1784.

1. In his letter of 28 Aug. 1783, GW asked Congress how he should respond to Jean de Heintz's letter to him of 13 May 1783 proposing that Congress select a number of Americans for admission to the Polish "L'ordre Institué en Honeur de la Providence Divine." Both GW's and Heintz's letters as well as a printed list of the members of the order (1778) are in DNA:PCC, item 152. Jean de Heintz is identified in the list as a chevalier of the order, a native of Poland, and a major in the service of the king of Poland. The resolution that Mifflin enclosed, adopted on 5 Jan. and signed by Charles Thomson, secretary of the Congress, reads: "On the report of a Commttee to whom was referred a Letter from the Commander in Chief of 28th August containing a proposal from the Secretary of the Polish Order of Knights of Divine Providence that Congress should nominate a number of suitable persons to be created Knights of the said Order.

"Resolved that the late Commander in Chief be requested to inform the Chevalier Jean de Heintz Secretary of the Order of Divine Providence, that Congress are sensible of the attention of that Order in proposing to them to nominate a number of suitable persons to be created Knights of the Order of Divine Prov⟨idence⟩ but that Congress cannot consistently with the principles of the Confederation accept of their obliging proposal." The resolution is also printed in *JCC*, 26:7.

In 1786, when writing about the opposition to the Society of the Cincinnati in 1783 and 1784, Jefferson reported: "No circumstance indeed brought the consideration of it [the society] expressly before Congress, yet it had sunk deep into their minds. An offer having been made to them on the part of the Polish order of divine providence to receive some of their distinguished citizens into that order, they made that an occasion to declare that these distinctions were contrary to the principles of their confederation" (Jefferson's Observations on Démeunier's Manuscript in Boyd, *Jefferson Papers*, 10:50). Boston's *Independent Chronicle, and the Universal Advertiser*, which led the fight against the Cincinnati in Massachusetts, printed this resolution of 5 Jan. on 1 April 1784.

From Lafayette

My dear General   Paris january the 10th 1784
The departure of the Washington Has Been So Sudden that I Could not get in time on Board the Particular letter which you ought to Have Received—So that My Correspondance Has Been Confined to an official Cincinnati letter, and a Bill of plated wares, which was not By Any means my intention[1]—inclosed I Send you a duplicate of the letter Respecting our Assossiation[2]—Major L'enfant tells me a tolerable Number of Eagles will Be made on thursday,[3] when After Having Called together the American officers Now Here, and Examined their Claims to the Marks of the Institution, We shall in a Body, and with ⟨our⟩ American Regimentals wait Upon Count de Rochambeau, and the Admirals of the french troops, and present them with the Badges they are to wear—You will Receive many Applications On that Subject, and I Need Not telling you old Rochambeau wants to Be as Conspicuous as He Can in that, as You Know He does in Every other Affair[4]—But as Nothing Can Be decided Before the Month of May I will timely write, and I Hope I will myself tell you my opinions in the Several instances that will Be Submitted to You—in Case the Badge is Multiplied, it will loose its price in Europe—and yet, there are some instances who are Entitled to Regard.[5]

By our last Accounts from America, my dear General, We Hear that Newyork is Evacuated, and that our Army, our Virtous and Brave Army Now are disbanded[6]—its dissolution, However Expected and proper it is, Has not Been Heard of By me Without a Sigh—How Happy I Have Been at the Head quarters of that Army! How Affectionately Received in Every tent I Had a Mind to Visit! My Most fortunate days Have Been Spent With that Army—and Now that it is ⟨no⟩ more, my Heart shall Ever Reverence and Cherish its Memory—God Grant our Brother officers May Be treated as they deserve! Will not the Country Remember what Evils that Army Have guarded Her Against, What Blessings they Have insured to them? I am told there is a peace Establishement of 800 Men—and My dear general Now is at Mount Vernon where He Enjoys those titles Every Heart Gives Him, As the Saviour of His Country, the Benefactor of Mankind, the Protecting Angel of liberty, the pride of America, and the Admiration of the two Hemispheres—and Among all those Enjoyements I know He Will Most tenderly feel the pleasure of Embracing His Best His Bosom friend, His Adopted Son, who Early in the Spring Will Be Blessed With a direct Course to the Beloved landing that leads to the House at Mount Vernon.

There are no Great News in France, But it is Not the Case in England Whose people Seem as it Were distracted—Pitt's party Have for the Moment Got in place, But the Majority in the Commons are So much Against them that it is Impossible for them to Remain in the Ministry—it is probable we will In a few days See Mr Fox and Lord North Restored to their former power, when they will Undo Every thing the others Have Done[7]—M[ess]rs Jay, Adams, and Laurens are Either at London or Bath, Mr Barklay is in England, and our old friend Doctor Franklin is Confined to His House By the Gravel[8]—Under those Circumstances I thought it My duty not to Neglect the Affairs of America—But as I Have no Instructions, Nor Any public Authority, I Can only Advise and influence Such Preparatory Measures, as I thing May Be Agreable to the United States—Some time Ago I presented a Memorial, Which, together With Some letters from the Ministers I Have on the 26th of last Month Enclosed to Mr Moriss[9]—in Consequence of those, and of Several Conferences I Had with the Ministers, they Have determined to put a final Hand to the Affair of L'Orient, which I Had long Ago taken Upon Myself to Begin, and which Wanted a definitive Conclusion—By a letter of this day to Mr Moriss I Send Him some further Parts of a Correspondance With the Ministry, Wherein it is officially Announced that Dunkirk, L'Orient, Bayonne, and Marseilles are the four free ports Given to the trade of America[10]—this Evening I Return to Versailles, where there is to Be a Conference Betwen the foreign affairs, Naval, and finances Ministers and Myself—As I Am little Acquainted With those Matters, I Consult upon them with Wadsworth[11]—in all this America Neither promises Nor Asks for Any thing, So that she Cannot Be Committed—and Her Ministers Being either Sick or Abroad, do not, *Betwen Us*, So much as to Mention an earnest Word of the Mercantile interest of America in France. European Affairs are about the Same as when I wrote You last—There is No probability of an impending War—at least for Next Year—The Emperor is in Italy as a traveller—Unless I Am Honoured With Some Particular Commands from Congress, I intend embarking for America Early in the Spring, and I Hope to Arrive in time for the Grand Cincinnati Meeting—Mde de Lafayette, Your Son George, and my daughters join in the Most Respectfull Compliments to You, and Mrs Washington[12]—I Give Her joy upon Your Peacefull Retirement into Private life—I Beg, My dear general, You will Remember me to George, Mead, Mr and Mrs Lund Washington, to all your friends and Relations[13]—Adieu, My dear general, Your Most Respectfull and affec⟨*mutilated*⟩ friend

Lafayette

ALS, PEL. The editor has adopted the reading of Lafayette's capricious capitalization that appears in Idzerda, *Lafayette Papers*, 5: 191–93.

Marie-Joseph-Paul-Yves-Roch-Gilbert du Motier, marquis de Lafayette (1757–1834), who left America for France in December 1781, did not land in New York on his return visit until August 1784.

1. The packet boat *Washington* arrived in Le Havre from New York on 8 Dec. 1783 with L'Enfant (see note 3) aboard. L'Enfant had two letters from GW for Lafayette, one dated 20 Oct. 1783 dealing with the Society of the Cincinnati and one dated 30 Oct. 1783 asking Lafayette to buy a large number of silver items, including trays, a coffeepot and a teapot, an urn, goblets, and candlesticks. Enclosed in GW's letter of 20 Oct. 1783 was a copy of the Institution of the Society of the Cincinnati. In Lafayette's response to GW on 25 Dec. 1783, he reported that the king had indicated he would allow Rochambeau's generals and colonels as well as the French admirals to wear the insignia of the Society of the Cincinnati. Lafayette promised to supervise the admission to the society of the men in Europe who, like himself, had served for at least three years as officers in the Continental army. For GW's unsuccessful effort

to withdraw his order for plate, see GW to Lafayette, 4 Dec. 1783 and 1 Feb. and 4 April 1784.

2. This is Lafayette's letter of 25 Dec. 1783. See note 1.

3. Pierre-Charles L'Enfant (1754–1825) was trained in Paris by his father, Pierre L'Enfant, who was a painter. Upon his arrival in America early in 1777, Congress made him a lieutenant in the corps of engineers. L'Enfant remained with GW's army until he went south in 1779 to participate in the siege of Savannah. After being wounded in the siege, he went to Charleston, South Carolina. He was captured there in 1780 and remained a prisoner of the British until January 1782. In May 1783 Congress promoted L'Enfant to brevet major in the engineers. GW on 16 Oct. 1783 gave L'Enfant permission to return to France to attend to his personal affairs. As president of the Society of the Cincinnati, GW commissioned L'Enfant to oversee while in France the making of the society's order, or badge, which L'Enfant designed in the shape of an eagle. After consulting with L'Enfant, Henry Knox on 29 Oct. 1783 wrote to GW: "In addition to the *medal*, which was finally determined to be *silver*, instead of *gold*, it was resolved that there should be a *diploma*, which, with the *silver medal* should be given to each member. The bald eagle of gold, *The Order* of the Society to be procured at the private expence of each member.

"*The diploma* and *silver medal* to be given at the expence of the Society. . . . Major L'Enfant has it in charge to get the *diploma* engraved, and the Die for the *medals* executed in the most masterly manner. He also will get *the order* for the subscribers" (DSoCi). On 30 Oct. GW instructed L'Enfant to have eight eagles made for him. For reference to the diamond eagle presented to GW, see d'Estaing to GW, 26 Feb. 1784.

4. In addition to the letter to Lafayette about the Society of the Cincinnati (see note 1), GW sent by L'Enfant a letter to Rochambeau, dated 29 Oct. 1783. Jean-Baptiste-Donatien de Vimeur, comte de Rochambeau (1725–1807), was commander of the French army that reached Rhode Island on 11 July 1780. A little over a year later, he and his army joined forces with GW for the siege at Yorktown, which culminated in the surrender of Lord Cornwallis on 19 Oct. 1781.

5. Lafayette was saying that nothing could be decided about disputed eligibility for election to the Society of the Cincinnati until the general meeting of the society in Philadelphia in May. For the decision reached at the meeting with respect to admitting French naval officers to membership in the society, see d'Estaing to GW, 8 Jan. 1784, n.1.

6. See Commissioners of Embarkation at New York to GW, 18 Jan. 1784, and Henry Knox to GW, 3 Jan. 1784, and notes.

7. William Pitt the Younger (1759–1806) succeeded Charles James Fox and Lord North after they were dismissed on 17 Dec. 1783. Pitt remained prime minister from the general election in 1784 until 1801.

8. John Jay (1745–1829), John Adams (1735–1826), and Henry Laurens (1724–1792), along with Benjamin Franklin (1706–1790), were the United States commissioners who negotiated the treaty of peace with Britain signed 3 Sept. 1783. Jay and Laurens were in England in January 1784, but Adams

had sailed on 5 Dec. 1783 from Harwich for Holland. Thomas Barclay (1728–1793), a Philadelphia merchant, was the United States consul general in France. Franklin lived at the hôtel de Valentinois at Passy; gravel was a sort of kidney or bladder infection or kidney stones.

9. Lafayette's letter to Robert Morris, 26 Dec. 1783, enclosing Lafayette's "Observations on Commerce between France and the United States" as well as letters from Calonne (Charles-Alexandre de Calonne; 1734–1802), 25 Dec. 1783, and Vergennes (Charles Gravier, comte de Vergennes; 1717–1787), 29 June 1783, are all printed in Idzerda, *Lafayette Papers*, vol. 5.

10. Lafayette enclosed in his letter to Robert Morris, 10 Jan. 1784, a letter from Calonne, the French comptroller general of finances, in which Calonne wrote that he was "authorized to notify you that it is His Majesty's intention to grant the United States the ports of Lorient and Bayonne as open and free ports in addition to those of Dunkirk and Marseilles." Calonne went on to say that he had "given orders to the Farmers General to offer preferential treatment and reasonable prices in purchasing tobacco from North America, and in addition the United States will be as favored in their trade in France as any other nation" (ibid., 189–90).

11. Jeremiah Wadsworth (1743–1804), who had been a sea captain and merchant in Connecticut before the war, acted as commissary to Rochambeau's army and in 1783 went to Paris to settle his accounts. He was there at this time.

12. The members of Lafayette's immediate family included Marie-Adrienne-François de Noailles, marquise de Lafayette (1759–1807), who was called Adrienne; Anastasie-Louise-Pauline (1777–1863), called Anastasie; George-Washington-Louis-Gilbert (1779–1849); and Marie-Antoinette-Virginie (1782–1849), called Virginie.

13. George Augustine Washington (c.1758–1793) was the son of Charles Washington, GW's brother, and of Mildred Thornton Washington. Lund Washington, GW's cousin, managed GW's estate during the war. As for "Mead," Lafayette may have been referring to GW's former aide-de-camp, Richard Kidder Meade (1746–1805), who, according to his son, received upon leaving GW's service these words of admonition: "Friend Dick, you must go to a plantation in Virginia; you will make a good farmer and an honest foreman of the grand jury of the County where you live" (Meade, *Churches of Virginia*, 1:295). Before the war, Meade lived in Prince George County, Va.; after the war, he settled on a plantation in Frederick County, Virginia.

To Robert Morris

Dear Sir,   Mount Vernon 10th January 1784
     I will thank you for putting the letter herewith enclosed into a proper channel of conveyance. The Count de Bruhl is informed by it that my Portrait (which I have begged the Count de Solms to accept) will be forwarded to his care by you, so soon

as it is finished, & I request the favor of you to do it accordingly. Mr Wright is desir'd to hand it to you for this purpose. & as he is said to be a little lazy, you would oblige me by stimulating him to the completion.[1] By promise, it was to have been done in five or six weeks from the time I left Philadelphia, near four of which are expired. I am sorry to give you trouble about trifles, but I know you will excuse it, in this instance. With sentiments of high esteem & regard I am Dr Sir Your most obt & affte servt

G: Washington

LB, DLC:GW.

1. See GW to Brühl, 3 Jan., GW to Solms, 3 Jan., and GW to Joseph Wright, 10 Jan. 1784.

From Henry Pendleton

Dear Sir   Charleston [S.C.] January 10th 1784

I take the Liberty of Introducing to you Mr Shuttleworth a Gentleman of very ancient Family and Large fortune in England who arrived here in his own Yacht about two months since and proposed to make a kind of maritime tour thro' America by sailing coastways and up the principal rivers as far as the Water will suffer his vessel to go; His Family in Yorkshire & Lancashire has several members in Parliament, all of whom have uniformly reprobated and opposed the Conduct of the English Ministers in the prosecution of the American War, and venerate the band of American patriots who have triumped over their flagitious designs, he is very desirous to pay his respects to the man who stands at the head of these, to whom he thinks England is nearly as much indebted for the preservation of her Liberties as America the loss of the Latter by Military Subjugation necessaryly producing that of the former by Ministerial power & Corruption. I have taken the Liberty to announce him, as he will sail up Potowmack by Mount Vernon as far as Alexandria.[1]

Amid the General Joy and Congratulations which every where meet you from an Empire, almost entirely owing its Political existence to your Courage and Virtues, I beg leave to add my own, and to wish you every happiness of which human Nature is Capable. I request the honor of my most respectfull

Complts to Mrs Washington, & to be permitted to assure you that I am with every Sentiment of Respect & Esteem Yr Mo. Obedt and Most Hble Servt

Hy Pendleton

ALS, PHi: Gratz Collection; Sprague transcript, DLC:GW.

Henry Pendleton, who died in 1788, was elected one of the South Carolina state judges in 1776. Chastellux on 30 Nov. 1780 had this to say about him: "Mr. Pendleton, a judge from South Carolina, a remarkably tall man, with a very distinguished countenance; he had the courage to hang three Tories at Charleston, a few days before the surrender of the town, and was accordingly in great danger of losing his life, had he not escaped out of the hands of the English, though included in the capitulation" (Chastellux, *Travels in North America*, 1 : 131). Pendleton was one of the few South Carolina leaders who in 1788 opposed the ratification of the federal Constitution. He was the nephew of GW's friend Edmund Pendleton of Virginia.

1. For the identity of Robert Shuttleworth, see Charles Cotesworth Pinckney to GW, 14 Jan. 1784, and note 1.

To Joseph Wright

Sir,   Mount Vernon 10th Jan. 1784

When you have finished my Portrait, which is intended for the Count de Solms, I will thank you for handing it to Mr Robert Morris, who will forward it to the Count de Bruhl (Minister from his Electoral Highness of Saxe at the Court of London) as the Channel pointed out for the conveyance of it.[1]

As the Count de Solms proposes to honor it with a place in his collection of Military Characters, I am perswaded you will not be deficient in point of execution. Be so good as to forward the cost of it to me, & I will remit you the money.[2] Let it (after Mr Morris has seen it) be carefully packed to prevent injury. With great esteem—I am Sir, Yr Most Obedt Servant

Go: Washington

ALS, PHi: Dreer Collection; LB, DLC:GW.

Joseph Wright (1756–1793) went in the early 1770s from New Jersey with his mother Patience Lovell Wright to live in London. Mrs. Wright became a secret agent for America during the war; her son studied with the painter Benjamin West and established a reputation as a portrait painter. In 1782 Joseph Wright went to Paris under the patronage of Benjamin Franklin and then sailed from Nantes to America. He remained in his native country, living in New York or Philadelphia, until his death from yellow fever in 1793. By tradition Wright's portrait of GW (see frontispiece) belonged to Francis

Hopkinson, signer of the Declaration of Independence, in whose family it descended until 9 Nov. 1891 when Oliver Hopkinson donated it to the Historical Society of Pennsylvania. Washington himself commissioned a copy (now unlocated) for the Graf zu Solms und Tecklenburg. Samuel Powel commissioned a copy which also is now in the Historical Society of Pennsylvania, and Thomas Jefferson commissioned still another copy to take with him to France in 1784. Wright painted only the head and outline of the body in Jefferson's copy (now in the Massachusetts Historical Society), and the work was finished in Paris by the artist John Trumbull. Jefferson wrote that he had "no hesitation in pronouncing Wright's drawing to be a better likeness of the General than Peale's" (Jefferson to Barré, 11 July 1785, in Boyd, *Jefferson Papers*, 8:281–82). The exact dates of Washington's sittings for the portrait are not known. See the references in note 1.

1. See GW to Brühl and GW to Solms, both 3 Jan. 1784. See also GW to Robert Morris, 10 Jan. 1784, Morris to GW, 14 Feb. 1784, and Wright to GW, 1 Sept. 1784, 30 Jan. 1785.

2. On 15 May 1784, in Philadelphia, GW paid Wright £18 "for Drawing my Picture for Ct DeSolm 40 Drs" (Ledger B, 199), even though the comte de Brühl had agreed to pay for it (Brühl to GW, 4 Sept. 1783).

From Elias Boudinot

Eliz[abe]th Town [N.J.]

My very Dear Sir   Jany 11th 1784

We have recovered the most sensible pleasure on the News of your safe return to Mount Vernon and your anxious family at it is with the Warmest affection & attachment, that rejoice the United Voice of your Country, in Congratulating your & our Mrs Washington on this happy & interesting Event—You must permit me sir—tho' it may be lost a midst the public Testimonies on this occasion from a thousand more important Sources[1] to add my individual, tho' most sincere & affectionate Wishes for your happiness & prosperity; for it would be doing violence to my feelings, while again enjoying the sweets of Domestic Life on my little Estate here rescued from the Hands of a Powerful Enemy after a seven year expulsion,[2] to perswade myself to be silent, however trifling the Tribute, or refrain from grateful acknowledging those invaluable & laborious services by which I am thus reinstated in the most essential and important Comforts of rational Life—I need not add the sense of obligation I feel myself under for the many kind marks of personal attention & confidence expressed towards me during the War, and I shall ever esteem it one of the greatest Honors on

my life that I have served my Country in conjunction with &
under the Direction of Genl Washington—You have our most
ardent Prayers to almighty God for your happiness & prosperity in this Enjoyment of the fruits of your own Labour and
of every domestic Bliss; and that after a long Period of extensive usefulness here, you may be prepared for & receive the
glorious reward of eternal Life in the World to come. Mrs B. &
Miss S., whose health is rather declining, join me in every respectful & Effectionate Wish, and beg to be very particularly remembered by Mrs Washington.[3] I have the Honor to be with
every sentiment of Esteem Dr Sir &c.

                                                      E. Boudinot

LB, NjP: Thorne-Boudinot Collection.

Elias Boudinot (1740–1821), president of Congress from November 1782
to November 1783, was married to Hannah Stockton (1736–1808). Her
brother, Richard Stockton, was married to Annis Boudinot, Elias Boudinot's
sister and GW's friend and great admirer.

1. Boudinot wrote "stources."

2. Before GW received this letter, Martha Washington wrote Hannah
Boudinot on 15 Jan., thanking her for her "polite and affectionate congrat-
ulatory Letter on the termination of our troubles, and the return of the General to domestic life," and offering Mrs. Boudinot her "compliments on your
restoration to your own House, after an exile of seven years" (owned by
Creighton Hart, Kansas City, Mo.).

3. "Miss S." is probably Boudinot's daughter Susanne Vergereau. See GW
to Boudinot, 18 February.

Letter not found: from James Nourse, 11 Jan. 1784. On 22 Jan. GW
wrote to Nourse: "Yesterday gave me the honor of your favor of the
11th."

From Simeon DeWitt

Sir   New Windsor [N.Y.] January 12th 1784
    I have enclosed to Your Excellency a Copy of a Letter to the
President of Congress containing such proposals respecting the
publication of Maps from the Surveys we have made during
the War As I thought would be the least objectionable—I wish
some Additions could be made to them, but as the Expence
which would attend them was probably the reason why my first
proposals were not accepted I have now made them otherwise.[1]
If any other mode practacable with me could be suggested I
would with pleasure adopt it.

I thought it necessary to give this information to clear myself in Your Excellency's Opinion if the Country loose the satisfaction of seeing our works published.[2] I am with the Greatest esteem Sir Your Excellency's Most Obedient Humble servant

S: DeWitt

ALS, DLC:GW.

Simeon DeWitt (1756–1834) became in 1778 an assistant to Robert Erskine, geographer and surveyor general to the Continental army. Following Erskine's death on 2 Oct. 1780, Congress on 4 Dec. named DeWitt "geographer to the army, in the room of Robert Erskine, deceased" (*JCC*, 18:1118), and on 16 Dec. GW informed DeWitt of his appointment as "Surveyor of the Army." Congress resolved on 11 July 1781 that the titles of both DeWitt and Thomas Hutchins, who was made geographer to the southern army on 4 May 1781, would be changed to "*Geographer to the United States of America*" (ibid., 20:738). After the war, on 13 May 1784, DeWitt replaced Gen. Philip Schuyler as surveyor general for the state of New York, a position he held until his death. He was one of the most important mapmakers in the early Republic.

1. After receiving a letter from DeWitt dated 4 June 1783, Jonathan Trumbull, Jr., talked to GW on behalf of DeWitt, "to obtain permission for publishing a Map of the Seat of War in America" (Trumbull to DeWitt, 8 June 1783). Trumbull on 8 June assured DeWitt of GW's strong support for the project. DeWitt wrote Elias Boudinot, president of Congress, on 17 June 1783, proposing that he use the surveys he had made for the army and make some additional ones for drawing a map of the region within "the Meridians of Philadelphia and Stanford in Connecticut And the Parallels of Philadelphia and Fishkills." Such a map, he said, would include the main actions of the war and yet be of manageable size. If allowed to hire two surveying assistants, he proposed to have his drawings of the maps ready for the engravers by winter (DNA:PCC, item 78). On 20 Oct. 1783, a committee headed by Hugh Williamson reported to Congress: "That though a map of the principal theatre of war in the middle states from actual surveys on a large scale is much desired, such a work cannot in prudence be undertaken at the public expence in the present reduced state of our finances" (*JCC*, 25:711). The text of DeWitt's letter to Thomas Mifflin of this date, which he enclosed in this letter to GW, is: "When His Excellency General Washington was the last time at West Point I requested a discharge from him in case the Public should not stand in need of any farther services from me, which I was inclined to Judge since I had not any hopes that Congress would accede to the proposals I made last summer respecting the publication of a Map from the surveys in my possession of the principal seat of the late war. He answered that the nature of my office being such as that Congress might possibly still have Occasion for my services he did not think himself Authorised to grant the discharge I requested but advised me to make a final Application to know if my proposals would be agreed to or my continuance in Office be any longer Necessary.

"If the expence of bringing my maps to a farther degree of perfection by additional surveys be Judged to be needless, I have this proposal to make. I will undertake to compleat in the best manner I can from the materials I have as much as shall be conveniently contained in one Plate and publish it at my own risque, provided I can be furnished with Cash from the Continental Treasury sufficient for the purpose on account of the pay now due to me from the United States. Probably a Thousand Dollars would be sufficient. I make this stipulation with the greater assurance as I have not had the indulgence extended to me by which Others of the Army Who like myself were not patronized by any particular State have recieved on the settlement of their Depreciation Accounts considerable proportions of the Balances due them. From the impressions of one Plate I shall be able to Judge whether it shall afterwards answer to undertake any more. At present it will be a precarious business on Account of the quantity of spurious productions which can be manufactured with such ease in Europe and are imposed on the ignorant here.

"If a New State is to be laid off adjoining Pensylvania and Virginia as has been expected I have hopes that from the parity of the Office I now hold and that of a surveyor general to such a State Congress will be inclined to transfer me to that Department, especially if it be allowable to suppose them influenced by a predelection in favour of their old servants who have done their duty with reputation under all the difficulties with which the American Army had to encounter, and Who have lost permanent places of employment by being engaged in a military Life—I would be willing to undertake the Surveying in a New State either under the denominat. of the Office of Geographer as I now possess it or simply with the emoluments of a Surveyor to the State if fixed in a permanent manner, for the two Offices so far from being incompatible would rather be assistant to each other.

"I must now Request Your Excellency to lay this before Congress and beg they may take the proposal I have made as well as my Application respecting the Surveyorship of a New state into consideration . . ." (DLC:GW). The ALS is in DNA:PCC, item 78. DeWitt's request for discharge is dated 16 Nov. 1783, and GW's response is dated 17 Nov. 1783.

2. GW wrote DeWitt on 3 Mar. 1784 heartily endorsing the project, and on the same day he wrote Thomas Jefferson in Congress commending both DeWitt and DeWitt's proposal. Jefferson replied on 6 Mar. that DeWitt's petition was being considered by a committee of which he was a member (see note 1).

From James Milligan

Sir   Comptrollers Office Philada 13th January 1784
I have the Honour, and the singular pleasure of transmitting, inclosed to your Excellency, copies of your Accots for family expences, Secret Services, and other Contingencies, commencing in June 1775 and ending Decemr 8th 1783, as officially Stated at the Treasury, By which it appears that a balance of Seven hundred and twenty Seven dollars & 7/10 of a dol-

lar Specie, is due by the United States to your Excellency on this Account.[1] For this Sum I have transmitted my Certificate to the Superintendant of Finance, who has assured me that he will direct payment of the Same to be made without delay.

You will be pleased Sir, to observe, that in the Account marked D, you are debited with Fifty Guineas paid to Doctor William Smith for his Bill of Exchange upon you, which Bill was transmitted you, as appears by the Superintendants letter to your Excellency, dated Decemr 26th 1782, to which, with Doctor Smiths letter accompanying it, I beg leave to refer. This Sum, Mr Morris informs me, was a Donation made by your Excellency to Washington College in Maryland. The manner of its having been paid, without going through your hands, and the Great attention you always gave to the more important duties of your high Station, Sufficiently Account for its escaping your notice at the time the Accounts were made up, but I doubt not, you will, upon this explanation, consider it as a proper charge.[2] Notwithstanding this debit, it is no unpleasing circumstance to me that I can inform your Excellency that the balance now Stated, still exceeds that Struck by yourself, by a fraction of $37/90$ths of a dollar. This is owing to your having on the other hand, omitted to charge Interest on Five hundred and Ninety one $31/90$ths dollars (paid by Colo. Baylor & Colo. Cary to Major Gibbs) from the 1st December 1776 to 1st July 1783, Which I am of opinion you are entitled to, as it appears you were that Sum in advance on the said 1st of Decemr over and above the Sum for which you had charged Interest.[3]

This being carried to your Credit, over balances the charge of Fifty Guineas, by the fraction mentioned.

As all Accounts, when liquidated, are regularly entered in the Treasury Books, and the original papers carefully filed, it is not customary or deemed necessary, for Accountants to receive any official papers, unless a Warrant for the balance, if any due; But your Excellency having in your Accounts, clearly displayed that degree of Candor and Truth, and that attention you have constantly paid to every denomination of Civil Establishments, which invariably distinguish all your actions, I could not resist the inclination I felt, of transmitting you these papers, in hopes that it may prove a matter of some Satisfaction to you.[4]

If it has this effect in the smallest degree, it will give me great pleasure. Sorry I am Sir, that I have not been able to do it so soon as I proposed; This unavoidable delay, I hope your Excellencys goodness will pardon.

As soon as you can favour me with your Account of Expences incurred after the termination of this, it shall be Expedited with all possible dispatch.[5]

To the universal congratulations of your applauding Country, and of an Admiring World, Suffer me Sir, to embrace this opportunity of offering to add the mite of a Sincere Individual, on the Great events that have taken place under your Auspicious Command. That Heaven may protect and preserve you long in happiness here, and at last Reward such Virtues as this World cannot, is the fervent prayer of Sir your Excellencys Most obt and Very Humble Servant

Jas Milligan Comptr of the Treasury

LS, DLC:GW.

James Milligan (d. 1818) was comptroller for Congress from the creation of the office at the time Congress reorganized the treasury for Robert Morris in 1781 until the office was abolished in 1787.

1. In his address to the Continental Congress, 16 June 1775, accepting command of the American army, GW wrote: "I do not wish to make any proffit from it: I will keep an exact Account of my expences; those I doubt not they will be discharged & that is all I desire" (*Papers, Revolutionary War Series*, 1:1–3). GW's own account of his expenses for the war until 1 July 1783 is in DNA: RG 56, General Records—Treasury Department. There is also a copy of the accounts, in GW's hand, in DLC:GW. The treasury's account of GW's receipts and expenditures from June 1775 to 8 Dec. 1783 (DLC:GW) that Milligan enclosed in this letter runs to twenty-four pages. For the correspondence leading to the adjustment of this account and its final settlement, see particularly Robert Morris to GW, 14 Feb., GW to Milligan, 18 Feb., Milligan to GW, 9 Mar., and GW to Milligan, 1 April 1784.

2. On 8 July 1782 William Smith (1727–1803) wrote GW that the Maryland legislature had renamed the Kent County School at Chestertown, of which he was rector, Washington College. In response, GW wrote on 18 Aug. 1782: "If the trifling sum of Fifty Guineas will be considered as an earnest of my wishes for the prosperity of this Seminary, I shall be ready to pay it to the order of the Visitors whenever it is their pleasure to call for it." On 23 Dec. 1782 Smith informed GW that he had drawn on Robert Morris in GW's name for "fifty Guineas" in order to buy "an Elegant Air-Pump & some optical Instruments" for the new college. Morris then wrote on 26 Dec. 1782: "I do myself the Honor to enclose to you a Bill of Exchange for fifty Guineas drawn by Doctor Smith upon yourself together with a Letter which I presume advises of it. Conceiving that a small Remittance might not be useless to your [military] Family I have indorsed it accordingly and of Course it will be chargable in the Public Books to your Household" (DLC:GW). There is this notation for

the entry in the account that Milligan enclosed here: "Amount of a Warrant drawn 4th December 1782 by the S. I. of Finance in favour of James McCall Esqr. for 50 Guineas, which Sum does not appear Credited in the Generals Account & being paid to Doctor Smith." GW readily conceded the correctness of the charge and apologized for having overlooked it (GW to Milligan, 18 Feb. 1784).

3. Richard Cary and George Baylor, both Virginians, were aides-de-camp to GW early in the war, Cary beginning 21 June 1776 and Baylor from 15 Aug. 1775 to 9 Jan. 1777. Caleb Gibbs of Massachusetts was a commander of GW's guards from 12 Mar. 1776 to 1 July 1781. During these years Gibbs handled the payment of GW's military household accounts. In his public accounts, June 1775–1 July 1783 (see note 1), GW has an entry dated December 1776 in which he enters 725½ dollars or £217.13 for "Household Expenses paid by Majrs Cary and Baylor in Octr & part of Novr while Captn Gibbs was absent with the Baggage." In explaining how he happened to overlook the interest upon the 591³¹/₉₀ dollars, GW wrote Milligan on 18 Feb.: "As the principal was rescued from error, & brought into a subsequent accot, I never thought about interest." One of Milligan's treasury accounts with GW, which he enclosed in this letter, credited GW with £45.13 from Baylor on 26 Nov. 1776 and £126 from Cary on 21 Nov. 1776, a total of £171.13 or 591³¹/₁₀ dollars, undoubtedly the principal "rescued from error," i.e. £217.13 or 725½ dollars.

From June 1775 to 1 Jan. 1777, GW himself bore a considerable part of his expenses, about 15 percent, for his military household. When he submitted his accounts for settlement on 1 July 1783, he entered £599.19.11 as the balance due him at the end of 1776, to which he appended the explanation: "This Balle arises from the Expenditures of my private purse—From which . . . my outfit to take the Command of the Army at Cambridge—The Expences of the Journey thither—and disbursements for some time afterwards were borne—It being money which I brought to, and recd at Philadelphia while there as a Delegate to Congress, in May & June 1775." In another entry, 1 July 1783, GW claimed interest on this amount that he was out of pocket: "To Interest of £599.19.11 being the Balle due me Decr 31st 1776—The amount having been applied to Public uses in the preceeding year—from whence to wit July 1st 1775 I charge Intt at 6 pr Ct pr Ann.— 288." Milligan's account with GW has an entry marked "Balance of Account Commencing June 1775 and Ending Decemr 1776 as ℔ Account herewith marked A," which allows GW's claims in dollars rather than pounds: 1,999-⟨³⁷/₉₀⟩ dollars, principal, and 959.89 dollars, interest.

4. The following item, from Boston, dated 5 Feb., appeared in the *Pennsylvania Gazette* on 25 Feb. 1784: "*Extract of a letter from Philadelphia, Jan. 8.* 'As every anecdote respecting great men is important, I will tell you one about General WASHINGTON.—While in town he delivered in his accounts to the Comptroller, in a book. It comprehends a period of 8 years, *all in his own hand writing*,—and every entry made in the most particular manner, stating the occasion of each charge, so as to give as little trouble as possible in examining them. In this you see he has been as exemplary as in every other part of his conduct. . . . '"

5. See GW to Robert Morris, 4 Jan. 1784, and note 1, and Milligan to GW, 9 Mar., n.3.

To Edward Hand

Dear Sir,   Mount Vernon Jany 14th 1784
    When I left Philadelphia I hoped to have had the pleasure of seeing you at Annapolis before my departure from thence, and to have had an oppertunity (previous to my resignation) of expressing to you personally, amongst the last acts of my Official Life, my entire approbation of your public conduct, particularly in the execution of the important duties of Adjutant General.
    Notwithstanding I have been disappointed in that expectation, & have it now in my power—only as a private character—to make known my sentiments & feelings respecting my Military friends; yet I cannot decline making use of the first occasion after my retirement of informing you, My dear Sir, how much reason I have had to be satisfied with the great Zeal, attention, and ability manifested by you in conducting the business of your Department; and how happy I should be in oppertunities of demonstrating my sincere regard & esteem for you; It is unnecessary I hope to add with what pleasure I should see you at this place—being with great truth My dear Sir, Yr real friend & most Obedt Servt

                                    Go: Washington

ALS, PHi: Dreer Collection; LB, DLC:GW.
    Edward Hand (1744–1802) was adjutant general of the Continental army from 8 Jan. 1781 to 3 Nov. 1783, after having served either in the Pennsylvania forces or in the Continental army beginning 25 June 1775.

To David Humphreys

My dear Humphrys   Mount Vernon 14th Jan. 1784
    I have been favored with your letter of the 6th—Be assured that there are few things which would give me more pleasure than opportunities of evincing to you the sincerity of my friendship, & disposition to render you services at any time when it may be in my power.
    Although all recommendations from me to Congress must now be considered as coming from a private character, yet I en-

ter very chearfully into your views; and as far as my suggesting of them to that Honble Body, accompanied by my testimonial of your competency to the execution of the duties of either of the Offices in contemplation will go you have them freely, & the enclosed letter, which is a copy of the one I have written to Congress on the occasion will be an evidence of my good wishes whatever may be the success.[1]

I cannot take my leave of you without offering those acknowledgements of your long & zealous Services to the public which your merits justly entitle you to & a grateful heart should not withhold—and I feel very sensibly the obligations I am personally under to you for the Aid I have derived from your abilities for the chearful assistance you have afforded me upon many interesting occasions, and for the attachment which you have always manifested towards me. I shall hold in pleasing remembrance the friendship & intimacy which has subsisted between us and shall neglect no opportunity on my part to cultivate & improve them, being with unfeigned esteem & regard Dr Sir Yr Most Affecte friend & obedt Servt

Go: Washington

ALS, Jagellion University, Poland; LB, DLC:GW.
1. See GW to Thomas Mifflin, this date (second letter).

To Thomas Mifflin

Sir,   Mount Vernon 14th Jany 1784
I have had the pleasure to receive your Letter of the 28th ulto by Mr Godin, & beg your Excelly to be persuaded, that I shall always be happy in opportunities of shewing every suitable attention to foreigners, & Gentn of such distinction, as those you do me the honor to introduce to my acquaintance.[1]

I am truly sensible Sir, that the Extract from the instructions of the Executive of Pennsylvania to their Delegates contains another most flattering proof of the favourable opinion they are pleased to entertain of my past services—Every repeated mark of the approbation of my fellow citizens (especially of those invested with so dignified an appointment) demands my particular acknowledgments. Under this impression I cannot but feel the greatest obligations to the supreme executive Council of the Commonwealth of Pennsylvania: But as my sentiments on the subject of their instructions, have been long & well known to the public, I need not repeat them to your Excellency on the present occasion.[2] I have therefore only to add that Mrs Washington joins me in presenting our best compliments to Mrs Mifflin, & that I have the honor to be, &a &ca.

G: Washington

LB, DLC:GW.

1. Mifflin wrote GW on 28 Dec. 1783: "This Letter will be presented to your Excellency by Mr Godin, Relation of Mr Van Berkel; who is on his Journey to South Carolina, with Mr Backer & Mr Barrow" (DLC:GW). Pieter Johan van Berckel (1725–1800) was minister from the Netherlands to the United States from 1783 to 1788.

2. In his letter of 28 Dec. 1783, Mifflin reported that "General Hand arrived here [New York] on Thursday and brought with him Instructions to the Delegates of Pennsylvania in Congress, from the Executive of that State—I have copied the first Part of the Instructions, which relate to your Excellency: & now enclose them" (DLC:GW). The copy that Mifflin enclosed to GW (DLC:GW) and the "Extract from the Instructions of the Supreme Executive Council of the State of Pennsylvania to their Delegates in Congress," dated 16 Dec. 1783 and signed by Thomas Mifflin, John Montgomery, and Edward Hand (DNA:PCC, item 19), are virtually identical. The extract reads: "Tho his Excelly Genl Washington proposes in a short time to retire, yet his Illustrious Actions & Virtues render his Character so Splendid & Venerable, that it is highly probable the Admiration & Esteem of the World may make his life in a very Considerable degree public. as numbers will be desirous of seeing the great & Good Man who has so eminently Contributed to the happiness of a Nation—his very services to his Country may therefore Subject him to expences, unless he permits her gratitude to interpose.

"We are perfectly Acquainted with the disinterestedness and generosity of his Soul, he thinks himself amply *rewarded* for all his labors and Cares by the love and Prosperity of his fellow citizens 'Tis true no rewards they can bestow can be equal to his Merits, but they ought not to suffer those merits to be burthensome to him—We are convinced the People of Pennsylvania would regret such a consequence.

"We are aware of the delicacy, with which this Subject must be treated: but relying upon the good sense of Congress, we wish it may engage their early attention."

To Thomas Mifflin

Sir,   Mount Vernon 14th Jany 1784

The goodness of Congress, in the assurances they were pleased to give me of charging themselves with the interests of those confidential Officers who have attended me to the resignation of my public Employments; and the request of your Excellency to Colonel Humphrys (after I had been honored with my public audience) that, if any thing should occur to him in consequence of what had just been suggested, that he would communicate it to you in a letter; induce me to take the liberty of bringing the wishes of that Officer before Congress.[1]

Having devoted the last Seven or Eight years to the Service of his Country, he is desirous of continuing in the walk of public life, although he is ignorant—as I also am—of the Offices which Congress have to bestow and may think him competent to—Two things however, seem likely to occur: either of which I am perswaded he would fill with as much advantage to the public as reputation to himself. The one is a Regiment; in case a Continental peace Establishment should be resolved on: The other, official Secretary to an Embassy abroad, if new appointments should be made, or a vacancy happen in the old ones.

There is a third thing which I barely hint at, with all possible deference, and with a diffidence which proceeds more from a doubt of the propriety of my suggesting it, than from any question which arises in my Mind of his competency to the duties; and that is Secretary of Foreign Affairs, if Congress should think it expedient to make another appointment; and should find all those requisites in him which are necessary to constitute a Minister for that department[2]—For his ability, integrity, punctuality, and sobriety I can fully answer.

If I have gone too far, Congress will please to excuse it; and attribute the error to my wishes to serve a worthy character. With great respect I have the honor to be Sir, Yr Excellys most Obedt & Hble Servant

Go: Washington

ALS, DNA:PCC, item 152; LB, DLC:GW. Endorsed "rec'd 29 Jany."

1. See David Humphreys to GW, 6 Jan. 1784.

2. For Jacob Read's query about Humphreys' qualifications for appointment as under secretary, see his letter to GW, 1 Feb. 1784.

From Charles Cotesworth Pinckney

Dear General,   Charleston [S.C.] Jany 14. 1784

The many favours I have received from you, emboldens me to take the Liberty to introduce to you Mr Shuttleworth an English Gentleman of Family & Fortune. I remember his Character at Westminster & Oxford, and it was in every respect amiable—He is visiting the Sea ports of America on a party of pleasure in a Vessell of his own, manned & fitted out at his private expence. He is Brother in Law to Mr Charles Turner who distinguished himself in the British House of Commons by his constant & strenuous opposition to the British measures in America. He is also Son in Law to General Desaguliers an Artillery Officer of considerable Merit. He is attended in his Voyage by the Revd Mr Perry (a Clergyman of reputation, whose amiable Character I also remember at Oxford,) & by his Physician.[1] They are anxious before they leave America to see your Excellency, the Admira—but I will not wound your Excellency's Feelings, by repeating to you those plaudits, which are the pleasing Theme not only of all your Countrymen but of all the World. I am convinced the most agreeable attention I can possibly shew these Gentlemen will be to give them an opportunity of delivering this Letter to your Excellency,[2] and if your Excellency will excuse the Liberty I take in doing so, you will add to the many obligations you have already conferred on Your Excellency's Most obliged & most humble Servt

Charles Cotesworth Pinckney

ALS, PHi: Gratz Collection.

Col. Charles Cotesworth Pinckney (1745–1825) of South Carolina joined GW's forces in the late summer of 1777. Before the end of the year he returned to his regiment in South Carolina where he took part in the southern campaigns during the next two years. By 1784 Pinckney had resumed his practice of law and other business activities in Charleston in addition to managing his plantations.

1. Pinckney accompanied his family to England in 1753, and upon his parents' return to South Carolina in 1758 he remained behind to continue his schooling for eleven years. He matriculated at Christ Church, Oxford, on 19 Jan. 1764, from Westminster School. Robert Shuttleworth (d. 1816), son of James Shuttleworth (1714–1773) of Gawthorpe, matriculated at Christ Church about two years before Pinckney. Sir Charles Turner, who was married to Robert Shuttleworth's sister Mary, was a member of Parliament for York City from 1768 to 1783. The Rev. Mr. Perry is probably Littleton Perry (c.1746–1816) who entered Magdalen College at Oxford in 1765, but he may be instead Thomas Perry, one of the three Perry brothers from Barbados who were at Oxford in the late 1750s and early 1760s. The father of Robert Shuttleworth's wife Ann, Lt. Gen. Thomas Desaguliers (c.1725–1780), colonel commandant of the royal regiment of artillery at Woolwich Arsenal from 1762 until his death, was a pioneer in the making of modern cannons.

2. Henry Pendleton also gave Shuttleworth a letter of introduction, dated 10 Jan. 1784.

To Samuel Vaughan

Sir,   Mo[un]t Vernon 14th Jany 1784

The torpid state into which the severity of the season has thrown things—the interruption of the post, occasioned by bad roads, and frozen rivers—& a want of other conveyance consequent thereof, must plead my excuse for not thanking you sooner for the polite attention you were pleased to shew me, while I was in Philada, & for the friendly offers you obligingly made me, before I left that city—But though my acknowledgements of them come late, I pray you to be persuaded that they are not less sincere, nor are they less gratefully offered on that account.

Colo. Humphreys (one of my late Aid de Camp's) who accompanied me to Virginia, & is now on his return home, will do me the favor of presenting this letter to you, & of handing Mr Higgins's observations on Cements, which you were pleased to lend me, & from which I have extracted such parts as I mean to carry into practice.[1]

I found my new room, towards the completion of which you kindly offered your house-joiner, so far advanced in the wooden part of it—the Doors, Windows & floors being done, as to render it unnecessary to remove your workman with his Tools (the distance being great) to finish the other parts;[2] especially as I incline to do it in s[t]ucco, (which, if I understood you right, is the present taste in England), & more especially as you may find occasion for him in the execution of your own purposes as the Spring advances. And now my good sir, as I have touched upon the business of stuccoing, permit me to ask you if the rooms with which it is encrusted are painted, generally; or are they left of the natural colour which is given by the cement made according to Mr Higgins's mode of preparing it? And also, whether the rooms thus finished are stuccoed below the surbase (chair high) or from thence upwards only? These are trifling questions to trouble you with, but I am sure you will have goodness enough to excuse, & answer them. Please to make a tender of my best respects to Mrs Vaughan & the rest of the family, & accept the compliments of the season from Mrs W——n & myself who join in expression of the pleasure we shou'd feel in seeing you under our roof. I am &a

                          G: Washington

LB, DLC:GW.

Samuel Vaughan (1720–1802), a supporter of the American cause during the Revolutionary War, came with his family to Philadelphia in 1783 from London where he had been engaged in the colonial trade.

1. David Humphreys wrote to GW on 6 Jan., perhaps before he left Mount Vernon. GW wrote Humphreys on this day, 14 Jan., but he did not refer to his letter to Vaughan as being enclosed. This and the notations on his letter to Bushrod Washington of 15 Jan. and to Clement Biddle of 17 Jan. (which see) suggest that GW arranged before Humphreys left Mount Vernon in early January to send his letters for Philadelphians to Humphreys for delivery. Benjamin Higgins's *Experiments and Observations on Cements* (London, 1780) was in GW's library at his death.

2. The "New Room" at the north end of the house was begun shortly before the Revolution after GW hired Going Lanphier (1727–1813) to extend the house at both ends. The library with a bedroom above it on the south end was completed after GW went to take command of the army in Boston, but as he indicates here, the interior of the two-story banquet (or new) room was still unfinished (*Diaries*, 3:246, 4:114–15).

From Dulau d'Allemans

Monsieur   a paris ce 15 janvier 1784

L'armée americaine vient de donner aux troupes francoises, qui ont eu L'honneur de Luy etre associée sous vos ordrès, une marque flateuse de bienveillance et d'estime. C'est a vous Comme a notre Commun général que nous devons temoigner notre reconnoissance, Le regiment d'agénois dont Javois L'honneur detre Colonel en Second pendant Le siege d'yorck y sera particulierement sensible, Ce regiment a été asses heureux pour s'y trouver sous vos ordrès et Cooperer a cette glorieuse expédition, moy seul ai été privé de cet avantage employé ailleurs pour Le service du roy, j'etais pendant Ce temps embarqué pour joindre Mon regiment a votre armée: contrarie par les vents, Jetté a La Martinique, cette occassion precieuse m'echapa, mes regrets furent dautant plus vifs que Je perdais Celle de servir sous Les ordres dun grand homme, et L'espoir den être connu personnellement. Je me plaindrois cependant moins de La fortune si je puis obtenir de Votre excellence une marque destime que Jaurois Jespere merité sans le contre temps.

Comme Colonel du regiment Dagénois, J'aurois été honoré de Lordre de Cincinnatus. mon absence forcée, ne permet pas a Monsieur Le Comte de rochambeau de my associer sans Votre aveu. Jose Madresser a votre excellence avec confiance, pour obtenir Cette grace, et vous prier de vouloir bien observer que Je ne dois pas être excepté de cette distinction accordée a mes Confreres Colonels, parce que dabord mon devoir, et ensuites des Contretemps malheureux mont retenu Loin de Mon regiment.

Je prie donc votre excellence de vouloir bien me faire Le mêmê honneur qu'aux autres Colonels, et m'accorder La marque de fraternité Militaire, qui Les associe, aux braves officiers qui sous vos ordrès ont sauvé Leurs patrie, mon zele, et mes regrets, sont mes droits, ils apuyent ceux que Les services de mon regiment doivent vous paroitre me donner cette grace que J'attens, et que je demande avec confiance pourra seule me consoler de navoir pas été asses heureux pour navoir pas besoin de La demander. J'ay L'honneur Detre avec respect De Votre excellence Le très humble et très obeissent serviteur

> Le vicomte Dulau D'allemans
> colonel du regiment de saintonge ⟨infanteri⟩.

Monsieur Le chevalier de La Luzerne qui vous remmetra Ma Lettre Voudra bien vous interesser a ma démande, vous en representer La Justice, et me transmettre Votre réponse, et si vous voules bien me Le faire accorder Le diplome de Lordre de Cincinnatus.[1]

ALS, PHi: Gratz Collection.

Pierre-Marie, vicomte Dulau d'Allemans (1752–1816), the second colonel of the régiment d'Agenois, was on his way to join his regiment at the time the regiment was fighting under GW at the siege at Yorktown in October 1781. His plea that GW advise Rochambeau to admit him to the Society of the Cincinnati was not successful.

1. Instead of translating this letter as he did many of those written to GW in French, David Stuart gave GW its gist in an undated letter, c.April 1784, printed below.

To William Hamilton

Sir,   Mount Vernon 15th Jan. 1784.

If I recollect right, I heard you say when I had the pleasure of seeing you in Philadelphia, that you were about a Floor composed of a Cement which was to answer the purpose of Flagstones or Tiles, and that you proposed to variegate the colour of the squares in the manner of the former.

As I have a long open Gallery in Front of my House to which I want to give a Stone, or some other kind of Floor which will stand the weather; I would thank you for information respecting the Success of your experiment—with such directions and observations (if you think the method will answer) as would enable me to execute my purpose. If any of the component parts are scarce & expensive, please to note it, & where they are to be obtained—& whether all seasons will do for the admixture of the Composition.[1]

I will make no apology for the liberty I take by this request, as I persuade myself you will not think it much trouble to comply with it. I am Sir Yr most obedt Hble Servt

Go: Washington

ALS, PWacD: Sol Feinstone Collection, on deposit PPAmP; LB, DLC:GW.

William Hamilton (1745–1813), of Woodlands, an estate near Philadelphia, was a noted horticulturalist with whom GW became friendly when he was in Philadelphia in 1774.

1. GW had extensive correspondence about the flooring for the gallery across the front of his house. See particularly GW to Clement Biddle, 17 Jan., 10 Mar. 1784; William Hamilton to GW, 20 Feb. 1784; GW to William Hamilton, 6 April 1784; GW to John Rumney, Jr., 3 July 1784, 22 June 1785, 18 Nov. 1785, 15 May 1786, 5 June 1786; John Rumney, Jr., to GW, 8 Sept. 1784, 9 Feb. 1785, 3 July 1785, 5 Sept. 1785, 16 April 1786; and Robinson, Sanderson, & Rumney to GW, 28 Jan. 1786.

Letter not found: from Richard Varick, 15 Jan. 1784. On 22 Feb. GW wrote to Varick: "The intemperate Season and irregularity of the Post, withheld your letter of the 15th Ulto from me 'till within these few days."

To Bushrod Washington

Dear Bushrod,   Mount Vernon Jany 15th 1784

I have received your letter of the 22d Ulto—the former one, accompanying my Trunks, also came safe.[1]

When I came to examine the Chimney pieces in this House, I found them so interwoven with the other parts of the Work and so good of their kind, as to induce me to lay aside all thoughts of taking any of them down—for the only room which remains unfinished I am not yet fixed in my own mind but believe I shall place a Marble one there. at any rate I shall suspend the purchase of any of those mentioned in your letter, & would not wish Mr Roberts to hold either of them in expectation of it.[2]

My best wishes attend you in which your Aunt joins—My Complimts to Mr & Mrs Powell.[3] With much truth & Affection I am Yrs

Go: Washington

ALS, PHi: Dreer Collection. GW wrote on the cover, "Favored by Colo. Humphreys."

Bushrod Washington (1762–1829) was the son of GW's brother John Augustine Washington. With GW's financial support and on his recommendation he had begun the study of law under James Wilson in Philadelphia. Later in this year Bushrod went with GW on his western trip. A United States Supreme Court justice at the time of GW's death, this nephew was heir to GW's papers and, at Martha Washington's death, to Mount Vernon.

1. Neither of these letters has been found.

2. Samuel Vaughan wrote GW on 5 Feb. that he was ordering a marble chimneypiece for GW's New Room, which later arrived and was installed in 1785. See GW to Vaughan, 8 April 1784. Mr. Roberts has not been identified.

3. Samuel and Elizabeth Willing Powel of Philadelphia were friends of GW.

Letter not found: from Charles Washington, 15 Jan. 1784. On 28 Feb. GW wrote Charles Washington: "Your Letter dated the 15th of January . . . came to my hands last Night." The letter may have been misdated.

To Clement Biddle

Dear Sir,   Mount Vernon 17th Jany 1784

On the 8th I wrote to you for 70 Yards of livery lace (red & white, ¾ or Inch wide, or any width between) to be sent by the Post; or any other safe & expeditious conveyance. Lest that letter should have miscarried I repeat my request, as I am in immediate want of the article. I did, at the sametime desire that one hundd weight, or a Barrl of good Coffee might be sent me by the first Vessel bound for the Port of Alexandria.

I pray you now, my good Sir, to send me as soon as a conveyance offers, four brass wired Sieves, of the common size in the rim, but exactly one eighth, one sixteenth, and one thirtieth of an Inch in the Mcshes—the fourth to be finer than the last mentioned—I want these to prepare materials to compose a Cement of which I propose to make some experiments—exactness therefore in the different sizes is required of the maker of them.[1]

I have seen rooms with gilded borders; made I believe, of Papier Maché fastned on with Brads or Cement round the Doors & window Casings, surbase &ca; and which gives a plain blew, or green paper a rich & handsome look—Is there any to be had in Philadelpa?—and at what price?—Is there any plain blew & green Paper to be had also?—the price (by the yd & width).[2] With great regard—I am Dr Sir Yr Most Obedt Servt

Go: Washington

ALS, PHi: Washington-Biddle Correspondence; LB, DLC:GW. GW noted on the cover, "favored by Colo. Humphrys."

1. For references to GW's plans for paving his gallery, see GW to William Hamilton, 15 Jan. 1784, n.1.

2. This is all concerned with the completion of the New Room at the north end of the house. See GW to Samuel Vaughan, 14 Jan., and GW to Biddle, 10 Mar. 1784.

From Commissioners of Embarkation at New York

Sir,   New York 18th January 1784

The british Troops being wholly withdrawn from this Place, it only remains to the closing the Business under your Excellency's Commission to us of the 8th of May Ulti.—that we should report our Proceedings.[1]

We presume it will be needless to recapitulate our former Communications, and therefore take the Liberty of referring to our Letters to your Excellency of the 30th of May, 14th and 18th of June last with their respective Inclosures.[2]

As Sir Guy Carleton did not, except in one or two instances, answer our Representations, we forbore to make further Representation. We interpreted his silence into a determination that all future application from us should remain equally unnoticed, and therefore presumed that they [would] be not only fruitless but also derogatory to the dignity of the Sovereignty by whose authority we were commissionated.

From our first arrival in this City hitherto we have whenever we were formally requested by the British Commissioners assisted them in superintending Embarkations. These Embarkations were always made in Vessels in the Pay and Service of the

Crown of Great Britain, and the superintendance consisted in visiting the Ships after they were laden and ready for sailing, and taking an account of the Negroes which the Captain informed us were on board, and which were also produced to us. The Captains were then asked whether they had any other american Property on board, they all answered in the Negative, and this was received as Evidence, without further Scrutiny, or Examination—A descriptive List of Negroes your Excellency will receive with this[3]—This List as to the names of the Negroes and places of residence of their masters is formed from the declarations of the Negroes themselves made to the british Commissioners in our presence.

We conceive it requisite to inform your Excellency that Sir Guy Carleton retained and exercised the authority of entering and clearing out Merchant Vessels, at this Port, which were never submitted to any Inspection, and Consequently it is impossible for us to determine for a certainty the number of Negroes or the Amount of other Property belonging to the Citizens of the United States which were carried away in those Vessels, neither do we know that any Measures were used by the british Government to ascertain these points—Sir Guy Carleton effected to distinguish between the Cases of such Negroes as came within the British Lines in Consequence of the Promises of Freedom, and Indemnity held out in the Proclamations of his predecessors, and such as came in, either previous to the Proclamations or subsequent to the Cessation of Hostilities. Negroes of the first Description he supposed not included in the Treaty, as the public Faith had prior to the Treaty been pledged to them for their Security against the Claims of their former Masters. Admitting this distinction to be just, We would mention a Circumstance to your Excellency which we suppose no otherwise material than to shew that Sir Guy Carleton, or at least that his subordinate Officers did not intend to observe the Treaty even agreeable to their own limited construction of it.

Whenever the Negroes at an Inspection of an Embarkation were examined, they always, except in a very few Instances, produced a printed Certificate from the Commandant of the City countersigned by his Secretary, purporting that they came within the british Lines in consequence of the Proclamations issued by Sir Henry Clinton and others. We were sensible as there was no mode prescribed for investigating these matters, that it was impossible the Commandant, or his Secretary could in every case have sufficient Proof of the time of the Negroes coming in, and therefore concluded there must be an abuse. In this we were not deceived, for it appears that Certificates with Blanks were given by the Commandant to Individuals to be filled up as their Convenience might require—One of these Blank Certificates have fallen into our Hands, and we transmit it to your Excellency.[4]

Sir Guy Carleton during the whole of the time from our arrival in this City until his departure on the 25th of November exercised the same kind of Jurisdiction in this City, and on Long Island and Staten Island, and as fully as his Predecessors in Command had at any Period of the War, and in the Exercise of this Jurisdiction he retained the Regulation of the Commerce of this Port, continued to Lease and receive the Rents of a number of Houses in this City which had been previously taken, and the Rents appropriated by the british Government here as belonging to persons residing without their Lines, and by them therefore declared as being in Rebellion, he refused, except in a very few Instances to restore Persons, who were desirous of returning to their former Habitations, the possession of their Estates, and caused several Citizens of the United States to be apprehended and tried by Courts Martial.[5] A Considerable Embarkation of Negroes took place the Day this City was evacuated—The hurry of business on the part of the Britons is the ostensible reason why we were not invited to the Inspection, as appears by a Letter from Captain Gilfillan.* We have the Honor to be, Your Excellency's Most Obedient Humble servants

Egbt Benson
W.S. Smith
Danl Parker

*Mr Gilfillan's letter to Col. Smith of 19th Feby 1784.[6]

Copy, MHi-A: William Stephens Smith Miscellany; LB, DNA: RG 59, Domestic Letters; copy, P.R.O., F.O., 116/1, ff. 54–58; LB, DNA: RG 59, Miscellaneous Duplicate Consular and Diplomatic Dispatches; LB, DNA: RG 46, entry 33; LB, DNA: RG 59, Reports of the Secretary of State to the President and Congress; copy, DLC: Jefferson Papers. Although dated 18 Jan. 1784 the report of the commissioners of embarkation could not have been written in the form that appears here (as well as in all of the other surviving copies) until after commissioner William Stephens Smith had received from London Thomas Gilfillan's letter dated 19 Feb. 1784 (see note 6). GW himself informed Charles Thomson on 5 April 1785 that he had received the commissioners' report "in the latter part of last Spring." The original report has not been found.

The three commissioners were all living in New York State when GW appointed them in 1783. Egbert Benson (1746–1833), a New York lawyer, was attorney general of the state from 1777 to 1787. Lt. Col. William Stephens Smith (1755–1816), also a New York lawyer, was an aide-de-camp to GW at the time of the Yorktown campaign. In 1786, as secretary to the United States legation at London, Smith met and married John and Abigail Adams's daughter, Abigail Adams. Daniel Parker, originally a merchant in Watertown, Mass., was a very active contractor for the Continental army and a trader with extensive interests not only in New York and New England but overseas as well. Parker and Company was already in serious difficulties when GW made Parker a commissioner of the embarkation in May 1783; before the end of 1784 Parker had fled to Europe to escape his creditors.

Guy Carleton, the new commander in chief of the British army in America, arrived in New York on 5 May 1782 with instructions to begin the withdrawal of British forces from the United States. Nearly a year later, on 14 April 1783, after learning that the preliminary articles of the treaty of peace had been signed in Europe, Carleton wrote Robert R. Livingston, secretary of foreign affairs, asking that Congress "empower any person or persons . . . to be present at New York, and to assist such persons as shall be appointed by me, to inspect and superintend all Embarkations which the Evacuation" of the city should require (DNA:PCC, item 78). The next day Livingston sent GW a copy of Carleton's letter along with a resolution of Congress: "That the Commander in Chief be, and he is hereby instructed to make the proper arrangements with the Commander in Chief of the British forces . . . for obtaining the delivery of all negroes and other property of the inhabitants of the United States in the possession of British forces" or of other British subjects (*JCC*, 24:242–43). GW met with Carleton on 6 May at Orange Town, N.Y. (see Substance of a Conference between General Washington and Sir Guy Carleton in Fitzpatrick, *Writings of Washington*, 26:402–6), and two days later he appointed Parker, Benson, and Smith commissioners to oversee the embarkation of the British at New York. Their instructions were "to attend particularly to the due execution of that part of the Article of the Provisional Treaty where it is agreed His Britannic Majesty shall withdraw his Armies &c. from The United States 'without causing any destruction or carrying away any Negroes or other property of the American Inhabitants.'" The United States commissioners went into the city on 10 May, and the three of them met with General Carleton on 15 May. On 22 May Carleton's adjutant general, Oliver Delancey, issued orders to the board created "to superintend all Embarkations" at New York, which was composed of the three Americans appointed by GW and four British officers (Capt. Richard Armstrong, Capt. Thomas Gilfillan, Maj. Nathaniel Phillips, and Capt. Wilbur Cook) appointed by Carleton, to meet at "Fraunces's Tavern every Wednesday at ten OClock" to hear "any Person claiming property embarked, or to be embarked." The board's instructions provided that "should any Doubts arise in Examination[,] the circumstances of the case" were "to be minuted down" for use in settling future claims. Furthermore, three of the commissioners were to examine every transport before it put to sea (MHi-A: William Stephens Smith Miscellany). By the end of May 1783 the American commissioners were fully aware of how limited a role they were to be allowed to play in preventing the removal of American property. On 23 June 1783, when he forwarded to Elias Boudinot, president of Congress, copies of reports from the commissioners dated 30 May and 14 and 18 June and copies of his correspondence with Sir Guy Carleton, GW expressed his doubts that "there will be much advantage in continuing our Commissioners any longer at New York" and raised the question "whether it would not be eligible to revoke the Commission." Benson, Smith, and Parker, however, continued to meet with their British counterparts (see note 3) until the final evacuation of the city on 25 Nov. 1783.

1. Sir Guy Carleton withdrew with his forces to Staten Island, completing his evacuation of New York City on 25 Nov.; and the last of the British transports and warships put to sea shortly after 4 Dec. 1784. It may be that it took several months after 18 Jan. 1784 to complete the report "closing the Business" because of the time required to compile the lists of the blacks who were taken away by the British. See the headnote and note 3.

2. These communications from the three commissioners are reports on their dealings with Sir Guy Carleton and the British commissioners of embarkation in which they discuss how severely limited their authority was. There are copies of the three letters in most of the repositories and collections where copies of this letter of 18 Jan. 1784 may be found, but the original letters to GW have survived and are in DLC:GW.

3. Copies of the individual inspection rolls made at New York by the British and American commissioners of the blacks who were transported from the city by sea between 23 April and 30 Nov. 1783 are in DNA:PCC, Miscellaneous Papers: Papers Relating to Specific States (ff. 21, 25, 26, 29, 30, 44, 47, and 52); other copies of these rolls are in the Guy Carleton Papers (photocopies), ViWC. The copies in DNA:PCC are probably copies of the ones that the commissioners enclosed in this report to GW dated 18 Jan. 1784. John Jay sent a clerk to Mount Vernon in September 1785 to make a copy of these rolls (see Jacob Read to GW, 9 Mar. 1785, n.2). In DNA:PCC there are ten separate rolls listing the blacks who were embarking from New York. The rolls indicate that between 23 April and 30 Nov. 1783 the commissioners made twenty-nine inspections of blacks boarding transports at New York. One or more of the commissioners appointed by GW signed each of the rolls except: (1) the roll for the six inspections made between 23 and 27 April 1783 before GW appointed the United States commissioners; this was signed by two of General Carleton's deputy quartermaster generals, Thomas Gilfillan and William Armstrong, and witnessed at General Carleton's request by the Americans Daniel Parker and David Hopkins (see Carleton to GW, 12 May 1783, DNA:PCC, item 52); (2) the roll of 25 June signed by the British commissioners of embarkation Wilbur Cook and Armstrong and the board's sec-

retary Samuel Jones; and (3) the roll of 30 Nov. 1783, which Gilfillan and Armstrong compiled after the evacuation of the city on 25 Nov. and which Gilfillan sent from London on 19 Feb. 1784 to the American commissioner William Stephens Smith. In the roll for the inspections of 5, 6, 8, and 13 Sept., it was noted that three blacks had been "returned to the owner"; but as the American commissioners reported to GW on 30 May and 14 June 1783 (see note 2), and as Sir Guy Carleton intended it should be, the board of commissioners for monitoring the embarkation of the blacks and Loyalists at New York largely confined themselves to questioning the departing blacks and recording what they said about themselves and their status. The columns in each roll have these headings: "Vessels Names and the Commanders," "Where bound," "Negroes Names," "Age," "Description," "Claimant's Names, Places of Residences," "Names of the Persons in whose Possession they now are," and "Remarks." Only rarely are names of claimants given. Under "Remarks," there is usually a statement about the black's place of origin, his or her past and present status, and how long he or she had been within British lines. According to the totals attested to in each of the rolls by the commissioners who signed, the commissioners listed and described in the ten rolls a grand total of 1,388 black men, 955 women, and 652 children who left New York by sea between 23 April and 30 Nov. 1783. The totals that Thomas Gilfillan gives in the last roll, dated 30 Nov. 1783, for the period from 26 April to 30 Nov. 1783 differ from these, but his grand total of 3,000 is very close. Three of these 2,995 blacks were identified as formerly belonging to GW: Daniel Payne, 22 years old, an "ordinary fellow" in the possession of Maurice Salt, who said he left GW "abt 4 years ago"; Deborah Squash, 20, wife of Harvey Squash, 22, both in possession of "Mr Lynch," who confessed she "came off [from GW] about 5 years ago"; and Harvey Washington, 43, a "fine fellow" who testified that he had left GW seven years before.

4. The copy of this letter of 18 Jan. 1784 in the Public Record Office (listed above in the source line) is followed by the clerk's copy of one of the "Blank Certificates," dated 23 April 1783, citing the proclamations of both "Sir William Howe and Sir Henry Clinton late Commanders in Chief in America."

5. Sir Guy Carleton made it clear as early as 6 May when he met with GW at Orange Town, N.Y., that according to his reading of the provisional articles of the peace treaty he was under no obligation to restore property to Americans, only to refrain thenceforth from either destroying it or carrying it away. It was on this basis that the three United States commissioners were restricted only to examining those blacks who were on the point of embarking so that American citizens in the future could make claims against the British crown if they had been wrongfully deprived of their slave property.

6. The British commissioner of embarkation Thomas Gilfillan wrote the American commissioner William Stephens Smith from London on 19 Feb. 1784: "My last Letter to you was from Simmersons Ferry Statten Island, Date 3d Decemr last, informing you of the Inspection made by Captain [William] Armstrong, and myself, of the Negroes on Board sundry Vessels then at Anchor near Statten Island, In which I gave you my reasons for not being able to transmit to you a Register of them previous to the time of my sailing for En-

gland, However since my arrival here, have got regular Registers made of them, & according to promise, a Copy of which I have herewith Inclosed, and in order to make it a Pacqet of moderate size, have caused it to be made on a smaller Paper, than that which we used at New York for that purpose, but upon the same Principle, with respect to the age, Description, &c. of the Negroes" (DNA:PCC, item 78). He concluded by explaining the meaning of the various initials in the roll of blacks dated 30 Nov. 1783. For the significance of this letter in setting the date on which GW received the letter of 18 Jan. 1784, see headnote. For references to the roll of blacks, 30 Nov. 1783, see note 3.

To Benjamin Harrison

My Dear Sir,   Mount Vernon 18th Jany 1784
    I have just had the pleasure to receive your letter of the 8th— for the friendly & affectionate terms in which you have welcomed my return to this Country & to private life; & for the favourable light in which you are pleased to consider, & express your sense of my past services, you have my warmest & most grateful acknowledgments.

    That the prospect before us is, as you justly observe, fair, none can deny; but what use we shall make of it, is exceedingly problematical; not but that I believe, all things will come right at last; but like a young heir, come a little prematurely to a large inheritance, we shall wanton and run riot until we have brought our reputation to the brink of ruin, & then like him shall have to labor with the current of opinion when *compelled* perhaps, to do what prudence & common policy pointed out as plain as any problem in Euclid, in the first instance.

    The disinclination of the individual States to yield competent powers to Congress for the Fœderal Government—their unreasonable jealousy of that body & of one another—& the disposition which seems to pervade each, of being all-wise & all-powerful within itself, will, if there is not a change in the system, be our downfal as a Nation. This is as clear to me as the A, B.C.; & I think we have opposed Great Britain, & have arrived at the present state of peace & independency, to very little purpose, if we cannot conquer our own prejudices. The powers of Europe begin to see this, & our newly acquired friends the British, are already & professedly acting upon this ground; & wisely too, if we are determined to persevere in our folly. They know that individual opposition to their measures is futile, & *boast* that we are not sufficiently united as a Nation to give a general one! Is not the indignity alone, of this declaration, while we are in the very act of peace-making & conciliation, sufficient to stimulate us to vest more extensive & adequate powers in the sovereign of these United States? For my own part, altho' I am returned to, & am now mingled with the class of private citizens, & like them must suffer all the evils of a Tyranny, or of too great an extension of fœderal powers; I have no fears arising from this source; in my mind, but I have many, & powerful ones indeed which predict the worst consequences from a half starved, limping Government, that appears to be always moving upon crutches, & tottering at every step. Men, chosen as the Delegates in Congress are, cannot officially be dangerous—they depend upon the breath—nay, they are so much the creatures of the people, under the present Constitution, that they can have no views (which could possibly be carried into execution), nor any interests, distinct from those of their constituents. My political creed therefore is, to be wise in the choice of Delegates—support them like Gentlemen while they are our representatives—give them competent powers for all fœderal purposes—support them in the due exercise thereof—& lastly, to compel them to close attendance in Congress during their delegation. These things under the present mode for, & termination of elections, aided by annual instead of constant Sessions, would, or I am exceedingly mistaken, make us one of the most wealthy, happy, respectable & powerful Nations, that ever inhabited the terrestrial Globe—without them, we shall in my opinion soon be every thing which is the direct reverse of them.

I shall look for you, in the first part of next month, with such other friends as may incline to accompany you, with great pleasure, being with best respects to Mrs Harrison,[1] in which Mrs Washington joins me, Dear Sir, Your Most Obedt & affecte hble servant

G: Washington

LB, DLC:GW.

1. Mrs. Harrison was Elizabeth Bassett Harrison (1730–1792), daughter of William Bassett (1709–c.1743), of Eltham, and sister of Burwell Bassett (1734–1793), the widower of Martha Washington's sister Anna Maria Dandridge Bassett.

To Thomas Mifflin

Sir   Mount Vernon Janry 19th 1784

In a Letter which I did myself the honor to write to your Excellency, on the 21st of Decr, amongst other matters which were submitted to the consideration of Congress, I mentioned the case of Brigr Genl Michael Jackson, and informed you that having mislaid the papers relative to it, I could only state the facts from my recollection—having now found the original documents I take the liberty to enclose them to Congress, and to submit the case to their decision.[1]

In the beforementioned communication, I believe I also omitted to include Capt. Houdin, (a french Gentleman who has served many years with reputation in the Masstts Line) amongst the Officers who were desirous of being arranged on any Peace Establishment that might be adopted—in that case, I beg leave to mention him as a deserving Officer, and to place him on the same footing with the other Candidates.[2] With great respect I have the honor to be Your Excellencys Most Obedt Servant

Go: Washington

LS, in David Humphreys' hand, DNA:PCC, item 152; LB, DLC:GW.

1. Michael Jackson (d. 1801), colonel of the 3d Massachusetts Regiment and brevet brigadier general, sent GW a memorial dated 18 Nov. 1783 "to lay before Congress" (Jackson to GW, 19 Nov. 1783, DNA:PCC, item 152). The memorial in part reads: "That your Memorialist began the war at the action of Lexington, on the nineteenth of April, 1775, and has continued in the Service of this Country ever since, in the Cause of which he has been in a number of severe actions; particularly one on the 24th of September, 1776 [at Montresor's Island, N.Y.], in which he received a wound; The pain which he has endured in consequence thereof, is beyond expression—more than thirty peices of bone have been extracted from him" (DNA:PCC, item 41). The doctors' certificate signed by John Cochran, D. Townsend, and Sam Adams confirmed that Jackson could "never expect to have the free use" of his leg again (26 Oct. 1783, DNA:PCC, item 41). GW's letter of 21 Dec. 1783 summarized all of this and reported that he had told Jackson that Congress was not likely to make provision for him alone but, instead, would do so in a general way when it provided for those similarly disabled from war wounds.

2. In his letter to Mifflin of 21 Dec. 1783, GW enclosed a list of sixteen officers who wished "to be on Peace Establishment" of the army, noting that "most of the Gentlemen whose names are on the list are personally known to me as some of the best officers who were in the Army." Michael Gabriel Houdin (d. 1802), who was a major by brevet, had been an officer in the Massachusetts forces since 1 Jan. 1777.

From Rochambeau

Dear Sir,   Paris 19th January 1784th
 I have received the letter which your Excellency honoured
me with, dated the 29th of last october Which Major L'Enfant
delivered me.[1] I can not better answer to the honourable invitation that you are willing to make me as well as to the general
officers and colonels of the french army auxiliary in America,
than by Sending you.
 1e. The answer of the marshal De Segur minister of war giving the Leave of our Sovereign to Join to this respectable
association.[2]
 2e. The list of the generals, Brigadiers, and colonels whom I
have admitted following litterally the powers with which I was
invested by the general Society.[3]
 3e. a List of Several Petitionors who entreated me to lay their
Claim before your Excellency, which Seems to me in the more
or less favourable case, according to my observations joined to
their Several articles, and for whom I ask a more explicit explanation to the general Society.[4]
 4e. A List of the Sums willingly and unanimously Subscribed
to concur to the benevolent views of this Establishment, and
given to the disposal of the general Society.[5]
 It is now my Duty to assure your Excellency in my name and
in the name of all the Cincinnati of the army under my command that this Institution may perpetuate, but will certainly
add nothing to the Warmth of the tender Sentiments of fraternity and friendship that we entertain for our Brothers of your
Army, and for the celebrated Chief whom we will respect and
Love till our last. it is in this profession of Sentiments that I
have the honour to be for all my Life of your Excellency The
most humble and obedient Servant

le cte de Rochambeau

LS, in English, DLC:GW; LS, in French, DSoCi; LS, translation, DSoCi; copy,
DSoCi. The two signed letters in DSoCi, both the one in French and the one
in English, were endorsed at the general meeting of the Society of the Cincinnati in 1784, probably by the secretary pro tem George Turner; and the English version of these was read at the meeting on 6 May. There is a translation
of each of the four enclosures both in DLC:GW and in DSoCi, and all eight of
these are initialed by Rochambeau. The original French version of enclosures

2 and 4, signed by Rochambeau, are in DSoCi. All of the documents in English, except the unsigned copy of Rochambeau's letter in DSoCi, are in the same hand. The documents in French are in a different hand.

1. The letter to Rochambeau of 29 Oct. 1783, going out under GW's signature to inform Rochambeau that "the Society have done themselves the honor to consider you and the Generals and Colonels of the Army you commanded in America as Members" (DLC: Rochambeau Papers), is a variation of GW's circular letter of the same date sent to the eligible French officers in the Continental army. For L'Enfant's mission to France, see Lafayette to GW, 10 Jan. 1784, nn.1 and 3.

2. Philippe-Henri, marquis de Ségur (1724–1801), a hero of France's mid-century wars, was made marshal of France and secretary of war in 1781. The translation of his letter dated 18 Oct. 1783 at Versailles reads in part: "I gave the King a full account of the letter that his excellency general washington has written to you, and of the proposal he has made you in the name of the american army as well as to the general officers and colonels who have been in america under your command, to join to the association which has been just now framed under the title of Cincinnatus. . . . His most Christian Majesty charged me with the direction of informing you that he gives you leave to yield to Such an honourable invitation: he desires you to acquaint his Excellency general washington with his Seeing allways with the greatest Satisfaction every things which may have any tendency to maintain and Strengthen the Connections formed between france and the United States. . . . you are then intitled, Sir, to acquaint the general officers and Colonels who have been in the army under your command, that the King gives them the leave to join to the association of the Cincinnati . . . as honourable by the motive of its Institution, as by the virtues and talents of the renown'd general who has been elected the president Thereof" (DLC:GW).

3. In addition to Rochambeau himself, the list includes five major generals, five brigadiers who became major generals on their return to France, three brigadier generals in America, and eighteen who "have acted all in america in the rank of colonel in the french army or in the detachme⟨nts⟩ coming from San Domingo to the Siege of york and gloucester" (DLC:GW).

4. The third enclosure is headed: "List of the officers whom may be the most intitled to pretend to the association of Cincinnatus whom the Count De Rochambeau could not admit following litterally the deliberation of the army, but for whom he takes the liberty to begg a more explicit explanation to the general Society." Ten are named in this list, all but one of whom was promoted from lieutenant colonel to colonel or brigadier general upon his return to France from America. The first two named, with an account of their service given, are L'Estrade and Lameth (see Lameth to GW, 6 Jan. 1784, and Rochambeau to GW, 1 Mar. 1784); Rochambeau inserted after these entries: "Those two seems to be in the most favourable ease to obtain this favour—le cte de Rochambeau" (DLC:GW). On 1 Mar. 1784 Rochambeau wrote GW that because of the king's opposition to enlarging the French society he was recommending that an exception be made only in these two cases.

5. The two English versions of enclosure 4 list the contributors in the same

order, and both show 42,000 livres having been given by twenty-five officers. Each version also lists eight other men who were expected to contribute a total of an additional 10,000 livres. Inserted at the bottom of both lists is the note initialed by Rochambeau: "The Sums which are not Settled are those of the officers who were not present at the assembly but who probably will accede to the ⟨same⟩ resolution." The French version, which does not have the notation and lists the contributors in a different order, shows a contribution of 44,000 livres from twenty-six officers instead of 42,000 from twenty-five. It also shows 7,500 livres expected from seven men instead of 10,000 from eight men. Rochambeau contributed 6,000 livres; Lieutenant General Vioménil, 3,000; the major generals, 2,000 each; brigadier generals, 1,500 each; and the colonels, 1,000 each. The American Society of the Cincinnati at its meeting in May 1784 voted not to accept gifts from foreigners.

Letter not found: from Boinod & Gaillard, 20 Jan. 1784. On 18 Feb. GW wrote to the firm: "I have been favored with your polite & obliging Letter of January the 20th."

To John Davidson

Sir,   Mount Vernon 20th Jany 84
    The address from the Yankee Club of Stewartstown coming through your hands to me,[1] I give you, without an apology for the trouble, the care of transmitting the enclosed answer to the Chairman thereof.[2] I am Sir Yr most Obt Humbe Sert
                                    G. Washington

LB, DLC:GW. Parke-Bernet catalog no. 1825 (29–30 April 1958, item 441) quotes from a letter of GW to Otho Holland Williams, 20 Jan. 1784: "The enclosed re [to] major Davidson containing an answer to the Address from the Yankee Club of Stewartstown, requests him to forward it to his brother, the Chairman thereof."

    John Davidson (1754–1807) was appointed naval officer at Annapolis in 1777 and was still in office on 2 July 1789 when he wrote GW asking to be reappointed. From 1783 to 1801 he was a member of the Maryland executive council. His brother Alexander Davidson was the chairman of the Yankee Club of Stewartstown.

    1. The text of the address, docketed by GW on 7 June 1783 "From the Yankee Club of Stewartstown in the County of Tyrone and Province of Ulster [in] Ireland," is: "At an early period of the contest in which you have been so gloriously engaged, our sentiments fully met those of the Americans, and tho' we long doubted the event, our warmest wishes were ever on the side of Freedom. Viewing with regret the oppressive scenes of misery under which our Native Country has long groaned without hopes of redress, & seeing the same direfull principle of Despotic sway pervading all the Courts and Countries of

the World; we rejoiced to hear that the spirit of America had risen superior TO THE PROUD MENACES OF BOTH Regal and Ministerial oppression; had thrown off THE GALLING YOKE of slavery & nobly spurned the fetters that were to bind her IN ALL CASES WHATSOEVER. Your situation however, compared with that of Great Britain, for a long time damped our hopes & caused many anxious fears. We could not conceive how an infant Country, scarcely known but as an appendage of a great Empire, unconnected among themselves, unprovided for War & without discipline could cope with an Ancient, powerfull & Victorious Nation; nor was it less difficult to imagine, who wou'd lead those unexperienced tho' zealous Bands to freedom & Independence against the Artfull maneuvres of experienced Commanders & the infernal schemes of the selfish & disaffected.

"But when we were informed that your Excellency, in obedience to your Country's call, had undertaken the Arduous task, & nobly embarked in the sacred cause of Liberty, rejecting every emolument which you might in justice have claimed for such signal & important services, such a singular and disinterested conduct, as an happy omen of American success, revived our Expectations & filled us with a kind of veneration for such a Character. And when you astonished the World by uniting the jarring interests & opinions of thirteen different States, ingaging by your manly prudence & mild address the affections of foreigners from various nations of Europe & even forcing approbation from the callous hearts of your invetrate enemies; your perseverence thro' the darkest scenes without despondence or murmuring combating every difficulty which inclement seasons and the wants of a brave but distressed Army could lay in your way, and at last rising victorious over the best appointed troops and Generals of high fame in the military line; we were lost in admiration of that Wisdom, magnanimity & perseverance which by TRIUMPHING OVER EVERY DANGER HAS ESTABLISHED the Liberties of the United States on the most honorable & permanent Basis. Upon this happy Revolution, we have embraced the first opportunity to convince you of our unfeigned Esteem & the particular share we take in whatever tends to the honor and happiness of N. America.

"But your exertions have not only vindicated the freedom of your Country but have also shed their benign influences over the distressed Kingdom of Ireland. To you Sir in the Course of a gracious Providence which in a conspicuous manner has protected your person & blessed your Counsels, do we acknowledge ourselves indebted for our late happy deliverance from as banefull a System of Policy as ever disgraced the rights of mankind.

"With the sincerest pleasure therefore we mention our affectionate congratulations on an event which has crowned America with Sovereignty & Independance, blessings so essential to the safety and happiness of a People, And humbly request that your Excellency will permit us to express the joy we feel on the happy return of peace & the sincerest wishes that your Country may become more & more prosperous, increase in lustre & glory & subsist to the latest ages.

"And that you Sir may long live to enjoy the fruits of your wisdom & magnanimity, to be a terror to Tyrants, & shine forth as a glorious example of disinterested virtue & future Patriotism is and will be the constant prayer of

Your much obliged most obedient & most devoted Humble Servants Sign'd in the name of the Society by Alexr Davidson Chairman" (DLC:GW).

2. A draft of GW's response dated at Mount Vernon, 20 Jan. 1784, is in David Humphreys' hand. It reads: "It is with unfeigned satisfaction I accept your Congratulations on the late happy & glorious Revolution.

"The generous indignation, against the foes to the rights of human nature, with which you seem to be animated; and the exalted sentiments of Liberty, which you appear to entertain; are too consonant to the feelings & principles of the Citizens of the United States of America, not to attract their veneration & esteem—did not the affectionate & anxious concern with which you regarded their struggle for freedom & Independence, entitle you to their more particular acknowledgments.

"If in the course of our successful contest, any good consequences have resulted to the oppressed Kingdom of Ireland, it will afford a real source of felicitation to all who respect the interests of humanity.

"I am now, Gentlemen, to offer you my best thanks for the indulgent sentiments you are pleased to express of my conduct; and for your most benevolent wishes respecting my personal wellfare, as well as with regard to a more interesting object—the prosperity of my Country" (copy, DLC:GW). There is also a letter-book copy in DLC:GW. A Presbyterian minister, the Rev. Thomas Birch of Saintfield, Ireland, sent copies of the exchange between GW and the Yankee Club to the press (see McDowell, *Irish Public Opinion*, 49).

From Jean Le Mayeur

Sir   New York janr 20. 1784

I have the honor of taking my pen to apologize to your Excellency for my not waiting on you in Virginia at so Early a period as I had stipulated.

the Extrime severe weather added to my not having fully Complited some private arrengements which are absolutely necessairy before I take my departure from this City have hitherto prevented a[n]d will for a few days Longer, delay my journey for your hospitable Mansion and rob my of the honor I have so happily proposed to myself in paying my personnel respects to your Excellency soon and viewing your Countenance and thro you a favorable Reception with your highly honored fello Citizens.

since your Excellencys much regretted departure from this City I have had the plaisure of gratifying tow Ladies and tow Gentleman who I believe have the honor of being personally known to your Excellency by furnishing them with good living teeth in the Room of those which were broken or otherwise decayed. Miss Ried of New Jersey—daughter of General Ried of the British army and Miss Shaw the sister of lady Wheate and a Relation of Colo. Varick lately a secretary to your Excellency have been furnished with to each and Colo. Warick himself has four fronts and one Eye tooth, th[r]ee of which were transplanted in december and are at this day perfectly secure and tow others which have been transplanted some days since are in a promising state and will be perfectly ferm at the period of my departure from this place[1] which is dependent on the completion of my arrengements first alluded to and which will positively take place in the Begining of february, when I have determind to proceed to the southward and honor myself with an immediate visit to Mount Vernon.[2] I pray my best Respects to Mrs Washington and have the honor to be with Great Consideration and profound Respects your Excellencys most obedt and humble serviter ⟨docr⟩

Le Mayeur

ALS, DLC:GW.

Jean-Pierre Le Mayeur was a French dentist who worked on GW's teeth at his headquarters in New York in 1783. See GW to Le Mayeur, 16 July 1783. For the dentist's visit to Mount Vernon later in 1784, see Le Mayeur to GW, 14 Aug. 1784. For Le Mayeur's visit in 1785 and a sketch of his life, see *Diaries*, 4:193–94.

1. Col. Richard Varick wrote a letter to GW on 15 Jan., which has not been found, testifying to the success of teeth transplants. See GW to Varick, 22 Feb. 1784. John Reed (1721–1807), who was second in command to Bouquet in Pontiac's War, was promoted to major general in the British army in 1781. Lady Wheate was Maria Shaw (d. 1856) of New York City. She was the daughter of David Shaw and married Capt. Sir Jacob Wheate of the Royal Navy.

2. The following item appeared in the *Virginia Journal and Alexandria Advertiser* on 22 April 1784: "Dr. Lamayner, Dentist from New-York, who transplants Teeth, is now in this Town, and may be spoke with by calling at Mr. Perrin's Store."

To Tankerville

My Lord,   Mount Vernon. 20th Jany 1784.

I do not know how it happen'd but the fact is, that your Lordships favor of the 15th of July did not reach my hands until the latter part of Decr whilst I was on my return to this Seat of retirement—The Letter however which I had the honor of writing to Lady Tankerville, duplicate of which, for fear of accidents, I now inclose; will have informed her Ladyship, & I persuade myself, you My Lord, of the impracticability of my taking an active & responsible part in the disposal of Mr Bennets Estate in this Country; but if my advice, & occasional assistance to the Gentlemen who accept the trust, can be of any avail, they shall be afforded with great pleasure.[1] Could I say more, without feeling conscious of giving assurances I should be unable to comply with, such is my willingness to serve your Lordship, & your right Honorable mother, I would do it most chearfully.

Much as I expected to find my own private concerns deranged; & intricately involved as I knew those of some others (which had been committed to my care) must be, I shall realize more trouble and perplexity than I apprehended (before I began the investigation) in restoring them, if it be practicable, to order. An almost entire suspension of every thing which related to my own Estate, for near nine years, has accumulated an abundance of work for me.

The second person named, My Lord, in the Power of Attorney, is miscalled: it should be Hooe, instead of Howe. Not adverting to the probability of this circumstance, at the time I was writing to her Ladyship, must account for, & will be received I hope, as an apology for that paragraph of my Letter which professed ignorance of such a person—So soon as I discovered the mistake I arrested the Power in its progress to the Attorney General, Mr Randolph & have now placed it in the hands of Colo. Hooe, who is an exceeding good man, & very competent to the execution of the trust which he accepts[2]—Mr Little, whose character I have enquired into since I came home, stands exceeding well in his reputation, & may from his peculiar knowledge of the Estate, be very serviceable in the disposal of it to the best advantage.[3]

I beg you to be assured My Lord, that no apology was necessary for the request you made to me—that I shall always feel pleasure in obliging your Lordship whenever it may be in my power: & that with great consideration & respect I have the honor to be Your Lordship, &a

G: Washington

LB, DLC:GW.
Charles Bennett (1743–1822) was the fourth earl of Tankerville.
1. Neither Lord Tankerville's letter of 15 July 1783 nor a letter of 21 June

1783 from his mother, Alicia Astley Bennett, the countess of Tankerville, has been found. It was in response to Lady Tankerville's missing letter that GW wrote her on 30 Oct. 1783: "It is painful to me to be under the necessity of declining the trust which the Earl of Tankerville & your other Son the Honble Mr Bennett have invested me with." The "other Son" was Henry Astley Bennett (d. 1815). Lady Tankerville's husband, Charles Bennett, third earl of Tankerville, became heir in 1755 in Virginia to thousands of acres of land, a share in a copper mine, slaves, and livestock, which were left to him by his mother's first cousin John Colvill (Fairfax County Will Book B-1, 97–101). The final settlement of John Colvill's estate, which was encumbered with debt, still had not been reached nearly thirty years after his death. The two executors of the will, Thomas Colvill, the decedent's brother and heir at law, who died in 1766, and the third earl of Tankerville, who died in 1767, were at the same time both John Colvill's chief heirs and his chief creditors. GW became involved in the affairs of the Colvill brothers in 1766 when he became an executor of Thomas Colvill's will. Thomas Colvill's affairs were deeply entangled with the unsettled estate of his brother John. For discussions of GW's involvement with the settlement of Thomas Colvill's estate and references to it throughout his correspondence, see the notes in GW to John West, Jr., December 1767, and in Thomas Montgomerie to GW, 24 Oct. 1788. Both this letter of 20 Jan. and Lady Tankerville's letter of 13 Feb. 1784 suggest that the third earl left most if not all of his Colvill inheritance in Virginia to his younger son Henry Bennett.

2. GW wrote the countess of Tankerville on 30 Oct. 1783: "Being altogether unacquainted with such a Gentlemen as Colo. Robert I. Howe of Alexandria (the second person named in the Power of Attorney) . . . I have sent it to Edmd Randolph Esqr. the Attorney General." Presumably GW was the first person "named in the Power of Attorney." The second was supposed to be Robert Townsend Hooe of Charles County, Maryland. A partner of Richard Harrison in the Alexandria firm of Hooe & Harrison, Hooe became mayor of Alexandria in 1780 and thereafter a member of the Fairfax parish vestry and of the Fairfax County court. See GW to Edmund Randolph, 10 Feb. 1784, and Randolph to GW, 19 Feb. 1784.

3. Mr. Little is undoubtedly Charles Little (d. 1813), a Scot who came to Virginia in 1768 and bought Cleesh, a plantation that John Colvill left to his brother for life, after which it was to go to Lord Tankerville (Fairfax County Will Book B-1, 97–101).

From James Tilton

Sir,   Annapolis [Md.] 20th Jany 1784.

It was with pleasure I received your communication of the 28 December 1783, appointing the city of Philadelphia to be the place for the general meeting of the society of Cincinnati, on the first monday in may next, agreeably to the original institution.[1]

I am convinced, sir, you may rely on the punctual attendance of the delegates of the delaware state society. It was not without mature deliberation in several meetings, that the officers of the delaware line entered into the association, and not before they had considered the objects of it as laudable, and the means of attainment as adequate to the ends proposed. I know therefore the delegates will consider themselves as inexcuseable for the least neglect. I have written a notification to Major James Moore (late Captn Moore) who is one of the two appointed to represent our little society.[2] He is a man of excellent character and can attend without inconveniency. And having myself the honor to be the other representative, I shall be ambitious to attend the first general meeting. I have the honor to be, sir, with all the respect that I ought, Your most obt servt

James Tilton

ALS, DSoCi.

James Tilton (1745–1822), an army surgeon during the war and a member of Congress from 1783 to 1785, was president of the Delaware Society of the Cincinnati.

1. See GW's Circular Letter to the State Societies of the Cincinnati, 1 Jan. 1784.

2. James Moore, who was promoted to captain in the Delaware State Troop on 5 April 1777, remained with the Delaware regiment until 1783. In 1778 and 1779 he was a prisoner of war. Moore attended the general meeting of the Cincinnati in May and remained active in the Delaware society.

To Heintz

Sir, Mount Vernon 21st Jany 1784

As soon as I had the honor of receiving your Letter containing a proposal of the order of the Knights of Divine Providence; I referred the subject of it to the decision of Congress, in my letter to that august Body dated the 28th of August last, a copy of which is enclosed. Whereupon the United States in Congress assembled, were pleased to pass their Act of the 5th Inst: which is properly authenticated by their Secretary, & which I have the honor of transmitting herewith.[1]

Notwithstanding it appears to be incompatible with the principles of our national Constitution to admit the introduction of any kind of Nobility, Knighthood, or distinctions of a similar nature, amongst the Citizens of our republic. yet I pray you will have the goodness to make known to the Illustrious Knights of the order of Divine Providence, that we receive with the deepest gratitude & most perfect respect this flattering mark of their attention & approbation. For the polite manner in which you have communicated the pleasure of the order, you will be pleased to accept my best acknowledgments. I have the honor to be with very great consid[eratio]n &ca

G: Washington

LB, DLC:GW. This letter was enclosed for forwarding in GW to Charles Thomson, 22 Jan. 1784, which see.

1. See GW to Thomas Mifflin, 9 Jan. 1784, and notes.

To Philip Schuyler

Dear Sir,   Mount Vernon 21st Jany 1784

Your favor of the 20th of December found me as you conjectured by that fire side, from which I had been too long absent for my own convenience; to which I returned with the greatest avidity the moment my public avocations would permit; and from which I hope never again to be withdrawn.

While I am here solacing myself in my retreat from the busy scenes of life, I am not only made extremely happy by the gratitude of my Countrymen in general, but particularly so by the repeated proofs of the kindness and approbation of those who have been more intimately conversant with my public transactions—and I need scarcely add that the favorable opinion of no one, is more acceptable than that of yourself.

In recollecting the vicisitudes of fortune we have experienced, and the difficulties we have surmounted, I shall always call to mind the great assistance I have frequently received from you, both in your public & private character. May the blessings of Peace amply reward your exertions, may you, & your family (to whom the compliments of Mrs Washington and myself are affectionately presented) long continue to enjoy every species of happiness this World can afford.[1] With sentiments of sincere esteem, attachment, & affection I am—Dr Sir Yr Most Obedt & very Hble Servant

Go: Washington

ALS, PPRF; LB, DLC:GW; copy, PWacD: Sol Feinstone Collection, on deposit PPAmP.

As one of the four original major generals under GW's command, Philip

John Schuyler (1733–1804) of New York organized Gen. Richard Montgomery's expedition into Canada in 1775–76. On 4 Aug. 1777 Congress replaced Schuyler with Gen. Horatio Gates. Schuyler was a member of Congress in 1779 and 1780.

1. Schuyler was married to Catharine Van Rensselaer (d. 1803) of Claverack, N.Y., by whom he had eight children who survived infancy.

To James Nourse

Sir,   Mount Vernon 22d Jany 1784

Yesterday gave me the honor of your favor of the 11th from Annapolis. I thank you for the trouble you have taken to bring me acquainted with the affairs of my deceased Brother of Berkly.[1]

It would give me great pleasure to render any service to his children; & as far as I can do it by paying attention to those two who are in my Neighbourhood with Mr Griffith, I will; but to concern myself in the smallest degree with the management of their Estates, I cannot.[2] It would be undertaking a trust which I could not discharge properly—consequently it would be wrong to engage in it. I have not only the derangement of nine years in my own private concerns to emerge from, but (what gives me infinitely more concern) those of others, for whom I have acted as Executor, by Powers of Attorney &ca to extricate also, if it be practicable—Here then it is evident I have sufficient employment (more indeed than comports with that ease & freedom from trouble & care which I wish to enjoy) without undertaking any new matter.

It gave me concern to hear that my Brothers Estate is so much involved, I had no conception of it. nor do I know upon what terms he obtained the Land I sold a Mr Pendleton. Not a farthing of the purchase money has ever yet been paid to me, nor have Deeds passed from me to any one[3]—I wish this may be all—it is to be feared many of my rents will be found in his hands when I come to a final settlement with my Tenants—they having been told, his receipts would exonerate them, while he has been requested to receive any rents which might be offered to him on my behalf.[4] If his Books are in your hands I shall be obliged to you for a transcript of the account between us, as it stands thereon.

I shall receive nothing which may fall to me as Heir at Law to his youngest son. But if the Lawyers are clear that the right is in me, it may not be amiss to consider, whether such property had best be given to any one, or to all his children in equal proportions—or whether still better pretensions may not be in some other.[5]

I thank you for your kind congratulations upon my return to domestic life, & am Sir, Yr most obedt servt

G: Washington

LB, DLC:GW.

James Nourse (1731–1784), a Londoner, settled in 1770 at Piedmont near Harewood, the house in Berkeley County, Va., where GW's brother Samuel Washington (1734–1781) lived until his death. Nourse and GW were executors of Samuel Washington's estate.

1. Nourse's letter has not been found. Samuel Washington was deeply in debt at the time of his death.

2. The two sons of Samuel Washington and his fourth wife Anne Steptoe Washington were George Steptoe Washington (c.1773–1808) and Lawrence Augustine Washington (1775–1824). The boys at this time were under the care of David Griffith (1742–1789), rector of Fairfax Parish and priest at Christ Church, Alexandria, Virginia. See Griffith to GW, 12 July, and GW to Griffith, 29 Aug. 1784. GW in fact did assume major responsibility for the education of his two nephews. See, for instance, GW to David Griffith, 29 Aug. 1784, and Charles Washington to GW, 7 Jan. 1789.

3. On 7 Dec. 1771 Philip Pendleton (1752–1802) signed a contract at Mount Vernon to purchase 180 acres of GW's Bullskin plantation in Berkeley County, Virginia. He agreed to pay GW £400 plus interest in two years and to pay one year's rent (*Diaries*, 3:37, 74). About a year later Pendleton decided to sell the land to GW's brother Samuel Washington, and in January 1773 GW transferred in his ledger the debt of £420, the purchase price of 180 acres plus one year's interest, from the account of Philip Pendleton to that of Samuel Washington (Ledger B, 22, 36). On 5 Oct. 1776 GW wrote to Samuel Washington from New York that he intended to "send a power of Attorney to Lund Washington to make a legal conveyance of the Land" that Pendleton "had of me, & sold you, upon the purchase Money being paid; not one farthing of which has yet been done." During the war Samuel Washington turned over the Bullskin tract to his son Thornton who at this time was living on it (see Thornton Washington to GW, 1 Aug. 1784). GW confessed to David Stuart on 21 Sept. 1794 that he had "never intended, under the view I had of his affairs, to ask payment"; and in his will GW specifically relieved "the Estate of my deceased brother Samuel Washington, from the payment of the money which is due me for the Land I sold to Philip Pendleton."

4. GW's accounts with his tenants in northern Virginia as recorded in his Ledger B reveal that they often made their payments to Samuel Washington. See also Battaile Muse to GW, 15 Nov. 1785, and GW to Muse, 4 Dec. 1785.

5. See Francis Willis, Jr., to GW, 24 Sept. 1788, and notes.

To Charles Thomson

Dear Sir,   Mount Vernon 22d Jany 1784

The original letter & other Papers from the Chevr de Heintz respecting the order of the Knights of Divine Providence, were transmitted to Congress without a Copy being taken; I am a little at a loss therefore in what manner to direct my letter to him, more especially as I have a feint recollection that their is a mode pointed out for the address by the Secretary himself— Let me pray you therefore, my good Sir, to examine into this matter, and after giving my letter another cover, to put it into the proper channel for conveyance.[1]

If my Commission is not necessary for the files of Congress I should be glad to have it deposited amongst my own Papers. It may serve *my Grand Children* some fifty or a hundd years hence for a theme to ruminate upon, *if they should be* contemplatively disposed.[2]

We have been so fast locked in Snow & Ice since Christmas, that all kinds of intercourse have been suspended; & a duty which I owed my Mother, & intended 'ere this to have performed, has been forced to yield to the intemperence of the Weather: but, as this again must submit to the approaching Sun, I shall soon be enabled, I expect, to discharge that duty on which nature & inclination have a call; and shall be ready afterwards to welcome my friends to the shadow of this vine & Fig tree; where I hope it is unnecessary to add, I should be exceedingly happy to see you, and any of *my late Masters*—now representatives.

Mrs Washington, if she knew I was writing to you in the stile of Invitation would, I am certain, adduce arguments to prove that I ought to include Mrs Thompson; but before she should have half spun the thread of her discourse, it is more than probable I should have nonplused her, by yielding readily to the force of her reasoning. With sentiments of sincere regd & esteem. I am—Dr Sir Yr Most Obedt Servt

Go: Washington

ALS, DLC: Charles Thomson Papers; LB, DLC:GW.

1. See GW to Heintz, 21 Jan. 1784.

2. On 29 Jan. 1784, before Thomson read GW's letter, Hugh Williamson of North Carolina offered a motion: "That his late Commission be returned to

General Washington in a neat gold box to be preserved among the archives of his family" (*JCC*, 26:54). The motion was referred to a committee headed by Thomas Jefferson. Despite the expectation that Thomson expressed in his letter of 7 Feb. of a prompt and favorable disposition of the motion, there is no indication that the committee ever reported; but an inventory of GW's papers dated 29 June 1904, made when the papers were transferred from the State Department to the Library of Congress, shows the commission among GW's papers. The commission is now in the Library of Congress.

From Barras

Sir   Paris Jany 23d 1784
   I receivd the Letter which you did me the honor to write me, as well as the institution of the Cincinnatus Society formd by the American Army, I am much flatterd to be comprisd in a military Society the members of which have with So much glory concurrd under the Orders of your Excellency to establish American Liberty, but it gives me great pain to See, that all the General Officers of the Sea, as well as the Captains of Ships of War, who have Cruisd and fought on the Coast of North America and particularly those who were employed under my Command do not partake with me the honor to be admitted in the Society.[1]
   I will not here Call to your mind the distinguishd Services renderd to America by the Naval Officers under the Command of Count d'Estaing and of Monsr de Grasse, I will confine myself to what regards the particular Squadron which I commanded, the frequent & honorable combats under the orders of Monr d'Estouches[2] the frequent Cruisings & bloody battles of the Frigates, for the protection of the American Commerce, the very dangerous junction formed with Count de Grasse in Chesapeak Bay, which insured the Success of the enterprise against York, are pretensions which may give to the Captains of this Squadron a right to the distinctions conferred on the Colonels of the Land forces, with whom they Cooperated. Persuaded, however, that to repair this ommission, the Members of the Society of Cincinnatus have only to Know the names of the General Officers and Captains of ships who Served on the American Coast—I have the honor to Send to your Excellency a list of those who were employed under my orders,[3] and I woud not myself accept the decoration of the Society, but that I

look on it as Certain that it will be very Shortly in Common with my Ancient Companions in Arms.[4] I am with respect and esteem, Sir &a

Barras

P.S. the Count de la Bretonniere has Communicated to me the Letter which he has the honor to write to your Excellency, in which he Setts forth the Services renderd by him, to the United States by Convoying American Fleets, he requests to be comprisd in the Society[5]—his request is well founded and I with pleasure join with this Officer and we pray that he may be Comprehended[6] with the other Officers—for whom I have made application.[7]

Translation, DSoCi; ALS, DSoCi. For the French text, see CD-ROM:GW. The English version was read at the general meeting on 11 May 1784. See Winthrop Sargent's Journal, doc. II in General Meeting of the Society of the Cincinnati, 4–18 May 1784. The handwriting of the translation indicates that it was not one of those done by David Stuart in April (see Stuart to GW, 25 April 1784).

Jacques-Melchior, comte de Barras-Saint-Laurent, commanded the *Zélé* under the comte d'Estaing in Rhode Island waters in 1778 and at Savannah in 1779. He became commander of the French expeditionary squadron at Newport, R.I., in May 1781 and reinforced Admiral de Grasse off Yorktown in September 1781.

1. GW wrote Barras on 17 May that the general meeting had altered the institution of the society to make the French navy captains eligible for election to the Society of the Cincinnati. See note 7.

2. Charles-René-Dominique Sochet Destouches (des Touches; 1727–1794), commanded the French expeditionary forces after the death of Ternay (Charles-Henri d'Arsac, chevalier de Ternay; 1723–1780) on 15 Dec. 1780 until he was succeeded by Barras in May 1781. After suffering heavy damage in an engagement on 16 Mar. 1781 with a squadron commanded by the British admiral Marriot Arbuthnot, Admiral Destouches and his squadron sailed to Newport, R.I., for repairs.

3. The naval officers listed by Barras in the enclosure were: Destouches; Charles-Marie, comte de La Grandière; Arnaud Le Gardeur de Tilly; Louis-André-Joseph, chevalier de Lombard; Isaac-Jean-Timothée Chadeau de La Clocheterie; Charles-Isamabart, comte de Médine; Augustin-Etienne-Gaspard Bernard de Marigny; Jacques-Aimé La Saige, chevalier La Villèsbrunne; Louis-Marie, chevalier de La Tanouarn; Maurice-Jean-Marie, chevalier de Launay de Tromelin; Louis-Josué Janvre, chevalier de La Bouchetière; Jean-François de Galaup, comte de La Pérouse; Louis-René-Magdelain Le Vassor, comte de La Touche-Tréville; Guillaume-Jacques-Constant Liberge de Granchain de Sémerville; Théobald-René, comte de Kergariou-Locmaria; and Jean-Marie, chevalier de Gillart de Villeneuve (Villeneuve-Gillart).

4. In the French text it is, "quelle me sera bientot commune avec mes anciens compagnons darmes."

5. "Comprised" in the French is "compris," here meaning "included." La Bretonnière's letter is dated 1 Feb. 1784.

6. "And we pray that he may be comprehended" is "et nous prie de le comprendre," translated "and ask you to include him."

7. The response from Philadelphia of the Society of the Cincinnati went out under GW's signature: "It was intended to comprehend in the original Institution of the Cincinnati, many Officers, who, through want of better Information, and a peculiarity of Circumstances, were omitted. The Institution as now amended and published, will fully include in the Society all the Generals & Captains of Ships of War, for whom you have applied to the President.

"The Count de la Bretonnière, having had the Command of a Royal Ship and rendered Services in America, is included without Doubt" (17 May 1784, DSoCi).

From Robert Stewart

Dear Sir   London Janry 23d 1784

As I purpose to do myself the Honour and great pleasure of writing to you soon, by a direct opportunity from hence to Virginia, in answer to the Letter which you did me the honr to write to me the 10th of last August, from the State of New York,[1] this only serves to entreat you will pardon the liberty I take in Introducing to Your Excellency, the Bearer Doctor Ross, who after a long residence [in] Turkey, and visiting many other Countries, intends going to America, and ardently wishes for the honr of being known to Your Excellency.[2] Docr Ross's great merit and extensive knowledge will, I hope in some degree, plead my excuse for the freedom I now presume on, at the earnest request of Mr Dempster, a Member of the British Parliament, a great admirer of yours, that has long honoured me with his particular Freindship & whose uncommon goodness of heart, distinguished abilities, and sterling worth render him, all partiallity aside, a valueable Member, and real ornament of Society.[3]

May I likewise beg you will do me the Honour to present my most respectfull Compliments to Your Lady and be persuaded of the high esteem and sincere attachment with which I have the Honr to be—My Dear General Your ever affectionate & faithful humble Servant

Robert Stewart

ALS, DLC:GW.

1. After GW left his Virginia Regiment at the end of 1758, Robert Stewart who had been his companion at arms since 1754 (see *Papers, Colonial Series,* vols. 1–5, *passim*) continued second in command of the regiment. For some years thereafter, the two men corresponded regularly. GW advanced Stewart money and did what he could to promote his military career (ibid., vol. 6). The last of their known pre-Revolutionary letters is a long one from Stewart written from Kingston, Jamaica, on 25 Jan. 1769. The next letter from Stewart was written on 19 April 1783 from London to renew his friendship with GW. In that letter, Stewart fills several pages with obsequious flattery and suggests that GW could make his old friend's declining years happy by securing for him an appointment from the new American republic to serve it in some capacity in England or France. In a coldly polite and brief reply on 10 Aug. 1783, GW expresses his surprise that Stewart is still alive after so many years of silence and informs Stewart that he does not concern himself with civil appointments which in any case should go to GW's fellow countrymen who had suffered the hardships of a lengthy war.

2. David Hartley wrote Benjamin Franklin on 28 Jan. 1784, at the request of Dempster, to introduce "Dr. Ross who . . . proposes with your permission to take your advice with respect to his proposed settlement as a practising Physician in America" (CtY: Franklin Papers). And on 1 Feb. 1784 William Strahan wrote Franklin: "My worthy Friend Dr. Ross is the Bearer of this Letter, has promised to deliver it into your own Hands" (CtY: Franklin Papers).

3. George Dempster (1732–1818), a man of great wealth and genuine distinction, was a member of Parliament from Perth and played the part of an independent whig in the House of Commons throughout the 1760s and 1770s.

From Vioménil

Monsieur   a paris Le 24 Janvier 1784

Le Baron d'angélly[1] qui ma Servi d'aide de camp pendant les campagnes que j'ay faites en amérique desirant tres vivement d'etre aggregé a la Société que préside Votre Exelence, cest avec la plus grande confiance que je la Supplie de vouloir bien luy procurer cet agrément, il étoit colonel attaché au corps de La marinne, L'orsque nous sommes arrivés a newport, m. le cte de barras La employé en cette qualité et cest avec Lagrement du ministre de ce departément que je prend La liberté de demander bonté, et protection a Votre Exelence pour le Succes de ma recomandation,[2] ma reconnoissance Sera vive et tout aussi durable que les Sentiments du tendre et respectueux attachement avec Les quels jay lhonneur detre Monsieur, De Votre Exelence Le tres humble et tres obeissant Serviteur

Vioménil

ALS, DSoCi.

Antoine-Charles du Houx, baron de Vioménil (1728–1792), came to America with Rochambeau as a brigade commander and second in command of the French army in America. He led an assault column at Yorktown in 1781 and assumed command of the French army at Boston in 1782 upon Rochambeau's departure.

1. François-Marie, baron d'Angély (1735–1808), a colonel in the legion of volunteers of the prince of Nassau-Siegen, was Vioménil's aide-de-camp in America.

2. As president general of the Society of the Cincinnati, GW signed in the general meeting at Philadelphia the following letter to Vioménil, dated 15 May 1784: "The Baron d'Angelly, for whom you ask admission into the Society of the Cincinnati, having been, as you inform the Society, a Colonel in the Auxiliary Army, is in consequence intitled to become a Member according to the Rules of the Institution.

"The Members of the Society in France will, in future, hold Meetings there, as we do in these States—Baron D'Angelly will please to make his Application to the former" (DSoCi).

From Thomas Walker

Dear Sir,   Castle Hill albemarle [Va.] Jany 24th 1784

The language I am acquainted with being in my opinion too poor to do justice to your merrit I shall be silent on that head.

The present business is respecting the Dismal, the Company having Shewed the value of those Lands, many are so mean as to wish for what is most undoubtedly their property.[1]

During Mr John Washintons mannaging for us he applyed to Mr Cooper the then surveyor to survey the Companys Lands which as I am informd he said was out of his power, this was sometime before the late grorius contest began, after that commenced it is well known that part of the Country was generally in the enemys possession of course no surveying could be done, since the return of Peace Mr Robert Andrews has by appointment made the survey,[2] the Company wish to have a meeting and have requested me as an old member & mannager to appoint one, your being as old a member & mannager and your character being the first at present in the world an appointment from you would in my opinion produce a full meeting,[3] the place & time I submit to your better judgment and convenience, the inclosed list will shew you the place of Residence of the different members.[4]

Possibly you may desire my opinion with regard to the time & place of meeting as you have been long employed gloriously in distant parts of the United states, I would not wish you to pay any regard to what is mention on this head unless it coinsides with your own Opinion.

Richmond espetially during the May assembly will be most convenient to a majority.

Fredericksburg the next most convenient, that will suit your self, Mr Page, Mr Lewis & Thomas Walker. Mr John Lewis of Fredericksburg informed me that he was impower by your Excellency & his Fathers Will to sell the Lands we held in partership in the dismal to which he wished my concurrence, I am willing to sell & have enquired of some gentlemen from that part of the state into the value, which they suppose fifteen Shillings Per Acre, far short in my opinion of the real value, that I submit to you and am willing to take any price for my part that is agreable to the other Par[t]ners.[5]

Your relation is very well and desires her best compliments [to] Your Lady and self, to which pleas ad mine to your Lady, Betsy & self should be extreemly happy to see you both any where but more particularly at this place.[6] I am Dear Sir with the greatest esteem your Excellencys Most Hble Servant

　　　　　　　　　　　　　　　　　　Thomas Walker

ALS, DLC:GW.

Thomas Walker (1715–1794) had been associated with GW since the 1750s at the time when GW was colonel of the Virginia Regiment and Walker was a commissary for the Virginia troops. By 1784 Walker had retired from public life and was living at his estate, called Castle Hill, near Charlottesville, Virginia.

1. In renewing the petition of 25 May 1763, William Nelson presented a petition to the Virginia council on behalf of himself and more than one hundred and fifty other men to take up and improve "a large Tract of waste Land lying in the Counties of Norfolk and Nansemond and commonly known by the name of Dismal Swamp." The council read the petition on 1 Nov. 1763 and granted Nelson and his associates each 1,000 acres of land on 2 November. On 3 Nov. 1763 the trustees, or managers, signed articles of agreement forming a company "for the purpose of taking up and draining a large Body of Land called the Dismal Swamp." The articles included a provision that the assets of the company could be divided only by a majority vote of the members in a general meeting. For details of the early history of the Dismal Swamp Company and the source of these quotations, see Articles of Agreement, 3 Nov. 1763, and notes in *Papers, Colonial Series*, 7:269–74.

2. John Washington (1740–1777) of Suffolk, Va., was the younger brother of Lund Washington, GW's wartime plantation manager. David Jameson wrote Walker on 25 Oct. 1784 that he was sending letters he had "recd in 1781 from Col. Henry Riddick who had been employed to superintend the Companys affairs after Mr Washington went away" (NcD: Dismal Swamp Land Company Papers). Apparently John Washington was a captain in the Virginia forces in 1775 and 1776. The Rev. Robert Andrews, professor of moral philosophy in the College of William and Mary, obtained a survey by county surveyors of 40,000 acres in Dismal Swamp (David Jameson to David Meade, April 1784, NcD: Dismal Swamp Land Company Papers). In 1785 Andrews was chosen to fix the route of an Elizabeth River canal, and he later became president of the Dismal Swamp Company.

3. David Jameson wrote to David Meade in April 1784: "After we had failed in a meeting [in November 1783] I wrote to Dr Walker as the oldest manager [of the Dismal Swamp Company], to appoint another, but he has not answered my letter. I imagine at the next setting of the assembly a meeting may be had of members sufficient to do business. And I hope Gen. Washington may be prevailed on to be there" (NcD: Dismal Swamp Land Company Papers). At the first meeting of the company more than twenty years before, on 3 Nov. 1763, GW, Thomas Walker, and Fielding Lewis volunteered "to attend the Surveying the Land" and to check the land grants in Nansemond and Norfolk counties and were appointed "Managers" of the company.

4. See enclosure.

5. John Lewis (1747–1825) was the oldest son of Fielding Lewis of Fredericksburg, Va., GW's brother-in-law and one of the original members of the Dismal Swamp Company. He was the son of Lewis's first wife.

6. Thomas Walker was married in 1741 to Mildred Thornton Meriwether, widow of Nicholas Meriwether. After the death of his first wife in 1778, Walker married Elizabeth Gregory Thornton, the widow of Reuben Thornton. As GW once explained, three daughters of his aunt Mildred Washington Lewis Gregory Willis named Frances, Elizabeth, and Mildred Gregory married three Thornton brothers, Francis, Reuben, and John Thornton, respectively. Francis Thornton's daughter Mildred in turn married GW's brother Charles, and John Thornton's daughter Mildred was the second wife of GW's brother Samuel. Walker's first wife, the Widow Meriwether, was a sister of the Thornton brothers; his second, the Widow Thornton, was GW's first cousin.

Enclosure
Members of the Dismal Swamp Company[1]

[24 January 1784]

David Jemeson for Samuel Gist & Self Shares[2]	1
David Mead for Self & Mr[s] William Waters[3]	1 ½
Mr John Lewis for his Father & Nathaniel Bacon[4]	2
Thomas Newton for Colo. Tucker & Major Fairly[5]	2

Mr Man Page of Mansfield[6]   ½
Mr William Nelson & Brother   1
Mr Secretary Thomas Nelson[7]   1
Your self   1
Thomas Walker & Joseph Hornsby[8]   1
                                                ———
                                                 1 1

David Jemeson york
David Mead near Westover
Mr Lewis Fredericksburg
Thomas Newton Norfolk
Man Page near Fredericksburg
William Nelson york
Secretary Thomas Nelson near Hanover Court House
Joseph Hornby Williamsburg
Thomas Walker Castle Hill Albemarle

AD, in Thomas Walker's hand, DLC:GW.

1. GW's copy of the Dismal Swamp Land Company's Articles of Agreement, 3 Nov. 1763, has the names of ten men signing as members of the company: William Nelson, Thomas Nelson, Robert Burwell, GW, Thomas Walker, Fielding Lewis, John Syme, Samuel Gist, Robert Tucker, and William Waters. John Robinson and Anthony Bacon & Co. were the other two original members, making a total of twelve shareholders. On 11 May 1771 John Robinson's share was surrendered to the company, leaving outstanding the eleven shares that Walker lists here. See an undated memorandum in NcD: Dismal Swamp Land Company Papers. See also note 1 in Walker to GW, this date.

2. David Jameson was a well-to-do planter and merchant living in Yorktown, Virginia. As lieutenant governor of Virginia he acted as governor in the summer and fall of 1781 during the absence from Richmond of Gov. Thomas Nelson. As his account with the Dismal Swamp Company suggests and as Thomas Walker confirmed, Jameson assumed the "cheif mannagment" of the company during the Revolutionary War years (see undated memorandum, NcD: Dismal Swamp Land Company Papers, and Walker to GW, 29 Aug. 1784). Samuel Gist (d. 1815) was a London merchant who owned property in Hanover County, Va., and was living in Virginia at the time the Dismal Swamp Company was organized. In 1782 the Virginia legislature vested all of his Virginia property in his daughter Mary, wife of William Anderson of Hanover County. Anderson became active in the company for Gist, who awarded him one quarter of his one share.

3. David Meade (b. 1744), originally of Nansemond County, lived at Maycox (Maycock), across the James River from William Byrd's Westover, in Prince George County, Virginia. He was married to the daughter of William and Sarah Prentis Waters of Williamsburg. Mrs. Waters was the daughter of

William Prentis (d. 1765). Her deceased husband William Waters (d. 1769) was for a time a partner in trade with John Blair. He also had large landhold-ings in York, Northampton, and Halifax counties in Virginia. William Waters transferred one-half of his share to his son-in-law David Meade on 27 April 1764, and in May 1766 Meade acquired one-half of Robert Burwell's share. See the undated memorandum cited above.

4. Anthony Bacon & Co. was one of the original members of the Dismal Swamp Company. Anthony Bacon (c.1717–1786) was a British merchant with whom GW briefly had dealings in the 1750s. He began as a ship captain and by this time was an important commercial figure in London. See *Papers, Colonial Series*, 1:218–19. Perhaps Walker intended to write Anthony rather than Nathaniel.

5. Thomas Newton, Jr. (1742–1807), who conducted business for GW in Norfolk in the 1780s, was the son of a merchant in Norfolk and was himself a Norfolk merchant as well as a leading citizen of the area. He was married to the daughter of Robert Tucker, Jr. (d. 1767), another Norfolk merchant, whose father (d. 1723) and son (d. 1779) were also Norfolk merchants and also named Robert. The mill owned by Robert Tucker, Jr., was on the north-eastern edge of the Dismal Swamp. Francis Farley of Antigua in the 1730s bought a tract of 26,000 acres in North Carolina from William Byrd II, and his son James Parke Farley married a daughter of William Byrd III. Francis Farley's plantation in Norfolk County, Va., was just to the north of the Dismal Swamp about fifteen miles east of Suffolk.

6. This is Mann Page (1749–1803), of Mannsfield near Fredericksburg, whose father, the former owner of the stock in the Dismal Swamp Company, was Mann Page (c.1718–1781) of Rosewell in Gloucester County, Virginia. The senior Mann Page acquired the one-half share from Robert Burwell in May 1766. See undated memorandum, cited above, but see also Appraise-ment of Dismal Swamp Slaves, 4 July 1764, n.1.

7. The original Nelson members of the Dismal Swamp Company were Thomas Nelson (1715–1787), known as the secretary, and William Nelson (1711–1772), president of the Virginia council. "William Nelson & Brother" listed here are presumably the two sons of President William Nelson: Gov. Thomas Nelson (1738–1789) and William Nelson (1754–1813). The Nelsons were merchants in Yorktown, Va., and the owners of numerous plantations and slaves in Hanover, Prince William, York, James City, and other counties.

8. Joseph Hornsby, like David Jameson, was not an original member of the Dismal Swamp Company but became one before the Revolution. The Joseph Hornsby named here is probably Thomas Walker's son-in-law. He may be, however, the son-in-law's English-born father who married Mary (or Marie) Rind of Williamsburg and reported for the tax roll of 1783 in Williamsburg ten slaves and a town lot. Thomas Walker transferred a one-half share to Hornsby in the 1770s, perhaps in 1775 (see the undated memorandum cited above).

From Walter Stewart

Dear Sir   Philadelphia January 26th 1784

Shortly before the Close of the War the House in which I am Connected sent a very large Property to the Havannah which went into the hands of a Merchant at that place. We have long, And with great Anxiety look'd for remittance, but none has Yet Arriv'd And the Silence of the Gentleman on the Subject Adds not a little to our Embarrasment And Apprehensions.

The Property is so Extensive And its Situation so delicate, that it has determin'd me to go there Previous to my Sailing for Ireland;[1] The Ship in which I shall go will leave this place in about Ten days, and I have to Entreat Your kindness in giving me a few lines of Introduction to the Governor, which I am Confident will be the means of Expediting my Business very much.

I hope your Excellency Will Excuse the Liberty I take in requesting this New Mark of Attention, but I am sure when you know that near Ten Thousand Pounds is kept from me You will have pleasure in being the means of having it restor'd, I Am well Assur'd getting properly Introduc'd to —— the present Governor will Occasion the Gentlemans Immediately Settling the Account.

Tis a distressing Circumstance my being Oblig'd to leave Mrs Stewart at this particular time, but as many of my future Prospects in life depend on My regaining this Property I must though unwillingly do it.

I Entreat Your Excellency's Answer as Soon as Possible, The Ship is Expected to sail by the 6th of Next Month, and As Your Letter will prove of the greatest Consequence to me, I Again request You will Excuse the Trouble I put You to.

Mrs Stewart Joins me in Affectionate Compliments to Mrs Washington & Yourself, And believe me to be with respect And Esteem Yr Excellency's Most Obedt Hble Servt

Walter Stewart

I take the Liberty to mention that the present Governor of the Havannah is Don Luis de Unzaga de Ameraga but his Usual Address is His Excellency the Governor & Captain General of the Island of Cuba &ca Havannah.[2]

Copy, in Stewart's hand, NjMoNP.

Walter Stewart (1756–1796) became a colonel of the 2d Pennsylvania Regiment during the Revolutionary War. In 1782 and 1783 he served as GW's inspector of the northern army. His father-in-law was the prominent Philadelphia merchant Blair McClenachan, and during the war Stewart became associated in business with Alexander Nesbitt.

1. Stewart returned from Cuba without going to Ireland. See Stewart to GW, 26 Oct. 1784.

2. Don Luis de Unzaga y Amézaga (c.1720–c.1790), governor of Louisiana from 1769 until the Revolution, became governor of Cuba in 1783. He remained in Cuba until 1785 and then he returned to Spain. See GW's letter of introduction to Unzaga, enclosed in GW to Stewart, 5 Feb. 1784, and Unzaga's acknowledgment, 26 August.

Letter not found: from Wakelin Welch, 26 Jan. 1784. On 27 July 1784 GW wrote to Welch: "Your letter of the 26th of Jany, & duplicate thereof, both coming by the way of James river, were long getting to hand."

From Elias Dayton

Sir,   Eliz[abe]th Town [N.J.] Janry 29th 1784

I have been honored with your Excellency's letter of the 28th Ult. appointing Philadelphia to be the place of meeting for the general society of the Cincinnati.[1]

I have since been particular in complying with your Excellency's request, by making that appointment known to the representatives of the society of this State and by urgeing in the most expressive terms, their punctual attendance. With the most sincere wishes that your Excellency may enjoy uninterrupted health & happiness I have the honor to subscribe myself with the greatest regard, Your Excellency's Most Obedt humb: servt

Elias Dayton

ALS, DSoCi. George Turner and GW, as secretary and president, respectively, of the Society of the Cincinnati, endorsed Dayton's letter, which was read at the general meeting on 8 May 1784.

Elias Dayton (1737–1807), a storekeeper in Elizabeth Town, N.J., fought in the French and Indian War. From 1776 to 1783 he was colonel of one or another New Jersey regiment. Dayton was president of the New Jersey chapter of the Society of the Cincinnati.

1. See GW's Circular Letter to the State Societies of the Cincinnati, 1 Jan. 1784.

From Rochambeau

Paris January 29th 1784.

Give me leave my dear Général to intrust you with friendship in one observation Which did not Escape to the regiments that composed our army. They find that the général society has given too much or too little extent to its favour, in granting it to all the Colonels and Stoping to them. I do not ask it for the Lieutenant colonels and majors because it is to the choice or favour that they owe their advancement as Well as the Colonels, but I think it Would be convenient to grant for ever and ever the marck of Cincinnati, not to the person, but to the office of the first Captain, actually in Service under the colours of every regiment Which has Served in america under your orders and mine.[1] I deliver up this reflexion, my dear Général, to your friendship, to use of it just as it will be most agreeable to you. I am With the most inviolable and respectfull attachment, my Dear Général your most obedient and very humble servant.

le cte de Rochambeau

LS, DSoCi; LS, DLC:GW. Both copies of the letter are in English and written in the same hand. They also are in the same handwriting as the two Rochambeau letters, in English, of 19 Jan. 1784. It is noted on the DSoCi copy that it was read on 11 May 1784 at the general meeting of the Society of the Cincinnati.

1. By "the office of the first Captain," Rochambeau probably meant regimental commander.

From Arthur St. Clair

Sir   Philada Janry 29th 1784

In Answer to your Circular Letter of the 28th ulto I have the Honor to inform You that Notice has been communicated to all the Delegates of the Society of this State (except Major Edwards) of the Time and Place which your Excellency has fixed for the general Meeting of the Cincinnati agreeably to the original Institution.[1]

It would be very proper that all the Delegates should attend, but I fear it will not be the Case—General Stewart will probably be sailed for Ireland[2]—Major Edwards is in Carolina, and may not be able to return in time, and it is doubtful as to myself. If a proper Number of the Society can be got together, a new Appointment in the Room of those who will necessarily be absent, may take Place; but the Members are now so dispersed, it is not easily done, besides that frequent Journeys to this City accord but ill with their Circumstances. It was a great Mistake to appoint any Person whose Attendance could not be relied on. I have the Honor to be Sir Your most obedient Servant

Ar. St Clair

ALS, DSoCi.

Arthur St. Clair (1736–1818), who became the first governor of the Northwest Territory in 1787, was president of the Pennsylvania Society of the Cincinnati. A former British officer who served in the French and Indian War, he settled in Pennsylvania and in 1776 supported American independence. He had risen to the rank of major general in the American forces when his abandonment of Fort Ticonderoga in 1777 clouded his military reputation, putting a damper on his military career.

1. See GW's Circular Letter to the State Society of the Cincinnati, 1 Jan. 1784. Evan Edwards was major in the 4th Pennsylvania Regiment when he retired on 1 Jan. 1783.

2. See Walter Stewart to GW, 26 Jan. 1784, n.1, and 26 Oct. 1784.

Letter not found: from Edward Newenham, 30 Jan. 1784. On 10 June GW wrote to Newenham: "I had the honor to receive . . . your favors of the 30th of Jany & 15th of March."

From Steuben

My dear General   [January 1784]
The letter of december 23d which I have had the honor of receiving from Your Excellency is the most honorable testimony which my serving could have received.[1] My first wish was to approve myself to Your Excellency & in having obtained it my happiness is complete.

The Confidence Your Excellency was pleased to place in my integrity & ability Gained me that of the Army & of the United States—Your approbation will secure it.

A Stranger to the language & customs of the Country, I had nothing to offer in my favor but a little experience & great good will to serve the United States, If my endeavours have succeeded I owe it to Your Excellencys protection, & it is a sufficient reward for me to know that I have been usefull in Your

Excellencys Operations—which always tended to the good of Your country.

After having studied the principles of the military art under Frederick, & put them into practice under Washington, after having deposited my sword under the same trophies of Victory with Yours, & finally after having received this last public testimony of Your esteem, there remains nothing for me to desire.

Accept my sincere thanks, My dear General for the Unequivocal proofs of Your friendship which I have received since I had first the honor to receive Your orders; & believe that I join my prayers to those of America for the preservation of Your life, & for the increase of Your felicity. with every sentiment of respect, I have the honor to be Your Excellencys Obdient

Copy, NHi: Steuben Papers.

Friedrich Wilhelm Ludolf Gerhard Augustin, Baron von Steuben (1730–1794), a professional soldier trained in the Prussian army of Frederick the Great, arrived as a volunteer in America on 1 Dec. 1777. Five months later GW asked Congress to make Steuben inspector general of the Continental army with the rank of major general, which was done. Steuben did not receive his final discharge from the army until 24 Mar. 1784. He settled in New York City.

1. GW wrote to Steuben on 23 Dec. 1783: " . . . I wish to make use of this last moment of my public life, to signifie in the strongest terms my entire approbation of your conduct, and to express my sense of the obligations the public is under to you, for your faithful and meritorious Services" (DLC:GW).

To Chastellux

My Dear Chevr   Mount Vernon 1st Feby 1784.

I have had the honor to receive your favor of the 23d of August from L'Orient. I hope this Letter will find you in the circle of your friends at Paris, well recovered from the fatigues of your long & wearisome inspection on the frontiers of the Kingdom.[1]

I am at length become a private citizen of America, on the banks of the Potowmac; where under my own Vine & my own Fig tree—free from the bustle of a camp & the intrigues of a Court, I shall view the busy world, "in the calm lights of mild philosophy"[2]—& with that serenity of mind which the Soldier in his pursuit of glory, & the Statesman of fame, have not time to enjoy. I am not only retired from all public employments;

but I am retireing within myself & shall tread the private walks of life with heartfelt satisfaction.

After seeing New York evacuated by the British Forces on the 25th of Novembr, & civil Government established in the City, I repaired to Congress, & surrendered into their hands, all my powers, with my Commission on the 23d of Decemr and arrived at this Cottage on Christmas eve, where I have been close locked up ever since in Frost & Snow. Mrs Washington thanks you for your kind remembrance of her, & prays you to accept her best wishes. With sentiments of pure & unabated friendship, I am My Dr Chevr Yours &ca

G: Washington

LB, DLC:GW; copy, ScC: Washington Letters.

François-Jean de Beauvoir, chevalier de Chastellux (1734–1788), the soldier and *philosophe*, landed at Newport, R.I., in July 1780 with the French army as one of Rochambeau's major generals. He remained in America for over a year after the victory at Yorktown, leaving for France in January 1783. Chastellux spoke English fluently, and GW was one among the many friends he made in the American army and with whom he remained in correspondence until his death in October 1788. The chevalier de Chastellux became the marquis in 1784 at the death of his brother.

1. Chastellux began his letter to GW of 23 Aug. 1783: "The King having honoured me since my return to Europe with a commission of inspector of his troops, and the Regiments I am to inspect being scattered through all the frontiers of this Kingdom, I am engaged in a progress of four thousand miles, but I find my self presently as near america as possible; and I wish heartily that instead of travelling on by land, I might embark at this place and proceed to Virginy where I am told your excellency is retired like an other Cincinnatus" (DLC:GW). Founded in 1664 by the French East India Company on an inlet of the Bay of Biscay and bought by the French government in 1782, Lorient was a free port and was to become an important station for the French navy.

2. The ending lines, in Addison, *Cato*, act 1, sc. 1, are:
> Thy steady temper, *Portius*,
> Can look on guilt, rebellion, fraud, and *Caesar*,
> In the calm lights of mild Philosophy.

From La Bretonnière

Monsieur   Paris Le 1er fevrier 1784
    Le Vte De La Bretonniere Capitaine des Vaisseaux du Roy à L'honneur de representer à Votre Excellence, qu'il comman-

dait La fregatte La Tourterelle En 1779, & 1780, Avec La quelle Il à d'abord Escorté Un convoy de Douze Batimens Americains, & plusieurs Batimens francois chargés De Munitions & d'officiers qui arriverent à Boston.

Ses ordres Luy prescrivoient de Se rendre directement à St Domingue D'ou Il Escorta au mois de Juin 1780 Un Second Convoy de Batimens Americains Jusqu'a la Bermude, ou Il S'Empara des Deux Corsaires Anglcois *La Bellone* de 28 Canons, & *L'Ambuscade* de 18, & de deux prises qu'ils avaient faites dont Il remit en possession les Proprietaires americains.

Il n'y avoit point D'Escadre francoise à L'Amerique à Cette Epocque dont La fregatte La Tourterelle fut Detachée, Ce qui met Le Sr Vte de La Bretonniere dans Le Cas de presenter Luy même Cette Adresse à Votre Excellence, Il Juge qu'elle Voudra Bien regarder Ses Services rendus au Commerce des Etats Unis avec La même faveur que Ceux des Capitaines Commandant Les Vaisseaux Des Escâdres En Station à L'Amerique, qui Comme Colonels reclament, & Sollicitent L'honneur d'Etre Associés à L'ordre de Cincinnatus.[1] J'ay L'honneur d'Etre avec respect Monsieur Votre trés humble & trés Obeïssant Serviteur

Vte de la Bretonniere

ALS, DSoCi. This is one of the relatively few letters to GW from French officers inquiring about membership in the Cincinnati for which no contemporary translation or English summary seems to have survived.

Louis-Bon-Jean de La Couldre, comte de La Bretonnière (1741–1809), later became known as the founder of the port of Cherbourg.

1. See the protest by Barras that the captains of French naval vessels were not made eligible for election to the Society of the Cincinnati, 23 Jan. 1784. Barras did not list Bretonnière among the captains who were eligible because, as Bretonnière explains here, his ship was not in the French squadron in American waters but instead escorted American ships in those waters in 1779 and 1780. When GW informed Barras for the Cincinnati on 17 May 1784 that French ship captains had been made eligible for election, he added that Bretonnière should be included "without Doubt." For GW's letter of 17 May, see Barras to GW, 23 Jan. 1784, n.7.

To Lafayette

Mount Vernon 1st Feby 1784

At length my Dear Marquis I am become a private citizen on the banks of the Potomac, & under the shadow of my own Vine

& my own Fig tree, free from the bustle of a camp & the busy scenes of public life, I am solacing myself with those tranquil enjoyments, of which the Soldier who is ever in pursuit of fame—the Statesman whose watchful days & sleepless Nights are spent in devising schemes to promote the welfare of his own—perhaps the ruin of other countries, as if this Globe was insufficient for us all—& the Courtier who is always watching the countenance of his Prince, in hopes of catching a gracious smile, can have very little conception. I am not only retired from all public employments, but I am retireing within myself; & shall be able to view the solitary walk, & tread the paths of private life with heartfelt satisfaction—Envious of none, I am determined to be pleased with all. & this my dear friend, being the order for my march, I will move gently down the stream of life, until I sleep with my Fathers.

Except an introductory letter or two, & one countermanding my request respecting Plate, I have not written to you since the middle of Octobr by Genl Duportail.[1] To inform you at this late hour, that the City of New York was evacuated by the British forces on the 25th of Novembr—that the American Troops took possession of it the same day, & delivered it over to the civil authority of the State—that good order, contrary to the expectation & predictions of G[enera]l Carleton, his Officers & all the loyalists, was immediately established—and that the harbour of New York was finally cleared of the British flag about the 5th or 6th of Decemr, would be an insult to your intelligence. And to tell you that I remained eight days in New York after we took possession of the City—that I was very much hurried during that time, which was the reason I did not write to you from thence—that taking Phila. in my way, I was obliged to remain there a week—that at Annapolis, where Congress were then, and are now sitting, I did, on the 23d of December present them my Commission, & made them my last bow—& on the Eve of Christmas entered these doors an older man by near nine years, than when I left them, is very uninteresting to any but myself. Since that period we have been fast locked up in frost & snow, & excluded in a manner from all kinds of intercourse, the winter having been, & still continues to be, extremely severe.

I have now to acknowledge, and thank you for your favors of

the 22d of July & 8th of September, both of which, altho' the first is of old date, have come to hand since my letter to you of October. The accounts contained therein of the political & commercial state of affairs as they respect America, are interesting, & I wish I could add that they were altogether satisfactory; & the Agency, you have had in both, particularly with regard to the Free ports in France, is a fresh evidence of your unwearied endeavours to serve this Country; but there is no part of your Letters to Congress My Dear Marquis, which bespeaks the excellence of your heart more plainly than that, which contains those noble & generous sentiments on the justice which is due to the faithful friends & Servants of the public; but I must do Congress the justice to declare, that as a body, I believe there is every disposition in them, not only to acknowledge the merits, but to reward the services of the army: there is a contractedness, I am sorry to add, in some of the States, from whence all our difficulties on this head, proceed; but it is to be hoped, the good sense & perserverance of the rest, will ultimately prevail, as the spirit of meanness is beginning to subside.[2]

From a letter which I have just received from the Governor of this State I expect him here in a few days, when I shall not be unmindful of what you have written about the bust, & will endeavour to have matters respecting it, placed on their proper basis.[3] I thank you most sincerely My Dear Marqs for your kind invitation to your house, if I should come to Paris. At present I see but little prospect of such a voyage, the deranged situation of my private concerns, occasioned by an absence of almost nine years, and an entire disregard of all private business during that period, will not only suspend, but may put it forever out of my power to gratify this wish. This not being the case with you, come with Madame la Fayette & view me in my domestic walks—I have often told you, & I repeat it again, that no man could receive you in them with more friendship & affection than I should do; in which I am sure Mrs Washington would cordially join me. We unite in respectful compliments to your Lady,[4] & best wishes for your little flock. With every sentiment of esteem, Admiration & Love, I am, My Dr Marqs Your Most Affecte friend

G: Washington

LB, DLC:GW.

1. Although GW wrote Duportail on 19 Oct. 1783, in his letter to Lafayette of the following day he indicated that his letter would be delivered to Lafayette by L'Enfant, not Duportail. It was on 30 Oct. 1783 that GW wrote Lafayette asking him to buy silver articles for him and on 4 Dec. 1783 that he wrote canceling his order (see Lafayette to GW, 10 Jan. 1784). GW's letter introducing the Rev. John Witherspoon is dated 9 Dec. 1783.

2. Lafayette's letters of 22 July and 8 Sept. 1783 are printed in Idzerda, *Lafayette Papers*, 5 : 145–47, 151–54. Lafayette enclosed in a letter to GW of 9 Sept. his letter to Congress dated 7 Sept. 1783, in which Lafayette reported on the French free ports: "Bayonne and Dunkirk Having Been Pointed out as American free Ports . . . I took Upon Myself to Represent the Harbour of L'Orient Was preferable to either of those Above Mentioned. It Has Lately Been Made a free Port, and I Now Wish the Affair of Bayonne May Be Again taken Up. Those three Ports, With Marsëilles, Would Make a Very Proper Chain, and in the Mean while I Hope L'Orient Will Prove Agreable to the American Merchants" (ibid., 148–50). With regard to what was "due to the faithful friends & Servants of the public," he had this to say, in part: "In the Difficulties Which a Patriotic, and Deserving Army Have Met With, Europeans Have Been Misled to See a Want of Public Gratitude. . . . In My Heart I Hope Every think Will Be Adjusted to the Satisfaction of that part of the Citizens Who Have Served in the Army, and that other Part in the Civil line who During the War Have Simpathised with their troops" (ibid.).

3. See Gov. Benjamin Harrison to GW, 8 Jan. 1784, and 3 April 1784, n.2. In a letter to Lafayette dated 4 Jan. 1782, GW enclosed a resolution and letter of the Virginia house of delegates thanking Lafayette for his contributions to the American cause and notifying him that the house had voted to have a bust of him made in Paris and presented to him. Lafayette wrote GW in his letter of 8 Sept. 1783: "it Would not Become me to Send to the Assembly House, (and to keep for me a Copy of) the Bust Which they Have Been pleased to Adorn With Honourable Inscriptions—So that I imagine Some Minister Here Will Be charged With the direction of that Monument of their Satisfaction, Which, I Confess, fills my Heart With a pleasing Sense of pride and Gratitude" (Idzerda, *Lafayette Papers*, 5 : 151–54).

4. The copyist wrote "Laday."

To Lauzun

My Dear Duke,   Mount Vernon 1st Feby 1784

I have had the pleasure to receive your favor of the 11th of Octor from L'Orient: every testimony which you give of my holding a place in your remembrance, is as pleasing as it is flattering to me; & I pray you not to deprive me of them.

After seeing the British forces withdrawn from New York, & Civil Government established there, I repaired to Congress (at

Annapolis) & surrendered into their hands all my public employments—I am now a private Citizen on the banks of the Potomac, meditating amidst Frost & snow (which at present encompass me) upon the structure of walks for private life; in any of which I should be happy to meet you, but in none with more pleasure than at this seat of retirement from the bustle of the busy world.

As I feel myself interested in every thing that concerns you, permit me to congratulate you with the warmth which friendship dictates, upon your late promotion; & to assure you that I derived much pleasure from the Accot you have given me of it.[1] Mrs Washington accepts your kind remembrance of her with gratitude, & offers best wishes in return. My Compliments are presented to Count Dillon, & the other officers of your Corps with whom I have the honor of an acquaintance; & with sentiments of the greatest regard & esteem, I have the honor to be Your Graces, &ca

G: Washington

LB, DLC:GW.

Armand-Louis de Gontaut, duc de Lauzun (later duc de Biron; 1747–1793), commanded Lauzun's legion at Gloucester during the siege at Yorktown and was chosen to take to Versailles the news of Cornwallis's capitulation. After Lauzun's return to America, he replaced Rochambeau as commander in chief of the French army in January 1783. Lauzun was a lieutenant general in command of one of the French armies in 1793 when he was arrested and, on 31 Dec., guillotined.

1. In his letter of 11 Oct. 1783, Lauzun reported that "the king has been so good to appoint me Major General and to keep my regiment in the peace establishment" (DLC:GW).

To Samuel Lewis

Sir,   Mount Vernon 1st Feby 1784

After an absence of near nine years I am returned to my own home again, & am begining to look into my private concerns, which have undergone an almost total suspension during that period.

In my researches after papers, I find Memorandums of warrants, which had been put into the hands of the Surveyor of Bottetourt to execute; particularly one in my own right, under the Royal Proclamation of 1763 for 5000 acres, which appears to have been executed in part on the 6th of Novr 1774 by a survey for 2950 on the Great Kanhawa, adjoining to (what is commonly called) the Pokitellico Survey for 21,941, acres.[1] And in a Letter of the 15th of Feby 1779, from Genl Lewis (whose death I sincerely regret) I find a paragraph containing these words:

"With regard to what you ask respecting Lands, no patents have been granted for any by the Proclamation of 63, but one which Doctr Connelly obtained by favor of Lord Dunmore, tho' there seems no doubt of our obtaining such rights, as soon as the Land office be opened, which is expected next meeting of the Assembly.[2] The burning Spring is surveyed in your & my names, I shall put the plat in the office, when opened, with some others I have in readiness.[3] It will, for the quantity, make a good stock place, as a great proportion may be turned into meadow. The ground off the river, from the mouth of Cole river up, & particularly about the burning Spring is very high, uneven & barren, so much so that no Settlement can be made off the low-grounds of the river."

I have now to beg the favor of you Sir, to give me such further information respecting the application of my warrants which have come into your office, as it may be in your power to do; & to inform me at the same time whether the Survey of 2950, acres made for my benefit, has ever been returned to the Secretarys office: Also, whether a patent for the Tract including the burning Spring has ever been obtained—for what quantity of acres—what improvements are on it, with such other particulars as may be interesting for me to know—particularly, in what County it lies—how far it is from the Kanhawa in the nearest part—& from the mouth of Cole river, where it forms its ju[n]ction with the latter.[4]

A Letter directed to any of your acquaintances in Fredericksburg or Richmond, with a request to put it into the post office, will be sure of getting to hand—other conveyances, more than probable will be precarious. I am—Sir Your most obt Servant

G: Washington

LB, DLC:GW.

Samuel Lewis, a son of GW's old friend and comrade Andrew Lewis (1720–1781), was the surveyor of Botetourt County, a position he had held since 1769 when the county was created from a part of Augusta County.

GW devoted a great deal of time and effort between 1769 and 1773 to securing for himself and other Virginians land promised to those who had fought in the French and Indian War. At the outbreak of that war, Robert Dinwiddie, lieutenant governor of Virginia, signed a proclamation dated 11 Feb. 1754 declaring that 200,000 acres would be set aside on the Ohio River for the officers and men who voluntarily served in the upcoming expedition to the Monongahela. Nine years later, in 1763, a royal proclamation instructed the colonial governors to reward the officers and men who had served in America in the recent war against the French with tracts of western land, ranging from 5,000 acres for field officers to 50 acres for privates. Because the transmontane west was closed to settlement after 1763, the Virginia veterans received no bounty land under either proclamation for nearly a decade after the war, but on 15 Dec. 1769 GW petitioned the Virginia governor and council on behalf of the officers and men of the Virginia Regiment of 1754 for the 200,000 acres of land promised them by Dinwiddie. The council consented to the survey of 200,000 acres, to be made in no more than twenty tracts, along the Great Kanawha and Ohio rivers for the benefit of the participants in the 1754 expedition (*Va. Exec. Jls.*, 6:337–38). William Crawford, who often served as GW's agent in the west, made the first survey in 1771. The initial allotment of land under this survey was completed on 6 Nov. 1772. GW received four tracts of land surveyed by Crawford, three on the Ohio River between the Little Kanawha and Great Kanawha rivers totaling 9,157 acres and one tract of 10,990 acres along the Great Kanawha. In the second bounty allotment under the Proclamation of 1754, made in November 1773, he secured a tract of 7,276 acres on the Great Kanawha, 3,953 acres in his own right and the rest by a trade with George Muse (ibid., 513–14, 548–49). See also *Papers, Colonial Series*, 8:passim, and, in particular, GW to George Mercer, 7 Nov. 1771, GW's Report on the Allotment of Bounty Lands, 23 Nov. 1772, GW to Charles Mynn Thruston, 12 Mar. 1773, GW's Advertisement, 13–15 July 1773, and GW's letter to Lord Dunmore and Council, 5 Nov. 1773.

On 6 Nov. 1773, after gaining the Virginia council's approval for the second allotment of land under the Proclamation of 1754, GW persuaded the governor and council to authorize warrants of survey on the "western waters" for those entitled to land under the Royal Proclamation of 1763 (7 Hening 663–69). GW had a right under this second proclamation to 5,000 acres for his own service as colonel of the Virginia Regiment, and by this time he had bought the shares of Capt. John Posey, who was entitled to 3,000 acres as a captain in the 2d Virginia Regiment in 1758, and the rights of Lt. Charles Mynn Thruston whose service as lieutenant in the 2d Virginia Regiment entitled him to 2,000 acres (see GW to James Wood, 13 Mar. 1773). With the Thruston warrant GW obtained a tract of 2,000 acres on the Great Kanawha at the mouth of the Cole (Coal) River (see GW to William Preston, 28 Feb. 1774, and Preston to GW, 7 Mar., 27 May, 15 Aug. 1774, and 27, 31 Jan. 1775; see also GW to Thomas Lewis, 1 Feb. 1784, n.6, and GW's grant dated 12 April 1784 in Vi: Va. Land Grants and Surveys, 1779–1800, Book I, pp. 540–41). GW used Posey's warrant for 3,000 acres to claim a tract of 2,813 acres surveyed by William Crawford on Millers Run at Chartiers (Shurtees) Creek and 187 acres of the 587 acres in a tract called Round Bottom on the Ohio River. For the Chartiers Creek tract, see GW to Thomas Lewis, this date, n.2; for the Round Bottom grant, see note 3 of that letter. Early in 1774 GW obtained the right to claim 3,000 more acres of bounty land under the Royal Proclamation of 1763 through his purchase of a warrant of survey from John Rootes, formerly a captain in the 2d Virginia Regiment. Sixteen years later GW used the Rootes warrant to claim three tracts of land on the Little Miami in the Northwest Territory (see GW to Thomas Lewis, 1 Feb. 1784, n.5).

As for the 5,000 acres GW was entitled to in his own right under the terms of the Proclamation of 1763, GW had the warrant for this acreage directed in 1774 to Botetourt County and to its surveyor Samuel Lewis (see William Preston to GW, 7 Mar. 1774, Andrew Lewis to GW, 9 Mar. 1774, GW to Andrew Lewis, 27 Mar. 1775). On 6 Nov. 1774 Samuel Lewis issued to GW a certificate of survey for 2,950 acres on the Great Kanawha, a tract first surveyed by William Crawford (see Vi: Va. Land Grants and Surveys, 1779–1800, Book 4, p. 444; GW to William Preston, 28 Feb. 1774; Preston to GW, 7 Mar. 1774; and Andrew Lewis to GW, 9 Mar. 1774, 27 Mar. 1775; see also note 1). Of the remaining 2,050 acres in GW's own warrant, a survey made on 26 May 1775 of the Burning Springs tract in Botetourt County accounted for 250 acres (Vi: Va. Land Grants and Surveys, 1779–1800, Book E, pp. 43–44). For correspondence regarding surveys of the 1,800 acres to which in 1775 he was still entitled by his warrant for 5,000 acres in Botetourt County, see William Crawford to GW, 7 Feb. and 6 Mar. 1775, and also, particularly, GW to Andrew Lewis, 27 Mar. 1775. Except for the Chartiers Creek tract, apparently no patents for any of the bounty land that he held under the Proclamation of 1763 were issued to GW before the Revolution. The grant for the Burning Springs tract was issued jointly to GW and Andrew Lewis on 14 July 1780 (see Vi: Va. Land Grants and Surveys, 1779–1800, Book E, pp. 43–44; GW to Andrew Lewis, 15 Oct. 1778; and Lewis to GW, 15 Feb. 1779; see also note 3). The two tracts on the Great Kanawha, for 2,000 and 2,950 acres, were granted to him on 12 April 1784; the Round Bottom tract, on 30 Oct. 1784; and the three Little Miami tracts, on 1 Dec. 1790 (Vi: Va. Land Grants and Surveys, 1779–1800, Book I, pp. 540–41, Book K, pp. 495–96, Book M, pp. 487–89, and Book 23, pp. 420–23).

1. The tract of 2,950 acres, downstream from present-day Charleston, W.Va., ran along the east, or south, bank of the Great Kanawha for about six miles in what was then Botetourt County, Virginia. GW claimed it in 1774 as a part of the 5,000 acres due him under the Proclamation of 1763 for his own service during the French and Indian War. The 2,950-acre tract was one of those that William Crawford had surveyed in 1771 for allotment under Dinwiddie's Proclamation of 1754, but it was not alloted to anyone in 1772 or 1773 after GW discovered that Crawford's surveys exceeded the authorized total of 200,000 acres. GW attempted without success in December 1773 to have a certificate of survey issued in Botetourt County for the tract on the strength of Crawford's 1771 survey and thereby obtain it for himself under the terms of the Royal Proclamation of 1763 (see GW to William Preston, 28 Feb. 1774, and, particularly, GW to Andrew Lewis, 27 Mar. 1775). GW secured Samuel Lewis's certificate of survey dated 6 Nov. 1774, but it was ten years later, on 12 April 1784, before Gov. Benjamin Harrison signed the

grant to GW of the 2,950 acres (Vi: Va. Land Grants and Surveys, 1779–1800, Book 4, p. 444). The Pocatellico survey of 1773 was William Crawford's second survey on the Great Kanawha for the soldiers' land bounty under Dinwiddie's Proclamation of 1754. It included 21,941 acres and bordered the river on the same side and downstream from GW's 2,950-acre tract and upstream of the tract that he acquired earlier on a warrant issued to him and George Muse jointly under the Proclamation of 1754 (see source note).

2. Dr. John Connolly (c.1743–1813), an explorer, land speculator, and trader living in Pennsylvania, acted as agent in the West for Virginia's governor, Lord Dunmore. He wrote to GW often in 1774 and 1775, before GW became commander in chief of the American forces and Connolly became a Loyalist.

3. In the spring of 1775 GW hoped to acquire 1,800 acres in the Ohio Country (see GW to Thomas Lewis, 1 Feb. 1784, n.7). With the 2,950-acre tract on the Great Kanawha, this would account for all but 250 of the 5,000 acres allowed him by his own warrant of survey issued to him under the Proclamation of 1763. On 27 Mar. 1775 GW suggested to Gen. Andrew Lewis that Lewis have a survey made of the final 250 acres at Burning Springs near present-day Charleston, W.Va., and that he and Lewis hold the tract jointly. Gov. Thomas Jefferson granted the tract to the two men on 14 July 1780 (Vi: Va. Land Grants and Surveys, 1779–1800, Book E, pp. 43–44). Thomas Hanson wrote in his journal on 15 April 1774: "the Burning Springs . . . is one of the wonders of the world. Put a blaze of pine within 3 or 4 inches of the water and immediately the water will be in flames and continues so until it is put out by the force of the wind" (quoted in Cook, *Washington's Western Lands*, 65).

4. No answer from Samuel Lewis has been found.

To Thomas Lewis

Sir,   Mount Vernon 1st Feby 1784

After an absence of almost nine years, & *nearly* a total suspension of all my private concerns, I am at length set down at home, & am endeavouring to recover my business from the confusion into which it has run during that period.

Among other matters which require my attention, indeed in which I need information, is the state of the Lands which I am entitled to in my own right, & by purchase under the Royal Proclamation in 1763, (west of the mountains). My papers are so mixed, & in such disorder at this time, occasioned by frequent hasty removals of them out of the way of the Enemy, that I cannot, (it being likely too, that some of them are lost) by the assistance of my memory, come at a thorough knowledge of that business. In a Letter which I have come across, from Capt.

William Crawford, who appears to have acted as your Deputy, dated the 8th of May 1774, I find these words—"Inclosed you have the Drafts of the round Bottom & your Shurtees Land, done agreeably to Mr Lewis's direction."[1] For the latter, I have found a patent signed by Lord Dunmore the 5th day of July 1774, for 2813 acres. but the other is yet in my possession[2]—& I am unable from any recollection I have of the matter to account for it, unless it should have been arrested there by some very ungenerous, & unjustifiable attempts of different people, at different times, to disturb me in my right to it—a right, I will venture to say, which is founded upon the first discovery of the Land—the first improvement of it; the first survey, & for ought I know the *only* report by authority that ever was made of it; which will be found in the words of the enclosed copy; the recital of which, if I mistake not, is in your own hand writing, & the whole with your signature.[3]

I have an imperfect recollection that in the year 1774 I sent a young man (of the name of Young, who at that time lived with me) to you on the business of these Lands; but not having as yet met with any letter from you, or report from him on the subject, I am unable with precision, to recollect the particular matters with which he was charged, or the result of his journey.[4] This then is one of the points on which I want information, & it is one of the inducements to my giving you the trouble of this letter. Another is, to know if I have any warrants in your hands unexecuted—it appearing from two Bonds in my possession, one from a Capt. Roots for 3000 acres;[5] the other from Lieut: (now, or lately the Revd Mr) Thruston for 2000 more;[6] that I ought (if I have not been neglectful in taking them out) to have warrts somewhere for 5000 acres under the proclamation of 1763—of which no locations, that have come to my knowledge, have yet been made.

Another thing of which I wish to be informed is, whether there are any surveys or locations in your Office, for the Land immediately at the point of fork between the little Kanhawa (upper side) & the Ohio; & in that case, in whose names they are made. The reason for the latter enquiry is, that Capt. Crawford in a letter of the 12th of Novr 1773, (an extract from which I herewith enclose, as I also do a copy of the survey, which he actually made at that place) proposed to locate this spot for his own benefit & mine. And I am the more sollicitous in this enquiry, as it appears by a subsequent Letter of his to me, that there was some difficulty in the way of his obtaining a warrant from Lord Dunmore for the part he expected to get himself[7]—If this difficulty continued to exist until his death, so as to prevent his location; & provided there are no better pretensions than mine; I should be glad to lay the two warrants before mentioned (to wit, Roots's and Thruston's) on this spot.[8] I would be understood however, explicitly to mean, that it is not my wish, in the smallest degree to injure my much regretted friend Crawford, or any person claiming under him by this application; but if the road is open, to learn only from you, by what mode I am to obtain it; having the above rights for 5000 acres, which were in whole or part designed for this very spot, yet to locate.

It might seem proper, before I conclude to make an apology for the trouble the compliance with these several requests will give you, but persuading myself you will consider the situation I have been in for many years, as a reasonable excuse, I conceive it is altogether unnecessary My good Sir to offer one. I shall only request the favor therefore, of an answer, & your care of the inclosed letter to your nephew, (who I find has made one survey for me in Bottetourt) or to the Surveyor of that County.

On the Death of your Brother, Genl Lewis, I most sincerely condole with you, as I had, while he was living a sincere friendship and regard for him. I am Sir Your very humble Servt

G: Washington

P.S. An answer under cover to some acquaintance of yours in Fredericksg or Richmond, with a request to put the Letter into the Post office, will be certain of getting to hand—otherwise, unless an opportunity shou'd offer directly to Alexandria, the chances are against my ever receiving it.

LB, DLC:GW.

Thomas Lewis (1718–1790), the older brother of Andrew Lewis, was the first surveyor of Augusta County, Va., serving from 1745 to 1777.

1. On 17 Feb. 1774 GW wrote Thomas Lewis about two tracts of land that he had had William Crawford survey for him, one at Round Bottom on the Ohio River about fifteen miles from present Wheeling, W.Va., and the other on Millers Run at Chartiers (Shurtees) Creek. Both tracts were considered to

be in Augusta County, Va., before the fixing of Pennsylvania's boundary placed them in that state. GW asked in his letter that Lewis make Crawford his deputy "to survey in the District between the Monongahela & Ohio, from Fort Pitt downwards, as far as you might choose to extend it." He also requested that Lewis certify for patenting the "Tract of 2,913 [2,813] acres" at Chartiers Creek. Lewis's response of 31 Mar. 1774 enclosing a letter to William Crawford has not been found, but when Lewis's letter arrived GW immediately wrote a letter (also missing) to William Crawford enclosing Lewis's letter to Crawford and "pointing out the necessity of his [Crawford's] attempting to qualify as your [Lewis's] Deputy, at your [Lewis's] Court for April" (GW to Thomas Lewis, 5 May 1774). See notes 2 and 3 below. See also William Crawford to GW, 8 May 1774, and Thomas Lewis to GW, 24 Feb. 1784.

2. The "Shurtees Land" was the tract of 2,813 acres on Chartiers Creek which GW secured on John Posey's warrant for 3,000 acres. GW's grant of the land from Lord Dunmore dated 5 July 1774 is printed in "Washington's Grants in West Virginia," 135–36. See GW to Samuel Lewis, 1 Feb. 1784, source note. GW was to have a great deal of trouble with settlers on his tract. See, in particular, GW's diary entries for 18–20 Sept. 1784, and the editors' notes (*Diaries*, 4:25–31). See also GW's correspondence in 1785 and 1786 with the Pennsylvania lawyer Thomas Smith who represented GW in his prolonged efforts to evict the settlers from his Millers Run land, and especially the editorial note in Smith's letter to GW, 9 Feb. 1785.

3. In his letter of 5 May 1774, GW wrote Thomas Lewis: "In the fall of the year 1770, when I went to view the Lands which have been since surveyed under the Proclamation of 1754 I made choice of this spot of Land (called the Round bottom) marked Trees, & directed Captn Crawford, when he went down the Spring following to survey it, which he accordingly did, as may appear by his certificate inclosed you by Mr [George] Young. Sometime after this, hearing that Doctor [John] Brisco had taken possession of it, & actually had, or was going to fix Negroes on it, I wrote him a letter [3 Dec. 1772], of which No. 1. is a copy, upon which I was informed he had quit it. Sometime after this again, I learned that Mr Michael Cresap had taken possession of it, built houses, & was working hands thereon, upon which I also wrote him a letter [7 Feb. 1775], of which No. 2 is the copy . . . receiving at the same time a message, by Capt. [William] Crawford, from Mr Michael Cresap, that if I would let him have the Land he would pay me what I thought the worth of it, to which, I returned for answer; that as it was the only piece of Land I had upon the Ohio, between Fort Pitt, & the Kanhawas, & found it very necessary as a Stage or Lodgment, in coming up the river, I could not agree to part with it, but again offered to pay for any labour or improvement, which he had made." GW had written Lewis earlier, on 17 Feb. 1774, about Crawford's survey of the 575-acre Round Bottom tract: "I am at a loss what to do about it; the quantity is too small to locate 1000 acres upon, and yet, rather than lose it, I must do so. Permit me to ask then, if the matter can be so managed upon your Entry book, as to secure this tract against the attempts of any other, upon condition of my surrendering one thousand acres of my claim for it, in

case of any other application; but yet for me to have the privilege, of redeeming it as it were, by purchasing up sundry small claims to the amount of the Tract, & locating of them upon that spot." The Virginia council had decided on 16 Dec. 1773 that an officer claiming land under the Proclamation of 1763 (see GW to Samuel Lewis, 1 Feb. 1784, source note) "be allowed a distinct Survey for every thousand Acres" (*Va. Exec. Jls.*, 6:553–54). On 22 April 1775 Fielding Lewis wrote GW that he had received for GW Thomas Lewis's survey of the 587-acre (mistakenly given as 578) tract on the Ohio.

In his response, dated 24 Feb. 1784, to GW's letter of 1 Feb., Thomas Lewis assured GW "that on Shertee & that at the round bottom on the Ohio, the Warrants with the assignments on which you right to both those are founded I have in Safe keeping, and they were all recited or Taken notice off in the Certificate of Location transmitted you by Colo. Crawford." Before getting Lewis's reply GW wrote a letter on 10 Feb. 1784 to the register of the Virginia land office, John Harvie, in which he described the location of the Round Bottom tract, complaining that Cresap had "arrested my survey of it for 587 acres." On 14 April 1784 John Harvie sent to GW the Chartiers Creek and Round Bottom grants, both dated 12 April 1784. GW's copies of the grants are in DLC:GW, and transcriptions may be found in CD-ROM:GW. The Round Bottom grant was made on a survey of 587 acres dated 14 July 1773. GW laid claim to it under several warrants he had bought: 187 acres of the 3,000-acre warrant that he got from John Posey, dated 25 Nov. 1773; a 200-acre warrant issued to Goodrich Crump on 14 Dec. 1773; and 50-acre warrants issued to Jesse Scott on 7 May 1774, to Marshall Pratt on 14 April 1774, to Robert Scott on 7 May 1774, and to John Poe on 10 May 1774. GW secured his grant to the Round Bottom tract in October 1784 (see Vi: Va. Land Grants and Surveys, 1779–1800, Book M, pp. 487–89; Book 4, pp. 417–18). On 31 May 1785, however, GW entered a caveat to block the issuing of a grant for the Round Bottom lands to the heirs of Michael Cresap, in which he gave the history of his own claims and of his troubles with Cresap. For a discussion of the claims of the young Michael Cresap, who was killed in 1775, and of his heirs to the Round Bottom tract, see GW to John Marshall, 17 Mar. 1789, n.2.

4. GW hired George Young in January 1774 for a year at an annual salary of £25 to make the improvements on his western landholdings required by law (*Diaries*, 3:226). Young moved to Mount Vernon from Bladensburg, Md., on 13 Jan. 1774, and shortly thereafter he went to the frontier to inspect GW's bounty lands and to deliver GW's warrants of survey to the surveyors in the western counties of Virginia (see Andrew Lewis to GW, 9 Mar. 1774).

5. As a captain in Col. William Byrd's 2d Virginia Regiment in 1758, John Rootes was entitled to a warrant of survey for 3,000 acres of bounty land under the Proclamation of 1763. On 14 Feb. 1774 John Page wrote GW that he had purchased from Rootes his warrant for 3,000 acres. It was undoubtedly this warrant to which GW was referring on 27 Mar. 1775 when he wrote William Preston, surveyor of Fincastle County, that he had a warrant for surveying 3,000 acres which had been mistakenly directed to Fincastle County rather than to Augusta County as it should have been. GW inquired about land in Fincastle County, and on 9 April 1775 Preston wrote him that John

Floyd was sending GW a description of a 3,000-acre tract in Fincastle which Floyd had recently surveyed. It was not until 1790 that GW secured under the Rootes warrant a grant of three tracts of land on the Little Miami: a survey of 839 acres dated 28 Dec. 1787, another of 977 acres dated 26 May 1788, and a third of 1,235 acres dated 27 May 1788 (Vi: Va. Land Grants and Surveys, 1799–1800, Book 23, pp. 89, 846–48).

6. GW in 1773 bought a warrant of survey for 2,000 acres which Charles Mynn Thruston was entitled to under the Royal Proclamation of 1763 for his service in 1758 as lieutenant in the 2d Virginia Regiment. The tract on the Great Kanawha that GW claimed with the Thruston warrant was across the river from the 2,950-acre tract that he claimed at the same time on his own warrant (see GW to Samuel Lewis, 1 Feb., n.1). These two tracts on the Great Kanawha were surveys that William Crawford made in 1771 but were not a part of the bounty lands assigned in 1772 and 1773 under the Proclamation of 1754 (see GW to Samuel Lewis, 1 Feb. 1784, source note). GW did not receive grants for these two tracts until 12 April 1784. See John Harvie to GW, 21 Feb., and 12 and 14 April 1784.

7. Neither the extract of William Crawford's letter nor the copy of his survey has been found. The tract of land at the forks of the Little Kanawha and Ohio rivers, the present site of Parkersburg, W.Va., contained more acreage than Crawford could claim under the Royal Proclamation of 1763. Crawford asked GW to "Joyn as much of your Officers Claim as will tak the hole survay . . . [and] you may Depend I will make any Equil Devesion you shall propose" (Crawford to GW, 12 Nov. 1773). This was not accomplished, however (see Crawford to GW, 10 Jan. 1774 and 6 Mar. 1775; see also John Harvie to GW, 21 Feb. 1784, particularly note 4).

8. For the military warrants GW secured from John Rootes and Charles Mynn Thruston, see notes 5 and 6.

From Jacob Read

Sir   Annapolis [Md.] 1st Feby 1784

By the post which arrivd from the Northward yesterday I had the honour to receive under Cover to myself the Letter I now do Myself the pleasure to inclose to you.[1]

As we have been for a Considerable time Without a post to or from the Southward I have preferred Sending this Letter to Mount Airy to be forwarded by any Conveyance that May offer from that place by a private hand and if none at present Shoud offer then to be put into the post office at Marlboro.[2]

By the desertion (for it deserves no other name) of one of the Delaware Delegates Congress are again left to do little more than meet and adjourn de die in diem. & I do not hear of any other Delegation Coming forward. Colonel Humphry's late of Your family is here—our Situation has not admitted of our thinking of any thing in behalf of that Gentleman and others in his Situation.[3]

Two very good and I think honorable places are now Vacant Vizt the place of Under Secr[e]tary of foreign Affairs and of Deputy Secratry of Congress. You know the abilities and genius of Col. Humphry's I wou'd be obliged to you for your Opinion Whether you think either of those wou'd Suit that Gentleman? and whether you Wou'd recommend his acceptance of either— The Latter is 1000 Dollars the former 800 per Annum.[4] Do me the honour to present my most respectful Compliments to your Lady and believe that I am with the gratest respect and Esteem Sir Your Most obedient and most Humble Servant

Jacob Read

P.S. The Minister of France Monssr Marbois are here. Also Genl Armand and a Number of other Officers asking what we cannot grant I pity & feel for them, but this is almost all than Can be afforded them.[5]

ALS, DLC:GW.

Jacob Read (1752–1816), a lawyer and planter in South Carolina, was a member of Congress from 1783 to 1785. He served as a United States senator from South Carolina from 1795 to 1801.

1. This was the letter from Elias Boudinot dated 11 Jan. 1784.

2. Mount Airy was the house where Benedict Calvert (c.1724–1788) lived in Prince George's County, Md., across from Mount Vernon. Upper Marlboro, Md., is a town on the western branch of the Patuxent River, also in Prince George's County.

3. The Congress finally on 14 Jan. reached a quorum of nine states in attendance and immediately ratified the definitive treaty of peace. Three days later Eleazer McComb (d. 1798), a delegate from Delaware, left for home. Not until the first of March were as many as nine states again present.

4. See David Humphreys to GW, 6 Jan. 1784, and note 2 of that document.

5. François Barbé de Marbois (Barbé-Marbois; 1745–1837) arrived in America with La Luzerne and became secretary to the legation in 1783. Upon La Luzerne's departure in June 1784, Barbé-Marbois became chargé d'affaires. For Armand's dealings with Congress at this time, see Armand to GW, 4 Feb. 1784, and notes.

To Rochambeau

My dear Count,   Mount Vernon Feby 1st 1784.

Having resigned my public trust, and with it all my public cares into the hands of Congress; I now address myself to you in the character of a private Citizen on the banks of the Potomack, to which I have been retired (fast locked in Frost and Snow) since Christmas Eve. The tranquil walks of domestic life are now unfolding to my view; & promise a rich harvest of pleasing contemplation—in which my dear Genl you will be one of my most agreeable themes—as I shall recollect with pleasure, that we have been Contemporaries & fellow-labourers in the cause of liberty, and that we have lived together as Brothers should do—in harmony & friendship.

I saw all the British forces embarked, and on the point of Sailing before I left New York about the 4th of December. I then repaired to Congress & surrendered all my public employments into their hands; and am now just beginning to look into the deranged situation of my own private Concerns which I did not permit to come in for any share of my attention during the last nine years of my life.

To see you at this seat of retirement from the bustle of the world, & the cares of public office is a pleasure too great to expect, tho' you must allow me to wish for it, because I can with much truth assure you that, I am with every sentiment of esteem, regard, and friendship My dear Count, Yr most Obedt & most Hble Servt

Go: Washington

Mrs Washington prays you to accept her Compliments.

ALS, owned by Paul Mellon, Upperville, Va.; LB, DLC:GW; French translation, DLC: Rochambeau Papers.

From Armand

Sir   anapolis [Md.] february 4th 1784

being intrusted by Grl duportail,[1] the officers of his corps & thoses of the legion with the management of their final settlement of accounts, I came to this place near three weeks ago; my intention was to lay our affairs before Congress, & while they had them under their consideration, to go and pay my respects to your Excellency.

I was to that point, when Colonel humphrey told us that you were Going to frederickbourg & to return only, in 10-or-12 days, during that time Congress have determined agreeable to our request, & the distressed Condition of the officers concerned in their resolve, oblige me to make all haste in my power towards philadelphia, less the thaw should prevent my being there for some weeks, which delay would be Extremely hurtfull to thoses Gentlemen who at this instant are destitute of resources.[2]

although thoses Circumstances deprive me at present of the honor to pay a visit to your Excellency, I am happy in the idea that as soon I have finally settled with the Superintendant of finance, I shall take a Journey to virginia, the whole purpose of which will be to see once more the man which I shall love, respect & admire all my days.

General mifflin who intended to pay you a visit with me has posponed the Journey & will go with the chevalier de la Luzern[3]—I inclose here a lettre that was Confided to my Care. I have the honor to be with the highest respect your Excellency's Sir—the most obdt hble st

　　　　　　　　　　　　　　　　C. Armand

ALS, DLC:GW.

Charles Armand-Tuffin, marquis de La Rouërie (1750–1793), used the name Armand as an officer in the Continental army after his arrival in America from France in 1777 until his final return to France in 1784. Made colonel commandant of the first battalion of Casimir Pulaski's Partisan Legion in 1777, he took part in GW's campaigns until 1779 when the legion joined the expedition against British-held Savannah. After Pulaski's death at Savannah, Armand assumed command of the Partisan Legion. In 1783 he was made a brigadier general and chief of cavalry in the Continental army. For further details of Armand's life and family, see Armand to GW, 18 May 1784, and notes and enclosure.

1. Louis Le Bègue de Presle Duportail (1743–1802) came to America as a captain of engineers in the French army in 1777, and Congress made him brigadier-general commandant of engineers for the Continental army. GW used him extensively in his campaigns, most notably as chief engineer at the siege at Yorktown. Duportail was a major general when he left the United States in 1783. He returned to America in 1793 to escape the Terror and remained until 1802 when he sailed for home and died on the high seas.

2. On 15 Jan. 1784 at Annapolis, where the Congress was sitting, Armand wrote Thomas Mifflin, president of Congress: "From the command & rank I held in the american army, I find my self at the head of the officers of the first partizan Legion & of the others french Gentlemen who continued in this service untill the end of the war, to represent their Circumstances to Congress & obtain from that hble body such sums on account of their pay & commutation as may Enable them to discharge their debts here & to return to Europe, and at the same time such terms for the payment of the interest & principal of what sums shall remain due to us as to render it practicable to negociate our notes without a material loss" (DNA:PCC, item 164). Armand went on to ar-

gue the justice of his claims, and on 22 Jan. the committee to which Armand's letter had been referred reported to Congress: "That the foreign officers lately in the service of the United States, who were not attached to the line of any particular State, complain of great and singular hardships under which they have laboured during the late war. The pay which they received for a considerable time in depreciated money, was very unequal to their actual expences, nor could they be profited by the recommendations of Congress on the subject of depreciation, which afforded immediate relief to the rest of the army, because there was no State to which they could look for the balance of their pay; hence it followed, that some of them have depended in a great measure for their support, on remittances from their friends in France, while others less fortunate, have contracted considerable debts in America. That in their present situation, they neither have the means of subsisting in America, nor of returning to their native country, unless some part of the money due them by the public shall be paid." Congress promptly voted to give the officers, "such sums on account of their pay as may be necessary to relieve them from their present embarrassments, and enable those in America to return to their native country" (*JCC*, 26:43). Four days later, on 26 Jan., Armand wrote Mifflin requesting Congress "to pass a resolve authorizing their financier to take such *measures* in the settlement of our accounts as will ensure us the punctual payment of the interest of the sums due to us." And on 3 Feb. Congress directed the superintendent of finance "to take measures, as far as may be consistent with the finances of the United States, for remitting annually to the foreign officers [as specified] . . . the interest of such sums as may remain due to them respectively, after the payments which shall have been made to them in consequence of the resolution of the 22d of January last" (ibid., 65–66). For a discussion of debts due to foreign officers, see La Radiere to GW, 26 April 1789, n.1.

3. Neither Armand, nor La Luzerne, nor Thomas Mifflin got to Mount Vernon at this time. Armand may have visited in April, La Luzerne did visit in April, and Mifflin was there in June. See Armand to GW, 14 Mar., La Luzerne to GW, 18 Feb., GW to La Luzerne, 5 May, and Mifflin to GW, 31 May 1784.

To Clement Biddle

Dear Sir,					Mount Vernon Feb. 5th 1784.

On the 8th of last month I wrote to you for 70 yards of Livery Lace, of which I was in immediate want, and requested to have it sent by the Post to Alexandria—As there is some reason to believe the Post has hardly gone *through*, yet, I beg leave to repeat my want of it, & to pray it may be sent as soon as possible—The lace should be red & white, Inch, or ¾ of an Inch wide, or any where between.

I would now thank you for sending me a two pole Chain,

exact in its length, & not too small, or weak in the links—this I wish to receive soon too.

The things you were to send by water, did not arrive before the Frost set in, & I have heard nothing of them since. I am with esteem & regard Dr Sir Yr most Obedt Servt

Go: Washington

ALS, PHi: Washington-Biddle Correspondence.

To Walter Stewart

Dear Sir,   Mount Vernon Feb. 5 [1784]

Your letter of the 26th Ulto did not reach me untill this day a little before dinner—The Servant says he was detained three or four days at George Town.[1]

If the letter herewith enclosed can be of any Service to you, it will afford me pleasure, as I wish you all imaginable success in your attempt to recover the property which has been withheld from your House at the Havana.[2]

The letters under cover with this (in answer to some which I have lately received from my friends in France &ca) I pray you to put into the proper channel of conveyance—by the Packet.[3] Mrs Washington joins me in wishing you a good & prosperous voyage, & in compliments to Mrs Stewart—tell her, if she don't think of me often, I shall not easily forgive her; & will scold at, & beat her soundly too—at Picquet—the next time I see her. With great esteem I am Dr Sir Yr Most Obedt Servt

Go: Washington

ALS, PWacD: Sol Feinstone Collection, on deposit PPAmP.

1. Georgetown, now a part of Washington, D.C., was in Maryland.

2. The text of GW's letter, dated 5 Feb., to Luis de Unzaga y Amézaga, governor of Cuba, is: "The Gentn who will have the honor of presenting this Letter to your Excellency, is Genl Stewart, an Officer of distinguish'd Merit in the American Army, having Embarked amongst the foremost in the cause of his Country, and persever'd in the Service of it, with equal honor to himself; and, advantage to her, Untill the happy reestablishment of peace, by the acknowledgment of our Independence & Sovereignty.

"He proposes soon to make a Voyage to Europe, but wishing, previously thereto, to Visit a place so celebrated & well known to this Country as the Havana, I have taken the liberty of introducing him to your Excellency's countenance & Civilities, during his stay there. He will repeat to you, the assurances of respect & consideration with which I have the honor to be, Yr

Excellys Most obedt & Most Hble Servt." Until the word "reestablishment," the text quoted here is taken from GW's letter-book copy (DLC:GW); the remainder from the photocopy of the ALS in American Art Association catalog (December 1925), item 460. A Spanish translation is in Archives General de Indias, Seville. Unzaga wrote GW on 26 August.

3. These undoubtedly included letters of 1 Feb. to Chastellux, Lafayette, and Lauzun.

Letter not found: from Samuel Vaughan, 5 Feb. 1784. On 8 April 1784 GW wrote to Vaughan: "Your favor of the 5th of Feby was long on its way to me."

From Charles Thomson

Dear Sir,   Annapolis [Md.] 7 Feby 1784

The bearer being just setting out for your seat I have detained him, till I could inform you that I have received the letter which you honored me with by Col. Humphreys. The letter enclosed therein for the chev. de Heintz I put under cover to Monsr Rothenbourg banquier a Danzic and sent the same to Mr R. Morris with a request to take the charge of forwarding it by a safe conveyance either with his dispatches to our Minister at the court of Versailles or the Hague or directly to the port of Dantzick.[1]

With respect to your commission I have to inform you that previous to the rect of your letter it had been in agitation among the members to have an order passed for returning it to you in a gold box A motion has accordingly been made to that effect wch was received with general approbation & referred to a comee to be drawn up in proper terms. The comee have not yet reported. But I have not the least doubt of its being returned to you in a way that will be satisfactory and I heartily wish that this sacred deposit may be preserved by your children & children's children to the lastest posterity and may prove an incentive to them to emulate the virtues of their worthy and great progenitor.[2] I thank you for your kind invitation & assure you nothing would give me greater Satisfaction than to be able to accept it. Mrs T. has not the least doubt of Mrs W.'s goodness in joining you in your kindness. & would be equally pleased in accompanying me to your seat. I hope in my next to be able to inform you not only of the return of the Commission but of measures taken to secure the papers in your possession.

We are here almost buried in snow. I have not time to say much of public affairs as Capt. Le Brun waits we have had 9 states only for 3 days since we came here.[3] Please to make my most respectful compliments to Mrs Washington. I am with the most sincere regard Dear Sr Your affectionate & most obt humble Ser.

Chas Thomson

ALS, DLC:GW.

1. For GW's dealings with the Polish chevalier Jean de Heintz, see Thomas Mifflin to GW, 9 Jan. 1784, n.1. It was Heintz's instructions that GW's reply should be sent to the Danzig banker Rothenbourg (Heintz to GW, 13 May 1783, DNA:PCC, RG 360).

2. GW wrote Thomson on 22 Jan. asking that his commission be sent to him. See note 2 of that document.

3. Capt. Jerome Le Brun de Bellecour of Pulaski's (later Armand's) Partisan Legion was one of the four French officers of the legion whom Congress, at Armand's behest, promoted by brevet on 3 Feb. 1784 before their discharge (Armand to Mifflin, 16 Jan. 1784, DNA:PCC, item 164; *JCC*, 26:66).

To John Harvie

Sir, Mount Vernon 10th Feby 1784

After an absence of almost nine years from home, & a total suspension, as it were to all my private concerns during that period, I am now endeavouring to obtain a knowledge of my Affairs & to put my business in some kind of order again. The deranged situation of my papers (occasioned by frequent hasty removals of them out of the enemy's reach) makes it more difficult to affect these, than it otherwise would be; but by some Memo[randu]ms I have lately met with, it would seem that several Land Warrants which I had obtained from Lord Dunmore in my own right, & by purchase from Capt. John Roots & Lieut: (now, or lately the Revd Mr) Thruston under the Royal Proclamation of 1763, amounting in the whole to 10,000 acres, have, or ought to have been placed in the hands of the Surveyor of Augusta, Bottetourt or Fincastle, or partly in all, for execution;[1] but having come across nothing as yet which points precisely to the appropriation of them, and as the offices for those Counties are at a great distance from me, & possibly the Surveyors of them unknown, as there may have been changes within the period above mentioned to which I am a stranger; I take the liberty to enquire of you, Sir, whether any Surveys, consequent of these warrants, have been returned to the Land Office since the beginning of the year 1774, in my name; besides one for 2813 acres which I have found a patent for, previous to that date[2]—There were many Surveys made by Capt: Wm Crawford, (specially appointed for the purpose) & for which Patents have issued; they being for the 200,000 acres granted by the Proclamation of Govr Dinwiddie in the year 1754; which I mention that you may not be misled in your researches, by a discovery of these.

If upon examination of the Surveyors reports you should find any Surveys subsequent to the above date, in my name, or in partnership with others, (for I expected to be joined with Genl Andrew Lewis in a small tract on the waters of the *Great* Kanhawa, including a burning Spring;[3] & with Wm Crawford in a tract at the confluence of the *little* Kanhawa & Ohio) I shall thank you for information thereof. And as there was some difficulty in the way of the latter, I shou'd be obliged to you for acquainting me if a survey of this spot has ever been returned, in the name of any other person, to the office—It being at the point of fork, will render the search easy, & as one Doctr Brisco set up a claim to it, his name, or that of Michael Cresap of Maryland who appears to have had pretensions of some kind or another to every good spot in the country, may render the search more easy.[4] You will please to advert to the circumstance of there being two Kanhawa's; & that this is distinguished by the appellation of the Little Kanhawa.

Having mentioned the name of Cresap, it reminds me of another matter which I must also request the favor of you to give me information upon—it is, whether if he has had any Surveys returned to the Land Office of this State, among them is one for about five or six hundred acres for a tract which is well known, & distinguished by the name of the round bottom on the Ohio, opposite to Pipe Creek, & a little above a creek call Capteening? He has, I find, arrested my Survey of it for 587 acres, made under all the legal forms & upon proper warrants, for no better reason that I could ever learn, than because it was a good bottom & convenient for him to possess it, & had it in his power to do it with impunity.[5]

The length of time which I have been out of the State, & the changes which may have happened in the Constitution of it since, may render these requests to you Sir, altogether improper; should this really be the Case, it makes an apology to you on my part necessary for the trouble of this application; but I must still pray your compliance with the requests; presuming, if the Land office should have been separated from that of the Secretary's, it is nevertheless kept at Richmond, where you can have recourse to the records of it without much trouble, the doing of which would save time to me, & render a second application from *me* to any other office unnecessary. I am Sir Your Most obt &c.

G: Washington

LB, DLC:GW.

John Harvie (1743–1807), son-in-law of Gabriel Jones, was register of the Virginia land office from 1780 to 1791.

1. For GW's earlier inquiry about the warrants for survey that he had acquired in 1773 and 1774 from John Rootes and Charles Mynn Thruston, see GW to Thomas Lewis, 1 Feb. 1784, notes 5 and 6 in particular. For a discussion of GW's acquisition of bounty lands under Dinwiddie's Proclamation of 1754 and under the Royal Proclamation of 1763, see particularly the source note in GW to Samuel Lewis, 1 Feb. 1784.

2. For Lord Dunmore's patent of the 2,813 acres of the Chartiers Creek land, 5 July 1774, see GW to Thomas Lewis, 1 Feb., n.2.

3. For the survey and grant of the tract called Burning Springs, see GW to Samuel Lewis, 1 Feb., n.3.

4. See GW to Thomas Lewis, 1 Feb., n.7.

5. For the Round Bottom tract, see GW to Thomas Lewis, 1 Feb., n.3.

To Edmund Randolph

Dear sir,   Mount Vernon 10th Feby 1784

A short time before I came home I received a power of Attorney from the Earl of Tankerville, & his Brother, the Honorable Mr Bennett; authorising Colo. Hooe, (miscalled Howe,) yourself & me, to dispose of property belonging to the latter in this State. Letters, from Lord Tankerville & the Countess his Mother, to me, accompanied the Power, expressive of their wishes that I would accept the trust; but the deranged situation of my own private concerns, which have in a manner undergone a complete suspension of almost nine years, and the intricately involved Affairs of some others, which, unfortunately for them, & painful in the reflection to me, were committed to my care; puts it absolutely out of my power to engage in any new matters, without violence to my own convenience, & injury to those I have in hand. Of this I have informed her Ladyship & my Lord; at the same time I assured them that the trust could not be reposed in better hands than Colo. Hooe's (who consents to act & has the Power) & yours, who I took the liberty to say, would either accept the appointment or inform them of the contrary.[1] Mrs Washington joins me in best respects to Mrs Randolph, & with great truth & sincere friendship, I am, Dear sir, Your most Obedt & affecte Servant

G: Washington

LB, DLC:GW.

Edmund Randolph (1753–1813) in 1784 was attorney general of Virginia. Until he became governor of Virginia in November 1786, he often handled legal matters in Richmond for GW. He was married to Elizabeth Nicholas, who died in 1810.

1. See GW to Tankerville, 20 Jan. 1784, n.1.

From William Smallwood

Sir,   Mattawoman [Md.] February 10th 1784

I was honored with your Letter dated the 28th December last,[1] and agreeable to your request, communicated the Objects contained therein to the Delegates of our State Society of the Cincinnati—and to obviate a possibility of failure in the communication, requested them to acknowledge the receipt of my Letters by the earliest Opportunity.

I have anxiously waited for an Opportunity of contriving an Answer to your Letter, but the extreme hard Weather still continuing to shut up the Communication, obliges me to lodge this at Piscattaway,[2] with directions to contrive it by the way of Alexandria or George Town, as I imagine Passengers cross over upon the Ice at one or both those Places without any risque or difficulty. I have the Honor to be with high Consideration & Regard your Excellencys Most Obed. Hble Sert

W. Smallwood

ALS, DSoCi.

Gen. William Smallwood (1732–1792), who lived on Mattawoman Creek in Charles County, Md., was president of the Maryland Society of the Cincinnati. He attained the rank of major general in the Continental army in 1780, and he served as governor of Maryland from 1785 to 1788.

1. See GW's circular letter, 1 Jan. 1784.

2. Piscataway is a town southeast of Mount Vernon in Prince George's County, Maryland.

From the South Carolina Legislature

Sir　　　　　　　　Charleston So. Carolina february 10th 1784

It is with inexpressible pleasure that we transmit your Excellency the Address of the Legislative body of the State of So. Carolina.[1]

We are peculiarly happy, in the Opportunity afforded us, of testifying the high sense we entertain, of the consummate abilities and unparalleled virtue, that you have displayed in a long, and arduous Contest—a Contest! that altho it often placed you, in the most dangerous, and difficult situations, served only, to discover the inexhaustible sources of your Genius, and invincible fortitude, and administer to you fresh occasions of Glory.

When we consider how much, the United States are indebted to your Excellency for their Freedom, Independence, and Peace; words are wanting to convey the warmth, and sincerity of our esteem, and grateful respect.

May you, Sir, ever possess the united affections of a Great, and free People, and long live to enjoy in domestick felicity, and tranquility, the pleasing satisfaction, of having conscientiously, discharged your duty, to your Country, in rescuing it, from Tyranny, and, arbitrary Domination. We have the honor to be, with the highest respect Your Excellency's most Obedient Servants

John Lloyd
President of the Senate
Hugh Rutledge
Speaker of the House of Representatives[2]

LS, DLC:GW.

1. The address, dated 10 Feb. and also signed by John Lloyd and Hugh Rutledge, reads: "The Senate, and House of Representatives of the State of South Carolina, now met in General Assembly, in their own names, and in the names of their Constituents, the free Citizens of this State, offer to your Excellency their warmest, and most sincere congratulations, on the restoration of Peace, and the happy establishment of the Freedom, and, Independence of the United States of America.

"To the distinguished, and, disinterested part you have acted during the course of a long, and arduous Contest, with the blessing of Heaven on your exertions, we greatly attribute our success in effecting a Revolution, glorious, in its progress, and, flattering in its Consequences; a Revolution; which has not only secured our own Liberties, but if we have wisdom to improve our present advantages, cannot fail of extending the blessings we enjoy, to our latest Posterity, and of making our Country an Asylum for the oppressed, and persecuted from every Quarter of the Globe.

"We rejoice at the Opportunity now afforded you of enjoying that domestick ease, and happiness, you so much delight in, and which, you have so long, and, so ardently wished for.

"May your valuable Life be long spared, to your Country, and Friends; May uninterrupted health be added to all your other Enjoyments; and when the Almighty Ruler of the Universe shall think fit to receive you to himself, Your Illustrious name, and, Character, will live in the Memories of our Countrymen, to the remotest period of Time" (DLC:GW). For GW's response, see his letter to Lloyd and Rutledge of 28 May 1784.

2. John Lloyd (1735–1807), a Charleston merchant and a planter in St. Bartholomew Parish, was president of the South Carolina senate from 1783 to 1788. Hugh Rutledge (c.1745–1811), one of the three politically prominent Rutledge brothers who also included John (1739–1800) and Edward (1749–1800), was speaker of the South Carolina house of representatives from 1782 to 1784.

To Jacob Read

Sir,   Mount Vernon 12th Feb. 84.

Sundays Post brought me your favor of the first; covering a letter from the late President—Mr Boudinot—for your care of which I thank you.

It is not in my power to speak to the question you have propounded respecting Colo. Humphryss Inclination to either of the Offices now vacant, but as he is at Annapolis he can answer for himself—I have no doubt of his abilities being adequate to the duties of either of the places, if Congress should offer & he accepts, because he is a man of erudition & judgment—of great honor & integrity—and equally sober & circumspect in all his conduct.

The intemperence of the Weather has obliged me to postpone from one day to another for more than a month—a visit which I am called upon by duty & inclination to make to my Mother—I am now however in the very act of setting off for Fredericksburg where she lives[1]—I expect to be gone 6 or 8 days—after which I should be happy to see you & any other Gentlem⟨en⟩ of my acquaintance in Congress at this place, in your hours of recess, or inactivity; of which, from your account, there are likely to be many—occasioned by the sudden—departure of one of your body—Mrs Washington is obliged by your kind remembrance of her and prays you to accept her Compliments. I am Sir Yr Most Obedt & very Hble Servt

Go: Washington

P.S. I will thank you for offering my best respects to the Chevr de la Luzerne, Mr Marbois & Genl Armand—I shall hope if the weather permits to see them here before they return to Phila.[2]

ALS, PWacD: Sol Feinstone Collection, on deposit PPAmP.

1. The entries in GW's cash accounts (Ledger B, 197) indicate that GW was at Colchester and Dumfries en route to Fredericksburg on 11 Feb. and in Fredericksburg on 12 February. He apparently misdated either his letter or the entries in the ledger. In any case, he was in Fredericksburg by 12 Feb., left there on 15 Feb., and was back at Mount Vernon on 17 Feb. (see GW to Gilbert Simpson, 13 Feb.; Citizens of Fredericksburg to GW, 14 Feb., n.1; and GW to Elias Boudinot, 18 Feb. 1784). See GW to Henry Knox, 20 Feb., and GW to Charles Washington, 28 Feb., for further indication that either GW wrote this letter before 12 Feb. or he wrote it after leaving Mount Vernon.

2. See Armand to GW, 4 Feb. 1784, n.3.

From Dolphin Drew

Sir   Berkeley C[oun]ty [Va.] Feby the 13th 1784.

Mr Albion Throckmorton a young Gentleman of my Acquaintance purchas'd late last Fall a Lease of one Collet one of your Tenants of about 200 Acres upon Bullskin. Since this Mr Throckmorton to his great Surprize has discoverd that Collet had no right to sell him the Lease, it being against one of the Covenants.[1] As however Mr Throckmorton has paid Collet his Money & enter'd upon the premises & made some preparations for a Crop, he requests that your Excellency will suffer him to keep the Lease; or if it be agreeable, he wou'd be very glad to purchase the same in Fee simple.[2] He likewise desir'd Me to mention to your Excellency that there is another Lease adjoining this originally leas'd to one Bowlie, which the Tenant wou'd sell him with your permission & he wou'd gladly buy; but this too he wou'd rather purchase in Fee.[3] As Mr Throckmorton is young & quite unexperienced in Matters of this kind, he desird that I wou'd write to your Excellency respecting the above & request an immediate Answer. I am, Sir, with great Respect Yr most ob. hble Servt

Dolphin Drew

ALS, DLC:GW.

Dolphin Drew began his practice of law in Berkeley County, Va., at the time it was formed in 1772.

Before his twenty-second birthday in 1754, GW had acquired seven parcels of land in Frederick County, Virginia. Four of these tracts totaling nearly two thousand acres were on Bullskin Run, which became a part of Berkeley County (now West Virginia) in 1772. For a full description of GW's early land acquisitions in Frederick County, see *Papers, Colonial Series*, 1:48. GW divided his Bullskin land into ten lots and in the late 1760s and early 1770s leased the lots to tenants. For GW's sale in 1771 to Philip Pendleton of 180 acres of his Bullskin holdings, see GW to James Nourse, 22 Jan. 1784, n.3.

1. Moses Collett leased a 200-acre section of GW's Bullskin land in 1773. On 1 Oct. 1783 GW's estate manager Lund Washington wrote GW: "Moses Collet is Dead and his family intends to move over the mountain in the spring they have sold their Lease, to a Mr Throckmorton and meant to give him Possession this Fall. . . . I did not see Mr Throckmorton but I desired some of his acquaintances to inform him if he had not already obtain your consent my opinion was that he never woud, and I told the Colletts, that you woud not agree to any such transfer" (ViMtV). Lund Washington went on to describe the ill consequences he envisioned should GW approve the transfer of the lease to Throckmorton. See also GW to Isaac Collett, 25 Feb. 1784. Albion Throckmorton (died c.1795) was originally from Gloucester County, Virginia. In 1785 he married Mildred Washington (c.1766–1804), the oldest daughter of GW's cousin Warner Washington (1722–1790). The Collett who was attempting to sell the lease was Isaac, the eldest and only surviving son of Moses Collett (see Isaac Collett to GW, 22 Feb. 1784).

2. GW responded on 25 Feb. to Isaac Collett's letter of 22 Feb., to say that he would not consider allowing Collett to sell his lease until Collett paid the back rent that he owed. On 27 April 1784 Lund Washington received from John Steen the £30 that Isaac Collett owed for the rent from 1780 through 1784, and in 1786 Steen paid for himself the £6 annual rent on the lot (Battaile Muse Papers, NcD).

3. For GW's explanation of his refusal to sell a part of his Bullskin land to Throckmorton, see GW to Dolphin Drew, 25 Feb. 1784. No one named Bowlie appears in GW's accounts as leasing his land on the Bullskin. Bowlie may be a misreading and misspelling of "Reiley" (see John Reiley, Ledger B, 71).

To William Drew

Sir,   Fredericks[bur]g [Va.] 13th Feby 1784

In the course of the last eight months, I have addressed two or three letters to you, praying an authenticated copy of the deceased Major Genl Lee's Will:[1] this I did consequent of a request from his Sister in England to me.[2] Not having received the copy wrote for, nor any acknowledgment of my Letters, I presume the latter have never reached your hands. I therefore give you the trouble of this Letter by Mr Throckmorton who has promised the safe conveyance of it to your office. I wish to be favored, as soon as convenient, with the Will in the manner she requires; the cost of which I will pay when you exhibit the charge. I wou'd send the money by Mr Throckmorton if I knew what would be the amount of the charge. I am sir Your Most Obedt servt

G: Washington

LB, DLC:GW.

William Drew, probably the brother of Dolphin Drew (see Dolphin Drew to GW, this date), was the first clerk of the Berkeley County court, a position he held from 1772 to 1785.

1. Only GW's letter of 10 July 1783 has been found, but on 15 April 1784 when writing to Sidney Lee, Gen. Charles Lee's sister, GW noted that William Drew had acknowledged receiving a letter from GW written in late December.

2. Miss Lee wrote GW on 14 Jan. 1783 from Newgate Street in Chester, England. As General Lee's sole surviving close relative, she asked GW to obtain for her a copy of the will her brother may have made in America before his death on 2 Oct. 1782 and to advise her "upon the steps necessary for her to take." GW on 20 April 1783 wrote agreeing to perform this service for the sister of his old colleague with whom he had broken after the battle at Monmouth, N.J., in 1778. On 22 April 1783 GW wrote to Jacob Morris asking him to obtain a copy of General Lee's will and send it to Miss Lee (see GW to Sidney Lee, 15 May 1783). Morris sent her a copy of the will, "but without the original or attested copy, and [without] receiving necessary powers from the Executors (from whom I have not yet heard)" (Sidney Lee to GW, 3 July 1783). William Drew did respond to this letter of 13 Feb. 1784, and GW probably sent it to Sidney Lee (see GW to Sidney Lee, 15 April 1784). Sidney Lee also received an attested copy of her brother's will (see Sidney Lee to GW, 23 May 1784).

From Samuel Low

Sir   Baltimore [Md.], Feby 13th 1784.

I beg leave to offer the enclosed piece to your perusal, requesting your Excellency's permission to publish the same with a Poem, intitled Winter Display'd your Excellency's immediate answer on this head will be very acceptable.[1]

I flatter myself, your Excellency will not be displeas'd with any commendatory expressions in the enclos'd, as I am confident of their truth, & be assured, sir, that my desire to inscribe this Poem to your Excellency is merely the effect of ardor & Sincerity; But shou'd your Excellency think proper to make any alterations, your noting the same to me will be an indelible favour.

I shou'd not have made bold to urge a reply on this Business with such haste, but the Manuscript is in the hands of the Printer in this Town, who only waits for your Excellency's permission to prefix the enclosed Dedication. I have the honour to be, with the profoundest respect & Veneration, Your Excellency's Mo: Obedt Hbe Servt

The Author

AL, DLC:GW.

1. The "enclosed piece" is printed in part in note 1 of GW to Samuel Low, 4 May 1784.

From Rochambeau

Paris february 13th 1784.

here is, my Dear Général, one demand for the order of Cincinnatus of the most remarkable Kind, and which appears to me deserve the attention of the Society. here is inclosed the letter that M. de Lilancourt, before a general commander in St Domingo, has wrote to me upon this Subject.[1] all the facts are exact in it, and you Know perfectly, well as me, how much obligations we owe to him for having Sent to us the detachment under the marquis de St Simon's orders, that he was Strongly authorised, by the Silence of his instructions, to refuse us.[2] I cannot then but particulary recommend his asking to your Excellency and to the general society. I am with respect Sir of your Excellency the most obeident and very humble Servant.

le cte de Rochambeau

LS, DSoCi. The letter is one of those read on 11 May 1784 at the general meeting of the Society of the Cincinnati in Philadelphia. See note 1.

1. The enclosure is a translation of Lilancour's letter to Rochambeau of 8 Feb. 1784, written in the same hand as this letter from Rochambeau to GW. Lilancour (Lillancour, Lilancourt) enclosed a copy of his letter to Rochambeau, in French, in his letter to GW of 20 Feb. 1784. The content of Lilancour's letter to Rochambeau is much the same as that of his letter to GW of 20 Feb. 1784, which see. Jean-Baptiste, comte de Lilancour-Taste, was governor of Santo Domingo and commander in chief of the troops there from 1776 to 1783. GW and the Cincinnati agreed with Rochambeau that Lilancour's cour-

age in providing de Grasse the Santo Domingo troops for the Yorktown campaign on his own responsibility made him eligible for election to the French Society of the Cincinnati. See GW to Rochambeau, 15 May 1784, printed below as Appendix IV, in General Meeting of the Society of the Cincinnati, 4–18 May 1784, printed below.

2. Claude-Anne de Rouvroy, marquis de Saint-Simon-Montléru (1743–1819), commanded the troops who went with de Grasse from Santo Domingo to Yorktown where Saint-Simon was severely wounded. He was an active Royalist during the French Revolution.

To Gilbert Simpson

Mr Simpson,   Fredericksbg [Va.] 13th Feby 1784

Having closed all my transactions with the public, it now behooves me to look into my own private business, no part of which seems to call louder for attention, than my concerns with you. How profitable our partnership has been, *you best can tell*; & how advantageous my Mill has been, none can tell so well as *yourself*.[1] If however I am to credit the report, not only of one, but every body from that country, I ought to have a good deal of wealth in your hands, arising from the produce of it; because all agree, that it is the best Mill, & has had more custom than any other on the west side the Alleghaney mountains; I expect something very handsome therefore from that quarter. I want a full settlement of this Account from the beginning, clearly stated. I also require a full & complete settlement of our Partnership accounts, wherein every article of debit is to be properly supported by vouchers; & the sums receivd to be mentioned for what, & from whom they were received. In a word I expect every thing relating to the par[t]nership, as well as my individual & separate interests, will appear clear & satisfactory.[2] And as I expect to leave home for a pretty long trip, before or at furthest by middle of April,[3] I think it incumbent upon you to make this settlement previous to it, especially as the world does not scruple to say that you have been much more attentive to your own interest than to mine. But I hope your Accots will give the lie to these reports, by shewing that something more than your own emolument was intended by the partnership; & that you have acted like an honest, industrious and frugal man for the mutual interest of us both, which will justify the opinion I entertained of you at the time of our Agreement, & would be complying with the conditions & professed intention of our associating together.

This Letter will be certain of getting into your hands in the course of ten or twelve days, as it goes by my Nephew, who I met with at this place, where I had come on a visit; & who is on his way to Fort Pitt &ca[4]—The enclosure for Major Stephenson (Brother to the late Colo. Crawford) I wish to have put into his own hands if living; if otherwise, into the hands of the Executor or Administrator of Colo. Crawford; as the contents of it relate principally to some matters between that deceased Gentleman & me.[5] I am, Sir Your humble Servt

G: Washington

LB, DLC:GW.

Gilbert Simpson, Jr., was the manager of GW's 1,644-acre tract, called Washington's Bottom, on the Youghiogheny River at present Perryopolis, Pennsylvania. GW claimed the tract in 1768, and in the fall of 1772 he entered an agreement with young Simpson to develop this land and build a gristmill on Washington's Run. Simpson was to develop a farm for GW, providing half the needed slaves, livestock, and supplies. He was the son of the man who for many years rented land from GW on Clifton's Neck at Mount Vernon.

1. For a description of GW's gristmill on Washington's Run less than a mile upstream from where it flowed into the Youghiogheny, see *Diaries*, 4:20–21. The mill was completed in 1775 at a cost of about £1,000.

2. Simpson defended himself in a letter of 27 April 1784, and GW wrote him on 10 July 1784 setting out the terms for the dissolution of their partnership. In the meantime GW prepared an advertisement, dated 24 June 1784, announcing that Simpson's farm would be offered for lease and that GW's share of the effects would be offered for sale. Simpson visited Mount Vernon in July 1784, and GW was at Washington's Bottom in September when the sale was held (ibid., 21–25).

3. GW left Mount Vernon on 26 April to travel to Philadelphia to preside at the first annual meeting of the Society of the Cincinnati, 4–18 May 1784.

4. See GW's instructions to John Lewis, 14 Feb. 1784, printed below.

5. See GW to John Stephenson, this date.

To John Stephenson

Dear sir,   Fredericks[bur]g [Va.] 13th Feby 1784

After condoling with you on the unhappy fate of your Brother William, which I do very sincerely; & upon the Death of your brother Valentine, I should be glad to get a copy from both their Books, or Memos. of the accounts as they stand between us; which are of long standing, & I fear not a little intricate. I write to you Sir, because I do not know (if you are not one yourself) who are the Executors or Administrators of those deceased Gentlemen. There were also some Land transactions, in partnership & otherwise between your Brother William & me, which I wish to have an account of. If it is in your power therefore, or you should have come across any warrants, Entries, Memoms or papers relative to this business, which can give me insight into the matter, I shall be much obliged to you for the information.[1]

There is also a Bond in my possession from your deceased brother Hugh (for whose Death I am also very much concerned) with your name, or that of your brother James's to it (I am not certain which as I am from home, & have accidentally met with this good & direct opportunity) for a Sum of money due to me from your Fathers Estate; which I wish to know when it can be settled & paid, as the situation of my private Affairs makes it absolutely necessary to close my Accounts & to receive payment as soon as possible.[2] I am, with great esteem Your very hble servant

G: Washington

LB, DLC:GW.

John Stephenson of Frederick County, Va., settled near the Great Crossing of Youghiogheny in the late 1760s. He was one of the younger half brothers of William (1732–1782) and Valentine (d. 1777) Crawford.

1. GW entered into an agreement with William Crawford in 1767 by which Crawford became GW's agent for surveying and claiming land in the West (see GW to Crawford, 17 Sept. 1767, and Crawford to GW, 29 Sept. 1767). All of GW's claims to land in the Ohio country in 1773 and 1774 under the proclamations of 1754 and 1763 were based on surveys or information provided by William Crawford (see the notes in GW to Samuel Lewis and GW to Thomas Lewis, both 1 Feb. 1784). GW's land dealings with William Crawford may be followed in the extensive correspondence between the two from 1767 to 1781, particularly in the years from 1769 to 1775. In 1774 GW sent William Crawford's brother Valentine out to his lands on the Ohio to establish legal right to the tracts that GW claimed by making clearings and building cabins on them (see particularly GW's instructions to Valentine Crawford, 30 Mar. 1774).

2. GW's bond of indebtedness from the Richard Stephenson estate was signed by his sons John and Hugh. Richard Stephenson died in 1765. He had five sons by Onora Grimes Crawford Stephenson (d. 1776), named Richard, James, John, Hugh, and Marcus. GW surveyed land for the senior Stephenson in 1752, and for the rest of that decade Stephenson was a fairly

regular supplier of provisions and services for GW in Frederick County. At his death Stephenson owed GW £70.10, most of it for "a Negro—named Fortune—sold him in 1763" (Ledger A, 3). By 24 Nov. 1771 the estate debt had grown to £85.0.2, mostly from unpaid interest (Ledger A, 331). GW credited William Crawford with paying on the account a total of £51 in 1772 and 1773; and in an entry in Ledger B, 38, GW closed the Stephenson estate account. There is this notation in the ledger: "By Ball[anc]e of this acct—in John and Hugh Stephensons Bond—wch was put into the hands of Thos Smith Esqr. of Carlisle (Pennsa) to bring suit after all the credits were made wch was accordingly done & £103.11.6¾ Pennsa C[urrenc]y was recd wch Ball[anc]es all accts with the Estate." For reference to Thomas Smith's collection of the bond of the two Stephenson sons, see GW to Smith, 23 Sept. 1789.

From Alicia Bennett, the Countess of Tankerville

Sir   upper Gros[venor] St. [London] febry the 13—1784
    I Am, favor'd with yours, and am very sorry it is not Convenient to you to Accept of the Trust, my Sons took the liberty of offering to you,[1] I wish'd to give you as little trouble as the Nature of the business wou'd admit of. the Chief thing I look'd to, was the Sanction and Honor it wou'd be to my Son Henry to be under your protection. I have for near twenty years had great trouble and Vexation About the Virginia property, and I did lately flatter myself, with your Assistance, I shou'd have the pleasure of seeing my Son Enjoy a good fortune independant, but how Vain are all our wishes & Expectations in this world. I have the Honor to be with the greatest Respect Sir your Most Obedient Humble Servant

A: Tankerville

ALS, DLC:GW.
    1. This was GW's letter of 30 Oct. 1783. See GW to Tankerville, 20 Jan. 1784, especially note 1.

From the Citizens of Fredericksburg

Sir   [Fredericksburg, Va., c.14 February 1784]
    While applauding millions were offering you their warmest congratulations on the blessings of Peace, and your safe return from the hazards of the Field, We The Mayor & Commonalty of the Corporation of Fredericksburg, were not wanting in Attachment and wishes to have joined in public testimonies of our

Warmest gratitude & Affection, for your long and Meritorious Services in the Cause of Liberty; A Cause Sir, in which by your examples and exertions with the Aid of your gallant Army, The Virtuous Citizens of this Western World, are secured in freedom and Independance. And altho: you have laid aside your Official Character we cannot Omit, this first Opportunity you have given us,[1] of presenting with unfeigned hearts, Our Sincere Congratulations on your safe return from the Noisy Clashing of Arms, to the Calm Walks of Domestic ease; and it affords us great joy, to see you Once more at the place which claims the Honor of your growing infancy,[2] the Seat of your venerable and Amiable Parent & Worthy Relations. We want language to express the happiness we feel on this Occasion, and which cannot be surpassed, but by Superior Acts (if possible) of the Divine Favor.

May the great and Omnipotent Ruler of Human events, who in blessing to America hath Conducted you thro: so many dangers, continue his favor and protection, thro: the remainder of your life in the happy society of an Affectionate and gratefull people. I have the Honor to be (in behalf of the Corporation) with every sentiment of esteem & Respect Your Excellencys Most Obt & most Hble Servant

William McWilliams
Mayor

DS, DLC:GW.

1. This was GW's first visit to Fredericksburg after his return to Mount Vernon at the end of December. See GW to Jacob Read, 12 Feb. 1784, n.1. The following account of the town's reception of GW, headed "Fredericksburg, *February* 15, 1784," is given in the *Virginia Gazette, or American Advertiser* (Richmond), 21 Feb. 1784: "On Thursday evening last [12 Feb.], our late illustrious Commander in Chief arrived in this Town from Mount Vernon, on a visit to his ancient and amiable parent—with every mark of heart-felt gladness, the Body Corporate, the next day waited on his Excellency with the following Address, as a public testimony of their grateful acknowledgments for his many services. . . .

"On Saturday at two o'clock, a Committee from the Common Hall, the late Officers of the army, and several Gentlemen of the Town and neighbourhood, waited on and conducted him to the Coffee house, where a public dinner was provided: On his approaching the place of entertainment, he was saluted with a discharge of twenty-one rounds from artillery—Language is too weak to express the heart-felt joy that appeared in the countenances of a numerous and respectable number of Gentlemen, who had assembled on this happy occasion. After Dinner the following toasts were drank, under the discharge of thirteen rounds of artillery to each toast.

1. The Thirteen United and Sovereign States of America.
2. The American Congress.
3. Our great and generous Ally, Louis XVI.
4. Our late virtuous and gallant army.
5. The American Ministers in Europe.
6. May commerce flourish, and the landed interest of America increase.
7. The Seven United Provinces, and other allies in Europe.
8. Unanimity in the Councils of America.
9. May the American revolution induce those oppressed, by tyranny, to imitate them; and may every success attend their virtuous endeavours.
10. The Volunteers of Ireland.
11. The Order of Cincinnati.
12. May the increase of the American navy be equal to the growth of her forests.
13. The memory of all our gallant heroes who have bravely fallen in defence of American liberty.

"The General was then pleased to honor the company with a toast: 'Fredericksburg; may it encrease and its commerce flourish'; thirteen rounds —— On the evening, an elegant ball was given at the Town-Hall, where a numerous and brilliant company of ladies assembled, who now in turn received the pleasure of beholding their great protector and virtuous defender. Joy sparkled in the eye, and every appearance was expressive of the animated feelings which warmed the hearts of all present. At twelve o'clock the General withdrew; and the next day left this place for Chatham, on his return to Mount Vernon, where, may he enjoy all the blessings this life can afford, and which his many virtues merit."

2. The text of the signed note by which Mayor William McWilliams sent his address to GW is: "I have made a small alteration in the enclosed address, instead of growing Nativity, I have said growing infancy. I have the Honor to be yr Excellency's Most Obt Servt" (DLC:GW).

To the Citizens of Fredericksburg

[Fredericksburg, Va., c.14 February 1784]
To the Worshipful the Mayor and Commonality of the Corporation of Fredericksburgh.
Gentlemen,

With the greatest pleasure, I receive in the character of a private Citizen, the honor of your Address.

To a benevolent Providence, and the fortitude of a brave and virtuous army, supported by the general exertion of our common Country, I stand indebted for the plaudits you now bestow.

The reflection however, of having met the congratulating smiles and approbation of my Fellow-Citizens, for the part I have acted in the Cause of Liberty and Independence, cannot fail of adding pleasure to the other sweets of domestic life; and my sensibility of them is heightened by their coming from the respectable Inhabitants of the place of my growing Infancy and the honorable mention which is made of my revered Mother; by whose Maternal hand (early deprived of a Father) I was led to Manhood.[1]

For the expressions of personal affection & attachment, and for your kind wishes for my future Welfare, I offer grateful thanks, and my sincere prayers for the happiness and prosperity of the Corporate Town of Fredericksburg.

Go: Washington

ADS (photocopy), ViMtV; ADfS, DLC:GW; LB, DLC:GW. Although GW docketed the draft 14 Feb., he did not write it until he had received William McWilliams's corrected copy of the address that had been delivered at Fredericksburg on 14 February. It may well be that he drafted his response after his return to Mount Vernon on 17 February.

1. Both GW's draft and the letter-book copy have "from Childhood" instead of "to Manhood."

To John Lewis

[Fredericksburg, Va.] 14th February 1784

G. Washington would be obliged to Mr Lewis for delivering or causing to be deliver'd by a safe hand, the Letter accompanying this, to Mr Gilbert Simpson, & if he goes by his house to Fort Pitt;[1] for observing the size, & condition of his Plantation: & the condition of the Mill—& for enquiring how many Tenants he has placed on the Land, for how long a term, & upon what Rents. Whether there is any person living upon a small Tract he holds at the Great Meadows—what sort of an improvment is thereon—of whom the person took it and upon what terms[2]—And should Mr Lewis have a favourable opportunity, the General would be obliged to him for informing those Settlers upon his tract West of the Monongahela, on the waters of Shurtee's & Raccoon creeks, that he has a Patent for the Land, dated the 5th day of July 1774—that he will most assuredly assert his right to it—but, in consideration of their having made improvments thereon ignorantly, or under a mistaken belief, founded on false assertions, that the Land did not belong to him; he is willing that they should remain upon it as Tenants, upon a just & moderate Rent, such as he & they can agree upon. The like may be said to any Person or Persons who may be settled at a place called the Round Bottom, on the Ohio opposite Pipe Creek & a little above a Creek called Capteening, which has been surveyed by the county Surveyor of Augusta upon proper Warrants from Lord Dunmore, ever since the 14th day of July 1773.[3]

If Mr Lewis can discover by indirect means who would be a fit Agent in the Neighbourhood of Fort Pitt to charge with the seating & leasing the Generals Lands in that country without holding up Ideas to them which may lead any one to expect the appointment; he would thank him for the information.

Such parts of these requests as can be complied with before his departure from Fort Pitt, the General would be obliged by receiving them (in a letter) from that place, as he is desirous of getting some knowledge of his affairs in that Country, as soon as possible.

LB, DLC:GW.

1. John Lewis, son of GW's brother-in-law, Fielding Lewis, was going to Pittsburgh. See GW to Gilbert Simpson, 13 Feb. 1784, and notes.

2. On 4 Dec. 1770 GW bought the tract of 234½ acres at Great Meadows, the scene of his defeat at Fort Necessity in 1754 (see *Diaries*, 4:20). For descriptions of this tract, see GW's advertisement, 15 July 1784 (printed in note 3, GW to Thomas Richardson, 5 July 1784), and GW to Thomas Freeman, 23 Sept. 1784, and 22 Sept. 1785.

3. For the "Shurtee's" (Chartiers) and Round Bottom tracts, see GW to Thomas Lewis, 1 Feb. 1784, nn.1, 2, and 3; see also editorial note in Thomas Smith to GW, 9 Feb. 1785.

From Robert Morris

Dear Sir   Philadelphia 14th February 1784

In acknowledging your Letters of the fourth & tenth of last month I must pray you to accept my Thanks for the Expressions of Kindness Contained in them. Mr Wright has promised that your Portrait should speedily be Compleated, but hitherto his Promise is unperformed. Whenever it shall be received I will obey your Orders in the Disposition of it. Your Accounts with the Explanation of them, were handed (in the usual

Course) to the Comptroller of the Treasury, and I have issued a Warrant for the Amount of his Certificate being Eight hundred and Fifty Seven Dollars and Fifty Two Ninetieths.[1] This Warrant is enclosed for you to put your name on the back of it and in the mean time Governor Clinton is informed that he may draw for the Amount and that his Bills shall be answered.[2] Mrs Morris joins me in presenting our warmest Respects to yourself and Mrs Washington, and I pray you to beleive that with every Sentiment of Friendship & regard I am Your most obedient Very humble servt

Robt Morris

LS, DLC:GW.
1. See GW to Morris, 4 Jan., n.1.
2. See George Clinton to GW, 27 Feb., GW to Morris, 3 Mar., GW to Benjamin Walker, 24 Mar., and Walker to GW, 3, 6 April.

From Nathanael Greene

Dear Sir,   Newport [R.I.] Feby 16th 1784
    I had the pleasure of receiving your letter of the 28th of December last,[1] and having had the Honor of being appointed President of the Cincinnati of Rhode Island, I embrace the earliest opportunity of giving you an Answer. General Varnum, Major Lyman, and myself, are in the appointment to attend the annual General meeting of the order. It is not expected more than One will attend the meeting. I intend to be in South Carolina before that time.[2]
    General Varnum or Major Lyman will attend, and I have the pleasure to communicate to your Excellency that the measures necessary for the establishment of the Order is fully gone into, and all the officers appointed agreeably to the Institution. With esteem and affection, I am, dear Sir, Your most obedient humble servt

Nath. Greene

LS, DSoCi; ADfS, RHi.
Maj. Gen. Nathanael Greene (1742–1786) was GW's most valuable general during the recent war. He was a Rhode Islander but was soon to return to the South where he had fought his greatest campaign. Greene died at Mulberry Grove, his plantation near Savannah, on 19 June 1786.
1. See Circular Letter to the State Societies of the Cincinnati, 1 Jan. 1784.

2. GW wrote Greene on 20 and 27 Mar. 1784 protesting the decision that only one of the three Rhode Island delegates should go to Philadelphia to the May meeting of the Society of Cincinnati. Greene responded on 22 April that his health made it impossible for him to travel to Philadelphia. On 6 May he wrote that he was still too ill to travel and that neither of the other elected delegates, Gen. James Mitchell Varnum (1748–1789) and Maj. Daniel Lyman, were going to the meeting but that he had persuaded Col. Samuel Ward (1756–1832) to represent Rhode Island. Ward arrived at the general meeting on 12 May.

To Boinod & Gaillard

Gentlemen,   Mount Vernon 18th Feby 1784

I have been favored with your polite & obliging Letter of January the 20th, & thank you for the many flattering sentiments contained in it.[1]

To encourage Literature & the Arts, is a duty which every good Citizen owes to his Country, & if I could be instrumental in promoting these, and in aiding your endeavours to do the like, it would give me pleasure.

Your Books being chiefly in a foreign Language (which I do not understand) & my Library containing the most valuable of those which are named in the English catalogue,[2] my demand will be small. but if those mentioned below are yet in your Store, they may be laid by, or sent to me as occasion offers, & the cost shall be paid to your Order.[3] I am Gentlen Your Most Obt &ca

G: Washington

An Accot of the New Northn Archipelago by M. J. Von Stræhlin 8Vos.
The Histy of the Ud Provinces of the Netherlands by Wm Lothian 4to
A review of the characters of the principal Nations in Europe— 2 Vols. 8vo.
Hermes, or a phlol enquiry, concerning Languages &ca by J.H. 8vo.
The true French master, or rules for the Fh tongue by Mr Cheneau of Paris, 8vo.
The New pocket Dicty of the Fh & Eng: langs. by Thos Nugent 2 vols. 8vo.

A course of Gallantries, translated from the Freh of Mr Duclos.
2 parts—8vo.
The rise, progress & prest state of the Northn Govts by J.
Williams Esqr. 2 Vols—4to.

LB, DLC:GW. Daniel Boinod and Alexander Gaillard, French booksellers,
issued two catalogs from Philadelphia in 1784. In the first, *Catalogue des Livres
que se Trouvent chez Boinod & Gaillard,* they wrote in the introduction of "the
Establishment we are now about to form" with "not so much the Desire of
Gain as that of living among a Free-People." Their advertisement of 3 Feb.
1784 in the *Pennsylvania Packet, and Daily Advertiser* (Philadelphia) indicates
that their store was on Second Street near Vine. Thomas Jefferson bought a
number of books from Boinod & Gaillard in the spring of 1784 before he left
for Paris. See Boyd, *Jefferson Papers,* 6:529–30, 541, 544, 7:280, 288, 290.

    1. Letter not found.

    2. In the *Catalogue,* cited above, the French titles run through page 81, the
Latin titles from 82 to 103, and those in English from 103 through 112.

    3. None of these titles appear in the inventory of GW's library which was
made after his death, and no record has been found in GW's cash accounts in
Ledger B of his having made any payments to Boinod & Gaillard in 1784 or
1785.

To Elias Boudinot

Dear Sir,   Mount Vernon 18th Feby 1784
    With equal emotions of pleasure & gratitude I received your
very polite Letter of the 11th ulto from Elizabeth-town, the late
acknowledgment of which is owing to the interruption of the
post, & a visit to my aged Mother; the last of which engaged me
several days, & from which I only returned yesterday.[1]
    The private congratulations of freindship, upon my safe re-
turn to a peaceful abode, & the sweets of Domestic retirement,
never can, with me, be lost in the midst of public ceremonies;
and they are received with more pleasure when they are known
to flow from a source which has always been the same. The affectionate terms therefore, in which your Letter is expressed,
could not fail to affect all my sensibility & to call for a return of
my warmest thanks—these I offer most sincerely.
    We have now a goodly field before us, & I have no wish supe-
rior to that of seeing it judiciously cultivated; that every Man,
especially those who have laboured to prepare it, may reap a
fruitful Harvest without the intermixture of Tares; the seeds of

which I am sure are too apparent to be sown by a skilful husbandman, who possesses a disposition to be honest.

It was with extreme pain I read that part of your Letter
which speaks of the declining State of Miss Boudinots health.
As the intemperence of the weather may have contributed
thereto, so it is to be hoped the approaching season will remove
the causes of her complaint, & restore her to good health, & to
her friends; in this wish, & in most affectionate compliments to
Mrs Boudinot and yourself, Mrs Washington heartily joins.
With the greatest sincerity & truth I am, My Dr Sir Your Most
Obedt &ca.

G: Washington

LB, DLC:GW.

   1. Jacob Read enclosed Boudinot's letter of 11 Jan. in his letter of 1 Feb.
which GW received at Mount Vernon on 8 February.

From La Luzerne

Sir.   Annapolis [Md.] Febr. 18th 1784.

I had flattered myself that my Stay in Annapolis would procure me an opportunity of waiting upon Your Excellency, but
the roads are so bad and the Snow so deep that I am obliged to
renounce to this happiness untill my return to this place, which,
I hope, will be towards the middle of next month.[1]

I hope then to take hold of the favorable moment, which I
have lost in this Season, and to enjoy longer Your Excellency's
Society in renewing the assurances of the respectful attachment
with which I have the honor to be, Sir, Your Excellency's Most
obedient and very humble Servant

le che. de la luzerne

P.S. I beg leave to enclose a Letter from the Marquis de la
Fayette. He gives me some hopes to be here in the Spring.[2]

LS, DLC:GW.

   Anne-César de La Luzerne de Beuzeville, chevalier (in 1785 marquis) de
La Luzerne (1741–1791), was the French minister to the United States from
1779 until his departure in June 1784, after which he became France's ambassador to Great Britain, a post he held until his death. La Luzerne was an effective supporter of the American cause during his tenure as minister.

   1. After La Luzerne's visit to Mount Vernon in April, the following item
appeared in the *Virginia Journal and Alexandria Advertiser* (15 April 1784): "On

Tuesday last [13 April] arrived in this Town, on his Return to Annapolis from a Visit to Mount-Vernon, his Excellency the Chevalier LA LUZERNE, Ambassador from His Most Christian Majesty to the United States, accompanied by his Excellency General WASHINGTON. They were received with repeated Discharges of Cannon from the Town and Shipping in the Harbor; and after dinner at Mr. Lomax's Tavern in Company with a Number of Gentlemen, were saluted with the like Compliments on their Departure."

2. This was undoubtedly Lafayette's letter of 11 Nov. 1783 which GW answers on 4 April 1784.

To James Milligan

Sir,   Mount Vernon 18th Feby 1784

The intemperance of the weather, & the great care which the Post riders seemed disposed to take of themselves, while it continued severe, prevented your Letter of the 13th of last month from reaching my hands 'till the 10th of this. I now acknowledge the receipt of it, with the accounts as they stand stated in the Treasury Books; for your trouble in transcribing which (it being unusual) you will please to accept my thanks, as the possession of them is pleasing, & may be useful to me.[1]

The charge of fifty Guineas paid James McCall Esqr. for the Revd Mr Smith, is perfectly just, & ought not to have been omitted by me, for I well recollect it was the desire of Mr Morris, that this sum might be carried to the credit of my public accots, & I certainly meant to do it, altho' it has been omitted.[2] For the act of justice which you have rendered, in allowing me interest upon 591 $3\frac{1}{90}$ Dollars, I am much indebted to you: the same reason which induced an allowance of interest on the Ballce of my Accot to Jany 1777, prevailed in this case also; but as the principal was rescued from error, & brought into a subsequent accot, I never thought about interest; & am altogether indebted to your attention & correctness for the discovery and credit.[3]

In the statement of my accots, I thought a note had accompanied the articles charged, where the money had been accounted for; but in this I am either mistaken, or do not perfectly comprehend your manner of entry; from which, to me it would seem, that Saml B. Webb, Ebenr Gray, Josiah Fessendon, Elijah Bennet, Capt. Calmly & John Philips in accot A—Colo. Weedon, for 500 Dollars (but this sum is again credited)—Wm

Dunn, Jos[ep]h Hunter, Hugh Mooney, John Miller & Chas Tatum, in Accot C—and Capt. Colfax & Lt Howe in Accot D, were to be charged in accots raised, or to be raised, with the several sums annexed to their respective names; whereas the money in every one of these enumerated instances has been paid for services actually performed, or upon accots which have been settled with me.[4] I am thus particular Sir, because it would give me pain, if thro' any inaccuracy in my statement, either of these persons should be involved in trouble, difficulty or expence, by a future call upon them. Captn Colfax, as you may perceive from his Accots which I render'd as vouchers to my own, gave the public credit for all the sums he stands charged with by me; among which is that for £171.18. & closes the whole with a transfer of the money in his hands to Mr Howe. Mr Howe also, as will appear in his accounts, settled the Expenditures for family purposes with me in November last; at the time I broke up House-keeping & discharged my household; & if I recollect right, was a Creditor instead of a Debtor to the public.[5]

I shall take notice in this Letter, because it is not my wish to encrease the troubles of your Office by making a distinct application hereafter, that in Accot B. I stand charged with the sums of £124.7.8 and £133.16.0 which have no existence in the Treasury Books, or elsewhere. The first sum I well remember to have received; the time & circumstances of it being too remarkable ever to be forgotten by me.[6] But the other sum of £133.16—I must confess I have no recollection of the receipt of it; but having found in my pocket Memo. Book, a short & blind entry to that effect, I placed it to the credit of the public Acot, altho' no trace of it remained in my memory, or any Accot of it could be found elsewhere; with a request (in a Note at bottom) that the matter might be enquired into, & justice done. It occurs to me, that about the period of that credit, I borrowed a sum in specie of the Marqs de la Fayette (as I had done of others when the exigencies of the public pressed) & that he & my Nephew Geo. Augte Washington set off for Philadelphia a few days afterwards: 'tis *possible* therefore I might have written for money by him, & that that sum may have been charg'd to his accot—but if this is not the case, and no such sum can be found charged to me in any of the public Offices, of that date, under any form whatsoever—I submit it to the consideration of yourself, or to the Superintendant of Finance whether I ought to be debited with it at all: because it is as likely that the error may have originated in a wrong credit on my part, as in the omission to charge it, on that of the public—especially as I have received several sums at different times on my private account, as well as other sums for the use of Colo. Fairfax (whose business I had in my hands several years before the War), all of which I applied to public uses, whenever the public had a call for it, without attending to the property, or propriety of the measure. Upon this state of the matter, which is a very candid one, I should be glad to have your sentiments, & those of the Financr. I am perfectly willing to give the public credit for every thing that is due, but it does not comport with my circumstances to do more, or even to lie out of money which I may with propriety call to my aid.[7]

The Account of my expenditures in Philadelphia & on my return home, I transmitted many days previous to the receipt of your Letter to Mr Morris, & presume it is in your Office long before this; & that I shall have the pleasure of receiving, as in the case of the former, an official statement of it from the Treasury books.[8]

For the honor of your kind congratulations on the great events which have taken place, & my return to domestic life, be pleased to accept my grateful thanks, & best wishes, in return. I am, Sir, Your Most Obt &ca

G: Washington

LB, DLC:GW.

1. Milligan explained in his letter of 13 Jan. that he was sending to GW a copy of the treasury's statement of his military accounts, 1775–83, even though it was not customary to do so.

2. See Milligan to GW, 13 Jan., n.2.

3. See Milligan to GW, 13 Jan., n.3.

4. On 9 Mar. Milligan sent GW a revised copy of the treasury's statement of his military accounts (see note 1). In this revised statement, also dated 23 Dec. 1783, Milligan inserted on the cover of schedule A (1 June 1775–31 Dec. 1776): "Note—The Persons in the within Account to whose Names this mark * is prefixed, Vizt Saml B. Webb Ebenezer Gray Josiah Fessendon [Fessenden] Elijah Bennet Captn [Lt. Elijah or Miles] Oakley, or Calmly & John Phillips, Are not to be charged in the Books, nor held accountable, As appears by Genl Washingtons letter to the Comptroller dated Febry 18th 1784—J.M." Milligan makes a similar notation on the cover of schedule C (1 Jan. 1777–6 Sept. 1781), listing the names Dunn, Hunter, Mooney, Miller, and Tatum. On the cover of schedule E (1 Aug.–8 Dec. 1783), he notes that Capt. William Colfax and Lt. Bezaleel Howe "are not to be charged in the Books nor held account-

able." There is also this entry in the treasury's account: "No. 5 Colo. [George] Weedon for his Regt Feby 1777—500."

5. The entry in the treasury statement is: "Advances to Sundry Persons for defraying the Expences of his Household, for which said Persons are to accot—Vizt Capt. Wm Colfax ⟨ ⟩ No. 2—£171.18.0[;] Lieut. B. Howe—[No.] 4—170.18.0." As members of the commander in chief's guards, both Colfax and Howe received and disbursed funds for the support of GW's military household. Colfax was a lieutenant in the 1st Connecticut Regiment when he was assigned to GW's guards on 8 Mar. 1778. Howe, a lieutenant in the 1st New Hampshire Regiment, joined the guards on 5 Sept. 1778. Accounts of both Colfax and Howe of GW's household expenditures may be found in DLC:GW.

6. In his own copy of his accounts (Accounts, G. Washington—with the United States, Commencing June 1775, and ending June 1783, Comprehending a Space of 8 Years, DLC:GW), GW notes that in January 1777, which was immediately after the brief Trenton-Princeton campaign, he received £124.7.8 "By Cash of Robt Morris Esqr. in specie pr acct."

7. In his own accounts (see note 6), GW has an entry for 13 May 1780: "By Cash—133.16," in "Lawful" money. An asterisk by this entry refers to GW's notation: "This sum stands in my acct as a credit to the Public—but I can find no charge of it against me in any of the Public offices—where the Mistake lyes I know not, but wish it could be ascertained, as I have no desire to injure or be injured." Milligan explained to GW on 9 Mar. that the £133.16 was paid, on GW's instructions, to George Augustine Washington for him to repay a loan that Lafayette had made to GW; and on 1 April GW wrote Milligan accepting his explanation of the charges.

8. See GW to Robert Morris, 4 Jan., n.1, and Milligan to GW, 9 Mar., n.3.

To Annis Boudinot Stockton

Dear Madam,   Mount Vernon Feby 18th 1784

The intemperate weather, and very great care which the Post Riders take of themselves, prevented your letter of the 4th of last month from reaching my hands 'till the 10th of this.[1] I was then in the very act of setting of on a visit to my aged Mother, from whence I am just returned. These reasons, I beg leave to offer, as an apology for my silence until now.

It would be a pity indeed, My dear Madam, if the Muses should be restrained in you; it is only to be regretted that the hero of your poetical talents is not more deserving their lays: I cannot, however, from motives of false delicacy (because I happen to be the principal character in your Pastoral) withhold my encomiums on the performance—for I think the easy, simple, and beautiful strains with which the dialogue is supported, does great justice to your genius; and will not only secure Lucinda & Aminta from Wits & Critics, but draw from them, however unwillingly, their highest plaudits; if they can relish the praises that are given, as highly as they must admire the manner of bestowing them.[2]

Mrs Washington, equally sensible with myself, of the honor you have done her, joins me in most affectionate compliments to yourself, the young Ladies & Gentlemen of your family. With sentiments of esteem, regard and respect I have the honor to be Dr Madam Yr Most Obedt & Most Hble Servt

Go: Washington

ALS, NjMoNP; LB, DLC:GW.

Annis Boudinot Stockton (1736–1801), sister of Elias Boudinot, widow of Richard Stockton (1730–1781), and mother-in-law of Benjamin Rush (1746–1813), was one of GW's most ardent admirers. An earlier poem of hers "Addressed to general Washington in the year 1777 after the battles of trenton and Princeton" (NjP: Stockton Papers) was probably the one her brother sent to GW in 1779 (see GW to Elias Boudinot, 28 Feb. 1779). After GW stopped briefly at Mrs. Stockton's house Morven at Princeton, N.J., on his way to Yorktown in August 1781, she completed and sent to him a long pastoral poem in which Lucinda and Aminta, two shepherdesses, reviewed "'the events which had occurred since the beginning of the war'" (L. H. Butterfield, "Annis and the General: Mrs. Stockton's Poetic Eulogies of George Washington," *Princeton University Library Chronicle*, 7 [1945–46], 19–39). After GW moved his headquarters to Rocky Hill near Princeton, he and Mrs. Washington became friends of Mrs. Stockton.

1. Letter not found.

2. The poem that Mrs. Stockton enclosed in her missing letter to GW of 4 Jan. 1784 she called, "Peace: A pastoral dialogue part the second." It was a continuation of the conversation between Aminta and Lucinda (see source note). Like the letter in which it was enclosed, GW's copy of the poem is missing, but it may be found in the bound volume of Mrs. Stockton's poems in the Princeton University Library. The poem fills fourteen pages with about twenty lines on a page. At one point she writes of GW:

> Such magnanimity, Such public Zeal
> As did the breast of our great leader feel
> Was never equal'd in the historic page
> Of ancient druid or enlighten'd Sage.

And Lucinda's final speech ends with these lines:

> Pale man from a swain a paper took
> In which I read the solemn words he spoke
> When he his great Commission did resign
> Which marks his character in every line.

From Edmund Randolph

Dear Sir   Richmond [Va.] Feby 19. 1784.

Your favor of the 10th instant, which I this day received, is not the first information concerning Lord Tankerville's power of attorney. I was written to by Lady Tankerville and his Lordship, as early as November last: and immediately desired Colo. Hooe to state to me the particulars of this new office. He answered me, that he was ignorant of the duty, expected from us, and must remain so, until your return to Mount Vernon. I waited for a further communication with him before I resolved on the part, which I ought to take. As you decline the undertaking, I shall immediately acquaint Colo. Hooe with my determination, to join him, if the services expected from me can be performed here. For it is impossible, that I should be active in the affair. I shall address Lady and Lord Tankerville to the same effect.[1]

I had prepared a letter to you, on the subject of three petitions, now depending in the general court, in the name of Colo. Bassett against yourself. They were intended, I presume, to cover some forfeiture of lands for noncultivation, or nonpayment of quitrents. Will you be so good, as to let me know, how the cases are circumstanced, that I may be able to decide, what conduct I ought to pursue concerning them?[2]

I left the form of an answer in Savage's suit against you and Mr B. Fairfax with the latter gentleman, in hopes of receiving it executed in a proper manner, that I might put the most expeditious end to the business.[3] I am dear sir with the sincerest affection yr much obliged obt servt

                                        Edmund Randolph

ALS, DLC:GW.

1. See GW to Randolph, 10 Feb., and note 1.

2. An order signed by John Brown, clerk of the General Court in Richmond, Va., and dated 15 Dec. 1783 commands a sheriff to summon GW "to appear before the Judges of the General Court, at the courthouse in the city of Richmond, on the seventh day of April court next, to show cause why 2448 acres of land in the County of Botetourt granted to the said George by patent bearing the date the 15th day of December 1772 and by him forfeited for want of Cultivation as it is said may not be granted to Burwell Basset" (PWacD: Sol Feinstone Collection, on deposit PPAmP). For GW's explanation of why his brother-in-law Burwell Bassett laid claim to the Ohio lands that GW had secured under the terms of Robert Dinwiddie's Proclamation of

1754, see GW to Edmund Randolph, 18 Mar. 1784, and notes. See also Randolph to GW, 15 May 1784.

3. At the time of her marriage to William Savage, Margaret Savage was the widow of Charles Green, the longtime rector of Truro Parish in which GW lived. Under the terms of William Green's will, GW and Bryan Fairfax after Green's death were appointed trustees to pay from his estate an annuity to his widow. In April 1767, having married Mrs. Green, Dr. William Savage assumed control of the Green estate and gave bond to GW and the new trustee, Bryan Fairfax, to pay his new wife £100 a year. The next year Dr. Savage went with his wife to live in Ireland. The main outlines of the long struggle by GW and Bryan Fairfax to force Savage to pay his wife's annuities is given in note 1 of Henry Lee and Daniel Payne to GW and George William Fairfax, 24 April 1767. Savage's suit, it seems, was instituted to prevent the execution of the judgment against him which GW and Fairfax had secured in 1775. See the note cited above and Randolph to GW, 15 May 1784.

From William Hamilton

Sir   Bush Hill [Pa.] February 20th 1784

I receiv'd your favor of the 15th January, & shall be happy in affording you all the information in my power respecting its contents. Just before I had the pleasure of seeing your Excellency in philada I engaged a person of the name of Turner, newly arrived from England, to do some Stucco work at Bush Hill. It was not long before he proved himself a Master in that Business, & has since compleated a cornice & ceiling, which are allowed by all who have seen them, to be in point of taste & execution, far Superior to any thing of the kind that has been done in this Country.

While he was at this work I frequently talk'd with him about the different compositions now so much used in England, particularly that for covering floors, Roofs, & fronts of Houses. He profess'd to understand the method of preparing & applying it, & wished me to encourage him in giving a Specimen. To this, I at length consented; and he undertook to make a variegated floor in my Green House, one for an open portico in the front of my House on the Schuylkill, and to cover the flats of two Bow windows, that have for these ten years baffled every attempt to tighten them. The price agreed for, was at the rate of eight pence sterling for every square foot that should be of any one colour, and a Shilling sterling for the same quantity, done in compartments of different colours, he finding himself in provisions &c. & in all materials whatever.

The Winter soon after set in, & has since continued so extremely severe as to put a stop to the work for the present. I am however very sanguine as to the Success, nor do I found my opinion merely on the account given me by Turner himself I have enquired of Mr Vaughn & several other english gentlemen who say great things of it. I find it may be adapted to every kind of Ornament—can be done at any season of the year (*in dry weather*) & is impenetrable to Water, Heat, & frost. It would give me great Satisfaction to let you know what are the component parts of this Cement, & I have for that purpose taken all possible pains to obtain a knowledge of them from the man who has undertaken to make it, but he is determined to keep the matter secret, in expectation of thereby making a living. As soon as the Spring opens, & the Season will admit, I shall proceed in the experiments abovementioned, and the moment I can form a Judgement with certainty, shall give myself the pleasure to inform your Excellency of the result. If in consequence you should desire to have Mr Turners Assistance in any kind of work you wish to have done in his Business, he will chearfully attend you on the same terms, that he is now with me.[1] I have the honor to be with great regard & the most perfect respect Your Excellencys most obedt humble Servant

W. Hamilton

ALS, DLC:GW.

William Hamilton had recently inherited the Bush Hill estate from his bachelor uncle James Hamilton (c.1710–1783), who was twice lieutenant governor of colonial Pennsylvania and twice acting governor. The great house at Bush Hill, just to the north of Philadelphia, was built about 1740 by William Hamilton's grandfather Andrew Hamilton (d. 1740). John and Abigail Adams lived at Bush Hill during the first two years at Philadelphia of his vice presidency, and in 1793 during the yellow fever epidemic it served as a pest house and hospital for the city.

1. No evidence has been found of any dealings by GW with this Mr. Turner.

To Henry Knox

My dear Sir,   Mount Vernon Feby 20th 1784

The bad weather, and great care which the Post Riders take of themselves, prevented your letters of the 3d & 9th of last Month from getting to my hands 'till the 10th of this. Setting of next Morning for Fredericksburgh[1] to pay my duty to an aged

Mother, and not returning 'till yesterday, will be admitted I hope, as a sufficient apology for my silence 'till now.

I am much obliged by the trouble you have taken to report the state of the Garrison & Stores, together with the disposition of the Troops at West-Point, to me.—and think the allowance of Rations, or subsistence money to such Officers as could not retire at that inclement season, was not only perfectly humane, but perfectly just.—and that it must appear so to Congress.

It would seem to me, without having recourse to calculation, that the allowance of a Majr General in a seperate department, to the person who shall discharge the duties of Secretary at War, Master of Ordnance, & Commanding Officer of the Forces which may be retained, or Raised for a Peace Establishment is as low as it well can be. I expect the President & some Members of Congress here in a day or two, & will tell them so.[2]

It was amongst my first Acts after I got home, to write to the President of each State Society, appointing Philadelphia (& the first Monday in May) for the general meeting of the Cincinnati. Colo. Walker took with him all the Letters for those Eastward of this, before New Years day; the others for the Southward I dispatched by the Post about the sametime[3]—I have even sent duplicates for fear of miscarriage, yet, 'though it is the most eligable method, it is to be feared it will not prove so effectual a communication, as a general notification in the public Gazettes would have been—And, in case of failure, I shall be exceedingly concerned for not having adopted the most certain; as it would give me pleasure to have the first general meeting, a very full one.

I have named Philadelphia (contrary to my own judgment, as it is not Central) to comply with the wishes of South Carolina, who, being the most Southern State, have desired it. North Carolina I have not heard a tittle from, nor any thing Official from New Hampshire. all the other States have acceded very unaminously to the propositions which were sent from the Army.

I am just beginning to experience that ease, and freedom from public cares which, however desirable, takes some time to realize; for strange as it may tell, it is nevertheless true, that it was not 'till lately I could get the better of my usual custom of ruminating as soon as I waked in the Morning, on the business of the ensuing day; and of my surprize, after having revolved many things in my mind, to find that I was no longer a public

Man, or had any thing to do with public transactions. I feel now, however, as I conceive a wearied Traveller must do, who, after treading many a painful step, with a heavy burden on his Shoulders, is eased of the latter, having reached the Goal to which all the former were directed—& from his House top is looking back, & tracing with a grateful eye the Meanders by which he escaped the quicksands and Mires which lay in his way, and into which none but the All-powerful guide, & great disposer of human Events could have prevented his falling.

I shall be very happy, and I hope shall not be disappointed, in seeing you at the proposed meeting in Philadelphia. The friendship I have conceived for you will not be impaired by absence, but it may be no unpleasing circumstance to brighten the Chain, by a renewal of the Covenant. My best wishes attend Mrs Knox & the little folks, in which Mrs Washington most heartily joins me. With every sentiment of the purest esteem, regard and Affection—I am, My dear Sir, Yr Most Obedt & obliged Hble Servant

Go: Washington

P.S. I hope Genl Greene will be in the Delegation from Rhode Island—and that we shall see him at the Genl meeting of the Cincinnati—will you intimate this to him.[4]

ALS, MHi: Knox Papers; LB, DLC:GW.

1. This seems to confirm that in the heading of his letter to Jacob Read dated 12 Feb., GW wrote either the wrong date or the wrong place.

2. Thomas Mifflin delayed his visit. See Armand to GW, 4 Feb. 1784, n.3.

3. See Circular Letter to the State Societies of the Cincinnati, 1 Jan. 1784. Lt. Col. Benjamin Walker (1753–1818) of New York was GW's aide-de-camp from January 1782 to the end of the war. In a postscript to a letter, probably written to Henry Jackson, on 23 Jan. 1784, Walker wrote: "My Compts to Genl Knox—tell him I brought a Circular Letter from the Genl to the several Presidents appointing the General Meeting of the Cincinnati at Phila in May next" (DNA: RG 93, Manuscript File, no. 29234).

4. See Nathanael Greene to GW, 16 Feb. 1784.

From Lilancour

Monsieur   Par Bordeaux a Clairac Le 20 fevrier 1784.
L'admission dans La Confraternité de Cincinnatus, des officiers francais (jusqu'au Grade de Colonel) qui ont Eu Le bonheur de Contribuer au Succés des Armes Des Etats unis de

l'amérïque est trop honnorable pour eux; pour que ceux qui peuvent Etre auctorisés a y aspirer par Leurs Services, ne Les Recherchent pas avéc LEmpressement Le plus vif.

j'ai Lhonneur Monsieur, dEtre Brigadier des Armées du Roy, et j'avais celui de Commander en chef La Colonie de Saint domingue, Lorsque M. Le Cte de Grasse en 1781 Sur Les instances de Votre Excellence et celles de M. Le Cte de Rochembeau; vint au cap me demander Les Secours que LEtat des affaires vous Rendait Indispensables, et les porter au Continent.

trois cent Batimens chargés dans La Rade de cette ville plus que Susceptibles D'attirer Les forces Ennemies qu'il Laissait derriere Lui; ne me Permettaient de me démunir sans mexposer; et Rendaient ma Position dautant plus délicate que dénué D'ordres de la Cour, il fallait prendre Les Evenemens Sur moi. consultant cependant moins une timide Prudence que L'utilité de la Cause commune; je n'hëzittai pas a Lui fournir 3700 hommes dont je donnai Le Commandement a M. Le Mis de St Simon, votre Excellence est mieux Instruite que personne, Monsieur, de Lheureux Effet de cette Resolution combien elle a contribué a La gloire des Armes alliées et a la Paix honorable qui en a eté Le fruit.

tel est Monsieur, Le titre que j'ai prié M. Le cte de Rochembeau de vouloir bien Recommander a Votre Excellence, du moment que j'ai Eté Instruit de LEtablissement de La confraternité. La Reponse que j'En ai Recu jointe a La Lettre que je Lui avais Ecrit, dont jai Lhonneur de mettre Les copies Sous Ses yeux[1] me donnent tout Lieu Desperer que Lappréciation qu'il fait de ma Conduite dans cette Circonstance critique et Le soin quil veut bien prendre de vous en Rapeller Lutilité; disposeront favorablement Votre Excellence en faveur de ma demande; et quelle voudra bien me procurer—Lhonneur que je Sollicite de Sa justice. Je suis avéc Respect Monsieur De Votre Excellence Le Tres humble et tres obeissant Serviteur

Lilancour

ozerais je Monsieur Supplier votre Excellence de vouloir bien faire parvenir a M[onsieu]rs de la Societé Generale le pacquet je prends La Liberté de mettre Sous Son couvert.[2]

ALS, DLC:GW; ALS, DSoCi.

1. Copies of the letter that Lilancour (Lilancourt) wrote to Rochambeau on 8 Feb. and Rochambeau's response of 13 Feb. are in DSoCi. There is also a

copy of his letter of 8 Feb. to Rochambeau in DLC:GW. See Rochambeau to GW, 13 Feb. 1784, n.1.

2. In addition to the copies of the two letters cited in note 1, "le pacquet" consisted of three signed copies of a letter dated 20 Feb. from Lilancour to the members of the general meeting of the Society of the Cincinnati asking to be admitted to the Cincinnati.

From Winthrop Sargent

Boston Feby the 20th 1784

Desirous of contributing to the Amusement of your Excellency I do myself the honor to Transmit you a Poem of Eulogy on the Institution of The Society of Cincinnati—I hazard it to your Excellency's Judgment without more Preface than an Extract from its accompanying Letter.[1]

If your Excellency & Mrs Washington (to whom I beg Leave to present my Respects) deign to grant the approbating Smile I shall have great Joy in that Felicity which I know it will bestow on the fair Poetess—with Sincere & warm Wishes for your Excellency's Happiness I have the Honor to be Dear Sir your most obedient Humble Servant

Winthrop Sargent

ALS, DLC:GW.

Winthrop Sargent (1753–1820) of Gloucester, Mass., served in the Continental army throughout the war and was promoted to captain on 1 Jan. 1777. From 1787 to 1798 he was secretary of the Northwest Territory under Gov. Arthur St. Clair, and in 1798 he became the first governor of the Mississippi Territory. Thomas Jefferson's refusal to reappoint him governor in 1801 ended Sargent's public career, but he continued to write papers for the American Philosophical Society and the American Academy of Arts and Sciences on various natural phenomena that he had observed.

1. The poem that Sargent enclosed, which runs to about three hundred lines, was written by his sister, Judith Sargent Stevens (1751–1820), who in 1788 married the Universalist minister John Murray (1741–1815). Sargent also included an extract of Judith's letter to him, which reads in part: "The proposals for forming the Society are greatly worthy the amiable Character of Patrons of Liberty—May nought impede their Progress. . . . May their Order *indeed* endure as long as Nature herself shall endure—My Sentiments you will see more fully exprest in the Attempt at Poetry which I take the Liberty to transmit . . . Reading the Institution [of the Cincinnati] over last Evening I could not forbear seizing the Pen." She begins her poem with the lines:

> Hail glorious Period! Hail benignant Peace!
> Now dinning Arms their hostile Clamour cease!

And she ends with the promise that the "Goddess Fame":

> Shall own the Cincinnati's fairer Claim
> Its Right undoubted to the Gift of Fame
> And while her Plaudit thus bestows Renown
> With her own hand affix the blooming Crown.

A transcription of the poem is in CD-ROM:GW.

For the rest of her life Mrs. Murray wrote and published poems, essays, and plays. Both GW and Martha Washington were listed as subscribers to her collection of writings, *The Gleaner*, published at Boston in 1798 in three volumes under her pseudonym Constantia.

From John Harvie

Sir   Richmond [Va.] Feby 21st 1784

I have Caus'd the Records and Return of Surveys in the Land Office to be accurately Searched to Collect proper Information respecting the Tracts of Land you mention in your Letter,[1] and am sorry that my researches will produce you so little Satisfaction, amongst the Surveys (not patented) turn'd over to me by the Secretary, I find two of yours of which I inclose you Copys, they only wait your Orders for Grants to issue upon them,[2] I can discover no Survey of General Andrew Lewis that Includes a Bituminous Spring[3]—neither is there any Survey in this Office that I can find for the Land at the Confluence of the little Kanhawa and Ohio, yet I think I have heard that the Commissioners for adjusting the Claims to Unpatented Lands in the District of Monongahela Yohagany and Ohio gave Doctor Briscoe a preemption Certificate for that Tract of Land, but in this particular I may be Mistaken as it is only founded upon a faint Remembrance—there has been no Survey in the Name of Michael Cresap returnd to this Office.[4] it would have given me the greatest pleasure if I could have Satisfactorily traced out your Claims to Lands, under the several Rights you mention, as the long Inattention to your private property from the Motive of Publick Service so Eminently display'd, fills every Generous Mind with an alacrity on even the most trivial Occasion to pay you sir such Tribute of Gratitude and Esteem as only can be felt for a Patriot whose Virtues are Unrival'd under the Impression of these Sensations I have the Honour sir of Subscribing myself Yr most Obt & very Humble sert

John Harvie

ALS, DLC:GW.

1. See GW to Harvie, 10 Feb. 1784.

2. Harvie is referring to the certificates of survey of the tract of 2,950 acres on the Great Kanawha in Botetourt County, Va., signed by Samuel Lewis on 6 Nov. 1774 and of the 2,000-acre tract also on the Great Kanawha but in Fincastle County, Va., returned by William Preston, 18 April 1774. See GW to Samuel Lewis, 1 Feb., n.1, and GW to Thomas Lewis, 1 Feb. 1784, n.6.

3. For a description of the Burning Springs tract in Botetourt County, see GW to Samuel Lewis, 1 Feb. 1784, n.3. Title to the tract was not finally cleared and a division made between the heirs of GW and Andrew Lewis until 1820 (see "Washington's Grants in West Virginia," 130–32).

4. In 1783 Alexander Parker bought Robert Thornton's claim to 1,350 acres at the mouth of the Little Kanawha. No land at that place was granted either to Dr. John Brisco of Berkeley County, Va., or to Michael Cresap. See *Diaries*, 4:41–42.

From Henry Knox

Boston February 21, 1784

Agreably to my promise my dear sir, I write you from this place, and flatter myself with the hope, that although my letter contains no important intelligence, yet it may not be unpleasing to you.

Your calm retreat, of mount Vernon, must be a source of ineffable delight to you. you can from thence, take a retrospective view, of the critical exigencies of the War, and see a thousand ways, by which, the issue might have been the reverse of what it is. And your happiness, must be in proportion, to the extreme difficulties, and dangers, of the contest, and the immense blessings secured to your country, by the glorious peace, contrasted with the miseries consequent upon an unfortunate termination.

We have little or no politicks—all commerce frozen up, by the uncommon severity of the season, but better prospects in the Spring—These are now upon the stocks in different parts of the state, for the fisheries and other branches of trade, upwards of 800 Vessels which will be at Sea, early in the summer.

New Hampshire and this State have come into the impost exactly as proposed by Congress—and it appears to be pretty certain that Rhode Island and connecticut, will be induced to come into it. Many sensible men are for the powers of the union being Legislated but no measures are proposed to effect it.[1]

The Cincinnati appears (however groundless) to be an object of jealousy. The idea is, that it has been created by a foreign influence, in order to change our forms of Government and this opinion is strengthened by a letter from one of our Ministers abroad. Burkes pamphlet has had its full operation The cool dispassionately sensible men, seem to approve of the institution generally, but dislike the hereditary descent.[2] The two branches of the Legislature of this State vizt the Assembly, and Senate, have chosen a committee, "To inquire into any associations, or combinations,[3] to introduce *undue distinctions* into the community, and which may have a tendency to create a race of hereditary nobility, contrary to the confederation of the United States, and the spirit of the constitution of this commonwealth." They have not yet reported, and perhaps they will not[4]—The same sentiments, pervade New England—The society here have had a respectable meeting in Boston, on the 18th instant at which Genl Lincoln presided—Genl Heath was not present. A Committee was chosen to attend the General Meeting at Philadelphia next may. Genl R. Putnam—Colo. Cobb, Colonel Hull, Major Sargent and myself—probably only two will attend. It was thought prudent, not to make any honorary members at present—The officers and soldiers conduct themselves in an exemplary manner, and are generally as industrious as any part of the community.

I wrote your excellency from West point on the 3d ultimo enclosing the returns, and a particular account of matters there which I hope met your appprobation—and I also wrote You a line on the 9th of the same month the day I sat out from thence—We reside at Dorchester about five miles from *Town* & in a very agreable situation. I shall hope for the pleasure of hearing from you at your leisure. Mrs Knox presents her sincere and ardent affection to Mrs Washington, and proposes to write particularly to her soon, and I also beg my respectful compliments may be added—I am my dear sir Your truly respectful and affectionate humble Servant

H. Knox

ALS, DLC:GW; ADfS, MHi: Knox Papers.

1. In his circular letter of 8 June 1783, GW urged state approval of Congress's impost request of April 1783. See *JCC*, 24:257–61. The Massachusetts legislature accepted the proposed impost in the fall of 1783 as did New Hampshire in January and Connecticut in May 1784, but Rhode Island held out until February 1786. By "upon the stocks," Knox meant the vessels were at anchor.

2. Public opposition to the Society of the Cincinnati found expression in

New England early in 1784 and continued unabated until after the first general meeting of the society in Philadelphia in May 1784. Aedanus Burke's influential pamphlet attacking the Cincinnati, *Considerations on the Society or Order of Cincinnati* (1783), was reprinted in Connecticut and Rhode Island; and on 29 Jan. and 5 Feb. 1784 the editor of Boston's *Independent Chronicle and the Universal Advertiser* printed long excerpts from it in his paper. Both John Jay and John Adams disapproved of the Society of the Cincinnati; but Adams wrote Lafayette from The Hague on 28 Mar. 1784 that he had "written nothing to America upon the subject" (Adams, *Works of John Adams*, 8:92–93), and the earliest letter on the subject from Jay that has been found is one to Elbridge Gerry from Paris dated 19 Feb. 1784 (Morris, *Jay Papers*, 2:694–95). See note 4.

3. In his draft of this letter, Knox wrote "which have or may be formed" after the word "combinations."

4. On 16 Feb. 1784 the Massachusetts senate joined the lower house in forming a committee "to consider what measures are necessary to be taken in order to prevent the Ill consequences of any Combinations that are or may hereafter be formed to promote undue Distinctions among the Citizens of this Free State, and tending to Establish an Hereditary Nobility, contrary to the Confederation of the United States and the Spirit of the Constitution of this Commonwealth" (Journal of Massachusetts Senate). In conformity to the committee's report, on 26 Feb. 1784 a second joint committee was "appointed to enquire into the Existence, nature[,] object & probable tendency or effect of an Order or Society, called the *Cincinnati*" (Journal of Massachusetts Senate, 22 Mar. 1784). The committee's report of 22 Mar. condemned the Cincinnati as a threat both to "publick liberty" and to "the liberties of the State." The society was seen as likely to lead to the establishment of an hereditary nobility, "which is contrary to the spirit of free government." The Massachusetts legislature concluded "that the said Society, called the Cincinnati, is unjustifiable, and if not properly discountenanced, may be dangerous to the peace, liberty and safety of the United States in general, and this Commonwealth in particular" (quoted in Wallace Evan Davies, "The Society of the Cincinnati in New England, 1783–1800," *William and Mary Quarterly*, 3d ser., 5 [1948], 3–25).

Letter not found: from Clement Biddle, 22 Feb. 1784. On 10 Mar. 1784 GW wrote to Biddle: "I have received the Lace & two-pole chain, accompanied by your favors of the 22d & 29th ulto."

From Isaac Collett

Berkeley County head of Bullskin [Va.]

Sir,   February the 22nd 1784

I make free to trouble your Excellency with a few lines relating to the conveyance or transference of the lease or Tenement of Land Guaranteed to Moses Collett of sd Couty As he has some time been dead. his sons during the war has bee mutch in the Army, since that mutch dispersed into the back Country's. his only survivor his eldest son who was his chief Executor who held the place having failed been afflicted this long time by a lingering disorder—under these circumstances it being not convenient for us to hold it. The young Gentleman that has purchased congratulates you upon the same, your Excellency not being at home at the time to Obtain consent at the time And opportunity not permitting to send before though it being contrary to your lease to sell without. Yet I hope you will give your Approbation At this time. under the circumstances laid before your Excellency's consideration.[1] In assenting to the same you'll mutch favour your Excellency's very humbl. and most obt Servant

Isaac Collett

ALS, DLC:GW.

1. See Dolphin Drew to GW, 13 Feb. 1784, and notes. GW responded from Mount Vernon on 25 Feb.: "Mr Collett, It would have been quite as proper to have written about the payment of your Rents, as a transfer of the Lease.

"When the arrearages of the former are discharged, it is very probable I shall have no objection to the latter, provided it is to a purchaser who means to reside on, & will improve the Land. Until these happen I shall consent to no sale at all, and advise you to attend to the first, Your humble servant G: Washington" (LB, DLC:GW).

From Fielding Lewis, Jr.

Dr Uncle & Godfather Frederick [County, Va.] 22d Feby 1784

Inclosed I have Sent you my Fathers letters wharein you will See his intention Before his death, of releiveing me out of my distressis, Occasioned by my youthfull Folley.

Since which it has pleased God to take him out of this transetorey life, before he had Compleated his Intention, tharefore I have taken the Freedom and liberty, of beging of you to Assist me through them, for which Kinderness I shall be willing to give you A Mortgage on my land as Securety, for what Evor Sum or Sums you will be Able to lend me, And Shall Annually remitt you my Crops till the hole is Returned to you again, as Nothing I think in this life So disagreeable as to be drag'ed About by the Sherrifs, and being in Confinement, Which Situation I am in at preasent or Should have wateid on you in person, that I might have had the pleasure of Seeing you Since your returne, With my love to my Aunt, I remain yours with Evrey Esteem and Regarde

Fielding Lewis

N.B. The young man I have Sent down Is A Sober Carefull person, who May be trusted if in your power to Assist me, and Should be glad after your perrusal of the inclosed letters, you would return them by the bearer.[1] F.L.

ALS, ViMtV.

Fielding Lewis, Jr. (1751–1803), was the oldest son of Fielding Lewis (1725–c.1781) and GW's sister Betty Washington Lewis (1733–1797) of Fredericksburg, Virginia. Fielding Lewis, Jr., inherited from his father 1,000 acres in Frederick County, Va., where he was living with his wife Ann (Nancy) Alexander, daughter of Col. Gerard Alexander of Alexandria, and their children. Lewis was married before he was 19 years old.

1. GW did return the letters. See GW to Lewis, 27 Feb. 1784.

From Daniel McCarty

Dr Sir   Feby 22d 1784

Tomorrow is appointed for us to have a Vestry the Place of meeting is to be at Wm Lindsay's in Colchester by 11 Oclock,[1] it was attempted five or six times last fall, but you and Mr Hendersons, both being out of the County we never could get a Sufficient Number of the Gentlemen to meet to make a Vestry,[2] by Which means the Poor Suffers Very much, and Some of them must Inevitabley Perish without they Can have some assistance, I must therefore beg your attendance if you can Possibly make it Convenient, Mrs McCarty and family Joyn me in our best Respts to you, and your worthy Lady &c.[3] and I am with the greatest Esteem Dr Sir Yr most obet and Very Hble Servt

Daniel McCarty

ALS, NjMoNP; Sprague transcript, DLC:GW.

Daniel McCarty (d. 1792) lived near Mount Vernon at Mount Air, about three miles up Accotink Creek from the Potomac. See *Diaries*, 1:247–48. McCarty had been a member of the Truro Parish vestry since 1748 and GW since 1762.

1. Colchester, Va., was a settlement on Occoquan Creek about eight miles from Mount Vernon. William Lindsay operated a tavern.

2. Alexander Henderson (c.1738–1815), one of the leading Scottish mer-

chants in Colchester, was first elected to the Truro Parish vestry in 1765. The vestry had last met on 22 Nov. 1782.

3. McCarty and his wife Sinah Ball McCarty had six children, all grown but living nearby. See GW's biting response to this letter on this day.

To Daniel McCarty

Dr Sir,   Mount Vernon 22d Feby 1784.

It is not convenient for me to be at Colchester tomorrow; and as I shall no longer act as a vestryman, the sooner my place is filled with another the better. This letter, or something more formal if required, may evidence my resignation, & authorize a new choice.[1]

I shall be very sorry if your apprehensions on account of the poor should be realized—but have not the Church-Wardens power to provide for their relief? And may not those Vestrymen who do meet, supposing the number insufficient to constitute a *legal* Vestry, express their sentiments on this head to the Wardens? Nay go further, & from the exigency of the case, give directions for the temporary relief of the needy & distressed. As a Vestryman or as a private parishioner, I should have no scruple to do either under such circumstances as you have described.

Mrs Washington joins in compliments & best wishes for you, Mrs McCarty & family with Dr Sir Your Most Obedt &ca

G. Washington

LB, DLC:GW.

The Truro vestry met on the next day, 23 Feb., and immediately elected John Gibson vestryman "in the room of his Excellency General Washington who has signified his resignation in a Letter to Daniel McCarty Gent." During the meeting McCarty, as churchwarden, "exhibited an account of his transactions for the years 1782 & 1783" (Truro Parish Vestry Book). McCarty participated in the election of two new churchwardens as well as in the vestry's other business including the adoption of measures for the relief of the poor. He then resigned from the vestry, and Lund Washington was elected in his place. The vestry was dissolved the next year.

1. See McCarty's letter of this date.

2. The acerb tone of GW's letter may only reflect his resentment of the implied rebuke in McCarty's letter of this date, but Lund Washington's reference to McCarty in his letter to GW of 23 April 1783 is suggestive: "It was very tight Pole[in]g between Broadwater & Stewart the former carried it by only 3 votes, there were some who woud have Blushd to vote agst Stuart and there-

fore did not vote at all, by which means he lost his Election and among these were your old friend McCarty—" (DLC:GW).

To Arthur St. Clair

Dear Sir,   Mount Vernon 22d Feb. 1784

Your favor of the 29th of Jany in answer to my circular Letter of the 28th of Dec. is at hand. I am sorry to find by it, that so many Delegates from your State Society are likely to be Non-attendants at the General meeting in May. It would have an odd appearance (whatever may be the causes) for the Society of the State, in which the General meeting is held, to be unrepresented upon such an occasion; and it would give me concern I confess, to find any so; for it is my wish that the first meeting (at least) may be full.

Not only for the purpose of bare representation then, but that the abilities of the Society of Cincinnati may be convened at that time, I hope your business elsewhere may, without much inconvenience, be made to yield to this call for your attendance.[1] With great truth & sincerity—I am Dr Sir Your most Obedt & Affecte Hble Servt

                                             Go: Washington

ALS, DLC:GW; LB, DLC:GW.

1. St. Clair did not attend, but Pennsylvania was represented at the general meeting by John Dickinson, Stephen Moylan, Thomas Robinson, Thomas B. Bowen, and Abraham G. Claypole. St. Clair when governor of the Northwest Territory changed the name of an Ohio town from Losantiville to Cincinnati in honor of the society.

To Richard Varick

Dear Sir,   Mount Vernon 22d Feb: 1784.

The intemperate Season and irregularity of the Post, withheld your letter of the 15th Ulto from me 'till within these few days.[1] There needed no apology for the delay, in the adjustment of your Accts. Your punctuallity is too well known to admit a doubt that, this would happen without sufficient cause.[2]

I received great pleasure from the Acct which you have given me of Doctr La Moyeur's operations on you; and congratulate you very sincerely on the success. I shall claim your promise of relating the Sequel; for I confess I have been staggered in my belief of the efficacy of transplantation—being more disposed to think that, the *Operator* is partial to his own performances, and the *Operatee's*, in general, are inclined to compliment, or having submitted to the *Operations*, are somewhat unwilling to expose the truth—Your Acct I can—I shall rely upon.

If contrary to expectation this Letter should find Doctr La Moyeur in New York, let me pray you to present my Compliments to him; and tell him that, his Letter of the 20th is at hand.[3] That I should have answered it but for the information given therein, of his intention of setting off in a few days for Virginia—and that I shall, whenever it is convenient to himself, & not before, be very glad to see him at this Seat where he—as you would at all times—meet a cordial, & welcome reception.[4]

I thank you very sincerely for your kind congratulations on my return to the tranquil walks of private life. I shall always be glad to hear from you, and shall *depend upon you* for a relation of the remarkable occurrences in your Hemisphere. Mrs Washington joins me in best wishes for yourself, & compliments to the Governor Mrs Clinton & family. I am with great esteem & regard Dr Sir Yr Most Obedt & affecte Hble Servt

Go: Washington

ALS, CSmH; LB, DLC:GW.

1. Letter not found.

2. For Varick's role in organizing and transcribing GW's papers, see GW to Varick, 1 Jan. 1784, and notes.

3. See Jean Le Mayeur to GW, 20 Jan. 1784.

4. For Le Mayeur's spring visit to Alexandria, see his letter to GW, 20 Jan., n.2.

From Jedediah Huntington

Dear Sir,   Norwich [Conn.] Febrr. 23. 1784

Your Favor of the 28th of Decr did not reach me before last Week. I shall not fail to give Notice either by Letter or in Person, to the Delegates from this States' Society, of the time appointed for the general meeting of the Cincinnati.[1] I have the Honor to be, most respectfully, Dear Sir, your very humble Servant

Jed. Huntington

ALS, DSoCi.

Jedediah Huntington (1743–1818) of the Connecticut forces at the beginning of the Revolutionary War was made a brigadier general in the Continental army in 1777 and served until the end of the war. He was president of the Connecticut Society of the Cincinnati.

1. For the delegates chosen by the members of the Connecticut Society of the Cincinnati, see David Humphreys to GW, 20 Mar. 1784, n.2.

From Francis Johnston

Sir   Philada Feby 23d 1784.

At the request of Captain Paschke of the Light Dragoons and, Captains De Marcellin and Le Roy late of the 2d P. Regt; I beg leave to inform Your Excellency that they are going to Europe and are desirous of receiving from your own hand a Certificate of their being Members of the Cincinnati Society [1]—they have all signed the Institution in due form and lodged with me an Order on the Paymaster General for a Months-pay respectively—this being the case I hope they will not fail in their present application. My most respectful Compts attend Mrs Washington & am with the highest sentiments of Esteem Your Excellency's Most Obt & Very Hble Servant

F. Johnston Treasr of the Cincinnati Society
of Penna and Secy ℣ tem

ALS, DSoCi.

Francis Johnston (1748–1815), colonel of the 5th Pennsylvania Regiment until his retirement on 17 Jan. 1781, was assistant treasurer of the Society of the Cincinnati. In 1785 he was elected treasurer.

1. Frederick Christopher Paschke (Paschka), who served under Casimir Pulaski, was more recently deputy quartermaster in the southern department of the Continental army. Antoine-Claude de Marcellin and Nicholas-Georges Le Roy were both commissioned in the 2d Pennsylvania Regiment on 28 July, and both remained in the service until 20 June 1784, when they returned to France. See Marcellin and Le Roy to GW, 4 Mar. 1784.

From Fock

My Dear General   Paris the 24 fevr. 1784

The many favors, and particular marks, of His Excellencis Kindness, and oblidging conduct, towards me, during the whole time, I spent in America, Gives me reason, to hope You will honor me with the order of Cincinnatus, of wich Your Excellency is the President. As I was not a Colonel during the war, I cannot get the order, wich is Conferred only on Generals or Colonels in General Rochambeaus Army, without Your Excellencis interposition.

Count defersen, and I were the only two of our Nation, wich hat the Happiness, to be under His Excellencis command, therefore I hopes my request will be Most graciously granted, by His Excellency, and will be to me the Highest Satisfaction, in my Native Country, and an eternal remembrance, of His Excellency, for Whom I have the greatest regard and attachment.[1] All my wishes are, to be once my own master, to pay my respects to His Excellency in America, in the mean time, I pray Him, to give My most respectfull Compliments, to Your Lady Mrs Washington, and be sure that I am for Ever, with the Highest esteme and devotion Your Excellencis Most Obedient and Humble Sarvant

Baron de Fock

My direction are à Paris à L'hotel de Monsieur L'Ambassadeur de Svede, à la Cour de france, Que. de ⟨B⟩aque[2]

ALS, DLC:GW.

Jean-Henric, Baron de Fock (1753–1817), was a Swedish nobleman. Fock was a captain attached to the Schomberg Dragoons in 1779, and he served as an aide-de-camp to Lauzun in America.

1. Hans Axel von Fersen (1755–1810), a Swede of noble family and a captain in the Swedish army at the time of the American Revolution, was an aide to Rochambeau in America. Fersen rose in Sweden to become grand marshal in 1801. He was killed in 1810 after being accused of poisoning the prince royal Christian-Auguste.

2. GW sent from Mount Vernon by Lafayette a letter of acknowledgment to Fock dated 25 Nov. 1784. The operative sentence in GW's letter is: "At the General Meeting held at Philadelphia in May, general principles respecting the right to that order were established—and the members of it in the Armies & Navy of His Most Christian Majesty were requested to hold meetings in France—to examine rights—and decide upon the equity of claims" (ALS, DSoCi).

From Jean-Daniel de Gambs

General,   Metz [France] 24 Feby 1784

The kindness you were pleased to shew me, when we had the honor of being commanded by you, encourages me to claim your protection for admittance into the Order of Cincinnatus. I

should be much flattered with the honor—I have been the
oldest Major in Count Rochambeau's army, and in this quality
made three Campains in America as Major of Brigade: and independant of the siege of Yorck, fortune was so kind to me, as
to place me with the Marquis Laval aboard the Conqueror, in
the action in the Chesapeak the 16th of march 81; making part
of a detachment for Virginia—The success of this expedition
was not answerable to our expectations, but you are not ignorant Sir, that this vessel was much worse treated than any in the
Squadron—I have seized with eagerness the opportunity that
presents, of sending you a letter by General Roberdeau with
whom I have corresponded since his arrival in London:[1] having
first become acquainted with him on our journey through Philadelphia, and knowing well his relation, a Colonel who stays
with me, and has served the King a long time with great
honor—Without this opportunity, which I consider as the most
ready, I should have begged Count Rochambeau to have inter-
ceded with you and Congress for me, as I am well convinced of
this General's good inclinations towards me. As the stay I made
in America, and the time I served under your orders General,
will allways constitute an Epocha dear to me; you cannot doubt
of the pleasure it will give me to be honored with such an
Order, as that of Cincinnatus. I have the honor to be with the
most profound respect, General, Your very Hble servnt

Gambs

Major of the regiment of Bourbonnais

Translation, in David Stuart's hand, DLC:GW; ALS, DLC:GW. A transcription of the original French letter is in CD-ROM:GW. Gambs's letter was forwarded to GW by James Milligan, 4 June 1784.

Jean-Daniel de Gambs (c.1740–1823) arrived at Newport, R.I., in July
1780 with his régiment de Bourbonnais under the command of Anne-Alex-
andre-Marie-Sulpice-Joseph Montmorency-Laval, marquis de Laval (1747–
1817). Gambs fought at Yorktown in 1781 before returning to France. He was
made lieutenant general in the French army in 1787, and in 1799 he became
governor of Naples under Joseph Bonaparte. Because he did not hold rank
above that of major during his American service, Gambs did not qualify for
membership in the French Cincinnati.

1. Daniel Roberdeau (1727–1795), who was a Philadelphia merchant engaged in the West Indian trade before the Revolution, became a brigadier
general in the Pennsylvania forces in 1776. He was also a member of Congress from 1777 to 1779. After his return from a visit to Europe in 1783–84,
he settled in Virginia, living first in Alexandria and later in Winchester. When

Milligan forwarded this letter to GW (see source note), he also sent a copy of a letter from Gambs to Roberdeau, whom Milligan mistakenly believed to be lost at sea. The letter from Gambs to Roberdeau, dated 24 Feb., and David Stuart's translation is in DLC:GW.

From Thomas Lewis

Sir   Rockingham C[oun]ty [Va.] Feby 24th 1784
    Yours of the 1th Instant Came to hand this day. in Complyance with your request, I have Searched my offices, and find no other locations in your name Returned by Colo. Crawford but those you mention vizt that on Shirtee & that at the round bottom on the Ohio, the Warrants with the assignments on which you right to both those are founded I have in Safe keeping, and they were all recited or taken notice off in the Certificate of Location transmited you by Colo. Crawford, no other warrants of yours are in my Possession, it may be they were Sent to Some other County, or returned in Colo. Crawfords hands for Location as opportunities might present—as you have obtained a Patent for the tract on Shirtee I am Surprized you did not. the Same for that on the round Bottom unless as you observe Some person had Entred a Cavet against it, but in this Case I think it altogether Improbable that any Judgement could be obtained either for or against you, as all trials of this kind were Suspended with the Comencement of Hostilities that Soon took place after your Location, besides in Such a Case you would have been Sumoned to defend your Claim[1]—All that I remember tending this way was a mesage from on[e] Michl Cresop, of Some Claim or pretension he had at that place but how Circumstanced I cant now reccolect—but this was after your Survey—I think I have Some faint remembrance of writing to you on that Subject but Cannot be positive.[2] what remains for you as things Stand is to have enquiry made at the land office whether any Suit was ever Commencd there against the land in Question & to have your Survey entred in that office in order to obtain'g a Patent. I never heard of any other pretensions to that land but this of Cresops, As to the land at the mouth of the Little Kanaway that Colo. Crawford presented you a Draft of, he never made any return thereof to my office, nor Entred any warrant theron to my Knowledge. it is probable

that at the time of making the Survey He thought it Clear of other Claims[3]—I cannot inform you whether any other person may have had the land at that place Survey Since, for Surveying business was Impracticable in those parts from the Commencment of Hostilities till the latter part of the war—& Dureing this time Several new Countys were made that were formerly part of Augusta of which Number the County of mononghela was one & the land in Question mostly in that County— whereof John madison became Surveyor & who was some time ago killed by the Indians it might be proper for you to make Enquiry in the Surveyors office there for the information you want—I have not been Surveyor of Augusta Since 1777, where I live fell into one of the Division on the Eastern waters called Rockingham[4]—would it not be proper for you to write to the representative of the late Colo. Crawford to make Strick Search amongst his papers for any warrants of yours that might have been Intrusted to his Care.

It is propable that your messenger [Young] was here on Some business respecting lands but with you I cannot recolect particulars, but think it probable it was with the warrents that you find recited in both your Certificats of Location.[5]

The warrants by Messrs Roots & Thruston, I have not the least knowledge of, if warrants were never Isued on the Rights of those I am at a loss to advise how they Can be obtained now or if Isued, lost or misslaid how they Can be replaced I am at a loss to Know.[6]

In addition to what I have Said relative to the land at the mouth of the L. Kanaway I would observe that it must be known to Sundry people that Colo. Crawford made a Survey at that place the report would Spread & prevail—& it is not Improbable that Such report might prevent any Subsequent locations, & the more so as Colo. Crawford, was most of his time Convenient to get information of any Such thing being done[.] if you have any trusty aquaintance in that part of the world you might get Information on this head. I wish it were in my Power to have given you a more Satisfactor information in the Several points of your requst. if I could I asure you I should not have Considred it as a painfull office, nor Shall I think any thing in my power so that you think can Contribute to your Service or Satisfaction.

It now remains that thank you for the kind remembrance you have of my late Brother—Death has deprived of Severel valuable freinds amongst whom I have to lament with you my much Esteemed friend Col. Fielding Lewis.

Now Sir permit me to present you with my Compliments of Congratulation on your Safe arival at your Seat in your native Country, not only on Acount of yr Safe return but also on the wreath of Laural with which you are Crowned—a Crown the more Glorious as it is Gift of merit not bestowed on you by your Country only, but by the Sufferage of all Europe, but in a more peculiar manner by all who have a regard to libert & the Common Rights of mankind but I must not offend your Delicacy by Picturing to you the Overflowings of my hart on the various Objects that present themselves to my Imagination on this Ocassion—Permit me than to asure you that I am with the most profound regard & Esteem Your Excellencys most Obedient & most Humble Servant

Thos Lewis

P.S. When I set down to write I meant this as a Sketch or rough draft of what might occur, but finding an imediat Conveyance by Mr Jones to winchester from whence you probably will receive this with as much Expedition as any other way & not having time to transcribe it I have ventured to present you Just as it is &[7]

ALS, ViMtV.

1. For a summary account of the steps GW took between 1774 and 1784 to make good his claim to the tract of land at Chartiers (Shurtees) Creek and to the Round Bottom tract, see GW to Thomas Lewis, 1 Feb. 1784, nn.1–3.

2. Lewis is probably referring to his missing letter of 31 Mar. 1774. See GW to Thomas Lewis, 1 Feb. 1784, n.1. For Michael Cresap's attempts to assert his claim to the land at Round Bottom, see GW to Thomas Lewis, 1 Feb., n.3, and GW to Harvie, 18 Mar. 1784, n.5, and 31 May 1785.

3. For the tract at the forks of the Little Kanawha and Ohio, see GW to Thomas Lewis, 1 Feb. 1784, n.7.

4. John Madison (d. 1782) at the county's founding in 1745 became clerk of the court of Augusta County at the same time that Thomas Lewis became its surveyor. He was married to the sister of Thomas Lewis's wife.

5. GW sent George Young, who was in his employ at Mount Vernon, out to the Virginia frontier early in the spring of 1774 with messages to William Preston and to Andrew and Thomas Lewis, among others. The warrants to which Lewis is referring are those applied to the Round Bottom and Chartiers Creek tracts (see note 1).

6. For the land GW claimed under the rights purchased from John Rootes and Charles Mynn Thruston, see particularly GW to Thomas Lewis, 1 Feb. 1784, nn.5 and 6.

7. Mr. Jones was probably the prominent lawyer Gabriel Jones (1724–1806) who lived in Augusta County and was married to Thomas Lewis's sister-in-law. See GW to Charles Washington, 28 Feb. 1784.

From Henry Babcock

Stonington [Conn.] 25th Feby 1784

Great illustrious, Sir! I have for these several Years set down to my desk to congratulate Your Excellency, upon your unparreled Successes in Arms.

There is a Gentleman that lives in Northampton who studies under the great Doctor Stiles, President of Yale College, in the State of Connecticut; has a true Poetick Vain, superior to any Man, I am acquainted with, who would (if possible[)] do Justice to your matchless Achievements, perhaps equal to Alexander Pope, Swift or Driden, when arrived to the Years of Homer would equal his Poetry: I intend writing him upon the Subject—If he could be informed from your own Cabinet; it would be better Information; than any History yet wrote, not excepting Mr Gordons history of the american Revolution; It would be read with Great Avidity, thro out the Globe; If it could, as & if translated into the language of Ciceronian Latin, which, Mr Dwight could easily do. He certainly is one of the most learned Gentleman I am acquainted with.[1] I certainly should be greatly indebted to Your excellencey, for the acknoleding of my Letter. This I certainly can say that the Minister of Great Britain did send to America; the very best Generals they had: And notwithstanding there great Superiority in Numbers, of veteran Troops, your Excellency out generald them all. had General Bradock attended to your advise, he would with your Assistance been triumpant; and those that remained, owed their lives to your great Exertions; otherwise, there would scarce been a Messenger to inform the Pub[l]ick. I have the Honor to be with every Sentiment of Esteem, & profoundest Respect, Your Excellencys most obedient & most humble Servant

Henry Babcock

ALS, DLC:GW.

Col. Henry (Harry) Babcock (1736–1800), a graduate of Yale College

(1752) and colonel of a regiment at the attack on Fort Ticonderoga in 1775, was dismissed in 1776 from the command of the Rhode Island forces because of his "distemperd mind" (GW to Nicholas Cooke, 28 April 1776).

1. Timothy Dwight (1752–1817), one of the Hartford, or Connecticut, Wits, gave up his position as tutor at Yale College in 1777 to become an army chaplain. In January 1779 he returned to his home in Northampton, Mass., where he remained for five years. While in Northampton, Dwight composed an epic poem, *The Conquest of Canaan* (1785), in which he made many allusions to contemporary events in America.

To Dolphin Drew

Sir,   Mount Vernon 25th Feby 1784
   Yesterday evening brought me your favor of the 13th.

Two things induced me to Lease my Lands in small tenements; the first was to accommodate weak handed people who were not able to purchase, thereby inviting & encouraging a number of useful Husbandmen & mechanicks to settle among us: The other, that I might have them restored to me at the expiration of the term for wch they were granted, in good order & well improved—One step towards which was to prevent a shift of property without my consent, and a covenant was inserted in the Leases accordingly.

From the first I laid it down as a maxim, that no person who possessed Lands adjoining, should hold any of mine as a Lessee, and for this obvious reason, that the weight of their labour, & burden of the crops, whilst it was in a condition to bear them, would fall upon my Land, and the improvement upon his own, in spite of all the covenants which could be inserted to prevent it. Having no cause to depart from this opinion, & without meaning to apply the observation particularly to Mr Throckmorton, whose person & character are entirely unknown to me, he must excuse me for declaring in very explicit terms, that I will not suffer his purchase of Collet, to be carried into effect. of this, Mr Lund Washington who was acquainted with my sentiments on these matters, and who superintended my business, informs me he acquainted Mr Throckmorton (hearing he was about to purchase) either directly or by means of his acquaintance in September last: he has not paid his money therefore, or erred in this business, without warning of the consequences.[1]

A good price & ready money might induce me to part with

the fee-simple of Collet's Lot—perhaps of the other also. Without these I do not incline to sell as Lands are rising very fast in their price; which will be enhanced by the emigration of Foreigners, & the demand for them. I am Sir Your most Obt Servant

G: Washington

LB, DLC:GW.
　　1. See notes, Dolphin Drew to GW, 13 Feb. 1784.

To La Luzerne

Sir,　　　　　　　　　　　　Mount Vernon 25th Feby 1784
　　I have been honored with your Excellys favor of the 18th from Annapolis covering a letter from the Marqs de la Fayette, for the trouble of doing which be pleased to accept my thanks.
　　I regret exceedingly that the weather and roads shou'd have deprived me of the honor of seeing you at my retreat—I shall look however, with pleasure for your return to Annapolis, when I shall expect the fulfilment of your promise.[1] It would be a gratification to express to you under my own roof the great respect attachment & regard with which I have the honor to be &ca

G: Washington

LB, DLC:GW.
　　1. See La Luzerne to GW, 18 Feb., and notes.

From d'Estaing

Sir　　　　　　　　　　　　Paris 26th February 1784.
　　It is in the name of all the French Sailors that I take the Liberty to request Your Excellency to accept of an American Eagle, *expressed rather than embellished* by a French Artist.[1]
　　Liberty (of which it is the happy and august Symbol) has risen of itself, supported by Wisdom, talents, and disinterestedness, by every virtue—by Genl Washington; obstacles have only Served to increase its strength. The efforts of a patriot army are irresistible, Seconded by the King's Troops, who have shewn themselves by their discipline and conduct, worthy of the

choice of His Majesty, his Navy has made every thing possible—
It appears then to be lawful to one of those who unite the titles
of Soldier & Sailor to those Sentiments of the most profound
admiration and attachment which You inspire to intreat you to
receive with indulgence an homage which must cease to be trifling, when it Shall interest your Sensibility.

One who has had the happiness to be the first of those whom
the King Sent to America, & who has been the last of those who
were designed to lead thither the forces of two great Monarchs,
thereby acquires the happy prerogative of being entitled to express, tho' faintly, the Sentiments of all his fellow Sailors & Soldiers.[2] I have the honor to be with respect Sir Your Excellency's
Most obedient and most humble Servant

Estaing.

L, in English, DLC:GW; LS, in French, DLC:GW.

1. D'Estaing wrote La Luzerne on 18 Feb. 1784: "You will find, Monsieur le
Chevalier, faults and gallicisms in the private letter in English which I wrote
to General Washington. . . . The thought will always be understandable. I
have thought it my duty to use my mother tongue in official letters and in
Memoirs [which are sent to GW]. My second letter was accompanied by a trin-
ket. Learning by chance that an Eagle set with diamonds had been made for
General Washington, I won over the jeweler. I obtained this Cincinnatus; I
had a trophy and a banderole added, saying thereon that it was presented to
His Excellency General Washington by French sailors" (Hume, *Society of the Cincinnati*, 81–83). The translation of the letter from d'Estaing to La Luzerne is by
Hume. For an account of the adoption of the eagle as the symbol for the Society of the Cincinnati and L'Enfant's mission to France to have the eagle
medals made, see ibid., xii–xiv, and Lafayette to GW, 10 Jan. 1784, n.3.

2. GW responded from Philadelphia on 15 May 1784 in these terms: "Any
token of regard of whatever intrinsic worth in itself, coming from the Count
D'Estaing, must [be] stamped with dignity & respect; but when attended with
the esteem & regards of all the Sailors of your Nation—the companions of
your honorable Toils in America, is not only agreeably acceptable—it becomes absolutely inestimable—As such I receive the American Eagle, which
your Excellency has been pleased to present me in the name of all the Sailors
of the French Nation. And at the same time that I acknowledge myself hereby
inexpressibly honored by that most respectable Body of men—I beg you to
assure them in my name, of the very high estimation in which I shall ever hold
this particular mark of their regard & attention.

"To the Navy of France sir, this country will hold itself deeply indebted: its
assistance has rendered practicable those enterprizes, which without it could
not with any probability of success, have been attempted. I feel myself happy
in this opportunity, thro' your Excellency's favour, of paying to the Officers &
sailors of His Most Christian Majesty, this tribute of grateful acknowledge-

ment, which I beg you sir to be so obliging as to convey to them, & at the same time to assure yourself of possessing in my breast, every sentimt of inviolable attachment & respect, with which your character has impressed my mind" (LB, DLC:GW).

From George Clinton

My dear Sir   New York 27 Feby 1784
I with great pleasure embrace the first direct opportunity that has offered, to acknowledge the receipt of your Letters of the 15th and 28th December;[1] the former covering Mr Morris Notes to the amount of 2080⁸⁰⁄₉₀ Dollars.[2] Mr Gouv. Morris has also informed me that a Warrant in your favor for 857⁵²⁄₉₀ is lodged in the Office of Finance, with directions to transmit it to me[3]—I will take care to procure this money as soon as possible, and have both sums carried to your Credit.

It afforded me much pleasure to hear that after all the toils of a public life you was once more in the perfect possession of Domestic happiness, which that you may enjoy long and uninterrupted will be the constant prayer of every good Citizen of these States.

Altho the termination of the War has put a period to many of the fatiguing parts of my duty, I have still such a Croud of public business as to allow me very little time for private enjoyments, besides which, my ill State of Health (having had three returns of the fever) and the indisposition of my family, some of whom have been continually Sick through the Winter, has prevented my having much pleasure since I saw you—the family are now pretty well—except that I am laid up with a violent cold and Washington with a broken thigh—an accident he had the misfortune to meet with about a Week ago, I am however in great hopes it will not be attended with and bad consequences.

As I understand you propose being in Philadelphia in May next I am in hopes, you will find it not inconvenient to extend your journey as far as this place—I need not say how much satisfaction such a visit will give to all your friends.

Mrs Clinton joins me in our best Compliments to Mrs Washington. I am Dear Sir with the most perfect Respect & Esteem your Affectionate Humble Servt

Geo. Clinton

LS, DLC:GW.

In December 1782 while at Newburgh, N.Y., GW borrowed from Gov. George Clinton (1739–1812) £1,870, giving his bond for 2,500 dollars in New York currency. GW had for long been eager to add to his Mount Vernon estate the 543-acre French-Dulany tract on the neck at Dogue Run. He learned of the possibility that Benjamin Tasker Dulany and his wife Elizabeth French Dulany would be willing to exchange this for a 376-acre tract near Alexandria, owned by Adam, Dow, & McIver of Alexandria, provided that Mrs. Dulany's mother, Penelope French, could be persuaded to give up her life's interest in the place. With the loan from Clinton, GW bought the so-called Dow tract, but it was not until 1786 that Mrs. French consented to give up her claims to the land at Dogue Run. See particularly, GW to Lund Washington, 21 Nov. 1782 (two letters; DLC:GW), 25 Dec. 1782 (MiDbGr), and Lund Washington to GW, 20 Nov., 4, 11 Dec. 1782 (all ViMtV).

1. In his letter of 15 Dec. 1783, GW wrote: "I have been able to negotiate a matter with Mr Robt Morris by wch about Seventeen hundred pounds York Curr[enc]y will be thrown into your hands on my acct which sum, when received, I pray you to carry to the credit of my Bond." See note 2.

2. GW recorded in Ledger B, 206, payment to Clinton of 425 dollars (£127.10) on 1 Dec. 1783 in interest on his bond and, on 15 Dec., of 4,226$\frac{19}{90}$ dollars (£1267.16.8) paid through Robert Morris. For GW's explanation of this, in which he points out that the total of Morris notes was 4,226$\frac{19}{90}$ instead of 2,080$\frac{89}{90}$ dollars, see his letter to Clinton's secretary, Benjamin Walker, dated 24 March.

3. See GW to Morris, 4 Jan., n.1, and James Milligan to GW, 9 Mar., n.3. GW notes the payment of this amount to Clinton on 25 Feb. in Ledger B, 206.

To Fielding Lewis, Jr.

Dear Fielding,   Mount Vernon Feb. 27th 84

You very much mistake my circumstances, when you suppose me in a condition to advance money.[1]

I made no money from my Estate during the nine years I was absent from it, and brought none home with me. Those who owed me—for the greater part—took advantage of the depreciation & paid me off with Six pence in the pound. Those to whom I was indebted, I have yet to pay, without other means, if they will not wait, than selling part of my Estate—or distressing those who were too honest to take advantage of the Tender Laws to quit scores with me.

This relation of my circumstances, which is a true one, is alone sufficient, without adding that my living under the best œconomy I can use, must, unavoidably, be expensive, to convince you of my inability to advance money.

I have heard with pleasure that you are industrious—convince people by your mode of living that you are Sober and frugal also, and I persuade myself your Creditors will grant you every indulgence they can. It would be no small inducement to me, if it ever should be in my power, to assist you.

Your Fathers advice to you, in his Letter of the 8th of Octobr is worthy the goodness of his own Heart, and very excellent to follow. If I could say any thing to enforce it, it should not be wanting.

I shall always be glad to see you here; your Aunt joins me in best wishes, and I am your Affecte Uncle

Go: Washington

P.S. There was a great space between the 23d of Septr 1778 when you were called upon by your Father for a specific list of your Debts; and his death: How happened it, that in all that time you did not comply with his request? and what do they amount to now? His letters to you are returned, & I hope will get safe to hand.[2]

G. W——n

ALS, NN: Washington Collection; LB, DLC:GW.
    1. For Lewis's plea to GW for aid, see his letter of 22 Feb. 1784.
    2. Young Fielding Lewis's financial difficulties were not of recent origin nor were they near an end. His father wrote GW on 16 Sept. 1769: "I am allmost certain that he will in a year or Two spend every Shillg [of his young wife's fortune] as I cannot perceive the least amendment since his Marriage, nor has he the least regard to any advice I give him"; twenty-three years later, on 25 Sept. 1792, his mother Betty Washington Lewis wrote GW: "Fielding is so distrest that his Children would go naked if it was not for the assistance I give him" (ViMtV). GW himself was not so restrained in his criticism when he next wrote his nephew on 4 Dec. 1786.

To Charles Washington

Dear Brother,   Mount Vernon Feb. 28th 1784
    Your Letter dated the 15th of January (which I presume must be a mistake, as the bearer says he left your House the day before yesterday) came to my hands last Night. I thank you for your kind congratulation on my return to private life, which is highly pleasing to me.[1]
    Your Son George went down with me the 11th of this Month

to Fredericksburgh, where I left him. In a day or two after, he proposed going to Colo. Balls; and I am not certain whether from thence to Berkeley, or not—He wrote to you, I know, by a Mr Throckmorton, & no doubt informed you of his intentions. The uncertainty I am in where he may be, will, I believe, induce me to keep the Letters which are directed for him, 'till I see him; as I suppose he will not be long from this, if he should not go to your House.[2]

Such attentions, & pecuniary aids as it was in my power to afford him, were rendered with great pleasure, because I thought him very worthy of them; and went with no less chearfulness from his Aunt, who has a great regard for him. It is to be lamented that he cannot get restored to perfect health. He looks very thin, and is yet troubled with the pain in his Breast of which he has long complained. Tho' I think, as he does himself, that he is better.[3]

I shall be obliged to you for a Copy of the Acct, as it stands upon my deceased Brother Samls Books, between him & me; The Land I sold Mr Pendleton with a view of raising money, got into his hands, and I have never received a farthing for it yet—this is not all—it is to be feared that when I come to call upon my Tenants in Berkeley for Settlement, it will be found that many of their Rents have been paid to him—These things very illy agree with my present circumstances, and call for money.[4]

From Fredericksburgh, I wrote to Mr Thoms Lewis of Augusta, & sent the Letter by Mr Jno. Lewis, who was to put it into the hands of some one who would give it to Mr Gabl Jones at Fredk Court. If you should go to that Court next Month, or should see Mr Warner Washington before it (where I think it likely the Letter was left) I shall be obliged to you for enquiring after it, as it is of some consequence to me.[5]

Whenever the Weather, & your convenience will admit it, I should be happy to see you & my Sister.[6] Mrs Washington joins in best wishes to you both, and the family, with Dr Sir Yr Most Affecte Brothr

Go: Washington

P.S. When you see the Family at Fairfield, present my Compts & best wishes to them.

The inclosed for my Tenant on Bullskin, please to send by a safe hand, that he may be sure of getting it. & I shall be obliged to you for informing the others on the same Tract & those above Harewood that if they do not settle & pay up their arrearages of Rent very soon I shall use the most efficatious means to do myself justice.[7]

ALS (photocopy), InU: U.S. History Manuscripts; copy, DLC:GW.

Charles Washington (1738–1799), GW's youngest brother, lived in a new house, Happy Retreat, overlooking Evitt's Run in Berkeley County, Virginia.

1. Letter not found.

2. George Augustine Washington (1763–1793) was Charles Washington's oldest son and a favorite nephew of GW's. He served as an aide to Lafayette during the Revolutionary War. Colonel Ball was Burgess Ball (1749–1800) of Lancaster County, Va., who was married to Charles Washington's daughter, Frances (1763–1815). For the identity of Albion Throckmorton, see Dolphin Drew to GW, 13 Feb. 1784, n.1.

3. George Augustine Washington, who suffered from what was probably tuberculosis, sailed to the West Indies for his health in May 1784. No record of earlier gifts of money to George Augustine Washington from GW and Mrs. Washington has been found, but on 25 April 1784 GW gave him £140 "to bear his Exps. to the West indies" (Ledger B, 197).

4. For Samuel Washington's involvement both in GW's sale of land to Philip Pendleton and in the collection of rents from GW's tenants, see GW to James Nourse, 22 Jan. 1784, nn.3 and 4.

5. GW's letter to Thomas Lewis of 1 Feb. 1784 may have been the one that he sent to him from Fredericksburg by John Lewis on 14 February. See GW's instructions to John Lewis, 14 Feb. 1784, printed above.

Warner Washington, GW's first cousin, lived with his family at Fairfield, his house in Frederick County, Va., to which he moved before the war.

6. Charles Washington and Mildred Thornton were married in 1757.

7. This was probably GW's letter to Isaac Collett, 25 Feb. 1784. Harewood was the house in Berkeley County built by GW's brother Samuel, who died in 1781.

To John Harvie

Sir,   Mount Vernon 29th Feby 1784

I have received, & thank you for your obliging favor of the 21st in answer to my letter of the 10th—I will write to the Surveyors of Augusta & Botetourt for information in those matters which the Land office is unable to give me: for sure I am, I have warrants somewhere which ought, long 'ere this, to have been executed. The two Surveys of which you sent me copies, I should be glad to have patents for, reciting the right under which I hold them, as soon as it is convenient to yourself. I have the honor to be &ca

G: Washington

LB, DLC:GW.

Letter not found: from Clement Biddle, 29 Feb. 1784. On 10 Mar. 1784 GW wrote to Biddle: "I have received the Lace & two-pole chain, accompanied by your favors of the 22d & 29th ulto."

From Samuel Fraunces

Sir   [New York] March 1st 1784

I have the honor of Conveying by an unexpected opportunity my most sincere & dutifull respects to your Excellency & a gratefull heart that is Fully sensible of the innumerable obligations your unmerrited favours has laid me under, therfor your Excellency's native goodness will pardon any presumption that may seem in this; My prayers shall at all times be most devoutly, for the health & happiness of your Excellency & family[.] My Wife & Daughters begs to be remembered likewise with every sentiment of esteem—they send Mrs Washington a couple "utensils For cutting paste" the best that could be procured & hopes will meet with approbation—they present their most respectfull Compliments to her in the mean time I remain with unfeigned sincerity Your Excellencys Most obedient and most devoted Humble Servant

Saml Fraunces

ALS, DLC:GW.

Samuel Fraunces, who came to New York from the West Indies, was the owner and proprietor of a noted tavern at the corner of Broad and Pearl streets in New York City. During the war Fraunces occasionally performed services for GW, and it was from Fraunces's tavern that GW bade farewell to his officers in 1783. GW made Fraunces the steward of his household in New York after he became president. At his death in 1794, Fraunces was survived by his wife Elizabeth, two sons, and five daughters.

From Rochambeau

Paris March 1th 1784

You Will be, my Dear Général, Single confidant of this letter. I did foresee the ministry on the way Wherewith could be received here the defferent Demands that I have made to you, in order to increase or make Some additions in the Society of Cincinnatus, one did answer me that the King had a great repugnancy to permit to his Subjects any Stranger order, and it Was but by a particular consideration that he has for you and for the united States, he had permited to us to be aggregated in the form regulated by the général Society. but a considerable addition perhaps Would not be So Well received. as it is not convenient to me to engage you in one proceeding Which may be Would have not here a Kind reception, I beg to annul all the demands I have made to you by my foregoing letters,[1] and I recommend only to you the two cases following as an explication to the deliberation already Settled by the général Society and that do not Wants any other consent in this country but that Which has been already given.

The Baron de l'Estrade Brigadier of the King's armies. has marched, being L. Colonel, to the attack of the Redoubts of york town at the head of the first company of the french grenadiers, has been made Brigadier for this action on his return to St Domingo.[2]

The chevalier de Lameth aid quarter Master Général. has been Wounded by the two shots in the attack of the redoubts of york-town[,] has been made Colonel for this action, While he Was yet in his bed at Williamsburg in consequence of his Wounds.[3]

This two Caises appear to me alones Which may be comprised as an explication of the deliberation of the american army to Which the King has already given his consent, and Which consequently Will have no Want of New approbation of him, I am Sir With respect of your Excellency The Most obedient and Very humble Servant.

le cte de Rochambeau

LS, DLC:GW.

1. Rochambeau wrote to GW on 19 Jan. and 13 Feb. 1784. For the nominations he had made for membership in the Society of the Cincinnati, see especially the letter of 19 January.

2. Claude-Amable-Vincent de Roqueplan, baron de L'Estrade (1729–

1819), was the lieutenant colonel of the régiment de Gâtinais at the siege at Yorktown in 1781. Rochambeau singled out L'Estrade and Lameth in his letter of 19 Jan. 1784.

3. See Lameth to GW, 6 Jan. 1784. Both L'Estrade and Lameth were elected to the French Cincinnati.

From Benjamin Lincoln

Dear sir   Hingham [Mass.] March 2d 1784

Since I was honored with the receipt of your favor of [   ]¹ this State society of the Cincinnati have had a meeting & have made choice of General Knox Genl Putnam Colo. Cobb Colo. Hull & Majr Serjeant to represent them in the General Meeting to be held at Philadelphia on May next. they are notified to attend I expect that two or three or more will have the pleasure of meeting your Excellency then—Our Citizens seem alarmed at the constitution of the Cincinnati & our General Court have the matter now under consideration.² I will do my self the pleasure of communicating to your Excellency their doing. With great esteem I have the honor to be your Excellencys most ob. servant

B. Lincoln

ALS, DSoCi.

Benjamin Lincoln (1733–1810), a native of Hingham, was made major general in the Continental army in February 1777. Lincoln served with GW before being given command of the American army in the southern department in 1778. He surrendered his army at Charleston in May 1780 to Henry Clinton but was exchanged in time to participate in the Yorktown campaign in October 1781. From 1781 to 1783 he was secretary at war for the Congress. In 1791 he led the army that put down Shays' Rebellion.

1. GW's "favor" to Lincoln was his circular letter of 28 Dec. 1783. See GW's circular letter dated 1 Jan. 1784.

2. See Henry Knox to GW, 21 Feb. 1784, and notes 2 and 4.

To Simeon DeWitt

Dr Sir,   Mount Vernon 3d March 1784

By the interruptions of the post, your letter dated the 12th of Jany never got to my hands until Sunday last.

I have urged, not only in public, but private conversations with individual members of Congress, the policy, indeed necessity of having accurate Maps of the United States—& they know full well my opinion of your worth, and ability to execute them. All seem sensible of these, but the want of funds I suppose, stops this, as it does many other wheels which ought to move.

The propositions contained in your Mem[oi]r of the 12th to Congress, appear to me exceedingly reasonable & just: these sentiments I will express to a very valuable & much respected member of that Body to whom I am now writing.[1] I am, with great esteem Dr Sir Your Most obt Servt

G: Washington

LB, DLC:GW.
1. See GW to Thomas Jefferson, this date.

From Duportail

Dear general   Paris march 3th 1784

I Cannot let so fine opportunity as major l'enfants going escape without Recalling me to your excellency's memory—probably this letter will find you on the bancs of potoomak; after having ascertained the liberty of your Country, and the fame of your name, you enjoy the Tranquill pleasures of the Rural Life like the patron of our society which you Represent more than any defensor of the Country—however there are Certainly great differences between the dictator and your Excellency, and one of them is that the Country which he defended was not then so large as the smallest of the 13 united states, but I am sorry I Cannot wish these last should act in future so great a part in the world proportionnately as Rome did, for it Cannot be but at our own expence—but I hope the americains will be wiser and more moderate in their ambition than the Romans. they shall be happier too—I leave to marquis delafayette to tell your Excellency the news of this Country. the succes of the society of Cincinnatus—your Excellency will judge of it by the demands presented by the marquis as well as by Count de Rochambeau. I have been Requested by many to support their demands with your Excellency. but I Refused to do it as perfectly inutile. I know very [well] that if the demands are just or if the society is disposed to favours, your Excellency will follow equal principles, and so those who have the same Rights (or the same Rights to favours) shall be treated in the same manner.

I saw yesterday for the first time a man in the Clouds and with Colonel gouvion we Regretted that you Could not enjoy so extraordinary view. eight days ago I was busy about preparing a description of that new art for your Excellency and Translating what we have best in that Respect, but I met since with a description made in england and reported in the magazin, so I do not doubt that you shall have it in america et that will spare me the trouble which was indeed great.[1] Since I left america I had neglected to write or Read any thing in english and I am exceedingly surprised of the difficulty which I experience in writing english and for fear of fatiguing your Excellency with my bad Stile I must end this letter, in wishing you all the happiness you deserve so well. I have the honour to be with great Respect your Excellency's the most humble and obedient Servant

duportail

permit me dear general, to present my best Respects to Mrs Washington.

ALS, DLC:GW.

1. On 4 June 1783 the Montgolfier brothers, Jacques-Etienne and Joseph-Michel, sent up a hot-air balloon near Lyon; shortly thereafter the physicist Jean-Alexandre-Césare Charles released a hydrogen balloon in Paris. It was, however, only after Jean Pilâtre and the marquis d'Arlandes actually went up in a hot-air balloon over Paris on 21 Nov. 1783, followed shortly by the ascent over Paris in a hydrogen balloon of Charles and M. N. Robert, that the balloon craze spread from France to the rest of Europe. For Gouvion's identity, see GW to Duportail, 4 April 1784, n.4.

To Thomas Jefferson

Dear Sir,   Mount Vernon Mar. 3d 1784

The last Post brought me the enclosed letter, under cover from the Marquis de la Fayette.[1]

If you have any News that you are at liberty to impart, it would be charity to communicate a little of it, to a body.

It is unnecessary, I hope, to repeat to you the assurances of the pleasure I should feel at seeing you at this retreat, or of the sincere esteem & regard with which I am—Dear Sir—Yr Most Obedt & very Hble Servt

Go: Washington

P.S. Has not Congress received a Memorial from Mr DeWitt, now, or lately Geographer to the Northern Army? The propositions which are contained in the Copy, which he sent me, seem founded in equity. and with respect to himself, I can assure you that he is a modest, sensible, sober, and deserving young man—Esteemed a very good Mathematician, & well worthy encouragement.[2]

G.W.

ALS, DLC: Jefferson Papers; LB, DLC:GW.

1. Lafayette's letter to GW was probably the one dated 11 Nov. 1783. See GW to Lafayette, 4 April 1784, n.1. The enclosed letter, presumably from Lafayette to Jefferson, has not been identified, but see Boyd, *Jefferson Papers*, 7:7–8.

2. See GW to Simeon DeWitt, 3 Mar., and DeWitt to GW, 12 Jan. 1784.

From Frédéric de Kalb

General,   Alsace [France] 3 march—84

I have just recieved the honor of the Order of Cincinnatus; wc. is conferred on those who have distinguished themselves in the service of America—You honor me with it, as Heir of an unfortunate & respectable parent—I return you my warmest acknowledgments for it, & wish the distance of your Country, did not prevent me from paying my respects to you personally—I am Your Hble & Obt servant

Frederic de Kalb

Translation, in the hand of David Stuart, DLC:GW.

Frédéric, baron de Kalb (1765–1793), was taken into the French Society of the Cincinnati on 16 Jan. 1784 as the son and heir of Jean, baron de Kalb. The elder Kalb, a brigadier general in both the French and the American armies, was mortally wounded in the Battle of Camden in August 1780. The son Frédéric died on the guillotine.

To Robert Morris

Dear Sir,   Mount Vernon 3d March 1784

Enclosed is your Warrant on Mr Hilligas, endorsed—I thank you for the trouble you have taken to negotiate the matter with Govr Clinton,[1] & have the honor to be with all possible regard, Dr Sir Your Most obedt & affecte Servant

G. W——n

LB, DLC:GW.

1. See GW to Morris, 4 Jan., n.1, George Clinton to GW, 27 Feb., and James Milligan to GW, 9 Mar., n.3. Michael Hillegas (1729–1804) was United States treasurer.

From George Muse

Excellent Sir: Caroline County [Va.] March 3th 1784

I now being Destressed for cash must colicite your favour to settle with my son Laurence Muse for my Exspences in going to Pitsburge on my way Down the Ohio To secure my Titled to Certain Lands, Agreable to your Derections, my Exspences in going To Pitsburge, which is Computed To be three hundred Miles, and from home again with a servent and three Horses, cost me forty pounds, which your Excellency has Never been charged with. the inclemency of the weather Ocationed my Exspences to be Considerable it being in height of Winter. your Derections to me by letter was to attend in person or legally auther[ize] some person To attend To the Devision of lands we were intitled To on the ohio which agent could not have been imployed without a considerable Exspence To your Self. Agreable To your bond you Were To be at all the Exspences Occuring, to the saveing & secureing the Said lands, Seating and Setling only Excepted.[1] Your bond you will Receive of my son on Setling With him.[2] it would have given me infinite Satisfaction To have waited on your Excellency my self, but my infirmitys will not allow me at present. I flatter myself of haveing The Honour of being in your Excellency's Company in my Antient days. I am your Excellences Most Obt & very Hume Servt

Geo. Muse

LS, DLC:GW.

George Muse (1720–1790), the father of Battaile Muse (1751–1803) who was soon to become GW's land agent in northern Virginia (see GW to Battaile Muse, 3 Nov. 1784), had incurred GW's strong displeasure at least twice: in 1754 at Fort Necessity and in 1773 after the distribution of land under the Proclamation of 1754 (see *Papers, Colonial Series*, 1:77; and GW to George Muse, 29 Jan. 1774).

1. On 4 Nov. 1773, the Virginia council ordered a patent to be issued under Dinwiddie's Proclamation of 1754 for a "Tract [on the Great Kanawha] of 7276 Acres to George Washington, and George Muse, the former to have 3953, & the latter 3323 Acres." Adjoining the Muse-GW tract was a surveyed

tract of 7,894 acres for which the council ordered a patent to be issued to William Bronaugh (6,000 acres), Dr. James Craik (1,794 acres), and George Muse (100 acres). GW purchased from Bronaugh the right to 2,000 of his 6,000 acres; and in return for Bronaugh's right to 2,000 acres and for other considerations he secured for himself from Muse the 3,323 acres that Muse was entitled to in the Muse-GW tract (*Va. Exec. Jls.*, 6:548–49; see also GW to Samuel Lewis, 1 Feb. 1784, source note and note 1, Agreement with George Muse, 3 Aug. 1770, GW to William Bronaugh, 18 Jan. 1775, and Ledger B, 114). The "other considerations" included a cash payment of £20 for 182 acres on 2 June 1774 (Ledger B, 114) and an agreement entered into by Muse and GW on 3 Aug. 1770 that GW would pay "all the cost and charges which shall arise ⟨in *illegible*⟩ and securing the said Muses share of the above Grant [under the Proclamation of 1754] (the expense of Seating & Settling the same excepted)" (ViMtV). In a notation in Ledger B, 114, dated January 1775, GW confirms that he was under obligation to pay "All the Expences attending the Surveying, Patenting, &ca of Colo. Muse share of the 200,000 Acres of Land under the Proclama[tio]n of 1754," and that all such charges, including the £20 for 182 acres and £22.16.8 for Muse's share of Capt. William Crawford's surveying fee, had been paid "to this date."

In 1775 GW persuaded Muse, Craik, and Bronaugh to apportion the land in their tract of 7,894 acres between themselves by drawing "Tickets" for the first, second, and third surveys of their respective shares. See George Muse to GW, 6 Jan. 1775, and GW to William Bronaugh, 18 Jan. 1775. At some time subsequently, presumably not long afterwards, the three men made the division. Near the end of the war, on 8 April 1783, Muse wrote to GW: "You are Indebted to me £40.0.0 for mine and servants Expences to fort Pitt In consequence of the Land agreed on pr Bond and attending on the division with Doct. Craig and Capt. Bronaugh" (DLC:GW). After Lund Washington sent Muse's letter to GW, GW wrote Lund on 6 May 1783 about it and ended by observing: "His Letter, brings some recollection of the matter to my mind; with this circumstance, that He was drinking weeks together in a place—particularly at Charles Smiths—I am very willing however, to comply litterally with my agreement—& wish you to settle the matter upon terms of liberallity rather than otherwise with him, as he has lain out of his money so long" (NhD). No such bond has been found, but the land agreement of 3 Aug. 1770 between Muse and GW (note 1) was apparently attached to George Muse's bond for £1,000 sterling to guarantee GW's compliance with the terms of the agreement (ViMtV).

On 11 Mar. 1784 GW took further steps to settle matters with George Muse. See GW to Laurence Muse, 11 Mar. 1784.

2. The son to whom he is alluding is Laurence (Lawrence) Muse.

From Marcellin and Le Roy

Sir   Philadelphia March 4th 1784.

Having had the Glory of serving in the armies of the United States, for near five years; and having seen the happy termination of the War, we are now preparing to return to Europe, with the hearth Self satisfaction of having Contributed a share of Service under your auspicious Command in the Establishment of a revolution So Brilliant and Extraordinary.

As the society of Cincinnaty must be extremely respected in Europe, and as we Cannot Continue in america long enough to receive the Diplomas we take the Liberty to trouble your Excellency with our request that you will be pleased to sign the Certificates, which we have the honor to transmit as also that you Will Condescend to accompany those Sign'd by General St clair, with certificates of your honorable approbation of our services.[1]

We now beg permission to take leave of your Excellency with our most ardent wishes for a prolongation of your health and Most Valuable Life and are with every Sentiment of Esteem and Veneration Sir Your Excellencys Most obedt hble Servt

Marcellin
Le Roy

LS, DLC:GW.

1. Antoine-Claude de Marcellin and Nicholas-Georges Le Roy were original members of the Pennsylvania Society of the Cincinnati. See Francis Johnston to GW, 23 Feb. 1784, and GW to Johnston, 22 Mar. 1784.

From Thomas Bee

Sir   Charleston [S.C.] 5 March 1784

The Charleston Library Society desirous of Testifying their Esteem for your Excellency, and at the same time of having the Opportunity to Inroll your Name as one of their Members, Did, by an Uninimous Vote at their last Anniversary Meeting, Elect you, an Honorary Member of their Society, as will appear by the inclosed Certificates, which as their President, I have now the Honour of Transmitting to your Excellency.[1]

This Institution was formed about Thirty years ago, with an immediate view, to the Extension of Learning and Science amongst the Inhabitants of this New World, and ultimately, for the purpose of Endowing a College in the Neighbourhood of this City. The ravages of war have for a time suspended these Intentions, but the repose we have now the prospect of Enjoying, in the procuring of which, your Excellency has borne so distinguished a part, makes us look forward with pleasing satisfaction to the Completion of our Plan.

It is the wish of the Society that this Mark of their respect may prove acceptable to your Excellency, and it will be an infinite gratification for them to receive from you Sir, any hints or Observations for the improvement of their plan, or that may in any way contribute to the advancement of knowledge, or benefit of Mankind. with the most sincere respect and Esteem I have the honour to be your Excellency's most Obt & most humble Servt

Tho. Bee

ALS, DLC:GW.

Thomas Bee (1730–1812), a Charleston lawyer who studied at Oxford and became a federal district judge in 1790, was active throughout his adult life in public affairs in South Carolina. He was a member of the board that organized the College of Charleston in 1785.

1. The certificate of membership in the Charleston Library Society is dated 13 Jan. 1784 (DLC:GW). GW responded from Mount Vernon on 28 May: "I acknowledge the receipt of your favor dated the 5th of March, enclosing a unanimous vote of the Charleston library Society electing me an honorary Member of their body with the cert. thereof ⟨*illegible*⟩.

"For this mark of attention, and for the honor done me by enrolling my name as a member of so respectable a Society—formed for such generous & laudable purposes, I beg the favor of you, Sir, to present my gratitude & best wishes for the completion of its objects; which, from the repose we have a prospect of enjoying, is scarcely to be doubted.

"If it shou'd ever be in my power to offer any thing which may be useful, or that can afford the least satisfaction to the society, it will contribute not a little to my pleasure to do it" (LB, DLC:GW).

Letter not found: from Joshua Barney, 6 Mar. 1784. On 24 Mar. GW wrote to Barney: "Your Letter of the 6th only came to hand the 22d."

From Chastellux

Dear general   Paris March 6 1784

When major l'enfant leaves Europe a second time to go to america,[1] I cannot help troubling your excellency with a few lines. the further I find myself from the time I had the happiness of seeing you, the more also I feel a desire to tell you how much I am attached to you. I think, moreover, my dear general, that being retired for the future to mount vernon, and your modesty making you fear to look back upon what is vast, and which must appear to your eyes with all that bright glory with which you have covered your self, your mind may give it self up intirely to sentiments of friendship, and I flatter my self, you will then indulge me to retain the privileges you have granted me a right to. perhaps when this letter reaches you, it may find you sitting under the shade of those trees you have planted, surveying with delight the magnificent view of pa-tomack. Why cannot I partake of your leisure, as I have done with toils, and enjoy the company of the immortal Washington, who after having saved a whole nation, is contented with making the happiness of a few individuals? I have the honor to be dear general your most humble and obedient servant

le Chr de Chastellux

All the military gentlemen with the rank either of general or colonel, who have been to america, wear at present the order of Cincinnatus, and the nation sees the decoration with pleasure, as it recalls to their mind the most advantageous war, as well as the most valuable Alliance they ever made. I am persuaded that this establishment being confined in proper bounds, will tri-umph over all the enemies it meets in america and I hope your country will understand how to unite the glory of the military to the liberty of the citizens.

Permit me to present my compliments to Mrs Washington and to Mrs Custis as well as to all your family and friends who partake of my attachment for you.

ALS, DLC:GW.

1. L'Enfant arrived in Philadelphia from New York during the general meeting of the Society of the Cincinnati.

From Thomas Jefferson

Dear Sir   Annapolis [Md.] Mar. 6. 1784.

Your favor of the 3d is this moment put into my hands, and as the post does not usually stay here above an hour, it leaves me time to scribble a few lines only, scarcely admitting them to be prefaced with an acknowlegement of the pleasure it will give me to be permitted to communicate with you occasionnally. we received dispatches from Europe yesterday, by Capt. Barney.[1] there is no news but in one from Dr Franklin of Dec. 25.[2] and another from the Marquis Fayette of Dec. 26.[3] the Doctor tells us only of the movements of our ministers, that mr Laurence was about sailing from England for America, mr Adams about setting out from England for the Hague, and mr Jay at Bath. he gives a picture of the disposition of England towards us; he observes that tho' they have made peace with us, they are not reconciled to us nor to the loss of us. he calls to our attention the numerous royal progeny to be provided for, the military education giving to some of them, the ideas in England of distraction among ourselves, that the people here are already fatigued with their new governments, the possibility of circumstances arising on the Continent of Europe which might countenance the wishes of Gr. Britain to recover us, and from thence inculcates a useful lesson to cement the friendships we possess in Europe. The Marquis tells us the Turks & Russians will be kept apart for awhile, probably for another year, but that they must in the end come to decision. that mr Fox & Ld North were both out of the ministry, & this by a maneuvre of the king's, who got them compromitted fairly with their E. India bill & contrived to get it rejected in the Lords; & that mr Pitt & E. Temple would come in. The Marquis himself will sail for America in the spring. The present hurry forbids me to write to you on a subject I have much at heart, the approaching & opening the navigation of the Ohio & Patowmac. I will trouble you by the next post.[4] De Witt's petition happens to be in my possession as member of a committee who have not yet reported on it.[5] I was happy to learn from you something of the man. I have the honour to be with the most sincere esteem & respect Dr Sir Your most obedt & most humble servt

Th: Jefferson

ALS, DLC:GW.

1. This is the naval hero Joshua Barney. See GW to Barney, 24 Mar. 1784. Jefferson was a delegate to Congress, which was meeting in Annapolis.

2. See Benjamin Franklin to Thomas Mifflin, 25 Dec. 1783, DNA:PCC, item 82. Mifflin was president of Congress.

3. Lafayette's letter of 26 Dec. 1783 to Mifflin is in DNA:PCC, item 156. Lafayette gave the same news to GW in his letter of 10 Jan. 1784. See also GW to Jefferson, 3 Mar., n.1.

4. See Jefferson to GW, 15 Mar. 1784.

5. See Simeon DeWitt to GW, 12 Jan. 1784.

From William Gordon

My dear Sir   Jamaica Plain [Mass.] March the 8th 1784

It afforded me peculiar pleasure to learn, how your Excellency had secured your public character by your manner of retiring to the private walk of domestick happiness, after having been, in the hands of the Supreme Governor, a glorious instrument of establishing the rights of the American States. Your name will be mentioned with honor by all historians, whether Whigs or Tories: but my prayer is, that it may be found written in the Lamb's book of life.

I am pursuing my plan with as much speed as the times will admit. Next monday I go for Newport, to inspect the papers of Genl Greene, who wishes me to do it ere he sets off for the southward, that he may explain to me certain anecdotes. When the roads are settled I shall push for Annapolis. I have not heard whether any resolution has been yet taken with regard to my petition. There is nothing like being present to solicit: but long absence from my people when at Princeton, the approaching winter, & the removal of Congress would not admit of my tarrying then to complete my business. I was therefore necessitated to conclude upon returning the morning of Nov. 3d, & reachd home with Mrs Gordon on the 20th after an agreeable journey, two or three days excepted.

Intend myself the honor of visiting You at Mount Vernon after leaving Annapolis. Can I get out early enough in April shall hope for the pleasure of seeing You at Philadelphia the beginning of May. Whether present or absent while in life, You will have my sincerest wishes for your peace & comfort, & that when leaving this world becomes desireable You may set without a cloud to shine with answerable lustre in the world of Spirits. Pray my regards to Dr Craig.[1] Mrs Gordon joins in best respects to Self & Lady.[2] I remain with the greatest truth your Excellency's affectionate Friend & very humble Servant

William Gordon

The last saturday our Friend Col. Quincy of Braintree was buried.[3]

ALS, DLC:GW.

The Rev. William Gordon (1728–1807), a dissenting English clergyman who settled in Roxbury, Mass., in 1772, wrote to GW often during the Revolutionary War and in October 1782 began pressing him for access to his papers, "in order to perfect my historical collections" relating to the American Revolution (Gordon to GW, 2 Oct. 1782). Gordon's intention was to write a history of the winning of independence by the United States. GW replied on 23 Oct. 1782 that he could not make his papers available until after the war, "when Congress then shall open their Registers,—& say it is proper for the servants of the public to do so." On 8 July 1783 GW wrote: "I can only repeat to you, that whenever Congress shall think proper to open the door of their Archives to you, . . . All my Records & Papers shall be unfolded to your View." After receiving this letter from Gordon in 1784, GW wrote Gordon from Philadelphia on 8 May finally agreeing to allow him to see his public papers if Congress approved. On 17 May 1784 Gordon petitioned Congress for permission to use the records in the archives of Congress. Congress's journal for 25 May records that Congress agreed to allow Gordon access, with certain restrictions, and that "having the fullest confidence in the prudence of the late Commander in Chief," it had "no objection to his laying before Dr. Gordon, any of his papers which he shall think, at this period, may be submitted to the eye of the public" (*JCC*, 27:427–28). Gordon went to Mount Vernon in June and stayed for nearly three weeks. He wrote of his stay at Mount Vernon to Horatio Gates on 31 Aug. 1784: "I got to General Washingtons by breakfast on June the 2d; when he had read the Resolve of Congress, he told me that he should make no reserve and keep no papers back, but should trust to my prudence for the proper use of them. I sat [sic] into work and followed it closely, rising by day light and being at his books as soon as I could read, and continued it till evening, breaking off only for meals, and never went once to visit tho' invited. By the 19th about two o'clock I had finished, having searched and extracted thirty and three volumes of copied letters of the General's, besides three volumes of private, seven volumes of general orders, and bundles upon bundles of letters to the General" ("Letters of the Reverend William Gordon," 506). Gordon published, in four volumes, *The History of the Rise, Progress, and Establishment, of the Independence of the United States of America . . .* in London in 1788. A three-volume edition was published in New York in 1789. For further information on the preparation and publication of Gordon's *History*, see Gordon to GW, 24 Sept. 1788, source note.

1. Dr. James Craik (1730–1814), GW's friend since he joined the Virginia Regiment, acted as Gordon's agent in selling subscriptions to the London edition of his *History*.

2. Gordon's wife was Elizabeth Field Gordon.

3. Col. Josiah Quincy, of whom John Adams once wrote "he praises himself as much as other People censure him," was a Boston merchant and the father of the noted patriot of the same name (Butterfield, *Adams Diary and Autobiography*, 1:82).

From John Moriarty

Salem (N: England) [Mass.]
May it Please your Excellency 8th March 1784

The fame of your Character Emboldens me to address your Excellency, & make my Situation & Circumstances Known to you. I was bred up to business in the City of Cork (Ireland) from my Infancy, 'till the year 1777. I then took passage to the Continent; & arrived in this town, where I Immediately got Connected with the Inhabitants & met every reasonable Encouragemt, then Invested every thing I had or could Command in five Privateers & had good Success until 1780.—that year stripd of all, Except a little Schooner, which I Laded & Sent off to the Havanah; upon her return, Sold her Cargo of Suggrs in Boston for £35000, old paper Currency, all which died in my hands, & which I very lately sold for £49.18—then, I Laded my little Schooner with Lumber for the West Indies; which in fourteen days after her Sailing was Captured & Carried into Bermudas,[1] finding my affairs take a disagreeable turn, & my finances almost at an end, I Scraped up every thing left, for which I purchased a house, & a few acres of Ground near this town, on which I now reside & will be little Enough when Sold to Liquidate my Debts. Now that the War is over this is no place of Trade, & it is Mortifying to be Obliged to Seek for bread in a Wilderness, Considering that my Connections in France, Spain, Portugal, England & Ireland, are good & very Numerous. in order therefore to Continue my Commercial Connections with them I know no part of the Country So Calculated for it as your Country. I have not a friend or Acquaintance in all Virginia to whom I cou'd mention my present wants; what I want is a Farm with a house thereon, Convenient to a Navigable river; (where I may reside with my family; having here, a Son & Daughter & four Daughters in Ireland) & some Gentleman to Indulge me, by taking the purchase money by yearly payments.

I would also wish to be Connected with a Gentleman who may wish to go a little into Trade, who may be Inclined to give me an Interest in a small Vessel & a Cargo, & be paid from time to time, upon the returns, he Could run no risque, as the Pollicy of Assureance would Guarantee him & I would Engage to take the Burthen, & Transact the whole without giving him any trouble. I Should deem myself happy were I thus Circumstanced; & be under your Excellency's protection in Virginia. I could get Letters of Introduction from most parts of Europe (if necessary) one of which I beg leave to Inclose for your Excellency's perusal.[2]

No doubt but some friend or Relation of your Excellency's may deem it his Interest to Encourage me on this head, I dare say, he'd find his Accot in it; as this mode may, yearly take off the produce of his Estate, & answer Several other purposes. If I am Honour'd with your Excellencys Ansr & Sentiments on this Subject at any time before the later end of April, Shall deem myself happy—I have the Honr to Subscribe myself your Excellency's most Humble Servt

John Moriarty

P.S: the first Vessell that arrives here, after the harbour is Open, wth flour, will Come to a good Market, none here now, Sells in Boston @ 7 Dollars ℔ Barrel—2d quality will do best, say about 600 Barrells.

ALS, DLC:GW.

The Irishman and merchant of Salem, Mass., John Moriarty (d. 1797) is said to have been "a flamboyant type . . . remembered chiefly for his exploit of riding his favorite horse, for a boast, starting far down in the fields, through the back door and great entry [of his house], out the front door and up the opposite hill at top speed." This house in Salem, a large one "of fifteen rooms, with a gambrel roof and much fine panelling and carving," Moriarty bought in April 1782, but he had already sold part of his interest in it by 1784 and gave up the rest in 1785 (Buxton, "History of the South Church, Peabody," 354–55). No evidence has been found that GW ever responded to Moriarty's letter, but see Moriarty to GW, 2 Oct. 1789.

1. In 1781 John Moriarty was the principal owner of two privateers based in Salem: the 80-ton brigantine *Flying Fish* carrying twelve guns and fifty men and the 40-ton schooner called *Languedoc*. The *Flying Fish* was captured and taken to Halifax, Nova Scotia, in July 1782. In 1782 the galley *Harpey* was registered in John Moriarty's name, and a Moriarty of Salem was listed as owner of the brigantine *Nancy* in 1785 and 1786. See Allen, *Massachusetts Privateers*, 132, 201; DNA:PCC, item 196; and Phillips, "Salem Ocean-Borne Commerce," 262, 267.

2. No such letter has been found.

From Lafayette

Sir   Paris March the 9th 1784
Your Excellency Has Been Acquainted With my first Measures Respecting our Society—To My Letter Xbr the 25th[1] I Beg Leave Particularly to Refer and Entrust this with Major l'Enfant Who is Returning to America.

Having in a Body Waited Upon Count de Rochambeau, we delivered Him and His officers the Marks of the Assossiation—A Resolve of theirs for a Volontary Subscription Will Arrive in time to Be debated in the Grand Assembly.

Many Claims Have Been Raised By french officers, Which it is not My Business to Present—But I Beg Leave to observe that Some of them, Like in Chevalier de Lameth's Case, are Entitled to Consideration—Count de Rochambeau, I am told, is writing on the Subject.[2]

Former dispatches Have Apologized for the Part We Have taken Respecting Count d'Estaing's officers—The Neglect, We know, Was not Intended—and, as Also in Mr de Vaudreuil's Case, it Would Have Produced a Bad Effect.[3] The Captains in the Navy, Ranking as Colonels, Have Set up a Claim to the Assossiation—Some of them, la *Peyrouse*, la *Touche*, *Tilly*, Acted as Commodores[4]—it May Be Observed that American trade Will Have to do With Naval Officers.

At a Board of Officers Met at My House, the Claims of Several Gentlemen Were Introduced—Our Opinions are Submitted to the Assembly,[5] and With them I enclose a list of Members who Have Signed and Paid, or to Whom, on Account of their Dispersion, the Institution are Yet to Be Sent[6]—Clel du Plessis Convinced us He Had not Resigned.[7]

Our Brotherly Assossiation Has Met With General Applause—Not a dissenting Voice to Be Heard But on the Point of Heredity that Creates a debate Wherein Most of the Americans take the other Part[8]—Who Can Question But What We do not on Any Account Wish to Injure those Sacred Republican Principles for which We Have Fought, Bled, and Conquerd? and What Sacrifice Has not Been Made By us, in Support of those principles? which, I am Sure, we are Ready to Repeat Upon Every Occasion?

There is an Unanimous Opinion of the officers Here which they Beg Leave to Present, Viz.—that all American Officers in Europe Ought to Resort to a Committee of which this City is a Natural Center, and that the Committee Be Instructed to Correspond with the Grand Assembly.[9]

It Had Been My Fond Hope that I Could Have Arrived in time for the Begining of May—But American Concerns, an Account of Which I Give to Congress, detain me for a few Weeks—and Now When I think this Letter Will Be Read Among Representatives from all the lines of the Army,[10] My Heart is Glowing With all the Most Unbounded Sentiments of Affection and Gratitude—How Pleasing it is for me, to Recollect our Common toils, dangers, turns of fortune, our So Glorious Successes and that Lively Attachement Which United us With Each other Under our Beloved General—Never Can My Heart forget the Return of Affection I Have Particularly Obtained, the Numberless Obligations I am Under to My dear Brother Officers, and the Happy Hours, the Happiest in My Life, Which I Have Past in their Compagny—Before the Month of June is Over, I shall, thank God, Be Again With them, and Am Panting for the instant When I May Be Blessed with a Sight of the American Shore. With the Highest Respect and Unbounded Affection I Have the Honour to Be Sir Your Excellency's Most obedient Humble Servant

Lafayette

ALS, DSoCi.

1. Lafayette's letter to GW of 25 Dec. 1783 is printed in Idzerda, *Lafayette Papers*, 5:179–80.

2. See Rochambeau to GW, 19 Jan., n.4, and 1 Mar. 1784.

3. Louis-Philippe de Rigaud, marquis de Vaudreuil (1724–1802), took part in the siege of Savannah in 1779 under the comte d'Estaing as *lieutenant-général des armées navales*. His rank entitled him to election to the French Society of the Cincinnati with the original members. GW expressed his regrets at the oversight in a letter to Lafayette of 17 May 1784 (Appendix VIII in Winthrop Sargent's Journal, doc. II in General Meeting of the Society of the Cincinnati, 4–18 May, printed below).

4. See Barras to GW, 23 Jan. 1784.

5. See Lafayette to GW, 9 Mar. 1784 (third letter), n.7.

6. Lafayette's enclosed "Names of the American officers wearing now in France the badge of the society of the Cincinnati" included: "Mr genal Mis de la fayette, Col. Cambray [Louis-Antoine-Jean-Baptiste, chevalier de Cambray-Digny; d. 1822], Lt Col. Fleury [François-Louis Teisseydre, vicomte de Fle-

ury; b. 1749], Lt Col. Mauduit du plessis, Lt Col. du buysson [Charles-Fran-çois, vicomte du Buysson des Aix; 1752–1786], Lt Col. Tousard [Anne-Louis, chevalier de Tousard; 1749–1817], Maj. pontgibaut [Charles-Albert, comte de Moré de Pontgibaud; 1758–1837], capitaine la Colombe [Louis-Saint-Ange Morel, chevalier de La Colombe; 1755–c.1800], Majr gal Du portail, Br. genal de Laumoy [Jean-Baptiste-Joseph, chevalier de Laumoy; 1750–1832], Col. gouvion [Jean-Baptiste, chevalier de Gouvion; 1747–1792], Lt Col. Villefranche [Jean-Louis-Ambroise de Genton, chevalier de Villefranche; d. 1784], Majr Rochefontaine [Etienne-Nicolas-Marie Bechet, chevalier de Rochefontaine; d. 1814], and Majr L'Enfant." Also listed as having signed was Frédéric, baron de Kalb, son of the deceased Maj. Gen. Jean, baron de Kalb. Listed as not yet having signed because "now in the west indies" were "Lt. Col. Gimat" (Jean-Joseph, chevalier de Gimat) and "Lt. Col. Noirmont" (René-Hippolyte Penot Lombart de Noirmont; 1750–1792).

7. Thomas-Antoine de Mauduit du Plessis (Duplessis, 1753–1791), who came to America in 1777 and was brevetted lieutenant colonel in the Continental army for his services at Brandywine and Germantown, returned to France in 1779. He came a second time to America in 1780 as an aide to Rochambeau.

8. See Lafayette's private letters (letters 3 and 4) of this date for a less sanguine view of the opposition to the Cincinnati.

9. Lafayette makes clearer in his third letter of 9 Mar. that this committee for American officers who were temporarily in Europe was to have no connection with the French Society of the Cincinnati, unlike the Frenchmen who had been officers in the American army (see note 6).

10. GW wrote to Lafayette on 17 May 1784 (see note 3) that the letters addressed to him as president of the Society of the Cincinnati had been presented to the delegates of the general meeting then being held in Philadelphia.

From Lafayette

private
My dear General   Paris March the 9th 1784

Mr du Bouchet formerly a Major in our Service Having Presented me With His Claims to Our Assossiation, I found Myself Obliged to tell Him that His Pretensions Were Groundless—So far was He Convinced of it, that He did not think it Proper to Apply to our Committee, But Has determined Upon Going Himself to America—I Candidly Represented Him that there Was a Good share of Madness in His plan, and that a Refusal Will Set Him in a very disagreeable Situation—I Hoped He Was Converted When on a Sudden I Hear He Now takes up again His Resolution—and After I Have done My Best to discourage Him, I Cannot Refuse Him this Introductory letter to You, Least it might Be thought the Silence of the Committee is Owing to Particular Motives—Indeed, Mr du Bouchet's zeal is Great, and we Cannot But Be sensible of His Wishes to Become a Member of the Society—He is as Eager a Cincinnatus, as He Has Been a Rifleman in the Northern Army.[1] With the Highest Respect and tenderest Affection I Have the Honour to Be My dear General Your obedient Humble Servant

Lafayette

ALS, PEL.

1. Denis-Jean-Florimond Langlois de Montheville, marquis du Bouchet (1752–1826), was made a captain in the Continental army after his arrival in Philadelphia in 1777. He was promoted to major after the Battle of Saratoga and returned to France because of bad health. He came back to America in 1780 as an aide-de-camp to Rochambeau and was present at the surrender of Cornwallis at Yorktown in 1781. He was elected to the American Society of the Cincinnati on 17 May 1784 and apparently later also to the French Society. See Bouchet to GW, 17 May 1784. See also Lafayette's franker comments about Bouchet in his second private letter to GW of this date (third letter).

From Lafayette

My dear General　　　　　　　　　　　　Paris March the 9th 1784

Altho I Write You another Private letter, I Must Confidentially Let you know My opinion Upon Matters Relative to the Society.

The Captains in the Navy Have Been Much Mortified to be left out in the Institutions—they Rank as Colonels, they Have Rendered Great Services, and it is Expected Here they Will be Admitted into the Society—Some of them Came with Count d'Estaing Among Whom are Suffrein, d'albert de Rion, and Such other Great Characters—The Remainder Went Under Ternay, destouches, and Grasse—a few Have Been Sent to Carry Great News Such as the Treaty, or Have Actually Commanded in Chief, such as la peyrouse, la touche—I know they are Many, But How Can a Partial distinction Be Made—and As they Will Have Much to do with American Vessels, in preventing Contraband trade, I Suppose, or in Receiving American Ships into french Harbours, I think it Will Be Impolitic Not to put them in a Good Humour—in the Opinion I Give, I Oppose

My own interest, for the less Members there will Be in the Society, the More it is Valued—But I See a Substantial Public Motive to Be determined Upon, and As the *Capitaines de Vaisseaux* are dispersed throughout the Harbours, they Will not So much Crowd as land officers, Because they very seldom Come to the Capital—*M. d'albert de Rion*, la touche, la peyrouse, tilly Cannot But Have it, and I think it should Be general.[1]

As to the land officers Many Claims Have Been Raised—Some of them, I think, deserve Consideration—M. de l'estrade, M. de Menonville,[2] Such, in a word, as particular Reasons May Be Assigned for, ought to Be included—*Above all the chevalier de lameth* who Has Been So cruelly Wounded in the Redoubt, Who Was an aid de Camp, and two Months after was a Colonel—I think we must Avoid giving grounds of Complaint—inclosed is a letter Respecting Count Edward dillon who was Going to Savahana when Wounded in the Engagement at Sea, and Was then a Colonel—You will also find a Note from Mr de St Simon Respecting His Brother[3]—Menonville was His Adjutant General, and in that office they Have the Honours of Brigadier paid to them When Majors in the tranchees. Mr de Corny Has Applied to me, and I Could not Give Him the Badge—I promised Him I Would mention His Wishes, and Send You His petition—His claims are set up in the Capacity of an American officer.[4] inclosed you will find a petition from Mr de la Neuville and Mr de Vienne, the latter of Whom Has not the Shadow of a title, and if Such were admitted, the pretensions would Be Numberless, and Come from very disagreable Persons.[5]

Mr du Bouchet who, You know, is not a Wit, Has taken it in His Head to Go to America—Had I Refused a letter, it would Have killed Him, and out of pity I gave a private one to You, wherein I observe that He is Mad.[6]

in the Resolutions of our Committee,[7] You will find a Mention Made of gnl Conway which I am Going to Explain—I don't Say that I Have Merit—But I Say I Have in Consequences—viz.—Ennemies—My Popularity is Great throughout the Kingdom, and in this City—But Amongst the Great folks I Have a large party Against me, Because they are jealous of my Reputation—in a word, the pitt to one Man is for me—and in the Boxes there is a division—a Plot Was led to draw me into a snare, and Madame Conway was made a tool of to Give me and yourself the Air of an implacable Revenge Against that Man Who is Considered Here as Having Been Abandonned and Ruined By me in America—Secret Meetings were Held on the Occasion of which I Have Been Advised—I Have attended to my letters which I know Will Be printed—and to avoid the odium of Having stifled Connway's Claims, I Have not discouraged a Representation Being Made in His favor—the man is Not Worth troubling our Heads about Him—But as He will Become a Pretence to a sett who Have not Hitherto found Any Against me, it May Be Better either to Give Him the Badge, or if Refused to do it With that Secrecy and delicacy which will not Subject me to the Reproach of Having proposed him, in order that He May Be Humiliated—that Whole family is a Nest of Rogues—du Bouchet excepted who is Honest, But a fool.[8]

The french officers Have offered Monney—I Had Rather it Was not Accepted[9]—But at Such a distance I Cannot judge what is the Best to Be done—the formation of a Committee in Europe is very Necessary—But it must, for Reasons obvious, Be quite separated from any society the french officers may form as it is Calculated only for American purposes, and ought to Consist But of American officers for the time Being in Europe.

After proper allowances Have Been Made Both for the Navy officers, and particular Cases, I will Beg leave to Represent that the Members ought Not to Be too much multiplied—if a Greater facility takes place, the institution Will sink in proportion that it is Bestowed Upon too Many people, and our officers Must Be, Upon their Guard, not to give the Badge without proper Motives.

I Have Been Requested to present You with a New Model and Ribband—and from the persons that gave it Could not Refuse sending it to America. I need not saying this letter is Confidential. With the Highest Respect and tenderest Affection I Have the Honour to Be My dear General Your obedient Humble Servant

Lafayette

ALS, PEL.

1. For examples of protests at the initial failure to include French naval captains in the Society of the Cincinnati and for listings of the senior French naval officers who were in American waters during the American Revolution,

see d'Estaing to GW, 8 Jan., and Barras to GW, 23 Jan. 1784. See also notes in both documents.

2. François-Louis-Arthur Thibaut, comte de Ménonville (1740–1816), came to America with Rochambeau in 1780 as *aide-major générale* and distinguished himself at Yorktown as the commander of the detachment of the Soissonais Regiment that stormed redoubt no. 9. For the baron de L'Estrade, see Rochambeau to GW, 1 Mar. 1784, n.2.

3. Claude de Rouvroy, baron de Saint-Simon (1752–1811), was the younger brother of the marquis Saint-Simon-Montbléru. In a letter of 24 Oct. 1781 to the marquis de Saint-Simon, GW commended the brave service of both at the siege at Yorktown. Neither of the two enclosed letters has been found.

4. Louis-Dominique Ethis de Corny (1736–1790) did not arrive in the United States until April 1780, with Lafayette. Corny returned to France in February 1781 on a mission for Congress and then resigned his American commission on 1 Jan. 1782.

5. The petition from Louis-Pierre Penot Lombard, chevalier de La Neuville, has not been found. See note 7. The enclosed letter from Louis-Pierre, marquis de Vienne (1746–1812), asked GW to recommend to Lafayette that, "as an exception," Lafayette "enroll the Marquis de Vienne in the Society of the Cincinnati." Otherwise, "he dare not boast of having serv'd under the great General Washington," lest it "be inferred that he has not complied with his duty, that he has not shown the Spirit of a Soldier and a Gentleman." To support his claim, Vienne gave GW the following account of his service in America: "The Marquis of Vienne left France in 1778 to join the General the Marquis de la Fayette as Volunteer in America, to whome he was recommended. He embarked at Nants at his own expence on board a frigate belonging to the Congress, call'd the Queen of France, commanded by Captain Green. After a long and fatigueing voyage he arriv'd at Boston, where he remain'd only to make the necessary preparations. From thence he set off to join the Marquis de la Fayette, who was then at Vally Forge, where he arriv'd the day before the King's troops evacuated Philadelphia. He had the honour to be presented to your Excellency by the Marquis, who at the same time requested the permission of his serving under your immediate Command, to which you graciously condescended. He was of the detach'd party commanded by General de la Fayette to pursue the Enemy over Sandy-hook. The day before the Action of Mon-mouth, he was dispatch'd by the General de la Fayette with four Dragoons to reconnoitre the Enemy's march in their retreat, and to examine the position of their Camp. He pursued them with such speed, that they were no sooner encamp'd, than he thro' the favour of a Storm, pass'd between two of their advanc'd Guards into their very Tents, and took two English Grenadiers prisoners, whome he sent to General de la Fayette. He return'd shortly after to make his report of his expedition. He was the next day with the Marquis de la Fayette in the action of Mon-Mouth. The English having reimbark'd, the Marquis de la Fayette sent him from Brunswick to Philadelphia to be presented to the Congress, with letters of recommendation to the President Laurens. The Congress granted him the Degree

and rank of a Colonel. Shortly afterwds, he left Philadelphia and rejoin'd your Excellency at Old Plain, whence he set off the following day with the Marquis de la Fayette to march for Providence and Rhode-Island, where he serv'd during the time the Troops of the United States remain'd there, under the command of General Sullivan, and return'd not to the Continent, 'till after their retreat from Providence; at which time he was sent by the Marquis de la Fayette to carry dispatches to the Count d'Estaing. War being declared at this period in his Native Country, he demanded your Excellency's permission to serve under its Banners, to which you agreed, and sent him a discharge dated Fredricks-Bourg Octobr the 16th, 1778 together with a Certificate, both of which and one from the Marquis de la Fayette, he sends inclosed with this.

"The Marquis of Vienne set off at his own expence, and could not prevail on himself to receive any sort of recompence or appointment from the United States of America. His Name & Family are well known in France, and his Father is honour'd by his Sovereign with the Rank of Lieutenant General—Under these Circumstances it is plain he could have no Motives to be mercenary; nor any Desire that his Services should be recompensed with Money. He only sought the glory of spilling his blood, and exposing his life for the Cause and in the Service of the United States.

"That Campaign cost him more than Twelve hundred Guineas, out of a Fortune not the most considerable, nor entirely free from Embarrassments.

"He departed from Boston with M. le Comte d'Estaing, and wou'd certainly have return'd to America, had not both his health & fortune been impair'd, & render'd the Attempt impracticable" (translation, DSoCi). The contemporary translation has been corrected in another hand and the excerpts printed here incorporate the corrections. GW wrote a letter in response on 25 Nov. 1784 virtually identical to the letter he wrote Fock on that same day. See Fock to GW, 24 Feb. 1784, n.2.

6. See Lafayette to GW, 9 Mar. 1784 (second letter).

7. The enclosed resolutions are headed: "On a Board of American Officers held in Paris march the 8th 1784 Present Majir General Mis de la Fayette Majr general Duportail Colo. Gouvion Lt Col. Fleury Lt Col. Tousard Lt Col. Villefranche Maj. pontgibaut Maj. l'Enfant, the resolutions of another board held on January the 16th were retaken in consideration and confirmed. whereupon." Under this heading, there are "Petitions" listed in one column and "decisions of the Committee" in another. The petitions were from Thomas Mullens, "captain in the French army and Lt Col. by brevet in the united states," who served in America from 1776 to 1778; from the chevalier de Crenis, "captain of Dragoons in the French service and Lt Col. by brevet in the american army," who went to America in 1776 and stayed until 1779; Louis-Pierre, marquis de Vienne, "colonel by brevet in the united states army," who served in one campaign with GW's approval and that of Congress, at his own expense, and for the next three years suffered from "a very bad state of health"; and from Louis-Pierre Penot Lombart, chevalier de La Neuville, "Lt Col. in the French Service, and brigadier by brevet in the Continental army," who went to America in 1777 and a year later returned to France on a mission for Congress. The French committee decided that Lafa-

yette should present the case for the election of Mullens and La Neuville, that Crenis was not qualified for election to the Cincinnati, and that the committee "won't determine anything about the Marquis de Vienne." The docket on the document indicates that the French committee's resolutions were read on 7 May 1784 at the general meeting of the Society of the Cincinnati in Philadelphia.

8. In its resolutions, the committee expressed a wish "to represent to the general assembly that general [Thomas] Conway being now in the east indies, it has been impossible for him to make any application respecting the society." Thomas Conway (1735–c.1800), an Irishman reared in France, had reached the rank of colonel in the French army when Silas Deane in 1776 recommended him to Congress. After his arrival in America in the spring of 1777, Congress made him a brigadier general and in December 1777 promoted him to major general over GW's strong and open opposition. In the winter of 1777–78, Conway was in correspondence with Gen. Horatio Gates and others in opposition to GW's command. The so-called Conway Cabal was discovered and Conway's resignation from the Continental army was accepted in April 1778. In January 1778 Lafayette had refused to accept Conway as his second in command.

9. See Rochambeau to GW, 19 Jan. 1784, n.5. The Institution as adopted at the general meeting of the Society of the Cincinnati, 4–18 May 1784, provided that no donations would be received "but from citizens of the United States."

From Lafayette

My dear General   Paris March the 9th 1784

Had I Not So perfect a Confidence in Your friendship, I Would Very Much fear to tire You with My Scribbling of this day—But Cannot leave My Penn Before I Have Again Mentionned My tender Respectfull Affection to My dear General— I want to tell you that Mde de lafayette and My three Children are Well, and that all of us in the family Heartly join to Present their dutiful Affectionate Compliments to Mrs Washington and Yourself—Tell Her that I Hope Soon to thank Her for a dish of Tea at Mount Vernon—Yes, My dear General, Before the Month of june is over You will see a Vessel Coming Up Pottowmack, and out of that Vessel Will Your friend jump With a Panting Heart and all the feelings of Perfect Happiness[1]—I intended to Have Gone Sooner, But a few Commercial Matters still Keep me Here—for since no Body Middles With them, I Have Undertaken in My Private Capacity to do What is possible for one Who Has Neither Title, or instruction—it is at least a

Confort that in my Private Capacity I Cannot Commit Congress, and that I never speak But of What I Know—four ports Having Been declared free, I send Mr Morriss a Letter Respecting the duties to Be paid there—and I Hope Congress Will also publish that all duties Have Been Removed from the Exportation of Brandies.[2]

Most of the Americans Here are indecently Violent Against our Assossiation—Wadsworth Must Be excepted, and doctor Franklin Said little—But Jay, Adams, and all the others Warmly Blame the Army—You easely guess I am not Remiss in opposing them—and However if it is found that the Heredity Endangers the Free Principles of democrasy, I am as Ready as Any Man to Renounce it—You Will Be My Compass, my dear General, Because at this distance I Cannot judge—in Case Upon Better Consideration, You find that Heredity Will injure our democratic Constitution, I join with You By proxy in Voting Against it—But I so much Rely on Your judgement that if You think Heredity is a proper scheme I Will Be Convinced that Your Patriotism Has Considered the Matter in the Best point of View—*to You alone*, I would Say so much, and I Abide By your opinion in the Matter—let the foregoing Be Confidential, But I am sure Your disinterested Virtue Will Weigh all possible, future Consequences, of Hereditary distinctions.[3]

There are No News in this Moment that are Worth Relating—What Respects Balons, Mr l'enfant Will tell—the present English disputes are Some what Ridiculous—they Must end in a dissolution of Parliament or an Union Betwen pitt and fox. Adieu, My dear General, Accept with Your Usual Goodness the Affectionate tribute of a Heart So Entirely devoted to You that No words Can Ever Express the Respect, the Love, and all the Sentiments With Which You know it is glowing for You, and that Make me Untill my last Breath Your obedient humble Ser. and afectionate friend

lafayette

My Compliments Wait Upon George and all the family at Mount Vernon—Be so Kind My dear General as to Remember me to all our friends—I am very Sorry the Hurry I was in to leave You Occasioned My sending So Soon the plated wares— adieu, my dear General.[4]

I Had forgot to Mention that Major Lomagne is on Every Respect Entitled to Become a Member of the Assossiation—But Reports Having Been Spread Respecting the Manner in Which He left Armand's legion I Have Suspended Admiting of Him Untill He is Cleard By the information You May think proper to take—He Says Gnl Armand is His personal Ennemy.[5]

duplessis Has a little Surprised our Simplicity—I Wish He may Have Been Himself Mistaken—But He is gone out of Europe.

ALS, PEL.

1. Lafayette did not get to New York until early August and arrived at Mount Vernon on 17 August.

2. Lafayette wrote to Robert Morris on this date enclosing a letter from Calonne, comptroller general of finances, dated 8 Mar. 1784, concerning the fees to be paid by Americans at the four French free ports (Idzerda, *Lafayette Papers*, 5:203–5). For a discussion of the free ports, see Lafayette to GW, 10 Jan. 1784, nn.9 and 10.

3. For Lafayette's defense of his role in the forming of the French Society of the Cincinnati, see his letters to John Adams, 8 Mar. and 9 April 1784, as well as Adams's letter to Lafayette of 28 Mar. 1784 (Idzerda, *Lafayette Papers*, 5:201–3, 213–14, 211–12).

4. GW wrote Lafayette on 30 Oct. 1783 asking him to buy silverware for him. See Lafayette to GW, 10 Jan. 1784, n.1.

5. The vicomte de Lomagne was promoted from captain to major while in Pulaski's (later Armand's) Legion from February 1778 to September 1781.

From James Milligan

Sir   Comptrollers Office [Philadelphia] March 9th 1784

By last Post I was honored with your Excellency's favour of the 18th February, and have the pleasure of informing you that, As the Entry of your Accounts in the principal Books had been delayed, purposely until I should be favoured with your sentiments on the mode of the Statements transmitted your Excellency, it is still in my power to correct the impropriety of charging the persons, whose Names you have enumerated, with the Monies paid them; And you may rest assured Sir, that this matter shall be strictly attended to.[1] With respect to the Sum of £133.16 lawful in Specie, for which you had given Credit, and are charged in Account B. After some inquiry, I find in the Accounts of Thomas Smith Loan Officer for Pennsylvania, the following charge "May 20th 1780 Paid George A. Washington ℔ order of the Board of Treasury dated yesterday One Hundred and Sixty Seven Pounds 5/ Specie." this Sum in Pennsylvania Currency is exactly equal to the former in lawful, which you had Credited, and I have no doubt that it is the identical payment, for these reasons. The Sum is credited on the 13th of May. By a letter from your Excellency to the Board of Treasury dated the 14th you request that five hundred Guineas may be furnished the bearer Mr George A. Washington who will bring it to you: The order of the Board on Mr Smith was dated the 19th, and he paid it on the 20th. From these circumstances, and from your Excellencys recollection of having borrrowed money about that period, of the Marquis de la Fayette, it appears to me highly probable that the Sum borrowed of the Marquis was the £133.16 lawful, that you wrote the Board of Treasury as before mentioned, by your Nephew, who accompanied the Marquis to Philadelphia, That Specie, at that time of day, being difficult to obtain, the Board were unable to comply with your requisition for the five hundred Guineas; but upon Mr George A. Washingtons representing the circumstance of your having borrowed a Sum of the Marquis, they had enabled your Nephew to reimburse that Sum, by the order on Mr Smith for that Amount. The matter appearing thus so plain, I hope your Excellency will be of opinion with me that, the charge is well founded.[2] Although you have not been able Sir, to recollect every circumstance, you have pointed out a clue sufficient to unravel the whole, and instead of expecting that your Memory and attention could extend to every matter of this kind, it is to me a matter of astonishment, that you have been able to do so much.

The Accounts of the Loan Officers not having been Settled, and consequently, no final Entries made of them in the Books of the Treasury, is the reason why the charge could not be immediately found here. I have now the honor of enclosing an Offical Copy of the State of your Excellency's Accounts, Commencing the 13th and ending the 28th of Decemr 1783, by which it appears that there is a balance due you of Eight hundred and fifty Seven dollars and 52/90ths of a dollar. When this Account reached the office, I found that the Superintendant of Finance had not acted upon my Certificate of the balance due on the former Settlement: I therefore thought it best to recal that Certificate, and to carry the former balance to your Credit on this Settlement, and so to strike a New and final balance of the Sum above mentioned, for which Sum I transmitted a New Certificate to the Superintendant of Finance, who, I doubt not, will find means of remitting the money according to your direction.[3]

Although I am at present fully Satisfied of the propriety of the charge of £133.16 Specie, yet it would add to that satisfaction, to know your Excellencys opinion of the matter, when it may be convenient. I have only to add that, I am with the most perfect Respect and Esteem Sir Your Excellencys Most Obt & most Hume Servant

Jas Milligan Comptr
of the Treasy

LS, DLC:GW.

1. See note 4 in GW's letter of 18 February.

2. See note 7 in the letter of 18 February.

3. The enclosed statement from the treasury of GW's outstanding account with the United States (13–28 Dec. 1783) shows due him £212.2.6, carried over from the account of June 1775–8 December 1783, and £213.8.4 due him for the expenses of himself, his aides, and his guards while in Philadelphia and en route to Mount Vernon in December 1783 (£111.8.4), for payments to his aides to cover the cost of their returning home (£90), and for his steward Philip Walmsley's wages (£12). (For the 1775–83 account, see Milligan to GW, 13 Jan., n.1; for his account of 13–28 Dec. 1783, see GW to Robert Morris, 4 Jan., n.1; for the payment to his aides, see GW to Morris, 4 Jan., n.5.) The total owed him, £425.10.10, came to 1,438$\frac{4}{90}$ dollars, of which GW is shown having drawn 580$\frac{8}{90}$ dollars, leaving a balance due him of 857$\frac{52}{90}$ dollars. GW challenged the charge of 580$\frac{8}{90}$ dollars against his account, insisting to Milligan that 580$\frac{8}{90}$ dollars was what he drew in December 1783 to pay the back salaries of his aides and others and therefore should not be charged to him (see GW to Milligan, 1 April 1784).

To Clement Biddle

Dear Sir,　　　　　　　　　Mount Vernon 10th March 1784

Since last post I have received the Lace & two-pole chain, accompanied by your favors of the 22d & 29th ulto for which I thank you.[1]

From what you have written concerning the Sieves, it is to be feared I did not sufficiently explain myself in speaking to the sizes of the meshes[2]—You say, "the largest is of iron wire, as there was none of brass so coarse in Town"—& again, "the second & third are of brass wire, & there is no wire finer than of thirty meshes to an inch." The coarseness, or finess of the wire was not what I had in contemplation, but the size of the meshes which were to be formed by *that wire*: you therefore have misunderstood me, or I misunderstand you—unless (which is more probable, & if the case is so, all things are yet right), the wire being imported in its woven state, was only to be had of the sizes mentioned in your letter, & which, with as much of the kind for boulting (32 to the inch) as will make one sieve, will answer all my purposes very well. Be so good as to let me know what you call a *packet* of edging; which you say is at various prices, from one to three Dollars—& how many yards, that is, what length a packet will cover—also the price of the plain blue, green, & yellow paper pr piece, with the number of yards in a piece[3]—when I get your answer to these queries, I will determine at once whether to buy, or not to buy.

Mrs Washington joins in best wishes to Mrs Biddle & Mrs Shaw with, Dr Sir Your Most Obedt Servant

G: Washington

LB, DLC:GW.

1. Neither letter has been found, but see GW to Biddle, 5 Feb. 1784.
2. See GW to Biddle, 17 Jan. 1784.
3. See GW to Biddle, 6 May 1784.

Letter not found: to Robert McCrea, 10 Mar. 1784. On 13 Mar. McCrea wrote to GW: "I never open'd yours of the 10th Inst. till this Moment."

From Gerard Vogels

Sir   Philadelphia 10 March 1784.

Tho' personally unknown to your Excellency I have the Honor to inclose an Address in Verse sent by a Lady in Holland who never dedicated her Poems but to Virtue and Heroism, & who after having sung the great deeds of the Roman Warrior Germanicus in her Native tongue, thought it just to offer up her last poetical Breath in praise of an Hero who is esteemed by All to have equalled either ancient or modern Ones.[1]

Wishing the Remainder of your Excellency's days as well as

those of your amiable Consort may be as Happy as the former have been Glorious. I remain with the highest Esteem Your Excellency's Most Obedient & Most Humble Servant.

Gerard Vogels.

ALS, DLC:GW.

Michael Hillegas, a merchant in Philadelphia and treasurer of the United States, wrote GW from Philadelphia on 22 Mar. 1784: "I have the honor herewith of transmitting to you the inclosed Letter. It was delivered me for this purpose by a Mr Vogel a Gentleman from Amsterdam" (ALS, DLC:GW). After giving his letter and Lucretia van Winter's poem (see note 1) to Hillegas, Gerard Vogels wrote Nicholas van Winter that "Owing to the long winter and the severe frost on the river," he did not receive the poem enclosed in a letter of 19 Oct. 1783 until 2 Mar. 1784. "I handed it immediately to Mr. Hillegas," he wrote, "together with an address composed by my wife and myself. It is already on its way to H. Exc.'s country house in the care of a neighbor of the General who happened to be here and who will deliver it in person" (translated and quoted by Reitz in "An Unpublished Correspondence of George Washington," 48–50).

Gerard Vogels was a Dutch businessman who arrived in Philadelphia during the Revolution and fell in love with America and with Elizabeth Moulder, daughter of Col. Joseph Moulder, whom he married in 1784. Though he says here to GW that he was "personally unknown to your Excellency," Vogels wrote Lucretia van Winter and her husband at great length on 13 Dec. 1783 not only about GW's activities after his arrival in Philadelphia on 8 Dec. but also about being in his presence and conversing with him: "I saw the greatest man who has ever appeared on the surface of this earth. His Excellency arrived at 6(?) o'clock escorted by light cavalry. He passed the coffee house which is here the exchange. Everybody came to the door when Capt. [Robert] Morris rode up with the officers of the light cavalry. We all waved our hats three times over our heads. Then came the excellent Hero himself, riding an uncommonly beautiful horse which, proud of its burden, appeared to me like the horse of Germanicus. I don't know if in our delight at seeing the Hero we were more surprised by his simple but grand air or by the kindness of the greatest and best of heroes.

"To morrow we shall be introduced to General Washington, and next week we shall dine at the same table with His Excellency. Thursday by order of Congress is a general Thanksgiving day to be observed throughout all America.

"His Excellency promises to walk daily through the town to give the grateful Americans the pleasure of seeing him. Then he says farewell to all honors and the world's turmoil, to live quietly in retirement on his estate, his God-fearing C[h]ristian sentiments assuring him immortality here and in the hereafter. . . . This morning, while I was in the Ambassador's [Peter van Berckel's] sitting room reporting a certain matter to his Honor, General Washington came in and spoke to me. I said that I was a Dutchman and considered myself fortunate in seeing the Hero who had so gloriously given the Americans their precious liberty. H. Exc. bowed very kindly and said 'I hope the two Republics will always be of service to each other.'

"I have just come from the concert where the General has been the whole evening. He stayed till the song was going to be sung composed in his honor to Haendel's music, when His Honor departed. Evidently H. Exc. is above hearing his praise sung and retires before the just acclamations of his people. It was amusing to see how, in a place so crowded with the fair sex, everybody had eyes only for this Hero; indeed we only now and then stole a glance at our girls; H. Exc. drew everyone's attention. It was the most wonderful sight the world could produce, the noble virtues of the greatest and bravest hero crowned with supreme glory.

"At the end of the concert we sang the following verses, to the choice but very strong music of cymbals, kettle drum, trumpets, violins, oboes, basses, and flutes, in fact all instruments and all together, with deafening strength and feeling, followed by general shouting and clapping of hands. Everybody was in ecstasy.

> See the conquering hero comes,
> Sound the trumpets, beat the drums,
> Sports prepare, the laurel bring
> Songs of triumph to him sing. . . .

". . . This morning, General Thanksgiving day, I was in Christ Church and General Washington sat down in the pew next to mine. Mr. [William] White, the parson, gave an appropriate sermon. In a sentence of five or six words he gave the Hero well deserved praise and urged the Americans, now free in religion as well as in politics, to make good use of these noble gifts. After church His Honor came after me and addressed me, I thanked him for the short and beautiful sermon. His Honor asked me to dinner for Tuesday next week. 'You will be at table with General Washington. My brother-in-law Mr. Morris and my sister will come with H. Exc.' I said 'Your most obedient, Sir, I will.' Therefore I shall have twice the honor. If now I do not get vain I am not afraid that I ever shall" (ibid.).

1. The "Lady in Holland," Lucretia Wilhelmina van Winter, the Dutch poet, dated her poem 20 Oct. 1783 and addressed it to "A Son Exelence, Monseigneur le General Washington. Commandant en Chef de leur Hautes Puissances, les Treize Etats unis de l'Amerique Septentrionale, Etc. Etc. Etc." The poem is composed of twenty stanzas of four lines and ends:

> Et que votre Statue, au Conseil etablie,
> Soit par le grand Congres de ces nots honoré:
> Contemplez Washington, Pere de la Patrie,
> Defenseur de la Liberté.

David Stuart, who attempted a literal translation of the poem for GW, translated the stanza: "May your Statue established by Council, be honored by Congress, with these honourable words—Lo! Washington! the Father of his Country, the Protector of Liberty!" (DLC:GW). See the van Winters' letter to GW of 10 April 1784 and GW to Lucretia van Winter, 30 Mar. 1785.

To John Witherspoon

Revd Sir,   Mount Vernon 10th March 1784

The recourse which I have had to my papers since I returned home, reminds me of a question which you asked me in Philadelphia,[1] respecting my Lands to the westward of the Allighaney mountains; to which I was unprepared, at that time to give a decided answer, either as to the quantity I had to let, or the terms upon which I would Lease them.

Upon examination, I find that I have Patents under the signature of Lord Dunmore, (while he administered the Govermt of this State) for about 30,000 acres; & Surveys for about 10,000 more; Patents for which were suspended by the disputes with Gt Britain, which soon follow'd the return of the warrts to the Land office.[2]

Ten thousand acres of the above thirty lie upon the Ohio—the rest on the Great Kanhawa; a river nearly as large, & quite as easy in its navigation as the former—The whole of it is rich bottom land, beautifully situated on these rivers & abounding plentiously in Fish, wild fowl, and Game of all kinds.

The uppermost tract upon the Ohio (which I incline to lease) contains 2314 Acres, & begins about four miles below the mouth of the Little Kanhawa (there are two rivers bearing that name, the uppermost of which is about 180 miles below Fort Pitt by water) & has a front on the water of more than five miles. The next is 18 miles lower down, & contains 2448 acres; with a front on the river, & a large creek which empty's into it, of four miles & upwards. Three miles below this again (on the same river) & just above what is called the Big Bend in Evans's map, is a third tract of 4395, acres, with a river front of more than five miles.

Then going to the *Great* Kanhawa distant about twelve miles by land, but thirty odd to follow the meanders of the two rivers, and beginning within three miles of the mouth, I hold Lands on the right & left of the river, & bounded thereby, forty eight & an half miles; all of which (being on the margin of the river, & extending not more than from half a mile to a Mile back) is, as has been observed before, rich low grounds.

From this description of my Lands, with the aid of Evans's or Hutchins's map of that Country,[3] a good general knowledge of their situation may be obtained by those who incline to become adventurers in the settlement of them; but it may not be improper to observe further, that they were surveyed under the royal Proclamation of 1763 (granting to each commisioned & non-commissioned officer, according to his rank, & to the private Soldier, certain quantities)—and under a yet older proclamation from Mr Dinwiddie, then Lieutt Governor of the Colony; issued by the advice of his Council to encourage & benefit the military adventurers of the year 1754, while the Land office was shut against all other applicants: It is not reasonable to suppose therefore, that those who had the first choice; had five years allowed them to make it; and a large District to survey in; were inattentive either to the quality of the Soil, or the advantages of situation.

But supposing no pre-eminence in quality, the title to these Lands is indisputable; & by laying on the South East side of the ohio, are not subject to the claims of the Indians—consequently will be free from their disturbances; & from the disputes, which the settlers on the No. West side (when the Indians shall permit any), & even on the same side, lower down, will be involved in with one another; for it should seem, that there is already location upon location, & scarce any thing else talked of but land-jobbing & monopolies, before Congress have even settled the terms upon which the ceded Lands are to be obtained.

Having given this account of the Land, I am brought to another point which is more puzzling to me than description.

I have been long endeavouring to hit upon some mode, by which the Grantor & Grantees of these Lands, might be mutually considered, & equally satisfied; but find it no easy matter; as it is to be presumed that all adventurers, especially emigrants from foreign Countries, would not only *chuse*, but *expect* Leases for a long term. In this case, it is difficult in an infant Country, where lands rise progressively, & I might add rapidly in value, to fix upon a rent which will not in the first instance, startle the Tenant by its magnitude, or injure the Land-lord in the course of a few years by the inadequacy of it. What course then is to be taken?

To advance the rent periodically, in proportion to the *supposed* increasing value of the Land, is very speculative—And to leave it to the parties or their representatives—or to persons to be chosen by them, at like stated periods to determine the increase of it, would not only be vague & uncertain, but more than probable open a door for many disputes, & prove very unsatisfactory to both sides. Yet, difficult as the case is, private & public considerations urging me thereto, I have come to a resolution which I am going to promulge in the Gazettes of this Country, by inserting an advertisement, of which the enclosed is a copy[4]—leaving it optional in the Grantees to make choice of *either*.

Whether the terms there promulged, are sufficiently encouraging to the people of this Country, & inviting to strangers; or whether the latter might think so in the first instance, & change sentiments afterwards, upon seeing a wide, a wild & an extensive country before them, in which they may for ought I know, obtain good—tho' not so valuable & pleasant spots, upon easier terms; is not with me to decide—experiment alone can determine it—But it is for me to declare, that I can not think of separating forever, from Lands which are beautifully situated upon fine navigable rivers; rich in quality & abundantly blessed with many natural advantages—upon less beneficial terms to myself.

The Leases for short tenures, if these should be preferred to either of the other two, could be attended with no great injury to me, because the improvements which (according to the conditions of them) are to be made thereon, will enable me, if I am not too sanguine in my expectation, to rent them thereafter upon more lucrative terms than I dare ask for either of the other two at present.

It has been my intention in every thing I have said, & will be so in every thing I shall say on this subject, to be perfectly candid; for my feelings would be as much hurt, if I shou'd deceive others by a too favourable description, as theirs would be who might suffer by the deception.

I will only add, that it would give me pleasure to see these Lands seated by particular Societies, or religeous Sectaries with their Pastors—It would be a mean of connecting friends in a small circle, & making life, in a new & rising Empire (to the Inhabitants of which, & their habits new comers would be strangers) pass much more agreeably, than in a mixed, or dispersed situation.[5]

If a plan of this sort should be relished, it would be highly expedient for an agent, in behalf of such Societies, to come out immediately to view the Lands & close a bargain; for nothing is more probable, than that each of the Tracts here enumerated may, if the matter is delayed, have settlers upon it; an intermixture with whom might not be agreeable.

The number of Families which these tracts agregately, or each one separately would accommodate, depends more upon the views of the occupiers, than on any other circumstance. The soil is capable of the greatest production, (such as Europeans have little idea of): for *mere support* then, the smallest quantity would suffice; which I mention in this place, because a plan for the settlement of them (under the information here given of the quantity, quality & situation) can be as well digested in Europe, as on the Land itself—so far as it respects support only; & is to be prefered to a waste of time in ascertaining on the spot, the number it would receive, & what each man shall have, before the association is formed.

I will make no apology, my good Sir, for the length of this Letter; presuming from your enquiries, when I had the pleasure of seeing you last in Philadelphia, that you would not be displeased at the information I now give you, & might have a wish to communicate it to others—My best wishes attend you; with sentiments of great esteem & respect I am revd Sir Your most obt & very humble Servant

G: Washington

LB, DLC:GW.

John Witherspoon (1723–1794), the influential president of the College of New Jersey at Princeton whom GW had known since before the Revolution, sailed for England with Joseph Reed in December 1783 in order to raise money for his war-ravaged college.

1. Witherspoon sailed from Philadelphia on 20 Dec. in the *Washington*, after GW's arrival in the city on 8 December. GW's letter of introduction to Lafayette is dated 9 Dec. 1783.

2. For references to GW's landholdings on the Great Kanawha and the Ohio rivers, see notes, GW to Samuel Lewis and GW to Thomas Lewis, both 1 Feb. 1784. See also Enclosure: Advertisement: Ohio Lands, this date.

3. GW is referring to *A General Map of the Middle Colonies in America* (1755) by Lewis Evans (c.1700–1756) and to *A Topographical Description of Virginia, Pennsylvania, Maryland, and North Carolina* (London, 1778) by Thomas Hutchins (1730–1789). See GW to Benjamin Harrison, 10 Oct. 1784.

4. See Enclosure: Advertisement: Ohio Lands, this date.

5. GW clearly hoped that Witherspoon would be able to recruit religious

groups in Britain to come to America and settle on his Ohio land. See Witherspoon to GW, 7 June 1784.

Enclosure
Advertisement: Ohio Lands

Mount Vernon [c.10] March 1784

The Subscriber Would Lease about 30,000 acres of land on
the Ohio & Great Kanhawa, for which he has had Patents ten or
twelve years. Ten thousand of these, in three Tracts, lie upon
the Ohio, between the mouth's of the two Kanhawa's; having a
front upon the river of 15 miles, & beautifully border'd by it.
The remaining 20,000 acres, in four other Surveys, lie upon
the great Kanhawa, from the mouth, or near it, upwards.
These four Tracts (together) have a margin upon *that* river, (by
which they are bound) of more than forty miles.[1]

After having said thus much of the Land, it is almost super-
fluous to add that the whole of it is river low grounds of the first
quality—but it is essential to remark that a great deal of it may
be converted into the finest mowing ground imaginable, with
little or no labour. Nature, & the water-stops which have been
made by the Beaver, having done *more* to effect this, than years
of hard labour in most other rich soils; and that the Land back
of these bottoms, must forever render the latter uncommmonly
profitable for Stock, on account of the extensiveness of the
range; as it is of a nature (being extremely broken) not to be
seated or cultivated.

These lands may be had on three tenures: First—until Jany
1795, & no longer; Second—until Jany 1795, renewable every
ten years forever. Third—for 999 years.

The Rents, conditions & priviledges as follow. First, An ex-
emption from rent three years upon condition that five acres
for every hundred, & proportionably for a greater or lesser
quantity contained in the Lease, shall within that space be
cleared & tilled, or in order for the latter; and a house, fit for
the comfortable accommodation of the Tenant, erected on the
premises.

Second, That before the expiration of the term of the Leases
of the first tenure; or the first ten years of those of the second &
third; a dwelling house of Brick or Stone, or of framed work

with a stone or brick chimney; & a good Barn, suited to the size of the Tenement shall be built thereon—an Orchard of good fruit, to consist of as many trees as there are acres specified in the lease, planted & enclosed; And five acres for every hundred, & proportionably for a greater or lesser quantity, improved into meadow; which—or the like quantity, shall always be retained for mowing.

Third—The land to be accurately measured to each grantee; who will be allowed to take in regular form (with an extension back proportioned to the front on the river) as much as his inclination, & ability may require; which quantity shall be secured to him and his Heirs, by Lease in the usual form, with proper clauses binding on Landlord & Tenant, for the performance of covenants.

Fourth. A Spanish milled Dollar of the present coin, shall pass in payment of the rent for six shillings; & other current Gold & Silver coin, in that proportion.

Fifth—The Staple commodity, or other article of produce (for the greater ease & convenience of the Tenant) may be substituted in lieu of money rents in the Leases, if the Parties, at, or before the first rent shall become due, can agree upon a medium value for it.

Sixth. If the exigency or policy of the State in which these Lands lie, should at any time impose a tax upon them, or their appendages; such tax is to be borne by the Tenant.

Seventh. These conditions &ca being common to the Leases of the three different tenures, the rent,

Of the First. Will be four pounds per ann: for every hundred acres contained in the Lease; & proportionably for a greater or lesser quantity.

Of the Second—one shilling for every acre contained in the Lease, until the year 1795. one shilling & six pence for the like quantity afterwards, 'till the year 1805. two shillings afterwards 'till the year 1815. And the like increase per acre every ten years 'till the rent amounts to, & shall have remained at, five shillings for the ten years next insuing—after which it is to increase three pence pr acre every ten years for ever.

Of the Third—Two shillings for every acre therein contained; at which it will remain for 999 years—the term for which it is granted.

The situation of these Lands is not only pleasant, but in any point of view in which they can be considered, must be exceedingly advantageous—for if the produce of the country, according to the ideas of some, shou'd go down the Mississippi, they are nearly as convenient for that transportation, having the Stream without any obstruction in it to descend, as those which are now settling about the Falls of the Ohio, & upon Kentuckey, (to the choice of which, among other reasons, people were *driven* by the Grants to the Officers & Soldiers, of which these are part, in the upper country, & from the impracticability of obtaining Lands in extensive bodies elsewhere) If it shou'd come by way of Fort Pitt, to Potomac, (which is the most [   ] or to the Susquehannah—by the Great Kanhawa to James river—or by the Lakes Erie & Ontario to New York, they are infinitely more so—being, according to Hutchins's table of distances, 422 miles, all of which is against the Stream, nearer to those markets than the Settlements last mentioned—And what, in the present situation of things, is a matter of no triffling consideration, no other claims can interfere with these—patents having been long granted for the Land, & the property of it well known; and besides, by laying on the So. East side of the Ohio can give no jealousy to the Indians—the proprietors of it therefore, may cultivate their Farms in peace, & fish, fowl & hunt without fear or molestation.

Altho' I do not lay any stress upon it, the presumption being that the Indians during the late war, have laid all in ruins—yet it is of record in the Courts of Bottetourt & Fincastle (in which Counties the land did lay) that buildings, Meadows & other improvements which were made thereon in the years 1774 & 1775. designedly for the accommodation of Tenants, cost the subscriber, as appears by the oaths of sworn appraisers conformably to the directions of an act of the Assembly, of Virginia for seating and cultivating Lands, £1568:18:7½ equal to £1961.3.3—Maryland, Pennsylvania or Jersey currency.[2]

These Lands being peculiarly well adapted for small Societies who may incline to live detached & retired; any such applying in a body or by their pastors or Agents, shall have every assistance & encouragement, which can with convenience & propriety be given by,

G: W——n

LB, DLC:GW. GW sent a copy of this advertisement to John Witherspoon in Scotland on this day, and he subsequently sent copies to acquaintances in other states for their information or with a request that it be inserted in local newspapers. See, for instance, GW to Jonathan Trumbull, Jr., 4 April 1784, or to Rufus Putnam, 2 June 1784.

1. The three tracts on the Ohio and the four tracts on the Great Kanawha are identified in the source note in GW to Samuel Lewis, 1 Feb. 1784.

2. GW seems not to have succeeded in leasing any of his lands on the Ohio or the Kanawha on these terms in the 1780s.

To Laurence Muse

Sir,   Mount Vernon 11th March 1784

Having luckily found some printed blank Deeds, I am enabled to dispatch your business sooner than I expected.

The return of these Deeds to me, executed before proper Evidences, will entitle you to receive the Sum I expressed a willingness to pay you, on Accot of your Fathers expences to the Ohio.

Should Deeds (which I do not believe is the case) have been executed before for the 3323 acres specified in those now sent, no bad consequences can follow the second signing of them, as both would express the same thing but it would induce, & warrant my paymt of the above mentioned money, from which good may result.[1]

I hope the Witnesses will be such as expect to attend the next Generl Court, that there may be no hazard of the proof—& the sooner I can get them returned to me the better, as the time is now short. or, instead of bringing them back to me, a letter from my friend Colo. Edmd Pendleton, assuring me that they are in his hands, properly executed, & that he will carry or send them to the Court for recording, will be preferable.[2]

If no Deed should have passed for the 2000 acres in the other tract adjoining (which I am entitled to by purchase from Mr William Bronaugh) & which was to have been in exchange, with other considerations for the 3323 herein mentioned, I will, without delay, cause them to be executed; and, in the mean time, pass my Bond for the title. But from what you said respecting this matter, and from the tenor of your Fathers Letter to me of the 6th of Jany 1775—which I shewed you, there can be little doubt of its having happened already.[3] I am, Sir Your very humble Servt

G: Washington

P.S. Not knowing whether your father has a wife living or not, I have drawn the release on that supposition.

LB, DLC:GW.

1. For a discussion of GW's land dealings with Laurence Muse's father, see George Muse to GW, 3 Mar. 1784, n.1.

2. See Edmund Pendleton to GW, 9 April 1784.

3. George Muse wrote GW on 6 Jan. 1775: "I rec'd your letter dated the 5th Decr. . . . I approve of the method for dividing the land between Capt. Brenau Doctor Craig & my self; and instead of deeds being made to me for the 2100 acres of land, You will please to make them in the name of my son Battaile Muse." GW's letter to George Muse of 5 Dec. 1774 has not been found, but GW wrote William Bronaugh on 18 Jan. 1775 that George Muse and James Craik had agreed to draw "Tickets" for the first, second, and third survey of their respective shares in the 7,894-acre tract on the Great Kanawha.

From James Hanna

Sir,   Quebec March 12th 1784

Youl Excuse the liberty I take in incloseing the inclosed[.] sume years past a Baron von Lorch formerly in the Prusian Service went of from this place in the winter the same Rout Arnold Came to Joine you I know he got safe throe as G. Carelton Sent a party after him Comman[d]ed by a Captn Lonear whom got to the first inhabitants in Newingland wherein the Baron had Slept in the night before but Lonear fetchd in two of the inhabitants to convince the Genoral he had don his ⟨justy⟩ was his Excuse as the Genoral was grately displeasd with him he acting furder than his orders the Genoral asurd them they should go back. Early in the spring one of them not being content lept over Board and was lost, this Gentleman Baron Delorch I have in Care sum Litle property such as Arms & Cloathing Books and Papers which I took under my Care from the Person he left them with he Being afraid to have them in his care for fear of a discoverry if this Gentleman is to the fore he shall have his property By writeing to mee and if he is kild it is but proper his Relations should have it. I have wrote fully to Collonel Udny Hay Conserning this Gentleman to whom I Refer you and to the inclosed Commetion and two leters I took out of his trunk[1] and am Sr with the Gratest Respect your Very Hmble Servt

James Hanna

N.B. I had Som conversation with Collonl Mel⟨ch⟩ere on this afair which I refer you to.[2]

ALS, DLC:GW.

Neither James Hanna nor the Baron von Lorch has been identified. Hanna's letter is endorsed on the cover: "Mr James Hanna. Enclosing a Commission & 2 letter of a Baron Deloch in the Prussian Service July 1785." In DLC:GW there are two letters in German, one dated 23 Dec. 1768 and the other 31 Aug. 1772, both to Lorch. There is also a commission dated 25 May 1764.

1. Udny Hay (d. 1806) was deputy quartermaster general of the Continental army when the war ended.

2. Isaac Melcher (Melchior; 1748–1790) held the rank of colonel as barrack master general of the Continental army. See Charles Lee to GW, 29 Feb. 1776, n.3.

From Francis Lightfoot Lee and Ralph Wormeley, Jr.

Sir—   Mount Airy [Va.] 12th march 1784

The inclosed letters were received last summer, but, as your public engagements, at that time, did not permit your return to Mount Vernon, nor give you leisure to advert to transactions of private concernment, we postponed laying them before you, till you had withdrawn yourself from those public and official engagements.

we are totally ignorant of the part Col. Tayloe took in this affair,[1] which is the subject of Mr Montagu's letter:[2] we know the estate was sold, but, how it has been paid for; in what money; what has not been paid; and whether, any of the purchasers, may not have paid, be men of responsibility, are what we know not of; we should therefore esteem it a favor, if, you would inform us, as fully as you can, relative to this business, that from your knowledge and authority we may give Mr Montagu every light, that they may diffuse. we are with every degree of respect, and the highest esteem, Sir, your most obedient and most humble Servants

Francis Lightfoot Lee
Ralph Wormeley junr

LS, in Francis Lightfoot Lee's hand, MA. The enclosures have not been found.

Francis Lightfoot Lee (1734–1797) of Menokin, Richmond County, Va., and Ralph Wormeley, Jr. (1744–1806), of Rosegill, Middlesex County, Va., were married to daughters of John Tayloe (1721–1779) of Mount Airy, Richmond County. Lee and Wormeley were two of the executors of Colonel Tayloe's will.

1. The "affair" was the sale of George Mercer's American landholdings in November 1774; John Tayloe, George Mason, and GW were empowered to make the sale. For GW's explanation of his and Tayloe's role in the Mercer sale and its complex aftermath and for references to documents relating to GW's involvement, see GW's response to Lee and Wormeley dated 20 June 1784, and notes.

2. Edward Montague served as attorney for two of George Mercer's British creditors. See GW to Montague, 5 April 1775.

From John Sullivan

Sir　　　　　　　　　　　Durham [N.H.] March 12th 1784
Your Excellencys favor of the 28th of December, respecting the attendance of our Delegates at the General Meeting of the Society of the Cincinnati on the first Monday of May; came to hand the first Instant—the Contents have been communicated & a Meeting appointed on the second of April, at which time I doubt not Delegates will be chosen & the proper steps taken to insure a punctual attendance.[1] I have the honor to be with the most perfect attachment Your Excellencys most obedt & very humble servant

Jno. Sullivan

ALS, DSoCi.

John Sullivan (1740–1795), the son of Irish parents, was one of the major generals in the Continental army. On leaving the army in 1779, he was elected to Congress from New Hampshire and continued to be a leading figure in state politics until his death. At this time he was the attorney general of New Hampshire.

1. Only Col. Henry Dearborn (1751–1829) attended the general meeting of the Society of the Cincinnati from New Hampshire in May 1784.

Letter not found: to Benjamin Walker, 12 Mar. 1784. On 3 April Walker wrote to GW: "Your favor of the 12th of March reached me the day before yesterday."

From Bartholomew Dandridge

Dear Sir   New Kent [Va.] 13th March 1784.

It has given me great pleasure to hear you are arrived at home in safety & good health, I most sincerely congratulate you on this happy Event, and all others that have contributed to it, and wish you a long continuance of every Happiness you can desire.

I have endeavored to arrange the Affairs of Mr Custis's Estate in such a manner as I judged most for it's Interest, but I must own I have not succeeded in it agreably to my wishes or expectations, but when I have done the best I could I hope I may not be blamed for Consequences that I could not guard against. I have from time to time informed Mr Lund Washington of every material Circumstance that has attended the Estate since I took charge of it, of which I doubt not he has informed you and from that and my present Letter to him, you will have a full view of the present situation of Mr Custis's Affairs. I endeavored to avoid troubleing you with them when you were at a distance and engaged in Matters of so much greater consequence, If you have now leisure to point out to me any thing that you think will be of advantage to Mr Custis's Estate or Family, I shall be much obliged to you and will endeavor to conform to your directions.[1]

I believe I can now spare the Young Stud Horse, & hope it will suit you to take him in part for your demand against Mr Custis's Estate. I don't doubt but we shall readily agree in the Price, and the Estate is not yet able to make you any other Payment.[2]

Posey has fully answered your predictions of him, he has long since lost all sense of shame, and altho I was guarded against him, yet I could not prevent (even with much trouble), his injuring the Estate greatly in many respects. I am still pursuing such methods as I can to bring him to Justice, but his cuning is considerable, and his villany more than I can describe or you can conceive.[3]

If you should ever Visit this part of the Country I hope for the pleasure of seeing you, if not I hope I shall be able to wait on you (about June next) when we may finally conclude what is best to be done with Mr Custis's Affairs. I have not heard from Doctor Stuart or his Lady since their Marriage. I have wrote to him & refered him to Mr Washington for an Account of the situation of the Estate, & expect soon to know his views & Intentions.[4] The Estate in Fairfax & all transactions there I have always left to the management & care of Mr Washington who has been kind enough to comply with every request I have found it necessary to make to him.

My Mother and all our Family desire to be joined with me in a tender of their Esteem, Respect & Affection for you. I am Dear Sir Your most obedt Servt

B. Dandridge

Sir I imagine you can tell Mr Custis's situation with Cary & Co. I have recd no Letter from that House.[5]

ALS, DLC:GW. The letter came by "Favour of Col. [Burwell] Bassett."

Bartholomew Dandridge (1737–1785), who lived in New Kent County, Va., was the brother of Martha Washington.

1. John Parke Custis died in New Kent County on 5 Nov. 1781 at the end of the Yorktown campaign. Dandridge wrote GW four days later offering in GW's absence to join his sister, Martha Washington, as coadministrator of her son's estate, but at GW's insistence he qualified in February 1782 as sole administrator. See GW to Dandridge, 19 Nov. 1781, and GW to Peter Wagener and others, 20 Nov. 1781, and Dandridge to GW, 22 Feb. 1782. The ravages of war, John Parke Custis's own ineptitude as a man of affairs (see, for instance, GW to Custis, 26 May 1778), and the malign influence of John Price Posey (see note 3) combined to bring the once great Custis estate to the brink of ruin and left it heavily burdened with debt. For GW's and Dandridge's comments on this sad state of affairs during the year after Custis's death, see Dandridge to GW, 7 Jan., 22 Feb., 20 Mar., and 5 Nov. 1782, and GW to Dandridge, 20 April, 13 May, 25 June, and 18 Dec. 1782. Apparently there was no correspondence between the two from December 1782 until March 1784.

2. In a long letter to Dandridge on 20 April 1782, GW gave him "every information in my power respecting the State of my Accts with Mr Custis." GW's account with the estate of John Parke Custis, including a record of the transactions between GW and Custis from 3 Nov. 1773 when the General Court approved the closing of GW's guardian accounts with his young ward until Custis's death in 1781, is to be found in Ledger B, 217–19, 224, 226, 272. GW's ledger indicates that at this time, in 1784, John Parke Custis's estate owed GW £5,360.9.11, current money. By June 1786 it had been reduced to £1,119.18. Most of the payment came in the form of Custis's accrued credits in London which Wakelin Welch, of the firm that had been Robert Cary & Co., assigned to GW. See note 5, and GW to Welch, 27 July 1784. But GW also

credited the estate with £300 for Leonidas, the young stud horse referred to here, and £500 for the well-known Arabian horse named Magnolio, when the two animals became GW's property.

3. John Price Posey, the son of GW's old companion and neighbor John Posey, was the boyhood companion of John Parke Custis. He followed Custis down to New Kent County to become the manager of Custis's plantations. Dandridge writing GW at great length on 5 Nov. 1782 descants on "the villany and cunning of Posey," who, with Custis "in his power," pushed him "to turn every part of the Estate he possibly could into Money." With Custis "keeping no Accounts of his transactions," what profits that did arise from the selling of Custis's property, both Dandridge and GW believed, went to Posey, not to Custis. Armed with Custis's "general Power of Attorney," Posey had, according to Dandridge, "disposed of at least 24 Negroes, several Horses & a number of Cattle without Mr Custis's consent or knowledge and without intending to render any Account of the Produce of them, besides this he has generally had the Crops, and I suppose many other Things." See also GW to John Price Posey, 7 Aug. 1782. GW continued to press Posey to render what was due John Parke Custis's little son and heir, George Washington Parke Custis, almost up to the time of Posey's death (see, for instance, GW to Posey, 12 Jan. 1787). Posey was hanged in January 1788 for having destroyed the New Kent County clerk's office and courthouse by fire.

4. Dr. David Stuart (1753–c.1814) was married late in 1783 to John Parke Custis's widow, Eleanor Calvert Custis. They lived at Abingdon near Mount Vernon, and he practiced medicine in Alexandria. At Dandridge's death in 1785, Dr. Stuart took over the complete management of Custis's business affairs.

5. GW received in 1784 from Wakelin Welch an accounting of what was owed to the estate of John Parke Custis by Robert Cary & Company. See GW to Wakelin Welch, 27 July, n.3.

From Robert McCrea

Sir   Alex[an]d[ri]a [Va.] 13th March 1784

I never open'd yours of the 10th Inst. till this Moment,[1] & all I can say relative to the contents, is That I observe those Letters for your Excellency from the genl Post office comes free, & therefore I shall send yours free from this office untill there is orders, or reason, to the Contrary.[2]

there was however one or two from other offices Marked, but have taken no Notice thereof. Your Dollar is returned by Your Excellencys Most obedt

Robert McCrea

One oClock
P.S. the post is Just Arrived from the South, but cannot proceed
North for the river.

ALS, DLC:GW.
   Robert McCrea (c.1765–c.1840), a Scot who became a merchant in Alexandria, was acting as postmaster in the town at this time.
   1. Letter not found.
   2. See Ebenezer Hazard to GW, 11 May 1784.

From Armand

Sir   philadelphia 14th march 1784
   I have received a lettre from Grl duportail dated from paris
the 24th decembre last in which, he gives me the following account of the succes which the order & society of the Cincinaty
have in france.
   The order of the Cincinaty has had great succes here, till this
instant, the king has permitted the french officers who belong
to it to wear the badge of it—every man would wishes to have it,
& thoses who have not served the necessary time in the ameri-
cain army endeavour to give a turn to their brevets & furlough
which may obtain them the honor of wearing it—I assure you
that it has made and make now more noise [t]here than it does
in america, & the fact is, that there are many more for it than
against—the officers of the french army are much flattered by
that honorable distinction, & the Count de rochambeau make a
superiore affair of it—the Mquis de la fayette who is Commissioned by the ordere to receive in it the french officers who
served in america, receive dayly applications on the subject
from persons who ought to be sensible that they have no right
to be admitted.[1]
   as the character of cincinatus, so well marked by nature, acquired habilities & succes, in that one of your Exellency is the
most part & honorable fundation of the order, I thought that
the relation of my friend would be agreeable to you—and indeed to say or do any thing that may be agreeable to your Exellency, is the superior wishe Governing in my heart.
   I have allmost finish'd & with succes the affaire of the legion
& ingeneers, which give me the Expectation of being able to go

soon & pay my respects to your Excellency—in all probability it will be towards the later end of this month.[2] I have the honor to be with the highest respect Sir Your Exellency's the most obdt hble svt

C. armand

ALS, DLC:GW. Armand's accents on English words have not been retained.

1. See Lafayette's letters to GW of 9 Mar. 1784 and the notes in these letters for the status of the French Society of the Cincinnati.

2. See Armand to GW, 4 Feb. 1784, n.3.

From de Grasse

My Dear General   L'Orient [France] the 15th March 1784

I can not at this time answer the friendship with which you honor me unless it is by a proof of my confidence in you and I give it with pleasure.[1]

I have the honor to send to you the memorials which I have submitted to the consideration of the Court Martial for their better information of my conduct.

The sincere desire I have to make you judge of this affair induces me to deviate from the order I have received not to communicate those memorials in print. I request you not to shew them to any body, or if you think proper to make use of them I wish you would have them transcribed.

I hope, my dear General that when you have read them with attention, you will be sensible that I have not deserved that you should change your opinion of me; But that all my fault on the 12th day of April 1782 was being unfortunate.[2]

The Court martial assembled in this place for the determination of this affair will, I hope, determine soon.

I request your leave, my dear General to acquaint you with the issue whatsoever it may be.

I am waiting to hear from you with that impatience arising from the most sincere friendship; Do me the favour to let me hear from you the soonest possible.[3] Depend always on the tender and respectful attachment with which I have the honor to be My Dear General Your Excellency's Most obedient Humble Servant

The Count De Grass.
Associated in the Cincinnati

Translation, DLC:GW; LS, DLC:GW. GW received the letter and read the translation in Philadelphia in May 1784. A transcription of the signed French version is in CD-ROM:GW.

François-Joseph-Paul, comte de Grasse, marquis de Tilly (1722–1788), the commander of the French fleet at the siege at Yorktown in 1781, met defeat off the coast of Martinique in 1782 at the hands of the British admiral Samuel Hood. Forced to surrender his flagship, *Ville de Paris*, on 12 April 1782 in Saints Passage, de Grasse was taken to London where he was a prisoner of war until allowed to return to France in August 1782.

1. De Grasse wrote to GW on 28 Jan. 1783 telling of his defeat in the waters of the Leeward Islands. GW responded on 15 May 1783 to assure de Grasse that "Altho the 12th of April 1782, was an unfortunate Day to your Excellency, yet it has not tarnished your Glory in the Minds of those who know your Character & have been justly informed [of] the Circumstances of that Days Action. . . . It only proves, what many a noble Hero has heretofore experienced, that Fortune is a fickle Mistress in the Distribution of her Favors— and that, like a true Coquette, she is often best pleased with giving pain to her most deserving and meritorious Gallants."

2. In 1782 de Grasse published a *mémoire* justifying his actions in the battle at Saints Passage and blaming his defeat on the failure of some of the captains in his fleet to follow his orders. On 29 April 1783 the king ordered a *conseil de guerre* to be formed to investigate de Grasse's charges. The council of war was not actually convened until early in 1784, and it was not until 21 May 1784 that it issued its voluminous report, for the most part exonerating de Grasse's captains and, by inference, placing the onus on de Grasse for making unfair or false charges against them.

3. GW acknowledged de Grasse's letter from Philadelphia on 15 May: "My Dr Count, It was at this place I had the honor to receive your favor from L'Orient of the 15th of March—The confidence with which you have honored me, is a pleasing testimony of your friendship—it shall not be abused. And the promise you have given me of transmitting the determination of the Court Martial, I shall look for the fulfillment of with impatience, but under full persuasion that the enquiry will throw additional lustre on your character—'It was not in your power to *command* success (on the 12th of Apl 1782) but you did more—you deserv'd it.'

"I thank you for the memorials you have had the goodness to send me—It is unhappy for me however, that I am not sufficiently Master of the French language, to read them without assistance—this, when fully obtained, will, I have no doubt enable my judgment to decide favourably as my wishes & expectations have already done; & these are such as might be expected from your warmest friend & greatest Admirer, G: Washington" (LB, DLC:GW).

To Thomas Jefferson

Dear Sir,   Mount Vernon March 15th 1784.

The Baron de Steuben informs me, that he is about to make a final settlement with Congress; and to obtain from them that compensation which his Services shall appear to have merited; having entered into no stipulation at the time he engaged in the Service either for Pay or emoluments; chusing rather to let his Services point to their own rewards (after they were performed) than to set a value upon them before hand—Wishing, on the one hand, for nothing more than they deserved—on the other, convinced that the honor & dignity of the Sovereign power of these States would do him justice, if our cause should be crowned with success—if not, he would share their fortunes, & fall with them.

What the Barons expectations are, if he should incline to make them known, can be best explained by himself; but this I have heard him say, that to be placed in the same situation he was when he came to this Country, would content him—What this was I know not, but it should seem that, if a Foreigner gets nothing by the Service, he ought not to loose by it.[1]

My Sentiments with respect to the importance of the Barons Services have been delivered to Congress in so many instances, and he himself has received such repeated testimonies of it,[2] that it is unnecessary for me, in this place (especially as I have laid aside my military character, and am disinclined to trouble Congress any longer with my application) to give fresh proofs of my approbation of his abilities & conduct, tending to the same points. But I could wish to see his merit, which is great; and his Services which have been eminent, rewarded to his satisfaction. I am with the most sincere esteem & regard Dr Sir Yr obedt & very Hble Servt

                                                 G: Washington

ALS, DLC: Jefferson Papers; LB, DLC:GW.

1. When Steuben resigned his commission as major general in the Continental army in March 1784, he renewed his campaign to secure from Congress the sort of monetary reward that he believed his contributions to the winning of American independence merited. Initially, on his arrival in 1777, Steuben offered his services to Congress without conditions as to rank or pay, but in December 1782, his "private resources being exhausted," he made his

"first direct application" to Congress for suitable recompense beyond his regular pay (6 Dec. 1777, 5 Dec. 1782, DNA:PCC, item 19). Alexander Hamilton reporting on 30 Dec. 1782 for the committee to whom Steuben's letter was referred, recommended that Congress pay Steuben 2,400 dollars to be charged to his account and also allow him 300 dollars a month in lieu of extra pay and subsistence (30 Dec. 1782, DNA:PCC, item 164). In 1784, on 21 Mar. two days before he submitted his resignation from the army, Steuben requested "the attention of Congress to a report of their Committee on my Claims, dated 30th December 1782" (DNA:PCC, item 164). A committee's report on Steuben's letter of 21 Mar. recommended on 1 April that Steuben be given 2,000 dollars along with the thanks of Congress and a sword. The report was recommitted and a second report was made on 12 April calling for a payment of 6,000 dollars. After the failure of Elbridge Gerry's motion of 13 April to postpone the motion of 12 April in order to consider a motion for issuing to Steuben certificates worth 45,000 dollars in full settlement, Congress two days later finally reached an agreement (*JCC*, 26:178–79, 216–19). On 15 April Congress accepted Steuben's resignation, expressed its appreciation for his services, and voted him "a gold hilted sword." It then rejected Jefferson's motion that "the sum of ten thousand dollars be presented to Baron Steuben" as well as Ephraim Paine's motion that it be 8,000 dollars, but in the end it unanimously accepted Roger Sherman's motion, "That the Superintendant of finance take order for immediately advancing to Baron Steuben, on account, the sum of ten thousand dollars" (ibid., 227–30). The United States did not reach a final settlement with Steuben until after the new government was formed in 1789 (see Steuben to GW, 25 Aug. 1789, n.1).

2. See, for example, GW to Henry Laurens, 26 July 1778.

From Thomas Jefferson

Dr Sir   Annapolis [Md.] Mar. 15. 1784

Since my last nothing new has occurred.[1] I suppose the crippled state of Congress is not new to you. we have only 9 states present, 8 of whom are represented by two members each, and of course, on all great questions not only an unanimity of states but of members is necessary, an unanimity which never can be obtained on a matter of any importance. the consequence is that we are wasting our time & labour in vain efforts to do business. nothing less than the presence of 13 states represented by an odd number of delegates will enable us to get forward a single capital point. the deed for the cession of Western territory by Virginia was executed & accepted on the 1st instant. I hope our country will of herself determine to cede still further to the meridian of the mouth of the Great Kanhaway. further she cannot govern; so far is necessary for her own well being. the reasons which call for this boundary (which will retain all the waters of the Kanhaway) are 1. that within that are our lead mines. 2. this river rising in N. Carola traverses our whole latitude and offers to every part of it a channel for navigation & commerce to the Western country: but 3. it is a channel which can not be opened but at immense expence and with every facility which an absolute power over both shores will give. 4. this river & it's waters forms a band of good land passing along our whole frontier, and forming on it a barrier which will be strongly seated. 5. for 180 miles beyond these waters is a mountainous barren which can never be inhabited & will of course form a safe separation between us & any other state. 6. this tract of country lies more convenient to receive it's government from Virginia than from any other state. 7. it will preserve to us all the upper parts of Yohogany & Cheat rivers within which much will be to be done to open these which are the true doors to the Western commerce.[2] the union of this navigation with that of the Patowmac is a subject on which I mentioned that I would take the liberty of writing to you. I am sure it's value and practicability are both well known to you.[3] this is the moment however for seizing it if ever we mean to have it. all the world is becoming commercial. was it practicable to keep our new empire separated from them we might indulge ourselves in speculating whether commerce contributes to the happiness of mankind. but we cannot separate ourselves from them. our citizens have had too full a taste of the comforts furnished by the arts & manufactures to be debarred the use of them. we must then in our own defence endeavor to share as large a portion as we can of this modern source of wealth & power. that offered to us from the Western country is under a competition between the Hudson, the Patomac & the Missisipi itself. down the last will pass all heavy commodities. but the navigation through the gulf of Mexico is so dangerous, & that up the Missisipi so difficult & tedious, that it is not probable that European merchandize will return through that channel. it is most likely that flour, lumber & other heavy articles will be floated on rafts which will be themselves an article of sale as well as their loading, the navigators returning by land or in light batteaux. there will therefore be a rivalship between the Hudson & Patowmac for the residue of the commerce of all the country westward of L. Erie, on the waters of the lakes, of the Ohio & upper parts of the Missisipi. to go to N. York, that part of the trade which comes from the lakes or their waters must first be brought into L. Erie. so also must that which comes from the waters of the Missisipi, and of course must cross at some portage into the waters of the lakes. when it shall have entered L. Erie, it must coast along it's Southern shore on account of the number & excellence of it's harbours, the Northern, tho' shortest, having few harbours, & these unsafe. having reached Cayahoga to proceed on to N. York will be 970 miles from thence & five portages, whereas it is but 430 miles to Alexandria, if it turns into the Cayahoga & passes through that, Big beaver, Ohio, Yohogany (or Monongalia & Cheat) & Patowmac, & there are but two portages. for the trade of the Ohio or that which shall come into it from it's own waters or the Missisipi, it is nearer to Alexandria than to New York by 730 miles, and is interrupted by one portage only.[4] nature then has declared in favour of the Patowmac, and through that channel offers to pour into our lap the whole commerce of the Western world. but unfortunately the channel by the Hudson is already open & known in practice; ours is still to be opened. this is the moment in which the trade of the West will begin to get into motion and to take it's direction. it behoves us then to open our doors to it. I have lately pressed this subject on my friends in the General assembly, proposing to them to endeavor to have a tax laid which shall bring into a separate chest from five to ten thousand pounds a year, to be employed first in opening the upper waters of the Ohio & Patowmac, where a little money & time will do a great deal, leaving the great falls for the last part of the work.[5] to remove the idea of partiality I have suggested the propriety & justice of continuing this fund till all the rivers shall be cleared successively. but a most powerful objection always arises to propositions of this kind. it is that public undertakings are car[e]lessly managed and much money spent to little purpose. to obviate this objection is the purpose of my giving you the trouble of this discussion. you have retired from public life. you have weighed this determination & it would be impertinence in me to touch it. but would the superintendance of this work break in too much on the sweets of retirement & repose? if they would, I stop here. your future time & wishes are sacred in my eye. if it would be only a dignified amusement to you, what a monument of your retirement would it be! it is one which would follow that of your public life and bespeak it the work of the same great hand. I am confident that would you either alone or jointly with any persons you think proper be willing to direct this business, it would remove the only objection the weight of which I apprehend. tho' the tax should not come in till the fall, it's proceeds should be anticipated by borrowing from some other fund to enable the work to be begun this summer. when you view me as not owning nor ever having a prospect of owning one inch of land on any water either of the Patowmac or Ohio, it will tend to apologize for the trouble I have given you of this long letter, by shewing that my zeal in this business is public & pure. the best atonement for the time I have occupied you will be not to add to it longer than while I assure you of the sincerity & esteem with which I have the honour to be Dr Sir Your most obedient & most humble servt

Th: Jefferson

P.S. the hurry of time in my former letter prevented my thanking you for your polite & friendly invitation to Mount Vernon.[6] I shall certainly pay my respects there to mrs Washington & yourself with great pleasure whenever it shall be in my power.

ALS, DLC:GW. GW docketed the letter 18 March.

1. Jefferson wrote GW on 6 March.

2. Jefferson listed the same seven points in his letter to James Madison of 20 Feb. 1784 (Hutchinson and Rachal, *Madison Papers*, 7:422–35; Boyd, *Jefferson Papers*, 6:544–51).

3. In his letter of 20 Feb. to Madison, cited in note 2, Jefferson observes that "Genl Washington has the opening of the Potowmac much at heart. The superintendence of it would be a noble amusement in his retirement and leave a monument of him as long as the water should flow" (Boyd, *Jefferson Papers*, 6:548). It was on 6 Mar. that Jefferson indicated to GW that he planned to write him about the navigation of the Potomac.

4. See map. See also GW's letter of 29 Mar. questioning Jefferson's figures.

5. See the letter to Madison cited in note 2.

6. See GW to Jefferson, 3 Mar. 1784.

From Le Gardeur de Tilly

a Son Exélance   Rochefort Ce, 15e mars. 1784.

agrée je vous prie L'homage De mon Respect et me perméte De vous Rappeler Les Sirconstances, qui Mont procuré La Satisfaction De méttre En Evidance tout Le zele et Lamprescement a Cegonder veaux vüe par mes Scitations Sur veaux Côttes Comendant Le vaisseau de Sa Majésté LEveillé et Deux frégate avec Lesquels je me Suis Rendüe Maitre Du vaisseau Le Romulusse, Le Duc De york, La Goilétte La Revange Et plusieurs Austre petits Batiments Dont je Remie Les prisoniers, au Commandant Demptone, qui men temoigna alors toutes Sa Satisfaction, par Les Déprédation quavoit Commies Ces Dernier, Surtoutes vos Côtte jovois désire mieux faire En Corre Sil mut Etée possible.

jay Egalement eü La Satisfaction, Descorter La Corvette Le Wasington Du Cap françois a Lavane, ou Elle prie un chargement En argent je Continues a lui Donner Lescorte jusque Sur Les Cotte de la Délavare, ou ayant Rencontré un vaisseau de Soixante et quatre Et Deux frégates Enemie je Crûe Devoir Combatre Les Deux frégates pour faciliter La Retréte De vôtre Corvétte, qui fut En, profiter avèc Succes Ce qui fait LEloge du Capitaine Dont les Differente Maneuvres pendant Le Cours De Nôtre Navigation merite Les plus Grand Eloge; je Novois jamais Rappelé a vôtre Exelance Daussy foible preuve De tous Mes Desir a Repondre a la Confiance Dont on mavez honnoré Sy jusse püe partager La joix et La Satisfaction quont tous Seux que vous avez Bien voulüe assossier a Lordre de Cincinatus je Ne peux Donc vous Dicimuler tout Le Desir que jay Di Estre assossie Comme un temoignage De Vôtre aprobation et Souvenir que me Cera toujour pressieux. je Suis avec Respect De Son Exelance Son tres humble et tres obeissant serviteur

Le Gardeur de Tilly Captin Des Vaux du Roi

p. S. Monsieur Le Comte De Barrasse Et Mr Le marquis De vaudreüille mon dit vous avoir fait part de Leurs Voeux a mon Egard[1]

ALS, DSoCi.

Armand Le Gardeur de Tilly (1733–1812) in command of the *Eveille* participated with the French fleet in the Battle of the Chesapeake and at the siege at Yorktown in 1781, first under Destouches and then under the orders of Vaudreuil.

1. Barras wrote about Tilly on 23 Jan., but no letter of recommendation from Vaudreuil has been found. Tilly became a member of the French Cincinnati along with the other qualified French naval captains.

Letter not found: from Edward Newenham, 15 Mar. 1784. On 10 June GW wrote to Newenham: "I had the honor to receive . . . your favors of the 30th of Jany & 15th of March."

To Steuben

My dear Baron   Mount Vernon 15th Mar. 1784
I have perused with attention, the plan which you have formed for establishing a Continental Legion, and for training a certain part of the Arms bearing men of the Union as a Militia, in times of Peace—and with the small alterations which have been suggested & made, I very much approve of it.[1]

It was no unpleasing and flattering circumstance to me, to find such a coincidence of ideas as appear to run through your plan and the one I had the honor to lay before a Committee of Congress, in May last.[2] Mine however, was a hasty production, the consequence of a sudden call, & little time for arrangement—Yours, of mature thought, & better digestion. I, at the sametime that I hinted the propriety of a Continental Militia, glided almost insensibly into what I thought would be, rather than what I conceived ought to be, a proper Peace establishmt for this Country.

A Peace Establishment has always two objects in view—the one, present security of Posts—of Stores—& the public tranquillity. The other to be prepared, if the latter is impracticable, to resist with efficacy the sudden attempts of a foreign or domestic Enemy. If we have no occasion for Troops for the first purposes, and was certain of not wanting any for the second; then all expence, of every nature & kind whatsoever, on this score, would be equally Nugatory and unjustifiable—but while men have a disposition to wrangle & disturb the peace of Society, either from ambitious, political, or interested motives, common prudence & foresight requires such an Establishment as is likely to ensure to us the blessings of Peace, altho' the undertaking should be attended with difficulty, and expence; and I can think of no plan more likely to answer the purpose, than the one you have suggested; which (the principles being established) may be enlarged, or diminished at pleasure, according to Circumstances.

It therefore meets my approbation, and has my best wishes for its success. I have the honor to be Dr Sir Yr Most Obedt and very Hble Servt

Go: Washington

ALS, DNA: RG 46, entry 7; LB, DLC:GW.

1. In the summer of 1784, Steuben printed his "plan" in a pamphlet entitled *A Letter on the Subject of an Established Militia, and Military Arrangements, Addressed to the Inhabitants of the United States.*

2. GW's "Sentiments on a Peace Establishment," 1 May 1783, were enclosed in his letter to Alexander Hamilton, 2 May 1783 (DLC:GW).

From Edward Carrington

Sir,   Richmond [Va.] March 18th 1784
Permit me to offer you my most sincere congratulations on your return from the Feild to those pleasing scenes of domestic life which you left with regret. In contemplating the great event which has closed your Military life, be assured that no Fellow Citizen is inspired with more gratitude towards you than myself—but to the Common feelings of my Countrymen, I have to add, as an individual, my acknowledgements of, and unfeigned thanks for, the several instances in which you have been pleased to honor me with your attention, but more particularly your polite invitation to partake of the Honors of your Family, fills me with such an abundance of gratitude that I cannot suppress my declaration of it. diffident as I was of my abilities to serve you effectually, be assured that nothing prevented my accepting the honorable and flattering invitation, but the engagements I was under to my very Affectionate freind Genl Greene.[1] In civil life which I now embrace with real satisfaction my prayers are that this great Empire may be managed with wisdom and Honor, equal to the pleasures you both feel in having contributed to its deliverance from Tyranny. I have the Honor to be Sir, with great Affection your Most Obt Servt

Ed. Carrington

ALS, DLC:GW.

Edward Carrington (1749–1810), who was a lieutenant colonel of the artillery in the Continental army from 1776, became in 1781 Gen. Nathanael Greene's deputy quartermaster general and chief of artillery in the southern campaign.

1. GW evidently retained his good opinion of Carrington, for in 1789 he appointed him United States marshal for the district court of Virginia and in 1791 made him the federal collector of the excise tax on liquors in Virginia. See also James Madison to GW, 21 Oct. 1788, n.5.

From Elbridge Gerry

Sir   Annapolis [Md.] 18th March 1784

By the last Post I received from the president of the Senate of Massachusetts a Letter, inclosing the papers herewith transmitted, & requesting me to write to your Excellency on the Subject.[1] As I have no other Knowledge of the Matter, than what is derived from Colo. Gridley's Letter & the Resolve accompanying it, I can only say, that when your Excellency is at Leisure, if You think it expedient to make any observations on the Subject or Answer to the Resolve, & should inclose them to me, I will direct them to Colo. Gridley.[2]

I flatter myself with the Hopes that since your Retirement from publick Life You have not only enjoyed, Health, peace & Competence, but Likewise the pleasure of seeing all your Friends in the same happy Circumstances.

My Respects to your Lady, & be assured Sir I remain with every Sentiment of Esteem & Respect your most obedt & very humble sert

E. Gerry

ALS, DLC:GW.

Elbridge Gerry (1744–1814) was at this time attending the Congress of the Confederation at Annapolis as a delegate from Massachusetts. In 1783 he had been one of the most effective opponents of Alexander Hamilton's proposals for a peacetime military establishment, and he strongly disapproved of the Society of the Cincinnati (see Gerry to John Adams, 23 Nov. 1783, quoted in Billias, *Gerry*, 110).

1. Samuel Adams was president of the Massachusetts senate. The enclosures have not been found. See GW to Gerry, 31 Mar. 1784.

2. In his letter of 31 Mar. to Gerry, GW indicates that the letter from Gridley to Adams which Gerry had enclosed was dated 21 Feb. 1784 and was written by one of the sons of Col. Richard Gridley (1710–1796). It was proba-

bly written by Maj. Scarborough Gridley, who was an officer in his father's regiment in 1775 (see General Orders, 2 Sept. 1775, n.1, printed in *Papers, Revolutionary War Series*, 1:397–98).

To John Harvie

Sir,   Mount Vernon 18th March 1784

By a further research into my papers, I have found—with a letter from Colo. Fielding Lewis (which it shou'd seem must have come *to this place* after I had accepted the command of the Army & was gone to Cambridge)—the Survey which I now enclose, as I also do the letter alluded to, as it will account for its delay in reaching the Land office 'till now.[1]

As I recollect well that Michael Cresap & indeed others were disposed to give me trouble about this bottom, I will thank you for examining if any Caveat to the issuing of a Patent has ever been entered in the Land office by him, Doctr Brisco, or Charles Smith, all of whom at times, without a shadow of right, possessed themselves of the Land. If there is not, and the Constitution admits of no arrest to the progress of my claim elsewhere—I should be glad to receive a Grant there for, as soon as you can make it convenient—& should be glad also, if there is nothing improper in it, if the Patent was to recite the date of the Survey & the right upon which it is founded, that it may not have the appearance of a recent transaction—new rights—or purchase under the present modes.[2] I wish this might be the case also with the Grant for the Survey made by Colo. Preston & Mr Saml Lewis, copies of which you were so obliging as to send me last month.[3] The first of these accounts for my warrants to Mr Thruston, as the latter does for 2950 acres of the one to myself; and having since found the one to Capt. Roots (assigned to me) for 3,000 unexecuted; I have now only 5,050 acres unaccounted for—with these I am at a loss what to do, or where to locate them.[4]

With respect to the Tract of 578 acres it may be necessary for me further to add, that neither myself, nor any person in my behalf has ever been notified of a Caveat—that I have never heard of one. In my letter of the 10th of Feby I intimated that Michael Cresap had impeded the Patent for it; & by a letter from Capt. Crawford it appears that he attempted to do it with

Lord Dunmore, when he was on the Indian Expedition, but the result he knew not.[5] And that I have requested an examination for no other reason than to prevent (in case such a thing unknown to me should be) unnecessary trouble & expence. One thing I am certain of, & that is, that neither of the persons who have discovered a disposition to give me trouble & vexation in this affair, saw or heard of the Land, 'till it was surveyed on my Accot—with great esteem & regard I have the honor to be &ca

G: Washington

LB, DLC:GW.

1. Fielding Lewis's letter about receiving the Round Bottom plat is dated 22 April 1775. See GW to Harvie, 10 Feb. 1784, and GW to Thomas Lewis, 1 Feb. 1784, nn.1 and 3.

2. The grant which Harvie eventually prepared and Gov. Benjamin Harrison signed on 30 Oct. 1784 includes the date of survey and lists the warrants with which GW acquired the Round Bottom tract. See GW to Thomas Lewis, 1 Feb. 1784, n.3.

3. See Harvie to GW, 21 Feb. 1784, n.2.

4. Of the 5,050 acres unaccounted for in the total of 13,000 acres for which GW secured warrants under the Royal Proclamation of 1763, 2,050 acres were in the warrant of 5,000 acres given GW for his own services in the war. A survey and grant of 250 acres at the Burning Springs had in fact already been made, leaving only 1,800 acres in his own warrant still unaccounted for. See GW to Samuel Lewis, 1 Feb. 1784, source note.

5. On his return from Dunmore's expedition against the Shawnee, William Crawford wrote that he had "Run your Land at the round bottom Again and will Send you a new Draft of it." He then wrote: "I spooke to Lord Dunmore about your Land at Charters [Chartiers Creek] and the round bottom and it hapned that Mr [Michael] Cresap was present when we spooke of it Cresap was Laying Down his Claim and I was walking by[.] Cresap wanted it run for him by a warrent which he had Purchest and [I] then told his Lordship the nature of your Claim before Cresaps farce upon which he Said no more at the time but wanted me to Survay it for him also and return it. I told him I cold not at any rate do such a thing as I had survayd it for you" (Crawford to GW, 14 Nov. 1774). See GW's caveat in his letter to John Harvie, 31 May 1785.

To Edmund Randolph

Dear Sir,   Mount Vernon 18th March 1784

I have seen the form of the answer which you have drawn in Savages suit, and approve of it; presuming the references are founded on facts. Mr Fairfax was to have compared these, & will prepare a fair copy. I will remind him of the matter, & have it sent to you as soon as I can.[1]

The case of the depending petitions, in the General Court, is as follows.

The Land was obtained under a Proclamation of Mr Dinwiddie; issued by the advice of his Council Feby 19th 1754, for encouraging the raising of Troops for an Expedition to the Ohio. It was surveyed pursuant to warrants granted by Lord Dunmore, & Patented Decr 15th 1772.[2]

For 10,990 Acres, in Fincastle

$$\left.\begin{matrix} 4,395 \\ 2,448 \\ 2,314 \end{matrix}\right\} \quad \text{in Botetourt}$$

In the month of March 1774, I encounter'd, *in preparation only*, an expence of at least £300; by the purchase of Servants, Nails, Tools & other necessaries for the purpose of seating and cultivating the above Lands, agreeably to our Act of Assembly; & for transporting the same over the Allighaney Mountains— but this was entirely sunk. The disturbances occasioned by the Indians, which immediately followed, put a stop to my proceedings. the Servants, some of them, engaged in the Militia— others squandered—& the whole were lost *to me*; while my Goods, as I am informed, were seized for the use of the militia & a fort which was built, upon the Expedition under Lord Dunmore, & no compensation made me for them—nor, if I am rightly informed, anything given upon which I can found a claim.

The March following I went thro' the second edition of a similar expence, & find by having recourse to my papers, (since I came home) the Certificates which I enclose herewith.[3]

Not knowing what had been, or might be done in this second essay to cultivate my Lands (for I left home in May, while my people were out)—I wrote from Cambridge (in Septr 1775) to Mr Everard requesting as a further security, that they might be covered by friendly Petitions; & presume I must have required Colo. Bassett to take measures accordingly. But never knew what, or whether any steps had been taken in this business, 'till Mr Mercer (whom I saw at Fredericksburg the other day) & your Letter of the 19th of Feby since, informed me of the depending Petitions.[4]

Under this information and what follows, you will be so good as to do what shall appear necessary & proper in my behalf— The Lands, by the Proclamation and Patents, are exempted from the payment of quitrent, 'till the expiration of fifteen years from & after the date of the latter: but my ignorance of the existing Laws of this State, since the change of its constitution, does not enable me to determine whether the old Act requiring cultivation & improvement, is yet in force, or not; consequently I can give no opinion upon the proper line of conduct to be pursued. Admitting however that this act is in force, so far as it may apply to Lands under the circumstances mine are—yet the two principal Tracts are nevertheless saved; as will appear by the records of Fincastle & Botetourt, where the agregate of the valuations amount to £1583.15.7½ & the sum required to save the number of acres contained in them amounts to no more than £1538.10.0—and had it not been for the hostile temper of the Indians towards the close of 1775 which rendered it unsafe for my people to remain out, & who were actually driven in, to my very great loss in other respects (besides the noncultivation) I should most undoubtedly, have saved the whole agreeably to Law.

Miss Lee, sister to the late Major Genl Lee, wrote, requesting me to obtain for her an authenticated copy of his will—the copy I have lately got, but Mr Drew thinks it may be necessary to affix the Seal of the State to it, as it is to go to England—I request the favor of you therefore to procure & send this to me by the Post—the cost when made known to me I will pay.[5] With very great regard I am Dr Sir Your Most Obt & affecte Servant.

G: Washington

LB, DLC:GW.

1. For GW's involvement in the affairs of Margaret Savage, see Randolph to GW, 19 Feb. 1784, n.3.

2. For information on GW's claiming of land in the Ohio country under the terms of Robert Dinwiddie's Proclamation of 1754, see GW to Samuel Lewis, 1 Feb. 1784, and source note.

3. For GW's first abortive attempt to people his lands on the Ohio with Valentine Crawford as his manager, see his instructions to Crawford, 30 Mar. 1774, and Valentine's reports of the outbreak of hostilities with the Indians, 6, 7 May 1774, and notes to these documents. For GW's second attempt to get settlers on his land, see his instructions to James Cleveland, 10 Jan. 1775; William Crawford to GW, 7 Feb. 1775; GW to James Cleveland, c.March 1775; William Crawford to GW, 6 Mar. 1775; instructions for William Stevens, 6 Mar. 1775; and Cleveland to GW, 10 April, 12, 21 May, and 7 June 1775. See also GW to Samuel Lewis and to Thomas Lewis, both 1 Feb. 1784, and notes.

4. See GW to Thomas Everard, 17 Sept. 1775. GW's letter to Burwell Bassett of the same date is missing, but see Bassett to GW, 6 Nov. 1775. Everard as clerk to the secretary of Virginia's General Court was in charge of issuing land patents. Randolph had inquired about Bassett's suits in his letter of 19 February.

5. For GW's dealings with Sidney Lee regarding the will of her brother Charles Lee, see GW to William Drew, 13 Feb. 1784.

To Nathanael Greene

My Dear Sir,   Mount Vernon Mar. 20th—84

From the purport of your letter dated at New Port Feby 16th which only came to my hands yesterday I have little expectation that this reply to it will find you in the state of Rhode Island—If however the case should be otherwise it is to express an earnest wish that you might make it convenient to take the general meeting of the Cincinnati in your way to So. Carolina.

I was concerned to hear you say "one of your delegates only was expected to be there"—It were to be wished on many accts that the ensuing meeting might not only be full in representation, but that the best abilities of it might also be present—there are, in my opinion, very important reasons for this—& I cannot avoid expressing an earnest wish that yours may be amongst them.

I would add more, were I not apprehensive that this letter will not meet you in time. I have received Letters from France on this subject, which, with the Sentiments which many seem disposed to entertain of the *tendency* of the Society make it, I repeat it again indispensably necessary that the first meeting should be full and respectable.

As there is time (supposing this letter finds you in Rhode Island) to give me an acknowledgement of it, let me entreat an answer.[1] My best wishes in which Mrs Washington joins attend Mrs Green, yourself, & family—Very sincerely & Affectionately I am—Dr Sir Yr faithful & Obedt

Go: Washington

ALS, DSoCi; LB, DLC:GW.

1. See Greene's letters of 3 and 20 April.

From David Humphreys

My dear General   New Haven March 20 1784

I arrived at this place just a Month from the time of my leaving Mount Vernon, perfectly free from Misadventures, altho' attended with disagreeable roads & the coldest weather I ever experienced—in my route I had the pleasure of executing all your commands, except that of delivering your verbal Message to Govr Clinton, this, the impracticability of passing the Hudson below Kings-ferry prevented; I have however written a private Letter to His Excellency on the subject.[1]

On the 17th inst. the Connecticut State Society of Cincinnati convened at Hartford; they appointed Generals Parsons, Huntington, & Swift, with Colo. Trumbull & myself to attend the General Meeting in May next as their Delegation—in consequence of which I expect the honor of seeing you at that time.[2]

It is with no small satisfaction I inform your Excellency that the disposition of the People of this State respecting political subjects seems to be changing for the better with great rapidity; there is scarcely a doubt but that the Legislature will adopt the Impost at their next Session—and I am told that the influence of General Greene is operating very favorably in the State of Rhode Island; so that I still hope (agreeably to your old prediction) that every thing will terminate happily.

Having an accidental conveyance for Annapolis, I have only time to add my best wishes for Mrs Washington & the family, and to assure Your Excellency that I have the honor to be My dear General Your faithful friend and Hble Servant

D. Humphrys

ALS, PHi: Gratz Collection.

1. Humphreys' letter to George Clinton has not been found, but for GW's present dealings with Clinton, see the references in Robert Morris to GW, 14 Feb., n.2. See also GW to Clinton, 25 Nov. 1784.

2. Samuel Holden Parsons (1737–1789), Jedediah Huntington, and Heman Swift all failed to attend the general meeting of the Society of the Cincinnati held in Philadelphia in May 1784.

To Henry Knox

My Dear Sir,   Mount Vernon 20th March 1784

Your Letter of the 21st ulto did not reach my hands 'till yesterday—Having the Governor here & a house full of company—& the Post being on the point of setting out for the Eastward I must confine the few lines I shall be able (at this time) to write, to the business of the Cincinnati.

From what you have said of the temper of your Assembly respecting this Society—from the current of Sentiment in the other New England States thereon—& from the official letter which I have lately received from the Marqs de la Fayette on this subject[1]—I am more than ever of opinion that the general Meeting at Philada in May next ought, *by all means*, to be full & respectable: I was sorry to find these words therefore in your letter, after naming the Delegates from your State—"probably, only two will attend."

I think, not only the whole number chosen should attend, but the abilities of them coolly, deliberately, & wisely employed when met, to obviate the prejudices and remove the jealousies which are already imbibed—& more than probably, through ignorance, envy & perhaps worse motives, will encrease & spread—I cannot therefore forbear urging in strong terms the necessity of the measure. The ensuing General Meeting, is either *useful* or *useless*; if the former, the representatives of each State Society, ought to be punctual in their attendance, especially under present circumstances—If it is not, all ought to be exempted; & I am sure none can give the time which this journey & business requires, with less convenience to themselves than myself.

By a Letter which I have just received from Genl Greene, I am informed that himself, Genl Varnum & Majr Lyman are chosen to represent the Society of the State of Rhode Island—that he intends to be in So. Carolina before the meeting, & it is not expected more than one will attend it![2] I wish this could be otherwise, & that General Greene would attend—private interest, or convenience may be a plea for many, & the Meeting thereby be thin & unfit for the purpose of its institution.

I have heard nothing yet from New Hampshire, New York,

or New Jersey to the Eastward—nor anything from the South-ward—to the last, duplicates have long since been sent.[3]

As there can be no interruption of the Post by bad weather, now, & there is time for it, pray let me hear more fully from you on the subject of this letter, by the return of it—particularly what the Committee's of your Assembly have reported. Mrs Washington joins in best wishes for Mrs Knox, yourself & the little folks, with Dr Sir Your most obedt & Affecte humble Servant

G: Washington

LB, DLC:GW.

1. Lafayette wrote GW on 25 Dec. 1783 about the Society of the Cincinnati: "Objections are Made, as is the Case in Every Novelty—the Hereditary part of the institution Has its Comments—But the General Voice is in favour of our Brotherly Society" (Idzerda, *Lafayette Papers*, 5:179–80).

2. See Nathanael Greene to GW, 16 Feb. 1784.

3. See the note in GW's circular letter, 1 Jan. 1784.

To Francis Johnston

Dear Sir,   Mount Vernon 22d Mar: 84

Inclosed you have the Certificates for Captns Pashke, De Mercellan[1] & Le Roy returned, with my Seal & Signature; but if I recollect right, they must be countersigned by the Secretary General to give them validity.

They only came to my hands yesterday, or you should have had them sooner.[2] With great esteem I am—Dr Sir Yr Most Obedt Servt

Go: Washington

ALS, owned (1979) by Mr. Steve Barnett, Provo, Utah; LB, DLC:GW.

1. Marcellin's certificate (in DSoCi), signed by GW, reads: "This Certifies, that Captain Claude Antoine Villet de Marcellin, of the Pennsylvania Line, being in virtue of his Services in the American Army, entitled to become a Member of the Cincinnati and having signed the Institution and complied with the Regulations therein specified, is accordingly admitted a Member, and is entitled to all the Rights, and Priviledges of the said Society of the Cincinnati. Given under my hand and Seal at Mount Vernon—this Twentieth day of March 1784."

2. See Johnston to GW, 23 Feb. 1784, and Marcellin and Le Roy to GW, 4 Mar. 1784.

To Joshua Barney

Sir,   Mount Vernon 24th March 1784.

Your Letter of the 6th only came to hand the 22d[1]—I thank you for your care of the Packages sent by the Marqs de la Fayette, for which I will send a Carriage in the course of two or three days[2]—In the mean while, if you would be so obliging as to have them deposited at the lodgings of Mr Jefferson, a Delegate in Congress at Annapolis, from this State, it would oblige me—If you will be pleased to let me know what expences have attended these packages, the money shall be paid to your order. I am Sir Yr most obt humble Servt

G: Washington

LB, DLC:GW.

Joshua Barney (1759–1818) of Baltimore, who despite his youth at the time was one of the naval heroes of the Revolution, was at this time still in the Continental navy. It was he who was chosen to command the *Federalist* when it sailed in June 1788 from Baltimore to Mount Vernon to be presented to GW in celebration of Maryland's ratification of the Constitution.

1. Letter not found.

2. GW wrote Barney on 29 Mar.: "The bearer is sent for the Packages you were pleased to inform me, were in your care, from the Marqs De la Fayette for my use" (ALS, owned [1969] by Victor B. Levit, San Francisco). GW wrote Lafayette on 4 April 1784 that he had received the silver "plate" brought from France by Captain Barney. See also GW to Lafayette, 10 Jan. 1784, n.1, and 1 Feb. 1784, n.1.

To Thomas Jefferson

Dear Sir,   Mount Vernon 24th March 1784

Your letter of the 15th came to my hands the 22d—at the moment the Governor & some other company came in.[1] I can do no more at present than to acknowledge the rect of it, but will take the first leisure moment to write fully to you on the points it contains. Capt. Barney informs me that he has two packages on board, from the Marqs de la Fayette; the enclosed to him contains a request to land them under your care 'till I shall send for them, which will be in the course of a few days.[2] They are valuable, & I pray you to give them house room. I am very truly &c. &c.

G: Washington

LB, DLC:GW.

1. GW indicated in his letter to Henry Knox of 20 Mar. that Gov. Benjamin Harrison was already at Mount Vernon on that date.

2. See GW to Joshua Barney, this date.

To Tench Tilghman

Dear Sir,   Mount Vernon Mar. 24th 1784

I am informed that a Ship with Palatines is gone up to Baltimore, among whom are a number of Tradesmen. I am a good deal in want of a House Joiner & Bricklayer, (who really understand their profession) & you would do me a favor by purchasing one of each, for me. I would not confine you to Palatines. If they are good workmen, they may be of Assia, Africa, or Europe. They may be Mahometans, Jews, or Christian of any Sect—or they may be Athiests—I woud however prefer middle aged, to young men. and those who have good countenances & good characters on ship board, to others who have neither of these to recommend them—altho, after all, the proof of the pudding must be in the eating. I do not limit you to a price, but will pay the purchase money on demand—This request will be in force 'till complied with, or countermanded, because you may not succeed at this moment, and have favourable ones here after to do it in[.][1] My best respects, in which Mrs Washington joins, are presented to Mrs Tilghman & Mrs Carroll[2]—and I am Dr Sir Yr Affecte Hble Servt

Go: Washington

ALS, PHi: Gratz Collection; LB, DLC:GW.

Tench Tilghman (1744–1786) was GW's trusted aide-de-camp throughout the war. From this time until his death in April 1786, Tilghman acted as GW's agent in business matters in Baltimore.

1. See Tilghman to GW, 29 Mar. 1784.

2. Anna Maria Tilghman and Margaret Tilghman Carroll were sisters. See Tilghman to GW, 11 Aug. 1784, n.1.

To Benjamin Walker

Dear Walker,   Mount Vernon 24th March 1784

I perceive by the Governors letter dated Feby 27th (which only came to hand yesterday—& learn also by a Letter from Colo. Varick) that you are of his Family.[1]

Let me entreat you therefore, without giving the Govr any more trouble in the matter than is absolutely necessary, to clear up a mistake which must have happened somewhere.

The Govr in acknowledging the receipt of my Letters of the 15th & 28th of Decr—adds—"The former covering Mr Morris's Notes to the amount of 2080^{8}%$_{90}$ Dollars." It ought to have covered (if any were enclosed) 4226 dollars & a fraction; arising first, from the balance of my warrant upon the Paymaster for 6000 Dollars, of which I recd 2500 only, taking Mr Morris's Note for the remainder, (to wit 3500)—& next, for the balance of the Accot I had then deposited in the Auditors Office, amounting to £217.16.8 (Dols. at 6/) which together made the 4226^{1}%$_{90}$ Dollars. This business was transacted by Colo. Cobb— the Notes, as I intended them for the Govr, never came into my hands, or only to look at—& to him, in the hurry we were all in, the morning of our departure from Philada, was given my letter to the Govr, open, with a request that the letter & notes might be delivered to His Excelly as he passed thro' New York—the former informing him, that I should throw into his hands about £1700 towards the discharge of my bond— whether the letter was left open to receive the Notes, or merely for him to seal, as I was hurried by the crowd of visitors which pressed upon us at that time, I do not now recollect—but certain it is, the Govr, by the means here mentioned, ought to have received Notes for 4226 Dolls. instead of 2080.[2]

The other sum of 8575^{2}%$_{90}$ Dollars (which is mentioned in the Govrs Letter) is a subsequent transaction altogether, arising from our Expenditures in Philada—on the road to Virginia &ca— a warrt for which on Mr Hilligas was drawn by Mr Morris & sent to me for indorsation, which it has accordingly received, & is sent back to him again for the Govrs use. Under this information you will confer a favor upon me by getting this mistake explained & rectified.[3] If the Govr received no more than 2080^{8}%$_{90}$ dollars, Colo. Cobb only can account for it; as the facts are literally as I have stated them.

I have obtained no answers yet to the circular Letters you took with you for New Jersey, New York & New Hampshire— the two first certainly must have got to hand; but it may not be amiss nevertheless for you to enquire (by a line) of the Presidents of those two (State) Societies, whether they have or have not got them—accompanying the enquiry with information of the time & place of the Genl Meeting.[4]

I understand the Society of Cincinnati is the cause of much jealousy & uneasiness in the New England States—Pray what is said of it in yours—& in the Jersey. Will you (for a letter may arrive at this place before I set out) be kind enough to give me full information on that head—who your Delegates are—whether they will attend &ca—It were much to be wished that the Genl Meeting might be full & respectable; that the several matters which may come before it, might be deliberately weighed, & wisely resolved on—A thin meeting will bring the Society into contempt.

Inclosed you have a letter which came under cover to me—My best wishes attend the Govr—I feel great concern for his own, & the indisposition of his Family, & very much so for the accident my namesake met with[5]—Mrs Washington joins me in these & Complimts to you. I am very truly Yours &a

G: Washington

LB, DLC:GW.

1. For Richard Varick's letter, see GW to Varick, 22 Feb. 1784. For Walker's status, see Walker to GW, 3 April.

2. See George Clinton to GW, 27 Feb., and notes.

3. See GW to Morris, 4 Jan., n.1.

4. See Walker to GW, 3 April.

5. For George Clinton's description of the accident that befell his little son, George Washington Clinton, see his letter of 27 February.

Letter not found: from Hugh Williamson, 24 Mar. 1784. On 31 Mar. GW wrote to Williamson: "The last Post brought me your favor of the 24th."

To James Craik

Dear Sir,　　　　　　　　　　Mount Vernon 25th March 1784

In answer to Mr Bowie's request to you, permit me to assure that Gentleman, that I shall at all times be glad to see him at this retreat—That whenever he is here, I will give him the perusal of any public papers antecedent to my appointment to the command of the American army—that he may be laying up materials for his work.[1] And whenever Congress shall have opened *their* Archives to any Historian for information, that he shall have the examination of all others in my possession which are subsequent thereto, but that 'till this epoch, I do not think myself at liberty to unfold papers which contain all the occurrences & transactions of my *late* command; first, because I conceive it to be respectful to the sovereign power to let them take the lead in this business—& next, because I have, upon this principle, refused Doctr Gordon & others who are about to write the History of the revolution this priviledge.[2]

I will frankly declare to you, My Dr Doctor that any memoirs of my life, distinct & unconnected with the general history of the war, would rather hurt my feelings than tickle my pride whilst I lived. I had rather glide gently down the stream of life, leaving it to posterity to think & say what they please of me, than by an act of mine to have vanity or ostentation imputed to me—And I will furthermore confess that I was rather surprized into a consent, when Doctr Witherspoon (very unexpectedly) made the application, than considered the tendency of that consent. It did not occur to me at that moment, from the manner in which the question was propounded—that no history of my life, without a very great deal of trouble indeed, could be written with the least degree of accuracy—unless recourse was had to me, or to my papers for information—that it would not derive sufficient authenticity without a promulgation of this fact—& that such a promulgation would subject me to the imputation I have just mentioned—which would hurt me the more, as I do not think vanity is a trait of my character.[3]

It is for this reason, & candour obliges me to be explicit, that I shall stipulate against the publication of the memoirs Mr Bowie has in contemplation to give the world, 'till I shou'd see more probability of avoiding the darts which *I think* would be pointed at me on such an occasion; and how far, under these circumstances, it wou'd be worth Mr Bowie's while to spend time which might be more usefully employed in other matters, is with him to consider; as the practicability of doing it efficiently, without having free access to the documents of this War, which must fill the most important pages of the Memoir, & which for the reasons already assigned cannot be admitted at present, also is. If nothing happens more than I at present foresee, I shall be in Philadelphia on or before the first of May; where 'tis probable I may see Mr Bowie & converse further with him on this subject—in the mean while I will thank you for communicating these Sentiments. I am very truly Your affectionate friend & Servt

G: Washington

LB, DLC:GW.

1. Mr. Bowie was John Bowie of Philadelphia. See GW to Witherspoon, 8 Mar. 1785, and Witherspoon to GW, 14 April 1785.

2. See GW to William Gordon, 8 Mar. 1784.

3. It is not known when John Witherspoon approached GW about Bowie's writing his biography, but the two conversed in Philadelphia when GW was there in December 1783. See GW to Witherspoon, 10 Mar. 1784. On 8 Mar. 1785 GW wrote to Witherspoon of "the cursory manner in wch you expressed the wish of Mr Bowie, to write the memoirs of my life," and reported telling, "Mr Bowie, when I saw him at Philada in May last, that I could have no agency towards the publication of any memoirs respecting myself whilst living."

To Nathanael Greene

My Dr Sir,   Mount Vernon 27th March 1784

A few days ago, by the post, on wch of late there seems to be no dependance, I wrote you a few lines expressive of an earnest wish that you could make it convenient to be at the Genl Meeting of the Society of Cincinnati, before you took your departure for South Carolina. I did not then, nor can I now, assign all my reasons for it; but to me it should seem indispensable, that the Meeting in May next should not only be full, but composed of the best abilities of the representation. The temper, of the New England States in particular, respecting this Society, the encreasing jealousies of it, a letter from the Marquis, & other considerations point strongly to wise determinations at this time.[1] If then private interest or convenience withhold the first characters from the Meeting, what may be the consequence?— 'tis easier, & perhaps better to be conceived than told. At any rate a *bare* representation will bring the Society into disrepute, & unfit it perhaps to decide upon the weighty matters which may come before it. besides, these excuses may be offered by one man as well as another, & sure I am none can urge them with more propriety than myself. I would add more, but that I fear this letter will not reach you in time & I am detaining a countryman of yours who has a fair wind, & I know is setting

upon thorns from his eagerness to embrace it.[2] Most sincerely &
Affectionately I am Yrs

G: Washington

LB, DLC:GW; ALS, advertised in October 1988 by Sotheby's catalog no.
5759, item 204, and in Paul C. Richards's catalog no. 235, item 198.

1. GW wrote Greene on 20 March. He is probably referring to Lafayette's
letter of 25 Dec. 1783.

2. The Richards catalog indicates that the foregoing sentence in the ALS
read: "I would add more, but that I fear this letter will not reach you in time,
and because I am detaining a Countryman of yours (who is to be the bearer of
it) with a fair wind, who is in as bad a situation as a man or Jester looks would,
be, from his eagerness to embrace it."

To Thomas Jefferson

Dear Sir,   Mount Vernon 29th Mar. 84

It was not in my power to answer your favor of the 15th by
the last post for the reason then assigned. I wish I may be able
to do it to your satisfaction now, as I again am obliged to pay
attention to other Company (the Governor being gone).

My opinion coincides perfectly with yours respecting the
practicability of an easy, & short communication between the
waters of the Ohio & Potomack, of the advantages of that communication & the preference it has over *all* others, and of the
policy there would be in this State, & Maryland, to adopt &
render it facile. but I confess to you freely, I have no expectation that the public will adopt the measure; for besides the jealousies wch prevail, & the difficulty of proportioning such funds
as may be allotted for the purposes you have mentioned, there
are two others, which in my opinion, will be yet harder to sur-
mount—these are (if I have not imbibed too unfavourable an
opinion of my Countrymen) the impracticability of bringing
the great, & truly wise policy of this measure to their view—and
the difficulty of drawing money from them for such a purpose
if you could do it. for it appears to me, maugre all the sufferings of the public creditors—breach of public faith—and loss
of public reputation—that payment of the taxes which are already laid, will be postponed as long as possible! how then are
we to expect new ones, for purposes more remote?

I am not so disinterested in this matter as you are; but I am made very happy to find a man of discernment and liberality (who has no particular interest in the plan) thinks as I do, who have Lands in that Country the value of which would be enhanced by the adoption of such a scheme.

More than ten years ago I was struck with the importance of it, & dispairing of any aid from the public, I became a principal mover of a Bill to empower a number of subscribers to undertake, at their own expence, (upon conditions which were expressed) the extension of the Navigation from tide water to Wills's Creek (abot 150 Miles) and I devoutly wish that this may not be the only expedient by which it can be effected now. To get this business in motion, I was obliged, even upon *that ground*, to comprehend James River, in order to remove the jealousies which arose from the attempt to extend the Navigation of the Potomack. The plan, however, was in a tolerable train when I set out for Cambridge in 1775, and would have been in an excellent way had it not been for the difficulties which were met with in the Maryland Assembly, from the opposition which was given (according to report) by the Baltimore Merchants, who were alarmed, and perhaps not without cause, at the consequence of water transportation to George Town of the produce which usually came to their market.

The local interest of that place (Baltimore) joined with the short sighted politics, or contracted views of another part of that Assembly, gave Mr Thomas Johnson who was a warm promoter of the Scheme, on the No. side of the River, a great deal of trouble. In this situation things were when I took command of the Army—the War afterwards called Mens attention to different objects—and all the money they could or would raise, were applied to other purposes; but with you, I am satisfied not a moment ought to be lost in recommencing this business; for I *know* the Yorkers will delay no time to remove every obstacle in the way of the other communication, so soon as the Posts at Oswego & Niagara are surrendered; and I shall be mistaken if they do not build Vessels for the Navigation of the Lakes, which will supercede the necessity of coasting on either side.[1]

It appears to me that the Interest & policy of Maryland is proportionably concerned with that of Virginia to remove obstructions and to envite the trade of the Western territory into the channel you have mentioned. You will have frequent

oppertunities of learning the sentiments of the principal characters of that State, respecting this matter, and if you should see
Mr Johnson (formerly Govr of the State) great information may
be derived from him.

How far upon more mature consideration I may depart from
the resolution I had formed of living perfectly at my ease—ex-
empt from all kinds of responsibility, is more than I can, at
present, absolutely determine. The Sums granted—the manner of granting them—the powers—and objects—would merit
consideration. The trouble, if my situation at the time would
permit me to engage in a work of this sort would be set at
naught; & the immense advantages which this Country would
derive from the measure, would be no small stimulus to the undertaking; if that undertaking could be made to comport with
those ideas, & that line of conduct with which I meant to glide
gently down the stream of life; and it did not interfere with any
other plan I might have in contemplation.[2]

I am not less in sentiment with you respecting the impolicy of
this State's grasping at more territory than they are competent
to the Government of. And for the reasons which you assign, I
very much approve of a Meridian from the mouth of the Great
Kanhawa as a convenient and very proper line of seperation.
But I am mistaken if our chief Majestrate will coincide with us
in opinion.

I will not enter upon the subject of Commerce—It has its advantages & disadvantages, but which of them preponderates is
not the question. From Trade our Citizens *will not* be restrained, and therefore it behoves us to place it in the most convenient channels, under proper regulation—freed, *as much as
possible*, from those vices which luxury, the consequence of
wealth and power, naturally introduce.

The inertitude which prevails in Congress—and the non-at-
tendance of its Members, is discouraging to those who are willing & ready to discharge the trust which is reposed in them;
whilst it is disgraceful, in a very high degree, to our Country.
but I beleive the case will never be otherwise so long as that
body persist in their present mode of doing business; and will
hold constant, instead of annual sessions; against the former of
which my mind furnishes me with a variety of arguments, but
not one—in times of peace—in favor of the latter.

Annual Sessions would always produce a full representation and alertness in business—The Delegates after a recess of 8 or 10 Months would meet each other with glad Countenances—they would be complaisant—they would yield to each other as much as the duty they owed their constituents would permit—and they would have oppertunities of becoming better acquainted with the Sentiments of them, & removing their prejudices, during the recess. Men who are always together get tired of each others Company—They throw of the proper restraint—they say and do things which are personally disgusting—this begets opposition—opposition begets faction—& so it goes on till business is impeded, often at a stand. I am sure (having the business prepared by proper Boards or a Committee) an Annual Session of two Months would dispatch more business than is now done in twelve; & this by a full representation of the Union.

Long as this letter is, I intended to have been more full on some of its points, as well as to have touched upon some others; but it is not in my power, as I have been obliged to snatch the moments which have furnished you with this hasty production from Company. With very great esteem & regd I am Dr Sir Yr Most obt & very Hble Servt

Go: Washington

Quære, have you not made the distance from Cuyahoga to New York too great?[3]

ALS, DLC: Jefferson Papers; LB, DLC:GW.

1. A move was afoot as early as 1769 for Maryland and Virginia to have another go at extending the navigation of the Potomac upstream from Georgetown and Alexandria, above the Great Falls. In 1770 GW became one of the leading proponents, on the Virginia side of the river, of the enterprise. See John Semple to GW, 8 Jan. 1770, Thomas Johnson to GW, 18 June 1770, and GW to Johnson, 20 July 1770. In February 1772 GW guided through the Virginia assembly a bill "for opening and extending the navigation of the river Potowmack from Fort Cumberland to tide water" (8 Hening 570–79), and he continued to be active in the affairs of the Potomac River Company until he left for Philadelphia and Boston in 1775. His involvement in the company's affairs may be traced in what survives of his correspondence with the Marylander Thomas Johnson (Johnson to GW, 26 Mar., 10 May 1772, 21 Feb., 28 June 1774, 17, 24 Jan., 25 Feb. 1775, and GW to Johnson, 5 Aug. 1774). For an earlier attempt by Virginians and Marylanders to join forces in making the upper Potomac more navigable, see GW to a Participant in the Potomac River Enterprise, c.1762, and notes, printed above.

2. GW's interest in improving the navigation of the upper Potomac, as Jefferson knew, was both long-standing and intense; but Jefferson's letter of 15 Mar. may have served to focus GW's attention, after his return home from the war, on the urgency of resuming efforts to open up the river. In any case, by the time he got back in early October from his trip to the wilds of Pennsylvania, GW was firmly committed to take immediate action for making the Potomac fully navigable as a part of a larger project to connect it by other streams and short portages to the Ohio River and the Great Lakes. See particularly GW to Benjamin Harrison, 10 October. As his correspondence from October 1784 through January 1785 documents, GW emerged from his short-lived retirement from the public stage to push through the Virginia and Maryland legislatures identical bills for creating the ambitious Potomac River Company, of which he became first president.

3. See Jefferson's letter of 15 March.

From Tench Tilghman

Dear Sir   Baltimore [Md.] 29th March 1784

I was yesterday honored with your Excellency's letter of the 24th and immediately applied to the Gentlemen who have the consignment of the Palatines, to know whether there were any among them answering the description of those you want—I am sorry to inform you there are not. There are no Bricklayers at all—There are Carpenters, but they are of the common kind—I cannot find that any more of these people are expected—The charges of bringing them are so enormous, that the profits are not by any means adequate to the expence—I shall however keep a look out as you desire—A few may come in by chance—I need not say how happy it will ever make me to receive your Excellency's commands, and Mrs Tilghman desires me to say to Mrs Washington, she hopes she will never make the least difficulty of calling upon her for the execution of any Commission in the line of the Ladies. I have the honor to be with true Respect and Esteem Your Excellency's Most Affecte Hble Servt

Tench Tilghman

ALS, PHi: Gratz Collection.

From William Fitzhugh

Dear General   Mount Washington [Md.] March 31st 1784

My delay to congratulate Your Safe return to Mont Vernon, after your long Absence, and the Eniment Services render'd Your Country—proceeded from my fixed Intention to do it personally, at your House soon after your arival there, of which, I recieved from my son Perry the pleaseing inteligence—But a Severe attack of the Gout, with eruptions in my Leg and foot, about the first of January, has confin'd me ever since until a few days ago—Permit me therfore at this late day Jointly with Mrs Fitzhugh, to Congratulate you, your Lady and friends, On the Happy Event—and to offer our warmest wishes for Health, and every other Felicity to you and yours. We still intend, so soon as the Season is favorable to the movement of Invaledes—to indulge ourselves with the Pleasure of Visiting Mont Vernon.[1]

The bearer hereof, Capt. Thomas Trueman Greenfield informs me, That having purchased a lease from a Tenant of yours in Berkley County, you wish'd to know his Character, previous to a confirmation of His Purchase—Capt. Greenfield has resided in Calvert County for many years past, & there commanded a Company of Militia during the War—He is of a reputable family, of good Character and Credit, & I believe may be relyed on as a man of Integrity and punctuallity.[2] My son William, who had the honor to serve in the Southern Army, under the Command of General Greene, was at Pitsburg the 8th of Febry on his way to Kentucki, there to Locate some Lands for himself and to compleat the Business on former Locations of mine—He Expresses an inclination to serve in the Military, If on the Peace Establishment, He can obtain an appointment in Virginia, or Maryland—He was a Lieutenant in the 3d Lt Dragoons—Baylors—& continued in the Service to the end of the War—The favorable testimony of General Green respecting His conduct and Service, Induces Me to recommend Him to your Excellencys Notice, but this is offered only as an introduction to what I shall say when I have the Honor to meet you.[3]

Mrs Fitzhugh Joins with me in respectful Compliments &

best wishes to you, Your Lady & Family. I have the Honor to be with every sentiment of respect & Esteem Your Excellencys Affectionate & Oblig'd Hume Servt

Willm Fitzhugh

ALS, DLC:GW.

Col. William Fitzhugh (1721–1798) of Stafford County, Va., moved to Rousby Hall in Calvert County, Md., shortly after his marriage to Ann Frisby Rousby in 1755. Rousby Hall was burned during the Revolution, and he subsequently lived at Millmont in Calvert County. Mount Washington has not been identified.

1. Capt. Peregrine Fitzhugh (c.1760–1811) was one of GW's aides-de-camp in 1781. His father, Colonel Fitzhugh, was in bad health and his eyesight was failing, but he did visit Mount Vernon on 7–8 April 1785 (see *Diaries*, 115–16).

2. Thomas Trueman Greenfield leased from GW 183 acres adjoining the land of Ralph Wormeley in Berkeley County, Virginia. He secured the lease from Samuel Bailey and paid £10 rent per annum. See Ledger B, 285.

3. William Fitzhugh, Jr. (1761–1839), served as a cornet and lieutenant in the 3d Continental Dragoons, from 1779 to 1783. He settled in Hagerstown, Md., where he remained until 1800 when he moved to Livingston County, New York.

To Elbridge Gerry

Sir,   Mount Vernon 31st Mar. 84.

Your favor of the 18th came to my hands last Week, but not in time to answer it by the last Post.

I have examined my Letter and orderly Books but find no such order as Mr Gridley alludes to, in his letter of the 21st of Feby, to you.

If his Father, or himself ever received such orders they are no doubt to be produced, and will speak for themselves. Mr Gridley never reported himself to the Chief Engineer (Genl Duportail) nor has he ever been returned to me by him, or any Senior Officer in that department that I remember as one of the Corps—in the Service of the United States—It is not in my power therefore, from any recollection I have of the circumstance he speaks of—or of his Services—to certifie anything on which his claim can be founded.[1]

It would give me pleasure, at any time when your leizure and inclination would permit to see you, or any of your Brother delegates at this retreat—being with great esteem Dr Sir Yr Most Obt & Most Hble Servt

Go: Washington

ALS, NN: Bancroft Collection; LB, DLC:GW.

1. Col. Richard Gridley was chief engineer for the Continental army in 1775 and 1776. Thereafter until 1780 he held the title of engineer general of the eastern department. In May 1779 General Duportail became the commandant of the corps of engineers and in November 1781, major general chief engineer. For the identity of Gridley's son, see Gerry to GW, 18 Mar. 1784, n.2. Probably at issue was something related to Gridley's pay as engineer general. See Congress's recommendations to the Massachusetts legislature, 26 Feb. 1781 (*JCC*, 19:197), the letter from Robert Morris read in Congress on 6 Mar. 1783 (ibid., 24:168), and Expenditures for Pensions, 30 Sept. 1785 (DNA:PCC, item 141).

From Thomas Jefferson

Dear Sir   Annapolis [Md.] Mar. 31. 1784.

Your servant delivered me your favor this morning; Capt. Barney is gone to Philadelphia and his vessel to Baltimore, having left with me one of your packages only. the persons who brought this could give me no certain account of the other package which you suppose to have been brought. this your servant now receives.[1]

Being obliged to seize a moment in Congress of writing you these few lines, I can only mention to you that late advices from Europe mention another revolution in the British ministry, Mr Pitt & his friends having resigned. no new ministry was formed. this does not come however authentically. I am with very great respect & esteem Dr Sir Your most obedt & most humble servt

Th: Jefferson

ALS, DLC:GW.

1. See GW to Jefferson, 24 March. GW noted an expenditure of twelve shillings in his cash accounts, 29 Mar., for "Exps. of a Servt to Annapolis" (Ledger B, 197).

To Hugh Williamson

Dr Sir,   Mount Vernon 31st March 1784

The last Post brought me your favor of the 24th[1]—The sentiments I shall deliver in answer to it, must be considered as coming from an individual only; for I am as unacquainted with the opinions, & know as little of the affairs & present management of the Swamp Company, in Virginia, (tho' a Member of it) as you do, perhaps less—as I have received nothing from thence, nor have heard any thing of my interest therein, for more than nine years.[2] I am equally uninformed of the motives which induced the Assembly of Virginia to open a Canal between Kemps, & the No. West Landing; but presume territorial jurisdiction must have been the governing principle.[3]

From an attentive review of the great dismal Swamp (and it was with a critical eye I examined it) I have been long satisfied of the practicability of opening a communication between the rivers which empty into Albemarle Sound (thro' Drummonds Pond) & the waters of Elizabeth or Nansemund Rivers. Once, for the purpose of forming a plan for reclaiming the Lands, more than with a view to the benefit of navigation, I traversed Drummonds pond through its whole circuit; & at a time when it was brim full of water. I lay one night on the east border of it, on ground something above the common level of the Swamp; in the morning I had the curiosity to ramble as far into the Swamp as I could get with convenience, to the distance perhaps of five hundred yards; & found that the water which at the margin of the Lake (after it had exceeded its natural bounds) was stagnant, began perceivably to move Eastward, and at the extent of my walk it had deepen'd—got more into a channel—& had increased obviously in its motion. This discovery left not a doubt in my mind, that that current was descending into one of the rivers of Albemarle Sound. To ascertain it, I directed our Manager to hire persons to explore it Fully; & to the best of my recollection he sometime afterwards informed me, that he had done so—that it was found to be the head of the Northwest river—that to where the water had formed a regular channel of considerable width & depth, did not exceed 4 miles—& that from thence downwards to the present navigation of that river, there was no other obstruction to small craft, than fallen trees. What I have given as coming under my own knowledge, you may rely upon—The other, I as firmly believe, & have no doubt but that the waters of Pequemins & Pasquetank, have a similar, & perhaps as close a connexion with Drummonds Pond as that of the No. West.[4]

My researches, at different times, into, & round this Swamp (for I have encompassed the whole) have enabled me to make the following observations—That the principal rivulets which run into the great dismal, if not all of them, are to the westward of it, from Suffolk southwardly—That Drummonds Pond is the receptacle for all the water which can force its way thro' the reeds, roots, trash & fallen timber (with which the Swamp abounds) into it—That to these obstructions, & the almost perfect level of the Swamp, are to be ascribed the wetness of it. That in wet seasons, when the banks of the pond are overborne by the assemblage of waters from the quarter I have mentioned, it discharges itself with equal difficulty, into the heads of the rivers of Albemarle, Elizabeth & Nansemond; for it is a fact, that the late Colo. Tucker of Norfolk, on a branch of Elizabeth river, & several others on Nansemond river, have Mills which are, or have been worked by the waters which run *out* of the Swamp.

Hence, & from a Canal which the Virginia company opened some years since,[5] I am convinced that there is not a difference of more than two feet between one part of the Swamp and another. That the East side, & south end are lower than their opposites; & that a canal of that depth when the water of Drummonds pond is even with its banks—& more or less in the proportion it rises or sinks, will take the water of it, & with the aid of one Lock, let it into either Elizabeth river, or Nansemond; neither of which, from the best information I have been able to obtain, would exceed six or seven miles. Admitting these things, & I firmly believe in them, the kind of navigation will determine the expence, having due consideration to the difficulty which must be occasioned by the quantity of water, & little fall by which it can be run off.

To attempt in the first instance such a Canal as would admit *any* vessel which the Bay of Albemarle is competent to, would in my opinion be tedious, & attended with an expence which might prove discouraging—whilst one upon a more contracted scale would answer very valuable purposes, & might be enlarged as the practicability of the measure, & the advantages resulting from it should unfold—appropriating the money which shall arise from the Toll, after principal & interest is fully paid, as a fund for the further extension of the navigation, which in my opinion, wou'd be exceedingly practicable, & would be found the readiest & easiest plan to bring it to perfection.

If this method should be adopted, I would very readily join my mite towards the accomplishment—provided the Canal which the State of Virginia is about to cut, should not render it an unnecessary, or unprofitable undertaking[6]—A more extended plan would be too heavy for my purse.

I agree in sentiment with you that whenever the public is disposed to reimburse principal & interest to the corporation & will open a free passage of the Canal, that the charter should cease; but I do not think eight Pr Cent is adequate, I mean sufficiently inviting, nor ten either, unless Governmt, in the act for incorporation, were to guaranty the expence, & be at the final risque of the success—and would have, tho' not an exorbitant, yet a fixed toll, & one which should be judged fully competent to answer the purpose; because it is not less easy than pleasing to reduce it at any time—but it would be found difficult & disgusting, however necessary and urgent, to increase it.[7]

In other respects my opinion differs not from yours, or the propositions you inclosed to Sir, Your Most obedient & very humble Servt

G: Washington

LB, DLC:GW.

1. Letter not found, but see GW to Thomas Walker, 10 April.

2. It was not until 8 April that GW received Thomas Walker's letter of 24 Jan. giving information about the Dismal Swamp Company and calling for a meeting of the stockholders.

3. "An Act for cutting a navigable canal from the waters of Elizabeth river to the waters of North river" (11 Hening 332–34), enacted by the Virginia general assembly in the October 1783 session, appointed trustees, or commissioners, to receive subscriptions for defraying the cost of cutting the canal, to supervise the work, and to receive the tolls that would be collected.

4. GW was a prime mover in the founding and early operation of the Dismal Swamp Company. Between 1763 and 1768 he visited the swamp six times or more. See Dismal Swamp Land Company: Articles of Agreement, 3 Nov. 1763, and notes. A journal of GW's tour of the area in October 1763 is printed in *Diaries*, 1:321–26.

5. This was known as Washington's Ditch and ran from Lake Drummond westward toward the town of Suffolk.

6. See note 3. In 1787, the Virginia legislature passed "An act for cutting a navigable Canal from the waters of Elizabeth river, in this State, to the waters of Pasquotank river, in the State of North Carolina" (12 Hening 478–94), but work on this, undertaken in cooperation with North Carolina, did not begin

until the 1790s, and the canal did not become operational until 1804. See Brown, "Dismal Swamp Canal."

7. The act authorizing the cutting of the Elizabeth River canal provided that tolls could not "annually exceed ten per centum on the amount of the money expended in opening the said canal" (11 Hening 332–34).

From Steuben

Sir   [March 1784]

On my arrival here I received a letter from Major L'Infant an extract of which I have the honor to present Your Excellency.

["]It is with the greatest satisfaction that I announce the success of the Cincinnati in France, the difficulties which it was supposed would attend the introduction of this order (as no foreign Orders are permitted to be worn with the Kings) are surmounted. His Majesty in his Council having decreed that this order shall be worn with the other orders of the Kingdom, willing by this to give to the Americans a proof of the friendship which he wishes to mentain with them.

"There are more wishes in France for the order of the Cincinnati than for that of St Louis."[1]

Major L'Infant proposed to leave France in Feby—so that we may expect him here the latter end of this month or begining of the next.[2] I beg Your Excellency will do me the justice to believe that I retain the most ⟨lively⟩ sense of the many marks of friendship which I have had the honor to receive from you, & especially of those so recently confered. I beg my respectfull Compliments may be offered to Mrs Washington, with the greatest respect I have the honor to be Sir Your Excellency's Obedient Servant

                                                                         Steuben

LS, DLC:GW. Steuben may have written this letter in April. According to the Alexandria (Va.) newspaper, Steuben left Mount Vernon on 17 Mar. after visiting GW, and this letter to GW appears to have been written at the end of his journey.

1. L'Enfant wrote GW on 25 Dec. 1783 about the reception of the Society of the Cincinnati in France and may have written again in January. See L'Enfant to GW, 29 April 1784, n.2.

2. L'Enfant did not leave France until after the middle of March and landed in New York on about 28 April. See letter cited in note 1.

To James Milligan

Sir,   Mount Vernon 1st April 1784

Your favor of the 9th of March came to hand last week. I am perfectly satisfied (from the circumstances you have related) that the charge of £133.16.0 is just—The manner in which you have accounted for it, makes the matter appear quite clear—It was the only channel thro' which I could have received the money unremembered, & it was from that consideration, I suggested the enquiry.[1]

I am obliged by the readiness with wch you adopt the alterations pointed out in my last[2]—& altho' I am unwilling to add to the troubles of your office, I must pray you to examine the warrant on which the charge of 580⁸⁰⁄₉₀ Dollars is placed to my debit. I drew no Warrt while I was in Philada for my own use, except for the balance of the Accot rendered Decr 13th, to wit £217. 16.8.—which amounting to 726¹⁰⁄₉₀ Dollars was credited in the subsequent Account of the 28th of the same month. It's true I drew a Warrant, (and I believe, for I cannot readily come at my Warrt Book, for the identical sum of 580 ⁸⁰⁄₉₀ Dolrs)—but this, if I recollect right was to give two or three months to each of my aids, & to a small party of Dragoons who were then with me. It was done with the consent, & (the mode) by the direction of the Financier: No charge of it was made by me, as will appear by a reference to my Accots—for I presumed the Paymaster General, would debit the persons for whose benefit the warrant was drawn with the respective sums annexed to their names. If however it is necessary that it should appear as an article of charge against me, in your Office, My Accot ought to have credit by these people, & they debited to the amount; as I only follow'd Mr Morris's direction in the business, without deriving any other benefit from the draft than the satisfaction of Servg those whom I knew stood much in need of the money.[3]

You will be so good as to excuse the trouble this alteration will make in your Accots—probably it is the last trouble I shall ever have occasion to give—You will receive at the same time, my thanks for your attention to my business, & the assurances of my being Sir, Your Most obt &c.

                                                    G: Washington

LB, DLC:GW.

1. See GW to Milligan, 18 Feb., n.6, and Milligan to GW, 9 Mar. 1784.

2. See GW to Milligan, 18 Feb., n.4, and Milligan to GW, 9 Mar. 1784.

3. See GW to Milligan, 9 Mar., n.3. There is in GW's papers a document, headed "Pay Office Philadelphia Feby 5th 1784" and signed by Philip Audebert, certifying "that His Excellency General Washington drew the following warrants on the Paymaster General:

"One dated 9th December 1783. for Contingent Expences	751.60
" " 15th ditto 1783 for his Own use	580.80
Dollars	1332.50"

The certificate has this endorsement: "By a letter from the Paymaster Genl to the Comptroller dated Decemr 24th 1783, it appears that his Excellency had transmitted him Vouchers for the Amount of the above warrant for 751⁶⁰/₉₀ Dollars having been paid as follows Vizt to Colo. David Cobb 225, Colo. David Humphreys 180, Colo. Edwd Walker 180, Van Hier's Corp 166.60—751⁶⁰/₉₀.

"These parties being respectively charged by Mr Pierce, The General is not now chargeable with the Amount of that warrant on the settlement now to be made with him—Comptrollers Office Febry: 5th 1784" (DLC:GW). See GW to Robert Morris, 4 Jan. 1784, n.1.

From Benjamin Harrison

My Dear Sir   Rich[mon]d [Va.] Apr. 3d 1784

The enclosed letter from the clerk of the H. Delegates will inform you that the marquess's thanks to the assembly have been presented.[1] The resolution directing the Bust was order'd to be carried into execution by the commercial agent who was soon after dismiss'd from office, it never came to my hands till I sent for it yesterday, I will endeavour to have it comply'd with tho' like other blunders of the assembly it was intended to be executed by their own officers.[2]

I am endeavouring to procure a copy of the tender law, if I obtain it I will forward it by the first safe private opportunity.[3]

Please to present my compliments to your good lady Miss Bassett and her Major let Fanny know her father has had the gout but is getting better.[4] I am Dr Sir your affecte & obed. Servt

Benja. Harrison

ALS, DLC:GW.

1. See Enclosure: John Beckley to Benjamin Harrison.

2. The resolution of the house of delegates of 17 Dec. 1781 reads: "*Resolved, unanimously*, That a bust of the Marquis de La Fayette, be directed to be

made in Paris, of the best marble employed for such purposes, and presented to the Marquis, with the following inscription on it:

"'This bust was voted on the 17th day of December, 1781, by the General Assembly of the State of Virginia, to the Honorable the Marquis de La Fayette, Major General in the service of the United States of America, and late commander in chief of the army of the United States in Virginia, as a lasting monument of his merit, and of their gratitude.'

"*Resolved*, That the commercial agent, be directed to employ a proper person in Paris, to make the above bust" (*House of Delegates Journal, 1781–1785*).

The governor and council received the resignation of the commercial agent David Ross on 2 April 1782.

On 1 Dec. 1784 the house of delegates voted to have two busts of Lafayette made, one to be presented to the city of Paris and the other to "be fixed in such public place at the seat of government [of Virginia] as may hereafter be appointed for the erection of the statue voted by the general assembly to general Washington" (11 Hening 553). Houdon's statue of GW and his bust of Lafayette are both in the rotunda of the Virginia state capitol in Richmond. See GW to Lafayette, 1 Feb. 1784, n.3.

3. GW may have asked Harrison for a copy of the tender law when Harrison was at Mount Vernon in March. See GW to Thomas Jefferson, 24 Mar. 1784, n.1. Harrison was probably referring to "An Act for calling in and funding the paper money of this state" enacted at the November 1781 session (10 Hening 456). The act was continued in the May 1783 session (11 Hening 193–94).

4. Frances ("Fanny") Bassett's "Major" was GW's nephew George Augustine Washington, whom she was to marry in October 1785. Her mother Anna Maria Dandridge Bassett, a sister of Martha Washington and wife of Burwell Bassett, died in 1777. Fanny Bassett was visiting Mount Vernon at this time; in December 1784 she returned to make Mount Vernon her home.

Enclosure
John Beckley to Benjamin Harrison

Sir,   [Richmond, Va.] Friday 2d April 1784.

I do myself the honor to enclose your Excellency a Copy of the resolution of Assembly, voting a Bust in honor of the Marquis Fayette, and to inform you that the Speaker communicated to both Houses of Assembly the Marquis's Letter of acknowledgment[1]—and am, with due respect, Your Excellencys Most obedt & humble servt

John Beckley.

ALS, DLC:GW.

John Beckley (1757–1807) arrived in Virginia from England in 1769 and became the young clerk of the botanist John Clayton. In 1779 Beckley, who already held several public clerkships, became clerk of both the Virginia house of delegates and the Virginia senate. When the first United States Congress met in 1789, it chose John Beckley to be its clerk, a position he held until his death.

1. For references to the Virginia assembly's resolution of 17–18 Dec. 1781, to Lafayette's letter of 8 Sept. 1783, and to other documents relating to the Lafayette bust, see GW to Lafayette, 1 Feb. 1784, n.3.

From Benjamin Walker

My dear General   New York 3d April 1784

Your favor of the 12th of March reached me the day before yesterday.[1]

Walmsley shall be spoke to on the subject you desire, tho' I believe he had no thoughts of returning to Virginia, he has his Wife here, and three or four days ago he informed me that he intended to quit Colo. Smith, with whom he has lived during the Winter, and commence Hair dresser in Town.[2]

I am surprized at your not having received any Answers to the Circular Letters. I kept those for the Eastward of this about a Week after I arrived here, when, finding no better conveyance, I forwarded them by the post;[3] least however any accident should have happend, I wrote yesterday, to the several persons to whom they were addressed, mentioning the purport of them, and desiring to know if they were received and if their Delegates will attend—the inclosed will shew you how far the Society in this State have proceeded.[4]

Our Legislature have been sitting here these three months, and have done little or nothing except the Impost bill (which is horrid imperfect) they have past no bill of any consequence—they had began a bill to raise Troops for their Frontiers, but the two Houses differed as to the Number, and now I believe the matter rests till they hear from their Delegates[5]—they must by this Time have arrived at Congress—Mr DeWitt and Judge Paine—are gone—the latter took it in his head to Preach in Mr Gano's Meeting the Sunday before he sat out—and a Motion was made in the Assembly to chuse another Delegate—as no Minister of the Gospel can hold an Office under our Constitution—but it failed.[6] The chief politics of the day here is whether the Tories shall be sent away or not—I was in hopes these matters would have subsided by degrees—but I see little prospect of it. The Tories have acted the most imprudent part possible—It never could be supposed that Men who during Eight Years have been taught to consider those people as their greatest Enemies, as the murderers of their Friends, and as the worst of people, could drop their resentments in a day, and receive them as their friends, time and a proper conduct on their part could alone work such a change, and this would have done it. If the Tories had kept themselves quiet and not interfered in public Matters, all the liberal and judicious of the Whigs, would have been so far their friends as to have assisted in burying animosities, and in the course of time, when their conduct had proved they might be trusted—they would have shared in the Government with their fellow Citizens: but instead of adopting such a Conduct, they no sooner got over the first impression of fear, than they laid claim to every attention—and very foolishly contested with the Whigs of the Church in the Election of a Rector supporting with all their influence Mr Moore against Mr Provost and such has their conduct continued[7]—the consequence is such as might have been expected—Resentments are rather heightend than decreased, and many of the most liberal of the Whigs, who came in with the most conciliatory disposition, are now their Enemies—it has helped to carry the spirit of Resentment against them into the Legislature, and two bills are going thro the House which if passed, must drive great part of them away.[8]

The Winter here has been exceedingly severe, much more so than in 1780—and the very great number of poor who had flocked from all parts into Town made it extremely distressing—the River was still close at Esopus a few days since, but a Rain we have now must Open it.

When I left Mount Vernon I mentiond my hopes of getting the appointment of Collector or Naval Officer for this port—but I found so many Candidates whose sufferings and large families gave them better claims that I dropped it—Genl Lamb has the appointment—Willet is Sheriff and Mr Benson Clerk of the City and County the best Office—Colonel Smith put in for it but failed—Till I can get into business which is my ultimate determination I have accepted the Governors invitation to be his Secretary[9]—a return of his fever has confined him these few days past to his Room and Mrs Clinton has also been unwell—Washington recovers fast—I beg my respectfull Compliments may be presented to Mrs Washington—and to the rest of the family and that you would believe me, your very obliged and affectte hum. Servt

Ben Walker

ALS, DLC:GW.

1. Letter not found.

2. Philip Walmsley was GW's chief steward in 1782 and 1783. He accompanied GW to Mount Vernon in December 1783 before returning to New York. See Walmsley's receipt, 27 Dec. 1783, DLC:GW. See also James Milligan to GW, 9 Mar., n.3. Colonel Smith is GW's former aide William Stephens Smith.

3. GW wrote Walker on 24 Mar. that he had just learned that Walker was one of Gov. George Clinton's "Family" and complained that he had "obtained no answers yet to the Circular Letters you took with you for New Jersey, New York & New Hampshire." See Circular Letter to the State Societies of the Cincinnati, 1 Jan. 1784, printed above.

4. See Walker to GW, 6 April.

5. The New York legislature, which convened in New York City on 21 Jan., remained in session until 12 May. It did not pass the bill "for raising Troops for garrisoning the Forts on the Frontiers of this State." See *Journal of the Assembly of the State of New-York, at Their First Meeting of the Seventh Session*, 2 April 1784, p. 106. See also Henry Knox, 26 July 1784, n.1.

6. The legislature of New York on 3 Feb. 1784 elected five men to represent the state in Congress. Only two attended: Ephraim Paine produced his credentials in Annapolis on 25 Mar., and Charles DeWitt did so two days later. When Paine was a member of the New York senate in 1782, Alexander Hamilton described him as "a man of strong natural parts and as strong prejudice." Hamilton also said of Paine: "his zeal is fiery, his obstinacy unconquerable. He is as primitive in his notions, as in his appearance. Without Education, he wants more knowledge, or more tractableness" (Hamilton to Robert Morris, 13 Aug. 1782, in Syrett, *Hamilton Papers*, 3:139). Charles DeWitt, of Ulster County, was one of the "popular Whigs" in New York politics. John Gano (1727–1804), a clergyman who in 1762 became pastor of the Baptist church in New York City, was a military chaplain during the Revolution but returned to his New York church at the end of the war and remained there until emigrating to Kentucky in 1788.

7. Samuel Provoost (1743–1815), from 1766 to 1771, and Benjamin Moore (1748–1818), from 1775 to 1783, were assistant rectors of Trinity Church in New York City. Provoost supported the American cause in the Revolution while Moore remained loyal to Britain. In 1783, shortly before the British evacuation of the city, Moore was made rector of Trinity Church. Early in 1784, after the evacuation, the vestry removed Moore and elected Provoost. Provoost soon thereafter became the first Episcopal bishop of New York state, and Moore became the second bishop after Provoost's resignation in 1801.

8. The New York assembly passed on 27 Mar. "An Act for the immediate Sale of certain forfeited Estates," which the council of revision rejected. At the end of the session the house passed, over the objection of the council of revision, a senate bill entitled "An Act for the Speedy sale of the confiscated and forfeited Estates. . . ." The other bill Walker is referring to was first entitled "An Act declaratory of Citizenship, and for the Naturalization of Foreigners." On 8 April the bill became "An Act declaring Descriptions of Persons without the Protection of the Laws of this State. . . ." The house finally passed this bill on the last day of the session, over the rejection of the council of revision, under the title "An Act to preserve the Freedom and Independence of this State . . ." (*Journal of the Assembly of the State of New-York, at Their First Meeting of the Seventh Session*, pp. 93, 115–16, 166–67).

9. General Lamb was the old Revolutionary John Lamb (1735–1800) who was brevetted brigadier general in 1783. He received GW's appointment in 1789 to continue as collector of customs in New York under the new government. Marinus Willett (1740–1830) served as sheriff of New York City and county until 1788. Egbert Benson also was attorney general of the state, from 1777 to 1787.

To Duportail

Dear Sir,   Mount Vernon 4th April 1784

At present I can do no more than snatch a moment to acknowledge (by Monsr Le Compte de laval, who is going immediately to Paris & gave me the honor of a call as he travelled from Charles town to New York)[1] the receipt of your letter of the 24th of Decr—to thank you for your kind remembrance of me—& to assure you that it will always give me great pleasure to hear from, or to see you in America.

Matters in this Country, since you left it, remain *nearly* in statu quo. It is said however, a more liberal sentiment is taking place in those States which were most opposed to commutation,[2] & the other interests of the army—& that the impost, which has laboured so long in them, will certainly pass this Spring—this will be a principal move towards restoring public credit, & raising our sinking reputation. More competent powers it is thought will also be vested, in a little time, in Congress— & that all things will come right after the people *feel* the inconveniences wch they might have avoided if they had not been too fond of judging for themselves.

I have only news paper Accts of the Air Balloons, to which I do not know what credence to give; as the tales related of them are marvelous, & lead us to expect that our friends at Paris, in a little time, will come flying thro' the air, instead ploughing the Ocean to get to America.[3]

Present me affectionately to Gouvernieur[4] (from whom I recd a letter just at his departure from Philada)—tell him he shall always have a first place in my esteem, & that whatever contributes to his happiness or interest will give me pleasure. With great esteem & regard I am Dr Sir Your most obedt & very humble Servt

G: Washington

LB, DLC:GW.

1. See GW to Thomas Mifflin, this date.

2. At the end of the Revolutionary War, there was a great deal of agitation among officers of the Continental army for Congress to grant them at the time of their separation from the army either half-pay for life or a lump sum payment, called commutation.

3. See Duportail to GW, 3 Mar. 1784, n.1.

4. The chevalier Jean-Baptiste de Gouvion, like Duportail a highly respected French engineer, came to America with Lafayette in 1777 and rose to the rank of colonel in the Continental army before resigning his commission in October 1783 to return to France. Gouvion's letter is dated 4 Nov. 1783.

Letter not found: from Henry Knox, 4 April 1784. On 12 April Knox wrote to GW: "I wrote your Excellency on the 4th of this month."

To Lafayette

My Dr Marqs—   Mount Vernon 4th April 1784.

I have no expectation, that this Letter will find you in France. Your favor of Novr to me, & of Decr to Congress, both announce your intention of making us a visit this Spring.[1] On this hope I shall fully rely, & shall ardently long for the moment in which I can embrace you in America. Nothing could add more to the pleasure of this interview than the happiness of seeing Madame la Fayette with you, that I might have the honor of thanking her in person for the flattering letter she has been pleased to write to me; and to assure her of the sincerity of my wishes, & those of Mrs Washington; that she wou'd make Mount Vernon her home, while she stays in America.[2]

Lest I should be disappointed of this gratification, I accompany this letter with another to the Marchioness; & if I could express to her half what I feel upon the occasion it would, if *twenty years* could be taken from the number of my days, make you diligent at your *Post*—Adieu—it is unnecessary to tell you how much I am Yours &a &ca

G: Washington

P.S. I have received the plate, you were so obliging as to send me by Captain Barney; and thank you for your great attention to my request though I endeavoured to countermand it. I shall be at Philada the first of May, when & where, I will buy a Bill, & remit you for the cost of it.[3]

G. W——n

LB, DLC:GW.

1. On 11 Nov. 1783 Lafayette wrote that it was "Certain I shall in a few Months Embrace My dear General, Spend with Him the Spring and Summer" (Idzerda, *Lafayette Papers*, 5 : 162–65).

2. Writing to his wife from Mount Vernon on 20 Aug. 1784, Lafayette told of his reunion three days before with his "dear general" and described the life that GW and his family were leading at Mount Vernon. "I have been asked," he said, "to send the fondest regards from the whole household, and Mrs. Washington was saying the other day that since they were both old, we must not defer the pleasure they would have in entertaining you and our whole little family here. On my earlier trip, my dear heart, I made the most solemn promise to bring you with me" (ibid., 237–38).

3. For GW's dealings with Lafayette regarding silverware, see especially Lafayette to GW, 10 Jan., n.1, GW to Lafayette, 1 Feb., and to Joshua Barney, 24 Mar. 1784. When Lafayette was at Mount Vernon in the late summer of 1784, GW paid him £129.7.6, "to Discharge 2 Accts for Plated Ware Amountg to 2214 livres" (Ledger B, 199).

To Adrienne, Marquise de Lafayette

Madam,   Mount Vernon 4th April 1784

It is now, more than ever, I want words to express the sensibility & gratitude with which the honor of your felicitations of the 26th of Decr has inspired me. If my expression was equal to the feelings of my heart the homage I am about to render you, would appear in a more favourable point of view, than my most sanguine expectations will encourage me to hope for. I am more inclined therefore to rely upon the continuence of your indulgent sentiments of me, & that innate goodness for which you are remarked—than upon any merit I possess, or any assurances I could give of my sense of the obligation I am under for the honor you have conferred upon me by your correspondence.

Great as your claim is, as a French, or American woman; or as the wife of my amiable friend, to my affectionate regards;[1] you have others to which the palm must be yielded. The charms of your person, & the beauties of your mind, have a more powerful operation—These Madam, have endeared you to me, & every thing which partakes of your nature will have a claim to my affections—George & Virginia (the offspring of your love), whose names do honor to my Country, & to myself, have a double claim & will be the objects of my vows.

From the clangor of arms & the bustle of a camp—freed from the cares of public employment, & the responsibility of Office—I am now enjoying domestic ease under the shadow of my own Vine, & my own Fig tree; & in a small Villa, with the implements of Husbandry & Lambkins around me, I expect to glide gently down the stream of life, 'till I am emtombed in the dreary mansions of my Fathers.

Mrs Washington is highly honored by your participations, & feels very sensibly the force of your polite invitation to Paris; but she is too far advanced in life, & is too much immersed in the care of her little progeny to cross the Atlantic.[2] This my Dr Marchioness (indulge me with this freedom) is not the case with you. You have youth (& if you should not incline to bring your children, can leave them with all the advantages to Education)—and *must* have a curiosity to see the Country, young, rude & uncultivated as it is; for the liberties of which your husband has fought, bled, & acquired much glory—Where every body admires, every body loves him—Come them, let me entreat it, & call my Cottage your home; for your own doors do not open to you with more readiness, than mine wou'd. You will see the plain manner in which we live; & meet the rustic civility, & you shall taste the simplicity of rural life—It will diversify the Scene & may give you a higher relish for the gaieties of the Court, when you return to Versailles. In these wishes, & in most respectful compliments Mrs Washington joins me. With sentiments of strong attachment, & very great regard I have the honor to be Madam Your most obedt & much obliged Servt

G: Washington

LB, DLC:GW.

1. In her letter to GW of 26 Dec. 1783, the marquise de Lafayette, "as a french as an american woman, as the wife of mr De la fayette," declared she shared in "the public joy" at GW's achieving a glorious peace (NIC: Department of Rare Books).

2. The marquise had written in her letter to GW of her "hope to see you both, in our Country, and to go and see you in america."

To Thomas Mifflin

Sir,   Mount Vernon 4th Apl 1784.

I take the liberty of introducing to your Excellency's civilities and attention, the Count de Laval Montmorency, Brother to the Duke de Laval, & Colonel in the Regiment of Royal Auvergne.[1]

This Gentleman is on a tour from Charles Town[2] to New York, where he proposes to embark for Europe.[3] His noble family, & personal merit, stand in need of no recommendation; but I could not with hold this testimony of my respect for him. I have the honor to be Yr Excellency's Most Obt & Most Hble Servt

Go: Washington

ALS, ViMtV.

1. Mathieu-Paul-Louis de Montmorency, vicomte (*puis* duc) de Laval (1748–1817), whose father Guy-André-Pierre, duc de Laval (1728–1798), maréchal de France in 1783, was himself the brother of Anne-Alexandre-Marie-Sulpice de Montmorency-Laval, marquis (*puis* duc) de Laval (1747–1817), the colonel of the régiment de Bourbonnais in Rochambeau's American army. His son Mathieu-Jean-Félicité de Montmorency-Laval was wounded in 1781 while serving in Destouches's squadron in the Chesapeake.

2. Benjamin Guerard (c.1733–1788), governor of South Carolina from 1783 to 1785, wrote GW from "Government House Charleston South Carolina" on 3 Mar. 1784: "I have the honor of addressing this to You by the particular wish & request of its noble Bearer Monsieur le Vicomte de Monmorency Laval Colonel Regiment d'Auvergne &c. who lately arrived here from Cape François to take the Tour of America accompanied by Monsieur le Marquis de Fontenille Colo. of Infantry in the Service of France as his travelling Companion. I hope that You will pardon the freedom which I shou'd not have presumed was it not proper and the Vicomte desirous from the Letter of recommendation he brought me of being mentioned by me to a Commander in Chief under whose Auspices his noble Brother the Duke has served" (LS, DLC:GW).

Fontenille was Pierre-Paul-Louis de La Roche, marquis de Fontenille (1757–1833), who served under d'Estaing as a captain in the régiment de Gätinais at the siege of Savannah in 1778. See Fontenille to GW, 20 Nov. 1784.

3. See Laval de Montmorency to GW, 27 April 1784. He wrote from New York saying he was sailing the next day.

To Jonathan Trumbull, Jr.

My dear Sir,   Mount Vernon 4th April 1784

The choice of your delegates to the General Meeting of the Cincinnati gave me pleasure, & I wish very sincerely that you would *all* attend;—Let me impress this upon you, with a request that you would impress it upon your Brothers of the delegation.[1]

This meeting, taking into consideration the prejudices and jealousies which have arisen, should not only be respectable in numbers, but respectable in abilities—Our measures should be deliberate & wise—If we cannot convince the people that their fears are ill-founded we should (at least in a degree) yield to them and not suffer that which was intended for the best of purposes to produce a bad one which will be the consequence of divisions proceeding from an opposition to the currt opinion, if the fact is so in the Eastern States, as *some* have reported. Independant of this there are other matters which call for attention at the ensuing meeting.

You will oblige me by having the enclosed advertisement inserted twice, (& as soon as convenient) in a Gazette of your State—The one which is most diffused among that class of people whose views it is most likely to meet will answer my purposes best.[2] Know the cost & I will pay it when we meet— Present my best regards to your good Father, whether in, or out of Office. Mrs Washington joins in best wishes for you & Mrs Trumbull[3] with Dr Sir Yr Most Obedt & Affecte Hble Servt

Go: Washington

ALS, NN: Emmet Collection; LB, DLC:GW.

1. Of the five men elected delegates, only Trumbull and David Humphreys attended the general meeting of the Society of the Cincinnati in Philadelphia in May. See Humphreys to GW, 20 Mar. 1784.

2. See GW's Advertisement, 10 Mar. 1784, in which he sets out conditions for leasing sections of his western lands.

3. Trumbull and his wife, Eunice Backus Trumbull, were married in March 1767.

From John Augustine Washington

Bushfield [Westmoreland County, Va.]

My dear Brother   4th Apl 1784

I had flattered myself long before this to have paid my respects to you at Mt Vernon, and some time in this Month my Family intended a Visit—but many things have hapned to prevent the execucion of my plan heatherto—first the Frost which continued very late, & when the weather was brakeing up a little, we got the Melancholy Acct of the untimely death of my Son Augustine, whose loss affected me a gooddeal, as I had entertain'd very high expectations from him, he had nearly finished his Education, was bless with abilities, to quallify him for any of the Learned Professions—and possesed as sweet a disposicion as ever a Youth did, I intended this fall or at the farthest next spring to have sent him to Edinborough to study Phisick[1]—I wish to God Mrs Washington could have borne this loss as well as myself—but the shock was too great for her infirm frame to bear with any tolorable fortitude, upon the first communication she fell into a Strong Convulsion which continued for some time, and when that went of, she lay for near four hours in a state of insencibility, when her reason returnd, her grief did also and she had a return of the Fit. she is now in a very low state both of Boddy and mind, I thought that the most likely way to quiet her mind, was to get her Children about her, Corbin has been down some time, and as soon as Potomack opened I wrote to Bushrod to come as far as Baltimore in the Stage where I would have horses sent (after allowing as many days as I thought it would take for my letters to reach him and for him to get to that place)[2]—my Servant and horses have been gone of three weeks this day, & I can hear nothing of them which has induced me to send of another messenger to inquire after the first. I was about 10 days past attacked with the Gout the Fit I believe has been slight, tho for part of the time it was with difficulty I could hobble across the Floor with the assistance of Crutches, at present my foot is easy, but I am not able to ware either Shoe or Boot—should Bushrod return shortly, as soon as he has spent some days with his Mama and recovered from the fatigue of his Journey, he and Corbin and my Self will do ourselves the pleasure of waitg on you, unless I should hear that you are gone to the northward, I think I have been informed you intended to Philadelphia this Month—if you do go, I should be happy to get information at Hooes Ferry or Mr Laur[enc]e Washingtons as I will regulate my comeing accordingly.[3]

I most sincerely congratulate you, on the suckcess that has attended your unw[e]aryed diligence for 8 Years past, and on yr retirement to domestic happiness—that you may long injoy good health and every blessing this world can affourd is my most ardent wish in which Mrs Washington most cordially joins me, as also in our Love and best wishes to my Sister—I am with every Sentimen of true Affection My dear Brother Sincerely Yours

John Auge Washington

ALS, PHi: Gratz Collection.

GW's favorite brother John Augustine Washington (1736–1787) lived at Bushfield.

1. George Augustine Washington, born in 1767, was the youngest of John Augustine Washington's three sons. On 16 Feb. 1784 the father wrote his oldest son Bushrod Washington (1762–1829), who was studying law in Philadelphia: "before this reaches you, you may have heard of the untimely and accidental death of yr poor Brother Augustine—a young Man at Delemans Academy trifling with a loaded gun ⟨she⟩ went of[f], and yr Brother setting before the fire recd the whole load in his breast of which he expired in a few minutes, this Acct was transmited [to] us by express on the 11th inst." (DLC: Bushrod Washington Papers). Hannah Bushrod Washington was the mother of the slain youth.

2. Corbin Washington (c.1765–c.1799) soon after this settled on Walnut Farm, originally a part of his father's Bushfield plantation. In 1787 he married Hannah Lee (1766–c.1801), daughter of Richard Henry Lee. John Augustine and Hannah Washington also had two daughters: Jane (1759–1791), the wife of William Augustine Washington (1757–1810), who was the son of GW's half brother Augustine Washington (1720–1762), lived at Blenheim in Westmoreland County; and the younger daughter Mildred Washington (b. 1760), who later married Thomas Lee (1758–1805), son of Richard Henry Lee, probably was living at home at this time.

3. John Augustine Washington was at Mount Vernon in early June. See GW to John Augustine Washington, 30 June. See also John Augustine Washington to GW, c.24 July. Hooe's ferry crossed the Potomac at Cedar Point. He

here is probably referring to Lawrence Washington (1728–c.1809) of Chotank; both the ferry and the Chotank area lay between Mount Vernon and Bushfield. In the McKay catalog no. 2723, there is listed as item 696 a letter from GW to John Augustine Washington dated 27 Mar. 1784.

From Rufus Putnam

Dear sir   Rutland [Mass.] April the 5th 1784

Being unavoidably prevented from attending the General meeting of the Cincinnati, at Philadelphia as I had intended; and where I once more expected the oppertunity in person to pay my respects to your Excellency: I cannot deny my self the honnor, of addressing you by letter; to acknowledge with gratitude the ten thousand obligations I feal my self under to your goodness, and most sincearly congratulate you on your return to Domestic happiness; to enquire after your health and wish the best of heavens blessings may attend you & your Dear Lady.

the settelment of the Ohio country engross[e]s many of my thoughts, and much of my time sence I left Camp has been Imployed in, informing my self and others, with respect to the nature, situation and circumstances of that country, and the practability of removeing our selves there: and if I am to form an opinion, from what I have seen and heard on the subject; there are thousands in this quarter will emigrate to that country, as soon as the honorable Congress, make provision for granting lands there and locations and settelments can be made with safety; unless such provision be too long delayed: I mean till necessity turns their views another way, which is the case with some already and must soon be the case with many more.

you are Sensible of the necessity as well as the propriety of both officers and soldiers, fixing them selves in business some where as soon as posable, especially as many of them are unable to lie long on their Oars, waiting the desition of Congress on our petition,[1] and therefore must unavoidably fix themselves in some other quarter, which when once don the Idea of removeing to the ohio country will probably be at an end with respect to most of them. besides the Commonwelth of Massachusetts have come to a resolution to sell their eastern country for public securities, and should their plan be formed and their proposition be made public before we hear any thing from Congress

respecting our petition, and the terms on which the lands petitioned for are to be obtained, it will undoubtedly opperate
much against the ohio scheme.[2]

from these circumstances and many others that might be
mentioned we are growing very Impatient to hear what our
prospects are.[3] among others who have agreed to accompany
me to the ohio the moment the way is open, are Brigdear Genl
Tupper[4] Lt Colo. Oliver[5] and Major Ashley.[6]

I should have hinted these things to some members of Congress but the Delegates from Massachusett, althoe exceeding
worthy men and in general would wish to promote the Ohio
settlement, yet if it should militate with the perticuler intrest of
this state by dreaning her of Inhabitants, especially at a time
when she is forming the plan of setteling the eastern country, I
doubt if they would be very warm advocates in our favor, and I
dare not trust my self with any of the New york Delegates because that goverment, are inviteing the eastern people to settle
in that state, and as to the Delegates from the other states I have
no acquantence with any of them.

these circumstances must apologize for my troubeling your
Excellency on this subject and requesting the favor of a line to
inform us, what the prospects are with respect to our petition
and what measures have been already, or are likely to be taken
with reguard to the ohio country.

I shall take it as a perticuler favor, sir if you will be Kind
enough to recommend some carractor in Congress acquainted
with, and attached to the ohio cause with whome I may presume to open a corrispondence.[7] I have the Honnor to be sir
with the highest respect your Excellency's Humble Servent

                                        Rufus Putnam

ALS, DLC:GW; ADfS, OMC: Papers of Rufus Putnam. Putnam sent this let-
ter to Henry Knox for Knox to take to Philadelphia and give to GW at the
Cincinnati meeting (Putnam to Knox, 10 April 1784, MHi: Knox Papers).
Knox did not give the letter to GW until shortly before GW's departure from
Philadelphia on 18 May (see GW to Putnam, 2 June).

Rufus Putnam (1738–1824), a colonel of engineers in the Continental
army during the Revolutionary War, became interested in western lands
while farming in Massachusetts before the war. In 1773 he was a member of
an expedition that went to search for lands on the Mississippi River. Congress
failed to act in 1784 on the officers' petition regarding the Ohio country (see

note 1), but in 1785 it made Putnam the surveyor of western lands. The next year Putnam organized the Ohio Company. After becoming the superintendent of the proposed Ohio colony in 1787, he went out in the following spring with the first party that settled at Marietta. GW in 1792 made Putnam a brigadier general to treat with the Indians and in 1794 appointed him surveyor general of the United States, a post that Putnam held until his dismissal by President Jefferson in 1803.

1. The petition to Congress dated 16 June 1783 and signed by nearly three hundred army officers, mostly from Massachusetts and New Hampshire regiments, asked for land, in the Miami country between the Ohio and Lake Erie, under the terms of Congress's proclamation of 20 Sept. 1776. For the petition, see DNA:PCC, item 42.

2. At the end of the war, Massachusetts turned to the selling of land in the District of Maine as a substitute for taxation. On 22 Mar. 1784 a committee of the General Court presented a comprehensive plan for laying out townships between the Penobscot and the St. Croix, the land that was to be sold. In July the legislature ordered that the townships be laid out and surveyed, and when this proceeded too slowly, it appointed Rufus Putnam surveyor, in November 1785. See Allis, *William Bingham's Maine Lands*, 25–27.

3. In his draft Putnam begins this paragraph: "Another reason why we wish to know as Soon as posa⟨ble⟩ what the intentions of Congress are respecting our petition is the effect Such knowledge will probably ⟨have⟩ on the Credit of the Certificates we have recived ⟨on⟩ Settlement of accounts those Securities are now Selli⟨ng⟩ at no more then 3/6 & 4/ on the pound, which in all probability might double if nomore the moment it was known that Goverment would recive them for lands in the ohio Country. from these circu⟨ms⟩tances."

4. Benjamin Tupper (1738–1792), an officer in the Massachusetts forces throughout the Revolution, was brevetted brigadier general in 1783. He was born in Stoughton, Mass., and died in Marietta, Ohio. Tupper was one of the organizers of the Ohio Company in 1785.

5. Robert Oliver (1738–1810), a lieutenant of a company of minutemen in April 1775, served until November 1783, when he retired as brevet lieutenant colonel of the 2d Massachusetts Regiment. He was born in Boston and died in Marietta, Ohio. Oliver was active in the affairs of the Ohio Company from its inception, becoming president in 1801.

6. Moses Ashley (1731–1791), a native of Stockbridge, Mass., served as a lieutenant in the Battle of Lexington in April 1775 and thereafter served in the Continental and Massachusetts forces until he retired on 12 June 1783 as major of the 6th Massachusetts Regiment.

7. See GW to Putnam, 2 June 1784.

From Edmund Clegg

At Thomas Francis: 2d street near Market street.
May it please Your Excellency   Philadelphia April 6 1784
I took the liberty to Address a Note to you when in this City, on the Subject of my Scheme, to establish the Weaving Manufactories of British Goods in these States[1]—I am happy to find the plan may be executed with greater Success than I did at first expect—I have got some Looms to Work & some Machines for Spining, and the Assembly have partly determin'd to Support the Undertaking—That is a Committe has been Appointed to Consider the Matter—and have brought in their Report to Assist with £400 Curency for 7 years, Intrest free[2]—I mean to do every thing in my power to render this Country Independant of Europe for Manufactured Goods in my Line, & if powerfull exertions were made I really think in 7 Years this might be accomplished—nor Need I say to You how much political Good would accrue thereby to these States—But I am of Opinion that only a very few in this State have a true Idea of the Effects of Such a scheme being executed—some of the Members told me as much, & desired my thoughts in Writing which I laid before the House and it was much approved of—and produced the above Mentioned Report, which was not Confirm'd by the House, being deferr'd 'till next Session—cheifly owing to the Warm disputes which arose upon a Bill for Emitting a Paper Currency.[3]

As I esteem the Proposed aid inadequate to a Spirited push to Effect my design I hope you'll pardon my freedom in sending You this Letter The object of which is to know if a more suitable support would be given under Your patronage.

If you honor me with Your reply please Inform me at what price Cacoons may be had per pound from the silk Worm & in what Quantities they might be had—I am—Hond sir Your Excellencys most obedient & very Humble sert

Edmund Clegg

ALS, DLC:GW.

1. The "Note" from Clegg to GW, presumably written when GW was in Philadelphia in December 1783, has not been found, nor has any response from GW.

2. The Pennsylvania house on 29 Jan. 1784 received and read "A petition from *Edmund Clegg*, late of the kingdom of *Great-Britain*, setting forth,

that the petitioner is a manufacturer of the wares of *Manchester*, and *Spit-talfields*, and proposing a plan for the establishing a manufacture of corduroys and fine jeans, to be carried on by the petitioner; therefore praying the encouragement of the House" (*Minutes of the Pennsylvania Assembly*). It was ordered that the petition "lie on the table." The petition was read a second time on 6 Mar. and referred to a committee of three who reported on 15 March.

3. The Pennsylvania house debated the proposed "Act for erecting and opening a Loan-office, and for emitting the sum of fifty thousand pounds in bills of credit . . ." on the last two days of the session, 31 Mar. and 1 April 1784 (ibid.). It voted to print the bill for public consideration.

To William Hamilton

Sir,   Mount Vernon 6th April 1784
I have been favored with your letter of the 20th of Feb. & pray you to accept my thanks for the information contained in it.

I expect to be in Phila. the first of May, but if, in the meanwhile, you should be perfectly satisfied of the skill of Mr Turner and the efficiency of his work you would add to the favor already conferred on me by desiring him not to be engaged further than to yourself until I see him.

I have a large room which I intend to finish in Stucco & Plaister of Paris—besides this I have a Piazza in front of my House (open & exposed to the weather) of 100 feet by 12 or 14 which I want to give a Floor to of stone or a cement which will be proof against wet & frost[1]—and I am, as you were, plagued with leaks at a Cupulo &ca which requires a skilful artist to stop. These, altogether, would afford Mr Turner a good job, whilst the proper execution of them would render me an acceptable Service. I have the honor to be Sir Yr Most Obedt Hble Servt
Go: Washington

ALS, PWacD: Sol Feinstone Collection, on deposit PPAmP; LB, DLC:GW.
1. For references to some of the correspondence GW had about the flooring of his piazza at Mount Vernon, see GW to Hamilton, 15 Jan. 1784, n.1.

From Thomas Jefferson

Dear Sir   Annapolis [Md.] Apr. 6. 1784.
I am obliged to you for your query as to the distance from New York to Cayahoga, as it has occasioned my reexamination

of that matter & detection of an error of 150 miles. the distances from New York to Niagara I collect from information as follows.

from N. York to Albany	164 miles
Oneida	165
Oswego	171
Niagara	180
	680
from Niagara to Cayahoga	140
	820

This last distance [from Niagara to Cayahoga] I collect by measuring on Hutchins's map & reducing that proportionably by the known distance from Niagara to Detroit which is 250 miles.[1]

The public papers confirm the resignation of mr Pitt & his friends. a ship arrived here, & some others in Philadelphia have brought us a riddle without a key. they received their bounties & drawbacks on clearing out from London as they used to do while we were colonies without any public act authorising it being visible. the custom house officers tendered them, & they were not so rude as to refuse them. the prohibitory proclamation they say is eluded & connived at by government.[2] we have 11 states in Congress & hope by the middle of May to adjourn to November. if any thing prevents this it will be the representation of 8 states of the 11 by 2 members each, who frequently dividing retard business extremely. the inclosed letter was put into my hands with a request to forward it to you. this will be delivered you by Monsr de Hogendorff, a relation of mr Van Berckel's. a very particular acquaintance with him here has led me to consider him as the best informed man of his age I have ever seen. nature & application seem equally to have concurred in fitting him for important business. he returns to Holland, his native country, in the summer, and cannot deny himself the satisfaction of paying his tribute of respect to you.[3] I have the honor to be with great esteem & attachment Dr Sir your most obedt & most humble servt

Th: Jefferson

P.S. The Minister of France arrived here to-day. I beleive he is on a tour through Virginia. but I have not yet learned when he sets out.

Since writing this I learn that the Minister has declined his tour through Virginia, but thinks to go as far as your house: perhaps within a fortnight.[4]

ALS, DLC:GW.

1. In his letter to GW of 15 Mar., Jefferson wrote that "to proceed on to N. York" from Cuyahoga would be 970 miles, and in a postscript to his letter of 29 Mar., GW asked Jefferson had he not made the distance "too great." Jefferson is referring to Thomas Hutchins's *A Topographical Description of Virginia, Pennsylvania, Maryland, and North Carolina* (London, 1778).

2. In the spring of 1783, the Fox-North ministry began its efforts to reestablish Britain's trade with its former American colonies in a series of orders relaxing the restraints placed upon that trade in 1775 by Parliament's Prohibitory Act. An order in council of 26 Dec. 1783 summed up what had been done to admit items from the United States at lowered duties and also listed additional items. William Pitt the Younger became prime minister on 19 Dec. 1783 at the age of 25.

3. Gijsbert Karel van Hogendorp (1762–1834), a 21-year-old Dutchman, landed in Boston in November 1783 and sailed from there back to Holland in July 1784. His purpose in coming to America was to study the republic, or republics, being formed in the New World. He arrived at Mount Vernon on 8 April (see GW to Jefferson, that day) and was back at Annapolis no later than 17 April (Boyd, *Jefferson Papers*, 7:82). For a sketch of Hogendorp's life and for references to his writings, see Howard C. Rice's introduction to Hogendorp's *The College at Princetown, May 1784* (Princeton, N.J., 1949).

4. La Luzerne came to Mount Vernon before GW left for Philadelphia on 26 April. See GW to La Luzerne, 5 May 1784.

From William Moultrie

Sir   Charleston South Carolina April 6th 1784

By comparing the date of the Letter with which you honored me as Senior officer in the state of South Carolina,[1] with the Period of Colonel Morris's arrival at Philadelphia it appears that the Dispatches from the Society of the Cincinnati of this State, with which he was charged came unfortunately too late to anticipate your Excellencys Enquiry concerning the Measures taken to Establish the society in South Carolina.[2]

The Dispatches alluded to have I hope removed every Degree of uncertainty on this Head, and I take the Liberty of enclosing herewith the proceedings of this Society from its formation to the last meeting.[3]

I have also to acknowledge the receipt of Your Excellency's circular letter of the 1st of January last, and in conformity thereto, The Delegates to represent this Society in the General Society are required to appear in the City of Philadelphia on the first Monday in May next—for which purpose Lieut. Colo. Washington has already sett out, and Colo. White will shortly follow—Lieut. Colo. Morris & Captn Turner, I am in hopes are in Philadelphia[4] therefore persuade myself that the Society of this State will be fully represented on the Meeting of the General society. I have the Honor to be with the greatest respect and Esteem Your Excellency's Obt servt

Willm Moultrie

LS, DSoCi. The letter appears to be in the hand of John Sanford Dart, the secretary of the South Carolina chapter of the Society of the Cincinnati. It is identified as a letter from John Allison in Hume, *Society of the Cincinnati*, 29–30.

After its successful defense of Charleston in June 1776, William Moultrie's South Carolina regiment became a part of the Continental line and Moultrie (1730–1805) himself was made brigadier general. He was captured at the fall of Charleston in 1780, and in 1782 he was exchanged for Gen. John Burgoyne and promoted to major general. At this time, in 1784, Moultrie was a member of the South Carolina house of representatives and president of the state Society of the Cincinnati. The next year he was elected governor of South Carolina.

1. GW sent a circular letter dated 24 Oct. 1783 to the "Senior Officer in each of the Southern States," asking that they inform him as president of the Society of the Cincinnati "whether the Establishment has taken place in your State, and what measures have been taken to effect it" (Fitzpatrick, *Writings of Washington*, 27:207–8).

2. Lewis Morris, Jr. (d. 1824), son of Lewis Morris (1726–1798), who was a signer of the Declaration of Independence for New York, went to South Carolina late in 1780 as brevet lieutenant colonel in the Continental army and aide-de-camp to Gen. Nathanael Greene. In 1783 he married Ann Barnett Elliott, daughter of William Elliott (1696–1766) of Charleston. Morris remained in Charleston after the war and became active in state politics in the 1790s as a Federalist.

3. The enclosures (SoCi) are copies of the proceedings of the South Carolina Society of the Cincinnati at its meetings in Charleston on 29 Aug., 3 Sept., 6 Oct. 1783 and on 5 Jan. and 5 April 1784. Forty-three officers attended the organizational meeting of 29 Aug. 1783, at which time General Moultrie was elected president. During this meeting, in acceding to the Institution of the Society of the Cincinnati the officers entered a "Declaration disclaiming all Intention of Interfering in any degree with the Constitutional powers of Congress or the Civil Authority of the State." It was at its "Anniversary Meeting" in the City Tavern in Charleston on 5 Jan. 1784 that the society chose its delegates to the general meeting to be held in Philadelphia in May. Elected were General Moultrie, Anthony Walton White, William Washington, Thomas

Shubrick, captain in the 1st South Carolina Regiment and aide-de-camp to Gen. Nathanael Greene, and Cornet John Middleton. After Moultrie and Middleton made known that they would not attend, the society elected Lewis Morris and George Turner in their stead; but Morris did not attend the general meeting in May, nor did Shubrick who was not even listed among the delegates elected (see Winthrop Sargent's Journal, doc. II in General Meeting of the Society of the Cincinnati, 4–18 May).

4. William Washington (1752–1810), GW's cousin, was born in Stafford County, Virginia. Before joining Benjamin Lincoln in the South in 1779, Washington rose to the rank of lieutenant colonel of the 3d Continental Dragoons. He was an important cavalry leader in the Carolinas until 8 Sept. 1781 when he was captured at Eutaw Springs, South Carolina. After being paroled, he married Jane Elliott, daughter of Charles Elliott (1737–1781) of Sandy Hill and Charleston, and soon became a South Carolina planter of great wealth. Anthony Walton White (1750–1803) of New Jersey, lieutenant colonel of the 1st Continental Dragoons, fought under Benjamin Lincoln in South Carolina. He and William Washington escaped from Banastre Tarleton in May 1780 at Linud's (Lanneau's) Ferry, S.C., by swimming the Santee River. George Turner (1750–1807) came to South Carolina from his native Ireland before the Revolution. During the war he was a captain in the 1st South Carolina Regiment. He was a frequent member of the South Carolina general assembly. Neither Lewis Morris nor Anthony Walton White are listed among those attending the meetings of the South Carolina society in 1783 and 1784 before the general meeting of the society in Philadelphia in May 1784 (see note 3).

From William Smallwood

Dr Sir,   Mattawoman [Md.] April 6th 1784

Commodore Brook[1] who will address this acquaints me that you desired him to request me to inform you of the Circumstances of Mr Stromats taking out a Warrant to affect Vacancy contiguous to your Lands on this Side the Patowmack[2]—I know very little of the Situation and Courses of your Lands or the adjoining Vacancy—but since Stromat took out his Warrant I have understood from Mr Dunnington the present Tenant who is an orderly honest Man, that there is some Vacancy.[3]

Mr Stromat also Obtained a Warrant for Vacancy adjoining my Land below yours, which joined his & which I had also made Application for before our Land Office opened—but Stromat made a prior Application for the same, upon which I waved mine—he has since promised to let me have such part of this Vacancy as his convenient to mine, and retain the Residue which may lye most convenient to his own Land—sometime before this, he made Application for the Courses of my Land adjoining yours and his, which I let him have—and afterwards he applied to me to get him the Courses of yours and other Lands from Annapolis, that he might also discover the Vacancy contiguous thereto, for which he informed me he had procured Warrants, which I then refused, and dissuaded him from executing them, & told him that I had understood he had taken possession of part of your Land under an Idea that the Courses of his own included it and yours left it out—which I urged he ought to have been very certain of, before he had taken such a Step, but he seemed very clear in the Matter, and Mr Dunnington informed me that he had understood that Stromats Father always claimed it—and that Majr Adams's Father applied to him to rent it.

Stromat urged that if he had not taken out a Warrant some other Person might have done it—and that if I wou'd not get him the Courses of those Lands when I went to Annapolis that he coud readily get them—I then signified that as he seemed intent upon the Matter, that he ought to let you and the others have upon the Office Terms such parts of the Vacancy as lay convenient to your Lands, which he agreed to—except with Respect to Mr Samuel Moore, who had never cleared out his Land—afterwards he wrote to me at Annapolis for those Courses, which I obtained for him, urging when I delivered them, again what is above recited—which he promised to comply with.

Mr Stromat by a private Survey has run out the Lands since he got the Courses, and your Lands include that part or most of it which he had taken possession of, and settled a Tenant on, who he immediately removed—this I lately had from Information, and believe it to be fact—If he shou'd execute his Warrants by the County Surveyor, before I go to Philadelphia, I will endeavor to inform myself, and let you know how it affects your Lands.[4]

I have received Answers to my Letters respecting the meeting of the Cincinnati in Philadelphia from Governor Paca and Colo. Ramsey (but none from Genl Williams whose punctual attendance you may depend on).

Accept and present my most respectful Compliments to Mrs Washington and believe me to remain with high Consideration and Regard Your most Obedt Hble Sert

W. Smallwood

ALS, DLC:GW.

1. Walter Brooke (d. 1798) was the son of Thomas Brooke (1706–1748) of Charles County, Md., and his wife Sarah Mason Brooke, the aunt of George Mason of Gunston Hall. He lived in Fairfax County, Virginia. During the Revolution, he was commodore of the Virginia navy, from 8 April 1777 to 30 Sept. 1778.

2. As the remainder of this letter makes clear, by "Vacancy" Smallwood means any land lying outside the tracts for which someone had legal title: in effect, unclaimed land. "Your Lands" in Charles County, Md., was the tract of 552⅓ acres that GW acquired from Daniel Jenifer Adams in December 1775 in partial payment of a debt. For this, see particularly GW's letter to Daniel Jenifer Adams of 8 Mar. 1775. "Stromats" was John Stromatt of Charles County, Maryland.

3. George Dunnington was the tenant on GW's land in Charles County, Maryland.

4. For GW's continuing dispute with John Stromatt over the boundaries of GW's property in Charles County, see GW to William Craik, 19 Mar. 1789, and note 4 of that document, which quotes from Craik to GW, 25 Jan. 1790.

To Samuel Vaughan

Sir,   Mount Vernon 6th April 1784

Your favor of the 5th of Feby was long on its way to me.[1] I scarcely knew in what terms to express my sense of your politeness, & the obligation you have laid me under by your order for the marble chimney piece & pair of glass Jarendoles;[2] but be assured Sir, this instance of your attention has made an impression, which never will be forgotten. You have much obliged me also by giving your sentiments respecting my room.

Altho' you have suspended your visit to Virginia, I would fain flatter myself that you have not laid it altogether aside. I expect to be in Philada about the first of May, when I shall have an opportunity of thanking you in person for your great politeness to me, & to assure you of the esteem & regard with which I have the honor to be Dr Sir Yr Mo[s]t obedt humble Servt

G: Washington

LB, DLC:GW.

1. Letter not found.

2. On 6 April 1785 GW had "the cases wch contained my Marble chimney piece" opened (*Diaries*, 4:114). Whether or not the girandoles, mirrors with attached candle holders, were sent is not known. If so, they either have not survived or have not been identified.

From Benjamin Walker

Dear General   New York 6 Apl 1784

Your favor of the 24 March was handed to me too late on Monday last to reply to it by that post.

The mention of 2080⁸⁰⁄₉₀ Dollars in the Governors Letter was a mistake it should have been 4080⁸⁰⁄₉₀—it was receivd in two Notes one are for 3500 Dols. & one for 580⁸⁰⁄₉₀ the last must have been for the ballance of your account but calculated in Pensilva. Currency instead of Lawfull Money.

I had the pleasure to write to you a few days ago & inclosed the by-Laws and proceedings of the Society of the Cincinnati for this State[1]—I have not heard of any objections to it, either in this State or in Jersey—and I am told the Jealousies that existed in the New England States begin to die away.

A certain Mr Williamos lately arrived from France mentioned to me yesterday that he had letters for you and some plants grape cuttings &c.—&c. that he should write to you by this Post—he was not determined whether he would send you the things from Philadelphia or from hence[2]—should he determine on the latter I shall be happy in giving him any assistance in shipping them and I hope that when at any time you wish for any thing from this place you will permit me to have the pleasure of procuring & forwarding them—I suppose that as Vessells do not frequently offer to Alexandria—any things shipped to Norfolk will not meet any difficulty in getting to you—I mean if committed to the care of a person there.

Our Assembly are busily occupied with a Bill to discriminate the Tories who are not to be allowed the Rights of Citizenship— a measure which I think can be attended with no good effect— a Bill for the Emission of Paper money is nearly passed—this and a bill for taking all kinds of Securities in payment for Confiscated Lands has reduced the Securities they gave their troops from 15/ to 9/ in the pound.[3]

The Governor is recovered from his late indisposition—& Washington recovers fast—both the Governor & Mrs Clinton desire me to tender their best Compliments to yourself and Mrs Washington & I beg that mine may accompany them.

Lt Colo. Talmadge, who has just married the eldest daughter of Colo. Floyd, desired me to present you his Respects.[4] With very great Respect I am Dear Genl Your very humble & Obedt Servant

Ben Walker

Mr Paine who is at my elbow & desires his Compts and says he intends to have the pleasure of writing you in a few days.[5]

ALS, DLC:GW.

1. See Walker to GW, 3 April.

2. Charles Williamos was a Swiss who served in the British army in America during the French and Indian War. He came to America from France in 1784 and became an intimate of Thomas Jefferson. For the details of his varied career and the breakup of his friendship with Jefferson, see the notes in Jefferson to Williamos, 7 July 1785, in Boyd, *Jefferson Papers*, 8:269–73. No correspondence between GW and Williamos has been found, but see GW to George Clinton, 25 Nov. 1784, n.5, and Clinton to GW, 5 Mar. 1785.

3. See Walker to GW, 3 April, n.8.

4. Maj. Benjamin Tallmadge (1754–1835), whom in 1778 GW employed in his secret service, married Mary Floyd, daughter of William Floyd of Mastic, Long Island, on 18 Mar. 1784.

5. See Thomas Paine to GW, 28 April.

To Thomas Jefferson

Dear Sir,   Mount Vernon April 8th 1784.

If with frankness, and the fullest latitude of a friend, you will give me your opinion of the Institution of the Society of Cincinnati, it would confer an acceptable favor upon me.[1] If to this opinion, you would be so obliging as to add the Sentiments, or what you suppose to be the Sentiments of Congress respecting it, I would thank you.

That you may have the best Materials on which to form a judgment, I send you a copy of the proceedings of the Society.[2] Consequent of their choice of me for Presidt Pro Tem and the direction therein, I sent the Institution to the French land & Naval Commanders—and to the Marqs de la Fayette—as the Senr French Officer in the American Army—whose proceedings thereon I also enclose to you.[3]

These Papers you will please to retain (for fear of accidents) 'till I shall have the pleasure (the Week after next) of seeing you in Annapolis on my way to Philadelphia; whither this, & other business, will take me; but the sooner I could receive your sentiments on this Subject, the more pleasing they would be to me.

The Pamphlet ascribed to Mr Burke, has I am told had its effect. People are alarmed, especially in the Eastern States.[4] How justly, or how contrary to the avowed principles of the Society and the purity of their motives, I will not declare, least it should appear that I wanted to biass your judgment rather than to obtain an opinion—which, if you please, might be accompanied with sentiments (under the information here given) respecting the most eligable measures to be pursued by the Society at their next meeting.[5]

You may be assured Sir, that to the good opinion, alone, which I entertain of your abilities & candor, this liberty is to be attributed; and I can truly add, that with very great esteem & regard I am—Dr Sir Yr most obt & Hble Servt

Go: Washington

P.S. I was on the point of closing this Letter, when Mr Hogendorff put your favor of the 6th into my hands.

ALS, DLC: Jefferson Papers; LB, DLC:GW.

1. For the extent of GW's involvement in the Society of the Cincinnati before this time, see the editorial note in General Meeting of the Society of the Cincinnati, 4–18 May 1784, printed below.

2. The Institution includes the record of the proceedings in establishing the Society of the Cincinnati on 10 and 13 May 1783 and the minutes of its first meeting on 19 June 1783. The Institution is printed in Hume, *Society of the Cincinnati*, 1–14.

3. There is nothing in the minutes of the meeting of 19 June 1783 when GW was elected president to indicate that he was given a "direction" to send copies of the Institution to the Frenchmen. For GW's doing so, see GW to Knox, 16 Oct. 1783, to Rochambeau and to Gérard, both 29 Oct., and to Lafayette, 30 Oct. 1783. GW had received a number of letters from the French officers reporting on the reception of the society in France; which of these he sent to Jefferson has not been determined.

4. For a discussion of Aedanus Burke's pamphlet and the opposition to the

Cincinnati in New England, see Henry Knox to GW, 21 Feb. 1784, and note 2 of that document.

5. Jefferson's reply is dated 16 April.

From Lafayette

My dear General   Paris April the 9th 1784

Among the Numberless Applications I Have Had for our Society, there is One which, in duty to My feelings, I Cannot decline to present. on my first Voyage to America, Monsieurs de Mauroy, Lesser, Valfort, and du Boismartin were with me, and Altho these Meritorious officers Had an Engagement with Mr Deane, Congress did not think it in their power to Employ them[1]—My instructions Being positive, I Have Answered them, that it was not within My limits to present them with the Badge of the Assossiation—But upon their Request for a Representation of their Case, I found it the More Impossible for me to Neglect it, As independant of their Great Merit, zeal, and Sacrifices, they Were My first Companions in the Voyage, and went over with me in a Manner that lays me Under particular obligations to them—Give me leave therefore, my dear General, to Present You with this Sollicitation of mine, which they will forward to Yr Excellency—With the Highest Respect and Most tender Affection I Have the Honour to Be My dear General Your Obedient Humble Servant

Lafayette

ALS, PEL.

1. In 1776 Silas Deane (1737–1789), the American commissioner in Paris, offered Charles-Louis, vicomte de Mauroy (Montroy; 1734–1813), the rank of major general; Jean Thevet Lesser (b. 1737), the rank of colonel in the *département de la marine*; Louis Silvestre Valfort (1727–1808), a colonelcy in the Continental army; and Boismartin, the rank of major. See A List of Officers of Infantry and Light Troops destined to serve in the Armies of the States General of North America, in Idzerda, *Lafayette Papers*, 1 : 18–19.

From Edmund Pendleton

Dear Sir   Edmundsbury [Va.] Apl 9. 1784.

Colo. Muse shewed me yr letter to his son requesting I would take charge of his Deeds to you, and procure them to be proved

and recorded in the General Court, which I would most cheer-
fully have done, but do not go to Richmond 'til after that Court
rises.[1] I have seen the Deeds Executed before 5 Witnesses, and
they are to be carried by one of them who is our Sherif & a careful man, to be lodged with the Clerk and proved as they come
in—so that I think you will run no risque in paying Colo. Muse
the money you mention, especially as there will be time enough
to compleat the proof in October, should any accident prevent
its being made by three now.[2] I have the honr to be with great
regard Yr Excellys mo. Obt Servt

Edmd Pendleton

ALS, DLC:GW.

    Edmund Pendleton (1721–1803) of Caroline County, Va., was president
of the Virginia Supreme Court of Appeals. Pendleton handled much of GW's
legal work in the years immediately preceding the Revolution.

    1. GW to Laurence Muse, 11 Mar. 1784.

    2. The deeds have not been found. The Caroline County sheriff was
William Buckner. By "three," he means three witnesses.

Agreement with Lewis Lemart

[Mount Vernon, 10 April 1784]

I hereby empower Mr Lewis Lemart to receive such Rents as
are due to me upon the Land tract on which he himself lives,
and which lyes partly in the County of Fauquier and partly in
Loudoun.[1] I give him the same powers with respect to my other
Tract on Goose Creek, near Mr Robert Ashby's—and I authorize him to make distress for the annual or Transfer Rents
which are reserved to me by the Leases.[2] and this he is in a more
especial manner to do from such persons as are about to remove from off the Land—He will see by the Lease (for I have it
not ⟨in⟩ My power at this moment, to make out the Accts for
each Man individually⟨)⟩) for many years they have been sub-
jec⟨t⟩ to the payment of Rent, and he will make no allowances
save such as appear by receipts from myself, Mr Lund Washington or any public Officer, by way of deduction without further
authority from me. He is not to detain any money which he receives under this power, in his hands longer than can well be
avoided; but shall transmit the same to me with an Acct of the
sums, from whom, and when received as soon as possible.

For his trouble in all these acts and doings, and in full compensation for all his expences, I hereby agree to allow him five prCent all the monies which he shall actually pay into my hands, or to any other person by my order—this power to remain in force till revoked by me. Given under my hand at Mount Vernon the 10th day of April 1784

Go: Washington

ADS, owned (1977) by Mrs. Robb A. Hake, Schenectady, New York.

Lewis Lemart served only briefly as GW's agent, for he died in the spring of 1785 (GW to Battaile Muse, 18 Sept. 1785). Lemart began in December 1772 leasing for £7 per annum 150 acres of the tract called Ashby's Bent, the 2,682 acres that GW bought from the estate of George Carter in November 1767 (see *Diaries*, 2:133, 3:239). It was located on the eastern slope of the Blue Ridge Mountains in Virginia.

1. After buying the Ashby's Bent tract, GW divided it into lots of 100 to 200 acres which he leased to tenants for periods ranging from ten years to three lives. See *Diaries*, 4:257, and Cash Accounts, November 1767, in Ledger A, 255.

2. GW acquired a 600-acre tract in Fauquier County on Goose Creek, usually referred to as the Chattins Run tract, from Bryan Fairfax in August 1772. When looking over the tract in May 1772, GW stayed at Yew Hall, the house of Robert Ashby (c.1707–1792) about eight miles south of Ashby's Gap on the road to Winchester, Virginia. In his cash accounts for April 1784, GW enters, on 10 April, £20, "To Edwd Phillips recd from him by Lewis Lamart for Rent of Lott No. 3 in Fauquier County leas'd Dulan," and £3, "To Henry Shaffar by Lewis Lamart in part of Rent for the Lott on which Michl Henry Liv'd" (Ledger B, 197).

From Nicholas Simon van Winter and Lucretia Wilhelmina van Winter

Honoured Sir   Leydan in Holland 10th April 1784
From the Extremity of the Earth, Deign to accept, the Sincere Hommages of Two Persons more closely united by the Bonds of Mutual Affection than by those of Hymen; Admirers of Virtue, we were impelled by an irrestistable desire to testify to you our Veneration, as Soon as we were informed that your magnanimity of Soul had Shewn forth So conspicuously, in your relinquishing the Honourable charge of the Chief Command in the Armies of the Thirteen United States of North America, & in Preferring a rural life, to all the Charms that could allure an ambitious mind, a resolution worthy of the Grand Liberator of

his Country, & which has raised you in the Eyes of the World above the most illustrious Monarchs. But how can we make you Sensible of our admiration Since probably you are a Stranger to the Dutch Language? The zeal of my Spouse has Surmounted that embarrassing obstacle. She has ventured for the first time of her life to make Verse in a foreign language,[1] for to make herself understood by the American Heroe, but She laments that She could not avail herself of her native language, Since in it She might have expressed herself with more Sublimity of Stile. Have the Goodness, Noble Sir, to let our Sentiments plead as an excuse for the faults of her Poetry; Last year about the latter end of Octr we Sent the original of the Inclosed Verses, to our Friend Mr Vogels, who Boasts an alliance with Mr Hillegas the Treasurer, & who has Since Married a Daughter in Law of Colo. Moulden's at Philadelphia,[2] but having never received any account of it from that time, we were apprehensive that the letter never arrived,[3] this Consideration has induced us to take the liberty of Sending this by another Conveyance, Wishing to lose no opportunity of Demonstratg the Veneration that your Virtue, & that of your Illustrious & Dear Companion, has inspired us with, & which we though far Behind, will endeavour to follow, Preferring it to all the Grandeurs of the Earth, being content with a Happy independance in our own Country, & having no other ambition but that of Boasting one Day, that the Illustrious Washington has Deigned to Receive the Sincere Hommages of two persons, who will always be with the Most Profound Respect Noble Sir Your Very Hble Servts

Nicholas Simon Van Winter
Lucretia Wilhelmina Van Winter

Translation, DLC:GW; LS, PHi: Gratz Collection; ADf, Amsterdam: Collectie Six. For a transcription of the LS, see CD-ROM:GW.

Lucretia van Mercken van Winter, who was married to Nicolas Simon van Winter and lived in Leyden, was a Dutch poet who wrote a number of popular tragedies in the late eighteenth century. In 1781 she published a poem of thirty-five stanzas, "To the British," which includes these lines:

> Oppressed America makes your glory fade,
> A new star is rising in our skies,
> Washington strong with his French allies
> Freed his country from your tyranny.

(Quoted in Reitz, "An Unpublished Correspondence of George Washington.") On 19 Oct. 1783 she sent a poem directed to GW and written in his praise to Gerard Vogels who forwarded it to GW through Michael Hillegas on 22 March. See Vogels to GW, 10 Mar., and notes.

1. The poem is written in French. See Vogels to GW, 10 Mar., n.1.

2. The van Winters wrote: "et qui depuis peù, comme nous croyons, s'est mairé a une des filles de feù Monsieur le Collonel Moulders."

3. See GW to Lucretia van Winter, 30 Mar. 1785.

To Thomas Walker

Dear Sir   Mount Vernon 10th of Aprl 1784

Your favor of the 24th of Jan: only came to my hands by the Post on thursday last—if this letter is as long on its passage to you, the May Session will have ended before it reaches you.

The favorable sentiments you have been pleased to express for me, deserve my particular acknowledgements; and I thank you for your kind invitation to Castle hill; which I certainly shall avail myself of, if ever I should come into that part of the Country. In return, I hope it is unnecessary to give you assurances of the pleasure I should feel in seeing you, and my cousin at this retreat from all my public employments.

I much approve the proposal for a meeting of the Swamp Company, but I pray *you* to issue the summons, and to name the time and place for holding it. Richmond appears to me to be the most convenient place, but any other, or any time, shall have my attendance when it may be in my power. The first of May I am called to Philadelphia on business of different kind [1]—how long I shall be absent is uncertain, for it is probable I may make a more extended tour, which would take much time to perform. I beg therefore that the meeting may not be delayed on my acct—Whatever resolutions the Company may come to, shall meet my concurrence.

Enclosed I send you the Copy of a letter from Doctr Williamson of North Carolina, who is a delegate in Congress, and member of a Company who holds that part of the Dismal swamp which lyes South of the Virginia line. I send it, that the proposition may appear before the next meeting of our Company, and be considered by it. [2]

With respect to the private purchase made conjointly by yourself, our deceased friend, and me, I can only say that I gave my consent to the Sale because Colo. Lewis desired his part to be sold; and indeed, because my own circumstances made it necessary for me to raise money by some such means; but I accompanied that consent with an opinion, that a Sale at this time would be premature, inasmuch as that the value of the Lands were not sufficiently known, nor had the spirit of emigration taken place in that extensive degree which was, and is, expected.[3]

In February last at Fredericksburgh, I had an oppertunity of seeing and conversing with Mr John Lewis on this subject, when it was our joint opinion, that it would be imprudent to precipitate the Sale, before a just value could be obtained—but that it might be proper to advertise the Land under just descriptions, in the several Gazettes, to see if offers equal to our expectations, would be made for them. If you approve of this measure for the Tracts in which you are concerned, it may be carried into effect along with that of Norfleets, which his father and I had between us in equal Moieties. Mrs Washington unites in best wishes for you and Mrs Walker with Dr Sir Yr Most Obedt Servt

Go: Washington

P.S. As it is now nine years since I have heard a tittle from the company, or how the affairs of it have been managed, if you would devote an hour for the purpose of giving this information I should receive it very kindly. I should be glad also to receive a copy of Mr Andrews Survey of the Company's Lands—or, if that would be troublesome, I should be very glad to know what quantity there is of it.[4]

Since writing the above, I find (as I mean to send this letter by Post to Fredericksburgh), that I have not time to Copy Doctr Williamson's letter to me, and therefore I give you the original.

Go: W——n.

ALS (photocopy), DLC:GW; LB, DLC:GW.

1. GW is referring to the upcoming first general meeting of the Society of the Cincinnati.

2. This is the letter from Hugh Williamson of 24 Mar. to which GW refers in his letter to Williamson of 31 March.

3. On 24 Mar. 1782 John Lewis wrote that his father, Fielding Lewis who died at the very end of 1781 or the beginning of 1782, directed in his will that in addition to his share in the Dismal Swamp Company, both the land that he and GW had bought from Marmaduke Norfleet and the land that he, Thomas Walker, and GW had bought from "Doctr Wright & Jones" be sold. On 17 April 1782 GW wrote to Lewis reluctantly agreeing to sell the two tracts that he owned jointly with his late brother-in-law, and added: "I have not a

sufficient recollection of them (especially the Tracts in which Doctr Walker holds a share) to describe any of them accurately. With respect to Norfleets, it is in No. Carolina, near the line, and upon the great road leading from Suffolk [Va.] to Edenton [N.C.]—abt 16 Miles from the former. . . . The Lands purchased of Jones & Doctr Wright lye betwn Norfolk & Suffolk, 6 or 8 M. from the latter and on or near Nansemond River." GW's account with Marmaduke Norfleet "of N. Carolina" (Ledger A, 239) shows that in October and November 1766, GW and Fielding Lewis paid Norfleet £90.10. It also shows that on 22 Nov. 1766 they agreed to pay Norfleet a total of £1,290.10 "for 1093½ Acres of Land lying in Pequemen County No. Carolina," in installments of £200 every October beginning in 1768 and running through 1773.

On 25 May 1788 GW consented to sell his half of the North Carolina land to John Cowper, subject to John Lewis's approval; and in May 1791 Lewis sold the Norfleet tract to Cowper (see John Lewis to GW, 7 Dec. 1788, n.1).

GW sold his own share in the Dismal Swamp Company in 1795 to Gen. Henry Lee, but when Lee could not make the payments, the share reverted to GW's estate in 1809.

The Nansemond tract was not sold. On 10 Oct. 1797 GW wrote Francis Walker that he had heard nothing about this property since telling John Lewis that he "would abide by" whatever "bargain for it" that he and Doctor Walker might make. GW in 1797 still held the title papers showing that he, Fielding Lewis, and Thomas Walker had bought, in the 1760s, a total of 1,210 acres in the county: 872 from Joseph Jones, 50 from Dr. James Wright, 100 from Stephen Wright, and 188 "King's Patent." In the schedule of his property attached to his will that he made in 1799 shortly before his death, GW made a notation on the entry relating to his Nansemond property: "These 373 acres are the third part of undivided purchases made by the deceased Fielding Lewis Thomas Walker and myself. . . . The land lyes on the Road from Suffolk to Norfolk touches (if I am not mistaken) some part of the Navigable water of Nansemond River. . . . the rich Dismal Swamp; is capable of great improvement; and from its situation must become extremely valuable" (ViFaCt).

4. See Walker to GW, 24 Jan. 1784, n.2.

To Robert R. Livingston

Dear Sir,   Mount Vernon 11th Apl 1784.

Give me leave to introduce to your Civilities the Marquis de Fontinelle, Colonel of Infantry in the Service of France and a Gentleman of Merit & Fortune.[1] The Marquis Was Aid to Count de Estaing at the Siege of Savanna and is now on a tour from Charleston to Boston—he is accompanied by Colo. Senf.[2] I am Dr Sir Yr most Obedt Hble Servt

Go: Washington

ALS, NHi: Robert R. Livingston Papers.

Robert R. Livingston (1746–1813) was at this time a chancellor of the state of New York. He became Congress's first secretary of foreign affairs in 1781. He later supported ratification of the United States Constitution but broke with Alexander Hamilton after the new government was formed and became an early supporter of Jefferson and Madison.

1. See Benjamin Guerard to GW, 3 Mar. 1784, in GW to Thomas Mifflin, 4 April, n.2.

2. Christian Senf (c.1754–1806), a Swede, was a captain-engineer in the Continental forces in South Carolina in 1778 and later reached the rank of lieutenant colonel. He was one of the officers attending the second meeting of the South Carolina Society of the Cincinnati in September 1783. After the war he became the chief engineer for South Carolina when the state became engaged in extensive canal building.

From John Harvie

Sir   Land Office [Richmond, Va.] April 12th 1784

Mr Griffith is so good as to present me an opportunity of answering your Letter of March the 18th. the Survey you Inclosed in it for 587 Acres call'd the Round Bottom must by Law lay in this Office Six Months before a Grant can issue upon it, at the Expiration of that time (unless a Caveat is hereafter Enterd) a Grant will be issued to you reciteing the date of the Survey and the Nature of the Right upon which it is founded agreable to your desire[1]—there being no Caveat or other Legal Arrest to your Title as I can find, either in the Name of Michael Cresap or any other person, yet nothing is more probable than that a Survey may have been returned to this Office for the same Tract of Land under a different Description, as practices of this kind frequently prevail in Order to Cover Surreptitious designs, however if I should make any such Discovery I will give you Immediate Information of it.

Grants are not yet fully Compleated upon your two Surveys that I sent you the Copies of, nor can they be made ready in time to be Convey'd to you by Mr Griffith, the next Gentleman I see from your Neighbourhood will do himself the pleasure to take the Charge of them to you.[2] I have the Honour to be Sir with every Sentiment of Respect & Esteam Yr Most Obt & Very Humble Servt

Jno. Harvie

ALS, DLC:GW.

1. For the Round Bottom grant, see note 2 in GW to Harvie, 18 Mar. 1784.

2. The two surveys referred to here are described in note 2, Harvie to GW, 21 Feb. 1784. Harvie enclosed the two grants in his letter to GW of 14 April 1784.

From Henry Knox

My dear sir.   Dorchester near Boston [Mass.] 12 April 1784

I received your favor of the 20th ultimo yesterday. I am fully persuaded of the importance of a general attendance at the meeting at Philadelphia, and I have now written to those concerned in this State, Rhode Island, Connecticut, and New Hampshire, urging their attendence to the utmost of my power. If General Greene shall not be gone before I reach Newport I will endeavor to bring him along.

I wrote your Excellency on the 4th of this month, and enclosed the report of the committee of the Legislature of this State, which was accepted by the Senate and assembly, but further measures were deferred untill the next session. This was supposed to be in tenderness to the members, to give them time to abandon so dangerous an association. The prejudices against the society have received great additional strength, by the thundering speech of the Governor of South Carolina.[1]

I shall set out for New York, from providence by Water on the 21 instant—The roads are too bad to go by Land. It is not very probable this will reach you before I shall have the pleasure of seeing you in Philadelphia.

Mrs Knox prays her affectionate compliments may be presented to Mrs Washington, and hopes that Mrs Custis and her little flock are well. I am dear sir with the most perfect respect and attachment Your humble Serv.

H. Knox

ALS, DLC:GW.

1. For the organizing of the South Carolina Society of the Cincinnati, see William Moultrie to GW, 6 April, n.3.

From John Harvie

Sir   Land Office [Richmond, Va.] April 14th 1784

Mr Griffith's staying a day longer in this City than he expected to do when I first saw him, has allow'd me time to make out and forward your Grants by him,[1] I am to Apoligize for there being on Common paper, by Assureing you that it was not in my power to procure as much Parchment at this place as was Sufficient to Contain the Grants, I have Written to Europe for a large Quantity of Parchment which I hope will Arrive this Spring. when that comes to hand if you then prefer it, by returning the Original Grants, I expect the Governour will have no Objection to Sign others on parchment and cancel those now made out upon paper.

You will find your Grants in the plainest Simplest Dress, without any addition to your Name or other Designation except the Seat of your Domestic Residence. when I first set down to Write these Grants this Simplicity of Expression did not Correspond with my feelings, and my Heart was about to Dictate to my pen a Long String of Illustrious Distinguishments, but in the Moment of Execution my mind felt such a Conviction that no Title that could be given you in the Grant could add Lustre to your Character, that I Concluded it best, and more Consistent with the Republicanism of your own Mind to leave out a plumage that could not Exalt a Character whose Dignity stands Recorded in the Warmest Corner of the Human Heart. I have the Honour to be Sir Yr most Obt & very H. Servt

             John Harvie

ALS, DLC:GW.

 1. See Harvie to GW, 12 April, n.2, and 21 Feb. 1784, n.2.

To Sidney Lee

Madam,   Mount Vernon 15th April 1784.

I fear you will think me inattentive to your commands—appearances are against me, but I have not been unmindful of your request, or my promise. During my continuence with the army, I wrote several Letters to Mr Drew, Clerk of the Court in which the Will of Majr Genl Lee was recorded; all of which I presume, miscarried; as the first Letter he acknowledges to have received from me, was written in Decr last, after I had retired to this Seat. His letter will account for the delay which took place afterwards[1]—& the sending to richmond (which is at a considerable distance from hence) to obtain the Governors certificate, has filled up the great measure of time which has elapsed since my promise to procure you an attested copy of the Will[2]—& will I hope, plead for my seeming neglect. Berkely is a remote county, much out of the Post road; which may accot for the miscarriage of my letters to Mr Drew—Your application to me, Madam, required no apology; I only regret that it has not been in my power to comply with your request sooner—if there is any thing further in which I can be serviceable, I pray you to command me. I have the honor to be &c.

G: Washington

LB, DLC:GW.

1. Neither GW's letter to William Drew of late December 1783 nor Drew's reply has been found, but see GW to Drew, 13 Feb. 1784, and notes.

2. See GW to Edmund Randolph, 18 Mar. 1784, and Randolph's reply, April 1784. Miss Lee wrote GW on 23 May 1784 that the executor of the will, Alexander White, had sent her a copy of the will but that she had received no word of the benefits she should have received under its terms.

From Thomas Jefferson

Dear Sir   Annapolis [Md.] April. 16. 1784

I received your favor of the 8th inst. by Colo. Harrison.[1] the subject of it is interesting, and, so far as you have stood connected with it, has been matter of anxiety to me: because whatever may be the ultimate fate of the institution of the Cincinnati, as in it's course it draws to it some degree of disapprobation I have wished to see you stand on ground separated from it; & that the character which will be handed to future ages at the head of our revolution may in no instance be compromitted in subordinate altercations. the subject has been at the point of my pen in every letter I have written to you; but has been still restrained by a reflection that you had among your friends more able counsellors, and in yourself one abler than them all. your letter has now rendered a duty what was before a desire, and I cannot better merit your confidence than by a full & free communication of facts & sentiments as far as they have come within my observation.

When the army was about to be disbanded, and the officers to take final leave, perhaps never again to meet, it was natural for men who had accompanied each other through so many scenes of hardship, of difficulty & danger, who in a variety of instances must have been rendered mutually dear by those aids & good offices to which their situations had given occasion, it was natural I say for these to seize with fondness any proposition which promised to bring them together again at certain & regular periods. and this I take for granted was the origin & object of this institution: and I have no suspicion that they forsaw, much less intended those mischeifs which exist perhaps in the forebodings of politicians only. I doubt however whether in it's execution it would be found to answer the wishes of those who framed it, & to foster those friendships it was intended to preserve. the members would be brought together at their annual assemblies no longer to encounter a common enemy, but to encounter one another in debate & sentiment. something I suppose is to be done at these meetings, & however unimportant, it will suffice to produce difference of opinion, contradiction & irritation. the way to make friends quarrel is to pit them in disputation under the public eye. an experience of near twenty years has taught me that few friendships stand this test; and that public assemblies, where everyone is free to speak & to act, are the most powerful looseners of the bonds of private friendship. I think therefore that this institution would fail of it's principal object, the perpetuation of the personal friendships contracted thro' the war.

The objections of those opposed to the institution shall be briefly sketched; you will readily fill them up. they urge that it is against the Confederation; against the letter of some of our constitutions; against the spirit of them all—that the foundation, on which all these are built, is the natural equality of man, the denial of every preeminence but that annexed to legal office, & particularly the denial of a preeminence by birth: that however, in their present dispositions, citizens might decline accepting honorary instalments into the order, a time may come when a change of dispositions would render these flattering; when a well directed distribution of them might draw into the order all the men of talents, of office & wealth, and in this case would probably procure an ingraftment into the government: that in this they will be supported by their foreign members, & the wishes & influence of foreign courts: that experience has shewn that the hereditary branches of modern governments are the patrons of privilege & prerogative, & not of the natural rights of the people, whose oppressors they generally are: that besides these evils which are remote, others may take place more immediately: that a distinction is kept up between the civil & military which it is for the happiness of both to obliterate: that when the members assemble they will be proposing to do something, and what that something may be will depend on actual circumstances: that being an organized body, under habits of subordination, the first obstructions to enterprize will be already surmounted: that the moderation & virtue of a single character has probably prevented this revolution from being closed as most others have been by a subversion of that liberty it was intended to establish: that he is not immortal, & his successor or some one of his successors at the head of this institution may adopt a more mistaken road to glory.

What are the sentiments of Congress on this subject, & what line they will pursue can only be stated conjecturally. Congress as a body, if left to themselves will in my opinion say nothing on the subject. they may however be forced into a declaration by instructions from some of the states or by other incidents. their sentiments, if forced from them, will be unfriendly to the institution. if permitted to pursue their own tract, they will check it by side blows whenever it comes in their way, & in competitions for office on equal or nearly equal ground will give silent preferences to those who are not of the fraternity. my reasons for thinking this are 1. the grounds on which they lately declined the foreign order proposed to be conferred on some of our citizens.[2] 2. the fourth of the fundamental articles of constitution for the new states. I inclose you the report. it has been considered by Congress, recommitted & reformed by a Committee according to the sentiments expressed on other parts of it, but the principle referred to having not been controverted at all, stands in this as in the original report. it is not yet confirmed by Congress.[3] 3. private conversations on this subject with the members. since the receipt of your letter I have taken occasion to extend these; not indeed to the military members, because being of the order delicacy forbade it; but to the others pretty generally: and among these I have found but one who is not opposed to the institution, & that with an anguish of mind, tho' covered under a guarded silence, which I have not seen produced by any circumstance before. I arrived at Philadelphia before the separation of the last Congress, & saw there & at Princeton some of it's members not now in delegation. Burke's peice happened to come out at that time which occasioned this institution to be the subject of conversation. I found the same impression made on them which their successors have received. I hear from other quarters that it is disagreeable generally to such citizens as have attended to it, & therefore will probably be so to all when any circumstance shall present it to the notice of all.

This Sir is as faithful an account of sentiments & facts as I am able to give you. you know the extent of the circle within which my observations are at present circumscribed, and can estimate how far, as forming a part of the general opinion, it may merit notice, or ought to influence your particular conduct. it remains now to pay obedience to that part of your letter which requests sentiments on the most eligible measures to be pursued by the society at their next meeting. I must be far from pretending to be a judge of what would *in fact* be the most eligible measures for the society. I can only give you the opinions of those with whom I have conversed, & who, as I have before observed, are unfriendly to it. they lead to these conclusions. 1. if the society proceeds according to it's institution, it will be better to make no applications to Congress on that subject, or on any other in their associated character. 2. if they should propose to modify it so as to render it unobjectionable, I think this would not be effected without such a modification as would amount almost to annihilation; for such would it be to part with it's inheritability, it's organisation & it's assemblies. 3. if they should be disposed to discontinue the whole it would remain with them to determine whether they would chuse it to be done by their own act only, or by a reference of the matter to Congress, which would infallibly produce a recommendation of total discontinuance.[4]

You will be sensible, Sir, that these communications are without all reserve. I suppose such to be your wish, & mean them but as materials, with such others as you may collect, for your better judgment to work on. I consider the whole matter as between ourselves alone, having determined to take no active part in this or any thing else which may lead to altercation, or disturb that quiet & tranquillity of mind to which I consign the remaining portion of my life. I have been thrown back by events on a stage where I had never more thought to appear. it is but for a time however, & as a day labourer, free to withdraw or be withdrawn at will. while I remain I shall pursue in silence the path of right: but in every situation public or private shall be gratified by all occasions of rendering you service & of convincing you there is no one to whom your reputation & happiness are dearer than to Sir your most obedient & most humble servt

Th: Jefferson

ALS, PHi: Gratz Collection; LB, DLC: Jefferson Papers.

1. This is probably Robert Hanson Harrison (1745–1790), a lawyer in Maryland, who held the rank of lieutenant colonel from 1775 to 1781 while GW's private secretary.

2. Jefferson is referring to a proposal made to GW in 1783 by the chevalier de Heintz that Congress select a number of Americans for induction into a Polish order, which Congress instructed GW to reject. For details of this incident, see Thomas Mifflin to GW, 9 Jan. 1784, and notes.

3. The report that Jefferson enclosed was a revised report of the committee of the Congress appointed to draw up a plan for the temporary government of the western territory, dated 22 Mar. 1784. The work of Jefferson himself, it set forth as number 4 of five principles: "That their respective governments shall be in republican forms, and shall admit no person to be a citizen who holds any hereditary title." When making his initial speech on 5 May at the general meeting in which he called for a drastic revision of the Institution of the Cincinnati, GW referred to this report as evidence of the depth of the opposition to the hereditary aspect of the society's Institution (see Winthrop Sargent's Journal, doc. II in General Meeting of the Society of the Cincinnati, 4–18 May 1784). Before the amended report was adopted on 23 April 1784 (the Land Ordinance of 1784), the Congress, on 20 April, voted to drop the words "and shall admit no person to be a citizen who holds any hereditary title" (*JCC*, 26:250–51). See Plan for Government of the Western Territory, 3 Feb.–23 April 1784, in Boyd, *Jefferson Papers*, 6:581–617.

4. The extent to which GW took Jefferson's strictures on the Society of the Cincinnati to heart is reflected in GW's Observations and in Sargent's journal, printed below as docs. I and II in General Meeting of the Society of the Cincinnati, 4–18 May 1784. On 7 May Elbridge Gerry wrote Samuel Adams from Annapolis: "G—— W—— on his Way to the Meeting of the Cincinnati

at Philadelphia, passed thro this place, and I am confidentially informed [by Jefferson; see Gerry to Stephen Higginson, 13 May, Burnett, *Letters*, 7:522], that he is opposed to recommend the dropping it altogether. This is communicated in Confidence to yourself to be imparted only to our Friends Mr. Higginson, Mr. [Samuel] Osgood, General [James] Warren and Mr. [James] Bowdoin" (ibid., 516). Jefferson later also recorded his recollections of GW's visits to him at Annapolis, first on his way to the meeting of the Cincinnati in Philadelphia when the two discussed further the points Jefferson had raised about the society in this letter, and subsequently, on his journey back to Mount Vernon after the meeting when GW, according to Jefferson, related how he had sought to have the society abolished and how he had failed (see note 16 in Winthrop Sargent's Journal, doc. II in General Meeting of the Society of the Cincinnati, 4–18 May). For an example of Jefferson's later heightened opposition to the Society of the Cincinnati, see his letter to GW, 14 Nov. 1786.

From Jethro Sumner

Sir   Hillsborough [N.C.] April 18th 1784
It was with pleasure, we recd your circular letter, the eleventh of March last,[1] and in a few days, a conveyance offered to the Gentlemen, Lt Col. Archd Lyttle, Majr Reading Blount, and Majr John Griffith McRee, who were appointed delagates in october last, to attend the Genl meeting of the Society of the Cincinnati.[2]

This states society, being appointed to meet on the second monday of this month, it was necessary that the delegates attend, on there way to the General Convention—when every measure were taken in our power to hasten there departure.

We Sir, beg leave to recommend to you these Gentlemen, whose services to the Country, has continued from the commencement of the late war. I am Sir, with Esteem and Respect, yr very Hble Servt

Jethro Sumner

ALS, NcRSC.
1. Sumner is referring to the copy of GW's circular letter of 1 Jan. 1784, addressed to him as president of the North Carolina Society of the Cincinnati. Perhaps Sumner is saying here that the letter was read by the state society on 11 March.
2. Reading Blount (d. 1807), former captain in the 1st North Carolina Regiment, and Griffith John McRee (1758–1801), former major in the state's forces, both attended the meeting in Philadelphia. Archibald Lytle served as a lieutenant colonel in the North Carolina regiments during the Revolution.

From Lachlan McIntosh

Dear General   Savannah in Georgia 20th April 1784.

Your Excellencys very obliging and kind favor of the 15th December last was delivered to me four days ago, inclosing Copy of the Letter you humanely wrote to the Minister of France in behalf of the unfortunate Captain DuCoins, who I hope through your Excellencys powerful Intercession may be restored again to his friends and Country & made happy.[1]

Please to accept my Sincerest Thanks for that as well as the concern you have been pleased to take in the injurys done to my own honor, altho' I have had no reparation for them yet, which probably may be owing as your Excellency observes to the Resolve of our Assembly of 1st Feby 1783 not being properly Authenticated—the Speaker and Clerk of our Assembly happening to be absent that time, as they are now. but I conceived 'twould be less Necessary as the Journals are always published in our Gazettes one of which that has the Resolve I have the honor of inclosing—wherein your Excellency cannot help Noticeing part of the Art and Management of Walton's party who composed the Committee, in softening as much as they could, and afterwards putting off their Report from day to day, keeping the House ignorant of it, untill they first Chose him Chief Justice to protect him from Insults, and which the Wretch still retains unmollested in Compassion to his Family.[2] I am with real Respect and Esteem Your Excellency's obliged & most Hble servt.

Lachn McIntosh

ALS, DLC:GW. The first of these two letters from McIntosh of 20 April is marked private.

Lachlan McIntosh (1727–1806), a Highland Scot who was brought to the colony of Georgia in 1736, assumed command of the Georgia battalion in 1776. After mortally wounding Button Gwinnett in a duel in May 1777, McIntosh left Georgia, and in December 1777 GW gave him command at Valley Forge of the North Carolina Brigade. McIntosh returned to Georgia in 1779 after the siege of Savannah, and in 1780 he was captured by the British at the fall of Charleston. This ended McIntosh's military career. He spent much of the rest of his life trying to repair his damaged reputation (see note 2) and, unsuccessfully, to restore his personal fortune in Georgia.

1. John Du Coin was the pseudonym of Jean-François Borigere de Costia. Borigere de Costia, it seems, had left France under a cloud when he joined a Georgia regiment in July 1777 as a lieutenant and then served until the end of

the war, reaching the rank of captain. GW wrote La Luzerne on 14 Dec. 1783 enclosing a letter from McIntosh (not found) describing Du Coin's "situation." GW confessed to being "unacquainted with the young Gentleman," but, GW wrote, since Du Coin had served "with Credit" during the war GW would be "obliged" to La Luzerne "by any thing your Excellency can do for him" (Arch. Aff. Etr.).

2. Just as McIntosh's involvement in Georgia's virulently factional politics had led to his duel with Button Gwinnett and his departure from Georgia in 1777, local political animosities accounted for "the injurys done" to McIntosh's honor when he returned to Georgia in 1779. After the failure of the siege of British-held Savannah in 1779 by French and American forces, McIntosh accompanied Gen. Benjamin Lincoln to South Carolina where he was given command of a body of South Carolina militiamen for the defense of Charleston. On 17 Mar. 1780, shortly before Charleston fell, McIntosh received a letter dated 15 Feb. 1780 from the president of Congress, Samuel Huntington, dispensing with McIntosh's services as a brigadier general in the army. Congress acted in response to a letter from Gov. George Walton of Georgia, dated 15 Dec. 1779, calling for McIntosh's removal because of "a general and settled Aversion" in Georgia to his having a military command (Hawes, *McIntosh Papers*, 115–16). The British granted McIntosh a parole in May 1781, and McIntosh persuaded Congress on 16 July to repeal its resolution of 15 Feb. 1780 suspending him from his command. McIntosh returned to Georgia in 1782 after the British evacuation of Savannah and mounted a campaign against George Walton and his political allies. At McIntosh's insistence the Georgia legislature appointed a committee to hear his charges against Walton. The committee, composed of William Gibbons, William Few, and young James Jackson, reported on 1 Feb. 1783 that Walton's letter to Congress regarding McIntosh was "unjust, Illiberal, and a misrepresentation of facts" (ibid., 117). George Walton, however, was not prosecuted as McIntosh hoped he would be. Instead, he was made chief justice of the state court the day before the committee issued its report and went on to become briefly in 1789 governor of the state for the second time, then a superior court judge, and in 1795 a United States senator from Georgia.

From Lachlan McIntosh

Sir,   Savannah in Georgia 20th April 1784.
    I had the honor of writing to your Excellency the 20th December in answer to your favor of the 24th October last which I hope you received[1]—and since, your Circular Letter of the 1st January with its duplicate came to hand at the same time, & only four days ago, which I laid before our State Association of Cincinnati whose Quarterly Meeting was held here Yesterday and this Day—and in Consequence, thereof, they have Chosen Majors Eustace, Lucas, Cuthbert and Captain Field to Repre-

sent them in the General Society, who are to proceed immediately to Philadelphia if we can possibly make out as much
Money as will bear their Expenses[2]—and to whom I begg Leave
to refer your Excellency for any information you may require
as they will go fully Instructed, & are directed to carry Copy of
all the Proceedings of our State Society from its commencement.[3] I have the Honor to be most respectfully Your Excellency's most obt Hble Servant

Lachn McIntosh
President of the Georgia Association of Cincinnati

ALS, DSoCi.

1. For GW's circular letter of 24 Oct. 1783, see William Moultrie to GW, 6
April 1784, n.1. In his letter of 20 Dec. 1783, McIntosh wrote GW that he had
directed "the Secretary of our State Association of the Cincinnati to copy such
extracts from the minutes of our proceedings as will give you all the information you require [about the establishing of the Georgia Society], which he will
inclose herewith."

2. Between 1776 and 1780 John Skey Eustace served as aide-de-camp to
generals Charles Lee, John Sullivan, and Nathanael Greene, successively.
John Lucas, who was McIntosh's aide at the siege of Savannah in 1779, was
captain in one or another of the Georgia regiments from 1777 to 1782. Alexander Daniel Cuthbert also served in the Georgia regiments, and Capt. James
Field was an officer in the South Carolina artillery in 1779 and 1780. Only
Cuthbert attended the general meeting in Philadelphia in May.

3. The instructions to the Georgia delegates included this sentence: "You
are also well acquainted with the Objections made to the whole of the Institution in our State, and the groundless fears of some Citizens which deserves
some Consideration, and if in any part of our Institution there is found upon
Mature deliberation a just Cause for such fears they ought to be removed, as
the greatest Glory of the Cincinnati is, that they were prime Agents in giveing
freedom to a great portion of the Globe, and leading the way for all the rest to
obtain it" (Hawes, *McIntosh Papers*, 131–32).

From Arthur St. Clair

Dear Sir   Philada April 20th 1784

I was favoured with Your Letter of the 22d of February—if
any thing could have induced me to postpone my Journey it
was your Wish that I should do so—indeed I should have been
extremly glad to have met the Society of the Cincinnati, but I
had made such Arrangements last fall, previous to my being
appointed a Representative, that I cannot dispense with going

to the back-Country at this time, without suffering very considerable loss.

Strong Prejudices are conceived against the Institution but as they are ill founded I doubt not but they will be got over—I own however that the hereditary Descent of the Medal appears to me an objectionable part, and could wish it might be altered in the Constitution; but I do not believe it is that has raised the cry so much as the Restriction with regard to honorary Members—had their number been left indefinite, or their proportion at least, it is probable they would never have exceeded that proposed in the Constitution. It would also have been well, perhaps, if all political purposes had been avoided—and it is probable some Alterations may take Place on these Points. It is surely ridiculous in the Legislatures to interfere, as, was there any thing Dangerous in the Society, that kind of opposition is the most likely way to establish it—but as the purposes are purely benevolent, and may have happy Effects too rigid an Adherence to the first outline should, in my Opinion, be avoided.

It would have aforded me a very singular Pleasure to have assured you personally with what sincere Respect and Esteem I Am Dear Sir Your Excellencys most obedient Servant

Ar. St Clair

I some time ago received a Letter from Capt. Paul Jones requesting that, at the general meeting he might be admitted a Member, and referring to Mr John Ross, for the Money to be paid. I cannot at present lay my hand on the Letter, but think I gave it to Coll Johnston—shall take the Liberty to request your interesting yourself in his Behalf.[1]

ALS, DLC:GW.

1. John Paul Jones's letter to St. Clair is dated 10 Nov. 1783 and is in CSmH. Francis Johnston was secretary of the Pennsylvania Society of the Cincinnati. John Ross may be Maj. John Ross of the 2d New Jersey Regiment, from which he retired in January 1780.

From Jonathan Trumbull, Sr.

Dear Sir   Lebanon [Conn.] 20th April 1784

Having had the satisfaction to accord with you in the Sentiment of retiring from the busy Cares of public Life, to the tranquil Scenes of private Enjoyment, I anticipate with much pleasure the Reflections which such a State will enable us to make upon the happy issue of those anxious & perplexing vicissitudes through which, in the Course of an Eight Years unusual War, you & I have had the Lot to pass, and in the Cares & solicitudes of which, we have born no ignoble part.

I felicitate you Sir! with great cordiality, on your having already reached the Goal of your wishes—and most devoutly invoke the divine Benediction on your Enjoyments & pursuits. A Month more I trust, will bring me to the Haven of retirement, in the Tranquility of which I hope to have leisure to attend to & cultivate those Seeds of private Friendship, which have been planted during the Tumults of War, and in the Cultivation of which I promise myself to reap much pleasure.[1]

Indulging these prospects, I am induced to wish, & even to hope, that the Correspondence between you and me, which commenced under the pressure of disagreeable circumstances, may not wholly cease when we find ourselves in a happier situation—Altho enveloped in the shades of retirement, the busy Mind cannot suppress its activity, but will be seeking some employment, which will indeed be necessary to dispel that languor, which a Scene of Inactivity would be apt to produce. Subjects will not be wanting; far different, & more agreable I trust, than those we have been accustomed to dwell upon: and Occasions will present, which may serve to beguile a lingering Hour, and afford some pleasing Amusement, or instructive Information.

Let not the Disparity of Age, or the idea of a Correspondent, *seventy three* Years advanced on his Journey through Life, chill your Expectations from this proposal; I promise you my best Endeavours; and when you perceive, as too soon alas! you may, that your Returns are not proportionate to your disbursments, you have only to cease your Correspondence; I shall submit.

The fruits of our peace & Independence do not at present, wear so promising an Appearance as I had fondly painted to my Mind. The Jealousies, the Prejudices & Turbulence of the People, at Times, almost stagger my Confidence in our political Establishment; and almost occasion me to think that they will shew themselves unworthy the noble prize for which we have contended, and which I had pleased myself was so near our Enjoyment. But again I check this rising Impatience, & console myself under the present prospect, with the consideration, that the same beneficent & wise Providence which has done so much for this Country, will not eventually leave us to ruin our own happiness, to become the Sport of Chance, or the Scoff of an admiring World. but that great things are still in store for this people, which Time & the Wisdom of the Great Director, will produce in its best season. In this better Confidence, I bid you Adieu for the present. wishg you every felicity, while I sub-scribe myself—with sincere Esteem & the most affectionate Re-gard Dear Sir Your most Obedient & most hume Servant

Jonth. Trumbull

ALS, DLC:GW; LB, Ct: Trumbull Papers.

1. For reference to the address written by Jonathan Trumbull, Sr., in Oc-tober 1783 declining reelection to the governorship of Connecticut, see Jonathan Trumbull, Jr., to GW, 5 Jan. 1784, n.2.

From Nathanael Greene

Dear Sir   Newport [R.I.] April 22d 1784

Your two letters of the 20th and 27th of March both came safe to hand. My indisposition is such I fear it will not be in my power to comply with your wishes if there was no other ob-stacle. I have a constant pain in my breast and am now so weak as to be incapable of bearing the fatigues of a Journey. Besides which the Doctor thinks it would be dangerous to go by water for fear I might burst a blood vessel as I am very subject to sea sickness and the Vessels of the stomach are exceedingly un-coated. And he thinks it equally dangerous to ride for fear of the same evil. My complaint arose from a strain I got in Provi-dence last Winter in making a violent exertion to save my self from a fall.

It was my intention to have been in South Carolina before this; but Mrs Greene not being put to bed as early as I expected I continued my stay until my own complaints forbids my going.[1] But was I well enough to travel I would certainly go by the way of Philadelphia notwithstanding it would be attended with no small injury to my private affairs; and my necessities on this head are far different from yours. In addition to my own em-barassments on this subject I am under such engagements to provide a Cargo for a vessel of my brothers expected in to Charleston that I should be at a loss how to accomodate that matter even if I had no calls of my own. And what makes me more anxious on this subject he has been unfortunate in trade at the close of the war which renders my obligation to fulfill my engagements the greater. You never felt embarassments in matters of interest and god grant you never may. No body can feel but those that experience It sinks the spirits and depresses the mind.[2]

The uproar that is raised against the Cincinnati makes me more anxious to be at the Meeting than I ever expected to feel. It was uninteresting to me before. Assuming honors hurt my delicacy; but persecution bannishes the influence. The subject is important and it may be equally dangerous to recede or push forward; but I am decided in my opinion not to abolish the order from the prevailing clamours against it. If this is done a way the whole tide of abuse will run against the commutation. The public seem to want somthing in New England to quarrel with the officers about, remove one thing and they will soon find another. It is in the temper of the people not in the matters complained of. I hope the meeting will not be hasty in their determination or in such a hurry to seperate. It is yet uncertain what the politicks of America will lead to if they are not influenced by some collateral cause. It is necessary to create a jealosy in the people to bind them together. If they are not afraid of the Cincinnati local policy will influence every measure. If Congress is silent on the subject as I hope they will it will be a convincing proof they both see and feel its advantages.[3] I am confident the tranquilaty of the public can only be preserved but by the continuance of the order. If I can come I will but whether I do or not I am for continuing the institution without alteration. To make any alteration in the present hour will be premature, injure its influence, and defeat all the good that may be expected from continuing it an object of public attention. My breast pains me so much that I cannot add only my good wishes for your health and happiness. Mrs Greene joins me in kind compliments to Mrs Washington and all the branches of the family. I am dear Sir with esteem and affection Your Most Obedt humble Sert

Nath. Greene

ALS, DLC:GW.

1. Catharine Littlefield Greene gave birth to their fifth child, named Louisa, in March 1784.

2. For information regarding Greene's financial difficulties arising both out of his wartime dealings with contractors to secure supplies for his army and out of his own recent shipping ventures with his brothers Christopher and Jacob Greene, complicated perhaps by Mrs. Greene's expensive tastes, see Greene to GW, 29 Aug. 1784, and notes. At his death in Georgia on 19 June 1786, General Greene left an estate still heavily encumbered by debt.

3. Thomas Jefferson held a quite different view of how his fellow congressmen regarded the Society of the Cincinnati. See Jefferson to GW, 16 April 1784.

From Timothy Pickering

Sir,   Philadelphia April 24. 1784
No opportunity having presented during the winter, of sending your barge to Potowmack; when last in New York I left fresh directions to find a conveyance by the first vessel bound to Alexandria. I have this moment received advice that such a conveyance is engaged. Captain Brothes has agreed to deliver the barge at Alexandria, to colonel Fitzgerald, for whom I left a letter, requesting him to pay the freight, and draw on me for the amount. Capt. Brothes' owners live at Alexandria. He intended to sail from New-York about the 25th instant.[1] I have the honour to be very respectfully Sir your most obedt servt
                                              Timothy Pickering
                                                        Q.M.G.

ALS, DLC:GW; LB, DNA: RG 93, Letters Sent—Col. Timothy Pickering.
Timothy Pickering (1745–1829) became quartermaster general of the Continental army in the summer of 1780 and was GW's choice in 1795 to succeed Edmund Randolph as secretary of state. In May 1783 Pickering formed a partnership with Samuel Hodgdon as commission merchants in Philadelphia.

1. GW as commander in chief in 1783 had a barge on the Hudson manned by a coxswain and eight oarsmen. See for instance, David Humphreys to John Pray, 9 April 1783 (DLC:GW). GW employed Pickering's partner, Samuel Hodgdon, to ship his personal effects by water from Philadelphia to Mount Vernon in December 1783 (see GW to Hodgdon, 13 Dec., and Hodgdon to GW, 11, 18, 20 Dec. 1783). No notice of the arrival at Alexandria of the barge or of GW's personal effects has been found; but in GW's account with Lund Washington there is this entry for 18 Mar. 1784: "By William Marbury Freight of 22 Boxes & other Packages of Goods from Phila. here" (Ledger B,

177). John Fitzgerald (d. 1800), an Irishman who settled in Alexandria before the Revolution and during the war was an aide-de-camp to GW, was a merchant in Alexandria. Captain Brothes has not been identified.

From Armand

[25 April 1784]
Armand request his Excellency to Compare the two inclosed papers then to send him the original in philadelphia at the french ministre & to keap the Copy by him—if his Excellency thought more proper to keap the original, armand request him to send him the Copy attested by his Excellency[1]—the purpose of armand in communicating thoses papers to his Excellency is to preserve his Esteem when he is gone from the Country if then attempts were made to diminish it.

AL, DLC:GW.
1. A notation on the cover, perhaps contemporary, indicates that the two enclosures were Armand's challenge of 19 Dec. 1782 to William Snickers and the account of the ensuing duel, which are printed below as enclosures I and II. On the cover GW wrote: "Note, the Original papers, of which the enclosed are copies, were returned to General Armand after comparing them. Go. Washington April 25th 1784." GW entered corrections, from the originals, in the copies that he retained. His corrections have been noted. See enclosures I and II.

Enclosure I
Armand to William Snickers

Sir   [19 December 1782]
I am going from this State & since your friends had too much respect for themselves to take your part or dares not take it openly, I find my self reduced to fight a man of your low character & the son of a man andighted for forgery[1]—I am on my march to the north & shall arrive at frederictown the 21st instant, & the 22d at eight o'clock in the morning I shall wait for you half a mile from the town on the road to sheperds town,[2] bring eight witnesses with you, each of them with a ⟨caise⟩ of pistols, bring more if you will, as for my part I shall have eight, bring allso throgmorton who whatsoever unworthy as well as your self he is of the major's or any man's notice, will find him disposd to fight him[3]—I have appointed the 22d because I shall

remains at frederictown that day but should it be impossible to you to be there at the time appointed, I shall remains till ten oclok the 23d at the place appointed—

his plantation xber 19, 1782

C. Armand ⟨Ms⟩ de la Rouerie

Copy, in Armand's hand, DLC:GW. He headed it: "Copy of a lettre dated the 19th decembre—1782."

1. See Edward Snickers to GW, 17 May, source note.

2. The duel was fought on 26 Dec. at Harpers Ferry, which is west of Frederick, Md., and downriver from Shepherdstown, West Virginia. See Enclosure II.

3. For "throgmorton," see Enclosure II, n.6. The "major" is George Schaffner (see Enclosure II, n.2).

Enclosure II
Account of Duel between Armand and William Snickers

Frederick town December the 26th 1782

We the Subscribers declare

That on the 21st instant we were called upon in fredericktown by Colo. Armand to be witnesses of the Conduct of the parties Concerned in a difference to be determined at Harpers ferry by 12' o clock the next day.[1]

Early in the Morning that day we sett out with the Colonel— Lieut. Fontevieux his Second, Major Schaffner & three other officers of the Legion who Considered themselves injuried by the adverse party and attended in Expectation of receiving Satisfaction[2]—when we had arrived abt a mile of the place appointed, by the desire of Colo. Armand we and his Second went forward and crossed the Ferry, where after being informed who made up the party of Captn Snickers Captn Morris recrossed the river and informed the Colonel they Consisted of Captn Snickers—Major Willis his Second—and Genl Morgan,[3] informing him at the same time that major Willis objected to any being present at the Combat but the principles and their Seconds—Lieut. Fontevieux said those Gentlemen being officers of the Maryland Line had attended at the instance of the Colonel as witnesses of the proceedings of the Day—Major Willis said he would acquaint Captn Snickers of it—on his return said the Captn would admit one of the Gentlemen, provided Colo. Armand had no objection to Captn Brady's[4] being present also—which on the Colonels landing was agreed to— the Colonel then Enquired after Mr Throghmorton and Major Nevil,[5] and was answeared they were not here to which he replied that he expected from what he had wrote they would have attended, but supposed they considered it more safe to stay away, that his injuried officers had Come to the other side of the River, and would Cross to receive satisfaction from Snickers or any Gentleman who would Stand in his place, Genl Morgan answeared he would evouch for Major Nevil's attending had he conceived himself under any obligation, the Colonel said he must know he is Charged with writing the piece, he was answeared by the General that the piece was acknowledged by its subscriber Captn Snickers to be his own[6]—well, well, we Shall soon see how it will be—replied the Colonel—Captn Morris then asked if there was no way of Settling the Matter without its being Carried to the greatest Extreems, was answeared by the Colonel with a degree of warmth, at the same time puting his hand into his pocket and taking out some Pistolballs, with Shewing his pistols, said these must Settle it[,] there is no other way—Major Willis replied take Notice the motion did not come from our Side.

the principles their Seconds and the appointed Spectators Captn Brady and Dyer, retired to the field, when after the Necessary preparations were made, and the distance of tenn paces prescribed—the Combatants took their Posts and fired—some thing though not material was said by Captn Brady for an accommodation, it not being attended to, they Called for their pistols for an other round, when the Colonel missed fire— Major Willis then proposed that an accomodation take place, and was answered[7] by Colo. Armand, if he Captn Snickers, will take in his publication he may go about his Bussiness, and I to my troop—Captn Snickers replied, if you will first acknowledge you treated me ill, I will withdraw the piece, the Colonel said— that can never be, come take your Pistols Sir—on which a third round ensued, the Colonels pistol again missing fire, when Major Willis renewed his good intentions for accommodating the Matter—which commenced and Continued through as in the last, when Captn Snickers proposed to Colo. Armand a settlement, by withdrawing that part of the publication that opperated against him, which he in plain terms rejected and desired him to take his pistol again, that as yet he had made but one fire, some altercation ensuing, when major Willis took possession of Captn Snickers Pistols, and declared they Should not further be used on this occassion—it was his opinion they had fought enough, to Continue it further he thought could be of no addition to the honor of Either, and at the risque of his reputation was determined to keep them, and Called on Genl Morgan, who at this time with the rest of the absentees were present, for his assistance as a superior officer, to prevent any further fighting—at this juncture the General and Major Schaffner were in Conversation when the later said if Colo. Armand was done with Captn Snickers, he would take the Colonels place, the General replied, he Snickers Should fight no more if he was done with the Colonel, the major Said he has injuried me, his fighting the Colonel is not giving me Satisfaction for if one Gentleman insults ten, he has ten Gentlemen to give satisfaction to, *or his friends must do it and I believe you to be his friend*, the General with a Shew of warmth asked him if he knew whom he was talking to, he said *he did, I know you are an Officer and I am an other*, to this was replied he would arrest both him and Colo. Armand if they persisted in Continuing the matter the Colonel answeared he Should obey no arrest from him on the Occassion, the General said, I am a General officer and will let you know you Shall obey any arrest from me the Colonel replied, I know you are a Genl officer, but you have on this occassion made void your authority by knowing and attending the bussiness of this day and more especially by admitting it to take place, which done, we may continue or decline on such principles as we may think proper[8] without paying any respect to your authority—the gentlemen present interposing the Dispute dropt—when Motion was made that although the principles had fought, the parties concerned in the Difference still remained in the same disagreable situation they were in, and recommended that four or five of the Gentlemen present should be appointed to settle the Dispute, which after some time was agreed to, and all adjourned to Captn Brady's an adjassant house, where the Matter was settled in the Manner and form of which you have a true Copy.

> Jona. Morriss Captn 1st Maryland Regt
> Edwd Dyer Captn 3d Maryland Regt[9]

D, DLC:GW.

Jonathan Morris was made a first lieutenant in the 7th Maryland Regiment on 10 Dec. 1776 and served in the Maryland forces until his retirement in April 1783. After making captain in April 1777, Morris was wounded at the Battle of Camden on 16 Aug. 1780, and then in January 1781 he was assigned to the 2d Maryland Regiment. Edward Dyer, a Marylander, became a second lieutenant in the Maryland 2d Regiment on 14 Jan. 1777, first lieutenant on 27 May 1778, captain lieutenant on 10 Sept. 1780, and retired on 1 Jan. 1783. In a letter to William Jackson on 20 Oct. 1783, Otho Williams referred to Dyer as "a plain, honest, poor man" with "a large, and an amicable family" (DNA:PCC, item 152).

1. Frederick, Md., is 22 miles from Harpers Ferry, West Virginia.

2. The aggrieved officers of Armand's Legion who were with him on the day of the duel were: Lieutenant Fontevieux, Lieutenant de Coutoures who acted as Armand's second in the duel, Maj. George Schaffner (Schaeffer) of Pennsylvania, Captain de Bert, Capt. John Sharp of Pennsylvania, and Cornet James McDougall.

3. William Snickers (b. 1759) was the son of Edward Snickers (d. 1791) of Frederick County, Va., with whom GW had had occasional dealings since 1756. Young Snickers survived the duel to have his horse Paul Jones win the Jockey Club purse in Alexandria on 10 Oct. 1786, in GW's presence, and to marry in 1793 GW's cousin Frances Washington (b. 1775), daughter of Warner Washington. Snickers held a captaincy in Charles Mynn Thruston's Additional Continental Regiment from March 1777 until the end of January 1778. Francis Willis, Jr. (1745–1829), held the rank of captain in William Grayson's Additional Continental Regiment from January 1777 to May 1778, was probably at this time living in Berkeley County, the location of Harpers Ferry where the duel was fought. For further identification of Willis, see Ralph Wormeley, Jr., to GW, 16 July 1784, n.1. Gen. Daniel Morgan left Gen. Nathanael Greene's army in February 1781 because of ill health and returned to Frederick County, Va., where he built his house, Saratoga, in 1782.

4. William Brady, former captain of the Berkeley County militia and of Stephenson's rifles, resigned his captaincy in the 11th Virginia Regiment in September 1778, when this notation was entered by his name: "Never done any duty, behaved infamously, and recommended to be struck off" (Heitman, *Officers of the Continental Army*, 96).

5. "Throghmorton" is probably Albion Throckmorton of Frederick County who married Warner Washington's daughter Mildred in December 1785 and so was to become the brother-in-law of one of the principals in the duel when Snickers married Mrs. Throckmorton's sister in 1793 (see Dolphin Drew to GW, 13 Feb. 1784, n.2). Presley Neville (1756–1818) and his father John Neville (1731–1803) left Frederick County, Va., shortly before the Revolution and built houses on either side of Chartiers Creek near Pittsburgh. The younger Neville, like his father, served with the Virginia forces during the Revolution. He was aide-de-camp to Lafayette in 1778 and was brevetted lieutenant colonel, the rank he held to the end of the war.

6. The "piece" that Snickers wrote has not been identified. Neville was General Morgan's son-in-law.

7. GW struck out what appears to be "assures" and wrote in "answered."

8. GW inserted "on such principles as we may think proper," which presumably he took from the original when he compared it with this copy.

9. Below this the copyist wrote "at your particular request we have been thus particular in our narrative state of this affair, which we think is correct—and have only to wish when requisit it may prove satisfactory," followed by "Jona. Morris[,] Edwd Dyer[,] Frederick town December the 26th 1782."

GW inserted "Sir," followed by a comma, at the beginning, and at the end, before the signatures, "we are Sir Yr Mo. Obt & very Hble Servt." He also added below the date line: "Colo. Armand," which seems to indicate that the narrative was written for Armand at GW's direction.

On another sheet the copyist wrote: "We the subscribers being Called upon to settle a dispute between Colo. Armand Major Schaffner—Captn de Bert—Captn Sharp—Lieut. decoutures and Cornet McDougle of his Corps on the one side and Captn Snickers and Mr Throgmorton of the other—are of Opinion that the Matter arose from a misunderstanding Colo. Armand and Captn Snickers who have been principles in this Matter by their Conduct at this meeting Evinced this opinion—we do therefore in the Names of those Gentlemen desire that an immidiate stop may be put to all publications on this head and that this unhappy dispute may be Buried in oblivion," signed by Edward Dyer, Jonathan Morris, "Wm Bready," and Francis Willis, Junior.

To David Parry

Sir,   Mount Vernon 25th April 1784

Altho' I have not the honor of a personal acquaintance with your Excellency, I take the liberty of introducing the bearer Major George Auge Washington, a Nephew of mine, to you. Bad health, & the advice of his Physicians induce him to try the Sea air, & a Vessel presenting from the port of Alexandria for Barbadoes he has taken a passage in her to that Island, from whence he may soon depart for some other, as it may not be proper for him to remain long in a place.[1] I have the honor to be &ca

G: Washington

Note—the above was written to the Governors of the several West India Islands.

LB, DLC:GW.

David Parry was governor of Barbados from 1784 until his death in 1793.

1. On 18 July Parry, writing from Barbados, thanked GW "for giving me an Opportunity of becoming Acquainted with so pleasant a man." It was not until 25 May 1785 that GW thanked Parry for his letter and for the attention he had shown George Augustine Washington. See also GW to George Augustine Washington, 27 June 1784.

From David Stuart

Dr Sir, Abingdon [Va.] 25th Apl 84
    I send you translations of two letters only—the third written
by a Merchant, is so full of the abbreviations in use by the
Gentlemen of that Profession, that I can only make it out, here
& there[1]—And from what I have been able to make out in this
manner, I imagine, you will not consider a translation very necessary—It begins with informing you, of his having been persuaded by his brother to come to America, with a venture of
goods; that the Country not agreeing with him he returned;
leaving his brother at Petersburg (the place they arrived at) to
dispose of the goods. It would appear, that not being able to get
any intelligence from his brother, respecting the sale of the
goods, in wc. they were jointly concerned, and being likely to
suffer in France by law, for the money, that enabled them to
make the venture of goods, he begs from your great acquaintance with every one, that you would be pleased to inform
him—if you can't do this, that you would cause an advertisement he gives (and wc. I cant find out) to be inserted in the
papers—He writes as if he had known you—His name is Dasmont[2]—Perhaps some of the French Gentlemen in Alexandria,
might give the information required—If you shall think so, I
will with pleasure lay it before them, and have the advertisement (as I suppose they may understand it) inserted in the
papers.[3]
    I beg Sir, you will continue allways to lay your commands on
me: as nothing I can perform, can be deemed in any sort an
equivalent, for what I stand indebted to you, as an American. I
am with the greatest respect, Yr very Obt Servt

                                      Dd Stuart

ALS, DLC:GW.
    1. None of these letters has been identified.
    2. Dasmont has not been identified.
    3. Stuart did show Dasmont's letter to an Alexandria merchant. See Stuart
to GW, April 1784.

From John Allison

Sir   Alexandria [Va.] April 26th 1784

At a meeting of the Officers of the Continental line in October last to appoint officers of the State Society of Cincinnati; It was there resolv'd, that no officer not holding a Continental Commission should be entitled to become a member[1]—As I saw it in a different light from the Gentlemen that compos'd that Body; I beg leave to lay before your Excellency the State & progress, of the Regiment to which I belong'd from its first rise to the close of the War.

April 1st 1776 an order passed the Committee of Safety for raising Nine Companies of Marines for the defence of the State; many of these Companys were compleated in less than a Month, & imeadeately enter'd upon Service.[2]

In the October Session following an addition was made of Six Regiments to the Continental Line, and three Regts of Infantry was likewise order'd to be rais'd for the defence of the State; In which three Regts was to be incorporated the Nine Marine Companies, they being found useless aboard small Vessels.[3]

May 1777 the Assembly finding they were deficient in their Continental Quota—Ordered that a Regiment of the State troops should imeadiately march to join the Continental Army under the Command of Genl Washington[4]—Which Regt was chiefly compos'd of the Marine Companies (who readily turn'd out Volunteers) And were put under the Command of Coll George Gibson.

The October Session of 1777 pass'd an act that the Regt of State troops under Colo. George Gibson, then in Continental Service, Should remain in place of the Ninth Virginia Regt Captured at German Town, to be considered as part of their Continental quota; And to be entitled to every previlige & emolument of Continental troops from this state, Which Act was coroborated by several others of a Similar Nature.[5]

In Jany 1779 an application was made to Congress respecting our Regiment, and receiv'd the following proceedings for Answer viz.—[6]

Sunday 31st Jany 1779

At a meeting of the Committee appointed by Congress to confer with the Commander in Chief—

Present   Mr Duane
          Mr Laurens   In Conference with the
          Mr Root   Commander in Chief
          Mr M. Smith

A letter from Coll George Gibson of one of the State Regiments of Virginia setting forth that he had recd no orders for re-enlisting that said Regiment, & that the time for which the men were enlisted is daily expiring—that very few of the men were enlisted to serve during the War; and that they are willing to enlist on the same terms as the troops from the State of Virginia, in Continental Service, was read; and the said letter being refer'd to this Committee with power to take such order thereon as they shall Judge proper; It is unanimously agreed that the Commander in Chief shall give orders for re-enlisting the men belonging to the said Regiment for the War, allowing them the Contl Bounty, & that if the State of Virginia shall incline to take the Regiments when so re-enlisted into its own imeadiate Service, it shall be at liberty to do so; and in that case, the Bounty money to be advanced out of the Continental Treasury together with the Expences of recruiting shall be return'd.

It is further agreed that if Colo. Smith & his Regiment rais'd for the service of the State of Virginia shall make a similar application to the Commander in Chief of the Army of these United States,[7] the same ⟨mea⟩sures in all respects to be pursued with Regard to that Regiment.

That a Copy of this resolution be deliver'd to the Commander in Chief, & the Original lodged with the Board of War.

Done in Committee of Conference with the Commander in Chief and Sign'd by their order—

(Copy)   James Duane Chair.

A Copy of the above proceedings was transmited to Virginia, whereupon the House of Delegates came to the following Resolution—

In the House of Delegates May 24th 1780

Resolved, that the officers of the first & Second State Regiments, having been employd for several years in the Continental Army, received by Congress as a part of the Quota of this State, and paid by the Continent as such, ought to have enjoyed equal rank privilege & emoluments, from the time of their being ordered to join the American Army, with the Continental Troops of this State.

Resolved, that the Congress by a Resolution dated the thirty first day of Jany 1779 have declaird their Willingness to take the said Regiments into the Continental line, it is expedient that the said Resolution be carried into execution, and that it be further recomended to Congress to give Rank to the Officers of these two state Regiments, having relation to the state of their State Commissions, Provided that such officers shall not be entitl'd to promotion except in the line of the said two regiments.

Resolved, that all disputes relative to rank or command among the officers of the said two Regiments shall be determined by a Board of Officers in like manner & under the same rules as given in the Continental Army.

⟨*illegible*⟩
John Beckley C.H.D.

26th May 1780

Agreed to by the Senate

(Copy)   Will. Drew C.S.

The Regiment in the Spring of 1780 consisting of 100 men for the War, Rendezvous at Petersburg; this number were properly officer'd & sent on to the Southard, where most of them ended their Military carreer in Continental Service; some of the Supernumerary Officers were incorporated with some troops then in the State & thrown into a Legion under Lt Colo. Dabney, which Legion existed to the close of the War.[8]

The proposals for establishing the Society of Cincinnati Says: All Officers of the American Army &c. &c. have the right to become parties to this institution—had the Gentlemen that compos'd the meeting of the Virginia line attended to the above circumstance; perhaps there might been no necessity of troubling your Excellency on the Subject—Though it was our missfortune throughout the course of the War, to labour under the disadvantage of State Commissions, (owing entirely to our own neglect at our first entering into Contl Service) I believe it is evident; we compos'd a part of the American Army as well as those that held Continental Commissions—To your determination we Submit the matter. In behalf of myself & the Officers of the first and Second State Regiments, I am your Excellencys most Obdt Hubl. Servt

John Allison Lt Colo. 1st S. Reg.

ALS, DSoCi.
John Allison, a merchant in Alexandria and an occasional visitor at Mount

Vernon, was major of the 1st Virginia Regiment when it and the 2d Virginia Regiment were transferred to Continental service in 1777, and he was its lieutenant colonel at the time of his retirement in February 1781. No letter in answer to this has been found, but GW may have responded in person.

1. At its initial meetings in October 1783 in Fredericksburg, the Virginia Society of the Cincinnati voted that the matter of "the admission of the Officers of the State Corps . . . should be refered to the decision of the General Meeting" (Edgar E. Hume, *Sesquecentennial History and Roster of the Society of the Cincinnati in the State of Virginia, 1783–1933* [Richmond, Va., 1934], 66). The delegates to the general meeting in Philadelphia in May decided that the officers of such state units were eligible for election to the society (see note 33, Winthrop Sargent's Journal, doc. II in General Meeting of the Society of the Cincinnati, 4–18 May).

2. See the proceedings of the Virginia committee of safety for 29 Mar. and 1 April 1776, printed in Scribner and Tarter, *Revolutionary Virginia*, 6:266–68, 295–303.

3. See "An Act for raising six additional battalions of infantry on the continental establishment" and "An Act for making a farther provision for the internal security and defence of this country" (9 Hening 179–84, 192–98).

4. The journal of the Virginia house of delegates for its May 1777 session has been lost.

5. Allison is referring to "An Act for speedily recruiting the Virginia Regiments on the continental establishment, and for raising additional troops of Volunteers" (ibid., 337–49). George Gibson (1747–1791) of Cumberland County, Pa., was colonel of the 1st Virginia State Regiment from June 1777 to January 1782. He returned to live in his native Pennsylvania after leaving the army.

6. Colonel Gibson wrote GW on 23 Jan. 1779: "The Assembly of Virginia in their late Act passed for the reinlistment of their Troops [9 Hening 565–67] have not taken any notice of the Two State regiments anex'd to the Continental Army." Gibson went on to point out that "His Excelly the Governor & many Gentn of the House of Assembly told me we were considerd as continental troops from the time we were taken into Continental Pay" (DNA:PCC, item 78). From 1777 on the 1st and 2d Virginia state regiments were in the Continental service, paid by the Congress, but they were not "on continental establishment" as were the regular Virginia regiments in the Continental army. GW gave Gibson's letter to Congress on 29 Jan., when it was referred to a committee. The committee's report as given here by Gibson has not been found in DNA:PCC.

7. Gregory Smith was colonel of the 2d Regiment of the Virginia state line from June 1777 until January 1779.

8. Gov. Benjamin Harrison in January 1782 ordered the formation of the Virginia state legion from the remnants of the 1st state regiment and of other units, and Lt. Col. Charles Dabney of the 1st Regiment was given the command of the legion.

From Laval de Montmorency

A Newyork le 27 Avril 1784.

je n'ai pas voulû quitter ce pays ci Sans témoigner a votre Excellence La reconnoissance que j'ai de Ses bontés, je regreterai toute ma vie de n'avoir pû en profiter plus Longtems. j'ai recû infiniment d'honnêtetés de la part des personnes pour Lesquelles Elle a bien voulû me donner des Lettres de recommandation, C'Est un remerciment de plus que j'ai a Lui faire.[1] je parts demain sur Le pacquebot francois pour me rendre en france, je ne manquerai pas de remettre moï meme Les Lettres dont Elle m'a chargé.[2] Si j'osois je prierois votre Excellence de présenter mon hommage respectueux a Madame De Wasington. j'ai l'honneur d'Etre avec un tres Sincere attachement, de votre excellence Le tres humble Et tres obeissant serviteur.

Le Vte de Laval

ALS, DLC:GW.
1. See GW to Thomas Mifflin, 4 April, and notes.
2. See GW to Duportail and GW's letters to Lafayette and his wife, all dated 4 April.

From John Lewis

Dear Sir,   Falls of Ohio 27 April 1784

According to your request I made every enquiry I cou'd when on the Monongahela and at Fort Pitt respecting the Situation of your Lands on the western Waters, as also of your Plantation under the care of Mr Simpson.[1] I cou'd get no satisfactory account of either indeed the short time I was in that Country put it out of my power to get the information I cou'd have wished, it being only four days from the time I got to Redstone till I left Fort Pitt for the falls of Ohio. But from the enquiry I made I think it wd be necessary to send some person, & as soon as possible, to make inquiry into the Situation of yr Plantation & Negro's. The information I got of some of yr Negro's is such as I chuse not to commit to paper, for fear of a Miscarriage of the letter. Not having an opportunity of seeing those persons who have settled on yr Lands on Raccoon and elsewhere, I thought it best to set up advertisements letting the people know your intentions respecting the Lands. I fell in with a Mr David Bradford a Gentleman of the Law, who was then on his way to Raccoon Creek, I got him to take advertisements with him, and a promise to make every enquiry into the situation of your lands there and give me information. A few days agoe I receivd a letter from him, a Coppy of which I inclose you by which you may Judge what step you'd best take for securing your Lands. Mr Bradford is a sensible Man of Good Character, livs on Shirtees Creek, & from the Conversation I had with him believe he'd undertake your Business in that part of the Country, and is I believe as proper a person as you could employ.[2] I have not been able to learn whether any persons have settled on yr Kanhaway lands, but believe there has been persons if not at this time settled on yr land on the Ohio, for this reason as I went down the Ohio I met two boat load of People going down, who told me they were from Washingtons Bottom, did not chuse to stay there any longer as they supposd they should be obliged to pay rent for the land. I have been inform that yr Land on the Ohio & Kenhaway have lately been survey'd, included within Larger Surveys by Persons from Pensylvania, with intent tis said to sell them in Philadelphia. There has been large Quantities of Barren Mountains lately Surveyd, that are not worth the Surveying fees, on purpose to sell in Philadelphia, 'tis pity some method should not be fallen on to Caution people against buying these Lands as they are altogether a fraud. I do not know when I shall be able to return, as yet have only got 32,000 Acres of My Lands Surveyd, but as soon as I can possibly get my business done shall leave this Country. My Compts to Mrs Washington I am & Sir Your Most Obdt Servt

John Lewis

ALS, ViMtV.

1. See GW to Gilbert Simpson, 13 Feb., and to John Lewis, 14 Feb., and notes.

2. Lewis is referring to GW's Millers Run, or Chartiers Creek, land near Raccoon Creek. David Bradford, a native of Maryland, settled in Washington County, Pa., shortly before the Revolution and was admitted to the Pennsylvania bar in 1783. He was to become a leader of the Whiskey Rebellion in 1794. See enclosure.

Enclosure
David Bradford to John Lewis

Sir   Washington County March 28th 1784

Agreeable to the Generals Wish, signified in his letter to you that the people who may have settled on his Lands shou'd be notified of his Intention of asserting his Claims, when out on racoon, I made out several Copies of your Advertisement & directed them to be set up on the Generals lands there, I have also directed some Copies to be set up on his Chirtiers land.

I conversed with several of those who have settled on the Genls Claims on racoon. they seem greatly alarmed indeed on being acquainted of the Generals intentions of asserting his Claim.

They seem'd to me previous to Your Advertisement to have been lulled under the Idea that his Claim wou'd never have made its appearance in this Quarter.

The strength & Justice of his Excellencys Title to those lands he has mention'd to you, will I am convinced induce the people, who have either Ignorantly or Audaciously settled themselves on his rights to Comply with any reasonable Terms the Genl may please to propose.

As it has been a considerable time since those lands have been surveyed, & at an early period of the settlement of this Country, the bounds, at this time cannot be easily ascertained. It cannot be known therefore with precision, who have settled themselves within those bounds.

To obviate this, it might not be improper to mention this circumstance to the Genl when you write to him on this Subject: And to recommend to him to send a Copy of the descriptive part of his patents to his Agent whom he may appoint to transact his Business. This will have a tendency in my Idea, of removing Doubts touching his bounds & also exclude the necessity of Instituting Ejectments which some of the Tenants might otherwise have the rashness to provoke.

I have taken the liberty of making these Observations under a desire of rendering every service to a Man who merits so much of every of his Countrymen. I am with much Esteem Sir Your Humble servt

David Bradford

ALS, ViMtV.

From Gilbert Simpson

Fayatte County Washingtons Bottom [Pa.] April 27th 1784
Sir
Yours of the 13th of February lays before me (and I shall Note its Contents) which did not come to hand till April the 8th my Self and Family laying down then in the Small Pox and not able to Read your Letter for Six days after which put it out of my Power to fulfill your Request to wait on You by the Time Present'd, at Present we have all got well over the Disorder and as Soon as I can get my Plantation in Order for Pitching my Crop I mean to wait on you and doubt not when I have layd before you a true Representation of Facts Supported by Men of Credit that you will still entertain the same Opinion of me that you are pleasd to express in yours that you have Formerly done and hold the Aspertions of your informers in their Proper Scale I shall now endeavour to inform you of the Cituation of the Premisses and Stock I consider I have been here Twelve Years I came into a Howling Wilderness continually apprisd for the first Year of the incursions of a Ravenous and Merciless Enemy which I was Obligd to fortify my Self on the Occasion and having the Mill on hand the same Year it could not be expected that much could be done on Either Plantation or Mill as we was often alarmd of the depredations committed by the Enemy People was Careless of turning out to work so that That Year was gone and but Little done but Since I have from a Wild Oponed a Beautiful Farm of One Hundred a fifty Acres of Cleard Land inder good Fences consisting of Meadow Pasture and Tillage—Land with a good Barn Stable a good Dwelling House Kitching and other Necessary Out Houses with a Good Orchard consisting of One hundred and Twenty Bearing Apple Trees as to the Peach Trees I Planted about 120 but last winter being so Severe I believe they are all Dead and now I think Proper to acquaint you concerning our Stock consisting as Follows 30 Head of Cattle 12 of Horses 50 of Sheep 30 Head of Hogs 6 Young Negroes and one more Expected in a Short Time all the Crops of Grain I shall Render a Proper Account for. I have found Two hands my self in the Crop since my being here which I intended should go for Part of the Provision for my Family, there is Sundry Accts Relating to the Estate that I could not Procure Receipts for such as Blacksmiths Shoe-

makers Weavers Midwifes and sundry others who went upon Campaigns and Never Returnd they was always paid in Grain the Produce of the Premisses which seemed to me altogether immaterial that had my Breast harboured the least Injustice it lay in my Power to take greater Advantages as to Converting of Emoluments to my own use Arising from the Premises to my own Use it has ever been far from me I ever held your Person and Interest in too Sacred a manner to Commit any such a Breach it's true I am a Poor man whom your Honor have known from a Child and Likewise the Family I derive from and I have with Permission till now been able to pass through the various Stages of my Life uncencered at least I never heard of it before but to Conclude on this Subject I trust when Maters are maturely canvasd on Adjusting of our Accts in spite of the Malicious Aspertions of ill designing men I shall be able to convince you of the wrong done me and Clear my Self with Honour Ive been well appris'd of one Grand enemy I have in your Parts from his own Sister, (I mean John Johnson who I doubt not have done his Utmost to injure my Character[)] but I defy his Testimony to Prejudice me before Judicious men that knows us both[1] You Perhaps might have expected more Land cleard in this Term of Time but I would have you Consider that I have but Two Hands except Children and one of them an Ordinary hand to begin to Clear Land in a Country where there is Such a Multitude of Heavy Timber and every Spring by the Timber Falling we have a Fresh Clearing we lay here under Several Emergencies that no Person can be a judge of without he was Spectator.

There is Five Plantations that I have Leasd out of the Tract with good improvements on them Four of which Containing 150 Acres each and one of 100 Acres as Conveniences did not Suit any further Addition to that[,] with a Meadow on each and an Orchard on two of them[.] Ive Receiv'd one Rent of £6 from the Leasd Land and £10 more I expect to Receive this Spring for Two Places one of 150 Acres and the other of 100 Acres and for three more Places Rent becomes due next Spring and now I have given you a Full Detail of Occurrencies concerning the Land and shall begin now to Inform you about the Mill which Representation I doubt not will be far different from what you have heard.[2]

I Grant that the Mill is Good but the Stream she lays on but very indifferent as it's Dry all Summer, and the Cituation of the Mill lays so that she is Frozen up the Chiefest Part of the Winter and now there is no less than Eight Mills and the Furthest of them not above Eight Miles apart from yours which takes great Part of our Custom away indeed was it not for our Boulting Cloth[3] which some of the above recited Mills is not Provided with the Mill would stand idle half her Time when well Provided with water my Self and hands have Lost above three Months of our Time in Repairing of the Dam and Digging a New Race I have Proper Accts to Lay before you Relative to the Mill properly attested by the Millers and you will find the Profits arising from her to be far Less than you may expect from the Information you have Receivd if Providence will permit me to come down[4] I shall bring the Opinions of the most Responcible Gentlemen in our Parts concerning the Profits arising from the Mill I wish Colll Crawford had been alive he could have given you a Different Account about the Mill[5] then what you have Receivd The Milwright I believe was an Excellent Workman and aimed at making her ⟨fly⟩ but did not consider other advantages I have Bonds and Book Debts by me now to the Amount of £150 due to the Estate and the Estate Owes £20.

The Report that you have heard of my having Cash in my hands Arising from the Profits of the Estate in General I acknowledge and heartily wish I never had for it's Bills of Credit which I am afraid will do neither you nor I any good[.] upon the whole I am determined never to live on a Place where I am Suspected as in such Cases I have a Spirit of Resentment as well as other Men and heartily wish for a Settlement and a Separation I am now a Growing in Years and Rather infirm and should it happen that I cannot wait on you I should be glad you would send an Attorney for you to Settle our Affairs by the Middle of July[6] and for the Present I shall conclude with wishing you and your Lady all the happiness that this world can afford you and when you are Removd home that you may both be wreathed with a Crown of Bliss and Felicity which doubtless will far Surpass the wreath of Lawrel that you have justly Acquired in defence of Your Country whose virtuous Deeds is not unoticed by all the Powers of Europe Please to accept of our kind Service to your Self and Lady and Remain Much Honourd Sir your Humble Servant

Gilbert Simpson

P.S. I should be glad you would send if you dont see me by the Middle of May A Person to settle with me by the Middle of July at Furthest that I may have time to dispose of my Part of the Stock.

ALS, DLC:GW.

1. Samuel Johnston (Johnson), who at the time of his death in 1769 was a tenant on GW's Clifton's Neck land at Mount Vernon, had a son named John and a daughter named Tamar Simpson, the one perhaps the brother-in-law of Gilbert Simpson, Jr., and the other his wife.

2. GW's diary entry for 16 Sept. 1784 states: "Continued at Simpsons all day—in order to finish the business which was begun yesterday. Gave leases to some of my Ten[an]ts on the Land whereon I now am" (*Diaries*, 4:24). For GW's troubled relations with these tenants, see particularly the editorial note in Thomas Smith to GW, 9 Feb. 1785.

3. For a description of the large stone mill at Washington's Bottom, see GW's diary entry for 13 Sept. 1784 and the editors' note in *Diaries*, 4: 20–21. Bolting cloth is used to sift ground grain.

4. For Simpson's visit to Mount Vernon, see his letter to GW of 31 July 1784.

5. William Crawford, the surveyor of the tract at Washington's Bottom for GW, was killed in 1782.

6. See GW to Simpson, 10 July 1784.

To Tench Tilghman

Dear Sir,   Annapolis [Md.] 27th Apl 1784

I came to this place to day, tomorrow (wind permitting) I shall cross the Bay on my way to Philadelphia—Hearing that a Ship with Servants is gone up to Baltimore, and fearing from your answer to my letter (written some time ago from Mount Vernon)[1] that I had not sufficiently explained my meaning I beg leave to inform you that tho' I should have preferred German Servants, yet I did not mean to exclude those from Ireland or any other Country, if good Tradesmen of the profession I designated, and of as good character as the nature of the case would enable you to obtain could be had.

With this explanation I pray your attention to my former request—If there is no coming at the characters of these people from such testimonials as the prudent part of them sometimes bring or the index of the countenance, I would if there is a choice prefer elderly to young men—they are not so vicious nor apt to run away, their professional knowledge is easier ascertained.

If you should buy, please to hire a person to carry them to my House in Virginia, the cost of which, with the price of the Servts I will pay to your Order in Philadelphia, or elsewhere. With very great esteem & regard I am, Dr Sir Yr Most Obedt & Affee Servt

Go: Washington

ALS, PHi: Gratz Collection.
    1. See GW to Tilghman, 24 Mar., and Tilghman to GW, 29 March.

From Thomas Paine

Dear Sir   New York April 28th 1784

As I hope to have, in a few days, the honor and happiness of seeing you well at Philadelphia,[1] I shall not trouble you with a long letter.

It was my intention to have followed you on to Philadelphia, but when I recollected the friendship you had shewn to me and the pains you had taken to promote my interest, and knew likewise the untoward disposition of two or three members of Congress, I felt an exceeding unwillingness that your friendship to me should be put to farther tryals, or that you should experience the mortification of having your wishes disappointed, especially by one to whom delegation is his daily bread.

While I was pondering on these matters, Mr Duane and some other friends of yours and mine, who were persuaded that nothing would take place in Congress; (as a single man when only nine States are present could Stop the whole) proposed a new line, which is to leave it to the States individually; and a unanimous resolution has passed the senate of this State, which is generally expressive of their opinion and friendship. what they have proposed is worth at least a thousand Guineas. Other States will act as they see proper. If I do but get enough to carry me decently thro the world and independantly thro' the History of Revolution I neither wish nor care for more, and that the States may very easily do if they are disposed to it. The State of Pennsylvania might have done it alone.[2]

I present you with a new song for the Cincinati, and beg to offer you a remark on that subject. The intention of the name, appears to me either to be lost or not understood. For it is material to the future freedom of the Country, that the example of the late Army retiring to private Life on the principles of Cincinatus, should be commemorated, that in future ages it may be imitated, Whether every part of the institution is perfectly consistent with a republic, is another question, but the precedent ought not to be lost.[3]

I have not yet heard of any objection in the Assembly of this State to the resolution of the Senate, and I am in hopes there will be none made. Should this method succeed, I shall stand perfectly clear of Congress which will be an agreeable Circumstance to me, because whatever I may then say on the necessity of strengthening the Union and enlarging its powers, will come from me with much better grace than if Congress had made the acknowlgment themselves.

If you have a convenient opportunity, I should be much obliged to you to mention this subject to Mr president Dickinson. I have two reasons for it, the one is my own interest and circumstances the other is on account of the State, for what with their parties and Contentions, they have acted to me with a Churlish selfishness, which I wish to conceal unless they force it from me.[4]

As I see by the papers you are settling a tract of Land, I enclose you a letter I received from England on the subject of Settlements.[5] I think Lands might be disposed of in that Country to advantage. I am Dear Sir your much Obliged and Obedient Hble servant

Thomas Paine

ALS, DLC:GW.

In the fall of 1783 shortly before GW left the army, Thomas Paine was living in some poverty in Bordentown, N.J., when GW, having learned of this, wrote Paine on 10 Sept. from his headquarters at Rocky Hill near Princeton to invite him to "come to this place, and partake with me." Paine made his visit during the fall before GW's return to West Point in November. Paine's most recent employment was in 1782 when he was being paid at the rate of 800 dollars per annum from secret service funds for "informing the People and rousing them" to action through his writings (see Robert Morris, Robert Livingston, and GW to the Continental Congress, 10 Feb. 1782). This employment came to an end after Robert Morris's resignation from the office of superintendent of finance January 1783. Paine wrote Elias Boudinot, president of Congress, on 7 June 1783 asking that Congress "direct me to lay before them an account of such services as I have rendered to America" (DNA:PCC, item 55). He wrote Boudinot again on 26 June expanding on his services to America and asking for a response to his letter of 7 June. Before closing, he wrote: "General Washington is the only Gentleman to whom I was ever fully explicit on the Circumstances of my Situation and that more particularly in a conference which he had with me at my Lodgings soon after my return from france [c.September 1781]. He felt for me because he felt for himself. and I owe something to the friendship of that Gentleman that I have been enabled to continue in America during the War" (DNA:PCC, item 55). Paine's request was referred to a committee of three, and Benjamin Hawkins reported for the committee on 18 Aug. 1783: "That it is indispensably necessary, a just and impartial Account of our Contest for public freedom and happiness should be handed down to posterity. That this can be best done by a historiographer to the United States of great industry and abilities; by one too, who has been and is governed by the most disinterested principle of public good, totally uninfluenced by party of every kind. That Thomas Paine Esqr. has rendered very essential services to the cause of America, from the commencement of the War to the conclusion thereof, without having sought, received or stipulated for any honors, advantages, or emoluments for himself. That a history of the American Revolution compiled by Mr Paine is certainly to be desired, Whereupon, the Committee recommend the following Resolution.

"That Thomas Paine Esqr. be appointed Historiographer to the United States. That his salary be [   ] dollars per annum" (*JCC*, 24:513). The report was referred to another committee on 31 Oct. 1783, where the matter seems to have ended.

1. Paine is alluding to the meeting of the Society of the Cincinnati to be held in Philadelphia in May.

2. For the action taken by New York, see GW to Patrick Henry, 12 June 1784, n.2. James Duane (1733–1797) was at this time mayor of New York City and a member of the state senate.

3. The only song written by Paine which has been found that is appropriate for the Cincinnati is called "Columbia" to be sung to the tune of "Anacreon in Heaven." It concludes with this sixth stanza (Conway, *Writings of Paine*, 4:488–89):

> Ye sons of Columbia, then join hand in hand,
> Divided we fall, but united we stand;
> 'Tis ours to determine, 'tis ours to decree,
> That in peace we will live Independent and Free;
> And should from afar
> Break the horrors of war,
> We'll always be ready at once to declare,
> That ne'er will the sons of America bend,
> But united their Rights and their Freedom defend.

4. John Dickinson (1732–1808) was president of the supreme executive council of Pennsylvania. Paine, who had been deeply involved in the turbulent politics of Pennsylvania in 1779, wrote Mathew Irwin on 27 Nov. 1784: "The President [Dickinson] has made me acquainted with a Conversation which General Washington had with him at their last interview respecting myself." On 6 Dec. the Pennsylvania council sent a message to the general assem-

bly stating that "the President having reported in Council a conversation between General Washington and himself respecting Mr Thomas Paine, we
have thereby been induced to take the services and situation of that gentleman at this time into our particular consideration." Its message went on to call
for "a suitable acknowledgement of his eminent services, and a proper provision for the continuance of them in an independent manner." The assembly
voted to pay Paine £500 (Conway, *Paine*, 208–9). For GW's unsuccessful
efforts to have the Virginia legislature come to Paine's aid, see GW to Patrick
Henry, 12 June, and notes, and Madison to GW, 2 July, 12 August.

5. The letter has not been identified.

From Pierre-Charles L'Enfant

Ser   new york april. the 29th 1784.

I take the liberty to inform your Excellency of my arrival at
this place after a passage of 43 days from france which I left on
the 16th of march last after having finished Every thing respecting the society, the diploma is Engraved and many prints
of it already drawn together with a number of stamps of the
bald eagle or sign of the association Exceeding by more than
two hundred the number for which I recived the money issuing
from the subscription which took place previous to my departure from america, those given to the french being included,
the die for the meadal is the only thing wanting, but will be
send after me.[1]

a letter which I had the honour to address to your Excellency
in junary last[2] will have acquainted you with the particulars of
my first Steps to bring to a proper issue the matter trusted to
me, with his must christian madjesty Kind reception, and gra-
ciouse assent to the wearing in his Kingdom the marks of an
association already beheld as one of the most recommendable
amongst those formed on similar occasions and of wich the
basis Established upon a characteristick Republican principle
will leave to posterity a respected monument of fraternity, and
a glorious testimony of a national and reciprocal union, never a
token of honor even the most illustrated in the different Kingdom of Europ could have fixed more the attention, and been
received with more gratitude than that which is Bestowed by
the american army on that of france. I will soon furnish your
Excellency with proofs a bundantly sufficient to vindicate my
assertion, and could have done it at this moment had not the

numbers of letters I am the bearer of been to voluminous to be sent by this opportunity[3] your Excellency will percive by thier defferent contents what sensation the cincinnati has caused in france and petition coming from different side⟨s⟩ will prove how much it has Excited the pride of Every persons who had the leist Share in the last contest with great Bretagne; and I am apt to belive that tho' the limited numbers of foreigners the american army has resolved to admit into thier Brotherly association seems to leave no Room for aditional members, yet the rank and distineguished merite, as well as the Eminante services Rendered to the united States, will be worthy of particular consideration and will move the society in favour of some gentlemen whose name can not but reflect honnour on the society, of this numbers are the captaine of the Roial navy who Rank as colonels in the armys, and some land officers whose particular Right are mentioned in the petitions formed in thier Bealf by the Counts dEsting and de Rochambeau, as for what concerns the officers who acted conjointly with us under the commande of general Count d'Esting and who were not personally named in the Resolve relative to foreigner, as it could not have been the intention of the society to cast any reflections upon gentlemen who nobly hazarded thier lives and shed thier blood on many occasions and of whom the galante Behaviour even in the much unfortunate attempt deserved the praise and gratitude of america. I thought it my duty to attend the purpose of the resolve as nearly as possible and construing its meaning to give the world a publick testimony of the american army's fraternal frindship and gratitude towards the french, I looked upon these gentlemen as having been tacitly comprehended under the more usual denomination as Expressed in the Resolve of the Cincinnatus, who said all the general and colonels who served america in the armys under the commande of general Counte de Rochambeau, your Excellency sensible how prejudicial such a forget-fulnes would have Been to the chief aim of the resolve, will I hope approve my Conduct towards those gentlemens to whom I presented the marques of the associations as being directed by special command from the society it self.[4]

previously to the day appointed to distribut the order of the Cincinnati general count de Rauchambeau communicated to the land officers the King his permission to thier acceptance of it, and after the Reading of your Excellency official letter together with the included Copie of the institution of the society those gentlemen being assembled made a motion to cause a sum of mony to be layd up by voluntary subscription the amount of to be thrown in to the funds of the general society, being acquainted with thier intention, I opposed it objecting that the title and marks of the Cincinnati were to be considered as freely allowed to foreigner, and that the american army had not meant to comprehend the french in the assessement required only from her continantal Bretheren, but they inssisted upon supporting thier motion by interpreting to its advantage the article of the institution which leaves a door open to donnation Even from personnes not reconised as members of the society, and arguing from this that it would be a Breach to the law of the association to oppose thier donnation they informed me of thier having unanimousely agreed to compleat a sum to the amount of *60000* Livres and deliver it up to me, which notwithstanding thier instances I refused to accept previousely to my reciving more particular direction from the general society to Whom I informed the Count de Rochambeau I Should transmit thier intention at the first general meeting and it as been agreed that until thier desisive Resolution the sayd mony should be deposited in the hand of the treasurer of his army,[5] after that matter had been setled in that way, al these gentlemen assembled againe on the 16 of junary last the day appointed for thier being admited amonght the Cincinnatus; on that morning I waited first on vice admiral Count desting and after having presented him with the marques of the association I procided from his hotel to that of the Count de Rochambeau were al those gentlemen were waitteing and they being there invested with the order, the ceremony inded with an Elegant Entertainement at which al the continantal officers Resident at paris were invasted, and at the issue of which, toast suitable to the occasion were drink until the compagnie divided. that very day I dispatched the same included in Letters, to the marin officers who were absent from paris and whose ansuerd I shal have the honnour to communicat to your Excellency.

as for what regards the french in the continantal service the marquis de la fayette Being at paris at the times of my arrival in that town I delivered up to him your Excellency dispatchis, and he will have accointed you with his prociding towards them, I am only to mentione some particular, which are that although from the terms of the association we did not think our selves hotorised [authorised] to Forme a regular assembly—yet many petition having been made from gentlemen who had not serve the times required to be reconised as members of our association we formed a comity to Examine thier particular pretention and some of themes being juged deserving to be distineguished from among the others, we agreed that they Should be recommanded to the general society, and the marquis de la fayette as Chief of the commity is to communicat this resolution to your Excellency.

having al so considered the advantages which Would result from aregular corespondence with our Brothers in america we al Expressed our wishis to obtaine from the general society the permission to name a president and to forme a society similar to that of the respective lignes of the Continantal army, upon what it as been agreed to hotorise me to informe your Excellency with our prociding and to solicite the general society to comply with our demande Requiering al so that three of thier representative be admited to set in the general assembly—living to your Excellency to choose amonght those who are stil in america—whaitting for your Excellency ansuerd to this account of my proceding in france I have the Honnour to be with great respect your Excellency most humble obeidient servant

P. L'Enfant

The name of the officers of count Desting army which were considered as comprehended into the resolve are
the marquis de Vaudreuil lieutenant general
de Bougainville Brigadier, & chef de cadre
Count Aartur dilon Brigadier Commandant
in second in his army at savana
de ⟨betisy⟩ suedois Colo. chef de division
de ⟨seting⟩ suedois Colo. idem
marquis de Rouvroy Col. idem—

ALS, DSoCi; copy, Digges-L'Enfant-Morgan Papers. The letter was read at the general meeting of the Society of the Cincinnati, 4–18 May.
    1. For L'Enfant's departure to France with letters to the French officers

about the Society of the Cincinnati and with instructions regarding the Cincinnati eagle and certificate, see especially Lafayette to GW, 10 Jan., n.3.

2. Letter not found, unless he is referring to his letter of 25 Dec. 1783.

3. Many of the French letters read in the general meeting and referred to in Sargent's journal were those brought from France by L'Enfant. See General Meeting of the Society of the Cincinnati, 4–18 May, printed below.

4. For the whole matter of membership in the French Society of the Cincinnati, see General Meeting of the Society of the Cincinnati, 4–18 May.

5. For a discussion of the money the French officers raised to be given to the American Society of the Cincinnati, see Rochambeau to GW, 19 Jan., n.5.

From Edmund Randolph

Dear Sir   [April 1784]

I have forborne to answer your late letter on the subject of the petitions, until I took the steps, which the case seemed to recommend. It is a point, on which the lawyers themselves are divided, whether a new petition can be now brought for a forfeiture before the 29th of Sepr 1775. Altho' I should not conceive such a petition very formidable, yet as there is a doubt, capable of being defended at least with plausibility, as the land is valuable, and as you have perfect confidence in Colo. Bassett, I thought it adviseable to confess judgments to him. I shall therefore return the certificates to the land office; and write to the Colo. for an order to procure fresh patents in your name.[1]

Some difficulty has occurred in the obtaining of an attestation of Gen: Lee's will: but I now have it in my power to inclose it to you.

I beg leave to remind you that the sooner your answer to Savage's bill comes in, the better. Believe me, my dear Sir to be with the sincerest affection yr much obliged and obt serv.

Edm: Randolph

ALS, PHi: Gratz Collection.

1. See GW to Randolph, 18 Mar., and particularly note 4 of that document.

From David Stuart

Dear Sir,   c.April 1784

I am sorry I was not at home yesterday, to have complied with your request, in sending a translation of the Chevalier's letter by Mrs Washington. You will now recieve one of that, and of

Crajenschot's[1]—Monsr Perrin, to whom I shewed Dasmonts letter, tells me, that the Brother enquired after by them, passed thro' town about a month ago—He took a minute of the Contents, to transmit, or take notice of to him, when he should have an opportunity; tho', he thinks from the time, (it being the flourishing period of paper currency) in wc. the venture was made, it has been an unfortunate one; and, that the Brother is unable to make any return[2]—The purport of the Vicounts letter, is, to inform you, that he was Coll of the regiment of Agenais, wc. acted with you at the siege of Yorck, and of the misfortune wc. detained him from being there; hoping you would be too just to add to this misfortune, by excluding him from the honor of an Order, that would be granted to so many of his regiment, and that Count Rochambeau would not admit him, without a line from you. He further adds, the Ch[evalie]r Lucern would interest himself with you, in his behalf his letter is dated at Paris, 15th January—84; and he signs himself Coll of the Saintonge infantry.[3] I am Sir, with the greatest respect Your Obedt Hble Servt

D: Stuart

ALS, DLC:GW.

1. A. J. Crajenschot's letter of 25 Aug. 1783 and Stuart's translation from the French are in DLC:GW. Crajenschot's letter was written from Amsterdam, covering a poem in two volumes *L'Amérique Delivré* by Chavannes de La Giraudière which Crajenschot had published. The "Chevalier's letter" has not been identified.

2. For Dasmont's letter, see Stuart to GW, 4 April. Perrin is Joseph-Marie Perrin, who was a French merchant in Alexandria.

3. The letter of Dulau d'Allemans, 15 Jan. 1784, is printed above.

To Samuel Low

[Philadelphia], Monday Evening 4th May 1784.
G: Washington presents his Compliments to Mr S.L. and begs leave to decline the honor of his dedication.[1] He would have answered the letter from Baltimore under the signature of the author long ago, if he had been informed to whom, or to whose Care he might have addressed it, but, as no direction was given in either case, the thing was not practicable.

Extreme hurry, at this moment, prevents his adding more

than thanks for the honor intended him by Mr S.L. If he had leizure; he would assign the Reasons.

AL, NNebgGW; LB, DLC:GW. The letter-book copy is headed, "To The anonymous author of a Poem."

1. The "dedication" was enclosed in a letter from Samuel Low, signed "The Author," and dated 13 Feb. 1784. The opening sentence (and paragraph) reads: "Being conscious of an unwarrantable presumption in addressing your Excellency, & impress'd with a thorough sense of the Striking contrast between the writer & the patron; the Merits in the one, which (without the smallest tincture of adulation) have excited the admi[ra]tion of men in all Nations, & the vast comparative demerits in the other, I was cautious of inscribing to your Excelly the following Poem, especially as I apprehended it might incur the imputation of a too great effrontery; But from the powerful consideration that there is no one so proper, so worthy to receive this weak (tho' sincere) tribute of gratitude as your Excelly to whom every American is indebted, as a part of that people, so wonderfully emancipated by your patriotic exertions; & convinc'd of that unparralel'd goodness of heart for which your Excelly is so justly celebrated, added to that endearing, that aimiable condescension to inferiors, which ever indicates the noble mind, I am embolden'd to present this poor production of an American Genius, to the perusal of one, whose innate understanding, joined to his Knowledge in the literary world, constitute no small part of his illustrious Character" (DLC:GW). It continues in this vein for several pages. A typescript of the complete letter is in CD-ROM:GW.

General Meeting of the Society of the Cincinnati

[4–18 May 1784]

I. Observations on the Institution of the Society, c.4 May 1784
II. Winthrop Sargent's Journal, 4–18 May

Editorial Note

The Society of the Cincinnati was instituted at Fishkill-on-Hudson on 13 May 1783 when a group of army officers adopted an Institution (or constitution) based on a draft drawn up by Henry Knox the month before. On 19 June 1783 the founders of the society elected GW its president. Although GW signed the Institution, he appears to have done nothing about the society until 23 Sept. 1783 when he wrote Knox to ask him to point out "in *precise terms*, what is expected from the President of the Cincinati previous to the general meeting in May next—As I never was present at any of your Meetings, & have never seen the proceedings of the last, I may, for want of information of the part I am to act, neglect some essential duty" (MHi: Knox Papers). The Institution of 13 May provided that officers of the American army who had served honorably in the Revolution for at least three years (and at their death "their eldest male branches") could become members of the Society of the Cincinnati in the state where they lived, "provided that they subscribe one month's pay" to be used for the support of needy officers and their families. The societies in each state were to meet each year on 4 July, and a general meeting would be held periodically to elect officers and to consider matters of general concern. The stated purposes of the Society of the Cincinnati were (1) "to preserve inviolate those exalted rights and liberties of human nature, for which they have fought and bled"; (2) "to promote and cherish, between the respective states, that union of national honor so essentially necessary to their happiness, and to the future dignity of the American empire"; and (3) "to render permanent the cordial affection subsisting among the officers" (DSoCi). In October 1783 GW sent copies of the Institution of the Society of the Cincinnati to some of the senior French officers who had served in America and received enthusiastic responses about forming a French society, which the king also promptly approved (see GW to Jefferson, 8 April 1784, n.3).

By the time GW arrived in Philadelphia for the first general meeting of the Society of the Cincinnati in May 1784, he had become convinced of the need for drastic action. See particularly note 16 in Winthrop Sargent's Journal. When the meeting convened, GW, as president of the society, sought first, in effect, to abolish the Society of the Cincinnati entirely. Failing that, he persuaded the members to alter the society's Institution radically, most notably in doing away with the provision for hereditary membership. In his Observations on the Institution of the Society of the Cincinnati, printed here as doc. I, GW sets down the alterations in the Institution which he insists upon in the meeting. Doc. II, Winthrop Sargent's Journal, provides the best surviving account of the proceedings of the meeting and of the role that GW played. Printed here as appendixes to Sargent's journal are letters directed to GW as presiding officer dated and received during the meeting itself and letters that went out during the meeting under GW's name as president of the society.

I
Observations on the Institution of the Society

[Philadelphia, c.4 May 1784]

Strike out every word, sentence, and clause which has a political tendency.

Discontinue the hereditary part in all its connexions, *absolutely*, without any substitution which can be construed into concealment, or a change of ground *only*; for this would, in my opinion, encrease, rather than allay suspicions.

Admit no more honorary Members into the Society.

Reject subscriptions, or donations from every person who is not a Citizen of the United States.

Place the funds upon such a footing as to remove the jealousies which are entertained on that score.

Respecting the Funds.

It would be magnanimous, to place them in the first instance, in the hands of the Legislatures for the *express purposes* for which they were intended. This would shew a generous confidence in our Country, which might be productive of favorable sentiments & returns.

If it should be thought that this wd be going too far—reserve them 'till our numbers are reduced to a certain ratio of what they now are—Or, for a certain number of years—then to be disposed of as above.

The disposal of them by Will, or Deed, is too unimportant an object, in my opinion, for any member to be tenacious of. The Sums Subscribed were, in that moment, consigned to charitable purposes—No one ever expected to receive a farthing of it back, unless haplessly he should become an object of its charity—and in this case whether he receives the benefits mediately or immediately from the Society the effect to him, and obligation to them are precisely the same.

Authorize the foreign Officers to hold Meetings in France (if it shall be permitted by their Government)—Empower them at these meetings to hear, & decide upon the pretensions of those, of their own body, who, under the letter, or spirit of the Institution, claim the priviledge of becoming members of the Cincinnati. As also the pretensions of foreigners not of any particu-[la]r State line whose claims are founded on being Officers in the American Army. Americans, in foreign Countries, who belonged to the line of any State, are to make application to the Society of that State, who shall hear, & decide thereupon.

Upon these principles Let the Institution be formed in as clear, distinct & explicit terms as language can convey. Let the Secret[ar]y transmit the same to the Senior Foreign Member in France, or the Senior Land & Naval Officer in that Kingdom (if it shall be adjudged better) for their government. Send copies also to the President of each State Society—Accompany all of these with a well composed letter, expressive of the reasons which induced us to alter the constitution.

Then Abolish the General Meetings altogether, as unnecessary; the Constitution being given, a continuation of them would be expensive, & very probably from a diversity of sentiment, & tenacity of opinion might be productive of more dissention than harmony; for it has been well observed "that nothing loosens the bands of private friendship more, than for friends to pit themselves agst each other in public debate, where every one is free to speak & to act." District meetings might also be discontinued as of very little use, but attractive of much speculation.

No alterations short of what is here ennumerated will, in my opinion, reconcile the Society to the Community—whether these will do it, is questionable. Without being possessed of the reasons which induce many Gentlemen to retain the order or badges of the Society, it will be conceived by the public that this order (which except in its perpetuity still appears in the same terrific array as at first) is a feather we cannot consent to pluck from *ourselves*, tho' we have taken it from our descendants—if we assign the reasons, we might I presume as well discontinue the order.[1]

ADf, DLC:GW.

On the second day of the general meeting of the Society of the Cincinnati, 5 May, GW spoke twice calling for a fundamental alteration of the society's

Institution, or constitution. These "Observations" are almost certainly notes that he made in preparation for his second speech of 5 May. Winthrop Sargent's journal of the general meeting indicates that GW again made most of these points in his long speech on 6 May. After hearing the report of the committee of twelve appointed to revise and amend the society's Institution in light of GW's criticism, GW on 10 May spoke at length against the committee's proposals, declaring that they retained too many features of the original Institution. A committee of five then undertook a second revision of the Institution, and, after further revision, its report was adopted as embodying the new Institution of the society. For GW's opposition to the original Institution and his role in having it altered, see Winthrop Sargent's journal (doc. II), and note 16 in particular.

1. For the crystallizing of GW's opposition to the original Institution of the Society of the Cincinnati as set out in these "Observations," see particularly his letter to Thomas Jefferson of 8 April and Jefferson's response of 16 April 1784, and notes of both documents.

II
Winthrop Sargent's Journal

[Philadelphia, 4–18 May 1784]

Tuesday the 4th of May. 1784.

⟨Assembled at the City Tavern, & after choosing a committee of three to examine the credentials of gentlemen who should present themselves as delegates to the General Meeting, adjourned till 9 o'clock tomorrow morning:—⟩

[Wednesday, May 5th, 1784.] Convened at nine:—Reced the report of the committee, as follows;

Properly elected[1] for

N. H. Henry Dearborn.[2]

Massachusetts. Henry Knox, Rufus Putnam, David Cobb, William Hull, Winthrop Sargent.[3]

Rhode Island Nathl Greene, James Vernom, Jeremiah Olney, Daniel Lyman, Samuel Ward.[4]

Connecticut Samuel H. Parsons, Jedediah Huntington, Heman Swift, David Humphreys, Jonathan Trumbul.[5]

New York. Phillip Cortland, Wm S. Smith, Nicholas Fish, James Fairlie.[6]

N. J. Elias Dayton, David Brearly, Jonathan Dayton, Aaron Ogden.[7]

P[ennsylvania] John Dickinson, Stephen Moylan, Thomas Robinson, Thomas B. Bowen, Abraham G. Claypole.[8]

D[elaware] James Tilton, James Moore.[9]

M[aryland] Wm Smallwood, Otho H. Williams, Nathl Ramsay, Wm Paca.[10]

V[irginia] George Wheedon, Wm Heth, Henry Lee, James Wood.[11]

N. C. Reading Blount, Archibald Lyghtle, Griffith J. McRee.[12]

S. C. Wm Washington, Walton White, Lewis Morris, George Turner.[13]

G[eorgia] John S. Eustace, Alexr D. Cuthbert, John Lucas, James Feilds.[14]

⟨*General Washington*, president genl and Gen. Knox, treasurer, beged leave to resign their offices. The President was then requested to resume his seat as a temporary appointment for the whole business of this general meeting; & Major Turner was desired to attend to the duty of scribe:[15] After which we resolved ourselves into a committee of the whole, Col. Ramsay in the chair, and the institution was read, agreeably to the general resolution. The President then arose—express'd the opposition of the state of Virginia and other states—observed that it had become violent and formidable, and call'd for serious consideration; desired of the members of the several states to declare the ideas which prevail'd in their country's with regard to our Institution, and the various manners which they had pursued to obtain this knowledge. *Connecticut*, by *Colo. Humphreys*; a very⟩ general disapprobation of the People—⟨*Masstts*, by *General Knox*; express'd⟩ similar sentiments—with this difference that some very sincerely wish its Existence, but with alterations material. ⟨*New York* by *Colo. Smith*;⟩ declared no opposition. ⟨*Delaware*, by *Mr. Tilton*⟩ inform'd that the principal and indeed only Enemies of the Cincinnati were amongst the Class of people denominated Tories. ⟨*Colo. White*, from South Carolina,⟩ gave it as his opinion, that almost all the various Classes in the State from whence he came were opposed to the Institution in its present form—⟨*Georgia*, by Major Cuthbert,⟩ declared the very opposite—⟨*Captn Dayton* arose and inform'd the meeting that he did not know the sentiments⟩ of the People generally in the State of ⟨*Jersey*, but that it was the determination of the Society to preserve and support its dignity. *Pennsylvania*, by *Governor Dickison*;—as⟩ an objection of the People's, pointed out the hereditary part—⟨*New Hampshire*, by *Colo. Dearbourne*, declar'd⟩

that the opinions of the State were very generally in opposition
to the Institution on its present Establishment.

⟨The President General arose, and acknowledged the infor-
mation⟩ from all the States—endeavoured to prove the disagreeable consequences which would result to the Members of
the Cincinnati from preserving the Institution in its present
form—illustrated the force & strength of opposition to it in a
variety of examples—supported by his own knowledge, &
⟨informations from confidential friends⟩—proposed as the
most exceptionable Parts & that required alterations in their
very essence—the following—Viz—⟨the hereditary part—interference with politicks—honorary members—increase of
funds from donations, and the dangers which would be the result to community from the influence they would give us⟩—declared that was it not for the connection which we stood in with
very distinguished Foreigners in this Institution he would propose to the Society to make one great Sacrifice more to the
World & abolish the Order altogether—the Charitable Part excepted—That considering the Connection which we stood in
with France—the particular situation which our Society had
placed some of their Officers ⟨he was willing, provided we could
fall on a middle way, that would neither lead us to the displeasing of them or encouraging the jealousies and suspicicions
of our countrymen, to adopt it—But he doubted if this was
possible, and if it should so appear on a full investigation he
was determined at all events to withdraw his name from
amongst us.[16]

The General here in confidence introduced a report of a
Committee of Congress that no persons holding an hereditary
title or order of nobility should be eligible to citizenship in the
new state they are about to establish, and declared that he knew
this to be levelled at our Institution—that, our friends had prevented it from passing into resolution, till the result of this
meeting should be known; but if we do not make it conformable to their sense of republican principles we might expect
every discouragement and even *persecution* from them and the
states severally—That 99 in a hundred would become our violent enemies.[17]

Here the General introduced a private letter from the Marquis *Lafayette*, objecting to the hereditary part of the Institution,
as repugnant to a republican system, and very exceptionable.[18]

Jersey and New York take the matter up on this letter, and in the strongest terms oppose the entire abolition of the hereditary rights and honors of the Society.⟩

Committee rose—President resum'd his Seat & the Chairman reported to have made some Progress in the Business before the Committee—beg'd Leave to sit again at 9 Clock to-Morrow Morng—to which time this meeting stands adjournd.

Thursday, May the 6th, 1784.

Met according to adjournment—The Proceedings of the preceding Day were read—Order of the Day moved for & the Meeting resolved into a Committee of the whole—a private Letter ⟨was introduced by *General Knox*, from the *Chevalier General Chateuxleau*, the sentiment of which seem'd opposed to the hereditary part of the Institution of Cincinnati.[19] General Washinton arose and again oppos'd this part as peculiarly obnoxious to the people. In a very long speech and with much warmth and agitation he express'd himself on⟩ all the Parts of the Institution ⟨deem'd exceptionable,⟩ & reiterated his Determination ⟨to vacate his place in the Society if it could not be accomodated to the feeling and pleasure of the several States[20]— *New York* spoke in favor of the present form of Institution—as perfectly consonant with the feelings of the people of their State.⟩

A final Report of the Committee being resolved the President resumed his seat & the Chairman reported that the Committee of the whole had taken into consideration the Institution of the Society of the Cincinnati & were of opinion, that it ought to be revised & amended:[21]—submitted for the Determination of the Meeting—whereupon 'twas resolved that a Committee, to consist of one Member from each State should be immediately appointed for this Purpose—The Ballots being taken by States (which is the mode of Voting determined in this Meeting) the following Election is declared duly made, viz.:[22]

New Hampshire Col. Dearbourne
Massachusetts Genl Knox
Rhode Island—
Connecticut—Col. Humphreys
New York—Col. Smith
New Jersey Cheif Justice Brearly
Delaware Doctor Tilton
Pennsylvania Governer Dickison

Maryland General Smallwood
Virginia General Wheedon
South Carolina Col. Washington
North Carolina—Major Blount
Georgia Major Cuthbert—

The Committee proceeded to Business—& House to the Reading of sundry Letters & Papers before them respecting the Society—some of which are refered to the Committee as connected with the Institution immediately & very materially.[23]

A number of Papers address'd to this Society being in the French Language a Committee is to be appointed to translate them—Genl Moylan & Genl Williams the Committee—They are desired to translate all the French & arrange them & other Papers properly for the Attention of this Meeting—adjourn'd to the Hour of 12 to Morrow Morng—

Friday May the 7th

Met agreeable to Adjournment—Major Blount a Delegate from North Carolina attended, produced his Credentials & took a seat with the committee of Revision—

The Committee for translating & arranging the Papers report that they have made some Progress & ask further Time for completing their Business: lay the Letters & Papers which are ready for Inspection before the Meeting—

The Committee for revising & amending the Institution also report—that they have made some Progress & ask Permission to sit again—

The Meeting proceed to the Reading of Papers laid before them respecting the Society—

Resolved that the President General have a Right "ex officio" to attend all Committees—debate & Vote—Adjourn'd to 12 oClock to Morrow—

Saturday Morning [8 May]

Assembled agreeable to the Adjournment of yesterday—Entered on the Reading of the Papers address'd to the Society, in the Order they were laid before the Meeting—[24]

Major Turner temporary Scribe to the Society begs Leave to resign which being granted Col. Trumbull is elected to that Office—

The Committee appointed to revise & amend certain Matters & things in the Institution of the Society of the Cincinnati report that they have finished their Business & and beg leave to lay their Proceedings before the meeting—Resolved, that they be read & lay on the table.

The Committee for arrangement of the Papers report that they have ready for inspection of the Meeting a part which they wish to lay on the table—& ask to sit again—

Resolved that this general Meeting will on Monday next go into a Committee of the whole, to take into Consideration the Alterations & Amendments of the Institution of the Society of the Cincinnati as proposed & reported by the Committee appointed for that purpose. Adjourned to Monday morning, at 9 o'clock.

The following is the form of the Institution, agreeable to the Alterations and Amendments proposed.[25]

1st It having pleased the Supreme Governor of the Universe in the disposition of human affairs, to cause the separation of the Colonies of North America from the domination of Great Britain, & after a bloody conflict of eight years, to establish them free, Independant, & Sovereign States, connected by alliances, founded on reciprocal advantage, with some of the great Princes & Powers of this Earth. Therefore—Gratefully to commemorate this vast event—to continue the mutual Friendships which have been formed under the pressure of common danger and in many instances cemented by the blood of the parties, & to inculcate the great social duty of laying down in peace the Arms assumed for public defence, by forming an Institution which recognizes that sacred and most important principle, and to effectuate those substantial acts of Beneficence dictated by the spirit of Brotherly kindness towards those Officers & their families, who unfortunately may be under the necessity of receiving them:

The Officers of the American Army do hereby in the most solemn manner associate, constitute & combine themselves into one society of Friends—having generally been taken from the citizens of America & holding in high veneration the Character of that illustrious Roman, Lucius Quintius Cincinnatus, whose example they follow by returning to their Citzenship, think, they may with propriety denominate themselves—The Society of the Cincinnati—

2d The Society shall be governed by the following rules & obligations—

3d All the Commissioned Officers of the Continental Army and Navy, as well those who have resigned with honour after three years service in the capacity of Officers, or who have been deranged by the resolutions of Congress upon the several reforms of the Army; as those who shall have continued to the end of the War, have the right to become parties to this Institution; provided that they subscribe one month's pay, and sign their names to the general rules in their respective State Societies on or before the fourth day of July, 1784—Extraordinary cases excepted, The rank, Time of service, resolutions of Congress by which any have been deranged, and places of residence, must be added to each Name—

4th Those Officers who are foreigners, not resident in any of the States, will have their names enrolled by the Secretary General, and are to be considered as members in the societies of any of the State in which they may happen to be—

5th The General society will for the sake of frequent communications be divided into State Societies, and those again into such districts as shall be directed by the State Society—

6th The Societies of the districts to meet as often as shall be agreed upon by the State Society; those of the States annually on such days and at such places as they shall find expedient; and the General society on the first Monday in May, annually, so long as they shall deem necessary, and after wards at least once in every three years—

7th The State Societies will consist of all the members residing in each State respectively, and any member removing from one State to another, is to be considered in all respects as belonging to the Society of the State in which he shall actually reside—

8th The State Societies to have a President, Vice President, Secretary, Treasurer & assistant Treasurer, to be chosen annually by a Majority of votes at the state meeting.

9th The Meeting of the General society shall consist of its Officers, and a representation from each State society, in number not exceeding five, whose expences shall be borne by their respective state Societies.

10th In the General meeting, the President, Vice President, Secretary, and assistant-Secretary, shall be chosen to serve untill the next Meeting—

11th Each State Meeting shall write annually, or oftener if necessary, a Circular Letter to the other State Societies, noting whatever they may think worthy of observation, respecting the good of the Society, and giving information of the Offices chosen for the current year; Copies of these letters shall be regularly transmitted to the Secretary General of the Society, who will record them in a book to be assigned for that purpose—

12th Each State Society will regulate every thing respecting itself & the societies of the districts, consistent with the general Maxims of the Cincinnati—Judge of the qualifications of the Members who may be proposed, and expel any Member, who by a conduct inconsistant with a Gentleman and a Man of Honour, or by an opposition to the interest of the Community in general, or the Society in particular, may render himself unworthy to continue a Member.

13th Each State Society shall obtain a list of its members, and at the next annual meeting, the State Secretary shall have engrossed on parchment two Copies of the institution of the Society, which every member present shall sign, and the Secretary shall endeavour to procure the signature of every absent Member, one of those lists to be transmitted to the secretary general to be kept in the Archives of the Society, and the other to remain in the hands of the State secretary.

14th From the State lists the Secretary General shall make out at the first General Meeting, a complete list of the whole society, with a Copy of which he will furnish each State secretary.

15th The Circular Letters which have been written by the respective State societies to each other, and the particular laws, shall be read and considered, and all measures concerted which may conduce to the benevolent Principles of the Society.

16th In order to form sufficient funds to assist the unfortunate, each Officer shall deliver to the Treasurer of the State society one month's pay—which shall remain for the use of the State society, the interest only, if necessary, to be appropriated to the relief of the unfortunate.

17th Donations may be received from members of the Society or others, for the express purpose of forming funds for the uses aforesaid, The interest of these donations to be appropriated in the same manner as that of the month's pay, Also monies at the pleasure of each member, may be subscribed in the societies of the districts, or the State societies, the whole whereof may be applied by the State society for the relief of the unfortunate members, or their Widows and Orphans.

18th And in order that there shall be at all times a sufficient number of persons in the society to take care of and manage the funds raised as aforesaid; each member shall have liberty to dispose of by deed or will, to take effect after his decease, his right or share in the said funds which persons so appointed shall have authority to act in managing and applying the interest of the funds agreeably to the principles of the institution. And in case any member should die without having disposed of his right in the said funds; the State society of which he was a member shall have power to elect a fit person in his place for the management thereof, untill charters can be obtained from Legislative authority for more effectively carrying into execution the humane intentions of the Society.

19th The Secretary & Treasurer of the State societies shall once in every year request permission of the Legislature of the State to which they severally belong, to lay before the same their books containing the proceedings of the said Societies, together with accounts of their funds & application thereof, and upon obtaining such permission, shall lay the said Books & accounts before such Legislature accordingly.

20th The Society shall have an Order, which shall be a bald Eagle of Gold, bearing on its breast the Emblems hereafter described, and suspended by a deep blue Ribbon edged with white, descriptive of the Union of America and France.

21st The principal figure, Cincinnatus; three Senators presenting him with a sword & other military ensigns; On a field in the background, his wife standing at the door of their Cottage—Near it a plough and instruments of husbandry.

Round the whole, Omnia Relinquit servare Rempublicam.

On the reverse—Sun rising; a city with open gates and Vessels intering the port—Fame crowning Cincinnatus with a wreath, inscribed—Virtutis Proemium. Below, Hands joining, supporting a heart, with the motto—Esto perpetua. Round the whole—Societas Cincinnatorum instituta. A.D. 1783.

22d A Silver Medal representing the emblems to be given to each member of the society, together with a diploma on parchment, whereon shall be impressed the figures of the Order & Medal as above mentioned.

23d The Society deeply impressed with a sense of the generous assistance this Country has received from France, and desirous of perpetuating the friendships which have been formed, and so happily subsisted between the Officers of the Allied forces in the prosecution of the War, having directed that the President General should transmit the Order of the society to each of the Characters hereafter named, viz:

His Excellency the Chevalier de la Luzerne, Minister Plenipotentiary.

His Excellency the sieur Gerard, late Minister Plenitpontentiary.

Their Excellencies the Count d'Estaing, the Count de Grasse, Count de Barras, The Chevalier Des Touches, Admirals and Commanders in the Navy.

His Excellency the Count de Rochambeau—Commander in Chief, and the Generals and Colonels in his Army.

Do now further direct that the President General also transmit the order as soon as may be to his Excellency the Marquis De Vaudreuil, and acquaint him that the Society do themselves the honour to consider him as a Member.

Monday morning, 9 oClock; 10th of May 1784. Met according to adjournment—The Order of the day being moved for, the Society resolved itself into a Committee of the whole—General Smallwood in the Chair—The Institution of the Cincinnati as revised and amended was read generally, and by Paragraphs particularly, that it might be debated on and more fully considered in every Point of View.

The Sentiments of the Majority of the Meeting appeared opposed to the Institution in its present alterations.

⟨The President General most expressly declared against it: gave it as his opinion that the 18th paragraph would be construed as intentional in us to make hereditary the Order, and only an alteration of the terms, but in fact expressing the same designs as held forth in the original Institution. He warmly and in plain language, or by implication seem'd desirous to expunge all the essentials with which the Society was endowed by those from whom it had its origin.⟩

Resolved, to take the sense of the General Committee of the Meeting on the several Paragraphs of the Institution as revised altered & amended in their order—Upon reading them, it is resolved to recommit all but the 1st—7th 8th 12th & 16th Paragraphs—The President resumed his Seat & the Chairman reported accordingly—The Report accepted by the Meeting & 'tis resolved that the Committee for altering & amending the Institution be excused further Proceedings thereon—Resolved also that a Committee of Five be appointed to take into Consideration the Institution & proposed Amendments & make such alterations as they may deem proper of which they are to report to this Meeting as soon as may be. Elected for this Committee; Governor Dickison—General Knox General Williams, Col. Lee & Col. Smith.

Laid before the Meeting & read a Letter from Genl Armand & other French officers—(Major L'Enfant particularly) requesting a Representation in this general Meeting or Society[26]—Resolved, that the Consideration thereof be referred to the Committee for attending to Foreign & other Letters & Papers address'd to this Meeting.

Adjourned till to-Morrow Morng twelve oClock.

Tuesday 12 oClock [11 May].

The Society met according to adjournment & went into the Reading of Letters & Papers before them—

The Committee for translating of the French & arranging all the Papers report that they have completed their Business & beg Leave to lay before the Meeting sundry Letters—

The Committee for altering cer[tain] Matters & things in the Institution report that they have made considerable progress in the Business—shall be able to make a final Report by to-Morrow Morng, & beg Leave to sit till that time—

Finished Reading all the Letters & Papers addressed to the Meeting & Resolved that they shall lay on the Table Until the final Report of the Committee, for altering & amending certain Matters & Things in the Institution—be made— [27]

Adjourned till to-Morrow Morning 10 oClock—
Wednesday Morning 10 oClock—12th of May—Met agreeable to Adjournment.

The Committee of five appointed to alter & Amend certain Matters & Things in the Institution of the Society of Cincinnati report—that they have Finished that Business; & lay their Proceedings before the Meeting—A Copy of the Institution as revised, altered & amended is in Page immediately succeeding the Alterations & Amendments as proposed by the Committee from the several States—

The form of Institution reported by the Committee of Five. [28]

1st.—It having pleasd the supreme Governor of the Universe to give Success to the arms of our Country & to establish the united States free & independent—Therefore, gratefully to commemorate this Event—to inculcate to the Latest Ages the Duty of laying down in Peace Arms assum'd for public Defence, by forming an Institution which recognizes the most important Principle—to continue the mutual Friendships which commenced under the pressure of common Danger & to effectuate the Acts of Beneficence dictated by the Spirit of brotherly Kindness towards those Officers & their Families who unfortunately may be under the Necessity of receiving them. The Officers of the American Army do hereby constitute themselves into a Society of Freinds & professing the highest veneration for the Character of that illustrious Roman, Lucius Quintius Cincinnatus, denominate themselves the Society of the Cincinnati.

2d The persons who constitute this Society are all the commissd and Brevet officers of the Army and Navy of the United States who have served three years & who left the service with Reputation—Officers who have been deranged by the several Resolutions of Congress upon the several Reforms of the Army—all such officers who were in actual service at the conclusion of the War & all the principal staff officers of the Continental Army.

There are also admitted into this Society the late & present Ministers of his most Christian Majesty to the United States—all the Generals & Colonels of Regiments & Legions of the Land Forces—all the Admirals & Captains of the Navy ranking as Colonels who have cooperated with the Armies of the United States in their Exertions for Liberty & other persons as have been admitted by their respective State Meetings.[29]

3d The Society shall have a President Vice President—Secretary & assistant Secretary—there shall be a Meeting of the Society at least once in three years on the 1st Monday in May at such Place as the President shall appoint. The said Meeting shall consist of the aforesaid Officers, whose expences shall be equally borne by the State Funds, & a Representation from each State Society—the Business of this general Meeting shall be to regulate the Distribution of surplus Funds—to appoint Officers for the ensuing Term & to conform the laws of State Meetings to the general Objects of the Institution—

4th The Society shall be divided into State Meetings & each Meeting shall have a President—Vice-President Secretary & Treasurer respectively to be chosen by a Majority of Votes annually The State Meetings on the Anniversary of Independence—They shall concert such Measures as may conduce to the benevolent Purposes of the Society. And the several States Meetings shall at suitable Periods make applications to their respective Legislatures for the Grant of charters.

5th Any member removing from one State to another, is to be considered in all respects as belonging to the Meeting of the State in which he shall actually reside.

6th No honorary members shall hereafter be admitted but upon election by the State Meetings, with permission of the Government of the State in which the Meeting is held, nor shall any member be elected but by the Meeting of the State in which he actually resides.[30]

7th The State Meetings shall judge of the qualifications of its Members, & admonish, or if necessary, expel any one who may conduct himself unworthily.

8th The Secretary of each State Meeting shall register the names of the Members resident in each State & transmit a Copy thereof to the Secretary of the Society.

9th In order to form Funds for the Relief of unfortunate Members, their Widows and Orphans each Officer shall deliver to the Treasurer of the State Meeting one month's pay. & donations may be received from members and others —the Interest of the Pay and Donations, if necessary, to be applied to the purposes before mention'd.[31]

10th No Donations shall be recd but from citizens of the United States—

11th The Funds of each State Meeting shall be loaned to the State by Permission of the Legislature & the Interest only annually to be applied for the purposes of the Society—& if in Process of Time, Difficulties should occur in executing the Intentions of the Society— the Legislatures of the several States be requested to make such equitable dispositions as may be most correspondent with the original design of the Institution.

12th The subjects of his most Christian Majesty, members of this Society may hold meetings at their Pleasure, & may form regulations for their Police, conformable to the Objects of the Institution & to the Spirit of their Government.

13th The Society shall have an Order, which shall be a Bald Eagle of gold &c.,[32] & as expressed in the original Institution, & in the Plan of Amendment proposed by the Committee of the States for revising the Institution which is annexed to these Papers in its order.

Upon this Report of the Committee & the Reading of the Institution the Meeting resolved itself into a Committee of the Whole—Genl Wheedon in the Chair, & with Freedom debated the Paragraphs as they were severally & repeatedly read. A considerable majority concurred in the 1st 4th 5th 7th 8th 9th 10th 11th 12th 13th 14th & 15th—determined to postpone the Consideration of the 2d:—the 3rd and 6th to be recommitted ⟨to the Committee of Five.⟩ The Committee rising report accordingly to the President who resum'd his seat.

This Meeting resolves to take up the Report of the general Committee to-Morrow Morning at nine oClock to which time it stands adjourned—

Thursday the 13th of May—Met according to adjournment & the Order of the Day being call'd the Meeting proceeded to the Consideration of the Institution of the Society of the Cincinnati as altered & amended by Paragraphs severally—Confirmed the 1st—made the alterations in the 2d Paragraph as annexed in their Order & page agreeable to the reference.

The Opinion of the Meeting was taken in Regard to the Admission of Officers of any Individual State to be Parties to the Institution of the Cincinnati, who had served in time and manner proposed—& in the affirmative—notwithstanding that part of the 1st Clause of the 2d Paragraph which appears to Limit the Right to officers of the Army & Navy of the United States collectively—[33]

The 3d Paragraph was confirm'd—4th also with the addition as in page [   ]³⁴—the 5th approved without any alteration— the 6th expunged—7th 8th 9th 10th 11th 12th 13th & all assented to.

Resolved that the Institution be styled—The Institution of the Society of the Cincinnati as altered & amended by the general Meeting held at Philadelphia, &c.

Resolved that a Committee of three be appointed to prepare a Circular Letter to the several State Societies with the Institution as now amended—setting forth the Reasons which induced this Meeting to make the alteration⟨s⟩ Governor Dickinson Cols. Lee and Humphreys the Committee The Institution is referred to the above Committee for critical correction & engrossment.

Resolved, that all the letters & papers addressed to this Meeting be refered to a Committee of Three to report thereon— Genl Knox, Col. Smith & Genl Williams, appointed—⟨The thirteen States concurred in the Institution as altered, &c. except New York, divided: Smith, for; Fairlie, against; Cortland absent.⟩

Adjourned till 12 oClock to-Morrow.

Convened according to adjournment Friday, 14th of May The Committee who were appointed to prepare the Draft of a Circular Letter &c. &c. &c. report that they have made some Progress in their Business & hope to be able to make a final Report by to-Morrow morng—ask Leave to sit again.

Resolved, that this Meeting will to-Morrow ballot for Officers to the general Society of the Cincinnati.

The Committee appointed to take into Consideration the Papers and Letters addressed to this Society report that there are some from France & one from Genl Armand that require Answers—others that ought to be refered to the Society in France—Resolved that a Committee of three be appointed to prepare Answers—Gens. Knox & Williams & Col. Smith. Resolved, that this Committee be authorized to confer with Major Lenfant on pecuniary & other matters & act thereon.

Resolved that a Committee of three be appointed to Draft the Form of a Diploma for the Members of the Cincinnati Major Turner Captains Dayton & Fairlie appointed—Adjourned till to-Morrow morning, 11 oClock.

Saturday 15th of May—met agreeably to adjournment.

The Committee for preparing Drafts of Letters reported & Laid on the Table a Draft of a Letter to Baron Viominel & one to B. General Armand.

They also reported that they had received & examined Major L'Enfant's Account for his Agency in France, which was Laid on the Table.

On motion, resolved that the officers of his most Christian Majesty's Army & Navy who have served in America & who were promoted to the Rank of Colonel, are comprehended in the Institution of the Cincinnati as altered and amended.[35]

The Committee on the Circular Letter & also for correcting & engrossing the Institution reported & Laid on the Table the Draft of a Circular Letter & also the Institution as amended fairly engrossed & corrected.

On motion the Draft of the Circular Letter having been read Paragraph by Paragraph fully considered & the same unanimously approved—Resolved, that the President of the Meeting be desired to sign & forward a Copy of the same to each of the respective State Meetings—[36]

A draft of a letter to Baron Viomenel—a draft of one to B. General Bogenville & one to B. Genl Armand having been read & approved are ordered to be transcribed signed & transmitted by the President.[37]

Ordered that a Committee of Two be appointed to superintend the Printing & publishing in Pamphlet the Circular Letter to the State Societies with the Institution as amended & altered by this Meeting—Mr. Humphreys and Mr. Turner chosen—

Ordered that the same Gentlemen procure the Circular Letter to be als[o] published—in the most public News Papers.

Agreeably to the Order of the Day the Members proceeded to ballot for the Officers of the Society for the ensuing term—when the ballots being taken—His Excellency General Washington was unanimously choosen President—Genl Gates was Chosen Vice President[38]—Genl Knox Secretary & General Williams Assistant Secretary—

Adjourned till Monday next 9 oClock.

Monday, 17th of May. Assembled agreeable to adjournment—A letter from General Gates was received & read signifying his grateful Acceptance of the Office of Vice President of the Society of the Cincinnati—

On motion, resolved—That Monsieur D'Tarle, Intendant &

second Officer of the French auxiliary Army & the Chevalier de la Meth Col. by Brevet—also the Count de Sonnovielle;—the Count la Touche—the Count de Kergariou—the Chevalier Ryguille—the Chevalier du Quesne—the Count de Trevalies—the Chevalier Manlivriers—the Chevalier de Vallonge—the Count de Capelles & Captains & Commanders of ships & Frigates of the French Navy who were employed on special Service on the Coast of America & who are mention'd particularly by his Excellency the Minister of France, are entitled by the Spirit and Intention of the Institution to become Members of the Society—[39]

On particular application by letter from Lt Col. De Bouchet—Resolved—

That 'tis the Opinion of this General Meeting that Lt-Cl De Bouchet is entitled from his Services to be a Member of the Society of the Cincinnati—[40]

Several drafts of letters, viz.—One to Chevalier La Luzerne—one to Count Rochambeau & one to Count Barras—one to Count De Estaing & one to Marquis La fayette being read and approved—Ordered, that they be transcribed signed & forwarded by the President—[41]

A draft of a letter to the Senior Land & Naval Officers & others Members of the Society of the Cincinnati being read was approved & is ordered to be transcribed sign'd and transmitted by the President—

From the General Meeting held in Philadelphia on the first Monday in May, 1784—To the Senior Land and Naval Officers and others, Members of the Society of the Cincinnati in France.[42]

Gentlemen

We, the Delegates of the Cincinnati having judged it expedient to make several material alterations & amendments in our Institution—& having thought it our duty to communicate the Reasons upon which we have acted in a circular Address to the State Societies, do now transmit for your Information—a Transcript of that letter, together with a Copy of the Institution as altered and amended.

Conscious of having done what Prudence & Love of Country dictated—we are persuaded you will be satisfied with the Propriety of our Conduct when you are informed, our decisions were influenced by a Conviction that some Things contained in our original System might eventually be productive of Consequences which we had not forseen, as well as, by the Current of Sentiments which appeared to prevail amongst our fellow citizens—Under these circumstances we viewed it as no Proof of Magnanimity to persist in any thing which might possibly be erroneous, or to conteract the Opinion of Community, however founded.

Nor were we displeased to find the jealous eye of Patriotism watching over those Liberties which had been established by our common Exertions—especially as our Countrymen appear'd fully disposed to do Justice to our Intentions, & to apprehend no Evils but such as might happen in Process of Time, after we, in whom they placed so much Confidence, should have quitted the stage of human action—& we flatter ourselves we felt not less interested in guarding against disastrous Contingencies, in averting present or future political Evils than the most zealous of our Compatriots.

For us then it is enough that our benevolent purposes of relieving the unfortunate should not be frustrated—that our Friendships should be as immutable as They are sincere & that you have received the Tokens of them with such tender Marks of Sensibility—For you, Gentlemen let it be sufficient that your merits & Services are indelibly impressed upon the Hearts of a whole Nation, & that your Names and Actions can never be lost in oblivion.

Cherishing such sentiments, & receiprocating all your affections, we pray you will have the goodness to believe, that altho' nothing could have increasd our friendship—yet by your Alacrity in associating with us you have taken the most effectual Measures for rivetting more strongly those indissoluble Ties. We have the honour, &c., &c."

The Committee for preparing the Form of a Diploma reported & lay on the Table the Draft of a Form which being read & considered was approved & is as follows:

Be it known—that W. L.—is a Member of the Society of the Cincinnati, instituted by the Officers of the American Army at the Period of its Dissolution—As well for the Commemoration of the great Event which gave Independance to North America as for the Laudable Purposes of inculcating the Duty of laying down in Peace Arms assumed for public Defence & uniting in Acts of brotherly Affection, & Bonds of perpetual Freindship the Members constituting the same—

In Testimony whereof I, the President of the said Society, having hereunto set my hand at Phi. in the State of P—— this 18th Day of May, in the Year of our Lord 1784 & in the 8th Year of Independance of the United States—

G. W——President

By order,
J. T. Secretary.

Major L'Enfant having produced his accompt for his Agency in France—Ordered that a Draft be made on Genl M'Dougal

Treasurer of this Society for the sum of six hundred and thirty Dollars to be paid to Major LEnfant as the Balance of his Accompt.[43]

On motion, resolved that Major Turner & Capt. Claypole be a Committee to Superintend & procure the Engraving on the Copper Plate brought by Major L'Enfant from France, the written Form of the Diploma, as approved by the Meeting—

On motion resolved;—That the thanks of this Meeting be presented to Major LEnfant for his great Care & Attention in the Execution of the Business of this Society committed to him to be transacted in France—[44]

Resolved, that a Committee of three to revise & correct the Proceeding of this Meeting & to make out the Extracts necessary to be sent to the Society in France & to the several State Societies—Members chosen were Genl Williams, Col. Trumbul & Col. Heth.[45]

Ordered that the Committee for procuring the written Form of the Diploma to be engraved on the Plate do, when the same is executed deliver the Copper Plate into the Hands of the Secretary or his Assistant to be placed in the Archives of the Society.

Adjourned till to-Morrow, 9 oClock Previous to this adjournment ⟨the matter of wearing the badge of our Order was agitated, as to time and place when it would be proper: and it appeared fully to be the sense of the Meeting that it should not be ostentatious and in common; and only on days of convention to commemorate the Institution, or when we were to attend the funeral of some deceased Member. Though no vote was called or taken (as it was thought improper so to do), yet this was understood to be a general sentiment, and meant for the government of every Member of the Cincinnati while residing in this country. In France, it is supposed that a different practice would prevail, and as the Bald Eagle is there held in high estimation, that it will generally be worn by Americans on their travels through that country:—at least, by all those who may be desirous of this distinction.⟩

Tuesday, the 18th of May Assembled agreeably to adjournment—

AD, DSoCi. Winthrop Sargent of Massachusetts kept this journal of the proceedings of the general meeting of the Society of Cincinnati in Philadelphia in

May 1784. The manuscript journal, now deposited in the archives of the society at Anderson House in Washington, D.C., was found among Sargent's papers in the nineteenth century by another Winthrop Sargent, who decoded the passages that Sargent had put in code and in 1858 published the entire journal in *Memoirs of the Historical Society of Pennsylvania*, 6:57–115. The order of the pages of the manuscript journal as now bound is different from the order in the printed version. The pagination in the printed version is clearly the original one and has been followed here. The passages decoded by the younger Winthrop Sargent are printed here within angle brackets.

The abbreviated official minutes of the proceedings of the general meeting of the Cincinnati, 4–18 May 1784, kept until 8 May by George Turner and thereafter by Jonathan Trumbull, also are in the archives of the Society of the Cincinnati at Anderson House, and there is a copy in DLC:GW. A slightly different version of the official minutes is printed in *Proceedings of the General Society of the Cincinnati, 1784–1884* (Philadelphia, 1887). Unlike the official minutes, Sargent's journal records the role GW played in the radical alteration of the Institution of the society, by which he sought to quiet the storm of controversy the original Institution had aroused (see Thomas Jefferson to GW, 16 April 1784, and notes).

1. Of the fifty men listed here as elected, thirty-four were reported in attendance by the press. See, for instance, the *Virginia Journal and Alexandria Advertiser*, 10 June 1784.

2. Henry Dearborn began his military career as captain of a company of minutemen in April 1775. He was a lieutenant colonel in the 1st New Hampshire Regiment when he left the army in 1782. Dearborn became Thomas Jefferson's secretary of war in 1801 and commander of the United States Army during the War of 1812.

3. Neither GW's former aide David Cobb nor Gen. Rufus Putnam attended. William Hull (1735–1825) at this time was lieutenant colonel in Col. Henry Jackson's Continental (or American) Regiment.

4. None of the Rhode Island members were in attendance at the opening of the meeting, but Samuel Ward arrived on 12 May. Nathanael Greene, James Mitchell Varnum, Jeremiah Olney (1749–1812), and Daniel Lyman did not attend.

5. Samuel Holden Parsons, Jedediah Huntington, and Heman Swift did not attend.

6. Philip Van Cortlandt (1749–1831), colonel of the 2d New York Regiment, was brevetted brigadier general in 1783; James Fairlie (d. 1830) was aide-de-camp to General Steuben; and at war's end William Stephens Smith was one of GW's aides. Nicholas Fish (1758–1833), a major in Van Cortlandt's regiment, did not attend.

7. All of the New Jersey delegation attended the meeting. David Brearly (1745–1790) was lieutenant colonel and then colonel of the 4th New Jersey Regiment, 1776–79. Capt. Jonathan Dayton (1760–1824) had most recently served in the consolidated New Jersey Regiment in 1783. Capt. Aaron Ogden (1756–1839) was in the 1st New Jersey Regiment when the war ended.

8. All of the members of the Pennsylvania delegation attended the meeting.

9. Both James Tilton and James Moore attended.

10. All of the Marylanders except Gov. William Paca (1740–1799) attended. Nathaniel Ramsay (1741–1817), lieutenant colonel of the 3d Maryland Regiment, was wounded and taken prisoner in June 1778 at the Battle of Monmouth.

11. The only Virginia member who failed to come to the meeting was the former colonel of the 8th Virginia Regiment, James Wood (d. 1813). George Weedon (c.1734–1793) was a brigadier general in the Continental army from 1777 to 1783. William Heth, who was colonel of the 3d Virginia Regiment in May 1780 when he was taken prisoner at Charleston, S.C., arrived on 6 May. Henry Lee, known as Light-Horse Harry and the leader of his Partisan Corps until the war's end, took his seat at the meeting on 7 May.

12. Lt. Col. Archibald Lytle of the 1st North Carolina Regiment did not attend. Reading Blount, former captain of the 1st North Carolina Regiment, arrived at the meeting on 7 May. Maj. Griffith John McRee arrived on 12 May.

13. Only Lewis Morris did not attend.

14. John Skey Eustace and James Field did not attend.

15. The society on 19 June 1783 at its first meeting asked GW to serve as president general and Knox to be treasurer general, until "the next general meeting." Upon giving up office on this day, 4 May 1784, GW "laid the original Institution of the Society on the Table with the Official Letters which he had written and received" (minutes, DSoCi). After securing GW's agreement to preside over the meeting, the delegates voted to defer the election of officers. They also agreed that they would vote by states.

16. GW's Observations on the Institution of the Society (doc. I) are notes he wrote either in preparation of this speech or as the record of what he had said in the speech. Thomas Jefferson, who helped form GW's resolve to seek radical reform of the society's Institution (see particularly Jefferson's letter of 16 April), wrote an account of GW's role in persuading the meeting to accept his recommendations. Jefferson did this in a series of comments in volume 5 of John Marshall's *Life of Washington*, published in 1807: "pg. 28. the member of Congress here alluded to was myself, & the extract quoted was part of a letter from my self [16 April 1784], in answer to one Genl Washington wrote [8 April 1784] . . . Genl Washington, called on me at Anapolis (where I then was as a member of Congress) on his way to the meeting of the Cincinnati in Philada. we had much conversn on the institution, which was chiefly an amplifier of the sentiments in our letters, and in conclusion after I had stated to him the modifications which I thought might remove all jealousy as well as danger, & the parts which might still be retained, he appeared to make up his mind, & said, no, not a fibre of it must be retained; no half way reformation will suffice. if the thing be bad it must be totally abolished and he declared his determination to use his utmost endeavor to have it entirely abolished. on his return from Philada, he called on me again at Annapolis, & sat with me till a very late hour in the night, giving me an account of what passed in their con-

vention. the sum of it was that he had exerted his whole influence in every way in his power to procure an abolition; that the opposition to it was extreme, & especially from some of the younger members, but that after several days of struggle within doors and without, a general sentiment was obtained for it's entire abolition. whether any vote had been taken on it or not, I do not remember, but his affirmation to me was that within a few days, I think he said it was 2 or 3 it would have been formally abolished. just in that moment arrived Major L'enfant, who had been sent to France to procure the eagles, & to offer the order to the French officers who had served in America. he brought the king's permission to his officers to accept it, the letters of thanks of these officers accepting it, letters of sollicitation from other officers to obtain it & the eagles themselves. the effect of all this on the minds of the members was to undo much of what had been done, to rekindle all the passions which had produced the institution, & silence all the dictates of prudence which had been operating for it's abolition. after this the General said, the utmost that could be effected was the modifications which took place & which provided for it's extinction with the death of existing members. he declined the presidency, & I think Baron Steuben was appointed" (undated, DLC: Jefferson Papers).

17. For the report of Congress, see note 3 in Jefferson to GW, 16 April 1784.

18. Lafayette refers to opposition to the "hereditary part" of the Cincinnati's Institution in his letter to GW of 25 Dec. 1783 and in his second letter of 9 Mar. 1784, but it is in his fourth letter of 9 Mar. that he expands on the opposition in France to the hereditary aspect of membership in the Cincinnati and expresses his own misgivings.

19. The letter from Chastellux has not been identified. Knox wrote Chastellux on 2 July 1784: "The Society of the Cincinnati has been misunderstood and occasioned clamours against the original institution to the popular opinion. we hope it will meet your approbation—and that of our other friends in France" (MHi: Knox Papers).

20. See note 16.

21. The committee of the whole was "unanimously of opinion that sundry matters and things" in the original Institution "ought to be corrected" (minutes, DSoCi).

22. It was decided by the general meeting "That a Committee be appointed to reconsider, revise, alter, and amend the General System of the Society of the Cincinnati, and to form a correct Institution or Code of principles and Obligations by which all the Members of the Society of Friends are to be united and governed in future, and to report their progress in that Business daily" (minutes, DSoCi). In the vote for the member of the committee from Connecticut, there was a tie between David Humphreys and Jonathan Trumbull, Jr. The latter arrived on this day.

23. Letters given to the committee included copies of those GW wrote on 29 or 30 Oct. 1783 to the French officers Gerard, d'Estaing, Barras, de Grasse, Destouches, Rochambeau, and Lafayette, enclosing copies of the In-

stitution of the Society of the Cincinnati. They also included letters dated 25 Dec. 1783 sent to GW, with enclosures, by Lafayette and L'Enfant.

24. Among these papers were the responses to GW's circular letter of 1 Jan. 1784 from the various presidents of the state societies of the Cincinnati: Arthur St. Clair and Elias Dayton, both 29 Jan.; William Smallwood, 10 Feb.; Nathanael Greene, 16 Feb.; Jedediah Huntington, 23 Feb.; Benjamin Lincoln, 2 Mar.; John Sullivan, 12 Mar.; William Moultrie, 6 April; and Lachlan McIntosh, 20 April.

25. GW strongly opposed this new form of the Institution when the committee of thirteen presented it on 10 May, and the meeting rejected most of it.

26. See Appendix II for Armand's letter to GW of 10 May.

27. Among the letters read were those to GW from Bougainville, 24 Dec. 1783, from Barras, with enclosures, 29 Jan. 1784, from Rochambeau, with enclosures, 19 Jan. and 13 Feb. 1784, from La Bretonière, 1 Feb. 1784, and a translation of a letter from La Luzerne.

28. The final form of the Institution as it appears in the minutes divides it into sections different from Sargent's division and numbering.

29. See note 39.

30. This paragraph was marked "expunged" and does not appear in the final Institution.

31. The second sentence of this section 9 is marked out here and omitted in section 10 of the final version.

32. The rest of this section is replaced in the final version with the words: "bearing on its breast the emblems hereafter described, suspended by a deep blue ribbon edged with white descriptive of the Union of America and France" (minutes, DSoCi). There follows in the minutes a detailed description of the badge.

33. With regard to section two, the minutes of the general meeting record that the members considered the question "whether by a Construction of the principles of the Institution, such Officers of the State troops as have served three years can be admitted or not" and decided in the affirmative.

34. The following clause was added to section three at this point: "and the several state meetings shall, at suitable periods, make applications to their respective legislatures for grants of charters."

35. A copy of this resolution of 15 May signed by GW is in NjMoNP, and a French translation is in DLC: Rochambeau Papers.

36. The circular letter to the state societies of the Cincinnati, which (like the new Institution adopted in the general meeting) was widely printed in newspapers, appears in the official minutes of the meeting (DSoCi). The text of the circular letter, dated 15 May 1784, is printed below as Appendix V.

37. For the letter to Vioménil, 15 May 1784, see note 2 of his letter to GW of 24 Jan. 1784. For the letter to Armand, 15 May, see Appendix II, n.2. The text of the letter to Bougainville, 15 May 1784, is: "The Letter which you wrote to the President of the Society of the Cincinnati relative to your Claim to become a Member [24 Dec. 1783, DLC:GW] has been read in this General Meeting: And it is their Opinion that Brigadier General de Bougainville is

comprehended in the Rules of Admission expressed in the Institution as amended and sent to the Society in France. Signed in Genl Meeting By Order" (Df, DSoCi). GW also signed a letter to Rochambeau dated 15 May. It is printed below as Appendix IV.

38. Gen. Horatio Gates (c.1728–1806), the victor over General Burgoyne in the Battle of Saratoga, 17 Oct. 1777, was president of the Virginia Society of the Cincinnati.

39. There is a copy of this resolution of 17 May, signed by GW, in Arch. Aff. Etr., Etats-Unis, vols. 5–6. A French translation is in the Rochambeau Papers, DLC. See Appendix III, below. "The count de Trevalies" and "the Chevalier Manlivriers" have not been identified, but the others are known to be members of the French Society of the Cincinnati. Lameth, La Touche-Tréville, Kergariou-Locmaria, and La Pérouse have been identified elsewhere. Benoît-Joseph de Tarlé (1735–1797) became *intendant en chef* of Rochambeau's army in 1780; Jean-Josse, chevalier de Tarlé (1739–1813), held the rank of lieutenant colonel in Rochambeau's army in 1780 as *aide-major-général de l'infanterie*. The chevalier de Sainneville; Louis Froger, chevalier de L'Eguille (1750–1795); Pierre-Claude, marquis du Quesne (1751–1834), who brought the news from Cadiz to Philadelphia on 24 Mar. 1783 of the preliminary articles of peace; Louis-Marie-Casimir, chevalier de Vallongue; and Hippolyte-Louis-Antoine, comte de Capellis, marquis du Fort (d. 1813), were all ship captains or senior naval officers who served in American waters between 1776 and 1783.

40. Bouchet wrote his petition (printed below as Appendix VI) in Philadelphia on this day, 17 May, and it was delivered to the meeting enclosed in L'Enfant's letter of this date.

41. A draft of the letter to La Luzerne, 17 May 1784, which was sent out under GW's signature as president general of the Society of the Cincinnati, is printed below as Appendix IX. For the letter to Barras of 17 May, see Barras to GW, 23 Jan. 1784, n.7. The letter to d'Estaing of 17 May is printed as Appendix VII. A letter to Lafayette, 17 May, is Appendix VIII.

42. A copy of this letter signed by GW and a French translation of it directed to d'Estaing and Rochambeau are both in DLC: Rochambeau Papers.

43. Alexander McDougall, president of the New York society, was the first treasurer general of the Society of the Cincinnati.

44. A copy of the resolution signed by GW is in DSoCi.

45. The official copy of the minutes and an abbreviated copy, which Otho Williams attests to be a "true copy," both in DSoCi, are in the same unidentified hand.

Appendix I
To Henry Knox

Dear Sir,   [Philadelphia, c.4–18 May 1784]
The names which follow, are those mentioned in the Marqs la Fayette's letter to me.

La' Peyrouse
La Touche
D'Albert de Rion*
Tilly*[1]

Enclosed it seems is the proper address to the characters therein mentioned, I send it that you may be governed thereby—pray return it to me again[2]—The enclosed private letters be so good as to include under cover of the public ones. Yrs affly

G.W.

*I am not sure that these two gentn may not be of the line, & thereby included in the genl descripn.[3]

ALS, NN: Emmet Collection. The letter is without date and without the name of the addressee. GW wrote this covering letter after receiving Lafayette's letters of 9 Mar. 1784, which L'Enfant brought with him from France. L'Enfant wrote from New York on 29 April that he had landed in New York with a packet of letters for GW relating to the Cincinnati that were "to voluminous to be sent." The letters, however, were in GW's hands at the opening of the meeting in Philadelphia, for on 5 May GW "introduced" to the meeting one of Lafayette's letters of 9 March. GW's letter printed here probably was intended for Jonathan Trumbull, Jr., or for Henry Knox. If the letter was directed to Trumbull, GW probably wrote it after 8 May when Trumbull was elected "scribe" of the meeting. If it was intended for Knox, as the Library of Congress indicates, it probably was written after 13 May when Knox was made chairman of a committee to receive "all the letters and papers addressed to this Meeting" (Sargent's journal, doc. II). In any case it was written in Philadelphia almost certainly during the meeting, not on 4 April as has been assumed.

1. See Lafayette's third letter of 9 Mar. 1784 to GW.

2. GW may be referring to the list of French officers that Lafayette enclosed in his first letter of 9 March. See note 6 of that document.

3. For Rions, see d'Estaing to GW, 8 Jan. 1784, n.1; for Tilly, see his letter to GW of 15 Mar. 1784.

Appendix II
From Armand

Sir   philadelphia may 10th 1784

When mr l'enfant returned lately from france, he communicated to me a lettre which he was to lay before the Grnl assembly of the Cincinnati & of which I have the honor to inclose an Extract[1]—as he does Express the desire of the Cincinnati in france to form a society there similar to those of the rcspectives states of america, & that their representatives a[t] this time, be taken from amongst the french at present here which belongs to the Cincinnati—myself & the other gentlemen in the same Circumstances who consist of 12th or 15th, thought it was proper we should wait in america for the answer which the gnl assembly would give to mr l'enfant's lettre, that in Case the Cincinnati in france were formed into one state society and of Course had representatives either by an appointment from your Exellency or an appointment by their own votes, we might be here to represent them.[2]

we do not presume to express here our desire to be admitted or not admitted as representatives of the Cincinnati in france. the gnl assembly has alone to determine on the alternative & we are sensible they will determine for the best, but it concern us much to know what is their determination, that in case the Cincinnati in france were not formed into a states society, or it should not be thought proper to admit at this time its representatives, we might be at liberty to go from here.

Having received no official lettre from france relative to the interest of the Cincinnati there, I do not mean to intimate here any desire or ideas of their own, further than what may be understood from the above mentioned lettre of mr l'enfant, the step I take here Concern more immediately the french officers who are present in philadelphia—they have desired me to state their ideas to your Exellency & request an answer. I have the honor to be with the highest respect Sir your Exellency's the most obdt hble srt

C. armand: Mqis de la Rouerie

ALS, DSoCi. Armand's acute accents on various and sundry *e*'s have been dropped.

1. Armand heads the enclosure: "Extract of a letter from Mr l'enfant to his Exellency gnl washington concerning the Cincinnati in france." It is in fact Armand's version of the last paragraph of L'Enfant's letter to GW of 29 April 1784.

2. The general meeting's response to Armand, dated 15 May, was: "The letter which was address'd by you to the President of the Society of the Cincinnati was read with attention the 10th Instant.

"As the revisions of the Institutions was then under consideration of a Committee no answer could be given to your letter until their report was made.

"The Society have not heretofore formed a meeting in france, and as there was no delegation from that Country, there could not, consistently, be any particular representation admitted into the general meeting—which, being a full representation of the Society at large, hath given due attention to the particular circumstances of the Members in france, who are provided for in the Institutions as amended by this meeting" (DSoCi).

Appendix III
From Pierre-Charles L'Enfant

Sir   Philadelphia 10th May 1784

As the reading of the Several Letters of Thanks & petitions which are now before you, may easily convey to you an Idea of the high consideration which the Cincinnati enjoy in Europe, give me leave in the name of all my countrymen to assure you of their sincere and heart felt gratitude, no pledge of friendship can be dearer to them than that which they have received at the hands of the Society of Cincinnati—I am particularly charged by them with supporting the Several demands which have been addressed to you: I shall not expatiate on the title which Several of them have to your consideration, being well persuaded of the equitable intentions of the Society, & not doubting that if you will weigh the merit which the French Navy has acquired in the service of the American cause, it will appear to you that they have an equal title with the Land Troops to your attention and favour.

Among the various demands which are addressed to you, there are undoubtedly Some which have no other foundation but the patronage of those who recommend them. The Society may easily judge, that altho' it might be easy to refuse to admit in France those who had no right to it by the Statutes of the Institution, it has been difficult to refuse complying with the solicitations of Several persons who wished to be recommended to your indulgence. You will no doubt give the proper weight to the claims of each petitioner.

The Captains of his Majesty's Ships who all have the rank of Colonels, have no doubt acquired a title to your favour, by their repeated services, on the different squadrons of Messieurs d'Estaing, de Grasse, de Barras, de Vaudreuil, & Destouches, & they hope that you will pay Some attention to their demands—Several Captains of Frigates who are designated by the Minister of France as having had particular commissions on the American coast, have acquired a title to be distinguished from those of the Same rank who have not rendered the Same Services—It is in order to enable you to attain the object which you have proposed to yourselves that the French General Officers have recommended the above mentioned gentlemen to your illustrious Assembly. It is with the Same views that the Counts d'Estaing and de Rochambeau have recommended to your favor the particular services of Some land Officers, who on account of those services & of their wounds have been promoted since the War to the rank required by our Institutions.

Permit me, Gentlemen, to observe likewise that altho' the opinion which appears to me to prevail in your Assembly be favorable to the

French, by considering them as on the same footing with the American members, yet I think it would not be proper to empower the former to admit or refuse the officers who have submitted their pretensions to the Assembly; because, it would be lessening the price of your favour, & because the French Naval Officers would be sensibly affected by not being *expressly nominated* by you which would seem as if you valued their merit at a less rate than that of the land Officers, On the other Side, if the French were to have it in their power to distribute an Order which excites general ambition, applications would be multiplied without end and denials (altho' authorized by our Laws) would bring ill will upon those who would be established Judges of the claims of the petitioners—These considerations, & the opinion I have founded thereupon, which I dare say is that of my Countrymen in general, induces me to request you to *nominate* or otherwise expressly designate the persons whose claims appear to you to be founded on Equity—Our sacred Laws, the respect due to the resolutions of an illustrious Assembly, the importance of giving up nothing which might hurt the integrity of our principles, all justifies the earnestness with which I solicit a nomination which at the same time that it satisfies the Candidates, may give no lawful cause of discontent to those whom the Laws may exclude.

If your opinion is favorable to the persons above designated, I would take the liberty to submit the following draught of a resolution:

"The Captains who commanded Ships being part of the Squadrons of Messieurs Le Comte d'Estaing, le Comte de Grasse, le Chevalier de Barras, le Marquis de Vaudreuil & le Chevalier des Touches, the Captains of frigates who have been employed on particular stations, & have combined their operations in concert with the Minister Plenipotentiary of his Most Christian Majesty with the United states, Those Land Officers who have been wounded, or who on account of their eminent services have been promoted to the rank of Colonels or Brigadiers before their return or immediately after, shall be considered as included in the Article of our Institutions which relates to the Officers of the French auxiliary Army. And our desire being to give to Officers of a rank inferior to that of Colonel a token of our Esteem, the order of our institution shall be granted to every one of the ⟨french⟩ Regiments who have served in America; including particularly the Regiment of Dillon as having been the most complete of all the detachments who have served with Count d'Estaing at Savannah—to be worn by the first Captain of the said Regiments & by him delivered to his successor in the same rank: Our intention being, that the 1st Captains only when in activity in the Said Regiments, (and who have Served in America) be authorized to consider themselves as

Members of our Institution, in the Same manner as the Generals &
Colonels &c. (This Article is put here only in case Genl Rochambeau's
letter & his ideas Shall have been admitted)."[1]

As to the Frenchmen who have served in the continental Army as
they consider none but the persons recommended by the resolution
of their Committee to be admissible, I beg the Assembly will be
pleased to grant a particular resolve, *nominating* the persons recommended without the least equivocation or shadow of claim to those
who are excluded. As to what concerns the establishment of the Continental society in France, it is expected that this resolution taking
place before, will be no prejudice to the rights which you will be
pleased to grant them.[2] I have the honor to be with the highest respect
Sir and Gentlemen Your most obedient & most humble servant

P. L'Enfant
major of the ingineer

LS, DSoCi. This letter was composed by someone with a better command of
the English language than L'Enfant. See, for comparison, L'Enfant's letter to
GW of 29 April from New York, which covers much the same ground as this
one addressed to GW as president general of the Cincinnati.

1. For the general meeting's endorsing the eligibility for membership in the
Cincinnati of French naval captains who had served in American waters, see
Sargent's journal for 17 May (doc. II). See also note 39 of that document.

2. See Appendix I, n.1.

Appendix IV
To Rochambeau

Sir   Philadelphia 15 May 1784

The letters with which you have honored the society of the Cincinnati have been read with attention, and the several subjects regarded
with the most respectful consideration.[1]

It is a circumstance pleasing to the society that the Count De
Rochambeau has so willingly become a member and interested himself in its reputation.

The very liberal subscriptions made by the gentlemen of the french
army merit our grateful acknowledgments—But as it is inconsistent
with the spirit of the confederation,[2] and contrary to the original intention of this society to receive sums of money from foreign nations
altho' in alliance, we trust the Gentlemen will not consider it any want
of our affection for them if we are obliged to decline the acceptance.

Your request in favor of the Count De la Lancour will be fully answered by a just construction of the Institution which includes all Offi-

cers of his rank who cooperated with the Armies of the United States, And the Count Manifestly cooperated by sending a considerable detachment of his command, from St Domingo to the Continent, at his own risque: and therefore the opinion of the society is that the Count De le Lancour is a member of right.

It is not in the ability of this meeting of the Society to comprehend the justice of all the claims which have been made, and therefore they are submitted to the meeting of the Society in france to be taken into consideration.

The several memorials, Petitions, and Letters relative to those claims will be transmitted to the society in france, together with a copy of the Institution, as it is amended, and a circular letter communicating the reasons for those amendments. Signed in general meeting

Go: Washington—Presidt

LS, DLC: Rochambeau Papers; Df, DSoCi.

1. Rochambeau wrote GW about the French Society of the Cincinnati on 19, 29 Jan., 13 Feb., and 1 Mar. 1784. He wrote again on 4 May 1784.

2. "Republican government" was struck out in the draft and "confederation of our States" substituted.

Appendix V
To the State Societies of the Cincinnati

Gentlemen,   Philadelphia, May 15th 1784

We the Delegates of the Cincinnati, after the most mature and deliberate Discussion of the Principles and Objects of our Society, have thought proper to recommend that the enclosed Institution of the Society of the Cincinnati, as altered and amended at their first Meeting, should be adopted by your State Society.

In order that our Conduct on this Occasion may stand approved in the Eyes of the World; that we may not incur the Imputations of Obstinacy on the one hand, or Levity on the other; and that you may be induced more chearfully to comply with our Recommendation, we beg leave to communicate the Reasons on which we have acted.

Previous to our laying them before you, we hold it a Duty to ourselves, and to our Fellow-Citizens, to declare—and we call Heaven to witness the Veracity of our Declaration—That, in our whole Agency on this Subject, we have been actuated by the purest Principles. Notwithstanding we are thus conscious for ourselves of the Rectitude of our Intentions in instituting, or becoming Members of this Fraternity; and notwithstanding we are confident the highest Evidence can be produced from your past, and will be given by your future Behaviour, that you could not have been influenced by any other Motives than those of Friendship, Patriotism, and Benevolence. Yet, as our Designs, in some Respects, have been misapprehended; as the Instrument of our Association was, of necessity, drawn up in an hasty manner, at an Epocha as extraordinary as it will be memorable in the Annals of Mankind, when the Mind, agitated by a variety of Emotions, was not at liberty to attend, minutely, to every Circumstance which respected our social Connexion; or to digest our Ideas into so correct a Form as could have been wished; as the original Institution appeared, in the Opinion of many respectable Characters, to have comprehended Objects which are deemed incompatible with the Genius and Spirit of the Confederation; and as, in this Case, it would eventually frustrate our purposes, and be productive of Consequences which we had not forseen: Therefore, to remove every Cause of Inquietude, to annihilate every Source of Jealousy, to designate explicitly the Ground on which we wish to stand, and to give one more proof that the late officers of the American Army have a claim to be reckoned among the most faithful Citizens—we have agreed that the following material Alterations and Amendments should take place: That the hereditary Succession should be abolished; that all Interference with political Subjects should be done away; and that the Funds should be placed under the immediate Cognizance of the several Legislatures; who should also be requested to grant Charters for more effectually carrying our humane Designs into Execution.

In giving our Reasons for the Alteration in the first article, we must ask your Indulgence, while we recal your Attention to the original occasion which induced us to form ourselves into a Society of Friends. Having lived in the strictest Habits of Amity, through the various Stages of a War, unparralleled in many of its circumstances; having seen the Objects for which we contended, happily attained; in the moment of Triumph and Seperation, when we were about to act the last pleasing, melancholly Scene in our military Drama—*pleasing*, because we were to leave our Country—possessed of Independence and Peace—*melancholly*, because we were to part—perhaps never to meet again; while every Breast was penetrated with Feelings, which can be more easily conceived than described; while every little act of Tenderness recurred fresh to the Recollection; it was impossible not to wish our Friendships should be continued; It was extremely natural to desire they might be perpetuated by our Posterity, to the remotest Ages. With these Impressions, and with such Sentiments, we candidly confess we signed the Institution; we know our motives were irreproachable—But, finding it apprehended by many of our Countrymen, that this would be drawing an unjustifiable Line of Discrimination between our Descendants, and the rest of the Community—and averse to the creation of unnecessary and unpleasing Distinctions, we could not hesitate to relinquish every thing, but our personal Friendships, of which we cannot be divested, and those Acts of Beneficence, which it is our Intention should flow from them.

With Views equally pure and disinterested, we proposed to use our collective Influence in support of that Government, and Confirmation of that Union, the Establishment of which had engaged so considerable a part of our lives: But learning from a Variety of Information that this is deemed an officious and improper Interference, and that if we are not charged with having sinister Designs, yet we are accused of arrogating too much, and assuming the Guardianship of the Liberties of our Country; thus circumstanced, we could not think of opposing ourselves to the concurring opinions of our Fellow-Citizens; however founded; or of giving anxiety to those whose Happiness it is our Interest and Duty to promote.

We come next to speak of the charitable part of our Institution, which we esteem the Basis of it. By placing your Fund in the Hands of the Legislature of your State, and letting them see the Application is to the best purposes, you will demonstrate the Integrity of your Actions, as well as the Rectitude of your Principles: And having convinced them your Intentions are only of a friendly and benevolent Nature, we are induced to believe they will patronize a Design which they cannot but approve; that they will foster the good Dispositions, and encourage the beneficent Acts of those who are disposed to make use of the most effectual, and most unexceptionable Mode of relieving the Distressed. For this Purpose, it is to be hoped that Charters may be obtained, in consequence of the Applications which are directed to be made. It is also judged most proper, that the Admission of Members should be submitted to the Regulation of such charters because, by thus acting in conformity to the Sentiments of Government, we not only give another Instance of our Reliance upon it, but of our Disposition to remove every Source of Uneasiness respecting our Society.

We trust it has not escaped your Attention, Gentlemen, that the only Objects of which we are desirous to preserve the Remembrance, are of such a Nature as cannot be displeasing to our Countrymen, or unprofitable to Posterity. We have retained, accordingly, those Devices which recognize the manner of returning to our Citizenship— not as ostentatious Marks of Discrimination, but as Pledges of our Friendship, and Emblems whose appearance will never permit us to deviate from the Paths of Virtue; And we presume, in this place, it may not be inexpedient to inform you, That these are considered as the most endearing Tokens of Friendship, and held in the highest Estimation by such of our Allies as have become intitled to them, by having contributed their personal Services to the Establishment of our Independence—that those Gentlemen, who are among the first in rank and reputation, have been permitted by their Sovereign to hold this grateful Memorial of our reciprocal Affections—and that this fraternal Intercourse is viewed by that illustrious Monarch, and other distinguished Characters, as no small additional Cement to that Harmony and Reciprocation of good Offices, which so happily prevail between the two Nations.

Having now relinquished whatever has been found objectionable in our original Institution; having, by the Deference thus paid to the prevailing Sentiments of the Community, neither, as we conceive, lessened the Dignity nor diminished the Consistency of Character which it is our Ambition to support in the Eyes of the present, as well as of future Generations; having thus removed every possible Objection to our remaining connected as a Society, and cherishing our mutual Friendships to the close of life; and having, as we flatter ourselves, retained in its utmost latitude, and placed upon a more certain and permanent Foundation, that primary Article of our Association, which respects the Unfortunate; on these two great original pillars, Friendship and Charity, we rest our Institution; And we appeal to your Liberality, Patriotism, and Magnanimity; to your Conduct on every other Occasion, as well as to the Purity of your Intentions on the present, for the Ratification of our Proceedings. At the same time we are happy in expressing a full Confidence in the Candour, Justice, and Integrity of the Public, That the Institution, as now altered and amended, will be perfectly satisfactory, and that Acts of Legislative Authority will soon be passed to give Efficacy to your Benevolence.

Before we conclude this Address, permit us to add, That the Cultivation of that Amity we profess, and the Extension of this Charity, we flatter ourselves, will be objects of sufficient Importance to prevent a Relaxation in the prosecution of them—To diffuse Comfort and Support to any of our unfortunate Companions who have seen better Days, and merited a milder Fate—to wipe the Tear from the Eye of the Widow, who must have been consigned, with her helpless Infants, to Indigence and Wretchedness, but for this charitable Institution—to succour the Fatherless—to rescue the Female Orphan from Destruction—to enable the Son to emulate the Virtues of the Father—will be no unpleasing Task—it will communicate Happiness to others while it increases our own; it will chear our solitary Reflections, and sooth our latest moments. Let us, then, prosecute with Ardour what we have instituted in Sincerity; let Heaven, and our own Consciences approve our Conduct; let our actions be the best Comment on our Words; and let us leave a Lesson to Posterity, That the Glory of Soldiers cannot be completed, without acting well the Part of Citizens.

Signed by Order
Go: Washington President

D, DSoCi; D, PPAmP: Benjamin Franklin Papers. The copy in DSoCi is a part of the minutes of the meeting.

Appendix VI
From Bouchet

sir, philadelphia. Mai. 17th 1784.

Being of all the petitioners for Becoming Members of the association of the cincinnati, the only officer Whose case stands so pecular as to advocate for an exception to the General Rules of the society, I ardently Beg your Excellency to Be pleased to Reccollect, that I have on no other purpose, that to Get admittance to the order, Cross'd the atlantick, and that Returning home disapointed in my expectation, Would ruin Both my Carracter and all prospect, I may have of prefference in the army.

am I, sir, so infortunate, as to have Been too sanguine and Confident in your Excellency's esteem and Goodness? am I so infortunate as to have Been in the Wrong, When I Indulged myself in the thought, that having since 1776 almost at any time, Being employ'd for the cause and more, Being the only french man Who Was at Both the surrenders of the two British armyes taken on this continent, you Would Graciously Look on and grant my petition? Disapointement Would Be a stain upon my honour, Wich could never Be Blotted out.[1] I am, sir With the highest Respect your Excellency's most humble and most obedient servant

Le chev. du Bouchet

ALS, DSoCi. This letter was enclosed in L'Enfant's letter of 17 May 1784.

1. See the resolution of the general meeting on 17 May as recorded in Sargent's journal granting Bouchet's request. A copy of the resolution extracted from the minutes and signed by GW is in PWacD: Sol Feinstone Collection on deposit at PPAmP. For Bouchet's military career in America, see note 40 in doc. II.

Appendix VII
To d'Estaing

Sir.   Philadelphia 17th May 1784

All the letters and memorials which have been sent by you addressed to the President of the Society of the Cincinnati have been laid before a general meeting now held in this City, and were conducive to the extensive latitude in that article of the Institution, (as amended) which denominates the characters to be admitted into the Society—"All the Admirals and Captains of the Navy, ranking as Colonels, who have co'operated with the Armies of the United States"—are litterally included, and it is the expectation also of the Society that it will effectually comprehend all the Officers of the French Navy who have been particularly recommended by your Excellency. The Generals and Colonels of the Land forces are provided for in the previous part of the same article: and the society, careful that those gentlemen who had already recd the order should not be omitted thro' mistake, have added "and such other persons as have been admitted &c.["]—The meetings of the Society in france is conceived to be in a situation Similar & parallel in all respects to those in the States of America, and as they are respectively empowered to judge of the qualifications of their members, this genl meeting are of opinion that they cannot do better than to refer all cases which require examination to the respective meetings to be held as well in france as in America.

Signed in general meeting.

Df, DSoCi.

Appendix VIII
To Lafayette

Sir   Philadelphia 17th May 1784

The Society of the Cincinnati in a general meeting, of delegates from the respective States now held in this city, have had before them the letters which were addressed by you to the President.

The measures you have taken to fulfill the intentions of the society are proofs of your attachment, and obligations on the Society.

The permission of his most Christian Majesty for His Generals, & Colonels and also for His Admirals to wear the order of the Cincinnati, is a real distinction to the society; and is considered as an obliging instance of his Majesty's condescension.

You will see Sir by the Papers which will be sent to the Society in france, that the Institution of the Society of the Cincinnati has necessarily undergone some alterations and amendments; and you will see also, in the Circular Letter, the reasons for such alterations being made.

By the Institution, as it is now recommended for concurrence and confirmation to all the State meetings and to the meeting in France, "It is provided that all the Generals and Colonels of Regiments & Legions of the Land forces, and all the Admirals and Captains of the Navy ranking as Colonels, who cooperated with the armies of the United States &c. are admitted into the Society["]: and it was so expressed as well to comprehend all the gentlemen mentioned in the Memorial of Count D'Estaing as several other commanders & Captns of Squadrans and Frigates who had done essencial service under the orders of His Excellency the Chevalier De La Luzerne; and also Mr De Tarlé and Colonel Lameth who here heretofore supposed not eligible to become Members—an explanatory resolve of the meeting hath been entered into purposely to express the sense of the society respecting the claims of those gentlemen—a Copy of which will also be sent to you with several memorials, upon which this meeting cannot decide—The meetings of the society in France being now distinctly considered in all respects of the same authority as the state meetings, no claims will in future be determined in the general meeting, and all claimants must apply to the meeting of the State, or Country, where they reside—Those meetings alone are to judge of the qualifications of members of this society and to execute the benevolent intentions of our Institution.

It is a subject of concern to this meeting that so good an Officer as Admiral De Vandreuil shod have been omitted by mistake—But as he is now included in the society, an error which we lament, should not induce him to decline the association.

You have the thanks of this meeting for your attention to the Honor of the Society,

Signed in general meeting.

Df, DSoCi.

Appendix IX
To La Luzerne

Sir,   Phila: May 17th 1784

The Letter addressed by your Excellency to the President of the Society of the Cincinnati, and the Memorials referred to that Body, have been laid before the General Meeting.[1]

The Institution, as it is amended, admits into this Society "the late & present Ministers of his Most Xian Majesty to the United States; all the Generals & Colonels of Regiments and Legions of the Land Forces; all the Admirals and Captains of the Navy ranking as Colonels, who have co-operated with the Armies of the United States in their Exertions for Liberty;—&c.["]

And, to testify to your Excellency, that it was the Intention of this Meeting to comprehend, in the Words "Captains of the Navy," those Officers who had the Command of Squadrons and Frigates, and who did essential Service on the Coast of America, they have entred on their Proceedings an Explanatory Resolve, which includes also Monsieur de Tarlé, second in the French Army, & Colo: Lameth, who, notwithstanding the peculiarity of their Cases, the Society consider as evidently included in the Association. Signed in Genl Meetg

G. Washington P.G.

Df, DSoCi.

1. La Luzerne's letter to GW, dated at Philadelphia, 6 May 1784 is in DSoCi. The text of the letter, which was read on 17 May, is: "Messrs les Comtes de Grasse et d'Estaing m'ont mandé qu'ils ont eu l'honneur de Vous faire parvenir les voeux de Messrs les Officiers de la Marine du Roi pour être admis dans la Societé des Cincinnati. Ces Messieurs ont joint à leurs lettres des Memoires dans lesquels ils font valoir les services des Officiers pour lesquels ils desirent d'obtenir cette faveur: Je connois trop la justice de Votre Excellence et celle de Messrs les Delegués qui composent l'Assemblée pour croire qu'il soit nécessaire de joindre mes sollicitations aux leurs.

"L'empressement des Marins françois à être admis dans la Societé des Cincinnati est bien naturel si l'on considere les principes d'honneur sur lesquels elle est fondée, ainsi que les vertus militaires et patriotiques qui distinguent les membres qui la composent.

"Les Amiraux qui ont commandé des flottes sur ce Continent demandent que les Capitaines de Vaisseau qui ont servi directement sous leurs ordres soient admis à porter la même decoration que Messrs les Officiers de terre du même grade, mais il est quelques Capitaines de fregatte qui n'ayant pas été employés dans de grandes Escadres ont cependant été très utiles à la cause commune, soit par les missions qu'ils ont remplies, soit par des combats qu'ils ont soutenus sur les cotes de l'Amerique. Ces Officiers ayant eu ordre de leur Ministre de concerter avec moi leurs operations je crois que c'est à moi à rapeller leurs services. Je prens donc la liberté d'adresser à Votre Excellence une notte qui les rappelle, en Vous suppliant de vouloir bien la recommander à l'attention du Committé chargé d'examiner les differens Memoires.

"J'ai aussi l'honneur de Vous recomander le chevalier de Lameth. Ses services Vous sont connus, il a été blessé très grievement au siege d'Yorck. Sa Majesté l'a recompensé en lui donnant le grade de Colonel, mais cette grace n'ayant cu lieu que deux mois après le siège il se trouveroît exclus de la Societé s'il n'y etoit admis par une grace particuliere. Ses blessures et son zele meritent quelque faveur et j'ose l'attendre des bontés de Votre Excellence et de celles de Messrs les Delegués.

"Je prens aussi la liberté de Vous adresser un Memoire pour le Sieur de Tarlé, Intendant de l'Armée; il est dans une circonstance particuliere que je crois meriter quelque consideration.

"Je supplie Votre Excellence de recevoir les assurances des sentimens d'attachement et de respect, avec lesquels je suis Monsieur Votre tres humble et très obéissant Serviteur."

Appendix X
From Pierre-Charles L'Enfant

Ser   philadelphi—monday may th17 1784

I take the liberty to adresse your Excellency with the inclosed letter from mr duBouchet, who his one of the officer whose particular cases have moved the french Comitee in favour of thier claimes, his suspecting that there as Been in the assembly some opposition to his claimes, is the accasion for is troubling your Excellency with a second adresse[1]—and I could not But Be Confident that your Excellency and the whole Communiti are dispose to render justice to his merite, and will considere How heurt full a dissapointement to his Expectation should Be to his military character, it is upon the same Considerations that I intreat your Excellency to Be favorable to the Wishes that the french continantal officer have Shew to protect the gentlemans whiche they have ⟨taken⟩ upon thems selves to recomande to the general society—and I will go as far as to assure your Excellency that those personnes are the only ones in whose Be[h]alf they intend to petition, and that from the communication of thier opinion they may Be considered as Being already name in france and from which idea the assembly not positively explaning thier intention would Be looked as if thier opinion was contrary to thier wishis.[2]

as I Expect your Excellency opinion will move the assembly in favour of those gentlemen, I Beg that in a view to prevent anny further application the assembly will Be pleased to personnally designate name By name those who shal have a sufficient suports for to merite so particular a proof of your attention and unapreciable favour— whose personnes names I Beg to Be mentione only in the ⟨ansuerds⟩ to the french continantal officer commitee held at the marquis De lafayette Hotel at paris. with great respect I have the honnour to Be sir your Excellency most obidient humble servant

                                                    P. L'Enfant

ALS, DSoCi.

1. See L'Enfant to GW, 10 May, printed as Appendix III above.

2. See Rochambeau to GW, 4 May 1784, for the second thoughts of the senior French officers on the election of specific individuals to the French Society of the Cincinnati.

From Rochambeau

My Dear Général   Paris may the 4th 1784.

The letter Which you have honoured me With, the 1st of february ultime, has made the greatest pleasure to me, and your title of particulary Citizen Cannot but increases the Sentiments of Veneration, and of the most tender affection that I have devoted to you for all my life. it is the finest End of the highest Employement that ever man has filled.

I owe to let you Know, my Dear Général, that the King has given to me the Command in chief of the province of the Picardy, and the town of Calais Will be my residence during the Summer. I Shall be very Neighbour With the people against Which we have had So much fighting: but What politeness Soever the commerce of the peace Will give me With them, my heart Shall be allways for the Général under the orders of Which I did fight them, and it Will be the height of the happiness for me, though I Cannot flatter myself of it, that to receive him in that residence.

You owe to have received, my dear Général, the little letter of Confidence by Which I did prevent you of all the repugnancy that the King has to admit Strange orders in his Kingdom, and that it Was only by an consideration for you and for the united States; he has permitted to us of being admitted in the Society of Cincinnatus.[1] if you admit all the demands that the officers of the navy make to you, as Well as that I Sent to you for my army, I fear that this great extension may displease to his majesty and I doubt he Will accept it. I think then it Would be convenient to Keep in two that I have designed to you, to Wit, The chevalier de Lameth and the Baron de L'Estrade, The first having been Wounded in the attack of the redoubts of york, and the Second having been ordered to march at the head of the first Company of Grenadiers as a Lieutenant Colonel in the Same attack. they have only been made, one Brigadier, and the other Colonel after the siege. They are both in So particulary Cases that if you grant that favour to them, I Shall not Want a new permission of the King and I Shall consider it as an explication of the first deliberation that his majesty has already approved of.

my most tender respects, I beseech you, my Dear Général to Madam Washington, Let me Know from you and from her as often as it will be possible to you, and be persuaded of the inviolable attachment and of the respect With Which I am My Dear Général Your Most obedient and Very humble servant

Le cte de Rochambeau

LS, DLC:GW.

1. See Rochambeau to GW, 1 Mar. 1784.

To La Luzerne

Sir,   Philada 5th May 1784

It was not until Capt: Hardwine deliver'd the Claret your Excellency was so obliging as to spare me, that I had the least knowledge of its being sent. In consequence of your kind offer to furnish me with three hogsheads, I wrote to Colo. Tilghman (at Baltimore) requesting him to receive & forward it to me; & obtained for answer, that before Your Excellys order had reached your Agent at that place, the Wine had been shipped for Philaa. In this belief & ignorance, I remained 'till the Wine was actually delivered to me when you were at my Seat in Virginia.[1]

I have given you the trouble of reading this detail to apologize for my not having paid for the Wine sooner. Colo. Biddle will now have the honor of doing it[2]—& I pray your Excelly to receive my thanks for the favor you did me by sparing this quantity from your own Stock. With the greatest personal attachment & consideration, I have the honor to be &ca

G. Washington

LB, DLC:GW.

1. La Luzerne visited GW not long before GW left for Philadelphia. See Armand to GW, 4 Feb. 1784, and La Luzerne to GW, 18 Feb. 1784.

2. See GW to Biddle, 6 May 1784.

To John Rodgers

Dear Sir   Philadelpa 5th May 1784.

The thanksgiving Sermon which you did me the favor to send me, I read with much pleasure; & pray you to accept my thanks for it, & the favorable mention you have been pleased to make of me therein.[1]

My Compliments await Mrs Rogers[2]—with great esteem and respect I remain Dr Sir—Yr most Obedt & Affecte Servt

Go: Washington

ALS, Brick Presbyterian Church, Park Ave. at 91st St., New York.

John Rodgers (1727–1811), a leading Presbyterian preacher in America from 1748 until shortly before his death, held a pastorate in New York City for forty-five years beginning in 1765. Rodgers delivered the sermon that he sent to GW in Trinity Episcopal Church in the city, which opened its doors to him and his congregation while their "New Brick Church" was being repaired after the British occupation.

1. Rodgers's sermon, printed in New York in 1784 by Samuel Loudon was entitled: *The Divine Goodness Displayed, in the American Revolution: A Sermon Preached in New-York, December 11th, 1783. Appointed by Congress, as a Day of Public Thanksgiving, throughout the United States.* Rodgers used as his text verse 3 of Psalm 126: "The Lord hath done great things for us, whereof we are glad."

2. Rodgers had been married since 1764 to his second wife, Mary Antrobus Grant Rodgers, the widow of a Philadelphia merchant.

From William Smith

Chester, Kent County Maryland

Most worthy & Hond Sir   May 5th 1784

In the Name & Behalf of the Visitors & Governors of Washington College and by their Order, I beg Leave to acquaint you that their annual Visitation is to be held on Tuesday May 18th instant. At that Meeting they hope for the Presence of the Visitors in General, who are Gentlemen of the first Distinction from every County on the Eastern Shore of this State. As the General Assembly have dignified this rising Seminary with your Name, & you are a Member of the Body Corporate, your Presence at some one Meeting, if you can make it convenient, is an Honour, which they most earnestly wish for, as it would give the highest Sanction to the Institution & be truly animating to a numerous Body of youth, who may, at a future Day, make a considerable Figure in the World.[1]

In Hopes of acquitting themselves with some Credit in your Presence, they have in Rehearsal the Tragedy of Gustavus Vasa, the Deliverer of Sweden from Danish Tyranny; & are to be otherwise examined in the Sciences &c.[2]

The Visitors & Governors of the College hope that your Excellency may now be able to determine nearly as to the Day of your Return Southward, and whether you could make it convenient to spend one Day with us in your Way. If Tuesday the 18 should not be the Day on which you could pass thro' Chester in Maryland or be at the College Visitation, we can by Adjournment make another Day convenient for us, either before or after the 18th.[3]

The Bearer Mr Page is one of the Visitors of the College & will transmit to me, as President of the Board of Visitors whatever Answer you may be pleased to Honour us with.[4] I am Sir, with the profoundest Respect Your most obedt humble Servant

William Smith

ALS, DLC:GW.

The Rev. William Smith, the first provost of the College of Philadelphia, had been both a prominent and a controversial figure in Pennsylvania for almost a quarter of a century at the time the legislature in 1779 revoked the college's charter and created the University of the State of Pennsylvania. Smith then became rector of Chester Parish in Kent County, Md., and there established Kent School which in 1782 became Washington College (see James Milligan to GW, 13 Jan. 1784, n.2).

1. GW did not return from the general meeting of the Cincinnati in Philadelphia by way of Chestertown.

2. Henry Brooke (1703–1783) published his tragedy *Gustavus Vasa . . .* in 1739, and it was produced in Dublin in 1744 under the title of *The Patriot*.

3. The ceremonies for the first graduates of Washington College were held in Chestertown on 14 May 1783.

4. This is probably John Page of Kent County, who subscribed £25 in 1782 to the founding of the college.

To Clement Biddle

Dear Sir   Phila. May 6th 1784

You will do me a favr by executing the enclosed Memms.[1]

The reason why I had rather the wine (had of the Chevr de la

Luzerne) should be paid for by a third person, shall be given to you when I see you.[2]

To send the articles wanted by the first Vessel bound to Alexandria, would be very convenient, & you wd do me a kindness to agree for, & express what the frieght shall be. I have suffered great impositions by the charges of some skippers, rather than enter into a contraversy, or dispute their Accts—I send you enclosed 250 dollars to pay the Chevr—& for the things now desired[3]—If Burgundy & Champaign is to be had *now*, as Cheap as I am told it sold at a while ago—or any other *good* wine of that sort *very* cheap, I should be glad to get, & send some round. but your previous information may be best.

If I could see a small slipe of the plain blew & green paper—with a sample of the paupier-Maché & gilded borders, I should be glad of it. In a hurry I am Yr obt & affe Servt

Go: Washington

My Letter to the Chevr is left open for your perusal—please to seal it before delivery—which I wish may be soon.

ALS, PHi: Washington-Biddle Correspondence.
1. The memoranda have not been identified, but see note 3.
2. See GW to La Luzerne, 5 May 1784.
3. The 250 dollars in bank notes that GW sent to Biddle came to (at 7/6) £93.15 (Ledger B, 198).

To Benjamin Franklin

Dear Sir,   Philadelphia May 6th 1784.

Mr Tracy the bearer of this, is a Gentleman of Fortune from Massachusettsbay—on a visit to Europe.[1]

His political character, and character for benevolence & hospitality are too well established in this Country to need any other recommendation, notwithstanding I have taken the liberty of giving him this letter of introduction to you.[2] With very great esteem and regard—I am—Dr Sir Yr Most Obedt Servt

Go: Washington

ALS, PU: Benjamin Franklin Papers; LB, DLC:GW.
1. Nathaniel Tracy (1751–1796) of Newburyport, Mass., made a large fortune in privateering and shipping during the Revolution and sustained great losses as well. In a letter dated 4 Aug. 1783 introducing Francesco, the count

dal Verme (1758–1832), GW asked Tracy to advance the nobleman money if he should need it. Tracy in May 1784 was preparing to go to Europe for the purpose of settling the accounts of his company, Jackson, Tracy, & Tracy, with the Gardoqui firm in Portugal. On 5 July he sailed from Boston for London, with Thomas Jefferson as a passenger, in his own vessel, the *Ceres*. Tracy failed in his mission, and not long after his return to Massachusetts in 1785 he was bankrupt.

2. GW also has in his letter book a letter of 5 May introducing Tracy to Lafayette: "Mr Tracy will hand you this letter—his character & worth you are not unacquainted with; yet, as he is about to undertake a Voyage to Europe, & proposes to make Paris a visit: I have taken the liberty of requesting you to give him an introduction into the circle of your acquaintance" (DLC:GW).

From Nathanael Greene

Dear Sir   Newport [R.I.] May 6th 1784

Since I wrote you by Col. Henley I took a ride to Boston to try my strength and see how traveling would affect me.[1] It increased my complaint but not so much as to discourage my attempting to be at the Cincinnati had not my complaint increased since my return. The Doctor thinks my life would be endangered by attempting to cross the Water and my pain in my stomach increased by riding by land. In this situation prudence forbids my coming; but that the Society may not be unrepresented Col. Ward has agreed to go altho not in the original appointment. He is sensible and prudent and deserves every degree of confidence you may think proper to repose in him. He is a young Gentleman of a liberal education and great observation.[2]

The clamour against the order rather increases in Massachusets and Connecticut States. In this little is said about it but in one County. Many sensible people are anxious for the continuance of the order—Many more wish the Heraditary part loped off as the most exceptionable part of the whole institution. others again are offended at the Heradatory part on account of the French Office[r]s. It is thought it may lead to an improper influence in our National affairs. But what ever objections are raised against the order it is evidently paving the way for the commutation. People begin to say they should have no objection to paying the commutation but for the dangerous combination of the Cincinnati[.] Drop the Cincinnati and the old question will revive; but continue the order and I am confident the commutation will go down. It is the wish of many that the order should be altered and admit no honorary members and terminate with the present Generation. But I fear any alteration in the present state of things would go far to defeat its influence upon the federal connection and the business of the commutation. It is worthy some consideration to attempt giving reasonable satisfaction to the apprehensions of the people; but I am at a loss to determin what will affect it. I hope the Meeting will not rise hastily and the Moment my health will permit I shall leave this for Philadelphia. My breast will not permit me to write more and I have written in much pain already. I am dear Sir with esteem & affection Your Most Obed., humble Ser.

N. Greene

ALS, DLC:GW.

1. See Greene to GW, 24 April 1784. "Col. Henley" is probably David Henley (1748–1823), who was colonel of one of the Massachusetts regiments when he retired from the service in April 1779.

2. Ward was also Catharine Greene's first cousin.

Letter not found: from Philip Schuyler, 6 May 1784. On 15 May GW wrote to Schuyler: "I cannot but thank you . . . for . . . your letters of the 6th & 12th Instt."

To Clement Biddle

Dear Sir,   [Philadelphia] May 7th 1784.

As the oppertunity to Potomack will be good, I return the Box you sent me the other day, in order that it may go by the Ship Fortune with the other things—As my purchase of any of the sorts of Wine (enumerated in my letter of yesterday) will depend upon the price, which *sometime ago* I heard was *incredibly low*, you would oblige me, if you know the rates they are at present, by the information—I have heard the same acct given of other articles, broad Cloths particularly, of which I would take a piece of my livery colore⟨d i⟩f it cd be had at the prices it has sold.

Upon second thoughts a dozn a⟨nd a⟩ half of Windsor Chairs will be suffict ⟨⟨I⟩ think my Memm requested two dozn) but ⟨I⟩

should be glad to have Almonds & other Nutts & a Box or two of Spirmi Citi Candles sent. I am Dr Sir Yr affecte Servt

Go: Washington

ALS, PHi: Washington-Biddle Correspondence. There is a tear in the manuscript. The letters in angle brackets are those missing from the manuscript.

Certificate for Louis-Joseph de Beaulieu

[Philadelphia, 8 May 1784]

I do hereby certify, that from Papers which have been produced to me, it appears that Mr Louis Joseph de Beaulieu has borne the rank of Lieutenant in the Service of the United States of America—that he has been appointed a Captn therein by brevet—that he has been dangerously wounded in several actions, in all of which he has behaved with great zeal and bravery—and in other respects has discharged the duties of an Officer & Gentleman to the approbation of all who are acquainted with him. Given under my hand this 8th day of May 1784.

Go: Washington—late comr in Chief Amn Army

ADS (facsimile), sold by Sotheby Parke-Bernet, no. 5097, item 104, 26 Oct. 1983; LB, DLC:GW.

Louis-Joseph d'Escudier de Beaulieu (b. 1753), lieutenant in Pulaski's Legion, was taken prisoner at Savannah in 1779 and later severely wounded at Charleston.

To William Gordon

Revd Sir,   Philada May 8th 1784.

Every aid which can be derived from my official papers, I am willing to afford, & shall with much pleasure lay before you, whenever the latter can be unfolded with propriety.

It ever has been my opinion however, that no Historian can be possessed of sufficient materials to compile a *perfect* history of the revolution, who has not free access to the archives of Congress—to those of the respective States—to the papers of the commander in chief, & to those of the officers who have been employed in separate Departments. Combining & properly arranging the information which is to be obtained from these sources must bring to view all the material occurrences of the War. Some things probably will never be known.[1]

Added to this, I have always thought, that it would be respectful to the Sovereign power of these United States, to *follow*, rather than to take the lead of them in disclosures of this Kind: but if there should be political restraints, under which Congress are not inclined at this time to lay open their papers; & these restraints do not in their opinion extend to mine—the same being signified by that honorable Body to me, my objections to your request will cease. I shall be happy then, as at all times, to see you at Mount Vernon, & will lay before you with chearfulness, my *public* papers for your information.[2] With great esteem & regard, I am Dr Sir Your Most Obt &c.

G: Washington

LB, DLC:GW; copy, DNA:PCC, item 19.

The copy is endorsed: "The Copy of Genl Washingtons Letter to the Revd William Gordon alluded to in the petition." See Gordon to GW, 8 Mar. 1784, source note.

1. After receiving this letter, Gordon petitioned Congress for access to its records. Congress granted this and indicated it had no objection to GW's making his papers available to the historian. See source note, Gordon to GW, 8 Mar. 1784.

2. Gordon took advantage of GW's invitation not long after receiving Congress's approval of his project. On the cover sheet of Benjamin Rush's notorious anonymous letter of 12 Jan. 1778 to Gov. Patrick Henry of Virginia (which Henry promptly sent to GW), in which Rush calls for GW's removal from the command of American forces, Gordon wrote: "Mount Vernon June 18, 1784. Before perusing the letter, I can take upon me to declare, that, From the knowledge I have of Dr. Rush's handwriting, I have not the least doubt but what it was written by him" (quoted in a footnote in Butterfield, *Rush Letters*, 1:185). In a private letter to Gov. Henry Lee of Virginia on 26 Aug. 1794 refuting charges that he was hostile to Patrick Henry and had recently spoken ill of him, GW commented: "I have conceived my self under obligations to him [Henry] for the friendly manner in which he transmitted to me some insiduous anonymous writings that were sent to him in the close of the year 1777, with a view to embark him in the opposition that was forming against me at that time" (ViHi). When discussing the anonymous letter, Gordon does not identify its author or mention Rush, but he does write: "Several members of congress were engaged in the business—some of the Massachusetts delegates—particularly Mr. Samuel Adams" (Gordon, *History*, 3:57). In a letter to Richard Henry Lee, 29 Aug. 1789, Adams has this to say: " . . . Dr Gordon in his History of the Revolution . . . has gravely said, that I was concerned in an Attempt to remove General Washington from Command; and mentions an anonymous Letter written to your late Governor Henry which I affirm I never saw nor heard of till I lately met with it in reading the History—" (Lee Family Papers, PPAmP).

From Ebenezer Hazard

Sir,   General Post Office, Phila. May 11th 1784.

The Secretary of Congress transmitted me a Copy of the enclosed Resolution, which I received with singular Pleasure as an Act of Justice due to your Excellency, and at the same Time relieving me, as I had desired, from the very disagreeable Situation with Respect to your Excellency's Letters to which I was reduced by the Ordinance for regulating the Post Office of the United States.[1]

The necessary Directions were forwarded, by the first Post, to Mr McCrea at Alexandria, and nothing on my Part shall be wanting to give this Act of Congress the most complete Effect.[2] I have the Honor to be, very respectfully, and with the most cordial Esteem, Your Excellency's most obedient and very humble Servant

Eben. Hazard

ALS, DLC:GW.

The historical editor Ebenezer Hazard (1744–1817) became postmaster general of the United States in 1782 and served until the new government was formed in 1789.

1. See Congress's resolution of 28 April printed below as an enclosure.
2. See GW's response to Hazard, 18 May 1784.

Enclosure
Resolution of Congress

April 28th 1784.

Whereas by the Ordinance for regulating the Post Office of the United States of America passed the 18th day of October 1782 it is ordained—That Letters, Packets & Dispatches to and from the Commander in Chief of the Armies of these United States on public service shall pass and be carried free of postage and whereas there is reason to apprehend that the numerous Letters and Packets addressed to the late Commander in Chief of the Armies of these United States in consequence of his late Command and on matters foreign to his private concerns will subject him to an expence in postage which it would be improper and unreasonable he should bear.

Resolved That all Letters and Packets to and from the late Commander in Chief of the Armies of the United States shall pass and be carried free of postage until the further orders of Congress and that the post master General be and he is hereby directed to refund to the said late Commander in Chief all the monies paid by him for the postage of Letters or packets since the time of his resignation.

Chas Thomson Secy

D, DLC:GW.

From John Jones

May it Please your Excellency   Curaçao May 12th 1784
I have taken the Liberty to Send you by the Brig Fairy Capt. Benjamin Croker which Sailed from hence for James River on the first Inst. a very fine fat Turtle with orders to the Capt. to Deliver the Same to ⟨Wm⟩ [&] Miss Armstead at Hampton, to be forwarded to you. It will give me great pride & pleasure to know you have received it Safe and that it is acceptable to yr Taste. I had the honor in a ⟨former⟩ war to be personally near you[1] & have Spent my time here during this war, wherein along with Yr Excellency's great Reputation, you have aided to raise a great Empire. your praises have been made by per⟨sons⟩ able to Do Justice to such a Character. I cant find powers to express my Sense of So great a one. but in an Humble Strain, let me have the honor to offer you any Services you may please to Command, in this Little remote Spot. Should I be Successfull in contributing to your pleasure or gratification no reward can be equal to the Satisfaction I Shall feel in an exertion of my greatest Care and Zeal in Doing you any good offices. I have the Honor to be with the greatest Defference, Your excellency's most faithfull & obedt Servant

John Jones

ALS, DLC:GW.
1. A John Jones, storekeeper in Conococheague, Md., on the Potomac, served as a commissary for GW's Virginia Regiment for a time in 1755 before becoming ill and being replaced. See GW to John Jones, 15 Sept. 1755, n.1.

Letter not found: from Philip Schuyler, 12 May 1784. On 15 May GW wrote to Schuyler: "I cannot but thank you . . . for . . . your letters of the 6th & 12th Instt."

From Lafayette

My dear General　　　　　　　　　Paris May the 14th 1784

To My Great Satisfaction, My departure is fixed Upon the tenth of Next Month, When I intend leaving paris, and Immediately Embarking for America—My Course will be straight to Pottowmack, and I do Most feelingly Anticipate the pleasure of our Meeting at Mount Vernon[1]—there is Nothing New in france, But that the Affair of the free Ports is Quite Settled, and that Nothing yet Has Been done Respecting the Intended Regulations for Commerce Betwen America and the West Indias—Governement are very friendly to the Interest of the United States, But labour Under Many difficulties, the Strongest of all is the Complaints of flour Merchants, Manufacturers, and Raisers in the Country Round Bordeaux—there Has Been a Pretention Set up a Vienna By the Empress of Russia, for a Preeminence of Her Ambassador over ours, Which is foolish and Groundless, and from Which She Must Certainly desist—some Portuguese Disputes Respecting a Settlement in Africa Have Been decided to the Satisfaction of france—Mr pitt's party will be the Stronger in the New Parliament—But Charles fox Comes in as a Member for Wesminster, and Will Head an Opposition—the Situation of Ireland is Critical, the lord lieutenant's Conduct Has Been foolish, and Some Resolutions of the people are very Spirited—A German doctor Called *Mesmer* Having Made the Greatest discovery Upon *Magnetism Animal*, He Has instructed scholars, Among Whom Your Humble Servant is Called One of the Most Enthusiastic—I know as Much as Any Conjurer Ever did, Which Remind's me of our old friend's at Fiskills Enterview with the devil that Made us laugh So Much at His House, and Before I go, I will Get leave to let You into the Secret of Mesmer, which, you May depend Upon, is a Grand philosophical discovery.[2]

Mr jay is Gone this Morning to Dover where He intends embarking for America—He Has taken Care of A family picture, including mde de Lafayette, our Children, and Myself which I Beg leave to Present to My dear General, as the likenesses of those Who are Most Affectionately devoted to Him.[3]

the Whole family join with me in the Most Respectfull Compliments to You, and Mrs Washington—Be so kind, My dear

General, to Remember me to the other Inhabitants of Mount Vernon, and to all friends that You May Happen to See— Adieu, My dear General, Be pleased With Your Usual kindness, to Receive the tender wishes of one who More than Any Man Existing May Boast of Being, Your excellency's Most Affectionate, Respectfull friend and Humble Servant

Lafayette

ALS, PEL.

1. Lafayette landed in New York in early August and got to Mount Vernon on 17 August.

2. Mesmer formed his Société de l'Harmonie on 10 Mar. 1783 and invited 100 members to join for 100 louis apiece. Lafayette joined on 5 April 1784 and took the oath of loyalty and secrecy. On 12 Aug. shortly after his arrival in America, Lafayette appeared before the members of the American Philosophical Society in Philadelphia and "entertained them with a particular relation of the wonderful effects of a certain invisible power, in nature, called *animal magnetism* lately discovered by Mr. Mesmer, a German Philosopher" (*Early Proceedings of the American Philosophical Society*, 126–27). See Friedrich Anton Mesmer to GW, 16 June 1784, and notes.

3. The portrait did not go with John Jay, and on 25 July 1785 GW wrote Lafayette: "The latter end of April I had the pleasure to receive in good order, by a Ship from London, the picture of your self, Madame la Fayette & the children, which I consider as an invaluable present, & shall give it the best place in my House." See also note 6, 5 : 218, in Idzerda, *Lafayette Papers*.

To d'Estaing

Sir,   Philada 15th May 1784

I cannot my dear General express to you all the gratitude which I feel for your very great politeness manifested for me in your letter of the 25th of Decr—which I now have the honor & pleasure to acknowledge.[1] The very tender & friendly regards which you are pleased to mention as possessing your mind, for my person & character, have affected me with the deepest sensibility; & will be forever remembered as a most agreeable token from the Count D'Estaing, for whose character as a Gentleman & a soldier, & for whose attention to the American interests & cause, I have ever been impressed with the highest veneration.

I feel myself happy that your Excellency countenances with so much cordiallity, the association formed by the Officers of the American army, a bond of cement Sir, which, if any thing could be wanting for that purpose, will I trust serve to render durable & permanent those mutual friendships & connections, which have happily taken root between the Officers of your army & ours. And I am peculiarly happy to be able to inform you that the wishes expressed in your letter are more than fulfilled; since by the institutions of our Society, as amended & altered at their General Meeting in this City held during the present month, & which will be officially forwarded to the Society in France, your Excelly will find that the honors of it are extended, not only to the few Gentlemen honor'd by your particular mention, but to all the Captns ranking as Colonels in your Navy—which, altho' not clearly expressed in the original Constitution, is now in the fullest terms provided for, & not left to doubtful implication.

I am much pleased with the prospect of soon having the pleasure of seeing in this country our mutual worthy friend de la Fayette. Be assur'd Sir, I shall be among the warmest of his friends who will welcome him to the American shore; & rejoice in an opportunity to embrace him in my arms. I am pleased that our confidence in Majr L'Enfant has been so honorably placed, & that the business entrusted to that Gentlns conduct has been executed to so great satisfaction. With the highest regard &c. I have the honor to be &c.

G: Washington

LB, DLC:GW.

1. For d'Estaing's letter of 25 Dec. 1783, see d'Estaing to GW, 8 Jan. 1784, n.1.

From Charles-Louis de Montesquieu

a Paris le 15 May 1784

Si mon Sang eut coulé, dans la guerre ou Votre Excellence assura dune maniere Si glorieuse la liberté de l'Amerique, je réclamerois avec plus de confiance les marques de l'association dont elle a décoré quelques Colonels francois.

j'appris en arrivant en france, que javois ete nommé Colonel en Second du Regiment de Bourbonnois, le 11 de novembre 1782. le vicomte de Rochambeau venoit detre nommé Colonel Commandant du Regiment de Saintonge, avant de passer à celui de Royal auvergne. j'etois à cette epoque en Amerique: le Regiment de Bourbonnois y etoit encore. j'ai été porté Sur l'etat de larmée, et j'ai touché les apointements attaches à mon nouveau grade en Amerique, ainsi jai été réellement Colonel avant la fin de la guerre, et Si ma comission fut arrivée plus tot, j'aurois pu Servir encore dune maniere active jusques à la paix.

Si je Reclame aussi tard une grace à la quelle jattache beaucoup de prix, Votre Excellence n'en doit pas être Surprise. Ce nest qu'apres avoir vu les marques de l'ordre de Cincinnatus à des Colonels arrivés en Amerique à la fin de la derniere campagne, que j'ai pu esperer de l'obtenir moi même⟨.⟩ j'ai l'honneur d'etre assés connu de Votre Excellence pour qu'elle ne doutte pas du Respect, de ladmiration et Si jose le dire, du tendre attachement que je conservérai toujours pour elle.

Montesquieu

P.S. je Serai vraisemblablement a Bordeaux quand votre Excellence reçevra ma lettre et Si elle me fait lhonneur d'y repondre je la prie davoir la bonte de me faire adresser Sa response *a Bordeaux.*

ALS, PHi: Gratz Collection; Sprague transcript, DLC:GW.

Charles-Louis de Secondat, later baron de La Brède et de Montesquieu (1749–1824), grandson of the author of *L'Esprit des Lois*, was aide-de-camp to Chastellux in America. He also commanded the detachment that accompanied Lauzun to Paris with news of the victory at Yorktown. Montesquieu was elected to the society.

From Edmund Randolph

Dear sir   Richmond [Va.] May 15. 1784.

Inclosed you will receive a letter, which fell into my hands from a gentleman, lately arrived from England.[1]

Colo. Bassett is here, and I shall prepare a deed to be executed for the whole of the lands, adjudged to him against you. I was not satisfied, that the proof, which you sent me of improvements, was agreeable to law, tho' the fact would certainly have acquitted some of the land: and therefore I thought it best to give him an order for the whole. I will have the deed recorded on the first tuesday in next month in the general court.[2]

Dr Savage is dead, and his suit has abated. If the injunction be not renewed by his executor, it will be in your power to proceed on the old judgment. I believe, that it will be necessary to give the executor time, until the succeeding court, to determine, whether he will revive it or not, such being the rule of the chancery.[3] I am Dr Sir with the greatest esteem and regard yr affte & obliged humble serv.

Edm. Randolph

ALS, DLC:GW.

1. This letter has not been identified.

2. See Randolph to GW, 19 Feb., n.2, GW to Randolph, 18 Mar., and Randolph to GW, April 1784.

3. See Randolph to GW, 19 Feb. 1784, n.3.

To Philip Schuyler

My dear Sir,   Phila. May 15th 1784.

It has long been my wish, and until lately my intention to have proceeded from this meeting of the Cincinnati to the Falls of Niagara—& probably into Canada.

Two causes however prevent it—My business is of such a nature that I cannot without great inconvenience, be long absent from home, at this juncture—it is indeed, exceedingly inconvenient to be away from it at all—the other is, that I am not disposed to be indebted for a Passport into that Country to the British whose *convenient speed* has not permitted them to surrender the Western Posts to us yet.

I cannot but thank you however, my good Sir, for the polite & friendly offers contained in your letters of the 6th & 12th Instt both of which are safe at hand[1]—if ever I should have it in my power to make an excursion of that kind nothing could add more to the pleasure of it than having you of the party.

We have been most amazingly embarrassed in the business that brought us here—It is now drawing to a conclusion—and will soon be given to the Public, otherwise I would relate it in detail—Mrs Washington is not with me at this place, otherwise I am sure she wd join me in best respects to Mrs Schuyler & yourself. With the great esteem and regard I am Dr Sir Yr Most Obedt & Affe. Servt

Go: Washington

ALS (photocopy), DLC:GW; LB, DLC:GW.

1. Letters not found.

To Jonathan Trumbull, Sr.

Dear Sir, Philada May 15th 1784.

It was with great pleasure & thankfulness, I received a recognizance of your friendship in your letter of the 20th of last month.

It is indeed a pleasure, from the walks of private life to view in retrospect, all the meanderings of our past labors—the difficulties through which we have waded—and the fortunate Haven to which the ship has been brought! Is it possible after this that it should founder? Will not the all wise, & all powerfull director of human events, preserve it? I think he will, he may however for wise purposes not discoverable by finite minds) suffer our indiscretions & folly to place our national character low in the political Scale—and this, unless more wisdom & less prejudice take the lead in our governments, will most assuredly be the case.

Believe me, my dear Sir, there is no disparity in our ways of thinking and acting, tho there may happen to be a little in the years we have lived; which places the advantages of the corrispondence between us to my acct, as I shall benefit more by your experience & observations than you can by mine—No corrispondence can be more pleasing than one which originates from similar sentiments, & similar conduct through (tho' not a long war, the importance of it, & attainments considered) a painful contest. I pray you therefore to continue me among the number of your friends, and to favor me with such observations as shall occur.

As my good friend Colo. Trumbull is perfectly acquainted with the proceedings of the meeting which brought us together—our embarrassments—& final decisions, I will refer the detail of them to him—With the most perfect esteem & regard I have the honor to be My dear Sir Yr Most Obedt & Very Hble Servt

Go: Washington

ALS, CtHi: Washington Letters and Papers; LB, DLC:GW.

Virginia General Assembly and George Washington,
15 May–15 July 1784

I.   Resolution of the Virginia Legislature, 22 June 1784
II. Address of the Virginia Legislature, 24 June 1784
III. Response to the Virginia Legislature, 15 July 1784

EDITORIAL NOTE

On 15 May 1784 the Virginia house of delegates agreed "to draw up an address to his excellency General Washington, expressive of the thanks and gratitude of the House of Delegates for his unremitted zeal and services in the cause of liberty; congratulating him on his return to his native country, and the exalted pleasures of domestic life." A committee of nine delegates was named, and the house instructed "the same committee, to consider and report what further measures may be necessary for perpetuating the gratitude and veneration of his country, to General Washington" (*House of Delegates Journal, 1781–1785*). The chairman of the committee, William Ronald of Powhatan County, on 5 June presented the text of an address to be given to GW and a report on "further means, to express the gratitude of this House" to him. Both were referred to the committee of the whole house. Two days later, on 8 June, the house voted to submit the address and the resolution of Ronald's committee to a new committee of thirteen delegates, including among others Patrick Henry, James Madison, and Richard Henry Lee. The new committee, "in concert with a committee of the Senate," was "to prepare an address and direct other testimonials of gratitude" to GW (ibid.). Ronald reported on 22 June that the house and senate committees had agreed on the text of a resolution calling for a statue of GW to be made (doc. I) and on the text of an address to be delivered to him (doc. II). The house promptly accepted both. Henry Lee, who at this time represented Fairfax and Prince William counties in the state senate, wrote GW on 4 July that the legislature's address would be delivered to him at Mount Vernon on 15 July. GW responded to the address on that day (doc. III).

I

Resolution of the Virginia Legislature

[Richmond, Va.] Tuesday June the 22d 1784
In the House of Delegates
Resolved that the Executive be requested to take measures for procuring a Statue of General Washington to be of the finest Marble and best Workmanship with the following Inscription on its Pedestal;[1] vizt

The General Assembly of the Commonwealth of Virginia, have caused this Statue to be erected as a monument of affection and gratitude to George Washington—who uniting to the endowment of the Hero the virtues of the Patriot and exerting both in establishing the Liberties of his Country has rendered his name dear to his fellow Citizens and given the World an immortal example of true Glory. Done in the year of Christ —— and in the year of the Commonwealth —— .

1784. June 24th

Teste

Agreed to by the Senate

John Beckley Clerk ⟨h.d.⟩
Will: Drew C.S.

D, DLC:GW. The text of the resolution is printed in *House of Delegates Journal, 1781–1785*, on 22 June 1784.

1. Gov. Benjamin Harrison wrote Thomas Jefferson in Paris on 20 July: "The Assembly of this State have voted a Statue of our late worthy commander in Chief General Washington, and have directed their intentions to be carried into execution by the Executive. . . . we have unanimously fixed on you and my friend Doctor Franklin . . . to undertake it. . . . To enable the Artist to furnish [sic] his work in the most perfect manner I have ordered Mr Peale to send to your address a full length picture of the general as soon as possible. The intention of the assembly is that the Statue should be the work of the most masterly hand. I shall therefore leave it to you to find out the best in any of the European States" (Boyd, *Jefferson Papers*, 7:378–79). See also Boyd's note. The *Virginia Gazette or the American Advertiser* (Richmond) on 28 Aug. reported that Harrison had written to Charles Willson Peale about sending a picture of GW to Jefferson. Jefferson wrote GW on 10 Dec. 1784 that he and Benjamin Franklin had chosen Houdon to make the statue.

II
Address of the Virginia Legislature

[Richmond, Va.] Thursday the 24th of June 1784
The Representatives of this CommonWealth would be unfaithful to the sentiments of their Constituents as well as do violence to their own, did they omit this occasion of congratulating you on the final establishment of Peace which has taken place since their last Meeting, and in the opportunity which this event has given for you to return to the felicities of private life. We shall ever remember, Sir, with affection and Gratitude the patriotic exchange which you made of these felicities, for the severe task of conducting the Arms of your Country through a Conflict with one of the most powerful nations of the Earth. We shall ever remember with admiration the Wisdom which marked your Councils on this arduous occasion, the firmness and dignity which no trials of adverse fortune could shake the moderation and equanimity which no scenes of Triumph could disturb, Nor shall we ever forget the exemplary Respect which in every instance you have shewn, to the rights of Civil Authority or the exalted Virtue which on many occasions led you to commit to danger, your fame itself, rather than hazard for a moment the true interest of your Country. In reviewing these merits we feel every Impression which they are calculated to make on grateful and affectionate Minds, and we fervently pray that they may be rewarded with every blessing of which this life will admit, and with complete happiness in that which is to come.

Archibald Cary S.S.
John Tyler S.H.D.

DS, DLC:GW; LB, DLC:GW. The text is printed in *House of Delegates Journal, 1781–1785*, 22 June.

III
Response to the Virginia Legislature

Gentlemen,   [Mount Vernon] Virginia 15th July 1784
With feelings which are more easy to be conceived than expressed, I meet, and reciprocate the congratulations of the

Representatives of this Commonwealth, on the final establishment of peace.[1]

Nothing can add more to the pleasure which arises from a conscientious discharge of public trust, than the approbation of one's Country. To have been, under a vicissitude of fortune, amidst the difficult and trying scenes of an arduous conflict, so happy as to meet this is in my mind to have attained the highest honor and the consideration of it, in my present peaceful retirement will heighten all my domestic enjoyments, and constitute my greatest felicity.

I should have been truly wanting in duty, and must have frustrated the great and important object for which we resorted to Arms, if seduced by a temporary regard of fame I had suffer'd the paltry love of it to have interfered with my Country's welfare, the interest of which was the only inducement which carried me to the Field—or permitted the rights of civil authority, though but for a moment, to be violated and infringed by a power meant originally to rescue and confirm them.

For those rewards and blessings which you have invoked for me in this world, and for the fruition of that happiness which is to come, you have Gentlemen all my thanks and all my gratitude—I wish I could insure them to you, and the State you represent, an hundred fold.

G. Washington.

LB, DLC:GW; ADf, DLC:GW.

1. The *Virginia Gazette or the American Advertiser* (Richmond), 14 Aug. 1784, reported: "A joint Committee of the two Houses of Assembly was appointed to wait on the General, and present the foregoing address [see doc. II] to wit: On the part of the House of Delegates, Mr [Joseph] Jones (of King George), Mr [William] Grayson, Mr [William] Brent, Mr [Alexander] Henderson, and Mr [Thomas] West. And on the part of the Senate, Mr [Burwell] Bassett, Mr [William] Fitzhugh, and Mr Henry Lee.

"The Joint Committee accordingly waited upon the General at his seat of Mount Vernon, and presented the Address, to which he was pleased to return the following Answer."

The text of GW's response followed.

From Armand

Sir   Philadelphia May 16th 1784
     nothing pain me more than to trouble so often your Excellency in requesting new favors while I feel shur if I live long

my days will hardly be sufficiant to thank you for thoses you have allready bestowed on me, more particularly thoses which were a proof of your friendship—every step I take now with your Exellency is ambarassing to me, and although I hope to succeed, my fear of displeasing is much greater than my hope, but after all I wrait & say, the general will do as he like & surely will be assured that my unlimited Confidence in him will never permit me to think that he has not acted properly, even in refusing my request—my friends wrait to me that from the Conduct of the ministre & his ansaeres on my subject, I may flatter my self to be made a brigadier in france at my arrival there & to have an agreeable Command—they tell me that a lettre from you to the ministre at war on the subject would fixe the matter, but that if you do not wishes to wrait to him—I am still assured to be placed on the above mentioned footing in our army if your Exellency would wrait to Count de rochambeau—mentioning that it would be pleasing to you to see me have the rank of brigadier in france & that having had the Command of a legion during all the time of my services here, Exept in 1777 that I commanded a Corps of light infantry, your wishes also to see me provided with a Command in france—Count rochambeau whose dispositions are friendly to me will by your lettre be authorised to speak officially to the ministre & mention the particulars it may contain of your satisfaction of my services—thus I am assured I will have the great pleasure of being once more indebted to your Exellency for my advancement.[1]

although when I had the honor to mention this subject to your Exellency you gave me Expectations that you would wrait—if from further Consideration it was displeasing to you— then do not wrait, I may run with a great deal of philosophy all chances in the world but that of displeasing you—I am going to europe in a week or two, may I beg leave to wrait some times to your Exellency—I am sure men of a much higher importance than I am are highly flattered by the liberty of a Correspondance with your Exellency, but I dare say non could be influenced to this request by stronger motives of attachement & respect than I am—I have the honor to be with thoses sentiments Sir your Exellency the most obdt hble srt

C. Armand

ALS, DLC:GW.

1. GW gave Armand a letter of recommendation addressed to Rocham-

beau on this day: "This letter will be handed to you by our mutual friend General Armand, Marqs de la Rouerie. The merits of this Gentleman, and his military Services in this Country, are too well known to you to require any recommendation from me—if they did he is possessed of the fullest testimony.

"He now wishes promotion & employment in the Service of his own Country; and, as he is deserving of it, so, I wish he could be endulged—but good wishes is all I can afford him, for it has been an established principle with me to avoid personal applications.

"The disposition of his Prince to reward the brave & meritorious—the justice of his government will, I am perswaded, confer those honors on him which he shall appear to deserve. And this, even if I was not restrained by the consideration just mentioned is all I could ask" (DLC: Rochambeau Papers). The letter is in GW's hand. There is also a letter-book copy in DLC:GW.

To John Foulke

[Philadelphia] Monday Morning [17 May 1784]
Genl Washington presents his Compliments to Doctr Foulke—thanks him for his polite Card, & Ticket—and would with great pleasure attend his Lecture on Pneumatics; but the business which brought him to this City does not leave him at liberty, as the Members of the Cincinnati are anxious to bring it to a close.

AL, DSI: National Air and Space Museum.
John Foulke (1757–1796), a graduate in 1780 of the University of the State of Pennsylvania, had returned from study abroad and was on the staff of the Pennsylvania Hospital.

To Rochambeau

My dear Count,   Philadelpa 17th May 1784
From the official letters and other proceedings of the general meeting of the Society of the Cincinnati, held at this place, and of which you have copies; you will obtain a thorough knowledge of what the Society have been doing, and the ground upon which it was done; to enter therefore into a further detail of the matter, in this letter, would be mere repetition—alike troublesome & unnecessary.

The Society could not go into too minute a discrimination of characters, and thinking it best to comprehend its members by general description, those who will constitute the Society in

France must, hereafter, decide upon the pretensions of their Countrymen upon the principles of the institution as they are now altered and amended.

I will detain you no longer than while I can repeat the assurances of sincere respect & esteem with which I have the honor to be My dear Count Yr Most Obedt Hble Servt

Go: Washington

ALS, DLC: Rochambeau Papers; LB, DLC:GW. See GW's official letter to Rochambeau, 15 May, printed above as Appendix IV, in General Meeting of the Society of the Cincinnati, 4–18 May 1784.

From Edward Snickers

Der Generale   May the 17. 1784

I fulley intendid to aweaighted on you to pay you the Respeckte Due you and to Do Sume bisnees but finding by the paper that you wase not at home and parte of my Bisnees wase to no hume is to make the Deeds for the Lande you Solde at Coll mercers Salle and I have gote the five Lotes that Mr James mercer Boughte and Lote number one that William Hickman Boughte and the Lote number 21 which Sedwicke Bought[1] and I have gote the Bonde you give Mr mercer and Mr Sedwick asighened to me but not hickmanes as he boughte two Lotes & peaid Mr Lunde washington the Cash for Sedwickes bonde by the hands of Mr John melton and he never Sighened the Bond to me and I Cane not now git the Cash of Sedwick with out Bringing a sut as I hade peaid him for the Lande before I peaid of his mande and am obliged to Bring Sute in youre name against him which I hope you have no obecksion to[.][2] the persones that Loves on youre 2 Lotes have peaid the Taxes on it quar. Since the yere 1778 agreabile to youre Dereckshones to me in 1779 and I thinke thay qoughte no[w] to begine to pay you Sumthing[3] thay Colde be Rented out now verey well I wase in hopes to aseene you upe in oure Country th⟨is⟩ time—and if you Do not when I heare you are Come home I will weaighte on you and aney thing that I cane sarve you in ples to Command and it will give me plesher to Do it[4] my Complementes to youre Ladey and am with Due esteme youre Sincere frind and moste obedente Humbile Sarvnt

Ed. Snickers

N.B. Sur if you will Calle to mind you and Mr James mercer told me at the Sale that if the Estate Solde for more than twelve thousand five hundrid pounds that I Shude be peaid whate Coll mercer wase in Due me I am yours E.S.

ALS, DLC:GW.

Horse trader, tavern keeper, wagoner, military supplier, plantation manager for others and planter for himself, and land speculator, Edward Snickers before his death in 1790 had become a well-to-do gentleman in Frederick County with extensive landholdings. GW used Snickers's horses and wagons to have supplies hauled between Alexandria and Winchester for the Virginia Regiment during the French and Indian War and for his own purposes thereafter. Beginning in the 1750s GW also sometimes stopped at Snickers's ordinary located near where Snickers's ferry crossed the Shenandoah River. Snickers became a commissary for the Virginia forces on the frontier early in the Revolution, but this came to an end in 1777 when he was accused of fraud. See Jones, "Snickers," in which the scattered references to Edward Snickers's multifarious business activities in the Frederick County records and elsewhere have been collected.

1. As one of the attorneys, or agents, appointed to dispose of George Mercer's Virginia property, GW in November 1774 held sales, on 21–22 Nov., of that part of Mercer's property lying in Loudoun and Fauquier counties and then, on 24–27 Nov., of his property lying along the Shenandoah River in Frederick county. GW himself ended up buying two of the lots in Frederick. In December 1774 he also acquired George Mercer's half of the Four Mile Run tract in Fairfax County. GW took this land in partial payment of the indebtedness of the John Mercer estate to the Daniel Parke Custis estate. For discussion of GW's continued involvement with the Mercers as a consequence of these sales, see GW to Francis Lightfoot Lee and Ralph Wormeley, Jr., 20 June 1784, GW to John Francis Mercer, 8 July 1784, and GW's Statement concerning George Mercer's Estate, 1 Feb. 1789, and the notes in the three documents. The advertisement, placed in Rind's *Virginia Gazette* (Williamsburg), 30 June 1774, by John Tayloe and GW, described the Frederick County tract of land as "5000 Acres on *Shenando* river . . . opposite to *Snicker's* Ordinary, and binding on the River about seven Miles." Before the sale, the tract was surveyed and divided into twenty-two lots of about three hundred acres each. Snickers seems not to have bought any land at the sale in 1774, but he subsequently had in his possession at one time or another a total of at least eight lots: lot no. 1 and those numbered 16 through 22. On 3 June 1777 Snickers sold lots 16, 17, and 19 in the eastern part of the Mercer tract, and not on the river, to Mahlon Taylor (see Frederick County Deed Book, 17:259); and by the time he made his will in 1790, he owned three adjoining lots along the river, nos. 18, 20, and 22. Five of these six lots were bought at the sale by George Mercer's brother James. Two other lots that Snickers owned and refers to here are lot no. 1, at the northwestern corner of the tract, which he bought from William Hickman of Frederick County, and lot no. 21 at the northeastern corner of the Mercer tract, which he got from Benjamin

Sedwick. Snickers still held lot no. 1 but not lot no. 21 in 1790. For Edward Snickers's will, see Frederick County Will Book, 5:296.

2. GW bought lots 4 and 5 on the river after the sale.

3. On 8 Aug. 1785 John Sedwick of Frederick County and GW exchanged letters about this piece of property. Sedwick wrote GW that his father, the late Benjamin Sedwick, bought lot no. 21 at the Mercer sale in November 1774 and in 1776 sold it "to Edward Snickers who by Agreement was to pay of the bond as a part of the Price. Mr Snickers in 1779 or 1780, Paid of[f] the Bond in your Absence to Mr Lun Washington and obtained the Bond, and though he has had the Land in possession ever since 1776, he has now brought A Suit in your Name, I dare say without your knowledge, on my Fathers Bond against his Executors and Security." GW assured Sedwick he knew nothing of the suit, and on 11 April 1786 John Sedwick wrote from Leesburg that Snickers did pursue his suit but lost and had withdrawn a similar suit that he had instituted in the Virginia General Court. For Snickers's holdings in the Mercer tract, see also Jones, "Snickers," 26–27, 40–41.

4. For GW's response to this, see his letter of 25 June.

From Armand

Sir   Philadelphia 18th May 1784

I take the liberty to inclose here a lettre from my mother to your Excellency.[1] I had it for some weeks past in my possession, but as she request in it your patronage of my services in america with the ministre in france, and knowing well as I do, that a tryal of any influence, stranger to your own knowledge of my Conduct would have been disagreeable to you; I did not wish to deliver it untill on my own request, you had honored me with a lettre for Count rochambeau.[2]

The profound veneration & respect my mother bears to your Excellency the tenderness I owe to her title & conduct with me, do not permit me to detain longer the Expression of her sentiments towards you—perhaps you will one day at your time of leisure, honor her with few lines in answer, I know too well how in that Case she will be happy, to deprive her of the hope by not delivering the lettre—I have inclosed in it a translation & her direction—I hope, from the great filial tendreness your Excellency has Evidenced, that you will forgive the liberty I take here.

farewell my dear General—at your service & command, armand is forever—may God allmighty bless me with the opportunity to evidence the unlimited Extent of the respect I have in my breast for you & with which I have the honor to be your Excellency's the Most obedt hble st

Armand

ALS, DLC:GW.

1. The translation of the letter from the marquise de La Rouërie, dated 12 Jan. 1784, is printed below as an enclosure.

2. See Armand to GW, 16 May 1784, n.1.

Enclosure
From the Marquise de La Rouërie

Rouerie [France] 12th Jany 1784

Will the heroe of our age, the man of all ages, the object of the admiration of all Nations, & Particularly of france, the theme of true enthusiasme, will the Great Washington allow a french woman, a Native of Britanny, too aspiring perhaps, but Still more an admirer of that Commanding Character, to Join with a feeble Voice in the tribute of praise which Everyone pays to that Great Man. some Compare him to Cezar, others to trajan, to alexander to fabius, to turenne & to Catinat among the ancients, & they take the talents & Virtues of Modern Characters, in order to form out of them a great Whole, but how Could they form one to resemble thee, Washington, here their art fails, forgive this familiar Language, it is that in which we Address the Gods.

Washington, I have a son, he Leaves thee, he has served under thy Command, fought under thy Eyes, thou Knowest him, thou dost More, thou honourest him with they Esteem, impart those flattering sentiments to our Ministers, the opinions of such a man as thou art hath an assendency which Gives it the force of a Law, what a title thy approbation ensures? he who hath acquired it hath obtained a right to that of Every other person.[1]

May the Parce[2] spare the thread of thy Glorious Day's Which are so precious to posterity such is the ardent wish formed for the sake of Both, by the humblest of thy servants.

The Mother of Armand

Translation, in Armand's hand, DLC:GW; ALS, CSmH. The original letter, in French, is dated 30 Jan. 1784, not 12 January. A transcription of it is in CD-ROM:GW.

The marquise de La Rouërie was born Thérèse de La Belinaze of noble family in about 1727. Her husband, Anne-Joseph-Jacques Tuffin, comte de La Rouërie, died in 1754 when their son Charles Armand-Tuffin (1750–1793), known in America only as Armand, was only 3 or 4 years old. The young comte de La Rouërie came under the care of his mother's brother the comte de La Belinaze (born c.1735). Armand and the Belinaze family were early opponents of the French Revolution, and the marquise de La Rouërie took refuge in London with other members of the family, probably shortly before or shortly after her son Armand's death in 1793.

1. See GW to the marquise de La Rouërie, 28 May 1784.

2. The marquise wrote "parques," meaning fates.

To Clement Biddle

Dear Sir,   [Philadelphia] Tuesday Morning 18th May 1784.

Rather than wait, & thereby hazard delay, I would purchase Copper at the present price for all the purposes mentioned in your estimate, the Spouts, or Trunks excepted—the want of these, as they do not retard the Work may remain a while longer.[1]

Pray let me have your Acct before Nine oclock, as I hope to set off soon after that hour & wish to pay the Balle before I go. I am Yr Obedt & affe Servt

Go: Washington

P.S.—As you forgot to put up the Bill for the Nuts I do not know [the] sorts you have sent.

ALS, PHi: Washington-Biddle Correspondence.

1. Neither GW's inquiry about the cost of copper nor Biddle's estimate of its cost has been found.

To Ebenezer Hazard

Sir,   [Philadelphia] 18th May 1784.

I have, before I leave the City, to thank you for the obliging expressions of your letter of the 11th.

I perswade myself you will have the goodness to notify the Postmasters in the different States, that letters franked by me are to pass free. otherwise, being unacquainted with the resolve of Congress, my corrispondents may incur the expence of Postage contrary to my expectation, & the good intention of Congress—and without any impropriety either on the part of the distant Postmasters. I am Sir Yr most obedt Servt

Go: Washington

ALS (photocopy), ViMtV.

From David Humphreys

My dear General   Philadelphia May 18th 1784

A few hours after your departure, I received a private communication from a friend in Congress informing me of my appointment as Secretary to the Commissioners for forming Commercial Treaties in Europe[1]—Tho' pleased with the information I considered myself as unfortunate in not having recd the Letter while your Excellency remained in Town—because I wished to avail myself of Letters of introduction or recommendation to some of your acquaintances & Correspondents, particularly to Doctr Franklin, the Count D'Estaing & such other Characters in England or France as you might think proper— Perhaps a general Certificate of my services & character, which I have never before solicited because I did not wish to give unnecessary trouble, would be of infinite consequence on some future occasion; and I trust you are persuaded my dear Sir, that I should not make an indiscreet or improper use of it— Nor must you think it less than the most serious truth, that in my opinion, nothing which I can possibly carry from this Continent will be of equal importance to my reputation, as to have it known that I have been an Aide de Camp to, & the friend of Genl Washington.[2]

Perhaps it is not yet too late; for I cannot but hope, that any Papers you might be pleased to address to me, or to Mr Jefferson for me at Boston, would reach that place before our embarkation, which will not be until between the 10th & 20th of June next.

I should not have presumed to ask these favors but for the former proofs I have had of your goodness—of which I shall never be unmindful in whatever climate or circumstances I may happen to be placed.

Wishing Mrs Washington & your Connections every possible felicity, I beg leave to add, that tho' others might be more lavish in their professions, none can ever be more sincere in their feelings of veneration, friendship & respect for you than My dear General Your very affectionate & most humble Servant

D. Humphrys

P.S. If I could have but a single line to shew that you presented me with the golden eagle it would be infinitely pleasing & useful.

Whether I should hear from you or not, I shall not fail to address your Excellency from the other side of the water.

ALS, DLC:GW.

1. On 12 May 1784 Congress elected Humphreys "Secretary to the Commission for negotiating treaties of Commerce with foreign powers" (*JCC*, 27:375). The plan was that he would sail to France with Thomas Jefferson whom Congress had chosen on 7 May to join the other two negotiators, Benjamin Franklin and John Adams.

2. See GW to Humphreys, 2 June 1784. Humphreys did not sail until July, and not with Jefferson.

To Elizabeth Powel

[Philadelphia] Tuesday Morning [18 May 1784].
G: Washington presents his most respectful compliments to Mrs Powell—he will be particularly careful of the letter and Box for Mrs Fitzhugh[1]—& only laments that it is not in his power to call & ask Mrs Powell's other commands—the Meeting of the Society will be at nine, immediately after wch the Genl will leave the City.

He prays Mr Powell to accept his best respects.

AL, ViMtV.

Elizabeth Willing Powel was the wife of Samuel Powel (1739–1793), a prominent Philadelphian with whom GW had frequent dealings in the years to follow. Mrs. Powel, who was the sister of William Byrd III's widow, Mary Willing Byrd, became a great favorite of GW's.

1. Mrs. Fitzhugh may have been Ann Frisby Rousby Fitzhugh, second wife of Col. William Fitzhugh of Maryland, but she probably was Anne Randolph Fitzhugh, the wife of William Fitzhugh (1741–1809) of Chatham in Stafford County, Virginia. It also is possible that she was the wife or widow of one of several other Fitzhughs with whom GW had an acquaintance. Mrs. Powel's letter to Mrs. Fitzhugh is dated 3 Mar. 1784 (ViMtV).

From Maithe

Sir, Toulouse [France] 19th May 1784

What higher honor, than the Cincinnatus of America, can be bestowed on the man, who, after avenging the cause of liberty, and establishing the supremacy of his country, by a voluntary act, reduced himself to the condition of a private man?

The discourse I venture to present you with, is infinitely below the greatness of the subject: but, it is at least, a sincere testimony, of the general admiration; excited by a revolution in wc. your virtues and exploits have had such a share[1]—I am with respect, Sir Your Hble & Obt servt

Maithe

Translation, in the hand of David Stuart, DLC:GW; ALS, DLC:GW. A notation on the cover identifies Maithe as "Avocat of the parliament of Toulouse." For the French version, see CD-ROM:GW.

1. GW responded from Mount Vernon on 25 Nov. 1784: "Your letter of the 19th of May from Toulouse, & the discourse which accompanied it, do me infinite honor. I lament that I am not sufficiently acquainted with the French language to make myself Master of the beauties of the latter; & equally so, that my expression will not do justice to my feelings when I confess to you my gratitude for the flattering sentiments you are pleased to entertain of me, in the former. But with a proper sense of the honor done me, I am Sir &c." (LB, DLC:GW).

From Sidney Lee

Sr Newgate Street Chester [England] May 23d 1784

The Very obliging Notice you did me the honor of taking of a former application of mine, added to the high opinion entertained by my most intimate friends and myself, of your generosity, encourages me again to beg your assistance & advice.[1] Have heard but twice from Mr Alexander White of Woodville Frederick County, the only ⟨act⟩ing Executor, of my late Brother General Charles Lee, since my brother's death.[2] His first letter dated July 10th 1783. The second September 25th 1783. In that of July he gave a great domestic loss, and a difficulty he had that with the prevailing with the Witnesses to the Will, who lived out of the State to repair to Berkeley County to prove it; and also the necessity he had been under to set out for Richmond to attend his duty in the Assembly as reasons for

not having Written earlier, and that I really thought very Sufficient. And indeed, as far as I could form a judgment from his
manner of Writing, beleived him to be a Man of integrity &
Sense. In his letter of September 25th he promises to go to
Congress to Settle an Open account that had for some time subsisted between that honorable Assembly & my brother. And by
which, he was of opinion I might be a considerable sufferer,
owing to my brother's carelessness of Vouchers on his part. but
as he gave the strongest assurance of every proper exertion in
my favor, and also hopeing from the knowledge several Members of the Congress must have had of Genl Lee's character in
all matters of business, they would act With some Indulgence to
his Sister;[3] gave myself no uneasiness upon the Subject before
the entrance of the present Month; when I began to think it
hard to be kept so very long in an utter state of ignorance,
whether or not I might ever receive any part of the fortune I
cannot have a doubt was intended for me. And now Sr strongly
suspect Mr White is no longer in the World, or render'd incapable by illness of transacting business. And upon that account
take this very great liberty of imploring I may be honor'd with
your advice, that I shall be happy to follow implicitly. Am the
more persuaded of the death or extreme illness of Mr White,
by having enclosed to him, by the first paquet that sailed after
receiving his last letter, a power of Attorney to enable him to
sell the land I had been informed I had a right to claim as heir
at law (from the States) to a Major General in their service [in]
the late War.[4] Of Which I have had no notice, no more than of
the very great mistake that I pointed out to him, in both the
Authenticated copies of the Will in my possession, that was
proved April 15th 1783, yet sworn to having been executed in
the presence of James Smith and another Witness (his name I
cannot make out) September 10th 1783, though my brother departed this life September 1782.[5] A mistake that from past
transactions it is impossible not to apprehend, the Leviathans
Muse & Atkinson will not (to gain time) avail themselves of; if it
pleases the Almighty I shall live, untill my affairs have past
through every difficulty that has, or may in future wish to impede them, on your great Continent. A Country that my most
zealous Wishes Will attend, as long as I am capable of distinguishing Virtue from Vice. And hope & beleive I shall With no

small pleasure to the end of my days declare myself (in my little circle) Sr With the truest respect your much obliged, & very obedient humble Servant

Sidney Lee

ALS, DLC:GW.

1. For GW's correspondence with Sidney Lee in 1783 concerning the will of her brother, Gen. Charles Lee, see GW to William Drew, 13 Feb. 1784, nn.1 and 2. GW had most recently written Miss Lee on 15 April 1784.

2. Alexander White (1736–1804), who lived in Frederick County, Va., and had taken care of business and legal matters for Charles Lee before Lee's death in 1782, was one of the beneficiaries of Lee's will as well as one of the two executors of the will. White was a representative from Virginia in the First Congress in 1789 and a commissioner in 1795 for laying out the new capital city named Washington.

3. White did present a petition to Congress, on 22 Dec. 1784, for the settlement of Charles Lee's account with the United States (DNA:PCC, item 48), and Congress acted affirmatively on his position two days later (*JCC*, 27:708–9). General Lee died heavily indebted to the government of the United States, and the specific bequests in his will to individuals in the United States included not only all of his land, slaves, and other personal property in Virginia but also cash bequests. Sidney Lee as the residuary heir of her brother inherited valuable property in England, but to make possible the settlement of his account with the United States (see *JCC*, 27:708–9) and the carrying out of his bequests in America, Sidney Lee found it necessary to send White £4,500 from England. For White's role in settling the estate, see Sidney Lee to GW, 5 April 1785, and notes.

4. When White requested from the state of Virginia a land warrant based on Lee's military service, Attorney General Edmund Randolph ruled that Lee's dismissal from the Continental army forfeited his rights to such a grant of land.

5. Lee signed the will in Baltimore on 10 Sept. 1782 while en route to Philadelphia. He died there later in the month. The witnesses were James Smith, Samuel Swearingen, and William Goddard. Lee concluded his will with these two oft-quoted provisos: "I desire most earnestly that I may not be buried in any Church or Churchyard, or within a mile of any Presbyterian or Ana-Baptist Meeting house, for since I have resided in this Country, I have kept so much bad company when living, that I do not choose to continue it when dead.

"I recommend my soul to the creator of all worlds and of all creatures, who must from his visible attributes be indifferent to their modes of worship or creeds, whether Christians, Mohomedans, or Jews; whether instilled by education or taken up by reflection; whether more or less absurd, as a weak mortal can no more be answerable for his persuasions, notions, or even skepticism in Religion, than for the color of his skin" (*Virginia Magazine of History and Biography*, 11:108–10).

Account of Expenditures in Attending the General Meeting of the Society of the Cincinnati

May 24th 1784.
The Society of the Cincinnati Dr to Genl Washington for his Expences attending the General Meeting in Philadelphia May—1784.

		Pensa Cury
Apl 26th	To ferriage—crossing Potomk River	9. 6
	Dining &ca at Upper Marlborh	19. 9
	Lodging &ca at Rawlins's[1]	2. 0. 7
27	To Ferriage at South River	9. 4
28	To Expences in Annapolis	4.11. 3
	Ferriages to Rock-hall pr [Gilbert] Middleton[2]	5.10.
	Oats &ca for the passage	8.
	Servants at Annapolis	3. 9
29	To Expences at [Richard] Spencers Tavern	2. 3. 4
	Ditto at New Town Chester[3]	1. 7. 6
30	To Ditto at the cross roads	1.19. 6
	Ditto at Middle Town	12. 9
	Ditto at New castle	1.11. 9
May 1	To Ditto at Wilmington	2. 1. 7
	Ditto at Chester	1. 4. 6
	Servants at difft Stages	7. 6
	Ferriage at Schoolkill	1. 8
17	To Barber sundry times	1. 5.10
	Washing—during my stay in Phila.	2.15. 8
	Livery Stable—Mr [Jacob] Hiltzhimer	16. 6. 7
	Servants Board	9. 3. 2
	Mr [Robert] Morris's Servants & other Exps. there	5.15.
	Exps. at the City Tavern[4]	3.10.
18	To Ferriage over the Schoolkill	1. 8
	Exps. at Chester	1. 1. 3
	Ferriage over Christiana[5]	2. 2

19	To Exps. at Newcastle	1.10.10
	Ditto at Middle Town	12. 9
20	To Ditto at New Town Chester	2.18. 4
	Ditto at Rockhall	3. 8. 4
	Ferriages to Annapolis	5.13. 8
22	To Exps. in Annapolis—pr Mr Mann[6]	3.17. 4
	To Ferriage over South River	8. 4
	Expences at Rawlins's Tavern	17.
	Ferriage over Patuxent	5.
23	To Ditto—over Potomack	9. 6
		£86. 4. 8

Errors Excepted Pr Go: Washington

ADS, DLC:GW. Vouchers are enclosed.

1. A tavern owned by Ann Gassaway Rollins (Rawlins, Rawlings) and her son Gassaway Rollins was near the South River in Anne Arundel County, Maryland.

2. Rock Hall is on the Chesapeake Bay in Kent County on Maryland's Eastern Shore.

3. This is Chestertown, Maryland.

4. GW had his first meal in Philadelphia while attending the Continental Congress at City (or New) Tavern on the west side of Second Street, above Walnut.

5. The crossing was at Wilmington, Delaware.

6. George Mann (1753–1795) kept a well-regarded tavern in Annapolis, sometimes called the City Hotel.

From Henry Knox

My dear sir   Annapolis 24[–28] May 1784

I had the mortification to find that you set out from this place about ten oClock of the same day I arrived here.[1] Our horses were injured on the road, which obliged me to halt one day at Baltimore. I am uncertain how long I shall stay, but I hope to set out on my return on Wednesday—You Know the state of things here—It is to be apprehended that all the necessary business will not be Finished before Congress adjourn.

Colonel Smith a day or two before we left the City of Philadelphia requested that I would mention to you an idea which seemed to prevail respecting Your recommendation to Congress, of the Gentlemen of your family, that it only comprehended Humphreys, and Walker and excluded the others, and himself among them—I promised that I would hint the matter to you but had not an opportunity.[2]

I send a letter from Colonel Humphreys, who is much pleased and satisfied with his appointment.[3]

I request that you would present my respectful compliments to Mrs Washington, and beleive me to be my Dear sir with the most perfect respect and affection Your Excellencys Most obedient Servant

H. Knox

28 May

I have now been here, nearly one week, and nothing of importance has been decided upon, owing to the contrariety of sentiments concerning the powers vested in Congress to raise troops in time of peace for any purpose—There appears but one sentiment respecting the necossity of having troops for the frontiers, but the difficulty is how to obtain them—The southern States are generally of opinion that the Confederations vests Congress with sufficient powers for this purpose, but the eastern States are of a different opinion.

The eastern delegates are willing to *recommend* th[e] raising troops for the Western posts—but the gentlemen from the Southward say this would be giving up a right which is of importance to preserve, and they cannot consent *to recommend*, when they ought *to require*, so that from this cause it is to be feared that there will not be any troops raised—and there are many difficulties to sending those which are raised and at West point &c.—I shall Stay untill the point is finally decided, or untill Congress adjourn provided it be on the 3d of next month, as is agreed.[4] I am my dear sir with the most ardent desires for your happiness Your sincerely respectful and affectionate

H. Knox

ALS, DLC:GW; ADfS, MHi: Knox Papers.

1. GW left Annapolis on 22 May when returning to Mount Vernon from Philadelphia where he and Knox had attended the general meeting of the Cincinnati.

2. In responding to Knox on 2 June, GW makes clear that his particular recommendation to Congress regarding his aides-de-camp encompassed all of those who were serving with him at the end of the war. See especially note 3 of that document.

3. See David Humphreys' letter of 18 May 1784.

4. For the votes on David Howell's motion, and amendments to it: "That there be inlisted, as soon as possible, to serve for the term of three years, unless sooner discharged, four hundred and fifty men, to be employed for defence of the northwestern frontier of the United States; and that the different States furnish their quotas in the following proportions," see the journals of Congress for Tuesday, 25 May 1784 (*JCC*, 27:428–29).

From Jonathan Boucher

Sir   Paddington, near London 25th may, 1784.

I will not affront You with any Apologies for this Intrusion: for, greatly altered as I am to suppose You are, since I had the Honour of living in Habits of Intimacy with You, it is not possible, You can be so changed, as that You would not feel Yourself hurt, & with Reason, were any Man, who had ever known You, to think it necessary to apologise to You for doing what He is prompted to do, only by a Sense of Duty; & what, moreover, He believes it to be no less your Duty to attend to, than it is his to suggest.

It is no Part of my present Purpose to trouble You with any Reflections of mine on the many great Events that have taken Place within the last Eight or nine years. You & I, alas! have not been the only Persons who have differed in our opinions; or who have found it impossible to agree. This is no Time nor Place for settling such Points: ere long We shall all have to answer For them at a Tribunal, where alone it is of infinite Moment that We should be justify'd.

How far You will agree with Me in thinking it in your Power to do something for the Religious Interests of your Countrymen, I undertake not to say; but, I assure myself, We shall not differ by your thinking it of little, or no, Moment. It cannot, I think, afford You Pleasure to reflect, how much has been done, through your means, for the Civil Concerns of your Country; & how little, as yet at least, for those of an higher Nature. That your Countrymen will be either better or happier by what has happened, permit me to say, remains yet to be proved: I am sure, You wish They should; but it can be no Matter of Doubt or Dispute with any Man, that They can neither be so good nor so happy as They have been, if They are not so religious. Many of the Speculations which the late unsettled Times have given Birth to, resemble your Persimmons before the Frost: They are fair to the Eye & specious; but really disgusting & dangerous. This, in my Mind, is the Case, in a particular manner, with many or most of the Utopian Projects, respecting Universal Equality on the Subject of Religious Establishments. I am unwilling to go deeply into the Investigation of this Question, though I want not Materials in Abundance to shew You, that it is romantic & mischievous in the Extreme; because such a Discussion must needs be tiresome & tedious to You: suffice it, for the present, to remind You, that the Practice of the whole World is against You. Similar attempts, in similar Times, were made in these Kingdoms & if I were very anxious to set You against such Projects, I certainly could take no more effectual Means, than by desiring You to remember what the Consequences of them were. In short, Sir, I hardly know a Point more capable of Demonstration—from History & Experience—than this is, that, to secure permanent national Felicity, some permanent national Religion is absolutely necessary.

I would hope, in Virginia & Maryland at least, this would not be an unpopular Opinion, as it certainly ought not: & I think certainly would not, if espoused & patronized by a Person that is popular. It is in this Light I view You; & this is the Reason of my having taken the Liberty to submit these Suggestions to your Consideration.

There are, at this Time, in this Country Candidates for orders in the Church of England both from Virginia & Maryland: it will not surprize You, that, from the Changes that have taken Place, They should meet with Difficulties; nor does it surprize, though it greatly grieves Me, that the Ill-willers & Enemies of our Church, Brittish as well as American, avail themselves of these unfortunate Circumstances, to discountenance & discourage our Church, if possible, still more than it is. Some of these Difficulties I hope, will be soon got over; & They all would, if the People of your States could think it right to shew a Desire only, that They might. It might perhaps, as yet, be too much to ask for a Restoratn of the old Establishment of the Church of England, though it be a Measure which sound Policy will sooner or later adopt, & the longer it is delayed, the worse it will be: but, I hope it is not too much, nor too soon, to hope that, even now, the Members of that Church may be put on a Footing with Christians of other Denominations; which They never can be, till all the Ordinances of their Church are in their own Power, independent of any foreign States: & among these Ordinances, that of ordination &c. is most essential. In short, both Justice & Policy require that You should have a resident Bishop of your own, that your young men may be ordained, as well as educated among Yourselves.

I have no other Interest in this Measure, than what my Zeal for the Church & the best Interests of Mankind give me: but, believing as I do, that it is of great Moment, the Thing should be attended to, & soon, & that You are particularly concerned to attend to it, because no other Man can do it with such Advantage. I could not be easy, till I had thus satisfy'd my Conscience. Three Years ago, I wrote You a Letter to the same Purpose; but my Friends within the King's Lines, thinking that neither the Times nor Yourself were then in a Temper to bear such applications, suppressed it. I have now done my Duty, & leave the Rest to Providence: & will add this only, that if, by any means, either as I have studied the Subject more than most Men, or as I happen to have Connexions in this Country, as well as Yours, who are sincere & may be useful Friends to such Measures, I beg Leave to make You a Tender of my best Services on the Occasion.

It was, no Doubt, a great Mortification & Calamity to me to have all my American Property torn from Me; the Loss of my Character in that Country, which I little deserved, affected Me much more, as You will allow, it ought: but, I have lately felt the utmost Edge of keen Sorrow, when it pleased Providence to deprive me of a true Friend, a most loving & beloved Wife, for whom I was indebted to her Country.[1] I pray God long to preserve You & Yours from this the heaviest of all Misfortunes. With respectful Compts to Mrs Washingn I remain, Sir, Yr most obedt & very Hble Servt

Jonan Boucher

ALS, DLC:GW.

Before sailing for England in 1775, the Rev. Jonathan Boucher (1738–1804) wrote GW, on 6 Aug., to renounce their friendship and to castigate the American Patriots. Boucher was a frequent correspondent of GW from 1768 to 1773 when he was John Parke Custis's schoolmaster.

1. Boucher's wife, Eleanor Addison Boucher of Maryland, died in his arms in London on 1 Mar. 1784. There is no evidence that GW responded to this letter.

From Reuben Harvey

Respected Friend   Cork [Ireland] 25th May 1784

I cannot sufficiently express the deep Sense I entertain of thy condescending marks of friendship for me, evinced by such peculiar marks as are contain'd in thy much esteemed letters, & in the Resolution of Congress which thou wert so kind as to obtain & forward to me; entirely unexpected & above any little Services that I had, in conjunction with a few other Friends to America, render'd to those poor People who experienc'd the effects of illiberal & unjust Persecution.[1] Our Nation is far from being a happy one, being under the power of a Parliament entirely sway'd by English Councils, which prevents salutary Laws from being pass'd that would materially advantage the Commerce of Ireland & America, particularly respecting Tobacco, Wheat, & Flour, Corn was never more wanted here than at this time, & Wheat can now be imported from any place, the price being much above 30/ ℔ barrel of 280 pounds, which is the standard price for it's admission from America & other Countrys, tho' it may be imported from Britain when the price is only 27/ the barrel; Thus doth our unwise Parlt make such a difference in this Article 'twixt American & English Wheat to the manifest injury of our numerous poor Inhabitants, who are emigrating from every Corner of the Island to your Land of Liberty having no employment & but little Food, even of the meanest Sort; Flour from America is rated at so high a Duty that it amounts to a prohibition, tho' from England it pays but 12d. ℔Ct. Tobacco pays 11d. ℔Ct duty, which is too high for importing any poor ordinary Tobaccos, however the Virginia very well affords this Tax, being worth 20d. to 22d. ℔ pound; It may seem improper for me to enlarge so much on Trade to thee but I flatter myself that a little information in that line won't displease, & it will probably serve for the knowledge of some Friends in thy part of the Country who are Planters & Farmers; Should any of such Gentlemen think of trying Cork with some James River or other Tobacco of good quality, & address it to me I shall use every endeavour to give them satisfaction And will chearfully honour their Bills for nearly the Amount of Tobacco, Wheat & other Articles when they ship them, And also will remit the proceeds of their Goods according to Orders &

with dispatch.[2] Please to excuse this liberty, & believe me to be with the most grateful feelings Thy sincere Friend

Reuben Harvey

ALS, DLC:GW.

Reuben Harvey was a Quaker merchant in Cork. He, along with several other men of the place, strenuously protested the mistreatment of the Americans, mostly seamen, who were held for several years during the Revolutionary War in the French prison at nearby Kinsale. He also extended aid to them.

1. Harvey first wrote GW on 12 Feb. 1783 when he enclosed copies of a number of letters "all relating to the poor Americans who were confined at Kinsale." In acknowledging Harvey's letter on 23 June 1783, GW expressed his appreciation for Harvey's aid to the American prisoners and informed Harvey that he had sent Harvey's letter with its enclosures to Congress. On 10 Aug. 1783 GW wrote again, to transmit the following resolution of Congress, dated 18 July 1783: "That his Excellency the Commander in Chief, be requested to transmit the thanks of Congress to Mr Reuben Harvey, merchant in Cork, in the kingdom of Ireland, and express the just sense Congress entertain of the services he has rendered during the late war, to American prisoners" (*JCC*, 24:440). Congress substituted "just sense" for "high sense" and deleted the rest of the original resolution: "by supplying them with clothing money and other necessaries, by promoting an inquiry into the treatment of those confined at Kingsale and in affording them every relief in his power. And to assure Mr Harvey that his exemplary conduct and liberality of sentiment has given him a distinguishing claim to the gratitude of his country" (ibid.).

2. Harvey also wrote GW a note from Cork, dated 24 May: "Reuben Harvey's respectful Compts wait on George Washington Esqr., Hopes he'l not be displeased at the liberty he has taken in sending for Family Use, a barrel of Cork Mess Beef, such as is cured for the West India Planters, & a ferkin of Ox tongues with Roots.

"They are on board the Ship Washington Enoch Stickney M[aste]r for Alexandria" (DLC:GW). Captain Stickney and his ship arrived in Alexandria on 29 July "with Redemptioners and Servants" (*Virginia Journal and Alexandria Advertiser*, 5 Aug. 1784).

On 25 Aug. GW acknowledged receipt by the captain of the mess beef and the firkin of ox tongues and of Harvey's letter of 25 May.

From Edmund Randolph

Dear Sir   Richmond [Va.] May 28. 1784.

Inclosed is the rough draught of a deed, prepared to be executed by Colo. Bassett. I send it to you for your satisfaction, with an assurance that I shall not fail to accomplish the business at the next general court.[1] I am Dear Sir with the greatest truth yr obliged and affte friend

Edm: Randolph.

ALS, ViMtV.

1. See Randolph to GW, 15 May 1784, and the references in note 2 of that document. See also Randolph to GW, 27 June and 3 July 1784.

To the Marquise de La Rouërie

Madam,   Mount Vernon 28th May 1784

The Letter which you did me the honor to write from Rouërie on the 12th of Jany came to my hands in the course of this month.[1] Language, or my ability, is too poor to express the sense of obligation I am laid under for the flattering sentiments contained therein—let your goodness then Madam, rather than a vain attempt of mine, speak my gratitude.

It is on the merits of your Son, not to any recommendation of mine, the Marqs de la Rouerie, must put in his claim to the smiles of his Prince, & the attention of his Ministers. For me it only belongs to do justice to his services by the most ample certificates of them, which he has obtained from me—and they are accompanied with my warmest wishes for his success. *He*, more effectually than *I*, can assure you of the great esteem, regard & veneration, with which I have the honor to be Madam &c. &c.[2]

G. Washington

LB, DLC:GW.

1. The marquise's letter is printed above as an enclosure in Armand to GW, 18 May 1784.

2. GW enclosed the original of this letter to the marquise in a note of this date to her son Armand: "If this Letter shou'd find you at Philada—or within the United States—or where, or whensoever it may reach you—it is to beseech your care of the enclosed. My best wishes always shall attend you, & nothing would give me more pleasure than to hear you had attained the summit of your desires, in whatever walk of life you may bend your course" (LB, DLC:GW).

To John Lloyd and Hugh Rutledge

Gentn   Mount Vernon (Virga) 28th May 84

It was not until the 24th Instt (after my return from Philadelphia) that I had the honor to receive your Joint favor of the 10th of Feby.

If the happiness I feel from the restoration of Peace, after a long and arduous struggle for the rights & liberties of our Country, sweetened by the enjoymt of domestic life, could be much encreased by any additional circumstance, it certainly would be so by the polite & flattering terms in which you, Gentn, have been pleased to mention my past endeavours, to effect the former.

I pray you, Gentlemen, to present the enclosed to the Honble the Senate & representatives of the Ho. of Assembly of the State of So. Carolina,[1] and to be assured, that with the greatest respect & consideration I have the honor to be Gentn

ADf, DLC:GW; LB, DLC:GW.

1. The text of a draft of GW's response of this date to the South Carolina legislature's address of 10 Feb. 1784 is: "It was with pleasure which is more easy to conceive than express I received your congratulations on the restoration of Peace, & the happy establishment of the freedom, and Independence of the United States of America.

"To meet the plaudits of my Countrymen for the part I have acted in the revolution, more than compensates for the toils I have undergone in the course of an arduous contest; and to have them expressed in such indulgent, and flattering terms as are contained in your Communication of the 10th of Feby, is not more honorable than it is pleasing to me.

"Permit me, Gentlemen, on this occasion of general joy, to congratulate you & your State in a particular manner upon its present repose, & recovery from these scenes of accumulated distresses for which it has been remarkable—and whilst we have abundt cause to rejoice at the fair prospect which a beneficent Provid[enc]e has l[ai]d before us to assure you of my entire beleif that the wisdom & liberallity of the People of So. Carolina will leave nothing unassayed to make the revolution as benefycial to mankind as it hath been glorious in the Accomplishmt.

"For the favorable wishes you have kindly bestowed on me you have all my gratitude; & my prayers for the welfare of your State, shall never cease" (ADf, DLC:GW).

To Tench Tilghman

Dear Sir,   Mount Vernon 28th May—84

As I am not yet supplied with such Tradesmen as I formerly wrote to you to purchase for me,[1] & the Baltimore paper swarms with advertisements of them, I should be obliged to you, if upon enquiry there is to be found a good joiner and

Bricklayer, or either of them, who are tolerable in appearance & character, that you would be so good as to purchase & send him or them to me at this place, with the cost, which shall be paid to your order.

It sometimes happens that very excellent Workmen—from folly & indiscretion, very often from an adiction to drink—indent themselves; if any such, skilled in Stucco work or Plaister of Paris should be found among those at Baltimore, or among the redemtioners, I should be glad to be the purchaser—but he must be a master workman to answer my purpose. If a good Bricklayer can not to be had, & a Stone Mason is to be bought who understands cutting & facing Stone for smooth Walls, or pavements perfectly I would take the latter. I am with great esteem & regard—Dr Sir—Yr most obt & affecte Servt

Go: Washington

ALS, RPJCB.
   1. See GW to Tilghman, 29 Mar. 1784.

From Thomas Mifflin

Sir,   Annapolis May 31st 1784
   Doctor Gordon having applied to Congress for access to their records and for their Countenance to his Admission to your Papers they have passed the enclosed Resolutions which I transmit to you at the request of the Doctor.[1]

On Friday I expect to have the Pleasure of seing Mount Vernon in Company with Mrs Mifflin and Mr Lloyds family—But there is a possibility that we shall not proceed farther than Alexandria on that day as the setting of Congress on thursday may be so late as to prevent my leaving Annapolis before friday Morning. at every event I have determined not to see Philadelphia before I have the Satisfaction of paying a Visit at Mount Vernon. I am with the greatest sincerity and Attachment Dear Sir Your Obedient humble Servant

Thomas Mifflin

LS, DLC:GW.
   1. See the source note in William Gordon to GW, 8 Mar. 1784.

Letter not found: from Samuel Vaughan, 1 June 1784. On 20 June GW wrote to Vaughan: "I have had the honor of your favor of the 1st instant."

To Chastellux

My Dr Sir,   Mount Vernon 2d June 1784.

I had the honor to receive a short letter from you by Majr L'Enfant[1]—My official letters to the Counts D'Estaing & Rochambeau (which I expect will be submitted to the members of the Society of the Cincinnati in France) will inform you of the proceedings of the Genl Meeting held at Philada on the 3d inst:; & of the reasons which induced a departure from some of the original principles and rules of the Society.[2] As these have been detailed, I will not repeat them, & as we have no occurrences out of the common course, except the establishment of ten New States in the Western Territory[3]—& the appointment of Mr Jefferson (whose talents & worth are well known to you) as one of the Commissioners for forming commercial Treaties in Europe; I will only repeat to you the assurances of my friendship, & of the pleasure I shou'd feel in seeing you in the shade of those trees which my hands have planted—& which by their rapid growth, at once indicate a knowledge of my declination, & their disposition to spread their mantles over me, before I go hence to return no more—for this, their gratitude, I will nurture them while I stay.

Before I conclude, permit me to recommend Colo. Humphreys, who is appointed Secretary to the Commission— to your countenance & civilities while he remains in France. he possesses an excellent heart, & a good understanding. With every sentiment of esteem & regard, I am My Dr Chevr Your Most affecte

G: Washington

LB, DLC:GW; copy, ScC: Washington Letters.

1. See Chastellux to GW, 6 Mar., and L'Enfant to GW, 29 April 1784.

2. See GW to d'Estaing, 15 May (second letter), and GW to Rochambeau, 17 May 1784.

3. GW is referring to Congress's passage of its territorial government ordinance on 23 April 1784.

To Benjamin Franklin

Dear Sir,   Mount Vernon 2d June 1784.

Congress having been pleased to appoint Colo. Humphrys Secretary to the Commissioners, for forming Commercial

Treaties in Europe, I take the liberty of introducing him to you.[1]

This Gentleman was several years in my family as an Aid de Camp. His zeal in the cause of his Country, his good sense, prudence, and attachment to me, rendered him dear to me; and I persuade myself you will find no confidence wch you may think proper to repose in him, misplaced. He possesses an excellent heart, good natural & acquired abilities, and sterling integrity—to which may be added sobriety, & an obliging disposition.

A full conviction of his possessing all these good qualities, makes me less scrupulous of recommending him to your patronage and friendship. He will repeat to you the assurances of perfect esteem, regard, & consideration, with which I have the honor to be Dear Sir, Yr Most Obedt & very Hble Servt

Go: Washington

ALS, PPAmP: Franklin Papers; LB, DLC:GW; copy, Bibliotheque Municipale, Nantes.

Benjamin Franklin remained in France for nearly two years after signing the Treaty of Paris on 3 Sept. 1783, not arriving back in Philadelphia until 14 Sept. 1785.

1. See GW to David Humphreys, this date, and notes.

From James Henry

Sir,   King and Queen [County, Va.], June 2d 1784.

I am under the necessity of giving you some trouble about an affair, which you could have no reason to suppose ever to hear of again. 'tis this.

When you executed a Deed to the late Mr J.P. Custis for the King and Queen Lands, where I now live, notwithstanding the Number of Gentlemen who were called upon to attest that Transaction, yet not more than one of them could be procured to prove the deed, 'till the limited time was past. in the meantime Mr Custis sold this Land to me and gave me a Deed with warranty, acknowledged and recorded in the Genl Court.

Thus it has happened, and the legal title to this Estate yet continues in you; and I was determined never to trouble you about it, while engaged in the important Business from which you are now so gloriously set free.

Mr B. Dandrige has been so kind as to take charge of the papers herewith sent, which will show you how the whole has been conducted, and will take care of the Deed of Confirmation which you may think proper to give me—I have indeed sent a blank deed for your conveniency, which I suppose may be unexceptionable: if however any other form would please you better, I'm contented, as nothing more is desired than a title to the Land, which has been paid for according to bargain, and which both Mr Custis and my self expected was sure to me when he acknowledged his Deed to me in the year 1779.[1] Had it been your hard fate to have been called away during the Contest, my determination was to risque my Chance with your Heir, rather than call off your attention but for a moment to such kind of unimportant Business; and tho your well earned Laurels will bloom long, very long, yet as life, however glorious, is short, in this I but imitate your example, in not putting off till to morrow what ought to be done to day.

I cannot, my Dear Sir, perswade my self to close this letter without adding my plaudit to the universal Voice. Were you at the head of a victorious Army, men of my turn would be silent; but to retire without Reward, perquisite or plunder has stamp'd a Seal of immortality on Genl Washington's Character; and to withold the small tribute of applause from living merit when there is not a possibility of changing our Sentiments, would be niggardly indeed. for posterity will surely do ample Justice.

May you live long, very long to enjoy that honest fame, which Virtue and honour may with the greatest propriety exult in without feeling a pang of remorse in secret. But whither am I running? You have had enough of this Stuff, but I will confidently affirm, the most fervent Wishes for your Glory and felicity, have not been made by any one living with greater sincerity than by Dr Sir, Your most obedt servt

Jas Henry

ALS, DLC:GW.

James Henry (1731–1804) returned to practice law in Accomac, Va., after receiving his education in Edinburgh, Scotland. He served in both the House of Burgesses and the house of delegates from Accomac County on Virginia's Eastern Shore. He was serving as a delegate from King and Queen County in 1782 when he was made a judge of the Virginia admiralty court. He was elected to Congress first in December 1779 and again in June 1780. In 1788 he became a judge of the Virginia General Court.

1. In 1774 GW bought from William Black two plantations for his ward, John Parke Custis. The one called Romancoke was a tract of 1,625 acres on Pamunkey Creek in King William County, Virginia. The other one nearby consisting of 1,981 acres in King and Queen County was the site of the house, Pleasant Hill, where Speaker John Robinson had lived until his death in 1766. For GW's purchase of the two estates for Custis, see GW to Robert Cary & Co., 10 Nov. 1773. GW conveyed both pieces of property to Custis in 1778, as he recalled in 1789: "I am much mistaken if I did not in the year 1778 convey both the King William and the King & Queen Lands to Mr Custis by Deeds executed at Camp before Colos. Harrison, Mead & many others as Witnesses to prove it in the General Court; and this in the presence of Mr Custis" (GW to David Stuart, 26 July 1789). GW bought Pleasant Hill with the notion that it would serve as a proper residence for John Parke Custis and his bride, but even before GW formally transferred the deed to him in 1778, Custis had put the estate up for sale. In October 1777 John Parke Custis placed this advertisement in the two Virginia gazettes: "*To be* SOLD *for ready Money*, THAT beautiful seat on *Mattapony* river, where the late Speaker *Robinson* lived. There are 1381 acres of high land and 600 acres of marsh, equal to any in the country, and may be reclaimed at a very moderate expense. Besides the marsh, there are twenty acres of swamp, which may easily be converted into a valuable meadow. On the above tract there is a mill, which is rather out of repair at present, but may be made, without much expense, as valuable as mills generally are. The plantation is under good fences, and in proper order for cropping, with a young orchard of choice fruit. The dwelling-house is of brick, as convenient and well built as any in the state, two stories high, with four large rooms and a passage on each floor, and good cellars under the whole, with a very convenient brick kitchen, servants hall, and wash-house. The stables, coach-house, granary, &c. are large, and in good repair, and there is a garden walled in with brick. No situation can exceed this in beauty, and few in convenience. Any person inclinable to purchase may be shewn the land and houses by applying to Mr. *Street*, who lives on the spot; and the terms of sale may be known by applying to *Burwell Bassett*, Esq; in *New Kent*, Mr *James Hill* near *Williamsburg*, or to the subscriber at *Mount Vernon*, near *Alexandria*" (*Virginia Gazette* [Purdie; Williamsburg], 17 Oct. 1777). James Henry bought the place and obtained a deed for 1,381 acres from John Parke Custis and his wife Eleanor Calvert Custis in 1779 (Vi, no. 24715, Va. Misc.). GW did not respond to Henry's letter for over six years, not until 20 Nov. 1790 when he confirmed that Custis held title to the property at the time Henry bought it. In 1778 GW also sold his dower property in York and King William counties and in Williamsburg to John Parke Custis (deed of release, ViMtV [photocopy], and bond to GW, ViHi, both 12 Oct. 1778).

To David Humphreys

My Dr Humphreys.   Mou[n]t Vernon 2d June 1784
    I very sincerely congratulate you on your late appointment—
It is honorable, & I dare say must be agreeable. I did not hear

of it until I arrived at Annapolis, where I remained but one day, & that occasioned by the detention of my Carrige & horses on the Eastern shore. Genl Knox not reaching that place before I left it—your letter of the 18th, only got to my hands on Sunday last, by the Post.[1]

I now send you, under flying Seals, letters to Mr Jefferson, Doctr Franklin & Count de Estaing—the letter to the Chevr Chastellux also mentions you & your appointment. My former corrispondence with England ceased at the commencment of hostilities, & I have opened no new ones since—but I enclose you a letter to Sir Edwd Newenham of Ireland, from whom I have lately received several very polite letters, & a pressing invitation to correspond with him. he has been a warm friend to America during her whole struggle—he is a man of fortune— of excellent (as I am told) character; and may, if you should go to Ireland, be a valuable acquaintance.[2]

It only remains for me now to wish you a pleasant passage, & that you may realize all the pleasures which you must have in expectation. It cannot be necessary to add how happy I shall be at all times to hear from you—You will have it in your power to contribute much to my amusement and information—& as far as you can do the latter consistently with your duty & public trust, I shall be obliged—further I do not require—and even here,[3] mark *private* what you think not altogether fit for the public ear, and it shall remain with me. Mrs Washington adds her best wishes for you, & you may rest assured that few friendships are warmer, or professions more sincere than mine for you. Adieu &c. &c.

G: Washington

P.S. Just recollecting my old neighbour Colonel (who may now be Lord) Fairfax—I give you a letter to him also, in case you shou'd go to England.[4]

LB, DLC:GW; ALS, sold by Thomas F. Madigan, item 94, 1921. The printed copy in the catalog was made from the ALS. It contains a few words, a phrase, and a clause not in the letter-book copy; a number of the abbreviations and contractions of the letter-book copy are spelled out in the printed copy as GW usually did. In two cases, which are noted, a difference in wording affects the meaning of the text. The "Certificate" appended to the letter-book copy, and printed here, does not appear in the catalog copy.

1. See Henry Knox to GW, 24–28 May 1784. The printed copy has this additional clause at the end of the paragraph, "and I am now writing by its return."

2. GW's letters to Thomas Jefferson, Benjamin Franklin, and Chastellux, all dated 2 June, are printed above and below. In his letter to d'Estaing of 2 June, he writes of Humphreys: "The zeal & intelligence of this Gentleman in the service of his Country; his good sense, prudence & attachment to me, has rendered him dear to me, & must be my best apology for the liberty I take in recommending him to your countenance & civilities, whilst he may remain in France" (LB, DLC:GW). To Edward Newenham he writes, also on 2 June: "This Gentleman is a particular friend of mine, and until I resigned my Military appointments, was one of my Aid de Camps. He has been uniformly a friend to the rights of mankind. He possesses in an eminent degree the social virtues. and is a man of integrity and worth. as such I take the liberty of recommending him to your Civilities if chance, or a visit to Ireland, should throw him in your way" (ALS, owned [1973] by Dr. Gilbert C. Norton, Endicott, N.Y.; LB, DLC:GW). And finally on 2 June he wrote about Humphreys to George William Fairfax: "He is a man possessing all the social virtues, & is of very great worth. As such, shou'd he ever come within your walks in England, (for he is lately appointed Secretary to the Commissioners for forming Commercial Treaties in Europe), I beg leave to recommend him to your favorable notice & civilities" (LB, DLC:GW). Humphreys was supposed to join Jefferson in Boston for their passage to France, but they ended up going separately (see Jefferson to Humphreys, 21 June 1784, in Boyd, *Jefferson Papers*, 7:311–12).

3. The printed version has "never have" instead of "even here."

4. See note 2. Immediately following in the letter book is a "Copy of a Certificate given to Colo. Humphrys," dated 2 June. It reads: "I do hereby certify, that Colo. Humphrys was among the first who embarked in the service of his Country, & that he continued therein to the end of the war—That from the early part of the year 1780 to the time of my resignation he was in my Family, and acted as one of my aid de camps with the rank of Lieut: Colonel. That during the whole course of his service he was actuated by an ardent zeal to promote the public weal—That his bravery, & spirit for enterprize were conspicuous on all occasions, and his intelligence, & attention to the duties of his office were of singular use to me—obtaining, as they justly merited, my highest regard & confidence."

To Thomas Jefferson

Dear Sir,   Mount Vernon 2d June 1784.

It was not until I had arrived at Annapolis, on my way home, that I heard of Colo. Humphrys's appointment as Secretary to the Commissioners for forming Commercial Treaties in Europe.

Permit me now Sir, to recommend him to your countenance and friendship,[1] which I would not do, did I not think him deserving of both. In him you will find a good Scholar, natural &

acquired abilities, great integrity, and more than a common share of prudence. I am certain he will abuse no confidence which may be reposed in him—that he will attempt to discharge the duties of his Office faithfully—and will make grateful returns for your Civilities.

I sincerely wish you a pleasant voyage, the perfect accomplishment of your mission—and in due time, that you may be restored to your friends in this Country; being with great attachment Dr Sir, Yr Most Obedt and Affecte Hble Servt

G: Washington

ALS, DLC: Jefferson Papers; LB, DLC:GW; copy, in David Humphreys' hand, Bibliotheque Municipale, Nantes.

1. See GW to David Humphreys, 2 June 1784, n.2.

To Henry Knox

My Dear Sir,   Mount Vernon 2d June 1784.

The inconvenience with which I left home, & my impatience to return to it, hastened every step I took back, & but for the delay I met with in crossing the Bay, I might have been at home with ease on the Friday after I parted with you. Before eight on thursday morning I was at Rock-hall, & not until friday evening could I get my horses & carriage over to Annapolis.[1]

It is a real misfortune, that in great national concerns, the Sovereign has not sufficient power to act—or that there should be a contrariety of sentiment among themselves respecting this power. While these matters are in litigation, the public interest is suspended—& important advantages are lost. This will be the case respecting the Western Posts.[2]

My address to Congress, respecting the Gentlemen who had composed my Family, went to two points, neither of which in my judgment could be misconceived; the first, was declaratory of the peculiar services & particular merits of those confidential Officers, who, during the war, had been attached to my person. The second, recommendatory of those who remained in that situation to the hour of my resignation. The latter was not confined to Humphreys & Walker who happened to be with me, but comprehended Cobb, Trumbull, & others who might come under *that* description, whose appointments terminated with my own existence as an officer.[3]

It would at this time, as it will at all others, give me singular pleasure to see you at this place; & I am sorry your anxiety to return would not permit you to extend your excursion from Annapolis.

Permit me to recommend the enclosed for Genl Putnam, to your care.[4] Mrs Washington joins in best wishes for you, Mrs Knox & family, with Dr Sir Yrs &c. &c.

G: Washington

LB, DLC:GW.

1. For GW's movements from the time he left Philadelphia on 18 May until his arrival back at Mount Vernon on Saturday or Sunday, 22 or 23 May, see Account of Expenditures in Attending the General Meeting of the Society of the Cincinnati, 24 May 1784, printed above. See also Knox to GW, 24–28 May.

2. See Knox to GW, 24–28 May, n.4.

3. See Knox to GW, 24–28 May. In his address to Congress upon resigning his commission at Annapolis, 23 Dec. 1783, GW declared: "While I repeat my obligations to the Army in general, I should do injustice to my own feelings not to acknowledge in this place the peculiar Services and distinguished merits of the Gentlemen who have been attached to my person during the war. . . . Permit me Sir, to recommend in particular those, who have continued in Service to the present moment, as worthy of the favorable notice & patronage of Congress" (DLC:GW).

4. See GW to Rufus Putnam, this date.

To Robert Morris

Dear Sir,   Mount Vernon 2d June 1784.

A brother of mine (Father to Mr Bushrod Washington, who studied Law under Mr Wilson) is desireous of entering his other Son in the commercial line; the inclination of the young Gentleman also points to this walk of life—he is turned of twenty—has just finished a regular education—possesses, I am told (for he is a stranger to me) good natural abilities—an amiable disposition, & an uncommon share of prudence & circumspection.[1]

Would it suit you My dear sir, to take him into your counting-house, & to afford him your patronage? If this is not convenient, who would you recommend for this purpose? What advance, & what other requisites are necessary to initiate him?[2] Excuse this trouble—to comply with the wishes of a parent, anxious for the welfare of his children, I give it, & my friendship prompted it; but I wish you to be perfectly unembarrassed by the application, on either accot.

If Genl Armand should have left Philada you will oblige me by placing the enclos'd in the readiest channel of conveyance.[3] My affectionate regards, in which Mrs Washington joins me, attend Mrs Morris, yourself & Family. With every sentiment of friendship & pure esteem, I remain Dr Sir &c.

G: Washington

P.S. The house I filled with ice does not answer—it is gone already—if you will do me the favor to cause a description of yours to be taken—the size—manner of building, & mode of management, & forwarded to me—I shall be much obliged— My house was filled chiefly with Snow. have you ever tried Snow? do you think it is owing to this that I am lurched.[4]

LB, DLC:GW.

1. John Augustine Washington was visiting Mount Vernon at this time. See his letter to GW, 4 April 1784, and GW's letter to him, 30 June 1784.

2. See Morris to GW, 15 June 1784, and enclosure.

3. The enclosure was GW's letters to Armand and his mother of 28 May 1784, which see.

4. See Morris's instructions for building an icehouse, in his letter of 15 June. In January 1785 GW records getting ice from the river to fill the "Well in my New Cellar" (*Diaries*, 4:74). "Lurched" is used in its sense of "discomfited" or "defeated."

To Rufus Putnam

Dear Sir,   Mount Vernon 2d June 1784

I could not answer your favor of the 5th of April from Philadelpa because Genl Knox having mislaid, only presented the letter to me in the moment of my departure from that place.[1] The sentiments of esteem & friendship which breathe in it are exceedingly pleasing & flattering to me—and you may rest assured they are reciprocal.

I wish it was in my power to give you a more favorable acct of the Officers petition for Lands on the Ohio, & its Waters than I am about to do—after this matter, & information respecting the establishment for Peace, were my enquiries as I went through Annapolis solely directed but I could not learn that any thing decisive had been done in either—On the latter I hear Congress are differing about their powers[2] but as they have accepted of the Cession from Virginia & have resolved to lay off 10 new States bounded by latitudes & longitudes it should be supposed that they would determine something respecting the former before they adjourn; and yet, I very much question it as the latter is to happen on the third—that is to morrow.[3]

As the Congress who are to meet in November next by the adjournment will be composed from an entire new choice of Delegates in each State it is not in my power at *this time* to direct you to a proper corrispondent in that body—I wish I could— for perswaded I am that to some such cause as you have assigned may be ascribed the delay the petition has encountered for *surely* if *Justice & gratitude* to the Army—& *genl policy* of the Union were to govern in this case there would not be the smallest interruption in granting its request—I really feel for those Gentlemen who by these unaccountable delays (by any other means than those you have suggested)[4] are held in such an aukward & disagreeable State of suspence; and wish my endeavors could remove the obstacles—at Princeton (before Congress left that place) I exerted every power I was master of, & dwelt upon the arguments you have used to shew the propriety of a speedy decision—every member with whom I conversed acquiesced in the reasonableness of the petition—all yielded, or seemed to yield to the policy of it, but plead the want of cession of the Land to act upon—this is made and accepted & yet matters (as far as they have come to my knowledge) remain in Statu quo.[5]

I am endeavouring to do something with the lands I now hold, & have held in that Country these 12 or 14 years—The enclosed contain the terms upon which I propose to Lease them[6]—I am not sanguine in my expectation that I shall obtain Tenants upon them in this Country; & yet, on Leases renewable for ever, or for the term of 999 years I will not (considering the advantages of these Lands, in quality & situation) take less—for a *short* term I care little about the Rents because knowing the value and convenience of the Land, I am certain that the improvements which are conditioned to be made thereon, will enable me thereafter to command my own terms—if you think the promulgation of the Paper enclosed can be of Service to others or myself it is optional with you to do it. I am—Dr Sir With very sincere esteem & regd Yr most obedt Servt

Go: Washington

ALS, OMC; LB, DLC:GW.

1. GW left Philadelphia on 18 May.

2. See the postscript in Henry Knox to GW, 24–28 May 1784.

3. Instead of "—that is tomorrow," the letter-book copy has "of next month," suggesting that the letter was drafted before 1 June.

4. The letter-book copy clarifies this sentence by having the parenthetical phrase follow "unaccountable."

5. See Putnam to GW, 5 April, and notes.

6. See GW to Thomas Richardson, 5 July, n.3.

From Hannah Crawford

Sr   Stuart Crossings [Pa.] June 4th 1784

After my Compliments to you I am now to Inform you that uppon Examining the accts of my Husbands do find that there is the Sum of one thousand one hundred Pounds Virginia Currency Coming from the State of Virginia to the Estate and as I am very much Harrased by the Credditors for debts due by the Estate—do now Sr beg and Entreat of you to Befreind me in Getting of that money although I must Confess it is too much of An obligation to Law uppon you But from my Husbands Connections with you in former times and your Considering the great disadvantages I am lying under will I hope make some attonement for offering to trouble you on any Such occasion and Indeed I did not know 'unto whome I Should apply to for a redress of Grievances[1] I Saw a Letter which you Sent to Brother John Stiphinson Conserning their accts between you and them as also conserning some transactions of Land which you are Conserned in we have not as yet got the Books all gathered together nor yet the papers but as Soon as we Can Get them you Shall have a Coppy of them[2]—I am dr Sr with Respect your Most obedt Humble Servant

                                              Hannah Crawford

ALS, DLC:GW.

Hannah Crawford was the widow of GW's old comrade in arms and business associate, William Crawford (b. 1732), who was killed by the Wyandot and Delaware Indians on the Sandusky River in 1782.

1. Mrs. Crawford's financial situation was acute by 1786. Both GW and the Virginia legislature came to her aid at that time. See GW to Thomas Freeman, 8 May 1786, and Hannah Crawford to GW, 16 Mar. 1787.

2. See GW to John Stephenson, 13 Feb. 1784, and notes.

From Henry Knox

My dear sir   Annapolis [Md.] 4 June 1784

I just write a line to inform you that I am just setting out for Boston—The president who has just gone for Mount Vernon, will inform you of the State of public matters—Things are not well and will probably be worse before they are better.[1]

I beg you to have the goodness to present my respectful compliments to Mrs Washington and beleive me my dear sir to be your truly affectionate

H. Knox

ALS, DLC:GW.

1. Thomas Mifflin visited Mount Vernon and was back in Annapolis by 11 June. See Samuel Hardy to Charles Thomson, 11 June 1784, in Burnett, *Letters*, 7:548.

From James Milligan

Sir   Philada June 4th 1784

I have the honor of enclosing a letter from Major Gambs of the Regiment of Bourbonnois, Addressed to your Excellency; together with duplicate of the same, and also copy of a letter from him to Daniel Roberdeau Esquire[1]—They came to my hand a few days ago, under covers to Mr Roberdeau, in whose absence, as his Attorney, I opened them, and as such, I take the liberty of troubling your Excellency on this occasion.

As the Ship in which Mr Roberdeau embarked at London, sailed from the Downs the 1st of March, and has not since been heard of; there is too much room to doubt of his safe arrival; and as the Major seems to have some relyance on Mr Roberdeau's good Offices in his behalf, I have conceived it proper to transmit the copy of his letter to my absent freind on the subject for your Excellencys fuller information. I have the honor of being with the greatest Respect and Sincerity—Sir Your Excellencys most Obedient and very humble Servant

Jas Milligan

ALS, DLC:GW.

1. See Gambs to GW, 24 Feb. 1784, and notes.

From I. Sailly

Philadelphia—4th June—84

Fully acquainted with the value of your Excellency's protection, in a Country, indebted to him for it's freedom; I was anxious before my departure from France, to procure an introduction to you—The Marquiss la Fayette entered into my views, and gave me the letter wc. accompanies this[1]—It is my design to procure uncultivated lands well loaded with wood, & intersected with rivulets and streams, and fix an establishment there, with many reputable families from France and Germany; and turn it to account, either by building forges & glass-houses, or attending to agriculture; and in short every thing that the situation of the place will permit—I have been informed that you have a great quantity of such lands in the back parts of the Country. If your Excellency has not yet disposed of them, and any part should suit me, I would be glad to treat with you for them; persuaded that no one is so able, and so disposed to encourage the settlement of honest, and industrious families, who will contribute to render the commearce of America flourishing by their various fabricks—If you shall condescend to honor me with an answer, be pleased to direct it to the care of Mr Bache Director of the Bank at Philadelphia[2]—at all events, I claim your protection—I have the honor to be with the most profound respect, Your Excellency's very Hble & Obent servt

I. Sailly

Translation, in the hand of David Stuart, DLC:GW; ALS, DLC:GW. A transcription of the French ALS is in CD-ROM:GW.

1. The enclosed letter from Lafayette has not been found.

2. GW wrote Sailly on 20 June. Richard Bache (1737–1811) was Benjamin Franklin's son-in-law. See Richard Bache to GW, 21 April 1789.

From William Duer

Sir.   New York June 5th 1784.

My Freind Mr Sayre, late Sheriff of the City of London, has Thoughts of Establishing himself in your State; and from his present Ideas, it is most probable his Choice will be not far distant from your Excellencys Seat[1]—My long Acquaintance with him in England (where he was beloved and Respected by an Extensive and polite Circle of Freinds) had riveted him deeply in my Affections; and I cannot but participate, in whatever may promote his Happiness—This Sentiment has acquired additional Strength from the Conviction I have that his Attachment to the Cause of Freedom has been the grand Source of his Persecution, and Consequent Misfortunes in England—a Circumstance which I trust will render him more acceptable, to Every liberal Character in this Country[2]—Your Excellency's Patronage (should he determine on Establishi[n]g himself in your Country) will undoubtedly be of Essential Service; and if it will add to your happiness to Contribute to the Success of an amiable, and deserving Character, you will Experience it in givi[n]g a Countenance to my Freind who I will venture to say will prove himself deserving your Esteem.

I hope your Excellency will Excuse the Liberty I take on this Occasion; I am tempted to use it from the happiness I have Experienced in Enjoying some share of your Excellency's Esteem, and Protection for, some years past: the Value of which has made too lasti[n]g an Impression to be Ever buried in Oblivion.

Lady Kitty, and Miss Browne Unite in the most Affectionate, and warm wishes for the happiness of yourself and Mrs Washington[3]—That it may at least Equal to the Anxiety you have felt for the welfare, and Honor of your Country is the sincere wish of Your affectionate and obliged Hble Servt

Wm Duer

ALS, DLC:GW.

William Duer (1747–1799), who was born in Devonshire, England, and settled in New York before the Revolution, was a very active speculator and a promoter of various business schemes in New York and elsewhere. In March 1786 he became secretary to the U.S. Board of Treasury, and he served briefly in 1789–90 as assistant secretary of the treasury under Alexander Hamilton. He died in prison in New York City. See William Duer to GW, 4 Nov. 1788, and notes.

1. Stephen Sayre (1736–1818) is described by his biographer as "soldier, merchant, ship-builder, politician, speculator, propagandist, diplomat, inventor, and occupant of prisons," who has also been characterized as "a most active gallant, a wicked schemer, a liar, a fool, a madman, an embezzler, and a traitor" (Alden, *Sayre*, 1). A New Yorker and a graduate of the College of New Jersey in 1757, Sayre went to England in 1766 where he became a colonial agent, a merchant, and in 1773 sheriff of London through the support of John Wilkes. Sayre spent most of the Revolution on the Continent, returning to New York from France in 1783. He was in Georgetown, Md., and Alexandria, Va., in the late summer and early fall of 1784 (see GW to Sayre,

15 July, 1 Sept., and Sayre to GW, 20 Aug., 15 Oct. 1784). Sayre did finally settle in Virginia, but only after GW had been dead for nearly two decades and shortly before Sayre's own death.

2. See Sayre to GW, 3 Jan. 1789, and notes.

3. GW was in attendance at Duer's marriage in 1779 to "Lady Kitty," the daughter of Maj. Gen. William Alexander (1726–1783) of Basking Ridge, N.J., who was known as Lord Stirling. Miss Brown is Anne Brown (Browne; b. 1754), daughter of William and Mary French Brown of Salem, Massachusetts. After her parents' death she lived with relatives in New York. In December 1773 she visited Mount Vernon with her half brother William Burnet Browne and, after GW became president, she occasionally was invited to various social functions. See *Diaries*, 5:448, 449. Miss Brown was a cousin of Lady Kitty Duer.

From John Rutledge

Dr Sir   June 5. 1784

Give me Leave to introduce, to your Acquaintance, Mr Brailsford, the Gentleman by whom this will be delivered.[1]

I shall be happy to hear, by him, of the Health of yourself & Family.

Mrs Rutledge joins with me, in respectful Complimts to Mrs Washington. I am with the greatest respect & sincerst Regard dr Sir yr most obedt Servt

J. Rutledge

ALS, DLC:GW.

John Rutledge and GW became acquainted as members of the First and Second Continental Congresses. Rutledge at this time was a recent governor of South Carolina and a leading member of the Charleston bar.

1. Rutledge was probably referring to William Brailsford who belonged to a prominent Charleston mercantile family. Brailsford formed with Thomas Morris a partnership that became one of the most active trading firms in the city in the 1780s. GW may have met Brailsford before, for on 12 Sept. 1782 GW wrote Thomas Bee of South Carolina: "Mr Brailsford did me the honor to present your favor of the 21st. Ulto. and I thank you for introducing so agreeable and well informed a Gentleman to my acquaintance" (Fitzpatrick, *Writings of Washington*, 25:150).

From James Wood

Sir   Richmond [Va.] 5th June 1784.

At the Arrangement of the Virginia Line made at Cumberland Old Court House[1] in the year 1782, a Number of Officers of Different ranks were Declared Superseded, which Bars such Officers from Obtaining Certain Portions of Lands under the Act of Assembly of this State,[2] Provided the Proceedings of the Board of Arrangement were Approved by the Commander in Chief. Applications are Daily Making by those Officers for Bounties in Lands, their right to which, Cannot be Determined by the Assembly till they are informed whether the Proceedings Were Approved by you. May I beg the favor of you, Sir, to give me the Necessary information by Post.[3] I Intended myself the Honor of meeting you in Philadelphia, but was prevented by the Advice of a Number of Officers, who were Anxious that I shou'd Attend the Assembly, and who Assured me there wou'd be a full representation from this State.[4] I am happy to inform your Excellency that the Alterations Made in the Articles of the Institution of the Society, meet with a very General Approbation here. My Best respects wait On your Amiable Lady. I have the Honor to be with every Sentiment of the most Perfect respect and Esteem. Sir Yr Excellency's Very Obt Servt

James Wood

ALS, DLC:GW.

James Wood, delegate from Frederick County to the Virginia house of delegates, was from 1776 to 1783 colonel of the 12th (later 8th) Virginia Regiment. He became governor of Virginia in 1796 and served until 1799.

1. After the eastern half of Cumberland County became a part of the new Powhatan County in 1777, the county courthouse was moved south from its old location near the James River to its present more central location. Cumberland County is east of the city of Richmond in Virginia.

2. The council of the state of Virginia on 18 Jan. 1782 decided that the remnants of that part of the Virginia State Line composed of the 1st Virginia Regiment should be combined with "Major [John] Nelsons Corps of Cavalry, Captain [John] Rogers's Company of dismounted Dragoons and part of a Company of Artillery under command of Captain [Christopher] Roan . . . and made a Legionary Corps, under the Command of Colo. [Charles] Dabney . . . consisting of three Companies of Infantry, two troops of Cavalry, and one Company of Artillery" (*Journal of Virginia Council*, 3:29–31). The governor was to direct Colonel Dabney to "call a meeting of the officers . . . to determine among themselves . . . who of them should retire, and who continue." Should they be unable to agree, "they shall then take place according to their seniority" (ibid.). An act of the Virginia legislature of October 1779 set the amount of land to be received from the state at the end of the war by "the officers who shall have served in the Virginia line on continental establishment, or in the army or navy upon state establishment to the end of the present war" (10 Hening 159–62). In May 1782 the Virginia general assem-

bly decreed "that any officer or soldier who hath not been cashiered or super-seded, and who hath served the term of three years successively, shall have an absolute and unconditional title to his respective apportionment of the land appropriated" (11 Hening 81–85).

3. GW responded to this letter on 12 June.

4. Wood was one of the Virginia officers chosen to attend the meeting of the Society of the Cincinnati in Philadelphia in May.

From Tench Tilghman

Dear Sir   Baltimore [Md.] 7th June 1784

Upon the receipt of your Excellency's favr of the 28th ulto giving me a greater latitude than you had before done, in re-gard to the qualifications of the Bricklayer and Joiner wanted by you, I went to the persons who have the disposal of the Irish Servants lately arrived, but found none of those Trades left upon hand. One or two more Ships are daily expected, and out of them you may be assured I will procure the best that are to be had. I shall attend to your direction of substituting a Stone Mason in the room of a Bricklayer, should circumstances re-quire it—I will also make enquiry for a Stucco Worker—but of him I almost despair—As your Excellency observes, he must be perfect, otherwise, like a bad Painter, he will deface what he ought to decorate.

I beg leave to take this opportunity of acknowledging the rect of your Excellency's letter of the 19th of May from Philada accompanied by a Badge of the Order of the Cincinnati, of which Society I have the honor of being a Member.[1] I pray your Excellency to accept my warmest and most grateful thanks for this distinguishing mark of your attention and regard. I had be-fore received many proofs of your Esteem, but I must confess you have, by this last instance of your goodness, made the most flattering addition—I shall now wear my Badge with a full conviction of having deserved it, or it would never have been presented by the illustrious hands of him, whose modest Vir-tue—unsullied honor—and true Glory it was the object of the Institution to commemorate.

I have the vanity to think that whatever contributes to the in-crease of my happiness will not be uninteresting to your Excel-lency—I therefore take pleasure in informing you that Mrs Tilghman presented me with a Daughter a fortnight ago, and

that she and her little Charge are both perfectly well—I entreat
your Excellency to make her and my most respectful Compliments to Mrs Washington—I have the honor to be Your Excellency's Most obt and hble Servt

                                        Tench Tilghman

ALS, DLC:GW.
   1. The text of the letter, dated at Philadelphia on 18 May, reads: "I pray
you to accept the enclosed (if a member of the Society of Cincinnatti)—I sent
for one for each of my aids de Camp" (*Tilghman Memoir*, 111).

From John Witherspoon

Sir   London June 7. 1784
   I was favoured with your Letter of the 10th of March just
three Weeks ago. I have considered attentively the Subject of it
& shall make a short Remark or two upon the Proposal. For
Reasons which I think are very good & which I have no doubt
of convincing you at meeting ⟨even⟩ so I have made & shall
make no Mention whatever of this Matter in England except to
a few Confidential Friends. The Disposition of the People in
this Country is very far from what my Friends, who pressed the
Voyage upon me, expected; though not different from what I
looked for my self. Having during the whole War abstained
from writing Politics as a matter of Prudence I have not yet begun it & therefore shall only say that Congress & yourself will
learn from Mr Laurens how things stand & in most of his Sentiments or perhaps all Mr Reed & I perfectly agree.
   In Scotland to which Country we propose to set off in a few
Days The better sort of People are even more set against America than here but the common sort much more favourable to it
& the Spirit of Emigration is very strong Some have corresponded with me & pressed me much to take some Measures to
assist them but I have hitherto declined. I shall however when
in that Country my self not only make known Your Proposals as
they stand & obtain the Sentiments of People upon them but
also hear their Observations & make my own upon any Alterations which might be made in their Terms.[1] I suspect that lease
holds will not in general be agreeable—the rather that all who
go to the Northern Parts purchase the Lands in fee Simple. Yet
the Reasons you give for not parting with it altogether are

good. However both Ends perhaps might be answered. How would it be for example to covenant with any body of Emigrants that a certain Tract should be surveyed & laid out in 100 Acre Lots which is the way in the Northern parts & then to sell the tract to them for what could be agreed for—conditioned that You should reserve a third part of the Lots either taken alternately or drawn by Lot & the improvement which they would receive would be a full Equivalent for parting with the rest. Or perhaps a Manner of holding well known in Scotland might strike many even to purchase the Land on a simple quitrent with fines of a years Rent of the real Value at the End of every Term suppose 19 years or at the Entrance of every Heir ⟨with⟩ something additional in Case of a Singular Successor as it is called in Scotland that is in Case of a Sale—This Method of a years Rent of the real Value at the Time the fines become due is more certain & Safe to both sides than a Rent rising in regular Proportions which you justly observe is a Speculative thing.

It is my Intention to commit this Short Letter to some Person who is going to America & I expect that Mr Reed & I will ourselves be there very soon if it please God to give us a safe Passage.[2] As soon as I arrive in America you may expect a Letter from me on the Subject of Emigrants & in the mean time with respectful Complements to Mrs Washington & best wishes for your self I am Sir your most obedient humbl. Servant

Jno. Witherspoon

ALS, DLC:GW.

1. For Witherspoon's trip to Britain and correspondence while in London regarding the emigration fever in Scotland, see Collins, *Witherspoon*, 2:138–43.

2. Witherspoon and Joseph Reed sailed in late July and reached New York on 11 Sept. 1784.

From Barbé-Marbois

Sir,   Philadelphia June 8th 1784.

I have received the Treatise upon the growth & management of tobacco for which I wish your excellency will accept my thanks. I know that Book will be very acceptable to M. Malsherbes.[1]

I have had So many proofs of your & Mrs Washington Kindness to me sir, that I am persuaded you'll take Some Share in the pleasure I feel in a connection intended with Miss Eliza moore the late Presidents daughter.[2] It is to take place on the 17. of this month; I hope it will make me perfectly happy & I am more particularly pleased as it Strengthen the ties by which I was allready connected with this continent, & its Citizens. The young lady presents you her respects. I think She is not a Stranger to your Excellency nor Mrs Washington: being So intimately connected I hope I will increase rather than diminish the Friendship with which you sir, have hounoured us both. I am with greatest respect Your very humble obedient Servant

De Marbois

Be so kind as to present my respects & compliments to Mr L. Washington & family.

ALS, DLC:GW.

1. See GW to George Clinton, 25 Nov. 1784, n.5, for an account of Malesherbes's sending grapevines to New York for GW in the spring of 1784.

2. William Moore (c.1735–1793), a wealthy Philadelphia merchant, was president of the Pennsylvania supreme executive council from 1781 to 1782. Elizabeth, his only daughter, did marry Barbé-Marbois, who first came to Philadelphia as secretary of the French legation in 1779.

From Simeon DeWitt

Sir   New York June 9th 1784

I am honored with Your Excellency's Letter of the 3d March—I write this to acquaint Your Excy that I am appointed Surveyor General of the State of New York in the room of Genl Schuyler who has resigned that Office; in consequence of which I shall make a resignation of my commission as Geographer, as soon as Congress have met again at Trenton; requesting at the same time permission to retain the papers I have, with the view of compiling them into a map or maps for publication as soon as I shall find it practacable. I have done part of a fair copy of one which shall include the Country between the meridians of Philadelphia and Norwalk in Connecticut and the Latitudes of Philadelphia and Fredericksburgh of a size of near 40 by 50 Inches. If the Congress allow my last request I have thoughts of sending it to France to be engraved, if not, I must think of other expedients.[1] St John the French Consul at this place has offered me his recommendations of persons to whose care designs of this nature might be entrusted, by which means I might have them executed with greater perfection and at less expence than can be expected in this Country.[2] I am with the greatest respect Your Excellency's most Obedient humble Servant

S: DeWitt

ALS, DLC:GW.

1. See DeWitt to GW, 12 Jan. 1784, and notes. The maps he retained in his possession were some of the rough military sketch maps that he helped make during the war. The maps eventually were presented to the New-York Historical Society and constitute the largest collection of maps prepared for the Continental army. See Walter W. Ristow, "Simeon De Witt, Pioneer American Cartographer," *Surveying and Mapping*, 30 (1970), 239–55. DeWitt never published the proposed collection of revised Revolutionary War maps.

2. Michel-Guillaume St. Jean de Crèvecoeur (1735–1813), himself a mapmaker, was a resident of the colony of New York from 1759 until his return to France in 1780. He came back to New York in November 1783 as the French consul in the city, a position he held despite frequent absences until his final departure in 1790. Crèvecoeur is best known for his *Letters from an American Farmer*, first printed in 1782.

Letter not found: from Clement Biddle, 10 June 1784. On 30 June GW wrote to Biddle: "Your favor of the 10th Instt . . . is come safe to hand."

To Caleb Brewster

Sir,   Mount Vernon 10th June 1784

I believe you have been misinformed as to a resolve of Congress, allowing officers on separate commands, extra-pay—I have heard of no such resolution—on the contrary, that these allowances were withdrawn. It was with great difficulty General Knox could obtain compensation for his extra-expences during his commd at the post of West-point—where, from the nature of it, he was absolutely obliged to encounter them, or turn strangers out of his house. I know also that application was made in favor of Lt Colo. Hull, who, whilst he was on the lines—exposed to the visits; and in a manner compelled to entertain a number of British officers, & had it not at his option to avoid expence—but with what success it was made I have never heard. this however I do know, that there were powerful objections made to both, lest it should open a door to a multitude of applications which Congress were determined not to comply with.[1]

Lest I shou'd be mistaken, in supposing there is no such resolve as you allude to, I enclose a Certificate which may be made use of, if there is.[2]

I hope you soon will be, if you are not already, perfectly recovered of your wound—my best wishes are offered for it; being with esteem & regard Dr Sir Yrs &c.

G. Washington

LB, DLC:GW.

1. It is not known when or by what means Caleb Brewster (d. 1827) made his inquiry, but GW's certificate (see note 2) makes clear its exact nature.

2. The text of the enclosed certificate, dated 10 June 1784, is: "I certify that in the year 1778, whilst the American Army lay at the white plains, it became necessary to station an officer & a few men, on the Sound to keep open a communication with the City of New York by the way of Long Island, for the purpose of my secret corrispondence: that Capt: Lt Brewster of the 2d regiment of Artillery was chosen for this service—that circumstances made it necessary to continue him therein until the close of the War—and as far as I know or believe—that he conducted the business with fidelity, judgment & bravery, having received a wound whilst he was on that duty, of which, I am informed, he is not yet recovered" (LB, DLC:GW). Brewster was wounded on Long Island Bay in December 1782 but remained in the Continental army until June 1783.

From George William Fairfax

My Dear Sir   Bath [England] 10th June 1784

I have been called upon very unexpectedly by a Gentn passing through this place to London, in order to Imbark for Virginia. So that I have scarcely time to say, that the Revd Mr B[r]acken of Williamsburg, has been so obliging as to take charge of a Case directed to your Excellency, containing two Prints, the best framed one for yourself, and the other for my Sister Washingtons kind acceptance of. before the Painting, from whence this was taken, was finished, I wrote two or three times to Colo. F. Lewis to endeavour to procure a minuture, or profile of you, in order to represent the first Figure, in the leading group, and was much disappointed as well as the worthy Artist, Mr Pine.[1] Our united Compliments and best wishes attend you, good Mrs Washington, and enquiring friends, and remain Dear Sir Your Excellencys ever Obliged, faithful Friend, and Obedt humble Servt

Go: Wm: Fairfax

ALS, DLC:GW.

In early July 1773 George William Fairfax and his wife Sarah Cary Fairfax left Belvoir. After visiting her relatives at Ceelys in Elizabeth City County, they sailed in August from Yorktown for England, where they remained for the rest of their lives. Fairfax wrote GW on 10 Jan. 1774 that the suit in chancery which he had come to settle would take years and that in any case he and his wife did not intend to return to their home in Virginia. Before his departure, Fairfax had given GW his power of attorney and had gotten GW to take on the general supervision of his affairs in Virginia. GW wrote Fairfax from Cambridge, Mass., on 26 July 1775 that his duties as commander in chief of America's military forces made it impossible for him to continue to see to matters in Virginia for Fairfax and urged him to appoint someone else to attend to his business there. See George William Fairfax to GW, 1 Jan., 5 Aug., 26 Nov. 1773, 10 Jan. 1774, 2 Mar. 1775; and GW to Fairfax, 19 Jan., 15 Oct. 1773, 10–25 June 1774, 31 May, 26 July 1775. See also George William Fairfax to GW, 23 Aug. 1784, and 30 June 1786. Despite the difficulties and the fact that many of Fairfax's letters were intercepted and never reached GW, the two men continued to write one another during the war and in 1783 resumed a regular correspondence which lasted until Fairfax's death in 1787. See particularly George William Fairfax to GW, 26 Mar. 1783, and GW to Fairfax, 10 July 1783.

1. For further description of the prints that Fairfax was sending to GW, see his letter to GW of 23 Aug. 1784. John Bracken, rector of Bruton Parish Church in Williamsburg from 1773 to 1818 and longtime master and briefly president of the College of William and Mary, was a visitor to London in the spring of 1784. Bracken was married in 1776 to Sally Burwell, daughter of Carter Burwell of Carter's Grove near Williamsburg. In a long and informative letter to Fairfax on 27 Feb. 1785 about the difficulties of the wartime correspondence between the two old friends, GW reported that he had seen Bracken in Richmond in November 1784. At that time, Bracken had told him that he would forward the pictures from Williamsburg by "the first safe conveyance" but that they still had not arrived. Fairfax's letter of 23 Aug. 1784 served as a letter of introduction for the English painter Robert Edge Pine (1730–1788) who arrived at Mount Vernon on 28 April 1785 "to take my [GW's] picture from the life" (*Diaries*, 4:129–30).

From Benjamin Hawkins

Sir,   North Carolina June the 10th 1784

I have the honour to enclose to your Excellency some acts passed the last Session of our Legislature—by which you will see in some measure the disposition of this State to comply with the views of Congress; as well as, to grant such further powers as may render the Confederation more competent to the purposes of the Union.[1]

The Act for levying our proportion of one million five hundred thousand dollars, exclusive of the impost, and impowering Congress to collect the same, will by no means raise so large a sum; it being only a land Tax, of six pence on every hundred acres of land, and a poll Tax of one shilling and six pence, on all white males from twenty one upwards, and on all slaves from twelve years old to fifty. it establishes the principle recommended by Congress, and I trust the good sense of this, and the other States, will soon (if they do not already) see the necessity of establishing solid a⟨*mutilated*⟩ effectual revenues to enable Congress to perform ⟨*mutilated*⟩ engagements.[2]

The members of the Legislature could not consent to vote the full sum required, after they had ceded all the lands westward of the Apalachian Mountain; they urged, it was not necessary, since Congress were in possession of the Cession of New York Virginia and North Carolina.

The Cession of our Western lands was much debated and opposed: The house of Commons were long divided, whether to make the Tenessee, Cumberland Mountain or the Apalachian our western boundary; but finally passed the act as you see it, fifty three against forty one: There are within our Cession more than three thousand men able to bear arms.[3]

The recommendation of Congress respecting the 5th article of the Treaty is not complied with nor is there any thing done to carry the Treaty into effect—and I suspect it will be difficult to induce us to think aright on this subject; (altho our Citizens seem well disposed) while we have ambitious, discontented spirits, whose popular existance depends on forming the passions of the common people against the refugees. the State cry of peculation and embezzlement of the public money, aided by complaints of hard times and heavy taxes, was never listened to with more avidity than the Clamours against the refugees and payment of British ⟨de⟩bts. and this too, by men, who cannot possibly be ⟨los⟩ers if all bona fide debts were wiped off with a sponge, but who most assuredly share in the disgrace of their country by such shameful unwarrantable conduct.[4]

I have not in this State heard a single objection to the commutation or rendering ample justice to the army. early in the spring there was circulated the pamphlet said to be written by Burk of South Carolina against the instituton of the Cincinnati which gave some uneasiness to some people, who were apprehensive the institution would be productive of an aristocracy dangerous to the principles of our Governments. but a little reflection with the remembrance of the patience perseverance and sufferings of the army in defense of their just rights and liberties has worn down the suspicions in some measure; and will I hope teach them to put their trust in those, who in the worst of times stood the constant centinals over the liberties of their Country, and to suspect those only who have screened themselves in the hour of danger and now step forth to revile the virtuous welldoer and his endeavours to adopt wise and equitable measures.[5]

The Legislation has changed the annual election from March to august, and the annual meeting will be in october.[6] I hope they then will amend such of our acts as are imperfect and pass such others respecting the treaty as may be consonant with the wishes of those who are for wise and equitable measures. I have the honour to be with great and sincere esteem sir your Excellencyes Most obedient and most humble servant

Benjamin Hawkins

ALS, DLC:GW.

Benjamin Hawkins (1754–1818), perhaps best known for his services as the agent of the United States in dealing with the southern Indians, was a member of Congress for North Carolina from 1781 to 1784, but he left Congress in the summer of 1783 and was elected to represent Warren County in the North Carolina house of commons. He was active in the recent session of the legislature that had met from 19 April to 4 June. He was one of the North Carolina senators in the First Congress and in 1796 GW made him superintendent of the Indian tribes south of the Ohio.

1. In addition to the acts cited in notes 2 and 3, Hawkins sent these acts passed in the April–June session of the North Carolina legislature: "An Act vesting a power in the United States in Congress assembled to levy a Duty on Foreign Merchandize, for the use of the United States"; "An Act for Authorizing the United States in Congress Assembled to Regulate the Trade of This State With Foreign Nations"; and "An Act to Impower the Delegates of this State in Congress to Assent to a Repeal of Part of the Eighth of the Articles of Confederation and Perpetual Union Between the Thirteen States of America, and to Subscribe and Ratify the Alteration Proposed in the Recommendation

of Congress of the 18th of April, 1783, in Place Thereof, as Part of the Said Instrument of Union." The last of these empowered the North Carolina delegates to approve Congress's proposal that requisitions upon states be proportional to population instead of land value as Article 8 provided (*N.C. State Records*, 24:547–49, 561, 564–65; copies of the acts are in DLC:GW).

2. See "An Act for Levying a Tax for the Purposes Therein Mentioned, and for Investing the United States in Congress Assembled With a Power to Collect the Same" (*N.C. State Records*, 24:557–59).

3. The vote was on "An Act Ceding to the Congress of the United States Certain Western Lands Therein Described, and Authorizing the Delegates from this State in Congress to Execute a Deed or Deeds for the Same" (ibid., 561–63). On 3 June William R. Davie entered in the house journal a lengthy protest to the passage of the cession act, which was signed by thirty-seven members (*Journal of N.C. House of Commons*, 69–70). The Congress received North Carolina's cession act on 3 June as it was on the point of adjourning and took no action. In October 1784 North Carolina repealed its cession act, and it did not cede the state's western lands until 1789.

4. Article 5 of the treaty of peace signed in Paris on 3 Sept. 1783 dealt with the restitution by individual American states of confiscated property belonging to British subjects. On 29 May the North Carolina house of commons rejected by a vote of 62 to 18 a first reading of a bill that would have paved the way for the restoration of some of the state's unsold confiscated Loyalist property to its owners. Hawkins was one of the eighteen men who voted in favor of the bill, and he signed a statement entered in the house journals on 3 June protesting the rejection of the bill. See *Journal of N.C. House of Commons*, 58, 69–71. The letters supplied in angle brackets are mutilated.

5. For a discussion of Aedanus Burke's pamphlet, see Henry Knox to GW, 21 Feb. 1784, n.2.

6. The act explains why the legislature chose to change the time of its election from March to August and its time of meeting from April to October, each year. See *N.C. State Records*, 24:547.

To Edward Newenham

Dr Sir,   Mount Vernon 10th June 1784.

At Philadelphia in the moment of my departure from it on the 18th of last month, I had the honor to receive (by the Convention, Captn Workman) your favors of the 30th of Jany & 15th of March; & I recollect to have received about three years ago, by the hands, if I remember right, of a Mr Collins, a short introductory letter of that Gentleman from you. If you have favored me with others, I have not been happy enough to have received them.[1]

For the honor of these letters, & the favorable sentiments they express of me, you have my sincerest thanks. To stand well in the estimation of good men, & honest patriots, whether of this or that clime, or of this or that political way of thinking, has ever been a favorite wish of mine; & to have obtained, by such pursuits as duty to my Country; & the rights of mankind rendered indispensably necessary, the plaudit of Sir Edwd Newenham, will not be among my smallest felicities. Yes Sir, it was long before you honored me with a line, I became acquainted with your name, your worth and your political tenets; & I rejoice that my own conduct has been such as to acquire your esteem, & to be invited to your friendship. I accept it Sir, with the eagerness of a congenial spirit, & shall be happy in every opportunity of giving you proofs of its rectitude; but none will be more pleasing to me than the opportunity of welcoming you, or any of your family, to this land of liberty—and to *this* my retreat from the cares of public life; where in homespun & with rural fare, we will invite you to our bed & board.

Your intention of making an establishment for one of your sons, either in Pennsylvania or this State, gives me pleasure: if it should be in the latter, or if you should come to this State first; every information or assistance which it may be in my power to give you, shall be rendered with great pleasure; & I shall have pleasure also in paying attention to your recommendation of others.[2]

This is an abounding Country, & it is as fine as it is extensive. With a little political wisdom it may become equally populous & happy. Some of the States having been misled, ran riot for a while, but they are recovering a proper tone again—& I have *no* doubt, but that our fœderal Constitution will obtain more consistency & firmness every day. We have indeed so plain a road before us, that it must be worse than ignorance if we miss it.

We have no distinct account yet how the Elections have gone in Gt Britain; consequently do not know the result of the Kings appeal to the people of that Country—it is a very important one, & shews that the affairs of that Kingdom are in a critical situation. This being the case also in Ireland, it would not be matter of wonder, if some important changes should take place in those hemispheres.[3]

I am much obliged to you for the Pamphlets, Magazines & Gazettes which you were so kind as to send me; & can only repeat to you assurances of the pleasure I shou'd have in seeing you under my roof. Mrs Washington joins me in best respects to Lady Newenham, to whom, for receiving—& the Marqs de la Fayette, for presenting my picture, I feel myself under grateful obligations.[4] You will please to accept my thanks for your friendly offers of service in Ireland—if at any time I should have any thing to do there, there is no person to whom I would so soon chuse to lay under the obligation. I have the honor to be &c.

G: Washington

LB, DLC:GW.

Sir Edward Newenham (1732–1814) became a regular correspondent of GW. A prominent member of the Irish Parliament since 1769, Newenham supported the American cause during the Revolutionary War with Britain and befriended the Americans held prisoner in Ireland. For further identification, see GW to William Persse, 11 Oct. 1788, n.1.

1. Newenham's letters of 30 Jan. and 15 Mar. 1784 have not been found. In a letter from Dublin, dated 6 June 1781, Newenham commended to GW, "Mr Collins the bearer of this letter," saying that he knew Collins and "his worthy brother" to be friends of American liberty. He added that they had recently been with "my most respected & worthy friend Doctor Franklin" who was equally persuaded of their "worth & integrity." Newenham held out the prospect that "in some time hence" the Collins brothers meant "to transfer their whole property, & settle in the land of freedom." Thomas Collins of Dublin was in Passy with Franklin, a letter of introduction in hand, in September 1780. On 30 Sept. 1780 he signed an oath of allegiance to the United States and received from Franklin a safe conduct of the cargo from England aboard the sloop *Newenham* (see Hays, *Calendar of Franklin Papers*, 3:296, 434, 5:43, 312). On 22 Feb. 1782 James Collins, "late of the Kingdom of Ireland, and lately come to this city from New York," subscribed to the Test Oath in Philadelphia (Campbell, *Friendly Sons of St. Patrick and the Hibernian Society*, 105). On 18 Mar. 1782 GW attended the dinner of the St. Patrick Society in Philadelphia where a Mr. Collins was listed as a guest. It seems likely that either Thomas or James Collins delivered the letter of 6 June 1781.

2. In his letter of 6 June 1781, Newenham spoke of his own wish to live in America and frequently mentioned this in his correspondence with Benjamin Franklin. On 5 Nov. 1780 he wrote Franklin that he hoped three of his five sons would settle in the United States. He had eighteen children.

3. George III dissolved Parliament on 25 Mar. 1784, and when the new Parliament met on 18 May, the prime minister, William Pitt (1759–1806), commanded a large majority in the House of Commons.

4. The portrait conveyed to Newenham by Lafayette has not been identified.

From Joseph Mandrillon

Sir   Amsterdam 11th June 1784

The happy and illustrious qualities with which Heaven has favoured you, merit without doubt, the confidence and the Love of all your Fellow Citizens—you have fully gratified their Hope, you have Sir, even surpassed it, by drawing on your Country All the prosperity which she enjoys—Before you, Sir, we had never yet seen a Great Man Universally admired, commended, respected and enjoy his immortality whilst living: you were born Sir to offer this lovely and rare Instance to your Age.

Permit me, Sir, to Present you an Exemplar of my Remarks, and of my Enquiries concerning America—Recieve them with that Bounty, that Indulgence which Constitutes the primitive basis of your Conduct—Pardon me for having traced the Portrait of your Excellency in the 5th Chapter of the 2d part of the Spectator, it is Sir too fare short of the Model to gain me any Merit.[1]

My Friend Mr E. Brush Merchant of New-York judging of my Soul by his Own has conceived that he could not better demonstrate his attachment, than by making me a present of your Portrait richly ornamented He is not decieved, and I possess nothing Sir which to me is more precious. This Portrait shall be to my Family and myself an inalterable monument of My Friends attachment, and of Respect to your Person.[2] I have the honor to be with the intimate Sentiment of Veneration which I have published Sir your Excellency's very humble and very Obt Servant

Jh Mandrillon

Translation, DLC:GW; ALS, DLC:GW. A transcript of the French ALS is in CD-ROM:GW.

Joseph Mandrillon (1743–1794) was a French banker in Amsterdam who retained a lively interest in America after visiting it before the Revolution. He wrote to GW often after GW acknowledged this letter on 25 Nov. 1784, and Mandrillon usually included samples of his poetry and prose. GW put an end to the correspondence in a letter of 30 June 1790 with the plea that the press of the business of the presidency made it impossible to carry on a private correspondence. Mandrillon returned to Paris at the outbreak of the French Revolution and died on the guillotine in January 1794.

1. Mandrillon's book *Le Spectateur Américain ou Remarques Généles sur L'Amérique Septentrionale et sur La République des Treize-Etats-Unis* . . . (Amsterdam, 1784) includes a "Portrait du général Washington" (pt. 2, pp. 45–50), which is

an unrelieved panegyric. In 1788 Mandrillon sent GW another of his books, *Fragmens de Politique et de Littérature, Suivis d'un Voyage à Berlin, en 1784* (Paris and Brussels, 1788), in which the essay on GW in *Le Spectateur* is reprinted. The latter work was in GW's library at his death. See Griffin, *Boston Athenæum Collection*, 134, and GW to Mandrillon, 29 Aug. 1788.

2. The portrait of GW that the merchant Ebenezer Brush sent Mandrillon has not been identified.

3. GW responded from Mount Vernon on 25 Nov. 1784: "I have had the honor to receive your favor of the 11th of June, accompanied with your remarks & enquiries concerning America. The honorable mention which you make of me in both is far above my deserts, & to be ascribed more to your politeness than to my merits: on my gratitude however you have a powerful claim; at the same time that it becomes matter of regret to me, that my want of knowledge in the French language will not allow me to become well acquainted with all the beauties of your Spectator" (LB, DLC:GW).

To David Stuart

Dear Sir, Mount Vernon 11th June 1784

A few days ago, I received the enclosed letter & copy of an intended address to be presented on thursday next[1]—I have drafted an answer which I pray you to look over, correct, and amend as you may find occasion, & think best.[2] Return it if you please by Austin, or Fanny Bassett.[3] I am glad to hear Mrs Stuart is better—my Compliments & good wishes to her. I am with very great esteem Dr Sir Yr most obt Servt

Go: Washington

ALS, PHC: Charles Roberts Autograph Letters Collection.

1. No such letter has been found. A committee of the Virginia house of delegates on 5 June presented to the house a draft of an address to GW, which was recommitted on 8 June and not approved until 22 June. See Virginia General Assembly and George Washington, 15 May–15 July 1784.

2. GW's reply to the address of the legislature is dated 15 July and is printed in the entry cited in note 1.

3. Austin, GW's "Mullatoe Man," died en route to Baltimore in December 1794 (Herman Stump to GW, 20 Dec. 1794; see also John Carlisle to GW, 21 Dec. 1794).

To Patrick Henry

Dear Sir, Mount Vernon 12th June 1784

After a long silence, more the effect of great hurry & business, than want of inclination; permit me to recall myself to your mind, by introducing to your recollection Mr Paine, the author of Commonsense, the Crisis &c.[1]

To say what effect the writings of this Gentleman has had on our public affairs at the epochas at which they were given to the world, would, to a person of your information, be altogether unnecessary; it is more for his interest, & to my present purpose to add, that he stands unrewarded for his exertions in the American cause—is poor, & I believe very much chagrined at the little notice which has been taken of him for his lucubrations.

New York, lately, has testified her sense of his merits by a donation which is very pleasing to him—& from individual States, rather than from Congress (for reasons which seem to have weight in his mind,)—he wishes they might be continued in this line. If his services appear in your eyes to merit reward, I am persuaded you will endeavor to do justice to them.[2]

I mention this matter to you equally unsollicited by, as unknown to him; for I never have heard that he has it in contemplation to bring himself before any State in the Union.[3] Convinced as I am of the efficacy of his publications, & of the little attention shewn him for them, I could not withhold this attempt to serve him, & to assure you of the esteem & regard with which I have the honor to be Dr Sir &c. &c.

G. Washington

LB, DLC:GW.

1. GW on this day wrote similar letters about Thomas Paine to Richard Henry Lee and James Madison.

2. On 16 June 1784, by gift from the state, Paine came into possession in Westchester County, N.Y., of "two hundred and seventy-seven acres, more or less, which became forfeited to and vested in the People of this State by the conviction of Frederick Devoe" (indenture, register's office, vol. T of Grantees, Westchester County, quoted in Conway, *Paine*, 1:203). For an explanation of the failure of Virginia to give financial aid to Paine, see James Madison to GW, 2 July and note 2.

3. For the action Pennsylvania took at GW's urging, see Paine to GW, 28 April 1784, n.4.

From La Luzerne

Sir, Philadelphia June 12. 1784

I cannot quit the Continent, without renewing my assurances of the esteem towards you, with wc. I am inspired—From the five years residence I have made in America, and the share I have had in business; I have had a better opportunity than most, of admiring your Military talents, and those great qualities wc. have secured for ever, the Independance, and liberty of your Country—I share in respect to this, the esteem and admiration wc. you have inspired into my whole *Country*—But I have this advantage over the greater part of my Fellow-Citizens, that I have lived in company with you, and enjoyed the Civil and Social virtues, that so particularly distinguish your Character—I beseech you to believe, they have impressed me with the greatest respect, and most sincere attachment.

I cannot renounce the hope of seeing you, one time or other, in France—I am sensible, how much your own affairs require you in America—I know too, how painful it would be to you, to be at a distance from a people, who feel as much attachment to your person, as admiration for your Virtues—But, I ought too, to aspire to give satisfaction to all France, & her sovereign, who are all singularly desirous of testifying to you, the esteem they have for you—If it was necessary to add other considerations to this; I might present to you the sentiments of all the French officers who served under you, and are attached to you by the most tender and respectful ties—I venture to join myself to them, and entreat you to be convinced, of the respectful attachment with wc. I am devoted to you for life—I have the honor to be your Excellency's very Hble & Obnt servt

C. de la Lucerne

May I beseech you to present my respects to Mrs Washington?

Translation, in David Stuart's hand, DLC:GW; ALS, MH: Jared Sparks Collection. A transcription of the ALS is in CD-ROM:GW.

To Richard Henry Lee

Dear Sir,   Mount Vernon 12th June 84.

Unsollicited by, and unknown to Mr Paine, I take the liberty of hinting the Services, and distressed (for so I think it may be called) situation of that Gentleman.

That his Common Sense, and many of his Crisis[e]s were well timed and had a happy effect upon the public mind, none I believe, who will recur to the epocha's at which they were published, will deny. That his Services hitherto have passed of unnoticed, is obvious to all. and that he is chagreened and necessitous, I will undertake to aver. Does not common justice then point to some compensation?

He is not in circumstances to refuse the bounty of the public—New York, not the least distressed, nor most able State in the Union, has set the example—He prefers the benevolence of the States individually, to an allowance from Congress, for reasons which are conclusive in his own mind, and such as I think may be approved by others. His views are moderate, a decent independency is, I believe, the height of his ambition; and if you view his Services in the American cause in the same important light that I do, I am sure you will have pleasure in obtaining it for him.[1] I am with esteem & regard Dr Sir Yr most obt Servt

Go: Washington

ALS, PPAmP: Correspondence of Richard Henry Lee and Arthur Lee; LB, DLC:GW.

1. See GW to Patrick Henry, this date.

To James Madison

Dear Sir,   Mount Vernon June 12th 1784

Can nothing be done in our Assembly for poor Paine? Must the merits, & Services of *Common Sense* continue to glide down the stream of time, unrewarded by this Country? His writings certainly have had a powerful effect on the public mind; ought they not then to meet an adequate return? He is poor! he is chagreened! and almost, if not altogether, in despair of relief.

New York it is true, not the least distressed, nor best able State in the Union, has done something for him.[1] This kind of provision he prefers to an allowance from Congress—he has reasons for it, which to him are conclusive, and such I think, as would have weight with others. His views are moderate—a decent independency is, I believe, all he aims at. Should he not obtain this? If you think so, I am sure you will not only move the matter, but give it your support.[2] For me, it only remains to feel for his Situation, and to assure you of the sincere esteem & regard with which I have the honor to be Dr Sir, Yr most obedt Hble Servt

Go: Washington

ALS, CSmH; LB, DLC:GW.

1. For New York's action with regard to Thomas Paine, see GW to Patrick Henry, this date, n.2.

2. For the attempt on the part of Madison and others to secure aid for Paine, see Madison to GW, 2 July 1784, and note 1 of that document.

To Edmund Randolph

Dear sir,   Mount Vernon 12th June 1784

At my return from Philada I met your favor of the 15th ulto—& since, have received that of the 28th. The rough draft of the conveyance from Colo. Bassett to me, appearing to be just in recital, &, I presume, legal in form; I return it with a wish that the business may be finally accomplished as soon as circumstances will permit.

With respect to the Suit of Doctr Savage, you will be so good as to inform Mr Fairfax or myself of the determination of his Executor (when he shall have taken it)—that we may proceed accordingly. With the sincerest esteem & regard I am Dr Sir &c.

G: Washington

LB, DLC:GW.

From Thomas Stone

Sir   Haberdeventure [Md.] June 12 1784

I have considered the Institution of the Cincinati as amended and am happy to find every Objection to the order removed by the late Alterations—It has given Me much pleasure to find all sensible Men with whom I have conversed on the subject concur in this opinion. with sentiments of perfect Esteem & respect I am Sir Yr most obt & most humble Sert

T: Stone

ALS, DLC:GW.

Thomas Stone (1743–1787) was a lawyer who studied under Thomas Johnson in Frederick, Md., and a planter who beginning in 1771 lived at his house Habre-de-Venture, Port Tobacco West Hundred, Charles County, Maryland. A signer of the Declaration of Independence, he was frequently elected to Congress and to the Maryland legislature. He was not a member of the Society of the Cincinnati.

To James Wood

Dr Sir, Mount Vernon 12th June 1784

In answer to your favor of the 5th, I have to inform you that I can find nothing in my letter or orderly books confirmatory or disapproving the arrangments which have been made of the Virginia line of the army in the year 1782—the presumption therefore is, if they ever came to hand, that they either obtained a silent acquiescence, or that I did not care to intermeddle in them at all, as part of the line was in So. Carolina, & the whole (by a resolve of Congress) were considered as belonging to the Southern army. If I should hereafter come across anything which can illucidate the point more fully, it shall be transmitted to you.

It gives me pleasure to hear that the alterations in the institution of the Society of the Cincinnati meets general approbation—if a sincere disposition in those who composed the general meeting to remove *all* the objectionable parts of it, & give satisfaction to their country, could have a claim to its approbation—their conduct cou'd not fail of this reward. With very great esteem I am &c.

G: W——n

LB, DLC:GW.

To Benjamin Harrison

Dr Sir, Mount Vernon [1]4th June 1784

Long as the enclosed letter & petition appear to have been written, they never came to my hands until thursday last; the latter, altho' called a copy, having the marks of an original paper; another copy accompanying it, inducing a belief that it is so, I delay not a moment to hand it forward.[1]

My being perfectly ignorant of the laws of the Commonwealth, & unacquainted, if such confiscations have taken place, with the principles upon which they are founded, must be my apology for taking the liberty of even bringing these papers before the Legislature, for it is not my wish to interfere in the politics of the State, nor desire, to see discriminations or departures from general principles, which are not warranted by Law or evident propriety; altho' in the present case, it should seem to me hard, to divest an Infant, under the circumstances young Bristow is described to be, of his partrimony.

As the petition is directed to the Governr the Senate & House of Delegates of the State of Virginia—I conceived it best to transmit it, & the Letters relative thereto, to your Excellency.[2] With great consideration & respect, I have the honor to be Your most Obedt humble Servant

G: Washington

LB, DLC:GW.

1. The enclosed letter from Mary Bristow, Spring Garden, London, is dated 27 Nov. 1783 (DLC:GW). It was sent to GW by George William Fairfax in a letter dated 9 Dec. 1783. There is another copy of Mrs. Bristow's letter, also in her hand, in the British Museum: Add. MSS 9828. The enclosed "Memorial & Petition address'd to the Governor, the Senate, and House of Delegates of the State of Virginia," as Mrs. Bristow described it, was signed by Mary Bristow "and the two Gentlemen who are joint Guardians with me" of Richard Bristow, her young son. At his death in 1779, Mary Bristow's husband, Robert Bristow, left to their infant son "sundry tracts of land and a considerable number of slaves" in Virginia. The Virginia property of the infant Richard Bristow was confiscated in 1779 under the provisions of "An act concerning escheats and forfeitures from British subjects" (10 Hening 66–71), passed in that year by the Virginia legislature. See Richard Marshall Scott to Gov. Henry Lee, 10 Mar. 1794, *Calendar of Virginia State Papers*, 7:63–64. Of the confiscated property, one tract of seven to eight thousand acres in Prince William County remained unsold in the possession of the state, which was collecting rents from tenants on the land. It was once a part of a larger tract of 30,000 acres bought in 1689 from Lord Culpeper by several men, among them Robert Bristow's grandfather, another Robert Bristow. Bristow's heirs continued to press their claims until their suit came to trial in 1806, but the Prince William tract remained the property of the state until the 1830s, at which time it was finally broken up and sold. See GW's comments in his letter to George William Fairfax of 27 Feb. 1785. See also John Dandridge to GW, 6 Dec. 1788, n.1.

2. See Governor Harrison's response, 2 July 1784.

To Mary Bristow

Madam,   Mount Vernon (in Virginia) 15th June 1784.

Your letter & the duplicate of it—dated the 27th of last November with the petition to the Assembly of this State, only came to my hands the 10th Instant. By the following Post I transmitted them to the Governor, as the Legislature was then sitting at Richmond.[1]

What effect the application may have on that body, is not for me, at this time, to announce; it is to be feared however, as the Lands were involved in the act of general confiscation—previous to the preliminary articles of Peace—that unless there is something in the case more discriminating than Minority (which I understand is not an exclusion in the Law) you will receive very little redress; but from any thing I know at present of the Issue (if a determination has been had upon the subject) I can furnish you with no information on which to ground either hope, or fear. If it were the latter, it would afford cause to regret, that Minors, & innocent persons who have not aided or abetted the Contest Should have become sufferers by it. This however is but too often the case in Civil, as well as other Commotions.

I have not delayed a moment, Madam, to acknowledge, after they came to my hands, the receipt of your letter & petition, & shall have great pleasure in announcing the favorable issue of the latter, if the fact will warrant it. With great respect I have the honor to be—Madam Yr Most Hble Servt

Go: Washington

ALS, British Museum: Add. MSS 9828; LB, DLC:GW.
1. See GW to Benjamin Harrison, 14 June, and Harrison to GW, 2 July 1784.

From La Touche-Tréville

Sir,   Paris 15th June 1784

The marks of kindness with wc. you treated me when in America, are too dear to me to be forgotten. It is impossible to have known the Country rescued by your brave efforts, without a wish to become a Citizen of it—Convinced, that it is in such a Country only, that I can meet with happiness; I claim by the Marquiss La Fayette your friendship; who will aid me I hope in obtaining it, & inform you of my situation—Your influence will I hope, smooth all difficulties with Congress, & the State, in whose bosom I mean to fix myself.[1] I am Your Excellency's Hble & Obt Servt

Ct de la Touche

Translation, DLC:GW; ALS, DLC:GW. David Stuart's translation is no more than a brief but accurate summary of the original French version, which may be found in CD-ROM:GW.

Louis-René Magdelain Le Vassor, comte de La Touche-Tréville (1745–1804), was a French naval lieutenant when he conducted Lafayette to America in 1777 aboard the *Hermione*. He was given command of a ship in 1780 and cruised American waters under the orders of La Peyrouse until he was captured by the British in 1782. La Touche-Tréville was a vice admiral in the French navy at the time of his death.

1. GW wrote La Touche from Mount Vernon on 25 Nov. 1784 while Lafayette was visiting him: "The Marqs de la Fayette presented me with the honor of your favor of the 15th of June. Let me beseech you to be persuaded sir, that I derived great pleasure from its contents, & shall think it a very happy circumstance if fortune should ever place it in my power to facilitate your views of settlement in a country which your personal services have contributed to free from those shackles which were forging for its bondage—The acquisition of such a citizen cannot be more pleasing, than honorable to America; & in whatever I can be useful towards the fulfilment of your wishes, you have only to command my best services" (LB, DLC:GW).

From Robert Morris

Dear Sir   Philada June 15th 1784

Having no Intention of entering again into the details of Mercantile Business, on the receipt of your Letter of the 2d Inst. I applied to those with whom I am Connected here, but found no Vacancy in their Counting Houses. And as I had announced to Congress my determination to quit the office of Finance during their recess, I had in Consequence of an Arrangement which I hinted to you when here, determined to establish a House of Business at New York. This is now fixed under the management of Mr Wm Constable & Mr John Rucker, two Gentlemen that have been regularly bred to business, are capable, active and Industrious; they have both had much Experience in Commerce, and their Honor and Integrity is unquestionable.[1] Mr Rucker is going to Europe immediately, Mr Constable whom I think is personally known to you, sets down at New York and is now about to enter on the execution of his Business to him therefore I communicated your Letter and herewith you have a Copy of his Letter to me Containing the Terms on which he is willing to admit your Nephew into the Counting House. He wishes for a speedy Answer as many others will be applying the moment the House is publickly announced. As to the Terms I have nothing to say. With respect to the place I can only say that if one of my Sons was old enough I should embrace the opp[ortunit]y of placing him. Your letter was immediately sent to Genl Armand who only left this place for Baltimore (where he is to embark) yesterday—My Ice House is about 18 feet deep and 16 Square, the bottom is a Coarse Gravell & the Water which drains from the Ice soaks into it as fast as the Ice melts, this prevents the necessity of a Drain which if the bottom was a Clay or Stiff Loom would be necessary and for this reason the side of a Hill is preferred generally for digging an Ice House, as if needful a drain can easily be cut from the bottom of it, through the side of the Hill to let the Water run out. The Walls of my Ice House are built of Stone without Mortar (which is called a Dry Wall) untill within a foot and a half of the Surface of the Earth when Mortar was used from thence to the Surface to make the top more binding and Solid—When this wall was brought up even with the Surface of the Earth I stopped there and then dug the foundation for another Wall two foot back from the first, and about two feet deep, this done the foundation was laid so as to enclose the whole of the Walls built on the inside of the Hole where the Ice is put and on this foundation is built the Walls which appear above ground and in mine they are about ten foot high, On these the Roof is fixed, these Walls are very thick, built of Stone and Mortar, afterwards rough Cast on the outside. I nailed a Cieling of Boards under the Roof flat from Wall to Wall, and filled all the Space between that Cieling and the Shingling of the Roof with Straw, so that the Heat of the Sun Cannot possibly have any Effect.

In the Bottom of the Ice House I placed some Blocks of Wood about two foot long and on these I laid a plat form of Common fence Rails Close enough to hold the Ice & open enough to let the Water pass through; thus the Ice lays two foot from the gravel and of Course gives room for the Water to soak away gradually without being in contact with the Ice, which if it was for any time would waste it amazingly. The upper Floor is laid on Joists placed across the top of the Inner wall and for greater security I nailed a Cieling under those Joists and filled the Space between the Cieling & Floor with Straw.

The Door for entering this Ice House from the north, a Trap Door is made in the middle of the Floor through which the Ice is put in and taken out—I find it best to fill with Ice which as it is put in should be broke into small peices and pounded down with heavy Clubs or Battons such as Pavers use, if well beat it will after a while consolidate into one solid mass, and require to be cut out with a Chizell or Axe—I tryed Snow one year and lost it in June—The Ice keeps untill October or November and I beleive if the Hole was larger so as ⟨to ho⟩ld more it would keep untill Christmass, the closer it is packed the bett⟨er i⟩t keeps & I beleive if the Walls were lined with Straw between the Ice a⟨n⟩d stone it would preserve it much, the melting begins next the Walls and Continues round the Edge of the Body of Ice throughout the Season.[2] Mrs Morris joins me in our best Compliments to Mrs Washington & yourself and I beg to return Mrs Washington my thanks for her kind present which will be very useful to me next winter. I am Dear Sir Your most Obedt hble servt

Robt Morris

P.S. Thatch is the best covering for an Ice House.

LS, DLC:GW.
    1. See enclosure.
    2. GW rebuilt his icehouse at Mount Vernon along the lines that Morris suggests here. See the *Annual Report* (1939), pp. 30–31, of the Mount Vernon Ladies' Association of the Union. See also GW to Morris, 2 June.

Enclosure
Constable, Rucker, & Co. to Robert Morris

Dear Sir   New York 12th June 1784
   I return you the Generals letter on the Subject of his nephew. Tho' a troublesome Charge to have the Care of a young man of Twenty distant from his parents, from the Character drawn of Mr Washington and from his Desire to learn Business I will take him as Apprentice.[1]
   I presume he will not serve longer than Three years, less will not suffice the fee One Hundred Guineas. Rather than the young Gentleman should lodge at a Boarding House where he may be liable to improper Company, he may live with me at One Hundred Pounds ℔ Annum, but should his friends have any eligible place in View, I would prefer his being fixed elsewhere. I am with much personal Regard Your obedt hule Servt For Constable Rucker & Co.

(Signed) Wm Constable

Copy, DLC:GW.

1. See GW to Morris, 2 June.

Letter not found: from Jean de Neufville, 15 June 1784. On 8 Sept. 1785 GW wrote Jean de Neufville: "your letter of the 15th of June last year indicated. . . ."

From Duportail

dear general [16 June 1784]

I thank you for the kind letter you have honored me with by Count de laval[1]—I wish I Could Carry you the answer my self and accompany the marquis, but I am detained here—however I do not renounce to the pleasure of seeing your Exellency again and my american friends, even if we are not happy enough to receive you here—in two or three years I intend to pay a visit to america.

I am Really sorry to hear that they go so slow in establishing a good interior administration. but the good sense of the americans is so well known to me that I have no doubt of their doing it sooner or later. I will see it with great satisfaction. having so great esteem and attachment for them I Cannot but wish to see them deserve the Regard and friendship of the world—Chr de la luzerne wrote to me that he had some hopes of having your Company in his journey to niagara. it is a new Regret for me.

I do not hazard, dear general, to say you any thing of what draws the public attention here either in politic or phisic ⟨as⟩ *balloons, magnetism.*[2] the marquis will give you a better account of it than I Can do. so permit me to end this with the assurances of the true respect and sincere attachment with w[hic]h I have the honour to be your Exellency's the most humble and obedient servant

Duportail

permit me to present my best Respect to Mrs Washington.

ALS, DLC:GW.

1. GW's letter is dated 4 April 1784.

2. For "*balloons*," see Duportail to GW, 3 Mar. 1784, n.1; for "*magnetism*," see Friedrich Anton Mesmer to GW, 16 June 1784.

From Friedrich Anton Mesmer

Sir,   Paris 16th June—1784.

The Marquiss La Fayette proposes to make known in the territory of the United States, a discovery of much importance to mankind. Being the Author of the discovery, to make it as diffusive as possible, I have formed a Society, whose only business it will be, to derive from it all the expected advantages—It has been the desire of the Society, as well as mine, that the Marquiss should communicate it to you—It appeared to us, that the man who merited most of his fellow-men, should be interested in the fate of every revolution, wc. had for it's object, the good of humanity—I am with the admiration & respect that your virtues have ever inspired me with—Sir Your Obnt Servant

mesmer

Translation, DLC:GW; LS, DLC:GW. David Stuart translated the letter for GW. A transcript of the ALS in French is in CD-ROM:GW.

Forced to leave Vienna in 1778, Friedrich Anton Mesmer (1734–1815) settled in Paris, where he became very popular for his treatment of patients through what he called "animal magnetism." In 1784 after being denounced by other doctors as a charlatan, he was investigated by a French governmental commission, which included Benjamin Franklin among its members. Its report led to Mesmer's retirement in Versailles.

From Rochambeau

paris ce 16 juin 1784

je ne veux pas, mon cher general, laisser partir le marquis de la fayette Sans Le charger de mes plus tendres complimens pour vous, et de vous renouveller les assurances de L'attachement le plus eternel que je vous ay voüé. je voudrois bien qu'il eut le talent de vous persuader de venir nous voir, et que tout cela put S'arranger Sans Se brouiller avec madame Washington.

nous avons icy le roy de Suede prince fort aimable, mais je ne luy pardonne pourtant pas de ne pas Souffrir que Ses Suedois qui etoient colonels a notre armée, portent l'ordre de cincinnatus, Sous le pretexte qu'ils etoient cy devant si républicains qu'il ne veut point d'ordre qui le leur rapelle.[1]

nous construisons un port a cherbourg dont La p[remi]ere pile a eté fondée par un apareil de nouvelle invention qui a eu Le succes Le plus complet, Les anglois le voyent avec beaucoup d'inquietude, ils travaillent avec beaucoup de vigueur a leur marine. le gouvernement est Le maitre, mais l'opposition est toujours forte plus en qualité qu'en quantité des individus.

revenés avec Le marquis, mon cher general, et le chr de la Luzerne, et Soyés bien pesuadé que quoique vous ne Soyés pas roy, vous Serés aussi bien reçu qu'eux. mes respects, je vous prie a madame Washington. je suis avec Le plus respectueux et Le plus inviolable attachement mon cher general votre tres humble et trè obeissant Serviteur

Le cte de Rochambeau

ALS, DLC:GW.

1. The two Swedish officers who were considered eligible to wear the badge of the Society of the Cincinnati were the noblemen Curt Bogislas Louis Christophe, Count von Stedingk (1746–1837), and Count Hans Axel von Fersen. Stedingk served with d'Estaing and Fersen with Rochambeau. It was Gustavus III who refused to give them permission to accept membership in the society.

From Adrienne, Marquise de Lafayette

sir   Paris 18 June 1784

if I ever had some right, to your indulgence, it's certainly in this moment; in which I am in the very moment to separate me from mr De La fayette, who is going to see you. I must hope for this indulgence, because I am not in a situation to write tolerably, but I cannot help myself from thanking you, for the kind Letter which you honoured me with.[1] the care of our children obliges me to stay here, and I believe that I could not be so good a mother if their father had not intreated me for. at Least sir I recommend my self to you for obtaining of him, his word to take me with him, at his first journey to america. you see what is my confidence in your Goodness.

accept my hommages, sir, and present them for me, to mrs Washington could I have the pleasure to see you both soon in your own Country, or in the our, and to offer my self to you the assurance of the Sentiment of the warmest esteem and regard, with which I am sir, your most humble and very most obedient servant

noailles De la fayette

ALS, PHi: Gratz Collection; Sprague transcript, DLC:GW.

1. GW wrote the marquise on 4 April 1784.

From Anastasie Lafayette

Dear Washington,   Paris the 18th june 1784
I hope that papa whill come back Son here, I am verry sorry for the loss of him, but I am verry glade for you self. I wich you a werry good health and I am whith great respect, dear sir, your most obedient servent,

anastasie la fayette

ALS, NIC: Arthur H. and Mary M. Dean Collection.

From Patrick Henry

Dear Sir.   Richmond [Va.] June 19th 1784
Your Favor by the post I have received.[1] I entirely accord in the Sentiments you express concerning Mr Paine, & I trust we may see some fit Testimonial of the public Gratitude towards him.

Had I consulted only my own Inclination, I should long 'eer this have done myself the pleasure to write you. The Scene of public affairs you have so gloriously closed, did not admit Leisure for the Correspondence of a person retired to the Degree I have been. I now embrace this first oppertunity that is presented to me, to bid you a cordial & sincere Welcome to your native Country. May your Retirement be happy, as your public Services have been great & glorious! and may you long live to enjoy in common with your fellow Citizens, those Blessings of peace Liberty & Happiness, for which they are so much indebted to you—Will you be pleased to forgive these Effusions from the Heart of one, fully impressed with a Sense of your exalted merit, but who most probably, may never have the pleasure to testify in person the high Regard & Esteem with which I am Dear sir your most obedient & very humble Servant

P. Henry

ALS, PHi: Gratz Collection.
    1. See GW to Henry, 12 June.

To William Herbert

Dr Sir,   Mount Vernon June 19th 1784
With pleasure I received the invitation of the Master & Mem-

bers of Lodge No. 39, to dine with them on the Anniversary of St John the Baptist; if nothing unforeseen at present interfere's, I will have the honor of doing it. for the polite, & flattering terms in which you have expressed their wishes, you will please to accept my thanks.[1]

Your Servant (who has been detained on Acct of some business in wch I was engaged) brings the bundle you enquired after for my Brother.

I heard yesterday of a Ship destined for Liverpool, from your port. I pray you therefore to give the Letter for Sir Edwd Newenham, herewith sent, into the particular care of the Captn—to be put into the Post Office on his arrival in England.[2] With esteem & regd I am—Dr Sir Yr most Obedt Servt

Go: Washington

ALS, ViAlL.

Lodge 39 (later 22) of the Grand Order of Masons in Alexandria was organized in February 1783. William Herbert (1743–1818), who came to Virginia from Ireland before the Revolution, was chosen secretary at the lodge's first election on 21 Dec. 1783. Herbert was married to Sarah Carlyle Herbert, the daughter of the Alexandria merchant John Carlyle, and was himself a merchant in the town.

1. GW's invitation has not been found, but the following notice appeared above Herbert's name in the *Virginia Journal and Alexandria Advertiser,* 17 June: "The Brethren of Lodge No. 39 are requested to meet at their Lodge-Room at Eleven o'clock, on Thursday the 24th Instant, to celebrate the Anniversary of St. John the Baptist." GW attended the dinner held at Wise's tavern in Alexandria.

2. GW wrote Sir Edward Newenham on 10 June.

To Barbé-Marbois

Sir   Mount Vernon 20th June 1784

It was with very great pleasure I received from your own pen, an acct of the agreeable, & happy connection you were about to form with Miss Moore.[1]

Though you have given many proofs of your predeliction & attachment to this Country, yet this last may be considered not only as a great & tender one, but as the most pleasing & lasting tie of affection. The accomplishments of the lady, with her connections, cannot fail to make it so.

On this joyous occasion, accept I pray you, the congratulations of Mrs Washington and myself, who cannot fail to participate in whatever contributes to your felicity & that of your amiable Concort; with whom we both have the happiness of an acquaintance, and to whom & the family, we beg leave to present our Compliments.

With very great esteem & regard and an earnest desire to approve myself worthy of your friendship I have the honor to be Sir Yr Most obedt Hble Servt

Go: Washington

ALS, Arch. Aff. Etr., vols. 5–6; LB, DLC:GW.
  1. See Barbé-Marbois to GW, 8 June 1784.

To Francis Lightfoot Lee and Ralph Wormeley, Jr.

Gentlemen,   Mount Vernon 20th June 1784
Your favor of the 12th of March with its enclosures were long getting to hand; and arrived on the eve of a journey I was about to make to Philadelphia. My stay at that place, a round of Company since, and unavoidable business, must apologize for my silence 'till this time.

For the satisfaction of Mr Montagu, I sincerely wish I could give a more pleasing detail of the proceedings under the Power of Attorney (transmitted Colonels Tayloe & Mason, & myself) and the decree of the Chancery Court thereon, than what follows.

Colonel Mason declined acting, Colonel Tayloe accepted the trust, but the whole weight of the business fell upon me until I left this Country, and took command of the American Army. Every transaction antecedent to that epocha Mr Montagu and Colo. Mercer were duly informed of, by me—and had an acct of the Sales, and the circumstances attending them, transmitted.[1] To collect the amount was all, (or nearly all) that remained to be done; and this ought to have taken place in November following my departure in May, 1775.

In December of that year, I wrote a letter to Colo. Tayloe of which the following, so far as it related to that business, is a copy.[2]

Dear Sir,   Cambridge 11th Decr 1775.
In a letter which I have received from Mr Lund Washington dated the 24th Ulto, are these words[;]

I got a letter the other day from Mr Mercer wherein he says that Colo. Tayloe and himself think, that the money due upon Bond for the Sale of Colo. Mercers Estate, or at least all those Bonds which are due from persons in Maryland, or near this, should be paid to me; those in Frederick & Berkeley, &ca to him, as he was going up there; and that they would advertize the people of it.

It is sometime ago since I desired Mr Washington to deliver all the Bonds, and other papers in my possesion relative to the Sales of Colo. Mercers Estate, and the Power under which we acted, to you, in person, or to your written order, as I found it would not be in my power to return to Virginia this Fall; & consequently, that it would be impracticable for me to be of any further assistance to Colo. Mercer & his Mortgagees; of this he informs me he has advised you.

From henceforward then, the matter rests *wholly* with you; but as a friend to you; to Colo. Mercer; and even to Mr James Mercer, I must express my entire disapprobation of the latters having any share in the collection of the debts arising from the Sales of the Mortgaged Estates. . . .

But Sir, after having declared that I can no longer consider myself as Colo. Mercers Attorney, it is presumption to give my opinion of this matter so freely, and yet, as I wish a happy conclusion to it, I shall take the liberty of suggesting, whether it would not be better to appoint Colo. Francis Peyton Collector of the whole Debt? He was at the Sale—privy to every transaction attending it—acquainted with the People—Centrical—and would, I dare say (upon Mr Mercers application) undertake it for a small compensation.

As to Mr Lund Washington's collecting a part, it would be injurious to him, & to me, unless the money was brought to him, he therefore must be an improper person for this business, and I hope will not be thought of for it.

Finding that Colo. Tayloe had adopted no measures for collecting the money, and that the interest of *all* concerned would suffer very considerably by a further neglect of it, I wrote him the following letter.[3]

Dear Sir,   New York Augt 19th 1776

A Letter which I received from Mr Lund Washington by the last Post informs me, that no person (by your order) has yet applied for Colo. Mercers Bonds in his hands. That frequent tenders of money in discharge of them are made to him—and that he thinks, if it was agreeable to you & me, he could collect the debts which are due, without much difficulty, or neglect of my business.[4]

I have never had a wish that this business should be placed in his hands, not so much because I was fearful of its interfering with my business, as because I was unwilling to have it thought I had a mind to favor a relation or friend with the Commission—& therefore recommended Colo. Peyton—but as the latter has not entered upon the collection (from what cause I know not) I shall have no objection to Mr Lund Washington's doing it if you desire it, and he will do it upon as easy terms as Colo. Peyton, or any other proper person would undertake it for.

From the purport of these letters, it must evidently appear that I was anxious to have the business executed, though from my then engagements—my absence from Virginia and the little prospect I saw of rendering any further Service to Colo. Mercer or his Mortgagees, I had determined to withdraw myself from the trust. I called upon Colo. Tayloe in decided terms to fulfil what remained to be accomplished under it; which indeed was no more than to collect the Bonds, & make report to the Court for a final decree respecting the priority of Mortgages; if the sum arising from the Sales should have been found insufficient to discharge *All* of them.

Continuing invariably in this determination, I listened to no application which could renew my Agency in the business, until Colo. Tayloes[5] death rendered it indispensibly necessary for me to report to the Court my proceedings on, & previous to, the Sales; with the circumstances of the different parts of the Estate, which I had sold.

This I acordingly did sometime in the Fall of the year 1779— And afterwards, upon finding that the business had come to a total stand—and all parties were suffering by means of the depreciation of the paper Bills of credit, and that a final decision, or *some* direction of the Court on the premises, was indispensably necessary, I wrote the letter which follows to the Attorney General, Edmund Randolph Esqr.[6]

Dear Sir,   Morris Town 12th Apl 1780.
    I mean to address you on a subject in the line of your profession, & to request that you will undertake the business, & prosecute it to a final, and as speedy an issue as circumstances will admit.
    The business in which I would wish to employ you, is in a Suit in Chancery brought in the Honble the Genl Court by Richard Gravat & Mary Wroughton of London, & George Mercer—in whose behalf I act as an Attorney—against James & John Francis Mercer & Messrs Dick & Hunter. The enclosure No. 1 (the Copy of an Interlocutory

decree passed in the Suit in November 1773) will shew you on what footing the matter was then placed. and No. 2 (the copy of a report by me, dated the 15th of Decr 1774) the proceedings in consequence with respect to it, on my part.[7]

The papers concerning the Cause, antecedent to the Interlocutory decree, are lodged I presume in the Secretary's office, or will be found among your Fathers, as he was employed in it (there being none in my hands that I recollect) and to these I must refer you for obtaining such further & previous information of the nature of the dispute, & of the plaintiffs claims, as you may think it necessary to have; for at this distance of time my memory will not enable me to state them, with any degree of precision. I would mention however, that I believe the validity of the Mortgage, or deed from Colo. Mercer, either to Mr Gravat or Miss Wroughton—and of one executed by Mr James Mercer, under the idea of being his Attorney to Messrs Dick & Hunter, by way of counter-security for some engagements they had entered into on acct of John Mercer Esqr. his Father, who had charged a settlement made on his sons with the payment of a certain part of his debts & the preference of the respective claims of the parties, make a part of the material points in dispute. and the consideration of the above deed of settlement made by Mr John Mercer in 1779[8] to his sons George & James—their subsequent advances or engagements in consequence, and the accounts between them and his Estate, and themselves, another material part. You will observe that such accts are mentioned in the Interlocutory decree, and an adjustment of them directed by Auditors or Referees appointed for the purpose, by the Court.

This remains still to be done, and as it seems to be essential in order to a final decree (a matter for which I very sincerely wish) I must sollicit your good offices in expediting it as far as it may be in your power. In a point so interesting & intricate as this, and in which so much may depend—it may be necessary probably for Council to attend on the part of the pltffs: if it should, you will be pleased to act upon the occasion as circumstances shall require & permit, either by attending the referees yourself, or employing some Gentleman to do it in whose abilities and knowledge you can confide. To promote the Auditing of these Accts is the primary object of writing to you by the present conveyance, as I should be happy, if possible, to have the business brought to a conclusion at the ensuing Court, and as this appears to be the first step to put it in a proper train.

I shall take occasion in the course of a few Weeks to write you again, and will then (if I can obtain them) transmit you a particular acct of the Sales under the Interlocutory Decree constituting the total of the Sum mentioned in the copy of the report; Also a state of the transactions since, with respect to the business—of the Debts collected—of the application of the money—& what proportion still remains unpaid.

All this was done accordingly—but it was sometime before I was able to procure the necessary documents for the purpose.

I shall be very happy to hear from you, and to receive any instructions for the better conducting the business you may think proper to give me.

To this Letter I received the following answer.

Dear Sir,	Richmond Decr 1st 1780.

I omitted to answer your Excellys favor of the 12th of April last, from an expectation of hearing from you soon after on the subject of it—This hope I was led to entertain from an expression contained in it, and had therefore resolved to trouble you but once, by way of reply.

It is not perhaps the smallest evil, which Virginia has derived from the War, that the public papers & records, in being removed from the offices, exposed to danger, have undergone great diminution, and that even those parts, which survive the carelessness of Clerks, are not yet recovered from their confusion. This circumstance has hitherto rendered it difficult to lay our hands upon all the documents in Colo. Mercers case. The Clerk of the Chancery within whose province this business falls, is so much engaged in another line, that he is unable to make the necessary arrangements in his department of the Court. I do not question however, that I shall procure every thing, which may serve as a foundation for a final decree, as far as papers are concerned. But I fear, that the Sequestering Act forbids the Court of chancery to proceed in this cause. It provides generally, 'that all Suits, which were depending in any Court of Law or equity within this commonwealth, on the 12th day of April in the year of our Lord 1774 wherein British subjects alone are Plaintiffs, and any Citizen of this Commonwealth is a defendant, shall stand continued (unless abated by the death of either party) in the same state, in which they were at that time.' Now Mr Gravat, Miss Wroughton & Colo. Mercer come within the description of British subjects, and thereby have occasioned a suspension of the Suit. I will take the opinion of the Court at their next Session in April, whether an Interlocutory decree does not except your Situation from the restrictions of this Law. I should have mentioned, that my Father must have filed every paper in his posession, respecting this business, as not a trace is to be found of one in his Press. I am the rather too inclined to believe this, as all exhibits must have been before the Court at the time of the Interlocutory decree.[9]

After this intercourse by letter, I heard nothing more of the matter until Jany 1783, when I recd (under cover) the following Interlocutory decree—wch has been complied with on my part.

In the high Court of Chancery
Saturday the 9th of Novembr 1782.
John Francis Mercer——Plaintff
against
Richd Gravat, Mary Wroughton & Geo. Mercer
Defendants

On the motion of the Plaintiff by his Council, it appearing to the Court that his Excellency Genl Washington is the only Survivor of the Persons appointed to sell the Estate of the Defendt Geo. Mercer who acted therein under an Interlocutory decree of the former General Court betwn the said Richd Gravat &ca Plaintiffs agt the said John Francis Mercer and others defendts and the present public employ-ment of the said Genl Washington rendering it impracticable that he should continue the collection of the money produced by the said Sale, It is ordered that the Plaintiff be appointed receiver of the effects in the room of the said Genl Washington and that he do receive as well the Money which may remain in the said General Washingtons hands as the Bonds and other Securities which he may have for the outstanding Debts and collect the Money due thereupon; Provided that the said Plaintiff do execute a Bond with sufficient security to be approved of by the Court if sitting or any two Judges thereof in vaca-tion with condition for paying such money as may come to his hands in virtue hereof according to the future decree of the Court as well in this Suit as the Suit of the said Gravat and others Plaintiffs against the said John Francis Mercer and others defendts. A Copy teste—

John Beckley CHC.Ch.

Thus far is all that is necessary to relate of my own official transaction of this business—what follows is from information and report.

Sometime after my letter of the 19th of August to Colo. Tayloe, Mr Lund Washington received authority from that Gentleman (but of what kind, or date, I know not, never having seen it) to collect the debts—In consequence, he received in paper Bills of credit at different times (including interest £8622-16-9¼—£3480 of which was placed (I presume by Colo. Tay-loes order) in the Funds of the United States Novr 1777—and in Octr 1779 £5008-18-0 more was deposited in the State fund of Virginia—while £66-9-6 appear to have been employed in the payment of the Tax on money.

Thus were matters circumstanced when the Interlocutory decree took the Bonds & other Securities out of my hands— What has happened since I know not, nor can any person inform you, except the Gentleman who is now vested with collection of them—a copy of whose receipt to Mr Lund Washington is hereunto annex'd—to which might be added the amount of my purchase at the Sale—viz.—Four hundred and fifty one pounds ten shillings.[10]

What may be further necessary, on the part of Miss Wroughton & Mr Gravat, none can better determine than Mr Montagu—If it was in my power to render further assistance, I would, but it absolutely is not—Company—a thousand references of old matters (in the Military line)—Letters to answer— and other things, have put it entirely out of my power hitherto to give the smallest attention to the business which more immediately relate, and is interesting to myself—it would be folly in the extreme therefore (even if I did not wish for, & stand in need of relaxation) to attempt to manage that of others.

I have been more prolix in this recital, especially in some part of it perhaps, than you may conceive necessary; but it is my wish that the Agency I have had from first to last in the business may be fully understood by Mr Montagu from your report to him. I am Gentn Yr most obedt Hble Servt

Go: Washington

ALS (photocopy), DLC:GW.

In his statement concerning George Mercer's estate, 1 Feb. 1789, printed below, GW provides a cogent summary of his involvement in the sale of George Mercer's Virginia lands in November 1774 and its aftermath, and the editors' notes elaborate on and elucidate GW's summary of the complex affair. See also Edward Snickers to GW, 17 May 1784, and GW to John Francis Mercer, 8 July 1784, and notes. George Mercer (1733–1786), GW's boyhood companion and fellow officer in the Virginia Regiment, left Virginia for good in 1766 and was now living in England. After going there, he mortgaged much of his Virginia lands to Mary Wroughton of Bath and to Richard Gravatt and other London bankers; his brother James in Virginia, who held George's power of attorney, mortgaged some of the same lands to James Hunter and Charles Dick of Fredericksburg. In the summer of 1773 GW, John Tayloe, and George Mason received George Mercer's power of attorney to sell his land to satisfy his creditors. After Mason refused to serve, GW held sales first in Fauquier and Loudoun counties and then in Frederick County, in November 1774. The problem of the overlapping claims of those holding mortgages on Mercer's land was compounded from the start by the difficulty of collecting the money for the land and slaves bought at the sales and subsequently also by the outbreak of war between Britain and its colonies. This letter to Lee and Wormeley is GW's documentary record of what was done, and not done, about the Mercer estate during the war. For GW's correspondence before the war about the sale, see his letters to James Mercer of December 1773, 8 Jan., 28 Mar., 11 April, and 12, 26 Dec. 1774; to John Tayloe, 20 Aug., 10 Dec. 1773, 31 Oct., 30 Nov. 1774; to George Mercer, 5 April 1775; to Edward Montague, 5 April 1775; and James Mercer's letter to GW of 11 Aug. 1773. In addition to the letters that GW quotes here, letters written during the war alluding to George Mercer's sale include GW to James Mercer, 21 Feb. 1777, 14 Oct. 1779, 25 Feb. 1780; to John Tayloe, 12 Mar. 1776; to Lund Washington, 19 Aug. 1776, 17 Dec. 1778; from John Tayloe, 6 Feb. 1776; from Lund Washington, 8 April 1778; and from George Mercer, 28 Nov. 1778.

1. The only such letters known to have survived are those to George Mercer and to Edward Montague of 5 April 1775, but GW wrote James Mercer in December 1773 that he was writing a letter to Montague and on 26 Dec. 1774 he reported to James Mercer that he had written a "long one" to George Mercer about the sale. Montague was the attorney for those in England who held mortgages on George Mercer's Virginia property.

2. The ALS copy of this letter to John Tayloe, dated 10 Dec. 1775, is printed in *Papers, Revolutionary War Series*, 2 : 536–39, with notes. The portion of the letter we have not reprinted here contains GW's explanation of why he disapproves of putting in the hands of James Mercer the collection of moneys due from the George Mercer sale.

3. No other copy of this letter of 19 Aug. 1776 to John Tayloe has been found.

4. Lund Washington's letter has not been found, but see GW's letter of 19 Aug. 1776 to him.

5. John Tayloe died in 1779.

6. No other copy of this letter to Edmund Randolph of 12 April 1780 and of Randolph's reply of 1 Dec. 1780 has been found.

7. None of these documents has been found, but for GW's recollection of these court proceedings, see Statement concerning George Mercer's Estate, 1 Feb. 1789, nn.1 and 2.

8. GW wrote 1779 here, but it was a mistake: John Mercer, the father of George, James, and John Francis Mercer, died in 1768.

9. For GW's testimony in court proceedings in 1789 regarding his role in the sale of George Mercer's property, see note 1 in Statement concerning George Mercer's Estate, 1 Feb. 1789.

10. There is a draft of a letter from James Mercer to Lund Washington, dated 25 June 1783, in which Mercer accuses Lund Washington of "a very great overcharge in your Commission" for collecting payments. Mercer presents figures to back up his accusation, and there is also Mercer's summary account of his dealings with Lund Washington (ViHi: Mercer Papers). But see also Lund Washington's accounts, MdAN.

To I. Sailly

Sir,   Mt Vernon 20th June 1784

I have been favor'd with a letter from you dated at Philaa the 4th inst:—I cannot better answer the queries therein, than by sending one of my advertisements; which is not only descriptive of my Lands in the back parts of this Country, but fully explanatory of the terms upon which they are to be obtained. If any of these lands should suit you & such families as you might incline to bring from France & Germany, and the terms are convenient & agreeable, it would be pleasing to me, that I have it in my power to accommodate you and your friends.

I have no other untenanted Lands, than what are mentioned in the enclosed Advertisement, except about 1200 acres within five miles of Alexandria which is altogether in wood, & the soil not of the first quality. I am Sir &c.

G. Washington

LB, DLC:GW.

To Samuel Vaughan

Dr Sir   Mount Vernon 20th June 1784

I have had the honor of your favor of the 1st instant.[1] It gives me pain that you should think it necessary to apologize for the delay of the marble chimney piece. it gives me much more I confess, that you ever should have thought of depriving another house of it. If it is not too late, I wou'd yet pray you to countermand the order; if it is, I must view the act as a most striking instance of your politeness; & shall consider the fixture of it in my house, more as a monument of your friendship, than as a decoration of my room, (which, for want of workmen, remains in statu quo)—& value it accordingly.

I hope this will find you, Mrs Vaughan, & the young Ladies, in perfect health & spirits, and much pleased with the tour you were about to take when you wrote last: the next I hope, will be southwardly, where Mo[un]t Vernon will lay claim to the happiness of seeing you. With great esteem & regard I am Dr Sir, &c.

G. Washington

LB, DLC:GW.

1. Letter not found.

From Daniel Parker

Dear Sir   in Philadelphia June 21t 1784
I had the pleasure to receive your favor of the 28th Ulto respecting the Plate wrote for by my brother Dr Parker,[1] since his Arrival in England he wrote me that he should go to Birmingham on purpose to have that Order executed to his mind, & that he expected to Ship them in the Minerva for New York, since which the Minerva has arrived, but he had not return'd from Birmingham before that Ship left London, by the next Ship they will no doubt be sent, & I shall cause them to be forwarded to you, by the first safe Conveyance.[2] I am very truly, with great affection & respect, your Obedt Serv't

Danl Parker

ALS, DLC:GW.

1. Letter not found.

2. GW often used the merchant and army contractor Daniel Parker in 1783 to provide him with personal goods and services in New York (see especially his letters to Parker dated 18 June, 12, 18 Sept. 1783). Before leaving New York in late 1783, GW arranged with Parker to obtain for him from England a silver tea and coffee service engraved with the Washington coat of arms (see GW to Melancton Smith, 20 Dec. 1784). Not long after writing this letter, Parker fled the country to escape his creditors. It was not until December 1784 that GW received a letter from Melancton Smith, dated 27 Oct. 1784, enclosing an invoice from London of 28 April 1784 for GW's engraved silver service. It was headed: "Invoice of sundry Merchandize shipped by Joy & Hopkins ⅌ the Henry Capt. Rawson for New York consigned to Daniel Parker Esqr. for Acct and risque of Messrs Benjn & Daniel Parker" (DLC:GW). See Smith's letter of 27 Oct. and GW's response of 20 Dec. 1784, and notes.

To Edward Snickers

Dear Sir,   Mount Vernon June 25th 1784
Upon my return from Philada, I found your favor of the 17th of May at this place. For your kind intention to make me a visit, I thank you, & shall always be glad to see you when it is convenient. With respect to the other matters mentioned in your letter, all *that* business is now in the hands of the Honorable Mr John Mercer, by a decree of the high Court of Chancery of this State. I have nothing therefore to do with the settlement of accounts, transferences of Lands &ca. It is possible, tho' even of this I am not certain, that under the former power

of Attorney & decree of the Court, it may be necessary for me to sign the Deeds for such Lotts as were not conveyed at the time of sale; but before I do this, it must be certified to me by Mr Mercer, that the terms of sale are complied with, & that it is proper for me to do so. This, as I have long declined acting upon the affairs of Colo. Geo: Mercer & his Mortgages, is necessary for my own justification.[1]

Whatever Mr James Mercer may have promised respecting the payment of his Brother's Debt to you, I know not; but think there must have been a misconception with respect to my doing it; further than saying it was reasonable it shou'd be so & ought to be allowed. All I had to do in the matter, under the decree of the Court was to sell the Estate—the amount of which was to be subject to a future decree. If £12,500 was sufficient to discharge the several Mortgages upon it, the overplus undoubtedly would be subjected to the payment of all just claims against Colo. Mercer—but how this matter really is, I know not. The moment I found I could no longer discharge the duties of the power under which I acted, I wrote to Colo. Tayloe (the other Attorney) to take the business wholly upon himself as I should no longer act, or consider myself responsible for the management of the Trust.

I shall, as soon as I can make it convenient, divide the Lotts I bought at Mr Mercers sale, into proper sized Tenements, & let them for a term of years to those who will give the highest annual rent, when a day shall be fixed for that purpose.[2] if any persons should be making enquiries of you respecting them, you will be pleased to give them this information. I am Dr Sir &c.

G: Washington

LB, DLC:GW.

1. For Snickers's interest in the former property of George Mercer, see notes 1 and 3, Snickers to GW, 17 May. See also GW to Francis Lightfoot Lee and Ralph Wormeley, Jr., 20 June 1784.

2. For the land GW bought at George Mercer's sale in 1774, see particularly Snickers to GW, 17 May, n.1; GW to Francis Lightfoot Lee and Ralph Wormeley, Jr., 20 June, and notes; and GW to James Mercer, 18 Mar. 1789, n.4. The two lots on Four Mile Run were 378 acres and 790 acres.

From Edmund Randolph

Dear sir   Richmond [Va.] June 27. 1784.
The deed, of which I inclosed you the rough draught, has been duly executed and recorded. The register of the land-ofice has undertaken to have other patents made out in your name by the next week. I shall not however send them by the stage, which will be the first opportunity; but I shall defer it un-til the post.[1] I am dear sir with the sincerest respect & esteem yr obliged & affte humble serv.

Edm: Randolph

ALS, DLC:GW.
1. See GW to Randolph, 18 Mar., and Randolph to GW, 28 May 1784. Ran-dolph sent the patents on 17 July.

From Thomas Richardson

Sir   George Town [Md.] June 27. 1784
This day week I forwarded you a letter from Colo. Biddle covering Invoice of sundrys Shipd by him for your Accot by Colo. Hooes Brigg, this covers a Bill of 4 Mattrasses which he informs will be shipd by a Sloop belonging to Capt. De Gal-latheau that would sail soon.[1] I am with great Regard Your very hble Servt

Tho. Richardson

ALS, DLC:GW.
Thomas Richardson was a merchant in Georgetown, Md., with whom GW had been associated before the Revolution in a movement to extend the navi-gation of the Potomac above Georgetown and Alexandria.
1. Clement Biddle's letter has not been found, but the invoice in Rich-ardson's hand, dated at Philadelphia, 22 June, and signed by James White-head for Clement Biddle shows total charges of £49.10.2 for four "Ma-trasses," of which £37.11.2 went to Amelia Taylor for making the mattresses (DLC:GW). See GW to Richardson, 5 July 1784. Robert Townsend Hooe was a partner in the mercantile firm of Hooe & Harrison in Alexandria.

From George Augustine Washington

Honord Uncle   BridgeTown Barbadoes June 27th 84.
Information of The conveyance by which this goes for Phila-delphia being communicated to me so short a time previous to

the departure of it that I have time only to acquaint You of my arrival, which was not untill the 23d Inst.[1]—we had a tedious passage of 26 days from the Capes and I may truely say so fatigueing that I was scarcely able to support it—I arrived much exhausted and reduced and am sorry to say that the voyage had not the expected good effect in relieving my stomach; as on that I fear greatly depends the removeal of my other complaints— As yet I have not finally determind on any thing for my future government as I have not suffitiently inform'd my self what plan I had best adopt.

I visited the Physician Yesterday to whom Doctr Stuart was so good as to give me a Letter. He appears to be the worthy person He represented Him and by every one who I have heard speak of him, the most eminent of His profession—I had only an opportunity of a short conversation with Him, but tomorrow He accompanys me to wait on the Governor (who resides a little distance out of Town) when I shall be able to make every necessary inquiry[2]—I inform'd Him the plan I purposed when I left America of making transitory visits to the different Islands— which He disapproves of as the approaching season will render it very disagreeable and hazardous, and decidedly gives the preference to this in point of climate to any of the West Indie Islands, as many have tried them, and sufferd by the experiment—I saw a Letter from a Mr Henderson of Bladensburg, Maryland who came here for His health, He left this some time ago to pursue the plan I intended by visiting the Islands but mentions to have receiv'd great injury, I am thinking from the favorable accounts I have of the climate of Bermuda, from the People of this place who have frequented it, that should a good conveyance offer in the course of four or five weeks I shall be induced to visit it[3]—opportunities from this to America (owing to the restrictions, which are still continued,) are not so frequent as I could wish, but shall not omit writing by any that may offer—I sensibly feel the inexp[r]essible obligations I am under to You for Your unbounded goodness, and how I shall ever be able to acknowledge it I know not,[4] but should I be so happy as to [be] bless'd with a restoration of my health, nothing in the compass of my power shall ever be omitted—the parental affection I have ever experienced from Mrs Washington lays me under equal obligations and it will ever be my study to make Her amends. the hurry I am in will I hope excuse my not writing Her by this conveyance I wish to be rememberd to all inquiring friends in the most affectionate terms—may you experience the most perfect happiness this world is capable of affording, is the sincere wish of Your truely affectionate Nephew

Geo: A. Washington

The inclosed to my Father & Colo. Ball I will beg You to have forwarded.

ALS, PWacD: Sol Feinstone Collection, on deposit at PPAmP.

1. See GW to Charles Washington, 28 Feb. 1784, and notes.

2. The governor of Barbados, David Parry, wrote GW on 18 July 1784 about George Augustine Washington's visit. The Government House was on the eastern outskirts of Bridgetown, the principal town and port of Barbados.

3. See George Augustine Washington to GW, 25 July 1784.

4. See note 1.

Letter not found: to Thomas Richardson, 28–29 June 1784. On 5 July GW wrote to him: "This day se'night a letter for you covering Bank Notes for 150 Dollars was lodged in the hands of Mr Watson." On 10 July Richardson wrote: "Your favos. of 29th June & 5th Instant came to hand."

From Jacob Read

Sir   Annapolis [Md.] 29th June 1784

Mr Vidler the Architect of whom I had the honour to inform you when at Mount Vernon is the bearer of the present Letter. his Visit to Virginia is to inform himself from his own Observation of the best place in which he Can settle and exercise his trade. I find he has sent to Europe for a Considerable Number of hands and will be soon able to undertake any piece of Work that may offer.

Mr Vidler expressed a great desire to See a General who has made so great a Figure and in so few Years led his Country men to Freedom, and Will be particularly happy if he Can assist in perfecting any of your plans for improving or beautifying Mount Vernon, at his request I do myself the pleasure to address this Letter to you and to assure you that Capt. Stuart with whom he Came to this Country mentions him as a man of the most modest and respectful deportment and as Skilful in his business, he appears to be a man of Sense and is well recommended.[1]

I request the favour of you Sir to present my most respectful Compliments to Mrs Washington and Miss Basset & to inform the latter that I delivered her Commands Safe in Annapolis.

The Committee of the States were to have Assembled on the 26th but as yet we have but Six States represented, today we hope to be able to proceed to business as several members are expected—Mr Wilson of Philadelphia & the Atty Genl of Pensylvania Came to town Yesterday on the business of Wyoming but there being no Court and the other party not appearing they took wing again last night[2]—They inform that the Trial of Monsr De longchamp was over & that he had been found Guilty by the Jury on Three distinct Charges in an Indictment but his Sentence is not known. Yesterday was the day on which the Court had ordered him to be brought up for Judgement. The Minister of France is gone, and Monsr de Marbois Certainly Married[3]—I ask pardon for this intrusion on your time and am with the most perfect esteem and regard Sir Your Most Obedient and most obliged Servt

Jacob Read

ALS, DLC:GW.

1. Edward Vidler delayed coming to Mount Vernon until April 1785, when GW wrote in his diary: "A Mr. Vidler, to whom I had written (an Undertaker at Annapolis) came here and opened the cases wch. contained my Marble chimney piece—but for want of Workmen could not undertake to finish my New room" (*Diaries*, 4:114). The "Marble chimney piece" was sent to him by Samuel Vaughan (see GW to Samuel Vaughan, 8 April, 20 June 1784, and GW to Benjamin Vaughan and to Samuel Vaughan, 5 Feb. 1785).

2. In November 1782 James Wilson and William Bradford, Jr. (1755–1795), the attorney general of Pennsylvania, appeared before a congressionally constituted commission, or court, to defend Pennsylvania's claims to the Wyoming Valley against the claims advanced by the state of Connecticut. The commissioners ruled that Connecticut had no governing rights to the disputed territory and left it to the state of Pennsylvania to resolve the conflicting claims of private owners. On 23 Jan. 1784, in answer to a petition of Connecticut settlers in the Wyoming Valley, Congress asked the states of Pennsylvania and Connecticut to appear before its committee of states so that "the private right of soil within" the Wyoming territory could be determined (*JCC*, 26:45). Bradford, representing Pennsylvania, announced his arrival in Annapolis on 28 June, but when the committee of states met on 5 July, no one from Connecticut appeared (see DNA:PCC, item 49, and *JCC*, 27:567). The final resolution to the Wyoming dispute came on 26 May 1786 when Congress

resolved that Connecticut should relinquish all claims to lands in Pennsylvania in exchange for Ohio lands, known as the Western Reserve (see *JCC*, 30:310–11, 31:654–5).

3. Thomas Jefferson wrote Charles Thomson on 21 May in Philadelphia: "The principal interesting occurence here is a very daring insult committed on Mr. Marbois by a Frenchman who calls himself the Chevalr. [Charles-Julien] de Longchamps, but is in fact the nephew of the Minister's steward's wife. He obliged him in his own defence to box in the streets like a porter" (Boyd, *Jefferson Papers*, 7:281–82). The fight between the two Frenchmen took place on 19 May, the day after GW left Philadelphia. On 12 July Longchamps was fined and sentenced to twenty one months in jail by the Pennsylvania Supreme Court. The Longchamps-Marbois affair became a cause célèbre when the French government insisted that Longchamps be returned to France to be tried for infringing on the rights of a French diplomat. Barbé-Marbois did not mention the affair when he wrote GW on 8 June of his engagement to Elizabeth Moore of Philadelphia.

To Clement Biddle

Dear Sir,   Mount Vernon June 30th 1784

Your favor of the 10th Instt covering an Invoice of Goods shipped by the Betsey Captn Broadhurst is come safe to hand—the Vessel is also arrived at Alexandria; and I shall send up this day for the things—I wish the Mattrasses had *all* been among them as the Season is wasting fast in which they are most useful.[1]

I have perused the accts you have delivered in at sundry times and find the debits & credits to stand thus. If they are not all brought to view you will please to note it, and rectify the mistake.[2]

Tomorrow, in the hands of some person in Alexandria, I will deposit for the use of Mr Richardson One hundred and fifty dollars on your Acct—and I pray you to pay Mr Claypoole agreeably to the contents of my letter to him, wch is under cover with this, and left open for your perusal—as also the German Printer if he ever inserted the Advertisement respecting my Western Lands, and for the one now enclosed for *him*, to be done in the manner requested of Mr Claypoole. Whatever these Sums, with the price of the Mattrasses, may over run the deposit I am about to make for Mr Richardson I will pay to you, on your order upon demand.[3]

As the Price of the Hinges appear to me to be very high,

and I am not in immediate want of them (having been disappointed of workmen) I will postpone for the *present* employing the man Mr Rakestraw has found—If I should hereafter be under the necessity of giving such prices I will attend to the direction in your letter; for which I am obliged, both to you & Mr Rakestraw.[4]

I recollect, sometime in the course of last year to have begged you to purchase for me from the redemptioners or Indented (Germans or Irish) a House joiner and Bricklayer. Many I have seen Advertised for Sale in Philadelphia of late—should this happen again I would pray you attention to my former request—It might be well to have them examined by skilful workmen, for many will call themselves Bricklayers who have only been mortar makers—and others joiners who know little of the Trade—I would prefer elderly men to very young ones, if there is choice[5]—and their being sent by water (round) to any other conveyance—The Cost & expence of these if you should make a purchase shall be paid as soon as it is made known to Dr Sir Yr most obedt Servt

Go: Washington

P.S. I shall be obliged to you for sending me 70 yds of gilded Border for papered Rooms (of the kind you shewed me when I was in Phildelpa)—That which is most light and Airy I should prefer—I do not [know] whether it is usual to fasten it on with Brads or Glew—if the former I must beg that as many may be sent as will answer the purpose.

G.W.

ALS, PHi: Washington-Biddle Correspondence; LB, DLC:GW.

1. See Thomas Richardson to GW, 27 June 1784.

2. Biddle's account with GW showed the following charges for goods supplied by Biddle in 1783 and 1784:

1783

July 23	Ticklenburgh & Blankts pr Bill	£204.13.0
	Paid Carriage of Do	3.15.
Octr	Sundries pr Bills	201.19.7
	Stays Mrs L. Washington	3.15.
	Commisn 2½ prCt	10. 7.
		£424. 9.7

1784

Decr 19	Bringhurst Wheels &ca	15. 2.
March	Coffee, Sieves, & Lace	14.12.6

May	Chevr de la Luzerne	30.
	Cundries pr Cap. Hayden	44. 7.4½
June 9	Goods pr the Betsey. Broadhurst	50.18.7
		£579.10.0½

On the credit side of the account, GW notes having given Biddle £450 in 1783 and in 1784: "May 5 Cash sent you in a letter to pay the Chevr de la Luzerne &ca 250 dollrs," or £93.15, leaving a "Balle due CB" of £35.15.0½.

3. GW records in his cash accounts having sent on 29 June 150 dollars (£45) to Thomas Richardson "for the use of Colo. Biddle" (Ledger B, 199). The letter to David C. Claypoole has not been found, but see GW to Biddle, 1 Feb. 1785, nn.2, 3, 4. For the advertisement, see enclosure, GW to Witherspoon, 10 Mar. 1784.

4. In 1787 Joseph Rakestraw made the top of the cupola and the weather vane for the mansion at Mount Vernon. See GW to Rakestraw, 20 July 1787, and GW to Biddle, 7 Aug. 1787.

5. GW wrote Biddle on 4 Aug. 1784 to notify him that he no longer had a need for the workmen.

From Lee Massey

Dear Sir,   Occoquan [Va.] June 30th 1784.

I write to apologize for my not having waited on you since your Return from the War, and to assure you that it is not owing, either to want of Respect & Affection for the private Citizen, or Gratitude to the General, but to a Comparison of the Importance of my Visit with that of the Settlement of your Affairs both publick & private, of which you doubtless have a great deal on your hands, and, if I am rightly informed respecting the State of visiting of late at Mt Vernon, very little Time to despatch it in. My Unwillingness to encrease this Nuisance is my sole Reason for sparing you so long, and depriving myself of the Pleasure of seeing you after an Absence of eight Years, employed in every kind of Danger & Toil for the Benefit of me & my Descendants; the Obligation of which I most heartily acknowledge, and do by these Presents thank you for it in behalf of myself and my Heirs for ever. I shall wait on you and do this personally, when I can think you at leisure for the Entertainment of idle Visitants. In the mean time, as I know you do not estimate your Friends by the Quantity of your Provision they devour, I shall hope that you will admit of this Excuse, and take the Will for the Deed. I beg you to believe that I sincerely rejoice at your safe Return, and that there is not a Man living

more concerned for yr Happiness than myself. I am very respectfully, Dear Sir, Yr most obedt humble Servant

Lee Massey

ALS, DLC:GW.
    Lee Massey (1732–1814) began his adult life as a lawyer in Fairfax County,
but in 1767 he succeeded the Rev. Charles Green as rector of Truro Parish.
He lived in Occoquan, Virginia.

To Robert Morris

Dear Sir,   Mount Vernon 30th June 1784

Your favor of the 15th did not reach my hands 'till the 27th. I
will delay no time in communicating the contents of Mr Constable's letter to my brother; but as he lives at the distance of
near an hundred miles from me, & out of the Post road, it may
be some time before I can obtain his answer.

This being the case, as it may be some disadvantage to Mr
Constable to be held in suspence—& as the application to you,
originated with me under a mistaken idea of your intention, respecting the manner of carrying on business; I think I can venture to desire that Mr Constable may not suffer himself to
forego another choice on account of my Nephew, or to sustain
the least inconvenience from waiting the answer of my brother.[1]

When my brother talked of sending his youngest son to Philada, I advised the application I made to you—I recollected,
that either Mr Vanberkel or Mr Vaughan had told me that he
had fixed one of his sons in your Counting-house—your extensive correspondence & knowledge in trade I conceived might
introduce my Nephew (if, during the course of his appren-
ticeship, he should display a genious for it, & assiduity,) advan-
tageously into business, & that in so doing your own plans
might be subserved.[2] How far his engaging with Mr Constable
will open prospects of this nature, is not for me to determine,
tho' I could wish his Father may decide for the best, who is a
tender parent—has the welfare of his children much at heart,
& entertains sanguine hopes of his Son, whose inclination
prompts him to move on the mercantile stage.

I am very much obliged by the description of your Ice-house;
I will build one this summer or Fall, agreeably thereto, but
upon a scale some thing larger, if workmen can be obtained.

Mrs Washington joins me in affectionate compliments to Mrs Morris & yourself, whom we should be exceedingly happy to see here, whenever it can be made convenient to you both. With sincere esteem & regard I am Dr Sir &c.

G: Washington

LB, DLC:GW; partially burned AL, sold by Parke-Bernet Galleries, catalog 1190, item 1132, 30–31 Oct. 1950.

1. William Constable's letter to Morris of 12 June 1784 is printed as an enclosure in Morris's letter of 15 June.

2. Pieter Johan van Berckel came as minister to the United States from the Netherlands in 1783. His son, named Franco Petrus, succeeded him as minister in 1788. Samuel Vaughan had set himself up with his son John as a merchant in the city. Vaughan had other sons as well.

To John Augustine Washington

Dear Brother,   Mount Vernon June 30th 1784

On Sunday last, I received an answer from Mr Morris to the letter I wrote him whilst you were here. Enclosed is an extract of it with a copy of the letter referred to[1]—As there appears to be ⟨*mutilated*⟩ a diffe ⟨*mutilated*⟩ Whether the engaging ⟨*mutilated*⟩ Mr Morris at Second hand, will be attended with all the advantages I contemplated—whether new York would be equally as agreeable to you, and my Nephew, as Philadelphia— and whether the terms of Mr Constable are usual and pleasing, is with you to determine. and the sooner you can do this, the better.

Had Mr Morris carried on business in the manner I expected, and as he formerly did, the advantage of entering your Son with him, most undoubtedly would have been great because his Mercantile Knowledge & connections greatly exceed that of any other Person's upon this Continent and are perhaps equal to what can be found in any other Quarter. consequently many doors might open to him, wch to others w⟨oul⟩d hardly be known, through wch knowledge and profit might be acquired. Mr Constables *Person* is known to me, but to his character I am a stranger, & therefore suppose it to be such as Mr Morris has delineated—the nature & extent of the commerce he is about to carry on from New York, and how far the knowledge obtained of it, would comport with that kind of trade which is carried on from this Country where it is to be presumed Corbin would ultimately take his Stand in the Commercial theatre, are matters worthy of consideration. The ⟨*mutilated*⟩ in that particular branch which it is most likely for him to move in is not to be preferred? If this is granted, and we know that the Trade of this State and Maryland is & must be, similar.

There is a Gentleman there, also connected with Mr Morris in Trade, at Baltimore who I *know* to be as worthy a man in *every* point of view as any that lives; but whether he is moving upon a large scale or a small one; whether he has an opening that would admit a youth, and upon what terms, I am ignorant. The Gentleman I mean is Lieutt Colo. Tilghman, who was in my family as an Aide de Camp & Secretary the whole War; & in the mercantile line many years before it. If he can oblige me, with any kind of convenience to himself, I am sure he would; & if you approve it, & I should upon enquiry find he is not in a piddling way (which can scarcely be presumed from his connection with Mr Morris) I would write to him on the Subject & shall be sure of a candid decision.[2]

My family, at present, are all well but our intermittant Months are not yet arrived.[3] I have come to a determination if not prevented by unforeseen events, to make a visit to my Lands in the western waters this Fall; & for that purpose shall leave home the first of September. Many are hinting their wishes, and others making direct applications to be of the party, but as I neither ⟨*mutilated*⟩ others to follow me in these pursuits, nor satisfaction to myself to be in company with those who would soon get tired & embarass my movements besides rendering them inconvenient. Thus much in general—but if Bushrod's health will permit, & it does not interfere with his studies, or plan of Settlement for the practice of the Law, I would take him with me with pleasure—Only Doctr Craik besides, will go with me. He would require only a Servant & a Blanket or two—every thing else I shall provide unless he should chuse to carry a Gun for his amusement as he would, more than probably—see abundance of Game.

Mrs Washington & all here join me in best wishes for the health of yourself and my Sister & other connections I am Dr Sr Yr most Obedt Brother

Go: Washington

ALS, DLC:GW. The manuscript is faded and mutilated; for its transcription heavy reliance has been placed on the printed version in Fitzpatrick, *Writings of Washington*, 27:431–33.

On this day GW wrote to William Hunter, Jr. (1731–1792), a Scottish merchant in Alexandria: "Genl Washington presents his Complimts to Mr Hunter, and begs the favor of him to forward a letter herewith sent, to his Brother in Westmoreland. It is a letter of some consequence and requires (if it could be obtained) dispatch" (AL, DNGS).

1. See Robert Morris to GW, 15 June 1784, and enclosure.

2. See John Augustine Washington's response, 8 July 1784, and GW's letter to Tench Tilghman of 14 July 1784. Tilghman, who was Robert Morris's business associate in Baltimore, also served as chief agent for GW in GW's business dealings in Baltimore and environs until his death in 1786.

3. The "intermittant months" were those of the late summer and early fall when many Virginians suffered attacks of malaria.

From Benjamin Harrison

My Dear Sir   Rich[mon]d [Va.] July 2d 1784.

The great impositions that have been practiced on the country in the settlement of the depreciation accts of the soldiers, and the number of forged certificates of service that have been produced to the auditors and warrants obtain'd on them induced me to request the attention of the assembly to the subject; in consequence of which they have directed a revision of them, and in order to a full detection of what has pass'd and to prevent the like evil in future they have requested me to call on the board of war at Philadelphia for the pay or muster rolls of the virginia line if they can be spared, and if not send me a copy of them.[1] I take the liberty to enclose you a copy of my letter and shall take it as a great favor if you will look over it, and if you think it will be necessary to add any thing to it that you will be so obliging as to write to him or any other person that can throw light on the subject.[2] Two officers are appointed to do this business, and tho' they are clever yet they may stand in need of advice how to proceed. you will oblige me much if you will favor me with your opinion on the subject.[3]

I recd your favor enclosing the petition & letters of the guardians of young Bristow which I immediately laid before the assembly;[4] they have done nothing on them nor will they till they take up the subject generally, which I think is right, but I am afraid when they do enter on it the distresses of the country will put it out of their power to do that Justice to the claimants they may expect. It was a horrid law, and the manner of executing it was worse than the law itself, for before the money produced by it was paid into the Treasury it was in no instance worth half what it was at the time of the sales, and in many instances it was not worth the tenth part.[5] I am Dr Sir with perfect esteem your mo. affect. and obedient Humble servant

Benja. Harrison

ALS, DLC:GW.

1. On 26 June 1784 the Virginia house of delegates resolved: "That the Executive be empowered and directed to appoint two commissioners, for the purpose of examining into all impositions which have happened in the settlement of accounts of the officers and soldiers of the Virginia line on continental or State establishments, including the navy, with the auditors, for arrearages of pay and depreciation; . . . and that a report of all proceedings herein be made to the next session of Assembly" (*House of Delegates Journal, 1781–1785*, 26 June 1784).

2. In the enclosed copy of his letter to Henry Knox, dated 2 July, Harrison wrote: "The number of forged soldiers certificates of service that have been received by the Auditors of publick accounts for this state, and for which settlements for depreciation have been made and warrants for payment obtained, is so great and amounts to such a sum, that the Legislature have thought it advisable to have a revision of them, and that it may answer the intended purpose of detection have requested me to call on your board for the necessary papers that may be wanted for a full investigation of the subject; I have therefore to request you to forward me by the Stage as soon as possible, the muster rolls of all the Virginia Regiments on continental establishment from the first of January 1777 to the last of December 1781, also those of the two State Regiments whilst in continental service; the first Regiment of Artillery, the first & third Regiments of Cavalry & such parts of Lees and Armands Legions, Hazens regt, And other corps as have been credited to this state" (DLC:GW).

3. On 1 July Harrison appointed as commissioners Samuel Hawes, Jr., who at the end of the war was a lieutenant colonel in the 5th Virginia Regiment, and Thomas Meriwether, who was major of the 1st Virginia Regiment from 1778 to 1781. See note 1. On 2 July the commissioners asked "to be supplied with the Muster Rolls of the Virginia Line on Continental Estab'nt and for those of all Corps that have been credited to Virginia, from Jan'y, 1777 to Dec: 1781" (*Calendar of Virginia State Papers*, 3:596).

4. See GW to Harrison, 14 June, and GW to Mary Bristow, 15 June 1784, and notes.

5. The act under which Richard Bristow's property was confiscated is cited in GW to Harrison, 14 June, n.1.

From James Madison

Dear Sir   Richmond [Va.] July 2d 1784.

The sanction given by your favor of the 12th inst. to my desire of remunerating the genius which produced *Common Sense*, led to a trial for the purpose. The gift first proposed was a moiety of the tract on the Eastern Shore, known by the name of "the Secretary's land." The easy reception it found induced the friends of the measure to add the other moity to the proposition, which would have raised the market value of the donation to about £4000 or upwards, though it would not probably have commanded a rent of more than £100 per annum. In this form the bill passed through two readings. The third reading proved that the tide had suddenly changed, for the bill was thrown out by a large majority. An attempt was next made to sell the land in question and apply £2000 of the money to the purchase of a Farm for Mr Paine. This was lost by a single voice.[1] Whether a greater disposition to reward patriotic and distinguished exertions of genius will be found on any succeeding occasion is not for me to predetermine. Should it finally appear that the merits of the Man, whose writings have so much contributed to infuse & foster the Spirit of Independence in the people of America, are unable to inspire them with a just beneficence: the world, it is to be feared, will give us as little credit for our policy as for our gratitude in this particular. The wish of Mr Paine to be provided for by separate acts of the States, rather than by Congress, is I think a natural and just one. In the latter case it might be construed into the wages of a mercenary writer, in the former it would look like the returns of gratitude for voluntary services. Upon the same principle the mode wished by Mr Paine, ought to be preferred by the States themselves.[2] I beg the favor of you to present my respectful compliments to Mrs Washington and to be assured that I am with the profoundest respect & sincerest regard your Obedt & humble servant

J. Madison Jr.

ALS, DLC:GW; copy, in Madison's hand, DLC: Madison Papers.

1. For further details of the attempts of Madison and Patrick Henry on 28 and 30 June to have the Virginia legislature bestow land on Thomas Paine, see the notes in "Bill to Aid Thomas Paine," 28 June 1784, in Rutland and Rachal, *Madison Papers*, 8:88–89. See also note 2. The "Secretary's Land" was

500 acres on King's Creek Northampton County, the income from which, before the Revolution, had gone to the secretary of the colony of Virginia.

2. Fearing that GW had not received this letter, Madison wrote him again from Orange County, Va., on 12 Aug. conveying much the same information but in different words: "I had the honor of receiving your favor of the 12th of June during my attendance in the Legislature and of answering it a few days, before I left Richmond. Since my return home I have been informed that the gentleman into whose hands my answer was put has mislaid or lost it, and that I cannot rely on its ever finding its way to you. I have therefore to repeat, Sir, that the sanction which your judgment gave to the propriety of rewarding the literary Services of Mr Payne led to an attempt in the House of Delegates for that purpose. The proposition first made was that he should be invested with a moity of a tract of public land known by the name of the Secretary's lying on the Eastern Shore. The kind reception given to this proposition induced some gentleman to urge that the whole tract containing about 500 acres might be included in the donation as more becoming the dignity of the State, and not exceeding the merits of the object. The proposition thus enlarged, passed through two readings without apprehension on the part of its friends. On the third a sudden attack grounded on considerations of economy and suggestions unfavorable to Mr Payne, threw the bill out of the house. The next idea proposed was that the land in question should be sold and £2000 of the proceeds allotted to Mr Payne to be laid out in the purchase of a Farm if he should think fit. This was lost by a single vote. Whether a succeeding Session may resume the matter and view it in a different light, is not for me to say. Should exertions of genius which have been every where admired, and in America unanimously acknowledged, not save the author from indigence and distress, the loss of national character will hardly be balanced by the savings at the Treasury" (DLC: Madison Papers).

From Edmund Randolph

Dear sir   Richmond [Va.] July 3. 1784.
The register is now engaged in renewing your grants. They would have been prepared for this post, if the form had been the same, as that, which has been hitherto practised. I trust, that there is little doubt of their being forwarded by the next.[1] I am Dear sir yr obliged & affte friend

Edm: Randolph

ALS, MH: Jared Sparks Collection.

1. The correspondence between Randolph and GW regarding the grants to GW (made by Governor Dunmore on 15 Dec. 1772) of 10,900 acres on the Great Kanawha in Fincastle County and of 4,395 acres, 2,448 acres, and 2,314 acres on the Ohio in Botetourt County begins with Randolph's letter of 19 Feb. 1784 and GW's response of 18 March. Four new deeds, signed by Gov.

Benjamin Harrison, were dated 6 July 1784. Copies of deeds for the tracts of 4,395 acres and 2,448 acres in Botetourt County are in DLC:GW. The deed for the 10,900 acres on the Great Kanawha was advertised for sale in April 1891 by Thomas Birch's Sons, catalog 663, item 181.

To John Rumney, Jr.

Mount Vernon July 3d 1784.

General Washington presents his compliments to Mr Rumney—would esteem it as a particular favor if Mr Rumney would make the following enquiries as soon as convenient after his arrival in England, & communicate the result of them by the Packet or any other safe & speedy coveyance to this Country. 1st The terms upon which the best kind of whitehaven Flag Stone, black & white in equal quantities, could be delivered at the Generals landing or at the Port of Alexanda by the superficial foot—with the freight & every other incidental charge included—The Stone to be 2½ inches thick, or there abouts, & exactly a foot square each kind (i.e. black & white)—to have a well polished face & good joints, so as that a neat floor may be made for the Colonade in the front of his house—Stone thus prepared must be carefully packed, otherwise the face & edges would be damaged—the expence of which should also be taken into the accot—2d Upon what terms the common Irish marble, (black & white if to be had, & of the same dimensions) could be had, delivered as above. 3d As the General has been informed of a very cheap kind of marble, good in quality wch is to be had at, or in the Neighbourhood of Ostend in France, he would thank Mr Rumney, if it should fall in his way, to institute the same enquiry respecting this also, & give information thereon.[1]

On the report of Mr Rumney, the General will take his ultimate determination, for which reason he prays him to be precise. The Piazza or colonade, for which this Stone is wanted as for the purpose of a floor, is ninety two feet eight inches, by twelve feet 8 inches, within the border or margin, which surrounds it. Over & above this quantity if the Flag is cheap, or a cheaper kind of hard stone could be had, he would get as much as would lay the floors of the circular Colonades at the end Wings of the House, each of which in length at the outer curve is 38 feet, by 7 feet 2 inches in breadth within the margin.

The General being in want of a House Joiner & Bricklayer, who understand their respective trades perfectly, would thank Mr Rumney for enquiring into the terms upon which such workmen could be engaged for two or three years (the time of service to commence from their arrival at Alexandria)—a less term than *two* years would not answer, because foreigners generally have a seasoning, which with interruptions too frequent, wastes the greater part of the first year, more to the disadvantage of the hirer, than the hired. Bed, board & tools to be found by the Employer—cloaths by the Employed. If two men of the above Trades, and of orderly & quiet deportment could be obtained for twenty five, or even thirty pounds sterling pr annum each (estimating Dollars at 4/6) the General, rather than encounter delay, would be obliged to Mr Rumney for entering into proper articles of agreement on his behalf with them, & for sending them out by the Vessel to this port.[2]

LB, DLC:GW. This memorandum written for GW was copied in his letter book.

John Rumney, Jr. (1746–1808), was a partner in the mercantile firm of Robinson, Sanderson, & Rumney of Whitehaven, England. The firm at this time had a store in Alexandria on Fairfax Street.

1. The correspondence regarding the English flagstones with which GW in the summer of 1786 covered the floor of the gallery, or piazza, across the front at Mount Vernon, includes Rumney to GW, 8 Sept. 1784, 9 Feb., 3 July, 5 Sept. 1785, 16 April 1786; Robinson, Sanderson, & Rumney to GW, 28 Jan. 1786; and GW to Rumney, 22 June, 18 Nov. 1785, and 15 May, 5 June 1786. GW received the flagstones in April 1786. See *Diaries*, 4:313.

2. For Rumney's securing the joiner Matthew Baldridge for GW, see Rumney to GW, 9 Feb. 1785, and GW to Rumney, 22 June 1785.

From Henry Lee

Dear Sir   Leesylvania [Va.] July 4th 1784

It is with Particular Pleasure I communicate to you that the General Assembly have Appointed a Committee of both Houses, to present to you an Address Expressive of the high Sense they entertain of your Singular Services and Merits, in the late Glorious revolution. a Copy of Which the Committee have directed me to inclose and to Announce to your Excellency, their intention of Waiting upon you for this Purpose on the 15th Instant.[1] I am happy in this Opportunity of Expressing the great respect and esteem with which, I have the honour to be your Excellencys Most Obt humble Servt

Henry Lee

ALS, DLC:GW.

Col. Henry Lee (1729–1787) of Leesylvania was senator for Fairfax and Prince William counties in the Virginia legislature at this time.

1. See Virginia General Assembly and George Washington, 15 May–15 July 1784, printed above.

To Thomas Richardson

Sir,   Mount Vernon 5th July 1784

This day se'night a letter for you covering Bank Notes for 150 Dollars was lodged in the hands of Mr Watson.[1] Since (that is on Saturday last) I received your favor of the 27th ulto enclosing the cost of four Matrasses £49.10.2—a price which exceeds anything I had the most distant idea of; in a word it is an errant imposition of the workman—and therefore I hope Colo. Biddle will enquire into the matter before the accot is paid.[2] If, notwithstanding, other people pay at these rates, I must submit—tho' I could have bought in Alexandria as *large* & as *good hair* Mattrasses covered with ticking for £3.10., as the one which I have already received from Philada; but this I was unacquainted with until I returned from that place, & then it was too late I *thought* to countermand my order. Under this cover you will receive one hundred & twenty dollars more, in Bank notes for the use of Colo. Biddle, to whom, as I have not received a letter myself from him, I pray you to mention my sentiments respecting the mattrasses.

You would oblige me by causing one of the inclosed Advertisements to be affixed in George town, Bladensburgh, Fredericktown, Hagers-town, & any other place which you may think proper on the Maryland side of the Potomac—I shall put one of them in the Baltimore paper next week.[3] I am Sir, Yr Most obt Servt

G: Washington

LB, DLC:GW.

1. Richardson wrote GW on 10 July that he had received on 5 July GW's letters of that day and also one of 29 June. The earlier letter has not been found. Mr. Watson is probably the merchant Josiah Watson of Alexandria.

2. See GW to Clement Biddle, 30 June 1784.

3. On 15 July 1784 two advertisements dated 24 June appeared under GW's name in the *Virginia Journal and Alexandria Advertiser*. The one advertising "Washington's Bottom for lease" reads: "THE PLANTATION or FARM, on which Mr GILBERT SIMPSON, the Copartner, now lives, lying in the County of Fayette, State of Pennsylvania, commonly called and known by the Name of WASHINGTON'S BOTTOM.—The Lot contains 600 Acres (Part of a larger Tract) but may, if it should be found more convenient, be divided into two Tenements.—It is near the River Yohiogany, and on the great Road leading from Virginia and Maryland to Pittsburg, distant from the latter about 35 Miles.—Appertaining to this Lot are about 150 Acres of cleared Land in Meadow, Pasture and Tillage, under good Fencing, a good Dwelling-House, Kitchen, Barn, Stable, and other necessary Buildings, 120 bearing Apple-Trees, &c.—The Quality of the Soil is inferior to none in that Country, and the Situation advantageous for a Tavern.

"At the same Time and Place will be sold, the Stock, which is large, of Horses, Cattle, Sheep, and Hogs; and the Negroes, for the ensuing Year, hired, or otherwise disposed of.—Bond, with approved Security, will be required, and Twelve Months Credit given without Interest, provided the Principal is punctually paid at or before the expiration of the Year, otherwise to bear Interest from the Date of the Bond.

"A MERCHANT MILL on another Part of the Tract, distant about a Mile from the above Farm, will be let on the same Day to the highest Bidder, for a Term of Years.—This Mill is near the River, but not exposed to Freshes, works two Pair of Stones in a large Stone House, has Bolting Cloths and other Conveniencies for manufacturing.—It was built by the famous DENNIS STEPHENS, and grinds incredibly fast.—Grain may be received, and Flour transported to all Parts of that Country, by Water.—The Subscriber, or an Agent properly authorised to transact the Business in his Behalf, will be on the Premises at the Time of Sale."

The second advertisement, "Land to Lease at Great Meadow and Bath," reads: "At the Time and Place aforesaid, will be let to the highest Bidder, for the Term of Ten Years, a LOT of LAND at, and including the Great Meadow, or larger Part of it, situated on the main Road from Fort-Cumberland, to Pittsburgh, and about half Way between the Two.—On this Lot there either is or ought to be some Improvements; and it is calculated to reseive very many, being one of the best Stands on the whole Road for an Inn.

"At Bath, in the County of Berkeley, on Tuesday the 7th of September next, will be let to the highest Bidder for the Term of Seven Years, a small Peninsula (or Neck of Land, formed by a bend of the River) containing 240 Acres, near 200 of which is rich low Ground.—This Land is situated on Potomack River and bounded thereby 400 Poles, 12 Miles above the Springs or Town of Bath aforesaid, which affords a ready Market for grain and the smaller Articles of a Farm, whilst it is become highly probable that the Navigation of the River will be extended, and Water Transportation thereby made easy and cheap for the heavier and more bulky ones.—There are Improvements on the Place."

To John Rumney

Sir,   Mount Vernon 5th July 1784
I have been favor'd with your letter of July 1783. the business which gave rise to it, was settled before the letter came to my hands.[1] Having imbibed a warm friendship for your oldest Son while living,[2] any act by which I could consistently have given aid to your other son,[3] or that would render a service to you, would have afforded me pleasure: of this I pray you to be assured, as also of the sincerity of my condolence on the loss you have sustained in Colo. Rumney who was an amiable Man, & a worthy Citizen of this Country. I am Sir &c. &c.

G: Washington

LB, DLC:GW.
    1. Letter not found.
    2. GW's friend Dr. William Rumney, who died in 1783, was a surgeon in the British army during the French and Indian War. In 1763 at the end of the war, he settled in Alexandria and lived there until his death.
    3. His "other son" was John Rumney, Jr., whose English firm had a store in Alexandria. See GW to John Rumney, Jr., 3, 5 July 1784.

To John Rumney, Jr.

Sir;   Mount Vernen 5th July [1784]
As you pass by, Mr Lund Washington will put a sheep or two on Board your vessel in aid of your Sea Stores—My best wishes for a pleasant voyage & happy meeting with Mr Rumney & your friends attend you. I am with esteem Sir yr most Obdt Servt

Go: Washington

L (photocopy), DLC:GW. In October 1911 Goodspeed's catalog, no. 88, advertised an "autograph letter written and signed by Washington," with several words torn from the text, addressed to Mr. Rumney at Alexandria and dated 1784 at Mount Vernon. It quotes the first line of the letter: "As you pass by, Mr. Lund. Washington will put a sheep or two on board your vessel in aid of your sea stores." The letter itself has not been found. The Library of Congress has a photocopy of a would-be facsimile of the letter, mistakenly dated 1797 instead of 1784, which is reported to have appeared in an unidentified magazine in the middle of the nineteenth century. This is the letter printed here.
    1. See Rumney's letter of 8 Sept. 1784 in which he gives thanks to GW and Mrs. Washington "for the genteel Present of Sea Stock."

From William Skilling

Sir   Caroline County [Va.] July 5th 1784

I have been inform'd that you was disirous of seeing me but it does not lay in my power at present, as I have engag'd to do a peice of worke for Mr Coleman which will Keep me Employ'd till the fall Season I should be very willing to have Waited on you Immediately if I had not been Engag'd but If I can be of service to you after I have done Mr Colemans work I will then wait on you as I would rather work for you than any other person[1] Colo. Richd Randolph has wrote to me that he will give me thirty pounds Sterling & two pair of Shoes a year but I have not engag'd with him as Yet & shall wait till I can hear from you before I do as I shall prefer Waiting on your Excellency before any other person[2]—please to let me know as Soon as you can if youl want me & direct to me to be left at Mr James Head Lynch's & I shall be sure to Receive it[3]—I am Yr Excellencys most Obt Humbe Servt

                                            William Skilling

ALS, DLC:GW.

In 1775 GW engaged William Skilling, who had worked for him before, to conduct servants and slaves to his Ohio lands. See Articles of Agreement, 25 Feb. 1775 (DLC:GW). Skilling came to work at Mount Vernon as a hired hand, probably late in 1784, and continued there at least until the summer of 1785. See *Diaries*, 4:135–36.

1. GW wrote Skilling on 22 July offering him a job. On 28 July Skilling replied that he would begin working for GW in November. Mr. Coleman may be Daniel Coleman (1753–1817) who rose to a captaincy in the Caroline County (Va.) militia in 1782 and represented his county in the house of delegates from 1800 to 1815.

2. Richard Randolph, who died in 1786, lived at Curles in Henrico County, Virginia.

3. James Head Lynch of Caroline County, Va., owned a tavern.

To John Francis Mercer

Sir,   Mount Vernon 8th July 1784

Strange as it may seem, it is nevertheless true, that I have not had it in my power to transmit the enclosed Statement of accots between your Father's Estate & Brothers, & myself, before this;[1] & now it is possible there may be omissions, for I find my affairs (as far as the little leisure I have will enable me to look into them) in very great disorder, requiring at least a Winter's close application to assort papers & adjust accounts.

I send these accounts just as they stand upon my books—no credit I believe is omitted—if I am mistaken however, they may be allowed now, or whenever they are discovered. I am at a loss to know whether the three accots can, or ought to be blended in one; your brother & self may determine this point—I pray you & him to make such a general statement as will ascertain the balance, when all the credits are allowed. I know you will do me justice in this, & I want no more; but beg to have a copy of it transmitted to me as soon as convenient. I have not struck a balance on either of the accounts, because of Interest—& stopage of interest at proper epochas, which must come into the final settlement of all.

I can only repeat to you, how convenient it would be to me to receive that balance—I do assure you Sir, that I am distressed for want of money, & know not, as I never was accustomed to it, how to parry a dun—Nevertheless, I would not have you adopt measures, or precipitate a Sale which may be injurious to yourself.

Will you be so good as to ask your Brother in what manner I am to obtain Deeds for the two Lotts I bought at Colo. Mercers sale, & which are credited in his Accot? With esteem & regard I am Dr Sir &c.

G. Washington

LB, DLC:GW.

John Francis Mercer (1759–1821), the son of John Mercer, and the much younger half brother of George and James Mercer, was at this time one of the Virginia delegates to Congress.

1. The statement of accounts that GW enclosed has not been found, but see in Ledger B his overlapping accounts with the Mercers—with the John Mercer estate for the years 1772 through 1791 (f. 221), with James Mercer, 1773–75 (f. 84), and with George Mercer, 1774–75 (f. 129). The Mercer indebtedness to GW arose mainly from the £2,100 sterling that John Mercer (d. 1768) borrowed from Martha Custis in 1758 shortly before her marriage to GW (see note 29 in Appendix III-B of Settlement of the Daniel Parke Custis Estate, 20 April 1759–5 Nov. 1761, printed above). In 1772, after the death of young Martha Parke Custis, Mercer's £2,100 bond, with accumulated interest of £1,109.11.6, became a part of the dower property controlled by GW. Between 1773 and 1775 the Mercer brothers made substantial payments to GW in the form of wheat for GW's mill and of land that GW acquired in the sales of George Mercer's land in 1774, including two tracts on the Shenandoah River in Frederick County (see Edward Snickers to GW, 17 May 1784,

n.1). GW also got, in December 1774, one-half of the Mercers' Four Mile Run tract in Fairfax County (see GW to James Mercer, 12 Dec. 1774). James Mercer was the executor of his father's estate after his father's death in 1768, but his brother George Mercer, who since 1766 had been living permanently in England, in 1773 took the management of his own American property out of the hands of James Mercer (see GW to Francis Lightfoot Lee and Ralph Wormeley, Jr., 20 June 1784, source note). At this time in 1784, their half brother, John Francis Mercer, was handling the affairs of John Mercer's estate. George Mercer died in France in 1784. For GW's continuing efforts to collect what remained due him from the Mercer estate, see particularly his letters to John Francis Mercer of 27 Mar. and 20 Dec. 1785; 30 Jan., 6 Mar., 12 Aug., 9 Sept., and 5, 19 Dec. 1786; 1 Feb. and 5 Nov. 1787; and 11 Jan. 1788. See also Statement concerning George Mercer's Estate, 1 Feb. 1789, and notes (*Papers, Presidential Series,* 1:269–76).

From John Augustine Washington

Bushfield [Westmoreland County, Va.] 8 July 1784
My dear Brother
Your favour of the 30th of June with the inclosed extracts &c. I had the pleasure to recieve last night—I am under very great obligations to you for the trouble you have taken upon this occasion, and also for your kind intention of writing to Colo. Tilghman, if you can understand he is in such a way of business as to promise a youth of application a tolerable share of knowlededg in Mercantile business—you must be perfectly acquainted with this Gentlemans disposicion and abilities in General, and no doubt Mr Morris must be satisfyed of his Mercantile knowledg by his ingaging with him in trade[1]—I should therefore suppose it probeble that Corbin might do very well under his direction—in the first place Colo. Tilghmans regard and respect for you may induce him to take more pains in instructing my Son then could other wise be reasonably expected, in the next place, altho his trade may not be so extensive as some Houses in Philadelphia, yet if he has a good General Knowledg of trade he will have more leisure to communicate that knowledg to others—and I am convinced that more Genl knowledg of trade may be acquired from Conversacion then Study, tho both is necessary, as to the business of the Counting House there is no doubt but that may be acquired there as no doubt regular bookkeeping is observed—It would give me great pleasure if Corbin goes to Colo. Tilghman that he could board in his Family; there are many objections to a boarding House;

even if we were vainly & rediculously to suppose that a youths morals could not be corrupted, he must be rendered in some degree unhappy from not having it in his power to chuse his Company—Mr Constables proposicion, to say nothing of the extravigance of the demand (which is realy beyond what I could afford) would not in other respects answer at Corbins time of life—a youth of 14 or 15 years of age taken with all the indiffirence that Mr Constable expresses in his letter to Mr Morris[2] probebly would by the time they arived to Corbins age acquire all that could be learned in the Counting House, and in a few years after might with proper instruction make themselves acquainted with the Genl principles of trade—the case is different with Corbin, who must indeavour to carry on his inquiries in the misteries of trade at the same time he is acquiring a knowledg of the Counting house business, and this could not well be accomplished without the Friendship as well as the abilities of the person under whose care he is placed—Corbin can have no objection to laying himself under obligations to stay for three years if it is required, the only possable injury that I can foresee to him is, that in case his Mother should recover her health and spirits,[3] she might consent, and he might find it for his improvement and interest to go abroad for a year or two before that time might expire—Bushrod has wrote to you, and no doubt return'd you his thanks for your kind offer of accompanying you to the Western Country, he I hope will never be more at leisure then at present, that he is waiting the arival of his Law Library, nor can he ever see that Country under greater advantages then by accompanying of you—Bushrod is much recovered, Mrs Washington Better then when I had the pleasure of seeing you, tho but poorly yet—Corbin has been very unwell, and is still complaining—we are happy to hear that you and my Sister and the Family are well, that you may continue so, and injoy all the cumforts of this world is the sincere wishes of Mrs Washington as well as Your Sincerely Affe & Obt Brother

                                    John Auge Washington

ALS, MH: Jared Sparks Collection.
    1. See Robert Morris to GW, 15 June 1784.
    2. See enclosure in Morris to GW, 15 June.
    3. See John Augustine Washington to GW, 4 April 1784.

To James Craik

Dear Doctor,   Mount Vernon July 10th 1784.

I have come to a resolution (if not prevented by anything, at present unforeseen) to take a trip to the Western Country this Fall, & for that purpose to leave home the first of September— By appointment I am to be at the warm-springs the 7th of that month; & at Gilbert Simpsons the 15th—where, having my partnership accounts, with some of very long standing to settle, & things to provide for the trip to the Kanhawa, I expect to be by the 10th or 11th—that is four or five days before the 15th.[1]

It is possible, tho' of this I cannot be certain at this time, that I shall, if I find it necessary to lay my Lands off in lotts, make a day or two's delay at each of my tracts upon the Ohio, before I reach the Kanhawa—where my stay will be the longest, & more or less according to circumstances.

I mention all these matters that you may be fully apprized of my plan, & the time it may probably take to accomplish it—If under this information it would suit you to go with me, I should be very glad of your company—no other, except my Nephew Bushrod Washington, & that is uncertain, will be of the party; because it can be no amusement for others to follow me in a tour of business, & from one of my tracts of Land to another; (for I am not going to explore the Country, nor am I in search of Fresh lands, but to secure what I have)—nor wou'd it suit me to be embarrassed by the plans—movements or whims of others, or even to have my own made unwieldy—for this I shall continue to decline all overtures which may be made to accompany me. Your business & mine lays in the same part of the country & are of a similar nature; the only difference between them is, that mine may be longer in the execution.[2]

If you go, you will have occasion to take nothing from hence, but a servant to look after your horses, & such beding as you may think proper to make use of. I will carry a Marquee, some Camp utensils, & a few Stores—a Boat, or some other kind of vessel will be provided for the voyage down the river, either at my place on Yohoghaney or Fort Pitt, measures for this purpose having been already taken—a few Medecines, & hooks & lines you may probably want. My Complimts & best wishes in which Mrs Washington joins, are offered to Mrs Craik[3] & your family, & I am with sincere esteem & friendship Dr Sir, Yrs &c. &c.

G: Washington

LB, DLC:GW.

1. For GW's account of his trip into Pennsylvania in September, see *Diaries*, 4:1–71.

2. Like GW, Craik in 1772 received grants of land for his military service in the French and Indian War: 1,374 acres on Little Kanawha in Botetourt County and 4,232 acres on the Great Kanawha in Fincastle County. See GW to Lord Dunmore and Virginia Council, 5 Nov. 1773.

3. Craik married Mariamne Ewell (1740–1814) of Prince William County, Va., in 1760.

To David Luckett

Sir,   Mount Vernon 10th July 1784

If nothing, unforeseen at present, happens to prevent it, I propose to be at my plantation on Yohoghaney the 10th of September—which with my Mill & other matters will be disposed of the 15th as you may see by the enclosed Advertisements:[1] from thence I have thoughts of visiting my Lands on the Great Kanhawa, & on the Ohio between the two Kanhawas, if I can do it conveniently, & obtain the means for a water conveyance.

Let me request the favor of you therefore Sir, to inform me by a line to be left at my Plantation in the care of Mr Gilbert Simpson, whether there are any public Boats at the Post under your command, which might answer my purpose; if there are not, whether one or more could be hired from the Inhabitants in the vicinity of it, & at what price by the day, with hands to navigate her, as also without hands. whether you could spare me from the Garrison three or four trusty Soldiers (a Corporal one of them) for the trip—& whether provision for man & horse could be purchased at Fort Pitt, with liquor for such a jaunt, & on what terms. 'Tis probable I may want water transportation &c. for ten Horses.

I persuade myself you will excuse the trouble this application will occasion you, & think there is no impropriety in my request respecting the Boat & Soldiers; if I had thought there was, I pledge myself to you I should not have made it. I am desireous of meeting your answer at Mr Simpsons to *all* these queries by the 10th, because my ultimate measures must be decided on at that place the moment I arrive there, & no time ought to be lost in having recourse to other measures if I cannot be supplied with you. I am with esteem Sir, Yr &c.

G: Washington

LB, DLC:GW.

Lt. David Luckett, a Marylander, recently had assumed command of a small detachment of soldiers manning Fort Pitt. He remained in command of the fort until he retired from the army in the summer of 1785. GW saw Luckett at Washington's Bottom, at Gilbert Simpson's house, on 14 Sept., when Luckett helped persuade GW that the "discontented temper of the Indians" made it unwise for him to go down the Ohio (*Diaries*, 4:21).

1. The texts of GW's advertisements offering his Pennsylvania lands for lease are printed in note 3, GW to Thomas Richardson, 5 July.

To Lee Massey

Dear Sir   Mount Vernon 10th July 1784.

I have been favored with your letter of June 30th—I thank you for the friendly style of it, & pray you to be assured that I shall, at all times, be glad to see you at Mount Vernon.

Business, & old concerns of the War, with which I have *now* nothing to do, are still pressed upon me. This, and Company, has left me little liezure hitherto to look into matters which more immediately relate to myself. but finding it necessary, I mean to devote my forenoons to business, while I give the after part of the day to my friends, 'till I can [(]if that should ever be) bring my affairs into order again—With this indulgence from my friends, their visits can never be unseasonable—& none will be received with more pleasure than those of Mr Massey. With great esteem & regard I am—Dr Sir Yr Most obedt Servt

Go: Washington

ALS (photocopy), DLC:GW.

To Edmund Randolph

Dear Sir,   Mount Vernon 10th July 1784.

The last Post brought me your favor of the 3d—& the Post preceeding, that of the 27th ulto. My particular thanks are due for the attention you have paid to the renewal of my Patents—

Your Fees on this, & the other business you have had the management of for me, I would gladly pay, if you will please to let me know the amount. Whether it is to Mr Mercer (who by order of Court, has the property of his Brother George in his hands) or to me, you look for your fee in the suit depending between Gravat & others in the high Court of Chancery, I know not—if the latter, please to advise me that I may take measures to obtain the money.[1]

In looking over some of my papers the other day, I found a Memo[randu]m of a prize (half an acre) which I drew in Colo. Byrds lottery, in the Town of Richmond[2]—the number of the ticket is 4965 & that of the Lott, or prize 265. this is all I got for twenty tickets on my own Accot—The same Memodm informs me, that in partnership with Peyton Randolph (your Uncle), John Wayles, George Wythe—Richard Randolph, Lewis Burwell, William Fitzhugh (Chatham), Thompson Mason, Nathl Harrison Jur & Richd Kidder Mead Esqrs. (ten in all) I have, or ought to have a joint interest in the following prizes, the produce of an hundred Tickets which were purchased amongst us. Vizt

No. 3181—half an Acre	No. 270.
3186—Do—Do	138.
3193—100 Acres	823.
5325—half an Acre	237.
5517—100 Acres	751.
5519—half an Acre	257.

If it would not be inconvenient to you, it would oblige me to let me know (if you can) what is become of this property; & of what value it is—especially the Lott No. 265 which I hold in my own right—for I faintly recollect to have heard that the joint stock was disposed of to no great advantage for the company—for me, I am sure it was not, as I have never received an iota on account of these prizes[3]—With very great esteem & regard I am D. Sir &c.

G: Washington

LB, DLC:GW.

1. For the suit between Richard Gravatt "and others," involving the estate of George Mercer (1733–1784), see GW's Statement concerning George Mercer's Estate, 1 Feb. 1789, printed below, and the notes of that document. See also GW to Francis Lightfoot Lee and Ralph Wormeley, Jr., 20 June 1784, and notes.

2. In a vain attempt to stave off the financial ruin threatening to engulf him, William Byrd III (1728–1777) decided in 1767 to dispose by lottery of all his "LAND and TENEMENTS" forming the "entire towns of Rocky Ridge and Shockoe, lying at the Falls of the James River, and the land thereunto, adjoining." For information regarding Byrd's lottery, which was held at Williamsburg in November 1768, see note 10 in GW's Cash Accounts, May 1769.

3. See Randolph's answer of 20 July 1784 to GW's queries about the Byrd lottery. On 2 Aug. 1789 Randolph, apparently having forgotten this exchange with GW in 1784, wrote GW that "Sometime ago Mr Fitzhugh, of Chatham, gave me a list of tickets in Colo. Byrd's lottery, in which yourself, several other gentlemen, as well as my father or uncle (I forget which) were jointly interested," and asked if GW had further information. See GW's response of 8 Sept. 1789. See also GW's letter to Bushrod Washington of 29 June 1796, quoted in note 1 of Randolph to GW, 2 Aug. 1789. For the Byrd lottery held on 2 Nov. 1768, see Cash Accounts, May 1769, n.10.

From Thomas Richardson

Sir   George Town [Md.] July 10th 1784
    Your favs. of 29th June & 5th Instant came to hand on Monday last the first covering 150 Dollars the other 120 in Bank Bills for the use of Colo. Biddle of which have advis'd him & passd the money to your Credit, have also sent him a Copy of that part of yours of 5th which relates to the Mattrasses[1]—have put one of your Advertizements up in this Town, sent one to the Court House, one to Bladensbg & inclosd three to Mr Geo. Murdock in Frederick Town desiring him to put one up there & forward the other to Carlisle & Lancaster. I am with the Greatest regard Your very hble Servt

                                        Tho. Richardson

ALS, DLC:GW.
    1. GW's letter of 29 June 1784 has not been found, but see his letter of 5 July.

To Gilbert Simpson

Mr Simpson.   Mount Vernon 10th July 1784.
    This Letter & the enclosed Advertisements will be delivered to you, I expect, by Mr George McCormick. The like Advertisements are sent to many other parts, & will appear in the Philada, Baltimore and Alexandria News-Papers, that the most public notice thereof may be given. I have also sent one to Fort

Pitt. The six which are sent you, may be disposed of at such places over the mountains as you shall think best.[1]

My part of the Stock (except Negroes, which may be necessary to finish the crop)[2] will certainly be disposed of—Your half may also be sold, & you to purchase in what you like on your own account—or set apart by a fair & equal division before the sale, as may be agreed upon when I come up—The Land & Mill will also be let in the manner described; for I cannot in justice to myself, any longer submit to such management—waste of property, & losses, as I have hitherto sustained by my partnership with you.

I shall bring up all my accots & memorandums in order to have a final settlement,[3] & desire you will collect every paper & thing which can serve to put matters in a fair point of view; for tho' I do not expect to be compensated for my losses, nor mean to be rigid in my settlement, yet commonsense, reason and justice, all require that I should have a satisfactory account rendered of my property which has been entrusted to your care, in full confidence of getting something for ten or twelve years use of it.

The letter, which will accompany this, for the commanding Officer of Fort-Pitt,[4] I beg you to send by some person who will be pointed in delivering it to him: he is desir'd to lodge an answer at your house by the 10th, which you will keep 'till I arrive. I have wrote to know what things I can be provided with at Fort Pitt for a trip down the Ohio, that I may be enabled to determine the moment I get to your house, whether to build a Boat & hire hands or not. Let the materials, as I mentioned to you when here, for building a Boat be provided notwithstanding; because if they are not wanted, they can readily be disposed of; & if they are, it will facilitate my passage exceedingly.

You may also, without making an absolute purchase of anything, know where & upon what terms, provision for man & horse; & such other articles, Liquor—Butter—Cheese, Salt-meat, Salt &c. can be had, that no delay may take place in these enquiries after I get out, if they should be found necessary. I would wish to know also if a good Hunter and Waterman could be had, & upon what terms: and if you should see Mr Hite who formerly assisted Colonel Crawford in his Surveys of the land I hold on the ohio & Kanhawa, ask him if it would suit him to go down the river with me, in case I should find it necessary to take a surveyor—& upon what terms by the day or month; as I do not know what, or whether I shall have anything for him to do, more than to shew me the land[5]—'till I get upon it—or know what prospect there is of settling it. I am &c. &c.

                                                    G: Washington

LB, DLC:GW.

1. For the advertisements, see GW to Thomas Richardson, 5 July, n.3. See also GW to George McCarmick, 12 July.

2. For the fate of these slaves, see *Diaries*, 4:326–27.

3. After putting Washington's Bottom up for lease on 15 Sept., GW wrote in his diary on 17 Sept. that he was "Detained here by a settled Rain the whole day—which gave me time to close my accts. with Gilbert Simpson, & put a final end to my Partnership with him" (ibid., 25).

4. See GW to David Luckett, this date.

5. John Hite was employed by William Crawford in 1773. See William Crawford to GW, 15 Jan. 1774. The copyist wrote "Lite."

From Gimat

Dear General   fort royal [Martinique] 12th jully 1784.

I embrace with the highest pleasure the opportunity of my friend comte de Kersaint[1] commanding a small fleet bounding to cheaseapeak bay, to present the hommages of my heart to your Exellency and to renew the respectful attachement which has devoted for ever to you. I Wished most ardently to follow comte de Kersaint for enjoing the happiness of paying a visit to you dear general, to offer you my best thanks for all the Kindness I have So often experienced from you, and to See once more my Brothers Soldiers of america, the remembrance of them being always very precious to me and will be the Same as long as I live. it is to you dear general and to the honor of having Served under the Standards of the american army that I am indebted of my promotions in our french army, the last flaters me above all I can express it and I like very much of repeating to Your, Exellency, that I feel better then I can't explain it here the acknowledgment that I owe to your Kindess & that I Shall be jaloux at any time and in all the circumstances you would be pleased to preserve them to me.

in the last letters I received from paris it was repported the marquis de la fayette intended to go again to america it was given to me by the duc de castries[2] as a certainty, I wish he would pay a visit to the west indias in going to america and get Leave from the governor of martinico to attend him in his voyages trough a contry where he will meet with So many friends and the first of all your Excelency.[3]

if I can be any ways Serviesable to you dear general, here or elsewhere I beg you will command me—being most Sincerely & affectionately with a respectful attachement your very humble and obedient Servant

Gimat.

Colonel du regt de la martinique

Give me leave to beg of you to present my best compliments to mistress Washington.

ALS, DLC:GW.

Jean-Joseph, chevalier de Gimat (d. 1793), arrived in America with Lafayette in 1777 as a lieutenant and Lafayette's aide-de-camp. He was made lieutenant colonel in the Continental army in 1778 and in 1782 became colonel of the régiment de la Martinique.

1. Armand-Guy-Simon de Coëtempren, comte de Kersaint (1742–1793), was captain of a ship in the French forces sailing in American waters during the Revolution.

2. This was either the minister of marine, Charles-Eugène-Gabriel de La Croix, maréchal de Castries (1727–1801), or his son Armand-Charles-Augustin de La Croix, comte de Charlus and later duc de Castries (1756–1842). The latter was the second colonel in the régiment Saintonge in Rochambeau's army in America.

3. Kersaint and GW missed connections. See Kersaint to GW, 12 Sept. 1784, n.2.

From David Griffith

Dear Sir,   Fairfax Glebe [Va.] 12th July 1784

Mr Nourse, an Executor of your Brothers will, and the guardian of your Nephews George & Lawrence, has given me instructions to furnish them with clothing and every necessary, without any restrictions, and discharges the Bills brought him, for this purpose, with very great punctuality. It is true, they were but badly supply'd, in many respects, when they first came to me; but I have the satisfaction to inform you that, at this time, they have a sufficiency of clothing for growing Boys, & that, in that respect, they are much better off than any of the young Gentlemen who are with me. The whole of Mr Nourse's conduct, towards his Wards, seems friendly and affectionate—manifests a disposition to do them all the Justice in his power, and an earnest sollicitude for their improvement in Morals Manners and learning.[1] With great truth and Sincerity I am, Dear Sir Your most huble Servt

David Griffith

ALS, DLC:GW.

    1. See GW to James Nourse, 22 Jan. 1784, and notes.

To George McCarmick

[Mount Vernon] 12th July 1784

Genl Washington requests Mr McCarmick to set up the Advertisements herewith enclosed at the following places. Leesburgh—Shepherdstown—Hagerstown—Martinsburg— Warm springs, and the Oldtown, or thereabouts. The above to be of those which have the writing in the Margin. The others to be set up along the road above the Oldtown, and at such other places over the mountains as Mr McCarmick may think best— letting Mr Simpson know the places, that he may not send those which are inclosed to him, to the same.[1]

The letter to the Commanding officer at Fort Pitt to be sent by Mr McCarmick or Simpson as they may agree—it ought to go safe & soon.[2]

Mr McCormick will please to inform those persons, or the leaders of them who are settled upon the Generals Land on Millers run, that he, McCor[mic]k, has seen & read his Deed for it—that the said Deed bears date the 5th day of July 1774—& the Survey the 23d of March 1771—that this Land was granted in virtue of the Kings Proclamation in Octor 1763 & is part of 3000 acres bought of Capt. Posey (an officer) who was entitled to so much under the Proclamation, as is recited in the Deed— that the agreement between the States of Virginia and Pennsylvania secures this right to the General, who did, at their first settling upon the land, & at sundry times since, which is easy to be proved, give them notice that it was his, & forewarned them of the consequences of persevering in an error; & lastly, it may be neighbourly & friendly in Mr McCormick to advise them, if they have a mind to avoid all the expence, & all the disagreeable consequences which may result from the prosecution of his right to the highest Court it can finally be determined in; it might be well for them to think seriously of an accommodation, either by removing, or becoming Tenants—& that this is not to be delayed beyond the time the Genl has appointed to rent his Mill &c.[3]

If Mr McCormick shou'd see Mr Hite[4] who assisted Colo. Crawford in surveying the Generals Lands in the Ohio & Gt Kanhawa, he would be obliged to him for asking Mr Hite whether, in case the General shou'd find it necessary when he gets to Mr Simpson's, to take a Surveyor down with him, it would suit him to go; & upon what terms, by the day or month. The General does not [wish] Mr Hite engaged actually, because he does not, at this time certainly know whether he shall want a Surveyor or not.

G: Washington

LB, DLC:GW.

Maj. George McCarmick at this time lived in Yohogania County, Pa., not far from GW's Millers Run (or Chartiers Creek) property in Washington County. After GW won his suit in October 1786 against the settlers who claimed most, if not all, of his 2,813 acres at Millers Run (see note 3), he engaged McCarmick to act for him in treating with the squatters who remained (see McCarmick to GW, 31 Oct. 1786, and GW to McCarmick, 27 Nov. 1786).

1. The advertisements to lease Washington's Bottom on the Youghiogheny and the tract at Great Meadows and 240 acres at Bath in Berkeley County, Va., are printed in note 3, GW to Thomas Richardson, 5 July 1784.

2. See GW to David Luckett, 10 July.

3. For GW's acquisition of his Millers Run property, see GW's correspondence in 1772 and 1773 with William Crawford, who made the original survey for GW and sought to protect his claims. See particularly Crawford's letters of 1 May 1772 and 29 Dec. 1773. See also *Diaries*, 4:22–23. When GW met at Gilbert Simpson's place at Washington's Bottom in September with claimants to different portions of the Millers Run tract, he found them adamant in their insistence upon the legitimacy of their claims. GW employed the Pennsylvania lawyer Thomas Smith to institute suits of ejectment against the squatters. GW's own deep involvement in the prosecution of the suits may be followed in his correspondence with Smith and others over the next two years. His diary entries for 14, 19, and 20 Sept. 1784 (*Diaries*, 4:21–23, 26–31), with the editors' copious notes, provide an extensive summary of the entire proceedings; but see also, in particular, the editorial note in Thomas Smith to GW, 9 Feb. 1785.

4. The copyist wrote "Lite."

From Otho Holland Williams

Dear Sir,   Baltimore 12th July 1784

After I had the pleasure of seeing you in Philadelphia I made an excursion to New York, and from thence up the north river as far as Saratoga. One motive for extending my tour so far that course was to visit the springs in the vicinity of Saratoga which I recollected you once recommended to me as a remedy for the Rheumatism.[1] They are now much frequented by the un-civilised people of the back country, but very few others resort to them, as there is but one small hutt within several miles of the place. Coll Armstrong and myself spent one week there which was equal to a little Campaign, for the accomodations were very wretched and provisions exceedingly scarce.[2] The Country about the springs being uncultivated we were forced to send to the borders of the Hudson for what was necessary for our Subsistence.

During our stay we made a few little experiments upon the Waters—Bark of a restringent quality turned them to a purple color very suddenly, and we thought that Iron was discoverable even to the taste.

They have certainly a very great quantity of Salts—A quart of the water, boiled down, produced a spoonful which being diluted in common water there remained on the surface a quantity of insipid, tasteless, matter like chalk, which we collected; then pouring off the water into a clean Vessel we found remaining at the bottom some thing like slacked slime—The water in which the first production was diluted being boiled down produced half a spoonful of very acute salt; But that which distinguishes these waters, in a very conspicuous degree from all others is the great quantity of fixed air which they contain. They are exceedingly pungent to the taste, and after being drank a short time will often affect the nose like brisk bottled ale. The water will raise flour sooner than any other thing and cannot be confined so that the air will not some how or other escape—several persons told us that they had corked it tight in bottles and that the bottles brake. We tried it with the only bottle we had which did not break but the air found its way through a wooden stopper and the wax with which it was sealed. A trout died in the water in less than a minute, or seemed dead, but recovered in common water—This experiment was repeated with the same effect. We observed, in digging, that the rocks which are about the springs, and which in one or two places project themselves above the earth in a conic form, go not deep into the ground, but are formed by the waters which, (the man who lives at the place informed us) overflow once ♃ month when not disturbed, and the earthy parts being exposed to the air and sun petrefy, & increase—this opinion is strengthened by the shells and bodies of insects which we found in broken parts of the rock.

I have given you my observations because, I think, you told me what you knew of these extraordinary springs was from information.

At Clermont Mrs Livingston charged me with a letter for Mrs Washington and with her most respectful compliments to you Sir;[3] All that amiable family joined in affectionate compliments to you and to Mrs Washington: and I beg you will permit me to add my own, I am Dr Sir, most respectfully Your Most obedient Humble Servant

O.H. Williams

ALS, DLC:GW; LB, PHi: Dreer Collection.

1. GW briefly visited Saratoga Springs in New York in the summers of 1782 and 1783. In 1783 he and Gov. George Clinton made plans to buy the Saratoga springs but in the end were unable to do so (see GW to Clinton, 25 Nov. 1784).

2. This was probably the John Armstrong from North Carolina who served with Williams as deputy adjutant general to Horatio Gates during the southern campaign. Armstrong was a lieutenant colonel when the war ended.

3. Mary Stevens Livingston was the wife of Robert R. Livingston (1746–1813) of Clermont in New York.

To Tench Tilghman

Dear Sir,   Mount Vernon 14th July 1784

A nephew of mine, Brother to the young Gentleman who studied Law under Mr Wilson, is inclined to enter into a Mercantile walk of life, & his Father is desirous he should do so. He has just compleated a regular Education—is about twenty years of age—Sober & serious—sensible, and I am *told*, remarkably prudent & assiduous in the comple[tion] of whatever he takes in hand. This is the character he bears—personally, I know little of him.

I have expressed a wish to his Father that he might be placed under your care, & it is very pleasing to him[1]—let me ask then My D. Sir, if it would be convenient for you to take him into your counting House, & immediately under your eye. If I had not conceived, from the character he bears, that he would do you no discredit, but may, when he is qualified, subserve your views in Trade, while he is promoting his own, I do assure you that I am among the last men in the world, who would propose the measure. If you are inclined to receive him, be so good as to let me know on what terms, & the requisites to be complied with on his part. Mrs Washington joins very cordially in compliments of congratulation to you & Mrs Tilghman on the encrease of your family. With the usual esteem & regard I am Dr Sir &c.

G: Washington

LB, DLC:GW; ALS, offered for sale by Thomas Birch's catalog, 683, 5–6 April 1892. The letter as printed in the catalog varies little from the letter-book copy.

1. See John Augustine Washington to GW, 8 July 1784.

From Unknown Author

[The author, who was a planter, probably in Virginia but possibly in Maryland, and a man with some knowledge of the classics, rings all the changes on the declension of the American Revolution from its early days of glory to its present sorry state in 1784. His jeremiad on the corruption of American society and its institutions repeats things often said before and to be said again in the 1780s, but the letter constitutes the fullest indictment of the Revolution to be addressed privately to GW. It is also the first direct call to him after the war to step forth and save the Revolution.]

Sir   [c.15 July 1784]

Altho I am a plain man, yet being more used to the Plow of late than to the Pen, some appology seems necessary for intruding so abruptly, and perhaps unseasonably on your Retirement—especially too in this manner where I am so ill qualified to engage, being unable either to methodise my Ideas or to express them with ease and propriety—I have Sir, for several years past, taken it into my head to imagine, that our Civil matters have not been conducted with that Integrity and attention, which the Interest of the Public, and the Happiness of the People required, My wishing to address you is not a sudden impulse—I have repeatedly made the attempt, but as often desisted least I should offend, where I wish most to please, for I confess that I have generally found myself singular in sentiment—but perceiving, before I could relinquish my opinion, that I must have given up the evidence of my senses, confirmed too by the testimony and experience, of the wisest & most disinterested Men of different Ages, whom I have had an opportunity of consulting on similar occasions, and on whos Judgement I have established my own, and altho it is not likely that you could have obtained a true idea of our management, yet as I think it improbable that it should have escaped Your observation altogether, and deeming it a duty which I owe, as well to those who are dearer to me than Life, as to my Country, by whos fate they must abide—I am therefore, from a Conviction that the Present is a Critical moment for America, irresistibly impeled to address you Great Sir, not only as the fittest, but I fear the only Person on Earth, that together with the inclination, possesses the Probity and Abilities sufficient to avert the impending ruin—And it is from an assured belief, that this is yet in your Power, that I am induced to trouble You, humbly presuming, that as this address originates from the Purest Motives I shall not be deemed presumptuous and that Your generosity, will make every reasonable allowance for my inaccuracy—You Sir, like Cincinatus have retired, with the applause of every Good Man—and would to Heaven that you may enjoy that happiness, which every well disposed mind must feel from knowing that their labours for the Public have been completely successful but with the most Poignant distress I mentioned, there seems to be reason to fear, that spurning the happiness, which you have procured for us, the same vices which recalled the noble Roman from his Retreat, may be the means of disturbing that Peace and Happiness which you so well merite.

From whatever cause it may have arisen whether from weakness or design in Those Persons who have for years past conducted & still continue to direct our Civil Affairs, certain it is that our Situation, notwithstanding the very favourable Peace, which we have lately obtained is at present alarming enough to engage the attention of every honest Man—That we have it yet in our Power to be truly happy must be readily granted, but if we are judge of the future by the past, it is greatly to be feared, that we may not be in a disposition fit to bring about so desirable an Event—Our Statesmen & Legislatures, totally unacquainted with our true situation, and seemingly ignorant that our Sole merite is almost confined to that department which has been immediately under Your Excellencys direction could not it is evident, arrogate more to themselves, upon this happy occasion had it flowed intirely from Their wise disinterested and heroick management—It is therefore not unreasonable to conclude, that finding their Abilities equal to the Task of conducting us thrô a perilous War, with success, They will consider themselves Adequate to Government in time of Peace—But to discover whether we ought to bestow Praise, or inflict Censure, it would be sufficient barely to examine into the Prevailing Manners & Morrals of the People, which affords Strictures on Their Conduct severer than Language can furnish, for Perhaps there never was an Instance, especially when we reflect on the point of time (for we find that most States have ben best governed in their infancy) of a change in the Circumstances & Temper of a Whole People, so sudden, so alarming and so extraordinary as that which we have seen brought about seemingly by the misconduct of our Rulers within these few years, however Sir as Your attention has been otherwise importantly engaged, it seems necessary to recall to Your recollection a few Circumstances which may assist not only in discovering our Disease but the Source whence it has originated.

At the commencement of the War with Britain when we were by the most contemptuous treatment, reduced to the unexpected, & disagreeable necessity of Arming in deffence of our invaded Rights, so generally and highly were the People of all Ranks animated with the noble Glow of Patriotism that They evinced on every occasion the most determined Resolution to submit to any Duty, and suffer any Inconveniences rather than fail to obtain, and secure to Themselves & Posterity the Rights of freemen—With such generous Principles universally prevailing, the Resolves of Congress & of our Commitions deservedly held in the highest Respect, for at that time They plainly pointed out the Conduct which was to carry us through the Arduous Contest with Honour & Success. And the good effects of these Prudent Counsels was visible from an encreasing Publick Spirit whilst Internal opposition shrunk before it, or caught Fire in colision with its Virtue. Selfish views was then unthought of, or gave way to those of the Public—Wisely excluded from the only Market which we had ever been accustomed to, Frugality with an Active and laudable Industry began to spread universally over the Country, and as fortunately our happy situation afforded ample means, we seemed wisely determined to depend upon our own Resources to supply us with those necessarys during the Contest for which we heretofore, perhaps imprudently, depended too much on others. With dispositions so commendable together with many other favourable Circumstances concurring we could not have wished for a Crisis more favourable for improving the

Morrals and Manners of a People. And we may justly conclude that nothing more was wanting but Simplicity of manners in our Rulers together with an attention to the Business of the Public and a Rigid adherence to the Principles of our Government to have made Americans Vie in Love of Country with any of the Ancient Republics most famed for Heroick Virtues—And when we reflect on our numbers, the Resources which we possessed, together with the many splendid Military successes obtained under the Auspices of Your Excellency, even with our small bandfull of Patriots, who by their bravery & patient Perseverance in the midst of wants harder to contend with than the Enemy[,] would have done Honour to any Age or Country—We need have been little affected by the continuance of the War, as in all probability we should not have experienced many difficulties which a different Conduct has brought on us—The nature of the War would have remained unaltred—Our National Credit would have stood firm and immoveable—Many of us from the Example of your Excellency would have placed our chief Pleasure in serving the Public, and should have thought ourselves sufficiently recompenced in being instrumental in contributing to the happiness of our Fellow Citizens—Generous Americans would then have Gloried in standing forth in Defence of their Country, and instead of the disgraceful measure of soliciting Troops from our generous Ally, You Sir would never have felt the reluctant necessity of retreating before the Enemy for want of Soldiers—People would have been spared the sight of sudden Riches for the most part Invidiously amassed nor should we have been burthened with a greater Load of Debt than our ample resources would have easily extinguished—as with the assistance of Frugality our Industry in all probability would have kept pace with the expences of the War. We therefore should have increased in Union Wealth & Power, whilst our Enemys would have become Poorer and Weaker, which must have Ultimately conducted us to Liberty and Peace with Honour Safety & Happiness—Without refering to the disinterested and Heroick Ages of the Ancients, the Swiss & Hollanders neither of whom could boast Resources or Advantages from situation with America, Prove this assertion to be more than Speculation—We wanted only Rulers actuated by the same Disinterested Principles and Simplicity of Manners—Ours to do them justice were ready enough to quote those Instances of Patriotick Heroism, but surely it was not sufficient barely to hold forth these Examples to the People altho in fine turned Periods—It was undoubtedly Their Duty as Fathers of their Country to have enforced the Doctrine by practising it—Nor was there any need on this occasion to look back to other Ages for Examples—To Their eternal confusion They had One before their ⟨Eye⟩ of Attention as well as Disinterestedness equal to any on Record, and it became as much Their Duty to render the Manners of the People conformable to the Spirit of our new Governments, as it was Your Excellencys to Discipline Your Troops—Public Virtue we find is a self renunciation which is always Arduous and even painful something therefore more than dry reasoning is Requisite for the Multitude—On such occasions the Example of Superiours is strangely atractive—It expresses much in a little and carries a Conviction to the People beyond the Power of Argument even when recommended by the magick of Eloquence—It was not expected that our Rulers should Trudge to Congress or our Assemblys with their Knapsacks on their Backs or as there was no occasion for it, that They should convene under a Tree to transact the Public Business—Yet the time and Their Station seemed to require that They should have been Austere in their Manners as strict over Them-selves as over others, thereby setting Examples of Temperance & Disinterestedness above all respecting Themselves and their high Station by a Judicious & Rational expenditure of Their Time—what they had to spare after providing for the Exigencies of the Public ought to have been employed as was expected by every thinking Man in providing wise Regulations for improving the Morrals of the People, and encouraging a Laudable Industry, by promoting useful Improvements in Agriculture and Manufactures. We possessed every necessary Ingredient, nothing remained but to have kept us employd, to have supplyd our reasonable wants—The necessity of Labour is the greatest Blessing which God has conferd upon Man, and nothing can be more destructive, or pernicious in a Young State than to permit their laborious Citizens to be seduced from their honest & useful Avocations by views of Ease & Avarice—This simple Conduct was notorious to the weakest of us, and was indeed held forth, by our Rulers from the beginning as our Strength & Dependance, and the Progress we had made justified the measure, therefore no Effort of Genius or Abilities was required in our Rulers to persevere—The Emminence of their Stations surely gave them a commanding prospect of their Duty—The road which led to Honour was open to their View. As they had set out in it, they could not lose it by mistake, nor could there possibly be any temptation sufficient to induce a Liberal mind to depart from it by design—Certain however it is that these Measures so Salutary and These Principles so consonant to the form of our Governments and indeed so necessary for their Efficacy and very Existance were soon neglected and departed from, without any necessity, but as it would seem, merely to encourage an Interest, which ought to have been forever Excluded from the Councils of America, where the true Center of Dominion ought and must be Land—It is the monied or Trafficking Interest that is aluded to, an Interest, which has sooner or later brought ruin upon every Landed Republick where it has been fostered—The Effects of its influence on our Councils is ever to be lamented, and its ⟨Predominating⟩ throughout to the Visible ⟨Bane⟩ of the Country, and extinction of every Liberal & Noble Passion is truely astonishing—As Effects great in there consequences often flow from the most trivial circumstances—perhaps the Place of meeting, or rather the Place of residence of our Supreme Council—The turn of thinking in the Society they frequented, Their manner of living, may all have had their Share, in misleading Their understandings, Perverting Their Judgement & Seducing Their Attention from the Interest and Business of the Public—Certain it seems that no Trading Town can be a fit Place of meeting for our Legislatures—Congress particularly ought to have a Place set apart for Their Meeting at which no more Buildings, should have been permitted, than was necessary for Their Reception, and that of Those requisite to Transact the Public Business—It seems immaterial to say where this Pitiful Interest began to Influence our Councils—It became visible by our hasty declaration of Independence, for surely that Transaction however well timed it might be in some triffling matters was certainly Premature in others—Amongst those of the greatest nay of the utmost Consequence seems to be the terms of Confederation— The Powers and Priviledges of Congress together with the adjustment of the Teritorial bounds and Claims of the different States matters which required the most dispassionate & mature Consideration. As our understanding at this time was not perverted nor shackled with the Temptations which soon followed, the National Interest would have been easier discovered and pursued, and in place of encumbring themselves in the dangerous Manner some States did with an undefined Territory incompatible with Their own Safety and the Existance of the Union—it might have been found how much more consonant it was to the Principles of sound Policy and the Spirit of our Governments to have Contracted instead of Adding—We ought not to have considered ourselves merely as Representing This or That State, but on this most Important Occasion we should have done and Acted as become Citizens of the World—Had these weighty matters together with some others worthy of consideration been agitated and Defined at that Period there is reason to Presume from the Then prevailing disposition and the Situation of our Affairs that every Matter would have been wisely and amicably setled on the firm Basis of Reciprocal Justice—for let Illiberal ploding Statesmen say as they will, experience proves that the well known Adage holds true in Public as well as in Private Affairs—This seemed the Prelude to our Blunders,

for as that Groveling Interest gained Influence in our Councils, Our
Patriotism became Visibly Languid. Our inattention to matters of the
utmost National Importance and the encreasing Regard to our Particular Interests became truly alarming. Opportunitys were soon
made for gratifying Avarice and Pride, the Temptation proved Irresistible The Impulse of Primeval meanness prevailed over the practice
of asshumed Virtues and Public Regard which grasped the Fate of
Millions became lost in the sordid visions of Private Benefits and the
vain desire of establishing Families—The most essential Interests
of the Public remained unthought of, or were invariably Sacrificed
whenever They came in competition with views of Private Avarice,
and it seems difficult to recollect an Instance since where the Principles of our Governments has been attended to—Our Appointments
our Expenditures were unconstitutional and our Manners and Morrals soon came to be such as would disgrace a Monarchy. Our own
Systems of Probity Frugality and Industry were ridiculed & exploded
Fraud & Extortion countenanced to the decay of Private Faith & Ruin
of Public Credit, which was suffered to tumble into ruins without one
Manly Effort or single Exertion for its support unless our Lottery
Scheme, which ought to make us blush can be deemed such—a Measure shameful in any Government but Scandalous in a Republic But
in what Instance have we Profited from our Knowledge & Acquaintance with the Past—have we from the miserable & wretched Catastro-
phe of other Nations endeavoured to Avoid and Gaurd against Those
Causes which must invariably produce similar & unhappy effects in
every State to the end of time. The consequences which from such a
Conduct might have been expected has followed—Matters of the
utmost Import upon which our Existance as a People seemed to depend has been most shamefully neglected—The management of the
Public money with Fidelity & Disinterestedness becomes a matter of
the utmost importance in every State but particularly in a Republic.
therefore we find that every well regulated free State has taken care to
Provide for the Honest application of their Revenues by Punishing
Cappitally all wilfull Embezzlings and every species of Corruption,
knowing that with out Œconomy it is impossible for even the might-
iest States any more than Private Familys to subsist with any Prospect
of Durability. As disorder is always followed by distress, so whenever
Waste & Embezzlement prevails Poverty & Ruin are inseperable At-
tendants, nor is it possible for human wisdom to divide Companions,
who in the unalterable nature of Things are Eternally United. But
notwithstanding the evident necessity of the measure, and having before our Eyes the recent & notorious fatal Consequences of Public Peculation among the People we had just seperated from—Yet we see
ours Profusely Squandred and Dissipated, being freely entrusted in

every Venal hand, without one necessary Restraint having been Enacted to secure its honest & faithful Application as if on Purpose to
pervert our Principles—Nor has other matters been better attended
to—Contending as we are with the First Maratime Power in the
World, who not only blocked up our Ports with their Cruisers but
whos Fleets says Congress covered the Ocean which besides nearly an-
nihilating our Exports rendered Supplys from abroad not only Precarious but greatly inhanced the Price—Thus circumstanced Interest
& Necessity clearly Pointed out the Wisdom & sound Policy of encouraging our useful Manufactures and of Limiting our Imports to Supplys for the Army together with a very few necessary Articles which
we could not expect to furnish ourselves, and even this inconsiderable
Business ought to have been transacted for and on Account of the
Public, Or by our Allys—But instead of Rational Schemes for Promoting Industry & Frugality a Gambling Traffick was Countenanced &
Encouraged altho visibly Ruinous in its Principles and most Baneful
in its Consequences. Trade Sir is the Golden Ball the Ignis Fatuus
after which we all seem Eagerly contending and to which we, it is to be
feared have Sacrificed every valuable Consideration. Nor can there be
a more Melancholy and Convincing Proof of the weakness & Partiality
of our Councils than the unremitting Ardour with which we have pursued this Phantom to our Destruction—Trade Sir is an Edged Instrument that requires to be managed with address to Prevent it from injuring those who handle it hence Commerce has generally ended in
bringing Ruin on every free State where it has flourished to any Extent—Yet under Wise Restrictions and when transacted upon liberal
Principles it may be productive of many Advantages to a Country—
Altho to investigate this important Subject fully is remote from our
Purpose, yet it seems necessary to observe that a Trade may enrich
Individuals and at the same time bring Poverty & Ruin on the State
and as the sole Pursuit of most Traders is their own Gain, and so that
succeeds they are careless of little else—It is therefore not to be won-
dred at that we see them confound the one with the other and there is
scarcely one of ours to be met with but is ready to assert that we have
derived great and considerable Advantages from our Traffick during
the War. Such Prejudices in minds so confined is excusable when we
reflect, however impiously Arrogant it may appear that we have seen
a day set apart by our Piddling Rulers for the People solemnly to address the Divinity with Grateful Thanks for the Success and Advantages derived from their Commerce—What in reason can be expected from such men whos Stations ought to have set them above the
low dirty Prejudices of the Vulgar, whom we find evidently making
the Public Interest to consist in their Private Advantage & the Success
of their Pitiful Lousey Schemes and Presumptuously ordering Public

Thanks To that Pure and Awful Fountain of Truth in whos all Pircing Sight the Wealth of Worlds is a Trash, for that which in all human Probability has been if not the sole at least the chief cause of our Wretchedness—To render Commerce of advantage, nay to prevent it from being injurious it became necessary to distinguish between the Profit of the Merchant & the Gain of the State—Inattention to this important Distinction has Produced many errors relating to Trade which having been adopted without consideration are become Proverbial. from hence it may be seen how necessary it becomes in our Legislation to inspect narrowly into the Nature & Consequences of their Trade and points out the danger of Permiting Traders to become Legislatures—Commerce being instituted for the Advantage of the Community ought to be made subservient to the Interests of the Whole, and when found Prejudicial to the Public Good ought to be subjected to such regulations as are sufficient to remove the Evil, or if necessary totaly restrained. The Epidamnians perceiving their morrals depraved from their Intercourse with Foreigners, Chose a Magistrate for making all Contracts, & Sales in the Name & Behalf of the State—Commerce then as Montesquieu observes, does not Corrupt the Constitution, and the Constitution does not deprive the Society of the Advantage of Commerce—Besides our having, this best of all Reasons as well as the Epidamnians, we had another, interesting enough to be taken notice of. Our Traffick besides Debauching our Principles robed us of our Wealth & Strength—For besides enriching our Enemys with our Specie, it contributed to furnish them at our expence, with an essential article of Provisions, at the same time dipriving us of numbers of our labourious Citizens, and by exciting a Spirit of Speculation, alured many of them that remained, from their honest Industry, to Prey on their Neighbours in the more easy and lucrative Business of Pedling—As Extortion was unrestrained, it soon became boundless, and the necessarys of Life, by passing thro' a variety of hands, the Extortion was accumulated to such a Degree as to become insufferable—The lucrative Effects of these exactions was manifested by the dissipated change in the manners of the Hucksters, and as there was nothing to be made from any Species of Agriculture, the Spirit of Adventure, and Dealing, encreased to an astonishing & an alarming degree to the great Prejudice of Religion Manners & Industry, and the encrease of Sensuality Idleness Fraud Villainy & all the licentious Disorders of a Corrupted People. The return for these Essential Sacrifices, have been chiefly Articles of Luxury, Superfluitys which we could & ought to have done without—But such was our infatuation, that this Set of Drones was encouraged to the Countrys Ruin, whilst the Spirit of the People (for of all Arts to reduce the spirit of freemen none has proved more effectual than Usury and Extortion) was unfortunately worn out before their Patience, in daily expectation, that Their Legislatures, profiting from Experience, would have put a Stop to measures so evidently destructive, whilst They, sharers in the Plunder, or intent on other schemes of Interest or Pleasure, beheld with the utmost unconcern that set of Men, making a Property of their Constituents and wallowing in the fruits of their Extortion, for it is evident, that nearly the whole Profit of this Baneful Traffick, was raised on the Articles imported, little of our Produce having been carried abroad—It has been computed, by those who Pretend to know, that our Exports in one Year before the War, were nearly equal to the whole, except Specie during its continuance—It has also been proved, with as much Satisfaction as the nature of the case will admit, that had Those who have been taken off, in Building & Navigating the Trading Vessells, together with the numerous Army of Retailers, Pedlars, and other Idlers, about our Sea Ports & else wher, who were ever accustomed to labour, been steadily employd, that we could have manufactured double the Quantity of Useful Articles that has been imported—From these calculations if but nearly accurate some Idea may be acquired concerning the nature of our Dealings, it scarcely deserves the name of Trade, and the considerable loss we have sustained from it. That however with Industry may soon be regained, But our Lost Principles are infinitely more to be regreted as not being so easily restored—That many of our Adventurers have amassed Propirty is certain—yet what they have been able to Retain bears no proportion to That which they have fleeced from the Country. Our Poverty & scarcity of Specie must demonstrate this to every impartial Enquirer—They have indeed proved but the Agents of the Enemy to fill their Coffers with the Specie & their Jails with the Citizens of their Country and to do our Piddling Patriots justice it must be allowed that no Servile S(*illegible*)ded Scots factor who has left his Conscience with his Religion on his native Shore, could have been more industrious or shown less Squimish remorse at the methods which has been employed in Gleaning up the Wealth of their Country. But the long indulgence which this set of men have been used to, has set them above every sense of Shame & Feeling & encouraged them to deem themselves the only People of Consequence amongst us, and their attempts, as appears from some of their Resolves since the Peace, tending to continue their gainful monopolly of us is insulting to the highest degree.

The dissipated manners of the Traders had already become infectious, when the iniquitous and Impolitick measures, adopted respecting the ungranted Lands, in Conjunction with our Trade, the Expenditures & Depreciation of our Money furnished such extensive Opportunitys for Fraud extortion speculation & Venality as entirely corroded every Liberal Passion—The Contagion became general and infested all Ranks with a Cursed desire of becoming suddenly Rich, not by a commendable Industry but from the Ignorance and Necessities of our Neighbours—Little else was regarded but Schemes of Private Gain, every other obligation was sacrificed to that single Pursuit, for so entirely had this degrading Passion engrossed our attention, that our Religious & Public obligations were unthought of, and our family Duties all comprozed in Providing a little wealth, or a few useless Acres. It was the very Delirium of Riches, and our Infatuation beyond what the most extravagant imagination can conceive, Its baneful consequences having exceeded what we are told, of the Misisipi & South Sea Schemes, their Effects being chiefly confined, to Those of a Particular Rank, with us the whole Mass of the People seems Infected, and we are evidently labouring under the pernicious Consequences of Wealth, whilst our Gambling Traffick & our Dissipation leaves us in all the wretchedness of Poverty—We may indeed defy History to instance a People, Pretending to Civilization, so miserably Poor, and at the same time so Wretchedly Depraved—Nor was the change by imperceptible degrees but most rapid—It was but the other Day, we pretended to Emulate the Heroick Virtues, of the Benevolent Numa and the Disinterested Curius, and already we Vie in Avarice & Dissipation, with the Covetous Crassus & the Proffligate Anthony, for we seem to have accomplished in a few Years, what has generally taken other Nations as many centurys—And had not the Sufferers found an Asylum in the Southern States, and the Country to the Westward, it is more than Probable, that the Consequences would have been felt in a very different manner—was Liberty but established amongst us on Liberal Principles no Man possessed of Health, with an Independant Spirit could possibly be Ruined.

Had our Enemys directed our Councils, they could not possibly have pointed out Measures more Pernicious for us, or more likely to have Effected their Purpose & our Destruction, as our Public Disipation, our destructive Trade and the impolitick Conduct pursued with the ungranted Lands—It indeed seems difficult to conceive any measure more justly deserving Censure, than our Conduct relating to the Unsettld Country—It is as infamous as Impolitick, Besides the ample field which it furnished, at the Public Expence, for Speculation & Embezzlement it alured our attention from the main object, and by dividing our Strength, & opening ⟨lur⟩king places for all who chose to Shrink from their Duty, evidently endangered the Cause—But in every point of view it appears Detestible, and must entail Infamy on the Authors—At the commencement of the War & for a considerable time after these Lands were Unreservedly held up, as in Justice in they ought as a National fund for defraying the Expences of the War, and when their Value & Extent is considered, surely it affords reason to imagine, that had they been wisely & honestly managed, they would even at a Price favourable for the Actual Seller, undoubtedly less than they are to be had for of the Land Jobber or Huckster, have proved, nearly sufficient to have answered every just Debt, which it was necessary to have incured, most certainly they would, had our National Expenditures been attended to, with that Disinterestedness & Œconomy, which we had reason to expect—Yet Sir enormous as this loss is to the Public, there seems still another Circumstance most interesting to every Friend of Liberty, and which makes this conduct more deeply to be regretted—There could not Posibly have happened a more favourable opportunity for Erecting a Number of States, fortunate in being formed on the Principles of Equality, by an equitable and generous Agrarian, a Regulation deemed from the Experience of States and the Testimony of every Political Writer, the most necessary & essential for the happiness prosperity & Duration of every Landed Republic—The loss of this most salutary measure is the more to be lamented as our Rulers on this occasion cannot plead Ignorance, Our Situation, our Circumstances nay our Safety, rendered it as plain & obvious, as it was wise & honourable, being not only consonant to the Spirit of our Governments, but most advantageous & glorious in its Issue and must Ultimately, have added a considerable degree of Safety & Stability to the Confederacy—for supposing these new States, from a more equal Division of Property, & a Wise System of Laws, formed on the true Principles of Democratic Liberty, as they are further removed from the means of Luxury, & other obvious Causes of Corruption, it is reasonable to presume that the Spirit of Liberty, would have continued longer uncontaminated amongst them, than it may chance to do in the old States, where a more unequal division of Property, and a freer intercourse with Foreigners, may Probably, soon produce a total change of Manners, the fattal consequences of which upon every Free State are too notoriously known.

But no thoughts like these for the honour of the Public. No great Designs for the Benefit of Posterity—Such has been our Sordid Illiberal System of Politicks, that to gratify the most Odious & Contemptible Passion, we have Risked, not only our own Liberty and Happiness, but evidently hazarded the Success of the Noblest Cause, and from our Local Situation, of the greatest Magnitude in its Consequences to Mankind in General of any Temporal Prize that ever was or will be contended for—Who that is interested for the happiness of Mankind, but must Regret the loss of this most favourable opportunity. Had Liberty been established upon Noble & Generous Principles nothing was too great to be expected—not only the Freedom & Happiness of America but in half a Century We might have defied the Tyrants of the Earth Combined—But alas these Men in Place of living Esteemed & Revered as Beings of a Superiour Species and of being Celebrated to all Future Ages amongst the Illustrious Patrons of Liberty & Founders of States are Execrated & Rendered Odious for thus meanly Sacrificing so Noble so Favourable so Godlike an Opportunity for Securing & Extending the Liberty & Happiness of Mankind at such an Œra as the Revolution of Centuries may not again Produce— Surely Sir if the Private Offender—But let us not arrogate the Bolts of the Almighty, for certainly no Temporal Sufferings can atone for such Villany and such Folly—Thus the Love of Money when ever it takes Possession of the Heart declars War against all Human Nature and there can not Posibly be a Lesson more humiliating to our boasted Superiority then to see Men evedently Possessing Abilities so far lost to every Sense of their Duty of which their Exalted Stations ought to have inspired them with the most Noble & Disinterested Ideas and the Occasion and Opportunity stimulated to the most Heroick & Zealous Exertions—Bartering every Thing worthy of Attention for a Phantome a Shaddow which even when obtained is surely accompanied with Solicitude & Discontent—It is presumed that enough has been said to answer the Purpose intended without prolonging a disagreeable detail of other Instances of our imprudence of which there seems no Lack—such as our vain Efforts towards establishing a Navy, our no less Don Quixotical Conduct, & Expeditions against the Indians, our Burthensome & inadequate Mode of Recruiting our Army, the manner of disposing of Confiscated Property, which in most States proved only a Job for the Money Brokers—together with many other Matters, Monuments of our Folly & Sinks to our Credit—I pretend not to be wellinformed, neither do I claim any greater share of abilities than my Neighbours. I may have thought a little more on our Situation than many others, and it seems not unreasonable to suppose that when matters of such Moment & Public Notoriety have been neglected that others of a more Private Nature have not been better Conducted—Those Instances which have been given of our Inattention were selected merely as their Consequences were obvious to the meannest Capacity and requiring neither Penetration to forsee nor Abilities to remedy and as being the Source from whence our Corruption seems Principally to flow—Congress it seems has complained that They have not been Properly supported by the People who They say has treated them Contemptuously—But Those who expect to be Revered merely from their Stations without doing any thing to deserve it must of course fall into Contempt—Those who would be respected by others must first Respect themselves a certain exteriour Purity or Dignity of Character commands Respect Procures Credit and invites Confidence. But the Public Exercise of, and ostentation of Vice has the contrary Effect—Dignity does not consist in Extravagance nor Greatness in Dissipation. Has any of our Statesmen exceeded John De Wit in Fame or Reputation—of unwearied application and Assiduity in Public affairs—He acceded to the true Republican Principles of Frugality & Moderation kept only one Man & a Maid Servant, walked always on foot at the Hague whilst in the negotiations of Europe his name was ranked with the most Powerful Kings—But altho our Rulers have done little to merite either the Support or Confidence of the People it must nevertheless appear to every impartial Person that We entered into the Contest with a Spirit becoming the Cause and had not our Rulers put it out of our Power by their Conduct we should have continued to have done every thing that was expected from us for that They enjoyd our unreserved and unlimited Confidence seems apparent not only from our patient Sufferings under the longest & most unheard of Series of Extortion as well as from many other Circumstances. We therefore were in their Hands as Clay in the Hands of the Potter to have Moulded as they Pleased—accordingly we find honest Statesmen raising their People from the depths of Depravity to Virtue & Knowledge for in other States Liberty has been Productive amongst other accomplishments of Domestick Arts and of such Political Knowledge & Acquirements as are necessary to make States respected Abroad and to Preserve Equality Happiness & Security at Home—Mark the Contrast—with us it has been Productive of a Sordid Despicable Passion of acquiring Money in Pursuit of which every useful Study every necessary & Beneficial Improvement has been totally neglected—That there is an Active Principle in the Soul of Man which requires to be employ'd is certain but we find that it is almost a matter of indifference to happiness whether high Passions are to be gratified or Subdued and the chief merite of a Legislature seems to consist in giving this active Spirit a propper direction, for the Soul is pleased with its Efforts, and provided it is exerted it signifies little though its Activity should be turned against Itself—In all Institutions Civil as well as Religious History & Experience proves it to be a standing maxim that the Senses Passions Imagination as well as Reason ought to be influenced by Objects propper to incite the Mind to the Practice of every Virtue and with hold it from Vice—We on the contrary have expected all from Reason which we see is seldom attended to amidst the tumult of the Passions. It is therefore from the

Effects of Habit assisted by well adapted Laws that we find Passions inspired Actions performed & Sacrifices made which our Contracted Souls cannot comprehend—But your Excellency Conduct furnishes an ample commentary on this Text—Can all their Money induce a Man to make a certain sacrifice of his Life—No this is inconsistant with the nature of the Passion but when Love of Country has been inculcated Examples are not only common, but we find them emulous of Sacrificing themselves for the Benefit of their Fellow Citizens Accordingly the Greeks owed more to their Love of Country which animated them to the Service of it than to all their Philosophers—the Romans were fired to Action by the same incentive—What have we seen in almost our own times the Dutch performing Miracles of Valour & Disinterestedness to save themselves & Morasses from the Spaniard when Public Virtue in Poverty urged them to Action Now they are overwhelmed in Wealth as Private Men they would scarce move a finger to defend their Country from invasion because that Public Spirit is expired—How weak, nay how Criminal is it then in the founders of States instead of cultivating Ideas so essentially necessary for their Prosperity & Existence to Permit the Prevalence of them to be entirely effaced But ours has attended so little to these necessary parts of their Duty that it seems difficult to recolect an Instance from which we can suppose they ever once thought of it We find them indeed arrogating merite from the abilities which they have displayed in Constructing our Constitutions and it must be allowed that their Form is well adapted to the Spirit of Democratic Liberty had they taken Care at the same time to have furnished us with good Laws we might have been Happy under a worse and every School Boy knows the very best cannot do without them—To attempt it is ful as absurd as it would be to put to Sea in a Hulk with out Rudder or Sails, which altho constructed without a fault must become the Sport of the Winds & sooner or later as the Storm setts be wrecked on the first strand that takes her up—It is certainly not so much in forming a Government, as in framing a System of Wise & necessary Laws by which that Government is made to Act where a Legislator has occasion to Exert All Experience Abilities & Wisdom that by adapting his Principles to the Spirit of his Government and the Temper of the People He may form such a Code as may afford a Reasonable Prospect of Happiness & Duration to his State. Yet such seems to have been the Fatality attending all our Proceedings of a Public nature that even this very essential & necessary Part of their Duty has been overlooked and indeed the whole tenor of their Conduct proves that no set of Men has so manifestly mistaken the way of Governing or could have shown more indifference to acquire Dignity from their high & important Stations—Thro' the whole of their Administration has run a heedlessness which is not easy to be accounted for—They seem to have consulted hardly any thing but their Prejudices & Caprices, and Plunged themselves into needless Circumstances the infallible mark of a Narrow Mind seeing things only in Part and not capable of Comprehending the Whole for neglecting to avail themselves of every wise means of good Government their favourite Scheme seems to have been that of subduing all Hearts to the Influence of Money the Natural Enemy to every Liberal Emotion of the Soul Hence Riches has become the only Idol of worship, & Poverty the objects of Contempt, and the ridicule which has thereby been thrown upon Patriotism Honour Integrity & Religion has done more real mischief in a Political Sense than all the Money in the States, nay than any Sum can Compensate for as this contemptible Passion becomes general we seem threatned with a universal Reign of Ignorance from ⟨*illegible*⟩ extinction of every Noble & Generous Principle.

I wish not to distress your Excellency feelings by entering into a further detail of our Proflagacy & Misery, but if to be insensible to the Principles of Religion & the dictates of Social Justice, if Poverty with Inordinate Desires can make a People wretched we are truly so—I am aware that it has been a received opinion for the three or four Years Past and nothing was more common, not only with our Peddling Rulers but also with others who from duty & opportunity ought to have been better informed, to assert, that there never was so much Specie in the Country before, and in the same Breath complain of the astonishing scarcity, and that their Business was at a total stand for the want of a medium—As we are seldom at a loss to account for what suits us, this Contradiction was solved, by the Planting Farmers having locked it up—And even this opinion was adopted, altho so ridiculous, being it suited their Purpose—It saved them the trouble of thinking, furnished them with an excuse for some Proceedings, which cannot be justified upon any other Principles, than the People being possessed of Money—That Specie has been scarce, is evident from many stricking circumstances, for it is a truth that even their insignificant Traffick was often at a Stand for the want of it, but that much of it was laid up is improbable, as the unheard of Premiums given for money must have brought it forth. At any rate a very little reflection will make it appear that very few Land occupiers could possibly lay up money since the War—After paying Taxes & other Impositions the residue generally proved insufficient to procure Necessaries nor is this surprizing when the advanced price of Goods during the War is considered together with high prices of every species of Labour & low fluctuating Markets—Thus circumstanced, Industry was of little avail, at any rate it has been impossible for a mere land occupier to do more than procure more Necessaries—many have not been able to do that—therefore supposing his Landed Property to be of equal Value which does not seem to be generally the case at Present, besides losing Nine Years & his share of the Public Debt he is in a worse state than at the begining of the War—but what must be his situation, if he unfortunately happened to be in Debt before, with an accumulating Interest which it has not perhaps been in his Power to wipe off—That the People in general were much distressed for the want of Goods seems evident, from the Efforts which they made, to raise a little money to procure a few necessarys since the Price has fallen. This is confirmed by the large Sums which has been sent out since the Peace—If the best Mercantile authority is to be depended upon, from Virginia & Maryland it is very little if any short of Two Millions of dollars, a Sum truly astonishing, as well as alarming—and our former Drains & evident scarcity before considered exceeds what wuld reasonably be thought, was in Circulation, and must leave us nearly without Medium nor has this drain nearly reduced our reasonable wants. If to this reduced, and exhausted State of the Country, we consider we are overwhelmed with Debt, Public & Private, The People wihout Principle harassing & harassed by clamorous & impatient Creditors Dispirited & Disabled from the scarcity of money of availing themselves of their Property either by Sale or Cultivation to advantage—Involved in a Labyrinth of Contention & Law without a Medium sufficient to answer their Taxes & the fees of the Corr⟨o⟩ding Law—Their Councils without Wisdom Generosity or Justice—If it is possible for us to exist long in such a Situation and under such management, or any thing like it, we shall exhibit a New Phenomenon in Political Nature that can hold together without the uniting Principles of Religion & Government (for we cannot call the names of things their realities) most certain it is that the Active Powers of Both are almost totally annihilated—Nothing, if I am at Liberty to speak my Sentiments seems more desparate than the State of the Public, or more detestible than its Authors. You Great Sir by having done your Duty nobly has Demonstrated to the World that it is in our Power to be a free & a happy People—But alas when our true condition comes to be known we shall seem not to have been let down but, flung down from the firmament of Glory for our conduct must Prove us unworthy of Liberty & unfit to Govern ourselves—Did matters rest here yet still they have gone too far but the nature of things is such that they cannot rest—It is true the form of our Constitution remain, but the best cannot subsist long under an ill administration and we have lost what is more material the very Blood & liver—for how useful is it to consider that our Spirit is unbraced and our Virtue Stifled by Pride & Avarice—And we are as much like

Republicans as an unprincipled worthless Debaucher as like an Upright Virtuous Man. Never Sir was there an Instance of a People going so thoughtlessly so precipitately to destruction. When the Distresses of a People proceede from the Pernicious hand of Administration it is then that Their case becomes truly alarming as without a speedy Reformation it soon becomes desperate for such seems to be the fatality attending human affairs unless they speedily Recover they seldom or ever mend—But what hope to expect a Reformation flushed as we are with an advantageous Peace & when Those whos duty it is to set about it has no Idea of any being necessary nor are Those who want reformation likely to reform others—They may open the Gates to disorders & scatter the Plague they carry about them but will never Stop the Current of one Vice either by Counsel or Example—Whilst Thus Governed what Relief can we reasonably look for—But matters cannot long continue as they are—nay it is plain that even the little concern which we give ourselves about Public Affairs interferes too much with our Selfish Pursuits & frivolous employments that the Burthen of Government is become too heavy and rather than undergo the fatigue much longer ourselves we will very willingly shift it on the Shoulders of the first That offers—for it is evident that we are fast approaching to that Point of disorder & Confusion where the only remedy for the Present is the Supreame Authority of a Powerful Man is alone Capable of restoring Order & Regularity.

From these Premises, if true some Judgement may be formed of our Abilities in the Art of Governing and also some Idea of our Present Situation—I have not attempted to deceive Your Excellency—They appear to me in the very Light in which I have endeavoured to represent here—I have been at Pains by Reflection & every means in my Power to divert myself of Prejudice. But Errors & Habits are difficult to be vanquished If I am an enthusiast it is in the Cause of Liberty and when I consider that Our Rulers were not Born to Power and of no Consequence more than One of the People until they were confided in—when I see these Men insensible of the Honor confered upon them Prostituting themselves & Sacrificing those Sacred Rights which they were chosen to Protect when I consider what we ought to have been and what we are like to be my Zeal may at such times have got the better of my moderation—I hope it is but Seldom and I humbly submit my opinions to your juster decision who can so well distinguish between the Errors of inexperience and the impulse of a Depraved Inclination—Being neither Splenatick nor Moron, as it gives me Pain to have Cause to Censure—so it would afford me true Pleasure to have reson to Praise—But altho to agravate is not intinded yet it will answer no good end to deny the truth and boast of our Health when every Symptom of fatal disease seems manifest—Incredible as our Situation may seem to be we need only to enquire into the Characters of the Leading or Active Men the nature of their Views or Pursuits with their manner of transacting the Public Business and look no further for the cause of every Evil we complain of—Extortionors, Speculators, Hucksters & Practising Lawyers Have of all men proved themselves the most unfit to legislate for a Free People Ever intent on the acquirement of wealth the Public Interest in their interested Eyes becomes the success of their own Private Business—Deficient in liberal Knowledge & Blinded by their Avarice their sordid Souls contract as their Baggs or their dirty A⟨im⟩s. They would press us all to their Private Advantage & spread yet further the Thirst of Money & the fatal Effects which attend it—No Study can contribute more to expand the Mind & enlighten the understanding than that of Jurisprudence taken in an enlarged sense and I question not but that there are many Attorneys born with open & Honest hearts but their knowledge being generally limited & confined to the Practice of their Profession which exposing them to an indiscriminate defence of right & wrong contracts the understanding while it corrupts the heart, hence we find them Shameless & unfeeling Ignorant Illiberal Avaricious & Disinginious & ever ready to gratify their Dirty Passions—If there be any instances upon record as some then are undoubtedly of Genuis Morrality united in a Lawyer they are distinguished by their singularity & operate as an exception—As to the Landed Gentlemen who are as the true Owners of our Political Vessell, (the other as such being only Passengers) and who must constitute the majority they have surely sacrificed their better Judgements to the selfish views of the other—It is indeed much to be lamented that People of Real Property have not taken Pains to be as well informed as their Duty to their Country requires. As it is only from them that one can expect to reap essential Service—But certainly their Passions must have arisen more from want of attention & their Aversion to Business than from want of Abilities However from the sordid Schemes of the One set & the Propensity to Pleasure in the other it is easy to perceive that the Interest of their Constituents must be unthought of and neglected not that any extraordinary share of Abilities have been required to discover the true Interest of the Country. It undoubtedly required to be sought after, and as the well known address with which our Active Set of Rulers have conducted their own Concerns leaves us no room to doubt their abilities—Had they given equal attention to The Concerns of the Public we may venture to affirm No Country could have been better Governed—When it is true told by those who wish to screen their Negligence or Vilany That There is this and that Mystery in Government that it requires the most consumate Abilities the most refined Address, and from the frequent miscarriages, and Blunders, of Those who attempt it, we are readily induced to take for granted what they tell us. It undoubtedly requires Probity and application— but whenever we find a Man, Disinterested & Vigilant, Possessed of Mother Wit, we may Trust that He will make an Excellent States- man—This opinion may seem singular, but reason & observation, will, I trust, Prove it just, and we constantly find, that in the first & Illiterate Ages of States, Probity & Vigilance, formed better States- men, than Education & Refinements, in the more enlightned æras. not but that Experience & a Knowledge of Mankind, is not only of Benefit, but necessary but it Proves that Probity & Attention are the first & principle Qualificatons of a Statesman—and so firmly do I be- lieve, that no Abilities whatever can Atone for the want of Probity, that rather ⟨than⟩ any Slave of Avarice, whos narrow Soul can be shut up in a Snuff Bottle, should Legislate for me, I would prefer an Hon- est Negro of common Understanding—He might be improved—The other never—Surely we have reason to say, There can be no vice so infamous so pernicious in Persons of Trust & Office as Avarice. He is the Pest of Society, He is against every Man He is no mans Friend and is his own least of all—In such a Situation, & under such Guidance what is to be expected but Ruin, must we then continue tamely to view its approach, or Resolve by the most rational Means to avoid it— Thank Heaven & Your Excellency we have these means stil in our Power, but every man of reflection must be convinced, that the same supine inattention with which our Affairs has hitherto been Con- ducted, is no longer safe, and that without Superiour degrees of Pro- bity, Wisdom & Vigour, in our Political measures, every thing we have Gained will be infalibly lost—No man is more sensible how little is to be done, in our Present State of Depravation, when every thing is so much amiss, and the Public Good so little regarded. Yet surely it is the greatest of folly, to offer an expedient which altho Pursued will not answer the end—such measures proceede in part from our Igno- rance of the ill condition we are in, but principally from a Dread of Pitiful Consequences, which has hitherto hindered us, from applying the necessary remedies, if they are attended with the least appearance of difficulty, and nothing can more plainly demonstrate the Want of Good Sense, and Resolution in particular men, or the Weakness of our Councils, than to Content ourselves & Prosecute and considerable matter, by ineffectual means—Let us not therefore Sir in future, rest on what cannot support us—we seem to be nearly arrived, at that Cri- sis, when our Pitiful system of Expedients will no longer serve our

⟨turn⟩—Let us therefore, ere we fall never more to rise, embrace the means whilst in our Power—The Remedy, and the only Remedy in our Situation, is clearly Pointed out to us from the highest Political Authority. Or thus impressed as I am with my want of Abilities, I shoud not have Presumed to have offered my oppinion. "That when once a Republic becomes Corrupted, there remains no Possibility of remedying the Rising Evil, but by a Thorough Reformation of those Corruptions, which a loose Administration, and the Depravity of our Nature has introduced, and Restoring Virtue, with a Simplicity of Manners, every other Correction is useless, or a New Evil—and many memorable Instances are to be met with, in the rise of Popular Governments, of Thus Renewing their Constitution and Restoring it, to its first Principles. It cannot in fact be said that we ever had Right Principles to revert to, and this Neglect cannot be too much lamented—It was like an Error in the first Concoction, which cannot be Corrected in the Second—the foundation is weak & insufficient and whatever Structure is raised upon it must of necessity fall—But we have the Spirit of our Constitution to direct us, and no Radical Cure can take Place but by beginning anew & forming Principles Consonant to the Nature of our Goverment—It is full time to make some appology for the freedom of this address—I certainly ought for the Prolixity of it—I did indeed expect, and I suppose any other Person, might have put all I wished to say in half the number of Pages—as to Public appeals You see I am unfit—indeed were I never so well qualified, yet find so little notice taken of them, that they seem to answer no good purpose and altho we may have no reason to reverence the Persons of our Rulers, yet there is a Respect due to their Stations, which it is our duty to Preserve—besides I would fain hope against all hope that our Condition may not be so bad as I apprehend. at any rate it seems unknown to the World—I flatter myself that this application is judiciously directed You Sir are justly honoured with the Confidence of Your Country. The Business is every way worthy of your Character, and Presents as ample, and as fair a field for Fame, as that which you have so worthily Explored. It is perfectly adapted to your Talents—Your liberality of Sentiment Your love of Virtue Your Philanthropy, your Zeal for rational Freedom, your Vigilance and Penetration, are Qualities in dispensible on this occasion—You are now Solemly called upon, to exert those great abilities with which you are fortunately endowed, for the Benefit of Mankind—Remember Sir that the obligation under which we lie to do Good, increases in Proportion to the Rank we hold, but above all to the Talents, which God has given us to perform it. You have Sir, with gratitude I acknowledge it delivered us from our External Enemies—but before we can reap the full fruits of your Toils, you must deliver us from the Demon of

Avarice & the Dominion of our Illiberal Passions—The undertaking is most Arduous, but then the Reward is the greater, and is indeed become absolutely necessary, if you hope to see us maintain, the Rank & Importance amongst the Nations, which you have obtained for us, and wish us to do justice to those, who have so generously, & liberally assisted us in time of need—No Reputation can be lost much may gained by the Attempt, if successfull, it will Endear you still more to every honest Man, it will bring down upon your head the Blessings of Thousands, & transmit your Name thro' countless Millions made happy by your means—There never by Heavens, was an occasion so Important, so Big with the fate of mankind—The Liberty not only of America but Probably of the World is at Stake—This Sir, motives the strongest, that can affect Reason or the Passions, ought to engage you in this Noble this Godlike attempt—Altho a total Change of measures, is evidently so necessary for our Existence as a People, yet I will venture to Predict you much opposition from the Selfish Mercenary Tribe—But you will have the Unanimous attachment of the Land holders, altho a distressed, yet still a Respectable Body, with all Persons of Genuine Worth and Integrity, and of every Man, who has the true Interest & happiness of his Country at Heart—You will have more than this, the Consciousness of a Great & Virtuous Action—You will have, with Reverence I utter it, the Blessing of approving Heaven— Stand forth then Sir, & Surrounded with Your Noble & Generous Actions Arouse us from our Lethargy, give us a Sight of our Danger Light up in our Breasts a Spark of that Sacred flame which has animated You to Deeds of Immortal Fame. Show us the scandal and false policy of Prefering a private Interest before that of our country— Restore us to a Mode of thinking and pursuits becoming of Freemen that we may regain a Station of Security for the Common wealth ere it falls in ruins never to rise again.

I take my leave of Your Excellency with a Presumption that nothing I have advanced can be construed into a Wish to offend—But if contrary to Expectation any thing should incur your displeasure, You have but destroy this and the cause is removed for no Person on Ea[r]th can possibly know the Contents of this Address and nothing is further from the intention of the Writer to disoblige—for he will ever be ready, on every occasion gratefully to acknowledge the inestimable Services which you have rendered him & his in common with the rest of his Country men—Any Man is capable of doing a piece of Service to another but it is some what Divine to Contribute to the Happiness of Millions—I am Great Sir, and what in my oppinion is to Your Credit, Good Sir Your Sincere Friend and Obliged Servant One of the Most distressed altho the first of all Profesions a HusbandMan.

I have been guilty of too many ⟨Igotisms⟩ to give my name—It is of no importance as what is said is intended only to excite your Exellencys attention to our Civil Matters the Result being left to your better Judgement—It seems the fate of the fertile & Extensive Country to the N.W. of the Ohio is yet undecided—If we mean to do Justice to our Creditors it is to be hoped that we shall have no more Speculaton at the Public Expence—But if we are to judge by the past this may be expected without Your timely & spirited interposition—If nothing else will do why not associate for the Preservation of Our Governments the Support of Public Credit & the encouragement of Industry & frugality—The Respect & Confidence which you justly Possess will I am convinced enable you to carry through any Scheme you may adopt for our Preservation.

AL, DLC:GW. GW endorsed the letter: "From an Unknown Author without date—received 15th July 1784."

From David Humphreys

My dear General   New York July 15th 1784
    You may be surprised, tho I dare say you will not be displeased to receive a Letter from me, dated at a moment when you would have supposed I had already traversed at least one half of the Atlantic—The occasion of my having yet to embark is this—Governor Jefferson on his tour to the eastern States informed me (in Connecticut) of the arrival of a french Packet at New York, in which he proposed sailing, unless he should find in an eastern port a Vessel destined directly to France, in which case he was to give me notice—On his arrival in Boston he advised me he had not found a passage, but expected to set out for New York the 1st of July—After his return from Portsmouth Mr Nat Tracey (who was about to sail for England in a ship of his own) having offered to land him on the Coast of France if practicable, he took the resolution of embarking & gave me information accordingly; but it was so late before I received it, that I found it impossible to avail myself of the occasion, and therefore formed the determination of sailing in the french Packet, whose departure is fixed for this day—And excepting the loss of Mr Jefferson's company, I confess I am much better pleased with my accomodations, & opportunity of acquiring some knowledge of french on the passage—Gen. Koscuiszko & Col. Senf are to be my fellow passengers.[1]

Governor Jefferson acquainted me, in one of his Letters from Boston, with his having recd a Packet from your Excellency addressd to me, but as he supposed it required a safe rather than a speedy conveyance he chose to retain it until we should meet again[2]—this, my dear General, will account for my not having acknowledged the receipt of those favours which I find you had the friendship to grant in consequence of my Letter from Philadelphia. Your Excellency knows the sincerity of my heart & the warmth of my affections—tho' it will probably never be in my power to be useful or to render any compensation to so good a patron & friend; yet, I trust it will always be mine, to be faithful, to be grateful, & not to reflect disgrace upon that friendship, from which I derive so much satisfaction, glory, & support.

Having seen your Excellency reach the zenith of human greatness, an object than which none was ever nearer my heart; I should now be perfectly happy could I but see justice done to your character & actions—but there are many traits in the one & circumstances of the other, which I fear will be lost. Indeed I find it is the opinion of many Gentlemen of candor & information that a true account of the war, at least of your military transactions cannot be given but by yourself or some of those who have been about your person. The fact is, in my opinion, it is a most delicate subject, highly interesting not only to your reputation, but to the good of mankind at large—I only take the liberty to suggest the subject for your consideration & will do myself the pleasure of writing more fully by another occasion[3]—With my best respects to Mrs Washington & the family I have the honor to be yr Excys most obedt Hble Servt

D. Humphreys

P.S. The closing & superscribing this Letter is one of the last acts which I shall do previous to my leaving the Continent—it brings to my Mind a thousand tender ideas, & expands all my soul in the best wishes for your health & felicity—I expect momently the signal of departure & can say no more than adieu.

ALS, DLC:GW; ADf, CtY: Humphreys-Marvin-Olmstead Collection.

1. See Thomas Jefferson to Humphreys, 21 June, 4 July 1784, in Boyd, *Jefferson Papers*, 7:311, 363. Jefferson sailed from Boston on 5 July aboard Nathaniel Tracy's *Ceres*. Humphreys reported to GW from Lorient in France on 12 Aug. 1784 that he himself had "a most delightful passage of twenty four days." Tadeusz Andrzej Bonawentura Kosciuszko (1746–1817), a Polish

army officer, was in Paris at the outbreak of the American Revolution and came to the United States in August 1776. He served in the Continental army throughout the war, as a colonel of engineers under Gen. Horatio Gates from 1776 to 1780 and thereafter as an engineer and cavalry officer under Gen. Nathanael Greene. He and the engineer Christian Senf did not sail with Humphreys.

2. See Jefferson's letter of 21 June cited in note 1.

3. Humphreys recurred to the topic of GW's biography as early as his letter of 30 Sept. 1784. Humphreys made a start himself at writing a life of Washington after his return from France in 1786.

From Benjamin Lincoln

My dear General   Hingham [Mass.] July 15th 1784
I may not omit so good an opportunity as now offers ℔ Major Bayliss to inform your Excellency that at the meeting of the Cincinnati of this State they with great pleasure adopted the system as altered and amended by the general meeting and it appears to give great satisfaction to the citizens at large.[1]

I am pursuing the plan I mentioned to your Excellency the last fall of erecting mill for manufacturing flour I hope to have them running by the first day of November. Bayliss goes to Ascertain in what part of your country wheat may be purchased on the best terms—He is interested with me in business, and nearly connected in my family—Your Excellencys knowledge of him, makes it unnecessary for me to say more than to wish your advice to him in the execution of his commission and to assure you that every smile on his attempts will lay me under new obligations.[2]

He will give your Excellency the printers account—it far exceeds what I expected it would amount to. I complained but was informed it was agreeable to the rules of business.[3] My best regards to Mrs Washington And believe me my Dr General with the highest esteem your affectionate humble servant

                                              B. Lincoln

ALS, DLC:GW.

1. Hodijah Baylies (1756–1842), General Lincoln's son-in-law and former aide-de-camp, was GW's aide from May 1782 to 23 Dec. 1783.

2. In October 1783 Lincoln visited the Brandywine mills in Delaware with a view to erecting a mill of his own on his land near Hingham, Massachusetts. Much of his time in 1784 was taken up with the building of the mill and get-

ting a miller to operate it. See his correspondence with Samuel Hodgdon in the Lincoln Papers, MHi. Lincoln's mercantile connection in Alexandria was with William Lyles, who sent him 3,258¼ bushels of wheat in the fall of 1784 (see Lyles to Lincoln, 6 Nov. 1784, MHi: Lincoln Papers).

3. GW records in his cash accounts having paid Baylies £3.12 "for Gen. Lincoln Printg Acct Boston."

To Stephen Sayre

Thursday Noon [Mount Vernon] 15th July [1784].
General Washington presents his Compliments to Mr Sayre and requests the favor of his Company at Dinner tomorrow— and any Gentleman of his acquaintance in Alexandria he may incline to bring with him.[1]

AL, ViHi: James Ambler Johnston Papers.

1. Sayre was staying in or about Georgetown, Md., in the late summer and early autumn of 1784. See his letters to GW of 20 Aug. and 15 Oct. 1784. See also William Duer to GW, 5 June 1784.

From Tench Tilghman

Dear Sir   Baltimore [Md.] 15th July 1784.
Only one Vessel has arrived from Ireland since I had last the honor of writing to your Excellency, and she came in last Night. As she had 450 people on Board, I thought I stood a good chance of procuring the two Tradesmen you have commissioned me to purchase[1]—Upon enquiry, I found only ninety were servants—among them none who would suit you. The remainder were persons who paid their own passages. There was a Bricklayer, who could not say much for himself, and several Carpenters, but they would not engage for any certain time, neither would they take less than the high daily Wages given to such Tradesmen here.

Such is the demand for Carpenters and Masons, that the Master Builders in those Branches who are settled here, in order to intice the new comers to give them a preference, will agree to release a four years indented servant at the expiration of one year and an half—And as it is usual for the owner of Ships to permit the servants to chuse their own Masters, you may suppose few or none of such as you want, ever go out of this Town, but upon such terms as I have mentioned—Indeed there is something so alluring in a Town to people of that Class, that they would generally prefer it, with some disadvantages, to the Country. I shall however continue to look out, untill you inform me that you are supplied, and should such, as I think will suit offer I shall not hesitate to make them some allowance upon the term of their Indenture, if I cannot procure them otherwise.[2]

Mrs Tilghman wishes her Compliments to Mrs Washington and your Excellency may be joined with those of Dear Sir Your most obt and hble servt

Tench Tilghman

P.S. Mr Thomas Peters has requested me to find a conveyance for a wheat Fan which he procured in Pennsylvania for your Excellency. I shall ship it by the Alexandria Packet to the care of Colo. Fitzgerald.[3]

ALS, DLC:GW.

1. See Tilghman to GW, 7 June.

2. See Tilghman to GW, 27 July.

3. Thomas Peters (1752–1821) went in 1783 from Philadelphia to Baltimore where he built a brewery and established the mercantile firm of Thomas Peters & Company. John Fitzgerald (d. 1800), who arrived in Alexandria from Ireland in 1769, became one of the leading merchants in the town. See GW to Tilghman, 4 Aug., in which GW acknowledges the receipt of the wheat fan.

From Ralph Wormeley, Jr.

Dear Sir.   Berkeley Rocks [Va.] July 16, 1784.

I saw Major Frank Willis two days ago here & enquired of him, if he had paid you the Money for the land he bought of Colo. Mercers, that I was Security for. He tells me that he sent £700 & odd pounds to Mr Lun Washington for the principal & Interest & that he had his Receipt for it. As he is going out of Country, I shall be glad if you will favor me with the particulars of the Affair that I may take care of myself. I shd have been glad to have seen the Bond taken in. I know Mr Willis has sold the Land for £500. more than he was to give.[1] if you shd take a Trip up to the Springs this Summer I shall esteem it a great Favr to see you here. I shall stay here Till the Middle of Octr pray make my most Respectfull Compliments to your Lady. I have the Honr to be with the greatest Esteem & Respect Dr Sr your most Obdt Servt

Ralph Wormeley

P.S. a letter to me sent to Mr Daniel Mcpherson Mercht in Alexandria, will be forwarded in a few Days.

ALS, DLC:GW.

1. Francis Willis, Jr. (1745–1829), left Berkeley County, Va., at this time to settle in Georgia, where in 1790 he was elected to the United States House of Representatives. It is possible that Wormeley is referring to Francis Willis, Jr. (1744–1791), of Whitehall, Gloucester County, with whom GW also had business dealings.

From Edmund Randolph

Dear Sir   Richmond [Va.] July 17. 1784.

I received your favor of the 10th of July by the last post. You will excuse me, I hope, from accepting fees for any business, which I may execute for you in the line of my profession. It is indeed a poor mode of acknowledging the repeated acts of friendship, which I have experienced from your hands: but I beg to be gratified in this, the usual way, in which lawyers give some small testimony of their attachment.

The grants, which accompany this letter, are of a bulky nature: but I thought I ought to inclose them by the post, the stage having been found in one instance not to be the most certain conveyance.[1]

I have not had time to inquire into the events of the lottery. If I should be able to procure full information before the departure of the post, I will communicate it to you in another letter.[2] If I should not, you may be assured of my transmitting to you all that I can learn by the next mail. I am Dear sir with the greatest truth yr affectionate friend & servt

Edm: Randolph

ALS, DLC:GW.

1. See GW to Randolph, 18 Mar., and Randolph to GW, April, 15 May.
2. See Randolph to GW, 20 July.

From Jacob Read

Sir   Annapolis [Md.] 17th July 1784
The Bearer Mr Prager comes recommended in the Most handsome manner to the Delegates from the State of South Carolina to Congress, by The Honourable Mr Laurens from London.[1]

Mr Prager also bore Letters from Doctor Franklin and Several others of the Principal American Characters in Europe to the Gentlemen of Greatest Weight in Philadelphia.

Permit me to Introduce this Gentleman to your Acquaintance and to request for him that Polite attention that all Strangers of Merit ever receive at Mount Vernon.

The Object of my friend in Visiting Virginia after paying his respects to Yourself is to View with a correct Mercantile Eye Your Ports Harbours Warehouses &ca as he has established an Extensive Concern in Philada & may probably form Connexions in Some of the Neighbouring States.[2]

As the Cridit of Mr Pragers House is Unlimited and undoubtedly good their Establishment in the Unitd States Cannot but be of the greatest Commercial benefit.

I Shall offer no appology for the Liberty I take in this Introduction because I am Sure it Affords you pleasure to see men of Merit & Consideration arrive & Settle in these States.

Do me the favour to present my best respects to Mrs Washington & believe that it will always afford me the greatest pleasure to render you every Service in my power in My present and every other Situation. I am with the greatest respect & regard Sir Your most obliged & most Obedient Servant

                                                              Jacob Read

ALS, DLC:GW.

1. Mark Prager, a nonprofessing Jew from England, came to Philadelphia after the Revolution and with members of his family established in the city the important mercantile firm of Pragers & Company. See Joseph Mandrillon to GW, 25 Oct. 1788, n.3. On 21 June 1787 while attending the Constitutional Convention, GW had dinner at Prager's house in Philadelphia.

2. On 23 July 1784 GW wrote William Fitzhugh of Maryland introducing Prager in these terms: "The Bearer Mr Prager is a Gentln who is very extensively engaged in Trade, & a partner in several very capital Houses in Europe. He is taking a review of the state of our Trade & ports, & probably, if he find

them answerable to his wishes, will fix a House in this State" (LB, DLC:GW). On the same day he wrote Gov. Benjamin Harrison: "Mr Prager who will have the honor of presenting this letter to your Excellency, is a Gentleman deeply engaged in Trade, & is a partner in several very capital houses in Europe. He is taking a review of the Ports &c. of this State, before he fixes his commercial plans; which, while they subserve his own interest, may be beneficial to this Commonwealth" (LB, DLC:GW).

Index